W9-CQN-734

B41

The speaker's resource book

an anthology, handbook, and glossary

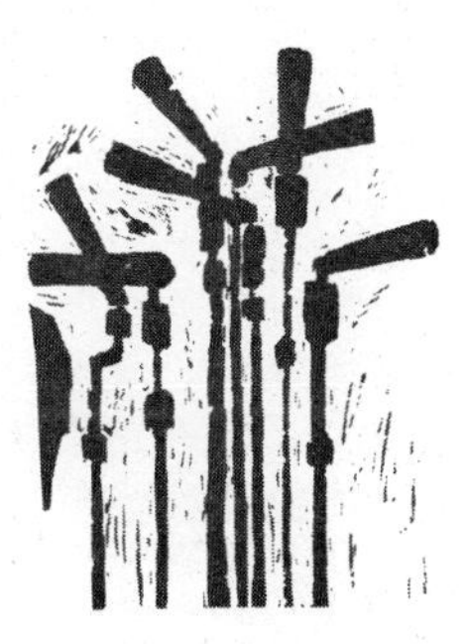

CARROLL C. ARNOLD
The Pennsylvania State University

DOUGLAS EHNINGER
State University of Iowa

JOHN C. GERBER
State University of Iowa

SCOTT, FORESMAN AND COMPANY

Chicago ▪ Atlanta ▪ Dallas ▪ Palo Alto ▪ Fair Lawn, N.J.

L. C. Catalog Card #61-8499

Foreword

The beginning student of public speaking will find that advice on how to make a speech is plentiful—and sometimes inconsistent. But he can be reasonably sure that all reliable advisers will urge him to listen to good speakers, read many speeches carefully, and practice making speeches as often as possible. *The Speaker's Resource Book,* based on these principles, combines the features of an anthology and a guidebook. It tries to serve college students of oral communication by making their study of speeches convenient and purposeful; furthermore, it points to ways of achieving challenging content in their own practice speeches. The book was planned for use either as a basic textbook or as an auxiliary work to accompany any good textbook on public speaking. It should also prove valuable in communication courses and, indeed, wherever public address is studied.

In coverage and organization *The Speaker's Resource Book* reflects the editors' conviction that whoever would learn the art of speaking must understand the social nature of speaking, must study models critically, and must carry content as well as method from his reading to his practice. Accordingly, this book provides a consideration of speech as a subject for study and as a social force; a collection of over forty speeches that can be used as models and as sources for ideas; guidance in analyzing speeches; suggestions on composing and delivering speeches; and information about the theory of oral communication.

The opening section, The Study of Speech, explores speech as an academic study and as a social art. Its four speeches and accompanying introductions and questions also serve to introduce the anthology proper—Speeches for Analysis and Ideas.

In choosing the selections in Speeches for Analysis and Ideas, the editors looked for materials likely to provoke discussion and to suggest ideas for students' speeches. To provide revealing comparisons and contrasts, they included some classic addresses, three essays, five student speeches, and two examples of public discussion. The selections are accompanied by (1) a brief introduction containing information about the speaker, the audience, and the occasion; (2) questions directed particularly to the ideas and form of the speech and additional questions inviting the student to probe the topic in search of new ideas for his own speeches; and (3) a reading list to assist those wishing to pursue the general subject further.

The last three sections summarize the leading principles of speech criticism, composition, and delivery. The section Analyses of Three Speeches suggests three methods of studying and evaluating a speech. The Student's Handbook of Public Speaking recommends procedures to be followed in composing and delivering a speech. The Glossary of Rhetorical Terms explains concepts and methods referred to in the introductions and questions and provides cross references to passages in the anthology that illustrate basic practices in speech composition. In effect, the Glossary is an inventory of the principal features of the theory of oral communication. Its main entries may be profitably used as the foci of classroom discussions.

Editorial responsibilities

The editors believe it is desirable to represent alternative approaches to the study of speeches, since no one mode of analysis is likely to reveal all the resources of an oral communication. Although they planned the book together, consulted frequently during its development, and read and criticized one another's materials, each editor took responsibility for specific parts of the volume and allowed his own approach to the problems of communication to be reflected in his work. In short, the editors have aimed at stimulating the reader through variety both in rhetorical materials and in editorial method.

Professors Arnold and Ehninger were responsible for The Study of Speech. In Speeches for Analysis and Ideas Professor Gerber was responsible for the sections on Education, The Arts, Science, and Ethics and Morals; Professor Ehninger for the sections on Social Problems and Business and Industry; Professor Arnold for The Media of Mass Communication and Politics. All three editors contributed definitions and illustrations for the Glossary, but Professors Ehninger and Arnold took major responsibility for its development and final form. The Student's Handbook contains the ideas and language of more than a dozen persons associated with the teaching of public speaking at Cornell University. The editors alone are responsible for the present form of this material, but they gratefully acknowledge their borrowings of thought and phrase. The analysis of Huxley's speech was prepared by Professor Walter Blair of the University of Chicago, General MacArthur's speech was analyzed by Professor Ehninger, and Jonathan Smith's speech by Professor Arnold.

Acknowledgments

For excellent suggestions and helpful advice, the editors are grateful to many persons. To the many speakers and teachers who furnished texts of speeches considered for inclusion in this collection, the editors owe a special debt. A number of addresses, thus generously offered and having intrinsic merit, fail to appear in the anthology because of considerations of space and subject matter. To the following persons who supplied us with texts or who graciously entered into correspondence about the book, we are especially grateful: Bower Aly, Albert A. Austen, Bruce Barton, Howard R. Bowen, Chester Bowles, Leo Burnett, L. Leroy Cowperthwaite, Robert R. Carson, Jack Douglas, Ralph T. Eubanks, Wilbur E. Gilman, James A. Grissinger, L. R. Hafstad, Margaret B. Hexter, Orville Hitchcock, William S. Howell, Robert B. Huber, Harry P. Kerr, Charles W. Lomas, Thomas E. Murray, Theodore R. McEldin, Robert P. Newman, Upton S. Palmer, H. G. Rickover, Frank Seiberling, Richard E. Singer, Wayne N. Thompson, Grace Walsh, C. Langdon White, and John F. Wilson. Others to whom we are indebted are identified elsewhere in this volume.

CCA
DE
JCG

Contents

part one THE STUDY OF SPEECH

part two SPEECHES FOR ANALYSIS AND IDEAS

1 / EDUCATION

2 / THE ARTS

3 / SCIENCE

4 / THE MEDIA OF MASS COMMUNICATION

5 / SOCIAL PROBLEMS

6 / ETHICS AND MORALS

7 / BUSINESS AND INDUSTRY

8 / POLITICS

ANALYSES OF THREE SPEECHES

The study of speech

Speech as a liberal study

CARROLL C. ARNOLD

The editors of *The Speaker's Resource Book* hope that those who read this volume will derive new insights into how speeches are formed and how composition helps to determine the effect of a speech. Some, we dare to hope, may even form a comprehensive view of that intricate occurrence, persuasion through oral discourse.

It is of practical importance to be able to compose a valid argument, to manage one's body while speaking, to make an acceptable "s" sound, and to acquire the many other specific skills that render one a competent communicator. But to learn such things as isolated skills without exploring the whole event of communication is to miss much that the study of speechmaking can reveal about mankind. There are large questions, as well as small ones, that need to be asked as one begins the study of speeches. What makes a speech different from other kinds of communication? Why do some speeches influence listeners and others fail? What are the differences among audiences, and how far do these differences control what speakers may or may not do with ideas? True, these are social and psychological questions, but they are intensely relevant to the study of speeches, for public speeches are always attempts at social control.

A speech may illustrate the devices of composition, but behind each choice of a compositional device there lies a bit of drama concerning the speaker's courtship of his reluctant listener. He pits his wish against the listener's inclination, chooses or fails to choose an action appropriate to the hearer's disposition, and thereby wins or loses much of his suit. Thus the scenes are played, the speaker's success hinging always upon the sureness of his adaptive skill and his understanding of his listener's nature. It is from observing such successes and failures that students of speaking begin to acquire the qualifications which Platc insisted the fully formed speaker must possess: "Such and such persons, he will say, are affected by this or that kind of speech in this or that way—and he will tell you why."

The selection "Speech as a Liberal Study" is placed at the head of this anthology of public addresses because it argues that all academic study of speech and drama should have as its ultimate goal the discovery of the kinds of effects speech may have—and why. This address was delivered to the General Speech Division of the Pennsylvania Speech Association, meeting in Philadelphia on October 17, 1959. It was the opening speech in a symposium-forum on the subject "Is Speech a Liberal Art?" Fred B. Millett, professor emeritus of Wesleyan University (Connecticut), replied to Professor Arnold's remarks, contending that speaking and writing are remedial studies unfortunately necessary in American colleges but without any "liberal" content of their own. Following the formal presentations, the two speakers engaged in informal discussion and debate, with members of the audience participating. Those attending the program were chiefly teachers and students of speech.

When reading this address, it is important to remember that the audience was presumably biased in favor of Arnold's general position. For this reason he chose not to anticipate Millett's specific arguments even though he was fully acquainted with them before the program began. Arnold tried instead to prod his listeners toward a critical evaluation of their own objectives in teaching and studying speech. Whether his "defense" of a somewhat sociological approach to the study of speech could affect his hearers as he intended is the kind of question Plato believed a qualified student of public speaking should be able to answer.

Carroll C. Arnold was born at Lake Park, Iowa, in 1912. He received his B.A. from Sioux Falls College in 1933 and his M.A. in 1940 and Ph.D. in 1942 from the State University of Iowa. From 1946 to June 1963, he was on the faculty at Cornell University, where he was Professor and Chairman of the Department of Speech and Drama. He is presently Professor of Speech at The Pennsylvania State University. Throughout his professional career he has been chiefly interested in the theory and criticism of speech composition; he has also written and spoken on such subjects as group discussion and general speech education.

Arnold's speech is printed here from the manuscript he used in delivering the address, edited to represent as exactly as possible the changes introduced in the actual presentation.

Good morning. I thank you for inviting me to join you in your convention. I especially thank you and Professor Millett for the privilege of appearing here with so distinguished a visitor. /1

I wish I were as sure about the meaning of our basic terms this morning as I am sure that Professor Millett and I enter this discussion sharing a strong allegiance to the educational aspirations that are always connoted by those sometimes imprecise phrases "liberal education" and "liberal arts." My view is that the academic study called Speech is capable of making major contributions to an undergraduate's understanding of what *he* is like, how he may constructively direct a significant portion of his energies, and what constitutes the social environment in which he lives. I tend to think these things make Speech a "liberal study," even though I despair of finding a neat and precise definition of what a liberal study is. /2

Let me make one other preliminary observation. When I speak of "speech" this morning, I have always in mind the full range of Man's speech behavior—the act of utterance, the symbol system of spoken language, the integration of matter and manner in spoken discourse, and dramatic communication in which discourse among characters is a central means of furthering the dramatic action. /3

Now, let me pose two elementary questions to open an exploration of how significant it may be to understand Man's speech behavior. When Man vibrates his glottal closure and manipulates his nasopharyngeal cavities in order to signal someone else, have these events psychological and social implications of a fundamental sort? Or are they events of marginal significance, comparable to manipulating the oral cavity and glottal closure in order to swallow? Again, when Man plans and personally executes sustained symbolic utterance in combination with symbolic action for the purpose of influencing the human forces in his environment, are these events capable of revealing fundamental truths about the human mind and the nature of social behavior? Or are they marginally significant like the bookbinder's execution of a book cover design? /4

Speech behavior is significant for the same reason other universally expressive behaviors are significant. No matter what aspect of speech you examine, you are always examining Man in the process of making what is, for him, an important adjustment to his surroundings as he perceives them. *This* is what makes his writing, his music, his painting—and his speech—important objects of study if we are to understand the marvelous complexity and the potentiality of Man's nature. Sometimes, indeed, it may be more important to understand *speech* behavior than the other modes of expression just because it is less self-conscious and more rapidly adaptable and consequently furnishes a more precise, though sometimes not very ennobling, insight into human nature. /5

There is also another way in which Man's speaking is uniquely significant. Speech is a *universal* fact of social environment. Men have lived, and some still live, innocent of writing or serious art. But so far as we know, speech is always one of Man's modes of dealing with the world about him. Thus, to know the influences under which a man or a society exists, one needs to know the contents, the forms, and the manners of the oral discourse that was a pervasive part of that man's or that society's conditioning environment. *If* there was writing, it must be known too. *If* there is serious art, it must be known. But there *will* be speech; it behooves us to know how to understand it. /6

Post-Gutenberg generations have, perhaps, been too impressed by the permanence of print. Often they have forgotten what Plato and, especially, Aristotle emphatically knew: that though speech is fugitive, it is a unique mirror of Man responding to his surroundings and, at the same time, it is a pervasive force regulating behavior in the human part of every environment. "To discern the nature of the soul and discover the different modes of discourse which are adapted to different natures" is the necessary aim of any true rhetoric, said Plato at the end of his *Phaedrus*. He was thinking of the speech event more than of the written record. When Aristotle observed that rhetoric and public address are always associated with ethics and politics, he seized upon the social force of all speaking and some kinds of writing. And when he insisted that in dramatic production Thought is usually conveyed through rhetorical-behavioral reflections of each character's moral and intellectual choices, Aristotle reminded his time and ours of the social readings which speech behavior always permits. These Greeks, and others, knew truths that the study called Speech amplifies: that Man's speech displays his nature in unique ways, and that its *immediate* influence is a different kind of influence from that which the remains of speech will have, however permanently sealed in written form. /7

By now you see my thesis. It is that every event of speech is in some degree a fundamental and socially significant event for the speaker, the spoken-to, and perhaps for those who come after. Whatever study, under whatever academic flag, will erode our ignorance about events of this kind will be a liberal and liberating study. Perhaps this is why Western Man has tried for at least 2500 years to subject his power of speech to systematic study. /8

I cannot pause to trace the triumphs and the miscarriages, the strokes of insight and the lapses into pedantry that have marked the human explorations of human speech. We ourselves are less than two generations away from some of the more bizarre episodes in Man's search for ways of understanding the nature and arts of speech. I think this is the chief reason we are today discussing the "liberality" of Speech as a study. /9

Happily for liberal studies, wisdom displaces error. Modern science is fortunate that Ptolemaic theories of the universe were laid to rest almost four hundred years ago. Ptolemy's ghost haunts no laboratory. It has been the misfortune of Speech that those eccentric mixtures of science and mysticism, Delsartian doctrines and Elocution, still linger in the folklore of the thoughtless and the misinformed. It is the misfortune of Speech that utterly mechanistic views of speech behavior did not disappear when surgeons ceased to "cure" stuttering with the knife. The naïve may even today buy mouth-machinery for the "cure" of lisping, stuttering, and like behaviors. /10

Admittedly, the sum of all our knowledge about speech is still expressed by a small fraction. But in the fifty years or so since Speech began, once more, to be accepted as a possibly liberal study, the fraction has grown. At least mechanics and mysticism no longer govern most undergraduate instruction. The undergraduate may, once more, find in studying Speech some of his most fruitful opportunities to explore the relationships between the different natures of men and the different manners and modes of discourse. /11

It is scarcely possible today for anyone to explore his own speech behavior under sensible guidance from persons who know what is now knowable about speech without making significant, intimate discoveries about the nature of Man—his infirmities and his potentialities. For this reason properly conducted speech rehabilitation consultations, properly taught courses in general public speaking or argument or discussion or rhetorical literature, and properly directed dramatic rehearsals and productions become liberal education of a most meaningful sort. Only laboratory experience in science and in creative writing equal the speech clinic, the platform, and the stage in producing personalized understanding of the self and the realities of the external world. And in addition there are the commonly admitted values of accumulating factual knowledge about human speech and the literary remains of Man's significant speaking efforts. /12

But, "What is the *content* of Speech?" The central and unique "content" of Speech is the range and consequences of the choices Man may make in influencing others through speech. Speech explores the potentialities of a pervasive medium of human expression; its special peculiarity is that the "choices" and intentions of Man, when using this medium, are always in some degree more *social* than aesthetic. /13

What William E. Gladstone paused in a busy political career to write to himself about the "content" of public speaking, he might have written about the entire study we now call Speech:

> "[T]he broad and essential difference between [the philosophical student] . . . and . . . the public speaker is this, that the latter is bound to have always alive in his mind as an original coordinate principle of his process, a regard to the mind of the hearer, its capabilities and its infirmities: how to avoid the aggravation of its defects by not giving them opportunity to work; how to secure encouragement . . . of its better tendencies by presenting them the . . . aid of opportunity."

"The mind of the hearer," the resources of Man's most personal mode of communication, and the methods of mediating between truth and Man Listening: these are the subjects central to all constructive study of speech and drama. /14

Speech can show to the youth bearing with him truths and aspirations derived from Philosophy and Literature and History and Science, the choices he must make if he would give his truths currency in a society that scrutinizes the spoken word confidently but often uninformedly. In the process of this showing, the youth will also learn much that he could not elsewhere discover about himself, his brothers, and their most basic form of public behavior. /15

Is this a liberal undertaking? Men have thought so, more often than not, perhaps for the good reason that few studies deal so fundamentally and directly with the vehicles of social experience. With or without the blessings of his academic proctors, Man has insisted upon exploring his speech as behavior and as a social force. Apparently, he has believed these studies could spur his judgment and imagination and enlarge his understanding. Perhaps then we ought to change our question and ask: "Will the college calling itself "liberal" organize and systematize the study of Speech, or will it have the subject studied piecemeal, narrowly, and anarchically in its porticoes?" This is about the only choice the liberal college has ever had since its conception. I think it is the only choice it has today. /16

For discussion

1. What is "speech"? Does it consist only of audible elements—word symbols, tones, and inflections produced by the voice—or are such visible elements as body movements, arm gestures, and facial expression also to be regarded as integral parts of "speech"?

2. If you decide to include visible elements in your definition of "speech," how would you classify talking done over the telephone or on the radio—in fact, in any situation where the speaker cannot be seen by the listener? Would you say that this sort of communication is not "speech"?
3. What is "good speech"—speech that meets certain predetermined standards of correctness and beauty, or speech that accomplishes its purpose by conveying the speaker's message clearly and convincingly?
4. To what extent do you believe a person's speech can be improved? What sort of training and practice are most useful for this purpose?
5. Distinguish between *self-expression* and *communication?* May a speaker express himself well and yet fail to communicate his ideas to another person? Conversely, may one communicate without expressing himself well? As a student of speech, which are you interested in: improving your ability to express yourself or improving your ability to communicate?
6. In what ways may a man's speech help us form a judgment concerning his personality, character, educational background, place of birth or residence, etc.?
7. Try to think of all the ways in which the speech of a national or cultural group may "mirror" the ethical, esthetic, and social standards by which that group is governed.
8. Arnold argues that the study of speech may properly be regarded as a "liberal" discipline because it helps a person understand (a) "what *he* [himself] is like," (b) "how he may constructively direct a significant portion of his energies," and (c) "what constitutes the social environment in which he lives." Would you agree that the study of speech, properly conceived and conducted, may indeed accomplish these ends? Why or why not?
9. If a man understands himself and his environment and if he habitually directs his energies toward constructive ends, would you regard him as "liberally" educated? What precisely does *liberal education* mean anyway?
10. On what grounds might it be argued that the study of speech is not a "liberal" discipline?
11. Cicero, the famous Roman orator, was in the habit of saying: The man who possesses knowledge and wisdom but does not know how to communicate them to his fellows is of little use in the world. On the other hand, the man who is a skilled and artful speaker but does not possess knowledge and wisdom is a danger to the state. Comment on this statement.
12. Justify Professor Arnold's assertion that speech is "a pervasive force regulating behavior in the human part of every environment." By what other forces is group behavior also regulated? Would you say that speech is more or less powerful and pervasive than these? Why?
13. What place do you think "liberal" studies should have in a college education? Which subjects would you classify as "liberal," and which would you exclude from this category? Why?
14. Explore the statement, ". . . the sum of all our knowledge about speech is still expressed by a small fraction." What are psychologists, speech pathologists, physicists, phoneticians, linguists, rhetoricians, anthropologists, etc., doing to extend this knowledge?
15. Arnold maintains that speech is one of the most important means man has for adjusting himself to his environment. What does he mean by this statement? In answering, give actual instances and examples.

Effective speech in a democracy

WILLIAM G. CARLETON

The cry that "oratory is a lost art" is often a hackneyed and thoughtless cry. Too often those who deplore the absence of Websterian and Lincolnian speaking think only of Webster's and Lincoln's memorable phrases and grieve that their like is not heard from contemporary politicians. Professor Carleton, on the other hand, offered a much more penetrating criticism of modern American public address when he spoke to the members of the Southern Speech Association in Gainesville, Florida, on April 5, 1951.

"Effective Speech in a Democracy" deserves close and thoughtful study for a variety of reasons. Among them is the fact that it diagnoses one of the chief causes of sterility in public address: the want of comprehensive, independent, adaptive mental activity. Carleton's proposition is that modern American speakers too often propound their conclusions without probing their subjects and fail to impose the stamps of their own minds on the discourses they compose and deliver. If this is right, the proof should be found

William G. Carleton, "Effective Speech in a Democracy," *Vital Speeches of the Day*, Vol. XVII, June 15, 1951, pp. 540-544. Reprinted by permission of the author.

in the addresses published in this volume and elsewhere. The speeches by Pericles (pp. 216-220), Emerson (pp. 36-46), Huxley (pp. 261-266), Theodore Roosevelt (pp. 102-107), Darrow (pp. 136-143), and Franklin D. Roosevelt (pp. 129-135) which appear here have achieved the status of classics in the literature of public address. To compare them with the less famous addresses on comparable subjects, also provided in *The Speaker's Resource Book*, should lend support or refutation to Carleton's characterization of public speaking today.

Equally important to students of public speaking is Carleton's emphasis on the speaker's unique opportunities to contribute original thought and independent influence in an industrial, metropolitan society. In such opportunities lie the special challenges for beginning and experienced speakers. The speaker's communication is uniquely his to control, as Carleton implies. From the first glimpse of his rhetorical purpose to the last phoneme of his final utterance, the speechmaker's speech is an intensely personal creation if he will make it so. Should it prove otherwise and the speech be imitative, timid, or bland, the mind and method of the speaker are at fault. He was not restrained from penetrating his subject nor from adapting his thoughts to the needs of his hearers. How highly society prizes such potential independence is shown by the fact that the speaker's right to speak the fresh results of his thought and the right of others to assemble peaceably to listen, are guaranteed by the first amendment to the Constitution of the United States.

Carleton's career as a student of political action in the United States gives him special authority when he discusses the political significance of popular discourse. He has been a member of the faculty of the University of Florida since 1927 and is now Professor of Political Science and Head of the Department of Social Sciences. He has studied and written much on American political parties and political activity in the nineteenth century. He was born at Evansville, Indiana, in 1903 and received his A.B. from Indiana University in 1926. He also received the degree of Doctor of Jurisprudence from the University of Florida in 1930 and an M.A. from Indiana University in 1934.

The audience that heard Professor Carleton in 1951 was composed largely of teachers and students of speech; however, the general appeal of the address was recognized by the editor's of *Vital Speeches of the Day*, who published it soon after its delivery.

Clear and effective speech in our American democracy is more necessary today than at any time in our history. A larger number of people participate in community and government decisions than ever before. Mass democracy, numerical democracy, the phenomenon so dreaded and so hoped for by people in the eighteenth and early nineteenth centuries, is here all about us. Wider and wider popular participation in government requires that the issues of the time be carried to all types and conditions of men, men who every day are contributing to the making of community and government decisions. /1

Moreover, not only do a larger and larger number of people participate in our elections and decisions, but the problems which must be considered and upon which judgment must be passed are more intricate and complex than they once were. And they are growing in intricacy and complexity all the time. In addition, American leaders increasingly must speak to win not only the attention and the understanding of American citizens but also of citizens in lands beyond the seas. All of this makes it imperative that in our oral and written speech on public affairs we strive more and more to practice rigorous integrity, intellectual clarity, and a lucid style. /2

Modern technology has made the mechanical tasks of today's speaker much simpler. The loudspeaker makes it much easier for the orator; it saves tremendous energy; it allows an effectiveness almost impossible for the unfortunate orator appearing before large audiences in pre-microphone days. For one Webster or one Bryan who could be heard by a large audience, there were a hundred speakers who could not be heard beyond the first rows. Indeed, quite frequently in the old days a speaker rose to prominence not because of his gifts of mind and expression but solely because nature had endowed him with leather lungs and a stentorian sound box. The radio and television have also added immeasurably to the opportunities of the contemporary speaker. Today the speaker can extend his mind and his personality into every nook and cranny of the world. A speaker in New York can come about as close to his physically remote audience sitting in San Francisco as an orator in the Ecclesia in Athens or a protest speaker in a New England town meeting ever came to his small and immediate audience. Today a speaker can literally bestride the world like a Colossus, and he can become as big an influence in the world as he has the mind and personality (and the social forces and pressure groups) to become. /3

However, in spite of the imperative need for effective speech today and in spite of the multiplying of mechanical aids, in my opinion there has been a decline in able public speech, a decline in the number of first class speakers and orators. True, more people participate in public speaking, more people are doers—and this is all to the good—but there has been a deterioration in the intellectual content, in the literary style, and in the method of delivering speeches, even among those who by reputation stand in the first rank of contemporary oratory and speech. There are, of course, notable exceptions to this general indictment. But the general indictment, I think, should stand, even when all due allowances are made for the tendency of contemporary man, in any stage of history to look back on the past with rose-tinted glasses, to romanticize it, to glamorize it, to dream of it as the golden age of oratory or literature or liberty or virtue or happiness or wisdom. /4

There has been a decline in the art of delivering a speech. There is the failure to convey a feeling of deep earnestness. (There is seriousness, yes, a simulated and stereotyped seriousness, the seriousness of dullness, of banality.) There is a lack of animation, of passion, of fire; a lack of rhythm and of music. The speaker today rarely communicates to his hearers the electric tension of a nervous system and a brain working at high gear—under control, of course, and always held in leash by reasonable and intellectual restraints—a nervous system and a brain working under immediate pressure, under the stimulation of having to think rapidly and out loud, and responding with flexibility, spontaneity, imagination, verve, vividness, and punch. /5

The truth is that too many speakers today are afraid to concede anything to the immediate occasion and to the moment. They perhaps come too well prepared. I do not mean, of course, the preparation of a well stored mind, which is the preparation of a lifetime. Nor do I mean the preparation which thinks out ahead of time the reasoned organization of a speech, an analysis of the propositions and the alternatives, how one topic will flow logically from the preceding one, and even many of the striking and quotable phrases. There can never be too much of this kind of preparation. But I do mean that speakers nowadays often come too well prepared in meticulous detail; they leave nothing to chance, to the occasion; they ignore the possibilities of cutting here and expanding there while in action; they do not yield sufficiently to the delights of spontaneous asides and anecdotes, of vivid illustrations thought of on the spur of the moment. Too many speakers use too many notes; the notes are too copious; and worse still, more and more speakers read their speeches. Even when notes or even manuscripts are in order, often the speaker does not know when to interpolate new material, when to depart from the too well prepared sheaf of papers he holds in his hand. /6

Much of this slavish dependence on notes and manuscripts is due to the radio. However, even when the speaker cannot be seen, his tell-tale manner lets the hearers know that the speech is being read and not delivered. A few speakers can read a speech *almost* as well as they deliver one—F. D. Roosevelt and Winston Churchill, for instance—but few are in the Roosevelt and Churchill class. /7

Most speakers—indeed, all speakers—need a little uncertainty to be at their best. There must be excitement, even actual stage fright, for a speaker to be stimulated to the point of brilliantly effective speech. Every great speech in history has been made under the impetus of stage fright. If the speaker or the actor does not experience stage fright—that last minute electrical charge of anxiety and challenge—there is something wrong. Speakers and actors know this. The story is told that Sir Robert Peel, for many years a leader in the British House of Commons, on important occasions was in the habit of letting a fellow member of the Commons take his pulse just before Peel was to rise in Commons to speak. Peel's racing pulses indicated that Peel was in good shape for a supreme forensic effort. /8

Even the most experienced speaker knows—indeed the more experienced he is the more deeply he is likely to know it—that there is always the possibility of failure in time of crisis. Who can forget the three or four awful minutes when Edmund Burke, with a long lifetime of superlative oratory behind him, faltered and failed when he faced a critical Scotch audience at the time of his inauguration as rector of the University of Glasgow? Yes, failure can come to the best and the greatest of them, and it is this possibility of failure which acts as a whiplash to the orator and the actor on critical occasions and produces the finest speaking and the finest acting in history. Present-day speakers rob themselves of this stimulus when they come to the loudspeaker too well prepared in details. /9

There has been a deterioration in the literary style of speeches. Politicians, lawyers, and ministers, the ranks from which most of our speakers are drawn, live in a busy and hurried age; they have less and less time for reading, reflection, and the maturing of their own literary styles; they do not read the masters and the classics as they once did. They are readers of newspapers and periodicals in an age when newspapers and periodicals are less literary and more journalistic. Practitioners of the art of public speaking today are apt to piece together a speech from newspaper clippings and current editorials. Or worse still, the busy public man, engrossed with a thousand and one duties and increasingly dependent upon experts in technical fields for the intellectual materials covering his job, calls upon numerous ghost writers to prepare his speeches. Paragraphs from many sources are then assembled and fitted together into a speech. /10

What is the result of all this? The result is the loss of honesty in style, even the disappearance of style altogether. The result is that too often our contemporary speeches are pallid, synthetic hodgepodges that might well be produced by public relations firms or advertising agencies, hodgepodges devoid of unity, philosophy, perspective, integrity, personality, or craftmanship. This results in productions without figures of speech and vivid illustrations, without cryptic phrases and terse aphorisms, without lights and shades, wit and humor, roll and rhythm. Even when speeches are not ghost-written, the ghost-written ones, representing as they do the speeches of our very highest politicians, are coming to set the pattern, and so today speeches that are not ghost-written are coming to sound ghost-written, synthetic, stereotyped. /11

There are exceptions, of course. A century which has produced a Jean Jaurès, an Aristide Briand, a Woodrow Wilson, and a Winston Churchill is not wholly devoid of oratory of the highest order. But the oratory of our run-of-the-mill politicians is not what it once was. One has but to read the Parliamentary Debates, the Congressional Globe, and the Congressional Record of the nineteenth century to be struck by the stylistic decline of much of the oratory and the public speaking of the twentieth century. /12

Now I realize, of course, that tastes in styles differ not only from individual to individual but from age to age. Much of the oratory and public speech of the nineteenth century would today sound pompous, florid, ornate. Even the sonorous, rolling, Romanesque style of Daniel Webster, so much admired in Webster's own day, often sounds to us today forced and artificial, and Stephen Vincent Benét, in his great American epic on John Brown, reveals how deeply a sensitive poet of our century can be offended by the Olympian periods of Webster. Even Webster was irritated by his many second-rate imitators, and he has recorded his own disgust at having to slay (that is, blue pencil) scores of Roman consuls and pro-consuls in editing the Latinesque inaugural address of President William Henry Harrison. And by the time the 1880's had been reached, much of American oratory had become so sickeningly sentimental as positively to revolt twentieth century taste. For 1880's sentimental oratory at its worst, take a look at James G. Blaine's funeral oration at the bier of James A. Garfield. Yes, we of the twentieth century have different tastes, and we demand styles that are more simple and direct. But—and this is the point—side by side with the rococo public speech of the nineteenth century there was also a style characterized by plain, clear, lucid, Anglo-Saxon address; many public men of that century used it and used it well; no one in the twentieth century—certainly not Woodrow Wilson or Franklin Roosevelt—can rival John C. Calhoun and Abraham Lincoln in the classic use of a simple, vigorous, and chaste style. /13

Most important of all, in our time there has been serious deterioration in the content of public addresses, but content cannot be separated from style, for style and content go hand in hand and it is difficult to distinguish cause and effect. /14

American speeches today, even those by leading statesmen, for the most part have ceased seriously to examine fundamental policy, to discuss first principles, to isolate and analyze all the possibilities and alternative courses with respect to a given basic policy. For the most part American speeches today assume a given policy; they proclaim it rather than debate it; they enumerate the "points of a program" necessary to implement the assumed policy and to reach the assumed goal; they confirm the faith of their followers in the assumed policy and goal; they rally enthusiasm; they exhort to action. The result is that speeches today are rarely intellectually comprehensive or cogently analytical. The result of this tendency toward mere enumeration and exhortation is to render formal public address superficial and arid; speeches sound like advertising copy in which one takes pains not to mention competing products (that is, competing ideas, competing alternatives of policy) for fear that the public might become acquainted with competing products (that is, competing ideas, competing alternatives of policy). One simply ignores competing ideas and alternative policies—or dismisses them with an epithet—and repeats the virtues of his own idea or his own policy. But things in this world are relative, and a given candidate, idea, or policy makes intellectual sense only in relation to other candidates, ideas, and policies. The failure in a single speech to examine, analyze, discuss, and debate alternative points of view with respect to a given policy robs that speech of deep intellectual content and conviction, and is not even fair to the point of view held by the speaker. Intellectually, the speaker is selling short his own point of view when he fails to examine it fairly in relation to other points of view. /15

The development of mass democracy and the growing complexity of public problems seem to have combined to give American politicians and other public speakers the idea that issues must be flagrantly over-simplified to reach the intelligence of the average citizen. This is a mistaken attitude and in many cases a cynical and snobbish one. Where speakers fail, they usually fail because they underrate the intelligence and maturity of audiences, because they "speak down" to audiences. Every great speech in history has aimed high; every great speech in history has assumed a generous degree of virtue, intelligence, and maturity in those to whom it was addressed. /16

Let me illustrate what I mean when I say that I believe that today's speeches should be intellectually more comprehensive and analytical. For five months now, since the November elections of 1950, we have been witnessing "the great debate" on foreign policy. We have *claimed* that we have been debating the fundamental alternatives of American foreign policy. But how many speakers in this "great debate" actually examined all the points of view, all the possibilities, all the alternatives, in American foreign policy? Very few. Almost every speaker *assumed* the course he favored, and proceeded to confirm that point of view in terms of itself, to set up a "point program" to achieve it, and to exhort to action. /17

What are the various possibilities in American foreign policy? There is the globalism of world federalism, at present hardly a practical alternative. There is the globalism of the United Nations, where the United States, although taking the lead, makes no important moves without carrying the support of the United Nations. There is the globalism of American imperialism, in which the United States takes the lead in Europe and Asia against Communism, and carries out its policies even though it does not have the backing of a majority of the nations or even of a majority of the important nations in the United Nations. There is the partial globalism of a federal state of the democracies or a federal state of the Atlantic community. There is the return to American isolation, in which the United States would withdraw from the leadership of the anti-Communist forces in both Europe and Asia. There is a partial American isolation, in which the United States would withdraw from leadership in Asia but not Europe, or from leadership in Europe but not Asia. There is the possibility of America's taking the lead to build up the social-democratic and democratic socialist forces in Europe and Asia to check the Communists. There is the possibility of breaking the current and dangerous polarization of power between the United States and the Soviet Union and returning to the old multiple balance-of-power system. Now it is quite possible that any given speaker will favor a combination of several of these possibilities, but by no stretch of the imagination could he favor all of them, for some of them are contradictory. To me, the intellectually convincing speech on American foreign policy would have to analyze and defend the course favored by the speaker, but it would also have to analyze fairly and combat the alternative courses the speaker opposed. /18

Will you permit me to illustrate my point by demonstrating for a moment how I would construct a speech on current American foreign policy? It so happens that I favor the following foreign policy: In the countries of Asia and Europe where the non-Communists are in control, I would, where conditions indicated, put the United States squarely behind a policy of social democracy or even democratic socialism as a way of combating Communism; and in the countries where the Communists are in control, I would play upon the nationalistic tendencies everywhere evident in Communist governments and Communist parties, to attempt to divide Communist countries from each other on national grounds and thereby contribute to the restoration of a multiple balancing-of-power system, a system which would prevent the Communists from acting together in a Communist front and threatening to upset the balance of power. For if we can remove the Communist threat to the balance of power we can remove the real cause of another great war. /19

In order to present effectively my point of view on the importance of playing wise social politics, it seems to me that I would have to show how and why conditions in Europe and Asia are converging to produce collectivist movements there and why laissez-faire capitalism there is not feasible; also I would have to show the difference between totalitarian socialism and democratic socialism and examine the reasons why I believe America's backing of social-democracy and even democratic socialism in Europe and Asia would check Communism and serve America's national interests. In order for me to present effectively my belief that nationalism within Communist countries and parties could be used to divide Communism and restore a multiple balance-of-power system, I would have to examine in some detail the degree to which Communist revolutions and movements are in fact nationalistic in aim, method, and development, and actually point out the specific grounds of possible national conflict between specific Communist countries. (In the main, Communism has spread not by international revolution but by a series of national revolutions; industrial revolutions are being built inside Communist countries on national patterns; potential national conflicts exist between Communist countries, as for example a possible future conflict between China and Russia over Manchuria.) /20

However, even when I had done all this my intellectual task would not be completed. I would have to point out why other courses in foreign policy would not serve America's national interests as well as the policy I favored. This would involve my examining the reasons why political isolation would not work today; why a policy of mere military containment of Communism through the United Nations would not be enough and would not work permanently; why even if it worked it would be the hard way to do something that could be done with less possibility of war and fewer long-time sacrifices; why a policy of mere military containment of Communism by the United States alone—a policy of American imperialism—would be even less workable and less desirable than a policy of military containment through the United Nations. In short, in order to carry intellectual conviction on so large and controversial a question, it seems to me I would have to construct a speech that analyzed critically all courses —those I oppose as well as those I favor. /21

In domestic affairs, too, the great issues of our time have never been adequately debated in public address. There is no great oration or debate to which one can point and say, "There is the preeminently able presentation of the case for the welfare state, with all alternative solutions weighed and examined." Neither can one point to any such oration or debate in opposition to the welfare state. /22

In the past the great issues of the day frequently have been debated in able and definitive fashion. Take for example Burke's pleas for British reconciliation with the American colonies; or Fox's appeal in 1800 for a cessation of the war with Revolutionary France; or the debate on the Reform Bill of 1832; or the arguments of Bright and Cobden for the repeal of the Corn Laws; or Gladstone's arguments for free trade or for Irish Home Rule. In American history, take for example the great debate over the adoption and ratification of the Constitution; or Calhoun's speech on the Independent Treasury; or Lincoln's cool and logical discussion of slavery from 1858 through the Second Inaugural of 1865; or even the debate of 1919-1920 over the League of Nations. Read these and then ask yourselves whether the great issues of our time are being debated with equal vigor, insight, comprehensiveness, and analytical power. I think you will be forced to agree that the issues of today are not being debated with equal ability. /23

The truth is we are in somewhat of a crisis in the practice of human communication, both written and oral. Technical and specialized subjects of all kinds are effectively communicated to technicians and specialists in the technical, scholarly, and professional journals. But where can the average citizen go to get an intelligent approach to a question, an approach intellectually competent and related in a comprehensive way to the average citizen's needs and experiences? If our speeches have become more platitudinous and aridly categorical, our printed matter in editorials and articles has also suffered. /24

Current periodical literature in America suffers on many counts. Our magazines of large mass circulation, those upon which the average man relies, increasingly have shied away from serious articles and given more and more space to "human interest" material. The digest magazines, for instance, with their huge circulations, boast of reproducing articles of permanent and lasting interest, but most of their articles deal with peripheral, marginal, and miscellaneous topics, and only about one article in twenty deals seriously with an important political, economic, or social question. Even when serious and important questions are dealt with, they have tended to become more superficial, more platitudinous, more pat, and more "humanized." Today a "profile" or character sketch of some public figure is often published as a substitute for a more solid approach to a political campaign or a political question. Publicity is more and more centralized; the costs of production reach staggering sums; an eye must be kept constantly on circulation and advertising figures. Magazines are more and more inbred and staff-written; articles of intrinsic intellectual merit and sound originality are passed over because they do not fit the "editorial needs" or conform to the personal views of the editors. (Perhaps I should say here that personally I have no grievance with editors; they have been generous with me; but as a citizen I resent the increasingly slick and stereotyped material I am forced to read. A few days ago I chanced to see a British periodical of last summer which contained an article by Bertrand Russell. The editor explained that while he personally differed from Russell's conclusions, he was publishing the article for its intrinsic intellectual content; that the article was a vivid illustration of how a first class mind operated on important subject matter in a comprehensive way vital for the average reader. There is too little of this sort of thing, particularly in the United States.) /25

The chief enemy of clear thinking and communication is the development of a stereotyped public opinion. Our agencies of news and information are highly centralized. Our economic and social life has become closely interwoven and interdependent. A mass impression is made rapidly and stereotyped for short periods, and then the first mass impression is followed by a second. Intellectually, we have become the victims of the stereotype of the week or the stereotype of the month or the stereotype of the year. Publishers are fearful of going against mass opinion because circulation and advertising are involved, and circulation and advertising are more and more important as production costs go up. Editors are afraid to go contrary to the stereotypes, and as a result they demand intellectual conformity and discourage intellectual individuality. Thus stereotyped thinking produces the periodicals, and the periodicals reinforce stereotyped thinking. It is a vicious cycle. /26

We have come to think too exclusively of political and governmental centralization as the producer of conformity and the enemy of freedom. But our problem is much broader than this. Conformity is the result of political centralization, but it is also the result of economic centralization and social centralization and publishing centralization and literary centralization and artistic centralization and intellectual centralization. And all of these flow from the machine and modern technology and the growing interdependence of industrial and metropolitan civilization. (However, this should not be considered an indictment of the machine or of industrial or metropolitan civilization; the machine releases human energies as well as curbs them; and there are many forms of administrative and managerial and group-life decentralization possible and yet to be explored—forms of decentralization that are consistent with a machine and an industrial civilization—but that is not my topic today; that is another story, and I have dealt with it on other occasions.) /27

We practitioners of public speech can do much to break the trend toward stereotyped thinking. It is easier for us to be original and to depart from the current mode of thinking than it is for publications of mass circulation. We do not have a huge capital investment to consider or a large payroll to meet; we need not keep our eyes on the cash register. The public will listen to our views, all the more so if our views are original and fresh, if we come with something to say and say it well; if we avoid the methods of the smart aleck and the exhibitionist; if we speak out of knowledge, understanding and conviction; if we present our own and conflicting points of view with fairness and insight. /28

Let us do our part to prevent the world of complete conformity, the nightmare world of George Orwell, from coming to pass. Let us be broad, comprehensive, and pluralistic in our intellectual approach; let us avoid the dogmatic, the doctrinaire, and the absolute; let us keep alive in our speeches a large measure of respect for diversity, individuality, and originality—even when we ourselves happen to be on the popular and winning side of the day—for it is from these sources that flow the springs of human freedom. And let us all take a turn now and then at using freedom, at differing from the majority and from the stereotype of the time, for freedom withers and dies when it is not used. /29

For discussion

1. While modern means of mass communication may have greatly increased the size of the audience a public speaker can reach, as is frequently pointed out, such an enlarged audience also imposes upon a speaker many restraints and limitations unknown to the orators of a century ago. What are these restraints? How and why do they arise? What, if anything, may a speaker do to overcome them?
2. Describe in some detail the role which public speaking plays in the life of a democratic society. By what ethical and social standards should speech in a democracy be governed?
3. Why are public choices and decisions more difficult to make today than ever before? Why is it more important that as a nation we choose and decide wisely?
4. Admitting the validity of Carleton's criticisms of the read speech, can you think of any occasions on which it might still be preferable for a speaker to read from a manuscript rather than speak extemporaneously?

5. Consider the statement: "Most speakers—indeed, all speakers—need a little uncertainty to be at their best. There must be excitement, even actual stage fright, for a speaker to be stimulated to the point of brilliantly effective speech." Do you agree or disagree? Defend your answer.
6. How much conscious attention should the average public speaker pay to the language or "style" in which his ideas are expressed—to the choice and arrangement of words, the use of figures of speech, epithets, antitheses, alliteration, etc.? What are some of the dangers of giving too much or too little attention to certain aspects of style?
7. In your judgment, are there significant differences between good oral and written style? If so, what are they, and why are they important?
8. Are you willing to accept Professor Carleton's contention that contemporary speakers are less "comprehensive and analytical" than the speakers of earlier generations? Base your answer not upon opinion or guesswork but upon careful research into several of the speeches to be found in this and other collections of speeches.
9. What, as you see it, causes styles and tastes in oratory to change? In view of these changes, can we ever hope to determine the essential qualities of truly great speaking?
10. What do you think of the widespread current practice of ghostwriting speeches? In framing your answer, pay special attention to the ethical as well as to the purely rhetorical problems involved.
11. Evaluate the receipt or formula that Carleton believes a speaker should follow in presenting his views on foreign policy. Would this formula make for a fair and rounded discussion of the subject? Would it make for a rhetorically effective speech? Can you think of any objections which might be raised against this recommended pattern?
12. Investigate some of the speeches given by the four modern speakers that Carleton regards as "great" (Jean Jaurès, Aristide Briand, Woodrow Wilson, and Winston Churchill). What dominant traits or characteristics do you find in their speaking? Would you agree that they deserve to be classified as "great"?
13. Who was the most effective public speaker you ever heard? Explain why he was effective.
14. Do you agree with Carleton's assertion that our present-day newspapers and periodicals foster "the development of a stereotyped public opinion"? What do you think about radio and television in regard to this statement?
15. What, specifically, can you as a student speaker do to help break "the trend toward stereotyped thinking"?

Demagogues, "good" people, and teachers of speech

W. NORWOOD BRIGANCE

"Demagogues, 'Good' People, and Teachers of Speech" was presented before the twenty-second annual convention of the Southern Speech Association, Jackson, Mississippi, April 2, 1952. It is at the same time an "occasional address" and a lecture on public speaking as a medium of mass communication. It is occasional in that it was intended to intensify speech teachers' pride in their profession; hence, one finds statements that directly or indirectly magnify the importance of speech and the teacher of speech. But the address has much more than ceremonial significance and purpose. Professor Brigance aimed at the "watering and cultivating of ideas" that would give his listeners a fuller, wiser understanding of their subject and the purposes of teaching it. Thus he had, as he said all speakers have, a "short-range purpose" and a "long-range purpose."

To study public speaking or to make informed judgments about speeches, one must recognize that practical effect is the goal of virtually all speechmaking. Those who speak do so from social motives; what they say can affect society for good or ill. The most important questions about a speech are therefore social questions. Is influential speech the gift of nature bestowed without price? Is speech so completely the product of habit and impulse that its power to influence is beyond the reach of artistic discipline? Is the public speaker's behavior so automatic a reflection of his intelligence and personality that he cannot control his speech consciously without destroying his own truthfulness? Brigance tried to answer such questions in his thoughtful, deeply informed comments on the history of speechmaking as an art, the ways speeches influence men and societies, and the responsibilities that go with the freedom to speak. And his speech, itself, illustrates how interest and meaning are enhanced when a public speaker does conform to intelligent principles of both rhetorical art and social responsibility. "Demagogues, 'Good' People, and Teachers of Speech" is reprinted here because it is a good model of effective speechmaking and a wise treatise on the social nature of public speaking.

W. Norwood Brigance, "Demagogues, 'Good' People, and Teachers of Speech," *Speech Teacher*, Vol. I, September 1952, pp. 157-162. Reprinted by permission of the *Speech Teacher* and the Speech Association of America.

William Norwood Brigance was born at Olive Branch, Mississippi, in 1896 and died in Crawfordsville, Indiana, on January 30, 1960. He received his B.A. from the University of South Dakota in 1916, his M.A. from the University of Nebraska in 1920, and his Ph.D. from the State University of Iowa in 1930. From 1922 until his death he was a member of the faculty of Wabash College, Crawfordsville, Indiana, and for most of this period he was Chairman of the Department of Speech.

This speech reveals two of Brigance's most impressive qualities: the breadth of his reading and information and his devotion to the objectives of liberal education. Long before he addressed the Southern Speech Association in 1952, he had established a national reputation as a teacher, scholar, and public speaker. He was author or coauthor of a dozen textbooks, wrote a biography of the famous nineteenth-century legal orator Jeremiah S. Black, edited a two-volume *History and Criticism of American Public Address,* was editor of *The Quarterly Journal of Speech,* and in 1946 served as president of the Speech Association of America. He was popular among his professional colleagues as a speaker and lecturer. They soon learned to expect his addresses to exhibit the unique combination of learning, originality, vigor, and color that distinguishes "Demagogues, 'Good' People, and Teachers of Speech."

There are two interesting attitudes toward speechmaking. The first comes from that frustrated minority who are unhappy about it. They say it is "medieval," "outworn," "a lost art," and "there is no place for it any more." Typical of these laments is that summarized by Edward T. Channing, onetime Boylston Professor of Rhetoric and Oratory in Harvard University. "But oratory, now, is said to be almost a lost art. We hear constantly how it has fallen from its old supremacy."[1] That was the lament of 1819, the year that Clay was 42, Calhoun and Webster were 37. Lincoln was ten, Douglas and Beecher were six! Over a century has past, yet the tune does not change. Frederick C. Irion, in examining the various media that influence public opinion, dismisses public speaking with a lofty gesture: "Public speaking in the United States reached the peak of its importance about a hundred years ago."[2] Irion said that in 1950. In his lifetime had lived Woodrow Wilson, Wendell Willkie, and Franklin D. Roosevelt. In his lifetime radio and television had displaced print as the most influential media of communication. /1

In contrast with this school are those who hail public speaking as "the key to personal success." For them it is "the magic formula for getting there," or "the way to dominate one person, or one thousand." It would be unfair to say that Lowell Thomas, exemplar of public address, holds this view. Yet its ghost is seen between the lines of his statement: "As I look back on it now, if given the chance to do it all over again, and if obliged to choose between four years in college and two years of straight public speaking, I would take the latter, because under proper direction it would include most of what one gets from a four-year Liberal Arts course, and then some." /2

Of these two schools, the first ignores the facts of life; and the second misses the true purpose of public address. If public address were outworn it would have gone out like the horse and buggy—or more literally like feudalism, isolation, and other institutions and culture patterns which have died, or are dying, however slowly and stubbornly. If public address were solely an instrument of personal power, it would long since have been put under control of a National Communication Commission which would license speakers to talk only in certain areas and only on certain subjects. /3

Neither has happened. Why? Because from the beginning of civilization speechmaking has been inherent in human society, and a free society cannot exist without it. Even primitive peoples had it. The American Indians, for example, were "natural orators," as I can vouch personally from having long lived among them. But their speaking led to nothing, for it lacked system. Early civilizations had it also, but there also it led to nothing, for again it lacked system. Not until the ninth civilization on this earth arose, that of the Greeks, did we have a system and theory of speechmaking. Not until then could it be reduced to a discipline and taught in schools. /4

Consider how and why this occurred. About 470 B.C. the Greek city-states began to throw off their dictators and set up a people's government. They now undertook to rule themselves. This was man's first democracy, his first free society. At once, these Greeks found they could not carry a democracy without a *system* of public address. A wronged citizen came to the new people's government and said, "The dictator took my land ten years ago. It's my land. I want it back." Land titles had been destroyed, yet justice required a hearing. So juries were set up—not juries of twelve good men and true, but

[1] Edward T. Channing. *Lectures on Rhetoric and Oratory* (Boston, 1856), pp. 10-11.

[2] Frederick C. Irion. *Public Opinion and Propaganda* (New York, 1950), p. 213.

one hundred, or five hundred, good men and true. The wronged citizen had to argue his case before these peers. He found unhappily that truth and justice were not enough. He needed also speaking skill. St. Augustine 800 years later was to put the problem in immortal words: "Who dare say that the defenders of truth should be unarmed against falsehood? While the proponents of error know the art of winning an audience to good will, attention, and open mind shall the proponents of truth remain ignorant?"[3] So these pioneers of democracy learned in the fifth century B.C. Not only in the courts did they need it, but also in the new legislatures. When the 500 or 5,000 freemen gathered to pass their laws, no one got a hearing unless he had the skill to hold attention, and no one got a law passed unless he had the skill of winning good will, and explaining clearly. /5

At once these people were forced into a systematic study of the science of speechmaking. Within some ten years the first book had appeared, written by a certain man named Corax. His book is now lost, and of the man himself we know nothing except that he is "the founder of rhetoric," and "the first who laid down the rules." But that perhaps is enough. It fixes the point of departure. /6

The sum of the whole is that systematic speechmaking grew out of the attempt of free people to govern themselves. That is why it is never "medieval," or "outworn." That is why you cannot restrict it, or license only certain people to practice it and forbid it to all others. That is why every citizen in every free society needs to be trained in its discipline. /7

Of course we hear it said that speechmaking nowadays is really useless, that it does not amount to anything because nobody is actually influenced by what the speaker says. (If this were true of speechmaking it would be equally true of other channels of communication like newspapers, magazines, and books. But we pass that by.) For example, the late Kurt Lewin, a most brilliant psychologist, observed that, "Lecturing may lead to a high degree of interest. It may affect the motivation of the listener. But it seldom brings about a definite decision on the part of the listener to take a certain action at a specific time. A lecture is not often conducive to decision."[4] Of this, three explanations are in order. First, it is true. Second, it has been known for twenty-three centuries. Third, it misses the purpose of speechmaking. /8

What, then, is the purpose of speechmaking? First is what may be called the *short-range* purpose. This is found in speeches given to courts, juries, legislatures, or groups already committed to action, but undecided on which action. It is also found in the speeches given during "times of decision" like a Presidential election, when people hear speeches this month and vote next month. The research showing that such speeches do win votes and influence human behavior is enormous and conclusive. It need not be reviewed here. We need only to remember that Dr. George Gallup said on the eve of the 1948 elections that the influence of speeches was "negligible," and remember his predicament on the morning after the election. We may with profit also remember the honest confession two months later of Archibald Crossley: "We were wrong. We *assumed* that speeches did not change votes and we stopped polling too early." The evidence is overwhelming. At "times of decision" good speaking, and sometimes not-so-good speaking, does change votes. But this is actually a minor purpose of speechmaking. /9

Second, is the *long-range* purpose. This, in a single sentence, is the watering and cultivating ideas. We live in a world that confronts us with many sorts of problems. We are beset by temptations. We are haunted by fears. We are uncertain of the future. We listen to speeches because we hope the speakers will give us new ideas, or new information, or will simply water and cultivate old ideas. We listen because we want to be given encouragement, to renew our faith, to strengthen our determination. /10

The speaking that counts with us takes up these problems that beset us. That is the kind of speaking that Aristotle said was important in 336 B.C. That is the kind that St. Augustine said was important in 397 A.D. It is the kind described by Viscount Morley in explaining the effectiveness of Richard Cobden: "He produced that singular and profound effect which is perceived . . . when a speaker leaves party recriminations, abstract arguments, and commonplaces of sentiment, in order to inform his hearers of telling facts."[5] It is the kind explained in the Instruction to Judges of the National Forensic League: "The orator should not be expected to solve any of the great problems of the day. Rather he should be expected to discuss intelligently, with a degree of

[3] St. Augustine, *De Doctrina Christiana*, Book IV.

[4] In T. M. Newcomb and E. L. Hartley, *Readings in Social Psychology* (New York, 1947), p. 336.

[5] *Life of Richard Cobden* (Boston, 1881), p. 119.

originality, in an interesting manner, and with some profit to his audience, the topic he has chosen." /11

The effect of such speaking is not immediate decision or change of attitude. It was rather described by Wilbur Schramm as "being like drops of calcarious water falling from the roof of a cave upon an ancient stalagmite. Sometimes an especially big drop leaves an especially large deposit, in such a position that it can be seen and actually appears to change the shape of the stalagmite. Usually the residue of each new drop simply merges with the other deposits, and the structure grows, almost imperceptibly, in the direction of the source of supply."[6] The validity of Schramm's analogy is affirmed by the research of the last quarter century. This research comes from many fields: from anthropologists, psychologists, sociologists, political scientists, as well as in the field of speech itself. It can be summarized as follows:

1. The cumulative effects of mass communication are powerful.

2. The radio is more effective than newspapers. Repeated experimental findings demonstrate that "the human voice is more persuasive, more friendly, more compelling than the written word."

3. Face-to-face speaking is more effective than radio. "The physical presence of a speaker establishes a more normal and satisfying social relationship than does the mere sound of his voice." /12

Everything said previously is merely the preface. We now come to the subject proper. *If speechmaking is inherent in a free society, then speech training is inherent in its educational system.* Reduced to simplest terms there are only two ways of settling differences: shoot-it-out or talk-it-out. To shoot-it-out is the method of totalitarian states. To talk-it-out is the method of free societies. Both requiring skill, training, and discipline. /13

Of course we have met the specious adage that "anybody can talk." It is a popular refrain of bird-witted minds who varnish nonsense with the charms of sound. Like most solecisms, it is not a falsehood. Rather, it is a half-truth. Everybody knows that anyone can "talk." In the same sense, anyone can "cut," but the child who can cut paper dolls cannot thereby cut out an appendix or trepan a human skull. There are various levels of cutting, some easy, and some difficult. So with "talk." Mere chatter is elementary. But formal speaking is difficult, very difficult. It is formal discipline that took centuries to develop. It is more complex than building dynamos or removing tonsils. It is not learned without sustained study and application. It is not learned by studying "English," or Turkish, or any language including the Scandinavian. It is learned by studying the formal discipline of speechmaking, which is older than any current living language. /14

Today we are witnessing the ill effects of our failing to train citizens in this essential of education. For example, the American Medical Association is one of the superbly trained professional bodies in the world. Since 1900 it has prolonged human life in this country by some fifteen years. But its appointed leaders lacked skill in public discussion, and for the past twenty years they have engaged it in dangerous and needless controversy. American business leaders have developed a dynamic capitalism that has come nearer to abolishing poverty than in any country or any time since man emerged on this planet. But most of its leaders are inarticulate, and are reduced to hiring "speechwriters" to represent them. As Smith, Lasswell, and Casey point out, this is "risky tactic," for these hired spokesmen may some day in the future decide to take over the power for themselves. American labor leaders, unable to get their training in school, turned perforce to night classes and short courses, where they learned "practical speaking" that too often was limited to teaching the effective use of invective and half-truth. American schools, in short, have failed to qualify citizens in this essential of democracy, and we are paying the price for that failure. A democracy, then, lives in constant danger unless its leaders are trained in speechmaking. "Talkers always have ruled; they will continue to rule. The smart thing is to join them," said Bruce Barton. Hitler knew this, but German educators did not. Every demagogue knows it. Only "good" people are stupid enough to believe that it takes skill, training, and discipline in order to shoot-it-out, but none at all in how to talk-it-out. /15

But what kind of speech training is needed in a democracy? The answer is obvious. The kind needed to promote the welfare of a free society. The kind that disciplines people in how to talk-it-out. The kind that definitely discourages the demagogue technique of shooting-it-out with a war of words. These are the standards to which students ought to be held accountable:

1. Does the speaker give accurate and significant *information* on his subject?

2. Does he give significant *ideas* about it?

3. Does he arouse listeners to *think* profitably about the subject?

[6] "The Effects of Mass Communications." *Journalism Quarterly* (December, 1949), No. 4, p. 397.

4. Is he *responsible* for what he says:

a. Responsible for speaking the truth?

b. Responsible for being intellectually honest?

c. Responsible for avoiding reckless assertion, for avoiding evidence which, though perhaps accurate, misleads by exclusion?

d. Responsible for lifting the tone of discussion above the level of name-calling? /16

Today two kinds of student speeches, including contest speeches, violate these standards. The first is the *Glittering Generality* speech. Here the student takes his place on the edge of created space and shoots at all eternity. He covers most, or all, the problems of man in a single speech. He solves each in a single sentence. He never walks on earth among mortals. He dwells in the stratosphere of thin air and dim thoughts. In plain language, he is "full of sound and fury signifying nothing." I say that enough of this is heard in the market place from self-made speakers. In the classroom we should require that speakers use words that have meaning. /17

Second is the *Hatchet Speech.* In this the speaker discusses an evil committed by people who are certain not to be in the audience. It may be slums—if he is speaking in a small town. Or liquor—if the audience is safely prohibitionist. Or oppression of the Negro in the South—if the listeners live in the North. With sinners at a safe distance, the speaker decapitates them in effigy before the eyes of his non-sinning audience. I insist that this kind of speaking only incites people to violent thoughts. It does not solve problems, nor does it water and cultivate thoughts. It has no place in the educational system of a free society. /18

Face the situation frankly. It is not easy for teachers of speech to stand courageously against such speeches. Students will ask, "But don't public men give such speeches?" and the answer must be "Yes." All over the land there are speakers who utter hollow banalities, or who try to make the eagle scream whenever they can get in proximity to a water pitcher and the American flag. Some go even further, and resort outright to the Big Lie Repetition of the Communists. We have them today even in the United States Senate, and you know who they are. But teachers of speech must see to it that we do not have them in the classrooms of the American schools. /19

I have no formula for preventing this, but I have been experimenting the past few years with the following set of standards, placed in the hands of every student at the beginning of the course: /20

Memorandum to students: You are to begin the study of speechmaking. Bear in mind that most speeches given by mine-run untrained speakers are inept, and altogether too many backfire. Persuasive speaking in one sense is like piloting an airplane: better learn the techniques, or don't try it. In this course you are to learn something of its techniques. Therefore, get set to learn them: /21

1. In persuasive speaking you don't punch people in the nose. Nor do you try to make people suddenly give up old beliefs and attitudes. Instead, you water and cultivate ideas just as people water and cultivate crops. You are to be a cultivator of ideas, then, not a human bull who bellows defiance and tries to gore. /22

2. Don't use your speaking as an excuse for airing thinly-veiled prejudices. Don't damn or praise indiscriminately, Congress, the President, Russia, Labor, Capital, Private Enterprise, or anything or anyone. Instead, get your facts and present your case. Hit as hard as you want with facts, but don't make reckless assertions, and don't name-call. No question is too controversial to discuss, but give listeners light and not heat. /23

3. One highly important factor of persuasive speaking (long suspected, but finally proved scientifically in the 1940's) is information. But it must be specific information, and honest information, and the listener must be made to believe it is honest. Therefore, brace yourself to the duty of testing, processing, and arranging honest and trustworthy information. Especially be suspicious of what you read in propaganda magazines and books. Learn how to use standard references in the library to check information and to fill in missing parts. /24

4. Don't try to be an authority on government, politics, or what-have-you. If you need it, get authority, and tell when and where your authority testified. /25

5. Don't pretend to have proved more than you have proved. In short, don't give hearers a chance to call you a braggart or exaggerator. Present your case in such a way that all who disagree will say, "Anyhow, he was fair." /26

This is not a success formula by any means. It will not automatically convert irresponsible sophomoric minds into responsible thinkers. Nevertheless, keeping this standard before the eyes of the class can lift the level of class thinking and speaking. Especially when a classroom demagogue tries buckshot techniques, it enables the class, rather than the instructor, to fence him in. /27

It may be, in that distant Utopia the public will fence in its demagogues, and by force of public opinion the only effective talk will be reasonable talk. It may be. It is enough if today we measure up to the duty of teaching the kind of speechmaking that gave birth to free societies, and without which they cannot survive. /28

For discussion

1. Why can a "free society" not exist without speechmaking?
2. Can a great orator develop in an authoritarian society, or does greatness as a speaker depend upon the atmosphere of freedom which only democracy provides?
3. Investigate further the beginnings of the systematic study of speechmaking in Greece and Sicily during the fifth century B.C. (In this connection, see R. C. Jebb, *Attic Orators*, Vol. 1; Lester Thonssen and A. Craig Baird, *Speech Criticism*; the article on "Rhetoric" in the *Encyclopaedia Britannica*, etc.)
4. How did Plato, Aristotle, Cicero, and St. Augustine contribute to the theory of speechmaking? (Again, see Thonssen and Baird, *Speech Criticism*.) What can you find out about the Roman teacher of rhetoric Quintilian?
5. Distinguish between the "short-range" and "long-range" purposes of speechmaking, as Brigance explains them. Which does he consider more important? Why? Do you agree?
6. How would you account for the following statements? ". . . the human voice is more persuasive, more friendly, more compelling than the written word." "The physical presence of a speaker establishes a more normal and satisfying social relationship than does the mere sound of his voice."
7. Why does Brigance believe that "talking-it-out" requires just as much "skill, training, and discipline" as "shooting-it-out"?
8. Review and explain the four "standards" to which student speeches "ought to be held accountable."
9. Describe a "glittering generality speech." A "hatchet speech."
10. Does Professor Brigance's condemnation of the "hatchet speech" mean that a student speaker never has the right to criticize a person, practice, or institution? If not, under what conditions is that criticism to be made?
11. What role does information or factual knowledge play in effective and responsible persuasive speaking?
12. According to Brigance, what ill effects may follow our failure to train citizens in "the formal discipline of speechmaking"?
13. Why is the systematic study of speechmaking "*never 'medieval,'* or '*outworn*' "? Why can it not be restricted or licensed?
14. Does Brigance set up an impossibly high standard for student speakers to meet? Do you agree with the five rules or principles which he thinks should govern all student speeches?
15. Have the world's "great" orators invariably adhered to the standards which Brigance recommends? If so, was this the reason they were "great"? If not, would you conclude that the "standards" are false or meaningless?

Four ways of looking at a speech

IRVING J. LEE

Irving J. Lee of Northwestern University delivered this address at the annual convention of the National Association of Teachers of Speech (now the Speech Association of America) on December 30, 1941. His discourse succinctly describes the chief ways of analyzing and evaluating the texts of speeches. Each method can reveal different facets of the speeches assembled in this volume. But, as Lee implies, one learns most by looking at speechmaking in several ways. The editors of *The Speaker's Resource Book* suggest that the speeches published here can be studied most profitably by raising the rhetorician's, the semanticist's, the logician's, and the general semanticist's questions in that order. To do so will bring successively to the mind the psychological and literary, the linguistic, the logical, and the sociological significance of these public addresses.

Lee's remarks are also worthy of study as an example of a "convention paper." Convention papers and their cousins, research reports, are not fundamentally different from lectures or other formal, expository speeches. Their uniqueness lies in the fact that they are discourses prepared for audiences of experts. Usually, too, they are presented at meetings to which the experts-as-listeners bring a special sense of professional responsibility. Such papers are usually

---

Irving J. Lee, "Four Ways of Looking at a Speech," *Quarterly Journal of Speech*, Vol. XXVIII, April 1942, pp. 148-155. Reprinted by permission of the Speech Association of America.

read, for precision is what such listeners demand of their reporters. But good convention papers and good research reports are not just "essays on their legs." Although the speakers may assume extraordinary knowledge and unusual powers of attention on the part of the audience, good papers of this kind still accommodate to listening man's limited span of attention, to his difficulties in remembering what he hears, to his gratefulness for topical allusions and touches of humor and human interest, and to his need for clear organization. That technical papers are written and delivered from manuscript makes it all the more important that learning by listening be made as easy and efficient as the subject will allow. Listeners do not become readers, with leisure to reflect and re-examine, just because a subject is difficult or a speaker decides to write out his speech.

"Four Ways of Looking at a Speech" was in many ways a model convention paper. It nowhere sacrificed the accuracy and precision that the subject and the audience of experts demanded; yet in composing it, Lee rendered the labor of analytical listening humanly possible—even pleasurable. The rhetorical means by which he did this can be discovered by reading the text carefully as Lee's rhetorician would read it. On December 30, 1941, in the Statler Hotel in Detroit, Michigan, these rhetorical designs turned into *events* as Lee began to read his address. They bound the speaker, his subject, and his listeners in a lively, human relationship as the subject unfolded; in that way they made a speech out of the paper Professor Lee had brought from Evanston, Illinois. To a lesser extent these same rhetorical procedures become events again as we read the printed version today. They still tell us we are reading a *speech*—not a soliloquy, or a thesis, or the typical sort of essay. Whoever would understand the art of public address must learn by what means speakers achieve or miss such effects. Lee and the other speakers whose addresses appear in this volume have furnished the laboratory materials for this kind of learning.

Irving J. Lee was born in New York City in 1909 and attended the public schools of Wharton, New Jersey. He received his B.A. from New York University in 1931 and his M.A. in 1935 and Ph.D. in 1938 from Northwestern University. From 1937 until his death on May 23, 1955, he was a member of the faculty of the School of Speech, Northwestern University. As a scholar and teacher he was especially interested in how meanings operate in public addresses; he published four books and numerous articles on this and related subjects. A considerable portion of his speaking, writing, and research was devoted to exploring the relevance of Alfred Korzybski's theories of general semantics to the study of public speaking. Lee also served a number of industrial corporations and governmental departments as a consultant on problems of communication.

The advance of any science becomes apparent first in a systematic refinement of its methods and then in the development and application of *new* methods. Thus, the history of internal medicine and psychiatry shows a steady movement from the rules of thumb of an earlier era to the specialized procedures of today. But unco-ordinated specialization can make for new confusion unless we are ever aware of relationships. /1

Something like this has been happening in the field of speech criticism in recent years. The development of new modes of analysis with varying terminology and apparatus has left some of us in need of reorientation. It is, perhaps, time to say with Lincoln, "If we could first know where we are, and whither we are tending, we could better judge what to do and how to do it." /2

Then, too, new methodologies are often introduced amidst attitudes of hostility and defensiveness. Students who have not been exposed to new doctrines seem inevitably to feel that their proponents come as legislators likely to repeal every last thing that is known. The unfamiliar procedures are looked upon as something antithetical, antagonistic, ready to replace the old and the presumably worn out. But new methodologies may well be not antithetical but complementary, not antagonistic, but additive. /3

Thus it is with some of the "new" ways in speech criticism. Students working entirely apart from each other have focused on perspectives which can throw light on particular areas in the speech process otherwise neglected by the others. It is my point that there are available today at least four different ways of looking at a speech which can be applied individually and co-operatively for knowledge about what goes on when someone speaks to someone else. My plan is to discuss in order the dominant concern of the rhetorician, the student of meanings or semanticist, the logician, and the general semanticist. In what way would each be interested in a public speech? What does each look for? What are the questions that each would ask? On what basis would each judge whether the speech was "good" or "bad"? /4

In this quest the analysis, if successful, could be used on the speech of any public figure, a radio commercial, a class assignment, this paper, or on any sort of connected discourse whatever. /5

Let me begin with the rhetorician. His first concern is the discovery of the effect of the speech. Did it make an impression? Was it accepted or rejected, approved or disapproved in varying degrees? Were audience attitudes solidified or changed? Modern techniques of direct polling, accompanied by tests of attitudes, make answers possible to these questions that are now more precise than ever before. But it is only after those findings are in that the rhetorician would get under way. His work would begin when he asked: What did the speaker do that got results? What did he say that influenced them? How did he say it? What strategies accounted for the acceptance of his argument? What peculiar tactics marked the method of his appeal? /6

Our rhetorician might be guided by the experience of students in the last 2,000 years. For observers of such processes have been all too numerous. They have noticed that minds were manipulated by an almost endless list of devices. We must be content here with a mere suggestion of the scope of the patterns of persuasion. The rhetorician would look for the attitudes of the speaker, the disguised or overt flatteries, the modes of insinuation, the sources of personal prestige. He would study the manifestations of voice, bodily movement, and gesture. He would analyze the progress and gradations of the attack, the lines of argument and the modes of support. He would be concerned with the specificity, the associational power, the interestingness, the varieties of suggestion, the spread or limitation of the *topoi,** the sources of humor, the paths of action, the impressions of universality. He would listen carefully for the colloquiality, the impersonality, the special adaptations, the turns and figures, the memorable phrases, the maxims, and the subtle devices of stylistic ingratiation. /7

In short, the rhetorician tries to overlook nothing that a speaker did that might affect his control of his audience. If, by chance, the speaker alienated his hearers, that, too, should be explained. And if ours was the complete rhetorician, he might then go on to generalize, to show us that the rhetorical performance was or was not the inevitable one, for when rhetoric will have become a science, rather than an art, the student will "be able to tell under what circumstances what devices will get what effects."[1] /8

The student of meanings, that is, the semanticist, has, however, an interest in other matters. His concern centers on these questions: What does he mean? Do I understand the speaker? How can I find out whether he is saying what I think he is saying? What, in other words, is being said? /9

For the ordinary business of living, in the daily round of domestic affairs, when dealing with the butcher or the newsboy, such questions seem pointless. Without too much effort we manage to take in and presumably understand whatever we hear. But as soon as we leave the ordinarily mundane, for talk of life and love, of purpose and significance, of use and method, of needs and programs, the old sureness is no more. What seems simple can often take on new complexity when disturbed by a question. Momentary doubt is often enough to reveal the tenuousness of one's grasp on an argument, for what appears inordinately clear on first hearing may, on further scrutiny, be susceptible to many diverse interpretations. /10

It is common knowledge that many a speech turns out to be all things to all men. The task of the semanticist is the reduction of this possible multiplicity to simplicity, the discovery of the sources of ambiguity, and the provision of the means whereby the speaker's intent may be faithfully reflected. /11

In this quest the semanticist is guided by three fundamental facts about the working of our language. /12

1. He starts with the fact of *ambiguity*. He knows that metaphor is not merely a decorative device but a necessary manifestation of language in use, insofar as a relatively small vocabulary must serve an inexhaustible number of purposes. It is small cause for wonder, then, if even our simplest words are ever turned to new uses. We learn very early that such a phrase as "he pinched her" may, on occasion, be used in a situation betokening social familiarity, an arrest, or a kidnapping. And that such a word as "operation" is used with by "no means the same 'working' in the technical vocabularies of theology, surgery, mathematics, and strategics."[2] When Secretary Knox said that the naval establishment in the Pacific was not "on the alert," he was not using that phrase in the sense of watchfulness or sleepiness, but in the technical sense that "certain essential preparations" should have been but were not made.* I. A. Richards[3] called attention to the lament of the philosopher G. E. Moore, "Why we should use the same form of verbal expression to convey such different meanings is more than I can say. It seems to me very curious that language should have grown up as if it were expressly designed to mislead philosophers; and I do not know why it should have." The diversity of interpretations, so characteristically common in discussion, may be cause for lamentation, but it is the work

* From the Greek; meaning here, the speaker's topics. *(Editor's note)*

[1] See Harwood L. Childs, *An Introduction to Public Opinion* (1940), pp. 89-102.

[2] Louis H. Gray, *Foundations of Language* (1939), p. 257.

* The reference is to the Japanese attack on the naval base at Pearl Harbor, Hawaii, with which the United States' active involvement in World War II began. Frank Knox was U.S. Secretary of War from 1940-1944. *(Editor's note)*

[3] *The Philosophy of Rhetoric* (1936), p. 96.

of the semanticist to take such difficulties as his province, to reckon with them, and then to help us find a way around them.[4] /13

2. *Generality* is the second important factor. A very large portion of the key terms of any speech will show such largeness of coverage that it is not always easy to discover which particular areas of human concern are being referred to. In a recent speech Robert Maynard Hutchins said, "Education implies teaching. Teaching implies knowledge. Knowledge is truth. The truth is everywhere the same. Hence, education should be everywhere the same." The very breadth and scope of these terms must give one pause. So much is included under their tentlike expanse, that the semanticist must needs wind in and through them lest he assume particulars not otherwise intended. Generality is not something to be stigmatized, but, rather, to be realized and analyzed anew. (Incidentally, with the coming of the censors, we may expect many an example of that maddening and sterile double-talk as the characteristic trade mark of most official public pronouncements—especially if the practice of the last war prevails.)* /14

3. The third focus of his attention involves a ferreting out of the terms which stand for *fictitious entities.*[5] Teachers of grammar have instilled the notion that "a noun is the name of a person, place, or thing," so religiously that speakers very often go on to use "any" and "all" nouns as if they were talking of similarly observable and verifiable matters. Such words as Right, Power, Obligation, Justice, Beauty, Art, Service, etc., which the semanticist calls "fictions" are to be understood as "mental inventions and abstractions" and not as the names of "direct and specific sense-experiences." In the warmth and immersion of the speech situation it is not difficult for a speaker to hypostasize,[6] to reify these "big words," endowing them with form and substance as if they necessarily stood for phenomena whose existence is readily manifest. The student of meanings, however, seeks to locate these fictions, warn us of their character, and determine in any case how they are being used. /15

Guided by the facts of ambiguity, generality, and fiction-making, the semanticist's task is set out: He must, by a process of "equivalent statement" somehow bring to earth, pin down, and *fix* the specific areas of reference. He must try to translate what was said so that the speaker's words are closely approximated in terms which dissolve the sources of confusion. When faced with a speech in which the opportunities for vagueness are exploited to the full, the semanticist, bent on clarity, does not dismiss the speech as a stupid mess of blabs, but, ever mindful that understanding is not quickly won, he systematically moves to his probing. For this work a battery of highly sophisticated procedures has been devised. There is space here to mention but a few. /16

1. He will investigate the key terms in their setting and context as the ground of meaning.[7] (To study them out of such focus is much as if one were to sing a bass accompaniment as a solo.) /17

2. He will analyze each metaphor into its tenor and vehicle.[8] /18

3. He will list the modes of definition which were used in the speech and those which may be applied in further clarification and explanation.[9] /19

4. He will provide the fictions with *archetypes,* as a way of fixing "the reference of words to observed entities."[10] /20

5. He will make use of an *analytical paraphrase,* by which the original sentences are translated into the simple 850 word vocabulary of Basic English. This kind of translation provides "a gauge by which to judge the original; by comparison of the two we have more chance of discovering what the original almost said, or might have said, or does not quite make clear whether it is saying or not."[11] /21

In short, then, when the semanticist has made his study, we should presumably know what the speaker has said. The nature of the symbolic process, making difficult the verification of any interpretation, will, of course, impose limits on the semanticist's knowledge. Whether or not we agree with the speaker is here not relevant. At least we should be clear on this, that we seek to know *what* it is about which a judgment must be made. /22

But it may be useful to raise the questions that are irrelevant in the analysis of "meanings." *Should* I agree with the speaker? Is what he said a sufficient

---

[4] See I. A. Richards, *Interpretation in Teaching* (1938), pp. 23-170; also James MacKaye, *The Logic of Language* (Hanover, N. H.: Dartmouth College Publications), Ch. V.

* The United States had entered the second World War only twenty-two days before this speech was made. Wartime censorship was thus a very new experience for Americans. *(Editor's note)*

[5] Hugh R. Walpole, *Semantics* (1941), Ch. 8. See also C. K. Ogden, *Bentham's Theory of Fictions* (1932), pp. 7-105.

[6] James W. Woodard, *Intellectual Realism and Cultural Change* (Hanover, N. H.: The Sociological Press), 1935, Chs. II, III and V.

[7] I. A. Richards, *The Philosophy of Rhetoric,* Chs. II, III, and IV. See the Report of the Committee on the Function of English in General Education, *Language in General Education* (1940), pp. 89-155.

[8] *Ibid.,* Chs. V. and VI. See *Interpretation in Teaching,* pp. 115-144.

[9] Hugh R. Walpole, *Semantics,* Ch. 6.

[10] *Ibid.,* Ch. 8. C. K. Ogden, *Bentham's Theory of Fictions,* 86ff, 105ff, 138ff.

[11] *Ibid.,* 234. See C. K. Ogden, *The System of Basic English* (1934).

statement of the case? Does his statement satisfy the requirements of valid demonstration? Was his argument adequately "reasoned"? With these questions we come to the province of our third student—the logician. His way of looking at a speech has little to do with the persuasiveness, the meaningfulness, or the scientific basis of the utterance, but in the main, with the way that the factual sentences of the speech are related one to another. Logic as a discipline gives the logician no way of testing the accuracy of the speech; it gives him nothing more than a set of rules by which to test the various *relations* between sentences.[12] What is involved here will, perhaps, be evident as soon as we see what the logician looks for. /23

1. The first step in his criticism requires the careful distinction between two kinds of sentences.[13] He gets at it by asking two different questions: First, which sentences in this speech say something about people, places, happenings, relationships, etc.? Are these sentences true or false and to what extent? Second, which sentences tell us not about the *outside* world but about the feelings, fancies, wishes, and imaginings *inside* the speaker? With the statements revealing the states-of-mind of the speaker, the logician has nothing to do. /24

When a man asserts something about the world-outside, others can go look, examine, test, and check. But when we are told *how he feels* about things, there is no further searching possible. We may wish, perhaps, that he "felt" otherwise, but his speaking now is in the realm of the non-logical. The logician is not surprised (though often distressed) when he finds that many public speeches (because of inside manifestations) are, thus, outside his field of study, for the expressive function is revealed in all pictorial descriptions, commands, pleadings, reveries, longings, urgings, hopes, fears, doubts, etc. Of all these the logician says simply, "These forms of utterance belong to poetry, and there is nothing I can do with them." Others, however, may ask: Are they sufficiently poetic? Could the sentiments be put with more fervor, more aptness, more adornment? Have others said them better? But in any case, such materials are incapable of logical analysis. /25

This distinction between factual and expressive sentences is often obscured by the fact that both may have the same grammatical form. The reporter's verifiable story of a wrestling match may, on paper, be filled with the same sort of declarative sentences which grace the lyric poet's "Ode to Melancholy." But when it is not clear that the one describes what can be seen, whereas the other expresses an inner-mood, we are ready for vast confusion. The next time you read a speech of Hitler's, blue pencil the mood-lines. Only what remains may be discussed as variants of the true and the false. To argue about the validity or relevance of the verbal products of his inner perturbation is not to understand how the logical discipline works. /26

2. The logician then inquires into the *condition of consistency*.[14] He wants to find out whether the assertions or suppositions of the speaker are consistent with each other. Do the views in the early part of the speech square with those of the later? Do the sentences follow one from another? Are they compatible? /27

There is nothing in logic which says that certain statements are to be accepted or rejected. There is merely the simple demand that a speaker does not at the same time accept and also reject his assertions. /28

At first glance the task of inquiring into consistency may seem trivial and simple. And yet the great contribution of symbolic logic in the last 100 years, in the writings of Boole, Peirce, Frege, Whitehead, Russell, and others, was (and is) to build up "a vast treasure of validating forms, conditioning valid inferences" entirely unknown to the traditional Aristotelian logic.[15] Students who would overlook this "instrument for exhibiting the relations of consistency and deducibility"[16] must be left with blunter tools and duller insights. /29

3. The third focus of study for the logician is the *adequacy of the evidence*.[17] He proceeds to ask: Is there "sufficiently secure empirical foundation" for the theorems and conclusions of the speaker? How well established in prior knowledge are the predictions which he makes? How many instances in support of his assertions are confirmed by observation? How meager or how exhaustive is the data on which the conclusions are based? /30

The answers to these questions are of tremendous practical importance. The discovery of the empirical basis of a speech (or its inadequacy) may have far-reaching consequences. We may well be reminded here of some of the effects on social legislation and human relationships of the highly questionable as-

[12] Rudolf Carnap, "Logic," *Factors Determining Human Behavior* (Cambridge, Mass.: Harvard University Press), 1937, pp. 107-108. The following analysis of the work of the logician draws heavily on this paper.

[13] *Ibid.*, pp. 108-112.

[14] *Ibid.*, pp. 112-115.

[15] *Ibid.*, p. 113. For further study see Willard Van Orman Quine, *Elementary Logic* (Boston, 1941).

[16] *Ibid.*

[17] *Ibid.*, pp. 115-117.

sertions that grew out of data obtained in the First World War. /31

"For example, the statistics of intelligence tests upon men drafted for army service have been used to bolster up the view that most men are slaves by nature, and to support the prediction that the run of mankind is incapable of higher forms of civilization."[18] /32

One may also be excused the passing reflection that the public soothsayers and pseudo-pundits, so much with us these days, too often honor this requirement of adequacy of evidence with but a passing nod. /33

The task of the logician, then, is to look at a speech with his tests of sentence function, consistency, and evidentiary basis. These conditions he establishes not because they have some "absolute metaphysical validity" or because they rest "on the will of God"—but very simply on the fact "that unless they are satisfied, thought and knowledge cannot perform their function as instruments for arriving at successful decisions in practical matters."[19] /34

I come now to the fourth critic, the general semanticist. His questions pick up at the precise point where the student of meanings and the logician leave off. He proceeds to elaborate their findings by a methodology which reveals the unnoticed nuances and subtleties of inaccuracy and misevaluation. He asks very bluntly: Does it make sense? Does the speech properly evaluate whatever the words are intended to represent? How does what is said correspond to what can be found in life? Both the student of meanings and the logician focus on verbal matters so thoroughly that both they and we may tend to forget that there is also a non-verbal world to be accounted for. Indeed, there are many today who would say with Plato, "But there is no use of our disputing about (words) when we have (life-) realities of such importance to consider." To correct this neglect, the general semanticist[20] starts with and keeps constantly uppermost the connections between two levels: the verbal and the non-verbal, the worlds of the speakable and the un-speakable. He seeks to check the language at every point for the relationship it has to the discoverable facts of life. He would stress what most students seem not to have realized: that language has no other function than to serve as a form of representation of something else. Let me summarize the direction of his attack in the following set of analytical questions: /35

1. Is the speech marked by elementalistic terms so that the speaker splits verbally what cannot be found so split in life? /36

2. Does his analysis encourage the view that things are ever static, when life manifests progress everywhere? Does he assume that the permanence suggested by the structure of his language is to be found as well in the life-facts his talk represents?/37

3. Does he suggest in his argument a sense of the uniformities in situations where novelty and variety are readily discernible? Does he obliterate differences in his gross formulations? /38

4. Has he sought the final causes of happenings, asking unlimited questions to which only limited answers are possible? /39

5. Is there sharp awareness that statements of fact are not the same as his statements about them, that his inferences and high order abstractions are not directly descriptive of happenings? Or does he act as if there is no difference between them? (A heightened understanding of this principle might have made some of our ubiquitous "experts" and commentators aware that their inferences about the coming of Mr. Kurusu* were not first order descriptions. Public policy based on the one as if it were the other must too often leave us a prey to disillusionment and tragedy.) /40

6. Is he oriented by the verbal definitions of "things," so that he deals in averages and properties, thus obscuring the sense of existing individuals which only can be found in life? (Have you noticed how the attempts to define the differences between the Chinese and the Japanese in terms of similarity-marking characteristics so often end in humorous futility, because in life there are only unique individuals? Averages by emphasizing similarities may apply to all but they cover no one.) /41

7. Does he lead us to assume that his views exhaust the details of happenings? Is he aware that one may have convictions without being overcome by the lust for conclusiveness? Or, in his speaking, does he remind us of the question posed by Lytton Strachey in his essay on Macaulay, "How can one fail to miss a great deal if one persists in considering

---

[18] *Ibid.*, p. 116.

[19] *Ibid.*, p. 117.

[20] Alfred Korzybski, *Science and Sanity, an Introduction to Non-Aristotelian Systems and General Semantics* (Lancaster, Pa., The Science Press, second edition, 1941), v-xlix. The index of this book will indicate paginations for the suggested formulations.

* Saburo Kurusu was one of two special Japanese envoys who came to Washington in November 1941, ostensibly to confer with U.S. officials on ways of easing the threat of war in the Pacific. The Japanese attack on Pearl Harbor on December 7 occurred during their negotiations. Predictions that the conferences would prevent American involvement in the war were thus brought to naught. *(Editor's note)*

the world from one side or the other of the House of Commons?" /42

8. Is the speaking the sort that produces automatic, signal reactions, or does he seek to orient his audience to delay, deliberate, and investigate? /43

9. Does his argument boil down the infinitely-valued and varied facts of existence into but few values? /44

10. How aware is he in his definition-making that any definition of words by words must be based ultimately on undefined terms? /45

11. Is he at all conscious of his verbalizing as verbalizing, so that at any moment he might stop for a look at things and people, and with Paracelsus cry, "Let us forget words and manners, and treat our patients." Or, with magnificent unawareness, does he try "to adjust the empirical non-verbal facts to his verbal patterns"? Or is he one of those about whom Montaigne was properly ironical? "Through presumptions they make laws for nature and marvel at the way nature ignores these laws." /46

In short, the probings of the general semanticist lead us to an index of the intelligence, to the "good sense" of the speech, to the nicety with which the speaker discriminates, to the degree with which we can, with security, rely on his evaluations, to the awareness that any utterance must be dealt with as a mode of behavior, as a living issue. If his language use is cluttered up with identifications, objectifications, distortions, oversimplifications—then for our survival, those evidences of immaturity and unintelligence must be revealed. If he is oriented in the patterns of the primitive, we must be protected, lest we succumb to counsel that may lead to disaster. /47

By way of perspective and summary, it may be useful to list the four basic questions which lead to these four ways of looking at a speech.

For the rhetorician—How did he get his effects?

For the semanticist—What, in other words, did he say?

For the logician—Is what he said a sufficient and consistent statement of the case?

For the general semanticist—Does he make sense, properly evaluating what it is he talks about? /48

It should be clear, of course, that my four experts are "fictitious entities," that men of such carefully circumscribed interests are nowhere to be found. Nevertheless, the emphases embodied in each are readily available for study. The following four books should be enough as a starter:

1. *The Rhetoric of Aristotle*
2. *The Meaning of Meaning* by C. K. Ogden and I. A. Richards
3. *The Logical Syntax of Language* by Rudolf Carnap
4. *Science and Sanity* by Alfred Korzybski /49

It may, perhaps, not be amiss here to suggest that speech teachers have too long and, perhaps, too carefully given themselves over with unselfish devotion to the rhetorical perspective. But in a world torn with the heated bludgeonings of oversimplifications, distortions, and prejudices, speech teachers who would help to preserve freedom of expression might well, before it is too late, begin the search for that more precious freedom—expression buttressed with maturity, adequacy, and good sense. /50

For discussion

1. What are the four ways in which Lee suggests a speech may be examined?
2. Look up in an unabridged dictionary the words *rhetoric, semantics,* and *logic.* Consult one or more encyclopedias in order to gain a clearer notion of the arts or sciences which these terms name.
3. What is the "first concern" of the rhetorician in studying a speech? What basic questions does he ask about the speech, speaker, and audience?
4. To what additional and more specific matters does the rhetorician also direct his attention?
5. What is the central concern of the semanticist when he evaluates a speech?
6. Compare the questions the semanticist asks about a speech with those asked by the rhetorician. Is there any duplication or overlapping? Are the answers to the rhetorician's questions in any way dependent upon answers supplied by the semanticist?
7. What three fundamental facts about the working of language guide the semanticist's "quest"?
8. Explain in your own words the "highly sophisticated procedures" the semanticist employs in probing a speech.
9. What does Professor Lee mean when he says, "The nature of the symbolic process, making difficult the verification of any interpretation, will, of course, impose limits upon the semanticist's knowledge"?
10. State the central concern of the logician when he examines a speech. To what three subsidiary matters does he direct his attention? With what sort of "sentences" is he especially concerned?

11. Compare the central concern of the general semanticist with those of the semanticist and logician. In what way does the general semanticist supplement and extend their findings?
12. In your opinion, does the rhetorician, the semanticist, the logician, or the general semanticist ask the most significant questions concerning a speech? Or does good rhetorical criticism entail approaching an address from all four points of view?
13. Distinguish between the "verbal" and "non-verbal" levels—between "the worlds of the speakable and the un-speakable."
14. Select one of the speeches in this book and apply to it each of the four methods of criticism which Lee describes. Compare the results.
15. How do the aims of the critic of speaking, regardless of the approach he may use, differ fundamentally from the aims of the critic of literature, art, or music?

Speeches for analysis and ideas

1 / EDUCATION

The place and the price of excellence

JACQUES BARZUN

Jacques Barzun, author, scholar, lecturer, and editor, was born in Paris, France, in 1907, but came to the United States in 1920. In 1923 he entered Columbia University, where he received his A.B. and Ph.D. degrees and subsequently became a member of the faculty. He was appointed Professor of History in 1945 and is now Provost and Dean of Faculties at Columbia. Among his best-known works are *Teacher in America* (1945), *Berlioz and the Romantic Century* (1950), *God's Country and Mine* (1954), and *The House of Intellect* (1959).

Barzun delivered the following address before the third convocation of the Graduate School of Cornell University in December, 1958. The convocation was held in the Alice Statler Auditorium on the Cornell campus, the audience consisting of between five and six hundred graduate students and members of the faculty. Barzun was introduced by the Dean of the Graduate School, John W. McConnell. The program consisted simply of the Dean's welcome to the new students and faculty and Barzun's address.

Published in pamphlet form by Cornell University, the speech was widely distributed on campus. The impact was remarkable. For example, the undergraduate organizers of the Cornell United Religious Organizations Program chose Barzun's speech as the basis of a panel discussion for incoming freshmen in the fall of 1960. One faculty member was so moved that he wrote: "I can think of no speech made here in the last half-dozen years that has received such continuing attention and restudy by the University community."

When asked about his training as a public speaker, Barzun replied, "I've been speaking since birth!" His philosophy of effective speaking rests on the notion that one should be heard and understood. He thinks a speech for a large audience should be written out but read as if it were impromptu. For smaller gatherings he thinks the speaker should carefully prepare the order of topics and memorize the opening and closing remarks word for word, but should speak without a script and without notes.

Although there are many subjects in which I am sure you take an interest comparable to mine, I have chosen one which (as I hope) is particularly suited to your present concerns and also to the times. You are students, presumably engaged in studying; you are graduate students, who may soon become teachers; you are parents or shortly to become parents; you are citizens, whose votes and whose taxes are being, or are going to be, solicited in the name of education. I am accordingly going to talk to you about education—or so it would seem. But as I have often said, talk about education bores me, so under guise of education I am going to talk to you about Intellect, and Intellect of the kind that is rarest and most excellent. I am going to use the facts and the follies of education to talk to you about intellectual excellence. /1

The word *excellence* has a pleasing sound. But it has been a long time since we in the United States have heard it from anybody but an advertiser. We associate excellence with the products of industry, not only because we are told they are excellent, not only because the price we pay and the effort we make to obtain these artifacts seem to justify our hope of their excellence, but also and, I think, chiefly, because we are very sure that, being artifacts, those which are declared excellent will not incur the resentment of the others. /2

If this is true, it means that we are still very much alive to the idea that underlies excellence—the idea of excelling, of raising oneself so as to be better or greater than, or superior to, another. We are alive to this idea at large, but we do not like to apply it to persons. We suppress it in our social life and even in our private thoughts, because it seems to run counter to another idea that we cherish more stubbornly—the idea of equality. We find it repugnant

By permission of Dr. Barzun. From a reprint of his address issued by Cornell University.

to our political professions and our democratic manners that anyone should be believed in any way better or greater than someone else, should know himself to be, or should act as if he were in any way superior. /3

Very recently, however, a public report on the state of education, prepared for the Rockefeller Brothers' Fund and drafted under the direction of Mr. John Gardner, the head of the Carnegie Corporation, was issued with the title: "The Pursuit of Excellence." In the light of our ancient prejudice about the word, the use of that phrase seems to me to mark a turning point in the national opinion. /4

The phrase did not, of course, provoke the change. Rather, it confirmed the fact that the change was taking place. For the change is not merely in education, any more than it is a rediscovery of excellence in living beings after a long siege of confinement in dead things. To talk of excellence in connection with education is much more momentous than appears on the surface. For what does excellence in education or learning really refer to? It refers to Intellect. To talk of excellence in education means to talk of the place of Intellect in the national life. And this is almost unheard of. Education with us has been for every good purpose, I will not say, *except* an intellectual purpose, but every good purpose *ahead* of an intellectual purpose. It has been for character, citizenship, health, social and individual adjustment, cultural assimilation, vocational aid, profitable friendships, marriage opportunities, and hobbies of distinction. The desire to raise the Intellect to new heights has not existed or been avowed. And we are still far from according Intellect a clear place; the Rockefeller Brothers' report seems to speak of it as if it were the same as creativity, which it is not; but even creativity they want to have thrive "in a context of concern for all." This is hedging: clearly we do not quite know what Intellect is, and what we do know we are afraid of. But we have at last come face to face with the fact that Intellect exists, and we mean somehow to come to terms with it. /5

The general public today probably thinks that the present agitation about education and the training of talents dates from the Russian success in launching rockets. But that is not so. The unrest and criticism came well before. Some of you will remember the reports of the President's Commission on Higher Education, the vogue of the book *Why Johnny Can't Read,* the mounting protest against so-called progressive methods, and the repeated exposures of folly and futility in our colleges and teachers' colleges. These and other like events show that the unassuming citizen has in the last few years been acquiring a new and well founded worry. /6

Still earlier, there had been a good deal of quiet self-scrutiny by professionals, usually encouraged by the foundations. The phrase "gifted child" emerged from these inquiries. The two most notable were perhaps the experiment in Portland, Oregon, which put the brightest children of all grades in speedier classes, and the advanced placement plan of acceleration devised by three colleges and three leading private schools in the East. The result of these pointed attentions that are paid to intellectual talent and have regard to the flight of time has been to make the American people recognize the inadequacy of their schools. The schools are inadequate because they culpably neglect the national resource of Intellect. /7

But this growing recognition, important as it is, does not bring us the remedy. Mere speed for the gifted is not enough. Larger doses of science and mathematics and American history will not change the strength and character of the instruction. If the diet is poor, undernourishment is not cured by larger amounts. Most important, inadequate arrangements cannot be bettered by people who have never found anything wrong with them. To put it more generally, the country is only beginning to perceive that its schools are not independent of the surrounding world: the world of parents, legislators, businessmen, journalists, and government officials. It is their ideas that have so far prevailed—ideas we need not scorn entirely, for they have made good up to a point the adventure of mass education. In 1900 no one believed that the free, public, and compulsory high school could work. Well, it does not work very much or very well, but it works. Enough to be imitated, right now, by most of the countries of Europe, which are cheerfully repeating our early mistakes: our colleges and universities are also semi-mass institutions, remedial institutions for high school deficiencies; and to this Europe has not yet attained. *We* are at the point of farthest advance, and we are dissatisfied. Looking back on half a century of improvisation, we begin to see that some of our deepest convictions will have to change if our various schemes of improvement are to make a difference. /8

For the admitted evil—the inadequacy of school and college, in particular the wastefulness of the high school—is not one that can be removed by once more tinkering at the curriculum and patting a few gifted youths on the head. The notion of the gifted is true and useful, but it stops short of the response to Intellect which we must make if, hand in hand with the Rockefeller Brothers, we are not only to pursue excellence but occasionally to catch up with it. /9

At the moment, the gifted child stands in the public mind as an agreeable freak of nature, hitherto undervalued but well worth cultivating, indeed, almost as interesting as the retarded child. The two types balance each other like a pair of exotic vases on a mantelpiece. Both types, we think, are given us plainly marked by nature, fated to be what they are. This may be true of the retarded; I am sure it is not true about the gifted. Their discovery, to themselves and by others, is not inevitable: it depends on the presence or absence of an intellectual atmosphere, on the awareness and acceptance of Intellect as a force. One of the most unexpected results of the Portland experiment was that, after a few months of the accelerated program, *those not in the program began to do better work.* Another startling result was that some notorious problem children, when given harder work to do, became good citizens. They had been bored, of course, and they had set fire to wastebaskets in order to have something to occupy their minds. Surely, in the light of such facts, we cannot consider the gifted child a natural species, which only requires the good treatment of a well-run zoo. We must on the contrary regard Intellect as potentially present in many individuals, and therefore as a power to be brought forth by making the school a place where intellectual effort and achievement are regarded as normal and necessary. /10

In the opposite outlook, which is still strong, I detect a secret desire to go on protecting equality, that is to say, to continue muffling excellence by showing, as is easy to do, that "Intellect isn't everything," that "to be smart isn't an unmixed blessing." Both propositions are true, but what have they to do with a school or university? As well argue in an opera house that "singing isn't all of life," and that Mozart's lot was not one of unmixed blessings. The equalitarian tradition, misapplied to our educational institutions, is still so powerful that even in our present anxiety about places for the new generations in school and college, there lurks a hope that the strict measures being advocated may be only temporary. When our own rockets are cutting figure eights around the Russians', we can go back to quietly neglecting all normal, healthy, unintellectual American boys, and to lavishing expensive care on our true favorite, the slow mind. ·/11

You will not, I am sure, suspect me of wanting to deprive unfortunate boys and girls of the least help which lovingkindness bestows upon them. I dwell on their situation because the country dwells on it, and in so doing creates the contrast I want to make clear. As regards the mind, the American school or college is, generally speaking, not an educational, but a *philanthropic* institution. It tries to reduce competition and abolish failure; it is interested in the sociable personality rather than the powers of Intellect; above all, it wants to preserve its own brand of happiness, in which everyone can—indeed must—participate. The worthy effort to make the handicapped feel that they are not outcasts but fully accepted members of the group—that effort is matched by another, directed at the gifted, superior, perhaps eccentric person, and intended to assimilate him—literally to make him similar, to rub down his natural contours till he, too, is spherical and smooth, fit to serve as an interchangeable part in the social machine. /12

The proof that this characteristic effort of our schools springs from philanthropic feeling and not from hostility to special talents is that our schools and colleges make a great point of self-development and the diversity of aptitudes. Teachers are instructed to watch for individual differences and to let each student develop at his own pace. That is why the idea of intellectual competition has nearly disappeared, why in many places numerical grades have been replaced by verbal accounts written like psychological novelettes, why courses once taken and credited are good forever, regardless of evaporation, and why the word and the fact of failure are forbidden as scandalous and destructive. The ideal modern school, as we all know, is one in which contentment reigns because the young person is steadily pleased both with what he does and with the fact that others are pleased with him. /13

Now if we step from this little utopia to the training quarters of a successful athletic team, we find a very different state of affairs. The boys being trained are indeed the same that we encounter in any of a thousand classrooms in the country; but on the field their view of life is suddenly and radically altered. To begin with, a special seriousness pervades the atmosphere; the boys are not contented but visibly anxious. One feels the concentration of many strong wills on one object. There is little aimless action. Everyone takes advantage of the intervals of free time to jump, swing, flex the muscles, to practice throwing, catching, running. The coach and his assistants are as much interested as the classroom instructor in individual development, and they are keen watchers of diverse aptitudes. But they clearly have in mind for each individual a fixed idea of what constitutes performance. Far from letting each set his own pace, they hold him to a standard of their own choosing. If he does not meet it, he fails. Let me make the point clear: if he fails, he fails. There may be reasons for the failure, but no excuse, and certainly no consolation prizes and no verbalized psycho-apologies to the parents. On the contrary, I am told that the verbalizing of football coaches in moments of stress is far from apologetic. /14

The reason for this atmosphere of the training quarters is quite simple: the game is serious business. It engages the minds, hearts, and passions of all concerned, from coach to player to spectator. Training is therefore serious too. And when people are serious, no confusion is tolerated between performance and failure. No amount of desire to make up for the accidents of birth would induce anyone to give a slow-footed or slow-witted youth a place on a team. Our philanthropic, remedial impulses do not stretch quite so far. Indeed, we would consider any such tempering of the wind either corrupt or stupid, and we would sack the coach. When, on the contrary, one of his athletes is named to the All-American team, after the most solemn screening by the best official and unofficial judges in the country, all those interested are confident that they have witnessed from first to last the true way of discerning, developing, and rewarding excellence. /15

The comparison I have just drawn, obvious as it is, contains the lesson American parents and teachers must learn. They must not say: "Yes, yes, we know it." They must believe it and act on it; they must do this no matter how strange it feels to believe what you say when you speak about education. /16

What the lesson tells us in familiar, unmistakable steps is what the definition of excellence implies: excellence means excelling, which means exerting the will to improve on nature according to rule. To squeeze high performance out of native ability, stern demands must be made by the talented on themselves, but these demands must come ultimately from the world that desires and rewards the performance. /17

And yet, and yet . . . simple and persuasive as is this set of specifications, it is likely that something more has to be said before we are finally convinced. The contrast between classroom and playing field seems to accuse us too easily of being serious about games and frivolous about brains. Not all Americans are lifelong children enamored of sports. Not even all Europeans, whose sporting fever is by now worse than ours, have lost their senses. Why then do we hear of Europe's growing difficulty in maintaining intellectual standards—in their schools, universities, and professions? Since European attempts at mass education are much more recent than ours, we are forced to conclude that a connection exists between the neglect of intellectual excellence and the culture of a thoroughgoing democracy. /18

Ask anybody why it is right that tennis players should be weeded out by ruthless public competition and why it is also right that Johnny, who cannot spell, should merely be asked to try again a little harder. You will be told that the object of tennis championships is simply to discover winners, whereas democratic schools have complex goals, of which supremacy in spelling is not even one. Schools are to keep children out of mischief and out of the labor market; they are to give the young of the country a common experience and a sense of their opportunities. The most taxing business of the modern school is to take the native and the foreign, the poor and the well-to-do, and induct them into the maze of industrial life. The school's primary aims are thus social and vocational rather than intellectual. And properly so, because the home is no longer an educational institution. It is at school that children must learn about hygiene and safe driving, about the machinery of local government and the problems of adolescence. On top of this, the majority will want to learn shorthand and typewriting, home economics and the shop techniques known as industrial arts. What is now going on in the schools of Western Europe is a reminder of our own past, an explanation of the natural law that, under the pressure of numbers, public schools will turn from being seminaries of Intellect to being social centers for multiple "adjustments." /19

Since this is true and since what we learned of the nature and conditions of excellence is also true, we would seem to have reached a deadlock. Or rather, our present desire to exploit the national resources of Intellect has brought us to see that there is a need, there is a place, for two markedly different institutions under the one name School. I also include under it college and university. We cannot do without the type of school or college I have described as a social center for assimilation and vocational guidance, and it is a safe guess that we shall continue to have it. The question is whether we want the other kind, the intellectual institution, which must take for granted much that the first kind is meant to impart. In other words, Intellect is a special interest requiring a special apparatus, a special nursery, if you will, though one which, to be effective, must not look like an isolation ward. /20

There is in fact no reason why the two types of school should not exist side by side in the same building, or on the same campus; nor why boys and girls with an intellectual bent should not share certain classes with others and attend special ones of their own. According to the National Defense Education Act (Public Law 85-864), the country needs linguists. Now, good linguists start young, and learned ones need to know many languages, including Latin, which the sales manager and the agriculturist do not need. Why not, then, have the future linguists go to Latin class by themselves and join their friends, the farmer and businessman, in the government class? The way the president is elected and the principles of public hygiene are the same for all, whereas the concern with deponent verbs is not. /21

In theory and practice, then, the country's desire to see some of its young pursue intellectual excellence does not imply any new and invidious segregation. Such separation as must come is exactly like that required by the pursuit of athletic excellence. There is a training table reserved for the fit competitors and denied to the rest. No choice is imposed by force or privilege. Nature, taste, and sometimes family tradition dictate the path. /22

Fortunately for our intellectual renascence, separations on intellectual grounds already exist or survive in rudimentary form. Certain high schools are noted for their excellence in art or in science or in the academic program generally. They serve communities where these accomplishments are valued. Certain colleges are renowned for their faculty and for the atmosphere of Intellect and the tradition of excellence which they have sustained for generations, since a time before mass education. The position of these schools and colleges makes them the natural leaders and best models of the School as an institution designed to nurture Intellect. They are free from close legislative control, free to choose their staff and students, free from irrelevant demands by militant and misguided taxpayers. All they have to contend with is lack of money and interference by militant and misguided parents and alumni. And by and large, thanks to intelligent and courageous leadership, they have resisted these errors born of meddlesomeness out of cultural conformity. /23

But this ever-present threat from the naive champions of thoughtless social pressures brings us back to the central issue: what should the cultural temper be to foster excellence, what price must we pay—quite apart from fees and gifts to endowment—to provide the favoring conditions? /24

Please note that I speak of providing *the favoring conditions.* Excellence cannot be bought or even asked for. You cannot without absurdity tell the waiter to bring you "an excellent cup of coffee." You can only ask him for a cup and hope that when tasted it will prove to be excellent. Similarly, the desire for intellectual excellence must begin soberly with the simple desire to establish and maintain the conditions of good work. Well, up to a point there is no lack of that desire. Those in charge of education, and the public too, acknowledge the need for good equipment. Modern seats of learning can generally boast a superb physique. But this is evidently not enough, or we should not be at the critical juncture we are discussing here. No one has ever believed that the high quality of the training table was the sufficient cause of a winning team. /25

Nor in scholastic work is the cause exclusively good teachers. You can anticipate what I am about to say: the conditions that favor excellence cannot work singly. If we cannot have them all, we must at least have several, and these must be bound together by the atmosphere of concentrated effort and high seriousness which we saw in the training quarters, the discontent and the will to excel which we find wherever achievement is preferred to pious hopes. /26

Once established, that atmosphere is not difficult to sustain. What is hard is to begin. The world is still amazed at the remarkable outburst of great painters in the small towns of Renaissance Italy. A glance at the history shows that after a school had got under way, thanks to the coming together of two or three geniuses, talent sprang out of the ground and rushed to the masters' ateliers. The concentration of eager minds, the intensity of their rivalry, and the awareness of an enthusiastic public, raised otherwise ordinary gifts to a higher power, to excellence. Atmosphere did it. /27

If, therefore, I am to answer literally the question implied in my title, the place of excellence is wherever there is the least glimmer of consciousness about its nature and requirements. If we grant that the country's main discovery and training of Intellect—for science, art, and public life—can be carried on only in school and college, in certain dedicated schools and colleges, these places will be hampered and diminished if they are not surrounded by an atmosphere in which excellence is a familiar spirit. The home must, before all others, give it thought and room. How can a child or youth strive to excel in study, if his parents in their unguarded moments show their indifference to Intellect, books, ideas, science, art—in a word, to the mind of man? /28

In the second place, the school or college must be staffed by men who recognize intellect when they see it, in one another and in their students. There is nothing automatic about this. Many teachers respect industry, politeness, and even flattery, who would be quite taken aback by an encounter with Intellect. For the young Intellect who is laboring to excel is quite different from the grind and the apple polisher trying to impress or to please. The test of Intellect is that its interest is genuine. It is indeed often necessary for a student to pretend an interest he does not feel: he *has* to do twenty calculus problems or write a 3000-word essay. But if he is ever to be educated, there must come a time when the problems grip him like a detective story and when he chafes at the 3000-word limit because he has so much to say. /29

Intellect, in short, is a passion like any other. We who teach acknowledge this when we say of a student that he has at last caught fire. This is the very reason why the young Intellect must not be isolated. He must have others of his age similarly engrossed, or the fire will be that of the single stick—a spark, a bit of smoke, and then blackness. Nor is it enough for him to be encouraged at home and by the masters. The regular fellows, with palpable muscles and wearing the right kind of disreputable clothes, must also feel the nascent intellectual passions before any one youth—and by extension any school or college—can tread firmly and with characteristic zest on the path of excellence. /30

These being the geographical conditions, so to speak, what are the emotional costs? And first of all, do we, for the sake of Intellect have to give up, two centuries after Jefferson's *Declaration*, the doctrine of equality? A few weeks ago in *Time* magazine there appeared a report that a new college for science and engineering was being sponsored by a group of midwestern businessmen. Seeking excellence, they said in commenting on the new college, they were bound to confess their disbelief in equality. The doctrine was false and must be given up. /31

If correctly reported, the statement is a foolish one. Equality has nothing to do with merit, talent, or Intellect. Equality is a social and political assumption necessary to a certain form of government and congenial to the citizens of the United States. When we say that we are all equal, we mean precisely that the possession of wealth, or physical stature, or mental powers will make no difference in law and in manners. Equality in this sense is the result of a deliberate choice which requires self-control and aims at social simplicity. /32

Consequently, the discovery that men are not equal because one is tall and the other short, one stupid and the other bright, is irrelevant. Equality simply enjoins that these obvious differences shall make no difference in rights and privileges—it is the way a host treats his guests. You may say that Jefferson believed we were "created equal," not simply endowed with equal rights. True, but if by analogy with a parent we try to imagine the point of view of the Creator, we see at once that our individual differences of talent or merit simply do not matter. That, if anything, is the meaning of the Fatherhood of God—in essence, stripped of local attributes, we are equal, if only because any virtue or power we may boast of implies no other. And who can add up all our traits and reach a total to compare with others? We are therefore equal in being incommensurable. /33

By the same token, when society incurs expense to develop intellectual power in those capable of it, the cost does not include giving up the principle of equality. Even now, the physician's education costs perhaps ten times as much as anybody else's. We think, rightly, that he amply repays the social investment, and we know that his difference from the rest of us does not make him a member of a dangerous elite. /34

No, the emotional price we must pay for intellectual excellence is not the loss of social equality. It is a more personal and intimate loss, to which I alluded earlier in speaking of competition and in contrasting our present philanthropic schools with the educational ones we are beginning to desire. The price of excellence is the acceptance of pain, error, failure, even, I dare say, cruelty. This we are not used to. We love the young and want to see them happy and successful. We understand so well their confused feelings, their good intentions, their seemingly limitless possibilities of worth, that we instinctively avoid dwelling upon their shortcomings. When rules are set up to guide their development and the rule makes them stumble, we bend the rule. This is undoubtedly proper at their first entrance into the world of obligation and responsibility, but we carry it so far that the very idea of effort and the fundamental difference between doing and failing to do are lost, forgotten alike by the teacher and by the student and absolutely unsuspected by the parent. /35

The moral is plain. It is hard enough to say: you have not done what you should have done; you have wasted your many chances; we have both warned and aided you, and you have given nothing of yourself: therefore find you own way outside the path that leads to praise and glory, and perhaps to wealth and power. Still harder, and indeed cruel, is to say: you have tried your best, but you are not made for the life you have chosen. Nature denied you the eye, hand, and brain. /36

But I submit that there is a cruelty far greater than either of these, an easy, indolent, irresponsible cruelty, which is to see the young, with their bursting energies and hopes and ambitions, flounder for lack of that special encouragement which is called Difficulty; to see them grow up full of fresh intelligence but with an Intellect like a garden full of weeds; to see them so naively pleased with their own accomplishments that the first stern demand, too long postponed, must be a shattering blow; to see them so accustomed to their own pace that they do not suspect the deep layers of grit and mother-wit they hold within; to see them, finally, when well past college age, discover with shame and remorse what they might have been if, instead of being neglected like mongrels or incubated like sickly growths, they had been urged and pressed and compelled to perform to the limit of their talents. /37

It is therefore not for the sake of turning out more engineers than Russia, not to manufacture as many linguists as the State Department wants, not to provide the colleges with enough teachers, it is not even to enable the du Pont Company to hire more chemists and produce the ultimate plastic which shall be food, clothing, and shelter all in one—it is not for these imperative or alluring prospects that this country must radically change its attitude toward scholastic excellence: it is simply and solely to put an end to the cruel injustice of letting rot, through protracted cowardice masquerading as kindness, the unimaginable endowments of youth and the tradition of Intellect which is their birthright. /38

The speech

1. What is the central issue discussed in this speech? Where is it best stated?
2. What does Barzun mean by "excellence"? What specific passages make this meaning most clear? What method or methods of definition does Barzun use?
3. What relationship between himself and his audience does Barzun establish in the introduction? Show how it might be a useful relationship for his purpose.
4. Is the organization of this speech an example of the motivated sequence? Develop your answer by making a careful analysis of the pattern of the speech's organization.
5. Do you find Barzun's evidence too general to be convincing? Support your answer with specific references to the text.
6. Do you believe that the contrast between what happens in the classroom and what happens on the athletic field is a valid one? An appealing one? Give reasons for your answers.
7. Does Barzun weaken his attack on schools for being philanthropic organizations by admitting that under the pressure of numbers public schools will inevitably become "social centers for multiple 'adjustments' "? Explain.
8. Cite examples of irony, sarcasm, and analogy. What effect do these devices have upon the style of the speech?
9. What precisely would Barzun do with our educational system? Is it a weakness in the speech that he did not spell out a series of specific changes he would favor? Explain your answer.

For further study and discussion

1. How do you define excellence in education?
2. Is it undemocratic to put the superior students in special sections where they get more demanding assignments?
3. Was your high school more of a philanthropic institution than one devoted to the training of the intellect? In answering this question, cite particular courses and activities.
4. How much time were your teachers forced to spend upon matters not concerned with the training of the intellect? Be as exact and specific as you can.
5. Does your community look to the schools as sources for adult entertainment? If so, give examples.
6. To what extent would you say your college is a philanthropic institution as Barzun uses that term?
7. What courses are you now taking, if any, that offer only feeble training for the intellect? Do you believe they should be eliminated from the curriculum?
8. In your opinion does a strong program in athletics contribute to excellence in education?
9. What conditions do you think are essential to creating an atmosphere in which excellence in education is properly valued?
10. Do you agree that pain and failure are the inevitable price of the pursuit of excellence? Cite personal experience to support your answer.

Suggestions for further reading

Arthur E. Bestor, ***The Restoration of Learning*** (New York, 1955)

James B. Conant, ***The Child, the Parent, and the State*** (Cambridge, Mass., 1959)

———, ***The Revolutionary Transformation of the American High School*** (Cambridge, Mass., 1959)

George S. Counts, ***Education and American Civilization*** (New York, 1952)

Benjamin Fine, ***Democratic Education*** (New York, 1945)

Robert M. Hutchins, ***The Conflict in Education in a Democratic Society*** (New York, 1953)

Alonzo F. Myers, ***Education in a Democracy*** (New York, 1954)

H. G. Rickover, ***Education and Freedom*** (New York, 1959)

David Riesman, ***Constraint and Variety in American Education*** (Lincoln, Neb., 1956)

George Zook, ***The Role of the Federal Government in Education*** (Cambridge, Mass., 1945)

What every Yale freshman should know

EDMUND S. MORGAN

The following speech, delivered at Yale University before the entering freshman class in September 1959, is in effect the personal manifesto of a professional scholar. Edmund Sears Morgan (1916-) has spent virtually his entire life engaged in scholarly pursuits. He has taught at the Massachusetts Institute of Technology, the University of Chicago, Brown University, and since 1955 has been a professor of history at Yale. He has published numerous articles and books on early American history, among them *The Puritan Family* (1944), *Virginians at Home* (1952), *The Stamp Act Crisis*, with Helen M. Morgan (1953), *The Birth of the Republic* (1956), and *The Puritan Dilemma* (1958). He is a member of various learned societies and has edited many scholarly magazines.

The students who heard this speech, like other "Ivy League" students, were from the top 10 percent of their high school classes. After graduation many of them will pursue scholarly careers. They will find Yale encouraging this, for the "elite" schools have become increasingly academic in character and are less inclined now than formerly to regard themselves as social training grounds. The students at Yale, for example, have recently insti little faculty assistance) a program known as "Ch a colloquium whose aim is to "confront individu the crucial issues of today's world." This program, and staffed by Yale undergraduates, brings world-fa figures to the New Haven campus for speeches and discussions.

Edmund S. Morgan, "What Every Yale Freshman Should Know," *Saturday Review*, January 23, 1960, pp. 13-14. Reprinted by permission of the *Saturday Review*.

The world does not much like curiosity. The world says that curiosity killed the cat. The world dismisses curiosity by calling it idle, or *mere* idle, curiosity —even though curious persons are seldom idle. Parents do their best to extinguish curiosity in their children, because it makes life difficult to be faced every day with a string of unanswerable questions about what makes fire hot or why grass grows, or to have to halt junior's investigations before they end in explosion and sudden death. Children whose curiosity survives parental discipline and who manage to grow up before they blow up are invited to join the Yale faculty. Within the university they go on asking their questions and trying to find the answers. In the eyes of a scholar, that is mainly what a university is for. It is a place where the world's hostility to curiosity can be defied. **/1**

Some of the questions that scholars ask seem to the world to be scarcely worth asking, let alone answering. They ask about the behavior of protons, the dating of a Roman coin, the structure of a poem. They ask questions too minute and specialized for you and me to understand without years of explanation. **/2**

If the world inquires of one of them why he wants to know the answer to a particular question, he may say, especially if he is a scientist, that the answer will in some obscure way make possible a new machine or weapon or gadget. He talks that way because he knows that the world understands and respects utility and that it does not understand much else. But to his colleagues and to you he will probably not speak this language. You are now part of the university, and he will expect you to understand that he wants to know the answer simply because he does not know it, the way a mountain climber wants to climb a mountain simply because it is there. **/3**

Similarly a historian, when asked by outsiders why he studies history, may come out with a line of talk that he has learned to repeat on such occasions, something about knowledge of the past making it possible to understand the present and mold the future. I am sure you have all heard it at one time or another. But if you really want to know why a historian studies the past, the answer is much simpler: he wants to know about it because it is there. Something happened, and he would like to know what. /4

All this does not mean that the answers which scholars find to their questions have no consequences. They may have enormous consequences; they may completely alter the character of human life. But the consequences seldom form the reason for asking the questions or pursuing the answers. It is true that scholars can be put to work answering questions for the sake of the consequences, as thousands are working now, for example, in search of a cure for cancer. But this is not the primary function of the scholar. For the scholar the consequences are usually incidental to the satisfaction of curiosity. Even for the medical scholar, the desire to stamp out a dreaded disease may be a less powerful motive than the desire to find out about the nature of living matter. Similarly Einstein did not wish to create an atomic bomb or to harness atomic energy. He simply wanted to find out about energy and matter. /5

I said that curiosity was a dangerous quality. It is dangerous not only because of incidental effects like the atomic bomb but also because it is really nothing more or less than a desire for truth. For some reason this phrase sounds less dangerous than curiosity. In fact, the desire for truth sounds rather respectable. Since so many respectable people assure us that they have found the truth, it does not sound like a dangerous thing to look for. But it is. The search for it has again and again overturned institutions and beliefs of long standing, in science, in religion, and in politics. It is easy enough to see today that these past revolutions brought great benefits to mankind. It was less easy to see the benefits while the revolutions were taking place, especially if you happened to be quite satisfied with the way things were before. Similarly it is not always easy today to see that the satisfaction of a scholar's curiosity is worth the disruption of society that may result from it. The search for truth is, and always has been, a subversive activity. And scholars have learned that they cannot engage in it without an occasional fight. /6

You may therefore find them rather belligerent toward any threat to the free pursuit of curiosity. They are wary of committing themselves to institutions or beliefs that might impose limitations on them or deliver ready-made answers to their questions. You will find them suspicious of loyalty oaths, religious creeds, or affiliations with political parties. In particular they will try to preserve their university as a sanctuary within whose walls *any* question can be asked. /7

This wariness of commitment can sometimes degenerate into a scholarly vice, a vice that paralyzes curiosity instead of preserving it. A scholar at his worst sometimes seems to be simply a man who cannot make up his mind. Every classroom from here to Melbourne has echoed with the feeble phrases of academic indecision: "There are two schools of thought on this question, and the truth probably lies halfway between them." When you hear this sentence repeated, or when you are tempted to repeat it yourself, remember that the truth may lie between two extremes, but it assuredly does not lie halfway between right and wrong. Don't short-circuit your curiosity by assuming you have found the answer when you have only made a tidy list of possible answers. /8

Dedication to curiosity should not end in indecision. It should, in fact, mean willingness to follow the mind into difficult decisions. /9

A second quality that makes a scholar has no apparent relation to the first and yet is inseparably connected to it. It is a compulsion to communicate. A scholar is driven by a force as strong as his curiosity, that compels him to tell the world the things he has learned. He cannot rest with learning something: he has to tell about it. Scholarship begins in curiosity, but it ends in communication. And though scholars may in a university take refuge from the world, they also acknowledge responsibility to the world, the responsibility to communicate freely and fully everything that they discover within the walls of their sanctuary. The search for truth needs no justification, and when a man thinks he has found any part of it, he cannot and ought not to be silent. The world may sometimes not care to listen, but the scholar must keep telling it until he has succeeded in communicating. /10

Now, there are only two methods of communication for scholars, writing and speaking. The scholar publishes his discoveries in books and articles and he teaches them in the classroom. Sometimes one or the other method will satisfy him, but most of us feel the need for both. The scholar who merely writes books falls into the habit of speaking only to the experts. If he works at his subject long enough, he reaches the position where there is no one else quite expert enough to understand him, and he winds up writing to himself. On the other hand, if he writes not at all, he may become so enamored of his own voice that he ceases to be a scholar and becomes a mere showman. /11

Communication is not merely the desire and the responsibility of the scholar; it is his discipline, the proving ground where he tests his findings against criticism. Without communication his pursuit of truth withers into eccentricity. He necessarily spends much of his time alone, in the library or the laboratory, looking for the answers to his questions. But he needs to be rubbing constantly against other minds. He needs to be tested, probed, and pushed around. He needs to be made to explain himself. Only when he has expressed himself, only when he has communicated his thoughts, can he be sure that he is thinking clearly. /12

The scholar, in other words, needs company to keep him making sense. And in particular he needs the company of fresh minds, to whom he must explain things from the beginning. He needs people who will challenge him at every step, who will take nothing for granted. He needs, in short, you. /13

You may have various purposes in coming here, and you may fulfill them: you may play football or tennis or the trombone; you may sing in the glee club, act in plays, and act up on college weekends. But what the faculty expects of you is four years of scholarship, and they will be satisfied with nothing less. For four years we expect you to join us in the pursuit of truth, and we will demand of you the same things we demand of ourselves: curiosity and communication. /14

Curiosity, of course, is not something you get simply by wishing for it. But it is surprisingly contagious. The curiosity we expect is more than a passing interest. We will not be satisfied by your ability to ask an occasional bright question, nor yet by your assimilation of a lot of predigested information. The accumulation of information is a necessary part of scholarship, and unfortunately the part most likely to be tested on examinations, especially those wretched ones called "objective examinations" where the truth is always supposed to lie in answer space A, B, C, D, or E, but never apparently in X, Y, or Z. But the curiosity we expect of you cannot be satisfied by passing examinations or by memorizing other people's answers to other people's questions. We do not wish to put you through a mere course of mental gymnastics. We want you to be content with nothing less than the whole truth about the subject that interests you. Which means that we want you to be forever discontent with how little you know about it and with how little we know about it. We want you to back us into corners, show us up, make us confess we don't know. Does this sound formidable? It is not. We may tell you what we know with great assurance, but push us and you will find the gaps. /15

Follow your own minds into the gaps. Follow your minds where curiosity takes them. You will not get the whole truth, not about protons, not about the structure of a poem, not even about a Roman coin. Nobody does. But if you learn anything, it ought to change your minds, and hopefully it will change ours too. It will be a sign that we have both wasted four years if you leave here thinking pretty much the same way that you do now or if you leave us thinking the same way *we* do now. /16

We expect of you, then, that you will be curious for the truth. We also expect that you communicate whatever truth you find, and that you do it both in speech and in writing. Many people suppose that they know something if they can stammer out an approximation of what they mean in speech. They are mistaken. It is extremely unlikely that you have thought clearly if you cannot express yourself clearly, especially in writing. Writing is more than an instrument of communication. It is an instrument of thought. You should have acquired some competence in its use by now. I suspect from past experience that you have not. But even if you have, you have a great deal more to learn about it. And if you do not know much more about it four years from now, it will again be a sign that we have failed in part of our job, the job of making you communicate clearly. /17

Communication is a two-way process, and a university is a community of scholars, where questions are asked and the answers communicated, your answers to us, ours to you. For the next four years we will be engaged as scholars together in this community. After the four years are over, most of you will leave Yale, but if our community is a successful one, if we really do communicate with each other, I believe that you will continue to be in some sense scholars, asking new questions, looking for new answers, and communicating them to the world. /18

The speech

1. How would the fact that the speaker is a professor of history at Yale affect the audience's attitude toward this speech? Why is Professor Morgan wise in not resorting too explicitly to ethical proof?

2. How does Morgan define *curiosity? University?* Are there any other key terms that must be understood in order to follow the argument closely?
3. By what means does the speaker catch the audience's attention in his introduction? What means does he use throughout in an attempt to hold it?
4. How many main divisions are there in the speech, and where does each begin?
5. In what way does Morgan believe that communication is "inseparably connected" with curiosity?
6. In attacking indecision, is Morgan arguing that a scholar should not look at both sides of a question?
7. What precisely does Morgan want Yale freshmen to know? Besides knowing, is there anything he wants them to do? What for you seems to be the central idea of the speech? Where is it best stated?
8. Would you say that the style of the speech is conversational? Explain your answer.

For further study and discussion

1. How do you define a university? A scholar? A student?
2. How do you account for the nonscholar's preoccupation with practical results and his disdain for scholarship for its own sake?
3. Can any curiosity properly be called "idle curiosity"?
4. What in your experience tends most strongly to stifle curiosity? To encourage it?
5. How do writing and speaking contribute to the development of a scholar? Are there significant differences in what they contribute toward his development?
6. What is "wretched" about objective examinations? Are they really objective? What do they demand of the student, and what do they not demand?
7. Which is more likely to encourage the development of a lively curiosity, the discussion-type class or the lecture-type class? Give the reasons for your answer.
8. What means of satisfying his intellectual curiosity are readily available to the college undergraduate? In answering this, give examples to support your main points.

Suggestions for further reading

Margaret E. Bennett and Molly Lewin, **Getting the Most Out of College** (New York, 1957)

Otto Butz, ed., **The Unsilent Generation** (New York, 1958)

Roger H. Garrison, **The Adventure of Learning in College** (New York, 1957)

Philip E. Jacob, **Changing Values in College** (New York, 1957)

Burges Johnson, **Campus Versus Classroom** (New York, 1946)

Agatha Townsend, **College Freshmen Speak Out** (New York, 1956)

Elton Trueblood, **The Idea of College** (New York, 1959)

The American scholar

RALPH WALDO EMERSON

Ralph Waldo Emerson (1803-1882) was the leading figure in the Transcendentalist movement in America. Viewed as a religious demonstration, this movement was a revolt against the Unitarian Church and its teachings which rested on a fundamentally rational basis. In its liberalism the Unitarian Church had argued away hellfire and damnation; but it had also taken away much of the warmth and mysticism normally found in religion. What had started out as a rational alternative to the excesses of Calvinism ended up in the opinion of the Transcendentalists as a sterile formalism, which in turn encouraged a dangerous complacency. The chief contention of the Transcendentalists was that everything and everybody are part of a great unity which they variously called God, the Absolute, the Over-soul, and the First Cause. Man, they believed, had access to the Over-soul directly through this intuition (which Emerson called the Reason) and indirectly through nature, which was the great physical symbol of the Over-soul. Thus, instead of emphasizing the importance of the rational faculty, they emphasized the primacy of the intuition which provided those mystical contacts with the Over-soul.

Emerson came from a long line of Puritan and Unitarian clergymen. His father was the pastor of the First Unitarian Church of Boston. Emerson, in turn, also became a Unitarian minister; by 1829 he was sharing the pulpit of the Second Unitarian Church with Henry Ware, a dynamic preacher of the period. By 1832, just as he was beginning to be recognized as a success in the pulpit, he resigned from the ministry because he felt he could no longer conscientiously perform the sacrament of the Lord's Supper. He also claimed (at a later date) that "in order to be a good minister it was necessary to leave the ministry." The breach with the Unitarian Church became complete when in 1838 he said before the Harvard Divinity School that "the idioms of his [Jesus'] language and the figures of his rhetoric, have usurped the place of his truth; and churches are not built on his principles, but on his tropes. Christianity became a mythus, as the poetic teaching of Greece and of Egypt, before."

Because of his views he was labeled an infidel by Professor Andrews Norton of the Divinity School. More calumny was to follow. It was only years later that the epithets ceased as people realized his teaching lent itself to virtue rather than to vice. Also, younger clergymen, more favorable to his views, had ascended to many of the pulpits in Boston. In short, the revolt was in time assimilated.

The Transcendental movement was not confined solely to religion. With its insistence on self-reliance, it inevitably concerned itself with other matters as well. The literary and scholarly aspects of American life especially came under close scrutiny. Emerson's sharpest criticism of American failings in these areas came in the following speech entitled "The American Scholar," which was delivered before the Phi Beta Kappa Society at Cambridge on August 31, 1837.

The speech was hastily composed because Emerson had been called on to substitute for the Reverend Dr. Wainwright. In spite of the short notice, the speech is well developed because Emerson had been thinking about its theme for a number of years and was greatly concerned about the lack of literary output in America.

The audience consisted of 215 members of Phi Beta Kappa as well as invited guests, who gathered in the meeting house near Harvard Yard. The rest of the program consisted of a poem read by the Reverend William Parsons Lunt, a few selections by a band, and a prayer. Emerson took one hour and fifteen minutes to read his oration.

The reception was mixed. Ralph L. Rusk, Emerson's biographer, reports that John Pierce listened impatiently. He was struck by Emerson's "misty, dreamy, unintelligible style" and credited it to "Swedenborg, Coleridge, and Carlyle." Long afterwards, James Russell Lowell summarized the conflicting moods of the listeners by saying, "What crowded and breathless aisles, what windows clustering with eager heads, what enthusiasm of approval, what grim silence of foregone dissent!" He also called the address "our Yankee version of a lecture by Abélard." Oliver Wendell Holmes didn't care for the esoteric passages but later referred to the speech as "our intellectual Declaration of Independence."[1]

Mr. President and Gentlemen, I greet you on the recommencement of our literary year. Our anniversary is one of hope, and, perhaps, not enough of labor. We do not meet for games of strength or skill, for the recitation of histories, tragedies, and odes, like the ancient Greeks; for parliaments of love and poesy, like the Troubadours; nor for the advancement of science, like our contemporaries in the British and European capitals. Thus far, our holiday has been simply a friendly sign of the survival of the love of letters amongst a people too busy to give to letters any more. As such it is precious as the sign of an indestructible instinct. Perhaps the time is already come when it ought to be, and will be, something else; when the sluggard intellect of this continent will look from under its iron lids and fill the postponed expectation of the world with something better than the exertions of mechanical skill. Our day of independence, our long apprenticeship to the learning of other lands, draws to a close. The millions that around us are rushing into life, cannot always be fed on the sere remains of foreign harvests. Events, actions arise, that must be sung, that will sing themselves. Who can doubt that poetry will revive and lead in a new age, as the star in the constellation Harp, which now flames in our zenith, astronomers announce, shall one day be the pole-star for a thousand years? /1

In this hope I accept the topic which not only usage but the nature of our association seem to prescribe to this day,—the AMERICAN SCHOLAR. Year by year we come up hither to read one more chapter of his biography. Let us inquire what light new days and events have thrown on his character and his hopes. /2

It is one of those fables which out of an unknown antiquity convey an unlooked-for wisdom, that the gods, in the beginning, divided Man into men, that he might be more helpful to himself; just as the hand was divided into fingers, the better to answer its end. /3

The old fable covers a doctrine ever new and sublime; that there is One Man,—present to all particular men only partially, or through one faculty; and that you must take the whole society to find the whole man. Man is not a farmer, or a professor, or an engineer, but he is all. Man is priest, and scholar, and statesman, and producer, and soldier. In the *divided* or social state these functions are parcelled out to individuals, each of whom aims to do his stint of the joint work, whilst each other performs his. The fable implies that the individual, to possess himself, must sometimes return from his own labor to embrace all the other laborers. But, unfortunately, this original unit, this fountain of power, has been so distributed to multitudes, has been so minutely subdivided and peddled out, that it is spilled into drops, and cannot be gathered. The state of society is one in which the members have suffered amputation from the trunk, and strut about so many walking monsters,—a good finger, a neck, a stomach, an elbow, but never a man. /4

Man is thus metamorphosed into a thing, into many things. The planter, who is Man sent out into the field to gather food, is seldom cheered by any idea of the true dignity of his ministry. He sees his bushel and his cart, and nothing beyond, and sinks

[1] Ralph L. Rusk, *The Life of Ralph Waldo Emerson* (New York, 1949), pp. 262-266.

into the farmer, instead of Man on the farm. The tradesman scarcely ever gives an ideal worth to his work, but is ridden by the routine of his craft, and the soul is subject to dollars. The priest becomes a form; the attorney a statute-book; the mechanic a machine; the sailor a rope of the ship. /5

In this distribution of functions the scholar is the delegated intellect. In the right state he is *Man Thinking*. In the degenerate state, when the victim of society, he tends to become a mere thinker, or still worse, the parrot of other men's thinking. /6

In this view of him, as Man Thinking, the theory of his office is contained. Him Nature solicits with all her placid, all her monitory pictures; him the past instructs; him the future invites. Is not indeed every man a student, and do not all things exist for the student's behoof? And, finally, is not the true scholar the only true master? But the old oracle said, "All things have two handles: beware of the wrong one." In life, too often, the scholar errs with mankind and forfeits his privilege. Let us see him in his school, and consider him in reference to the main influences he receives. /7

I. The first in time and the first in importance of the influences upon the mind is that of nature. Every day, the sun; and, after the sunset, Night and her stars. Ever the winds blow; ever the grass grows. Every day, men and women, conversing, beholding and beholden. The scholar is he of all men whom this spectacle most engages. He must settle its value in his mind. What is nature to him? There is never a beginning, there is never an end, to the inexplicable continuity of this web of God, but always circular power returning into itself. Therein it resembles his own spirit, whose beginning, whose ending, he never can find,—so entire, so boundless. Far too as her splendors shine, system on system shooting like rays, upward, downward without centre, without circumference—in the mass and in the particle, Nature hastens to render account of herself to the mind. Classification begins. To the young mind every thing is individual, stands by itself. By and by, it finds how to join two things and see in them one nature; then three, then three thousand; and so, tyrannized over by its own unifying instinct, it goes on tying things together, diminishing anomalies, discovering roots running under ground whereby contrary and remote things cohere and flower out from one stem. It presently learns that since the dawn of history there has been a constant accumulation and classifying of facts. But what is classification but the perceiving that these objects are not chaotic, and are not foreign, but have a law which is also a law of the human mind? The astronomer discovers that geometry, a pure abstraction of the human mind, is the measure of planetary motion. The chemist finds proportions and intelligible method throughout matter; and science is nothing but the finding of analogy, identity, in the most remote parts. The ambitious soul sits down before each refractory fact; one after another reduces all strange constitutions, all new powers, to their class and their law, and goes on forever to animate the last fibre of organization, the outskirts of nature, by insight. /8

Thus to him, to this schoolboy under the bending dome of day, is suggested that he and it proceed from one root; one is leaf and one is flower; relation, sympathy, stirring in every vein. And what is that root? Is not that the soul of his soul? A thought too bold; a dream too wild. Yet when this spiritual light shall have revealed the law of more earthly natures, —when he has learned to worship the soul, and to see that the natural philosophy that now is, is only the first gropings of its gigantic hand, he shall look forward to an ever expanding knowledge as to a becoming creator. He shall see that nature is the opposite of the soul, answering to it part for part. One is seal and one is print. Its beauty is the beauty of his own mind. Its laws are the laws of his own mind. Nature then becomes to him the measure of his attainments. So much of nature as he is ignorant of, so much of his own mind does he not yet possess. And, in fine, the ancient precept, "Know thyself," and the modern precept, "Study nature," become at last one maxim. /9

II. The next great influence into the spirit of the scholar is the mind of the Past,—in whatever form, whether of literature, of art, of institutions, that mind is inscribed. Books are the best type of the influence of the past, and perhaps we shall get at the truth, —learn the amount of this influence more conveniently,—by considering their value alone. /10

The theory of books is noble. The scholar of the first age received into him the world around; brooded thereon; gave it the new arrangement of his own mind, and uttered it again. It came into him life; it went out from him truth. It came to him short-lived actions; it went out from him immortal thoughts. It came to him business; it went from him poetry. It was dead fact; now, it is quick thought. It can stand, and it can go. It now endures, it now flies, it now inspires. Precisely in proportion to the depth of mind from which it issued, so high does it soar, so long does it sing. /11

Or, I might say, it depends on how far the process had gone, of transmuting life into truth. In proportion to the completeness of the distillation, so will the purity and imperishableness of the product be. But none is quite perfect. As no air-pump can by any means make a perfect vacuum, so neither can any artist entirely exclude the conventional, the local, the perishable from his book, or write a book of pure thought, that shall be as efficient, in all respects, to a remote posterity, as to contemporaries, or rather to the second age. Each age, it is found, must write its own books; or rather, each generation for the next succeeding. The books of an older period will not fit this. /12

Yet hence arises a grave mischief. The sacredness which attaches to the act of creation, the act of thought, is transferred to the record. The poet chanting was felt to be a divine man: henceforth the chant is divine also. The writer was a just and wise spirit: henceforward it is settled the book is perfect; as love of the hero corrupts into worship of his statue. Instantly the book becomes noxious: the guide is a tyrant. The sluggish and perverted mind of the multitude, slow to open to the incursions of Reason, having once so opened, having once received this book, stands upon it, and makes an outcry if it is disparaged. Colleges are built on it. Books are written on it by thinkers, not by Man Thinking; by men of talent, that is, who start wrong, who set out from accepted dogmas, not from their own sight of principles. Meek young men grow up in libraries, believing it their duty to accept the views which Cicero, which Locke, which Bacon, have given; forgetful that Cicero, Locke, and Bacon were only young men in libraries when they wrote these books. /13

Hence, instead of Man Thinking, we have the bookworm. Hence the book-learned class, who value books, as such; not as related to nature and the human constitution, but as making a sort of Third Estate with the world and the soul. Hence the restorers of readings, the emendators, the bibliomaniacs of all degrees. /14

Books are the best of things, well used; abused, among the worst. What is the right use? What is the one end which all means go to effect? They are for nothing but to inspire. I had better never see a book than to be warped by its attraction clean out of my own orbit, and made a satellite instead of a system. The one thing in the world, of value, is the active soul. This every man is entitled to; this every man contains within him, although in almost all men obstructed, and as yet unborn. The soul active sees absolute truth and utters truth, or creates. In this action it is genius; not the privilege of here and there a favorite, but the sound estate of every man. In its essence it is progressive. The book, the college, the school of art, the institution of any kind, stop with some past utterance of genius. This is good, say they, —let us hold by this. They pin me down. They look backward and not forward. But genius looks forward: the eyes of man are set in his forehead, not in his hindhead: man hopes: genius creates. Whatever talents may be, if the man create not, the pure efflux of the Deity is not his;—cinders and smoke there may be, but not yet flame. There are creative manners, there are creative actions, and creative words; manners, actions, words, that is, indicative of no custom or authority, but springing spontaneous from the mind's own sense of good and fair. /15

On the other part, instead of being its own seer, let it receive from another mind its truth, though it were in torrents of light, without periods of solitude, inquest, and self-recovery, and a fatal disservice is done. Genius is always sufficiently the enemy of genius by over-influence. The literature of every nation bears me witness. The English dramatic poets have Shakespearized now for two hundred years. /16

Undoubtedly there is a right way of reading, so it be sternly subordinated. Man Thinking must not be subdued by his instruments. Books are for the scholar's idle times. When he can read God directly, the hour is too precious to be wasted in other men's transcripts of their readings. But when the intervals of darkness come, as come they must,—when the sun is hid and the stars withdraw their shining,—we repair to the lamps which were kindled by their ray, to guide our steps to the East again, where the dawn is. We hear, that we may speak. The Arabian proverb says, "A fig tree, looking on a fig tree, becometh fruitful." /17

It is remarkable, the character of the pleasure we derive from the best books. They impress us with the conviction that one nature wrote and the same reads. We read the verses of one of the great English poets, of Chaucer, of Marvell, of Dryden, with the most modern joy,—with a pleasure, I mean, which is in great part caused by the abstraction of all *time* from their verses. There is some awe mixed with the joy of our surprise, when this poet, who lived in some past world, two or three hundred years ago, says that which lies close to my own soul, that which I also had well-nigh thought and said. But for the evidence thence afforded to the philosophical doctrine of the identity of all minds, we should suppose some pre-established harmony, some foresight of souls that were to be, and some preparation of stores for their future wants, like the fact observed in insects, who lay up food before death for the young grub they shall never see. /18

I would not be hurried by any love of system, by any exaggeration of instincts, to underrate the Book. We all know, that as the human body can be nourished on any food, though it were boiled grass and the broth of shoes, so the human mind can be fed by any knowledge. And great and heroic men have existed who had almost no other information than by the printed page. I only would say that it needs a strong head to bear that diet. One must be an inventor to read well. As the proverb says, "He that would bring home the wealth of the Indies, must carry out the wealth of the Indies." There is then creative reading as well as creative writing. When the mind is braced by labor and inventions, the page of whatever book we read becomes luminous with manifold allusion. Every sentence is doubly significant, and the sense of our author is as broad as the world. We then see, what is always true, that as the seer's hour of vision is short and rare among heavy days and months, so is its record, perchance, the least part of his volume. The discerning will read, in his Plato or Shakespeare, only that least part,—only the authentic utterances of the oracle;—all the rest he rejects, were it never so many times Plato's and Shakespeare's. /19

Of course there is a portion of reading quite indispensable to a wise man. History and exact science he must learn by laborious reading. Colleges, in like manner, have their indispensable office,—to teach elements. But they can only highly serve us when they aim not to drill, but to create; when they gather from far every ray of various genius to their hospitable halls, and by the concentrated fires, set the hearts of their youth on flame. Thought and knowledge are natures in which apparatus and pretension avail nothing. Gowns and pecuniary foundations, though of towns of gold, can never countervail the least sentence or syllable of wit. Forget this, and our American colleges will recede in their public importance, whilst they grow richer every year. /20

III. There goes in the world a notion that the scholar should be a recluse, a valetudinarian,—as unfit for any handiwork, or public labor as a penknife for an axe. The so-called "practical men" sneer at speculative men, as if, because they speculate or *see*, they could do nothing. I have heard it said that the clergy,—who are always, more universally than any other class, the scholars of their day,—are addressed as women; that the rough, spontaneous conversation of men they do not hear, but only a mincing and diluted speech. They are often virtually disfranchised; and indeed there are advocates for their celibacy. As far as this is true of the studious classes, it is not just and wise. Action is with the scholar subordinate, but it is essential. Without it he is not yet man. Without it thought can never ripen into truth. Whilst the world hangs before the eye as a cloud of beauty, we cannot even see its beauty. Inaction is cowardice, but there can be no scholar without the heroic mind. The preamble of thought, the transition through which it passes from the unconscious to the conscious, is action. Only so much do I know, as I have lived. Instantly we know whose words are loaded with life, and whose not. /21

The world,—this shadow of the soul, or *other me*,—lies wide around. Its attractions are the keys which unlock my thoughts and make me acquainted with myself. I run eagerly into this resounding tumult. I grasp the hands of those next me, and take my place in the ring to suffer and to work, taught by an instinct that so shall the dumb abyss be vocal with speech. I pierce its order; I dissipate its fear; I dispose of it within the circuit of my expanding life. So much only of life as I know by experience, so much of the wilderness have I vanquished and planted, or so far have I extended my being, my dominion. I do not see how any man can afford, for the sake of his nerves and his nap, to spare any action in which he can partake. It is pearls and rubies to his discourse. Drudgery, calamity, exasperation, want, are instructors in eloquence and wisdom. The true scholar grudges every opportunity of action past by, as a loss of power. It is the raw material out of which the intellect moulds her splendid products. A strange process too, this by which experience is converted into thought, as a mulberry leaf is converted into satin. The manufacture goes forward at all hours. /22

The actions and events of our childhood and youth are now matters of calmest observation. They lie like fair pictures in the air. Not so with our recent actions,—with the business which we now have in hand. On this we are quite unable to speculate. Our affections as yet circulate through it. We no more feel or know it than we feel the feet, or the hand, or the brain of our body. The new deed is yet a part of life,—remains for a time immersed in our unconscious life. In some contemplative hour it detaches itself from the life like a ripe fruit, to become a thought of the mind. Instantly it is raised, transfigured; the corruptible has put on incorruption. Henceforth it is an object of beauty, however base its origin and neighborhood. Observe too the impossibility of antedating this act. In its grub state, it cannot fly, it cannot shine, it is a dull grub. But suddenly, without observation, the self-same thing unfurls beautiful wings, and is an angel of wisdom. So is there no fact, no event, in our private history, which shall not, sooner or later, lose its adhesive, inert form, and astonish us by soaring from our body into the empyrean. Cradle and infancy, school and playground, the fear of boys, and dogs, and ferules, the love of little maids and berries, and many another fact that once filled the whole sky, are gone already; friend and relative, profession and party, town and country, nation and world, must also soar and sing. /23

Of course, he who has put forth his total strength in fit actions has the richest return of wisdom. I will not shut myself out of this globe of action, and transplant an oak into a flower-pot, there to hunger and pine; nor trust the revenue of some single faculty, and exhaust one vein of thought, much like those Savoyards, who, getting their livelihood by carving shepherds, shepherdesses, and smoking Dutchmen, for all Europe, went out one day to the mountain to find stock, and discovered that they had whittled up the last of their pine trees. Authors we have, in numbers, who have written out their vein, and who, moved by a commendable prudence, sail for Greece or Palestine, follow the trapper into the prairie, or ramble round Algiers to replenish their merchantable stock. /24

If it were only for a vocabulary, the scholar would be covetous of action. Life is our dictionary. Years are well spent in country labors; in town; in the insight into trades and manufactures; in frank intercourse with many men and women; in science; in art; to the one end of mastering in all their facts a language by which to illustrate and embody our perceptions. I learn immediately from any speaker how much he has already lived, through the poverty or the splendor of his speech. Life lies behind us as the quarry from whence we get tiles and copestones for the masonry of to-day. This is the way to learn grammar. Colleges and books only copy the language which the field and the work-yard made. /25

But the final value of action, like that of books, and better than books, is that it is a resource. The great principle of Undulation in nature, that shows itself in the inspiring and expiring of the breath; in desire and satiety; in the ebb and flow of the sea; in day and night; in heat and cold; and, as yet more deeply ingrained in every atom and every fluid, is known to us under the name of Polarity,—these "fits of easy transmission and reflection," as Newton called them, are the law of nature because they are the law of spirit. /26

The mind now thinks, now acts, and each fit reproduces the other. When the artist has exhausted his materials, when the fancy no longer paints, when thoughts are no longer apprehended and books are a weariness,—he has always the resource *to live*. Character is higher than intellect. Thinking is the function. Living is the functionary. The stream retreats to its source. A great soul will be strong to live, as well as strong to think. Does he lack organ or medium to impart his truth? He can still fall back on this elemental force of living them. This is a total act. Thinking is a partial act. Let the grandeur of justice shine in his affairs. Let the beauty of affection cheer his lowly roof. Those "far from fame," who dwell and act with him, will feel the force of his constitution in the doings and passages of the day better than it can be measured by any public and designed display. Time shall teach him that the scholar loses no hour which the man lives. Herein he unfolds the sacred germ of his instinct, screened from influence. What is lost in seemliness is gained in strength. Not out of those on whom systems of education have exhausted their culture, comes the helpful giant to destroy the old or to build the new, but out of unhandselled savage nature; out of terrible Druids and Berserkers come at last Alfred and Shakespeare. /27

I hear therefore with joy whatever is beginning to be said of the dignity and necessity of labor to every citizen. There is virtue yet in the hoe and the spade, for learned as well as for unlearned hands. And labor is everywhere welcome; always we are invited to work; only be this limitation observed, that a man shall not for the sake of wider activity sacrifice any opinion to the popular judgments and modes of action. /28

I have now spoken of the education of the scholar by nature, by books, and by action. It remains to say somewhat of his duties. /29

They are such as become Man Thinking. They may all be comprised in self-trust. The office of the scholar is to cheer, to raise, and to guide men by showing them facts amidst appearances. He plies the slow, unhonored, and unpaid task of observation. Flamsteed and Herschel, in their glazed observatories, may catalogue the stars with the praise of all men, and the results being splendid and useful, honor is sure. But he, in his private observatory, cataloguing obscure and nebulous stars of the human mind, which as yet no man has thought of as such,—watching days and months sometimes for a few facts; correcting still his old records;—must relinquish display and immediate fame. In the long period of his preparation he must betray often an ignorance and shiftlessness in popular arts, incurring the disdain of the able who shoulder him aside. Long he must stammer in his speech; often forego the living for the dead. Worse yet, he must accept—how often!—poverty and solitude. For the ease and pleasure of treading the old road, accepting the fashions, the education, the religion of society, he takes the cross of making his own, and, of course, the self-accusation, the faint heart, the frequent uncertainty and loss of time, which are the nettles and tangling vines in the way of the self-relying and self-directed; and the state of virtual hostility in which he seems to stand to society, and especially to educated society. For all this loss and scorn, what offset? He is to find consolation in exercising the highest functions of human nature. He is one who raises himself from private considerations and breathes and lives on public and illustrious thoughts. He is the world's eye. He is the world's heart. He is to resist the vulgar prosperity that retrogrades ever to barbarism, by preserving and communicating heroic sentiments, noble biographies, melodious verse, and the conclusions of history. Whatsoever oracles the human heart, in all emergencies, in all solemn hours, has uttered as its commentary on the world of actions,—these he shall receive and impart. And whatsoever new verdict Reason from her inviolable seat pronounces on the passing men and events of to-day,—this he shall hear and promulgate. /30

These being his functions, it becomes him to feel all confidence in himself, and to defer never to the popular cry. He and he only knows the world. The world of any moment is the merest appearance. Some great decorum, some fetish of a government, some ephemeral trade, or war, or man, is cried up by half mankind and cried down by the other half, as if all depended on this particular up or down. The odds are that the whole question is not worth the poorest thought which the scholar has lost in listening to the controversy. Let him not quit his belief that a popgun is a popgun, though the ancient and honorable of the earth affirm it to be the crack of doom. In silence, in steadiness, in severe abstraction, let him hold by himself; add observation to observation, patient of neglect, patient of reproach, and bide his own time,—happy enough if he can satisfy himself alone that this day he has seen something truly. Success treads on every right step. For the instinct is sure, that prompts him to tell his brother what he thinks. He then learns that in going down into the secrets of his own mind he has descended into the secrets of all minds. He learns that he who has mastered any law in his private thoughts, is master to that extent of all men whose language he speaks, and of all into whose language his own can be translated. The poet, in utter solitude remembering his spontaneous thoughts and recording them, is found to have recorded that which men in crowded cities find true for them also. The orator distrusts at first the fitness of his frank confessions, his want of knowledge of the persons he addresses, until he finds that he is the complement of his hearers;—that they drink his words because he fulfils for them their own nature; the deeper he dives into his privatest, secretest presentiment, to his wonder he finds this is the most acceptable, most public, and universally true. The people delight in it; the better part of every man feels, This is my music; this is myself. /31

In self-trust all the virtues are comprehended. Free should the scholar be,—free and brave. Free even to the definition of freedom, "without any hindrance that does not arise out of his own constitution." Brave; for fear is a thing which a scholar by his very function puts behind him. Fear always springs from ignorance. It is a shame to him if his tranquility, amid dangerous times, arise from the presumption that like children and women his is a protected class; or if he seek a temporary peace by the diversion of his thoughts from politics or vexed questions, hiding his head like an ostrich in the flowering bushes, peeping into microscopes, and turning rhymes, as a boy whistles to keep his courage up. So is the danger a danger still; so is the fear worse. Manlike let him turn and face it. Let him look into its eye and search its nature, inspect its origin,—see the whelping of this lion,—which lies no great way back; he will then find in himself a perfect comprehension of its nature and extent; he will have made his hands meet on the other side, and can henceforth defy it and pass on superior. The world is his who can see through its pretension. What deafness, what stone-blind custom, what overgrown error you behold is there only by sufferance,—by your sufference. See it to be a lie, and you have already dealt it its mortal blow. /32

Yes, we are the cowed,—we the trustless. It is a mischievous notion that we are come late into nature; that the world was finished a long time ago. As the world was plastic and fluid in the hands of God, so it is ever to so much of his attributes as we bring to it. To ignorance and sin, it is flint. They adapt themselves to it as they may; but in proportion as a man has any thing in him divine, the firmament flows before him and takes his signet and form. Not he is great who can alter matter, but he who can alter my state of mind. They are the kings of the world who give the color of their present thought to all nature and all art, and persuade men by the cheerful serenity of their carrying the matter, that this thing which they do is the apple which the ages have desired to pluck, now at last ripe, and inviting nations to the harvest. The great man makes the great thing. Wherever Macdonald sits, there is the head of the table. Linnæus makes botany the most alluring of studies, and wins it from the farmer and the herb-woman; Davy, chemistry; and Cuvier, fossils. The day is always his who works in it with serenity and great aims. The unstable estimates of men crowd to him whose mind is filled with a truth, as the heaped waves of the Atlantic follow the moon. /33

For this self-trust, the reason is deeper than can be fathomed,—darker than can be enlightened. I might not carry with me the feeling of my audience in stating my own belief. But I have already shown the ground of my hope, in adverting to the doctrine that man is one. I believe man has been wronged; he has wronged himself. He has almost lost the light that can lead him back to his prerogatives. Men are become of no account. Men in history, men in the world of to-day, are bugs, are spawn, and are called "the mass" and "the herd." In a century, in a millennium, one or two men; that is to say, one or two approximations to the right state of every man. All the rest behold in the hero or the poet their own green and crude being,—ripened; yes, and are content to be less, so *that* may attain to its full stature. What a testimony, full of grandeur, full of pity, is borne to the demands of his own nature, by the poor clansman, the poor partisan, who rejoices in the glory of his chief. The poor and the low find some amends to their immense moral capacity, for their acquiescence in a political and social inferiority. They are content to be brushed like flies from the path of a great person, so that justice shall be done by him to that common nature which it is the dearest desire of all to see enlarged and glorified. They sun themselves in the great man's light, and feel it to be their own element. They cast the dignity of man from their downtrod selves upon the shoulders of a hero, and will perish to add one drop of blood to make that great heart beat, those giant sinews combat and conquer. He lives for us, and we live in him. /34

Men such as they are, very naturally seek money or power; and power because it is as good as money,—the "spoils," so called, "of office." And why not? for they aspire to the highest, and this, in their sleep-walking, they dream is highest. Wake them and they shall quit the false good and leap to the true, and leave governments to clerks and desks. This revolution is to be wrought by the gradual domestication of the idea of Culture. The main enterprise of the world for splendor, for extent, is the upbuilding of a man. Here are the materials strewn along the ground. The private life of one man shall be a more illustrious monarchy, more formidable to its enemy, more sweet and serene in its influence to its friend, than any kingdom in history. For a man, rightly viewed, comprehendeth the particular natures of all men. Each philosopher, each bard, each actor has only done for me, as by a delegate, what one day I can do for myself. The books which once we valued more than the apple of the eye, we have quite exhausted. What is that but saying that we have come up with the point of view which the universal mind took through the eyes of one scribe; we have been that man, and have passed on. First, one, then another, we drain all cisterns, and waxing greater by all these supplies, we crave a better and more abundant food. The man has never lived that can feed us ever. The human mind cannot be enshrined in a person who shall set a barrier on any one side to this unbounded, unboundable empire. It is one central fire, which, flaming now out of the lips of Etna, lightens the capes of Sicily, and now out of the throat of Vesuvius, illuminates the towers and vineyards of Naples. It is one light which beams out of a thousand stars. It is one soul which animates all men. /35

But I have dwelt perhaps tediously upon this abstraction of the Scholar. I ought not to delay longer to add what I have to say of nearer reference to the time and to this country. /36

Historically, there is thought to be a difference in the ideas which predominate over successive epochs, and there are data for marking the genius of the Classic, of the Romantic, and now of the Reflective or Philosophical age. With the views I have intimated of the oneness or the identity of the mind through all individuals, I do not much dwell on these differences. In fact, I believe each individual passes through all three. The boy is a Greek; the youth, romantic; the adult, reflective. I deny not, however, that a revolution in the leading idea may be distinctly enough traced. /37

Our age is bewailed as the age of Introversion. Must that needs be evil? We, it seems, are critical; we are embarrassed with second thoughts; we cannot enjoy any thing for hankering to know whereof the pleasure consists; we are lined with eyes; we see with our feet; the time is infected with Hamlet's unhappiness,—

"Sicklied o'er with the pale cast of thought."

It is so bad then? Sight is the last thing to be pitied. Would we be blind? Do we fear lest we should outsee nature and God, and drink truth dry? I look upon the discontent of the literary class as a mere announcement of the fact that they find themselves not in the state of mind of their fathers, and regret the coming state as untried; as a boy dreads the water before he has learned that he can swim. If there is any period one would desire to be born in, is it not the age of Revolution; when the old and the new stand side by side and admit of being compared; when the energies of all men are searched by fear and by hope; when the historic glories of the old can be compensated by the rich possibilities of the new era? This time, like all times, is a very good one, if we but know what to do with it. /38

I read with some joy of the auspicious signs of the coming days, as they glimmer already through poetry and art, through philosophy and science, through church and state. /39

One of these signs is the fact that the same movement which effected the elevation of what was called the lowest class in the state, assumed in literature a very marked and as benign an aspect. Instead of the sublime and beautiful, the near, the low, the common, was explored and poetized. That which had been negligently trodden under foot by those who were harnessing and provisioning themselves for long journeys into far countries, is suddenly found to be richer than all foreign parts. The literature of the poor, the feelings of the child, the philosophy of the street, the meaning of household life, are the topics of the time. It is a great stride. It is a sign—is it not?—of new vigor when the extremities are made active, when currents of warm life run into the hands and the feet. I ask not for the great, the remote, the romantic; what is doing in Italy or Arabia; what is Greek art, or Provençal minstrelsy; I embrace the common, I explore and sit at the feet of the familiar, the low. Give me insight into to-day, and you may have the antique and future worlds. What would we really know the meaning of? The meal in the firkin; the milk in the pan; the ballad in the street; the news of the boat; the glance of the eye; the form and the gait of the body;—show me the ultimate reason of these matters; show me the sublime presence of the highest spiritual cause lurking, as always it does lurk, in these suburbs and extremities of nature; let me see every trifle bristling with the polarity that ranges it instantly on an eternal law; and the shop, the plough, and the ledger referred to the like cause by which light undulates and poets sing; —and the world lies no longer a dull miscellany and lumber room, but has form and order; there is no trifle, there is no puzzle, but one design unites and animates the farthest pinnacle and the lowest trench. /40

This idea has inspired the genius of Goldsmith, Burns, Cowper, and in a newer time, of Goethe, Wordsworth, and Carlyle. This idea they have differently followed and with various success. In contrast with their writing, the style of Pope, of Johnson, of Gibbon, looks cold and pedantic. This writing is blood-warm. Man is surprised to find that things near are not less beautiful and wondrous than things remote. The near explains the far. The drop is a small ocean. A man is related to all nature. This perception of the worth of the vulgar is fruitful in discoveries, Goethe, in this very thing the most modern of the moderns, has shown us, as none ever did, the genius of the ancients. /41

There is one man of genius who has done much for this philosophy of life, whose literary value has never yet been rightly estimated;—I mean Emanuel Swedenborg. The most imaginative of men, yet writing with the precision of a mathematician, he endeavored to engraft a purely philosophical Ethics on the popular Christianity of his time. Such an attempt of course must have difficulty which no genius could surmount. But he saw and showed the connection between nature and the affections of the soul. He pierced the emblematic or spiritual character of the visible, audible, tangible world. Especially did his shade-loving muse hover over and interpret the lower parts of nature; he showed the mysterious bond that allies moral evil to the foul material forms, and has given in epical parables a theory of insanity, of beasts, of unclean and fearful things. /42

Another sign of our times, also marked by an analogous political movement, is the new importance given to the single person. Every thing that tends to insulate the individual,—to surround him with barriers of natural respect, so that each man shall feel the world is his, and man shall treat with man as a sovereign state with a sovereign state,—tends to true union as well as greatness. "I learned," said the melancholy Pestalozzi, "that no man in God's wide earth is either willing or able to help any other man." Help must come from the bosom alone. The scholar is that man who must take up into himself all the ability of the time, all the contributions of the past, all the hopes of the future. He must be an university of knowledges. If there be one lesson more than another which should pierce his ear, it is, The world is nothing, the man is all; in yourself is the law of all nature, and you know not yet how a globule of sap ascends; in yourself slumbers the whole of Reason; it is for you to know all; it is for you to dare all. Mr. President and Gentlemen, this confidence in the unsearched might of man belongs, by all motives, by all prophecy, by all preparation, to the American Scholar. We have listened too long to the courtly muses of Europe. The spirit of the American freeman is already suspected to be timid, imitative, tame. Public and private avarice make the air we breathe thick and fat. The scholar is decent, indolent, complaisant. See already the tragic consequence. The mind of this country, taught to aim at low objects, eats upon itself. There is no work for any but the decorous and the complaisant. Young men of the fairest promise, who begin life upon our shores, inflated by the mountain winds, shined upon by all the stars of God, find the earth below not in unison with these, but are hindered from action by the disgust which the principles on which business is managed inspire, and turn drudges, or die of disgust, some of them suicides. What is the remedy? They did not yet see, and thousands of young men as hopeful now crowding to the barriers for the career do not yet see, that if the single man plant himself indomitably on his instincts, and there abide, the huge world will come round to him. Patience,—patience; with the shades of all the good and great for company; and for solace the perspective of your own infinite life; and for work the study and the communication of principles, the making those instincts prevalent, the conversion of the world. Is it not the chief disgrace in the world, not to be an unit;—not to be reckoned one character;—not to yield that peculiar fruit which man was created to bear, but to be reckoned in the gross, in the hundred, or the thousand, of the party, the section, to which we belong; and our opinion predicted geographically, as the north, or the south? Not so, brothers and friends,—please God, ours shall not be so. We will walk on our own feet; we will work with our own hands; we will speak our own minds. The study of letters shall be no longer a name for pity, for doubt, and for sensual indulgence. The dread of man and the love of man shall be a wall of defence and a wreath of joy around all. A nation of men will for the first time exist, because each believes himself inspired by the Divine Soul which also inspires all men. /43

The speech

1. What is the essential difference for Emerson between the thinker and Man Thinking?
2. What are the three important influences on the scholar? Would you say that Emerson discusses them in what for him is an ascending order? Give the reasons for your answer.
3. Explicate the statement: "In self-trust all the virtues are comprehended." What for Emerson is one really trusting when one trusts the "self"? Show how the whole argument depends upon the assumption that the source of man's power lies within the self.
4. What does Emerson find auspicious about the signs of the times? How do these auspicious circumstances reflect what Emerson believes to be a growing trust in the individual self?
5. Emerson has often been accused of delivering provocative but disorganized lectures. Is this one disorganized? If not, show what its organization is. If so, suggest a more coherent organization.
6. It is said that in his lectures Emerson seldom argued but only asserted his position. Is this true of "The American Scholar"? Find illustrations to support your answer.
7. What kind of proof or amplification is Emerson using in paragraph 13 to support the conclusions he draws in paragraph 14? Is this proof by reasoning? Suggestion?
8. By many Emerson was thought to speak at an inordinately high level of abstraction. Do you find this to be true of "The American Scholar"? Select two or three typical paragraphs and analyze them for their level of abstractness—or concreteness.
9. Emerson felt that we should not listen or read for systematized ideas but for isolated ideas that excite us to fresh vision. Show how he accommodates his own style to this theory.
10. In paragraph 31 Emerson describes what he believes to be the difference between the way a poet serves humankind and the way a public speaker serves them. Why do you agree or disagree with his description? It has been said that the passage of this paragraph beginning "The orator distrusts. . ." and ending "This is my music; this is myself" is a description of Emerson's personal experience when he lectured to audiences across the country. Can you find evidence that he may have had this kind of feeling when he delivered this lecture?

For further study and discussion

1. Define Transcendentalism, and tell how much of a Transcendentalist you are.
2. How do you account for the rise of Transcendentalism in this country? For its decline?
3. What do you believe is valuable in the study of history? To what extent can it help us to handle the present and to prepare for the future?
4. How do books serve you? Classify them according to their function in your intellectual development.

5. Do you consider yourself a student or a man studying? Develop your answer with examples.
6. David Riesman has said that whereas ours is an other-directed society, Emerson's was an inner-directed one (i.e., we get our values from listening to others; he got his values from reflection and contemplation). What are the advantages and disadvantages of each process? Which of the two is in your opinion superior?
7. To what extent do you find among your classmates the kind of scholar Emerson describes? Among the faculty?
8. What do you consider to be the chief functions of scholars in our modern society? Do you find that many of them fail to perform these functions adequately? If so, wherein does the fault lie?

Suggestions for further reading

Isaiah Bowman, ***A Design for Scholarship*** (Baltimore, 1936)
A. Whitney Griswold, ***In the University Tradition*** (New Haven, 1957)
Karl Jaspers, ***The Idea of the University*** (Boston, 1959)
Jose Ortega y Gasset, ***Mission of the University*** (Princeton, 1944)
Mark Van Doren, ***Liberal Education*** (New York, 1943)
Alfred North Whitehead, ***The Aims of Education and Other Essays*** (New York, 1929)

2/ THE ARTS

What is a classic?

T. S. ELIOT

Thomas Stearns Eliot (1888-   ) is considered by many to be the greatest living poet writing in the English language —and one of the greatest critics. He is a disciplinarian in his writing, believing in a controlled intelligence that can be molded according to the critical dicta he holds. Although there is emotion in his writings, it lies beneath the surface and is always subordinated to intellect. Starting out as a nonbeliever in religion, in 1928 he became an Anglo-Catholic, an event that had a strong effect on his poetry. Before his conversion, his works were an expression of the vacuity and sterility of a society without conviction or hope; his later work, however, has shown a belief in traditional religious values.

George R. Hamilton has said of Eliot:

"The poetry is inspired, not by people, but by the interplay of current ideas with traditional ideas, ways of thinking and feeling stored up in the written word. It rests on a background of wide personal reading, which extends to classics and religious works of many times and countries. The method is commonly to use the traditional ideas as a scaffolding, and actual terms or phrases are taken up into the fabric of the new building. The architecture, especially in the earlier work, tends to be an architecture of fragments; yet a whole is built up with calculated and severe economy, the syntax being oversimplified and relying on power of phrase, instead of a natural and varied structure of the parts of speech. It is highly allusive poetry and demands patient study."[1]

As a critic Eliot has been largely responsible for the present-day conviction that criticism should be an analytic study of esthetic values. He has insisted upon sense rather than sound and has roundly attacked what he has considered to be the vague sentiment and overblown rhetoric of the critics of the nineteenth century. One may properly say, therefore, that he has brought rationalism back into English criticism. As in poetry, his influence in criticism has been enormous. Largely as a result of his writing, most of us have come to value the Elizabethan poets more highly and to view with special favor the deliberately molded lines of writers like Donne, Dryden, and Pope. Conversely, we have come to see somewhat less value in Milton and in such nineteenth-century writers as Keats, Shelley, Byron, and Browning. Through Eliot, too, we have come once more to realize the remarkable achievements of a classical poet like Virgil.

Works of T. S. Eliot include: *The Use of Poetry* (1933), *After Strange Gods* (1934), *Murder in the Cathedral* (1935), *Collected Poems* (1936), *The Family Reunion* (1939), *The Idea of a Christian Society* (1939), *Practical Cats* (1939), *Four Quartets* (1944), *Notes Towards a Definition of Culture* (1948), *The Cocktail Party* (1950), *Poetry and Drama* (1951), *Selected Essays* (1951), *The Confidential Clerk* (1954), *The Cultivation of Christmas Trees* (1956), *On Poetry and Poets* (1957), and *The Elder Statesman* (1959). Eliot won the Nobel Prize for Literature in 1948.

In conversation Eliot's voice has been characterized as "both rich and dry, mellow and rasping." He has been described as "Tall, gaunt, with stooped, self-deprecating shoulders . . . [looking like] a trapped, graceful, long-legged bird."[2]

The following speech "What Is a Classic?" was the Presidential Address to the Virgil Society, October 16, 1944, a British organization of which Eliot was the first president.

The subject which I have taken is simply the question: "What is a classic?" It is not a new question. There is, for instance, a famous essay by Ste. Beuve with this title. The pertinence of asking this question, with Virgil particularly in mind, is obvious: whatever the definition we arrive at, it cannot be one which excludes Virgil—we may say confidently that it must be one which will expressly reckon with him. But before I go farther, I should like to dispose of

[1] George Rostrevor Hamilton, *The Tell-Tale Article* (New York, 1950), p. 84.

[2] Harvey Breit, "An Unconfidential Close-up of T. S. Eliot," *New York Times Magazine*, February 7, 1954, p. 16.

certain prejudices and anticipate certain misunderstandings. I do not aim to supersede, or to outlaw, any use of the word "classic" which precedent has made permissible. The word has, and will continue to have, several meanings in several contexts: I am concerned with one meaning in one context. In defining the term in this way, I do not bind myself, for the future, not to use the term in any of the other ways in which it has been used. If, for instance, I am discovered on some future occasion, in writing, in public speech, or in conversation, to be using the word "classic" merely to mean a "standard author" in any language—using it merely as an indication of the greatness, or of the permanence and importance of a writer in his own field, as when we speak of *The Fifth Form at St. Dominic's* as a classic of schoolboy fiction, or *Handley Cross* as a classic of the hunting field—no one should expect one to apologize. And there is a very interesting book called *A Guide to the Classics,* which tells you how to pick the Derby winner. On other occasions, I permit myself to mean by "the classics," either Latin and Greek literature *in toto,* or the greatest authors of those languages, as the context indicates. And, finally, I think that the account of the classic which I propose to give here should remove it from the area of the antithesis between "classic" and "romantic"—a pair of terms belonging to literary politics, and therefore arousing winds of passion which I ask Aeolus, on this occasion, to contain in the bag. /1

This leads me to my next point. By the terms of the classic-romantic controversy, to call any work of art "classical," implies either the highest praise or the most contemptuous abuse, according to the party to which one belongs. It implies certain particular merits or faults: either the perfection of form, or the absolute zero of frigidity. But I want to define one kind of art, and am not concerned that it is absolutely and in every respect *better* or *worse* than another kind. I shall enumerate certain qualities which I should expect the classic to display. But I do not say that, if a literature is to be a great literature, it must have any one author, or any one period, in which all these qualities are manifested. If, as I think, they are all to be found in Virgil, that is not to assert that he is the greatest poet who ever wrote—such an assertion about any poet seems to me meaningless—and it is certainly not to assert that Latin literature is greater than any other literature. We need not consider it as a defect of any literature, if no one author, or no one period, is completely classical; or if, as is true of English literature, the period which most nearly fills the classical definition is not the greatest. I think that those literatures, of which English is one of the most eminent, in which the classical qualities are scattered between various authors and several periods, may well be the richer. Every language has its own resources, and its own limitations. The conditions of a language, and the conditions of the history of the people who speak it, may put out of question the expectation of a classical period, or a classical author. That is not in itself any more a matter for regret than it is for gratulation. It did happen that the history of Rome was such, the character of the Latin language was such, that at a certain moment a uniquely classical poet was possible: though we must remember that it needed that particular poet, and a lifetime of labour on the part of that poet, to make the classic out of his material. And, of course, Virgil couldn't know that *that* was what he was doing. He was, if any poet ever was, acutely aware of what he was trying to do: the one thing he couldn't aim at, or know that he was doing, was to compose a classic: for it is only by hindsight, and in historical perspective, that a classic can be known as such. /2

If there is one word on which we can fix, which will suggest the maximum of what I mean by the term "a classic," it is the word *maturity.* I shall distinguish between the universal classic, like Virgil, and the classic which is only such in relation to the other literature in its own language, or according to the view of life of a particular period. A classic can only occur when a civilization is mature; when a language and a literature are mature; and it must be the work of a mature mind. It is the importance of that civilization and of that language, as well as the comprehensiveness of the mind of the individual poet, which gives the universality. To define *maturity* without assuming that the hearer already knows what it means, is almost impossible: let us say then, that if we are properly mature, as well as educated persons, we can recognize maturity in a civilization and in a literature, as we do in the other human beings whom we encounter. To make the meaning of maturity really apprehensible—indeed, even to make it acceptable—to the immature, is perhaps impossible. But if we are mature we either recognize maturity immediately, or come to know it on more intimate acquaintance. No reader of Shakespeare, for instance, can fail to recognize, increasingly as he himself grows up, the gradual ripening of Shakespeare's mind: even a less developed reader can perceive the rapid development of Elizabethan literature and drama as a whole, from early Tudor crudity to the plays of Shakespeare, and perceive a decline in the work of

Shakespeare's successors. We can also observe, upon a little conversance, that the plays of Christopher Marlowe exhibit a greater maturity of mind and of style than the plays which Shakespeare wrote at the same age: it is interesting to speculate whether, if Marlowe had lived as long as Shakespeare, his development would have continued at the same pace. I doubt it: for we observe some minds maturing earlier than others, and we observe that those which mature very early do not always develop very far. I raise this point as a reminder, first that the value of maturity depends upon the value of that which matures, and second, that we should know when we are concerned with the maturity of individual writers, and when with the relative maturity of literary periods. A writer who individually has a more mature mind may belong to a less mature period than another, so that in that respect his work will be less mature. The maturity of a literature is the reflection of that of the society in which it is produced: an individual author—notably Shakespeare and Virgil—can do much to develop his language: but he cannot bring that language to maturity unless the work of his predecessors has prepared it for his final touch. A mature literature, therefore, has a history behind it: a history, that is not merely a chronicle, an accumulation of manuscripts and writings of this kind and that, but an ordered though unconscious progress of a language to realize its own potentialities within its own limitations. /3

It is to be observed, that a society, and a literature, like an individual human being, do not necessarily mature equally and concurrently in every respect. The precocious child is often, in some obvious ways, childish for his age in comparison with ordinary children. Is there any one period of English literature to which we can point as being fully mature, comprehensively and in equilibrium? I do not think so: and, as I shall repeat later, I hope it is not so. We cannot say that any individual poet in English has in the course of his life become a more mature man than Shakespeare: we cannot even say that any poet has done so much, to make the English language capable of expressing the most subtle thought or the most refined shades of feeling. Yet we cannot but feel that a play like Congreve's *Way of the World* is in some way more mature than any play of Shakespeare's: but only in this respect, that it reflects a more mature society—that is, it reflects a greater maturity of *manners.* The society for which Congreve wrote was, from our point of view, coarse and brutal enough: yet it is nearer to ours than the society of the Tudors: perhaps for that reason we judge it the more severely. Nevertheless, it was a society more polished and less provincial: its mind was shallower, its sensibility more restricted; it has lost some promise of maturity but realized another. So to maturity of *mind* we must add maturity of *manners.* /4

The progress towards maturity of language is, I think, more easily recognized and more readily acknowledged in the development of prose, than in that of poetry. In considering prose we are less distracted by individual differences in greatness, and more inclined to demand approximation towards a common standard, a common vocabulary and a common sentence structure: it is often, in fact, the prose which departs the farthest from these common standards, which is individual to the extreme, that we are apt to denominate "poetic prose." At a time when England had already accomplished miracles in poetry, her prose was relatively immature, developed sufficiently for certain purposes but not for others: at that same time, when the French language had given little promise of poetry as great as that in English, French prose was much more mature than English prose. You have only to compare any Tudor writer with Montaigne—and Montaigne himself, as a stylist, is only a precursor, his style not ripe enough to fulfil the French requirements for the classic. Our prose was ready for some tasks before it could cope with others: a Malory could come long before a Hooker, a Hooker before a Hobbes, and a Hobbes before an Addison. Whatever difficulties we have in applying this standard to poetry, it is possible to see that the development of a classic prose is the development towards a *common style.* By this I do not mean that the best writers are indistinguishable from each other. The essential and characteristic differences remain: it is not that the differences are less, but that they are more subtle and refined. To a sensitive palate the difference between the prose of Addison and that of Swift will be as marked as the difference between two vintage wines to a connoisseur. What we find, in a period of classic prose, is not a mere common convention of writing, like the common style of newspaper leader writers, but a community of taste. The age which precedes a classic age, may exhibit both eccentricity and monotony: monotony because the resources of the language have not yet been explored, and eccentricity because there is yet no generally accepted standard—if, indeed, that can be called eccentric where there is no centre. Its writing may be at the same time pedantic and licentious. The age following a classic age, may also exhibit eccentricity and monotony: monotony because the resources of the language have, for the time at least, been exhausted, and eccentricity because originality comes to be more valued than correctness. But the age in which we find a common style, will be an age when society has achieved a moment of order and stability, of equilibrium and harmony; as the age which manifests the greatest extremes of individual style will be an age of immaturity or an age of senility. /5

Maturity of language may naturally be expected to accompany maturity of mind and manners. We may expect the language to approach maturity at the moment when men have a critical sense of the past, a confidence in the present, and no conscious doubt of the future. In literature, this means that the poet is aware of his predecessors, and that we are aware of the predecessors behind his work, as we may be aware of ancestral traits in a person who is at the same time individual and unique. The predecessors should be themselves great and honoured: but their accomplishment must be such as to suggest still undeveloped resources of the language, and not such as to oppress the younger writers with the fear that everything that can be done has been done, in their language. The poet, certainly, in a mature age, may still obtain stimulus from the hope of doing something that his predecessors have not done; he may even be in revolt against them, as a promising adolescent may revolt against the beliefs, the habits and the manners of his parents; but, in retrospect, we can see that he is also the continuer of their traditions, that he preserves essential family characteristics, and that his difference of behaviour is a difference in the circumstances of another age. And, on the other hand, just as we sometimes observe men whose lives are overshadowed by the fame of a father or grandfather, men of whom any achievement of which they are capable appears comparatively insignificant, so a late age of poetry may be consciously impotent to compete with its distinguished ancestry. We meet poets of this kind at the end of any age, poets with a sense of the past only, or alternatively, poets whose hope of the future is founded upon the attempt to renounce the past. The persistence of literary creativeness in any people, accordingly, consists in the maintenance of an unconscious balance between tradition in the larger sense—the collective personality, so to speak, realized in the literature of the past—and the originality of the living generation. /6

We cannot call the literature of the Elizabethan period, great as it is, wholly mature: we cannot call it classical. No close parallel can be drawn between the development of Greek and Latin literature, for Latin had Greek behind it; still less can we draw a parallel between these and any modern literature, for modern literatures have both Latin and Greek behind them. In the Renaissance there is an early semblance of maturity, which is borrowed from antiquity. We are aware of approaching nearer to maturity with Milton. Milton was in a better position to have a critical sense of the past—of a past in English literature—than his great predecessors. To read Milton is to be confirmed in respect for the genius of Spenser, and in gratitude to Spenser for having contributed towards making the verse of Milton possible. Yet the style of Milton is not a classic style: it is a style of a language still in formation, the style of a writer whose *masters* were not English, but Latin and to a less degree Greek. This, I think, is only saying what Johnson and in turn Landor said, when they complained of Milton's style not being quite English. Let us qualify this judgment by saying immediately that Milton did much to develop the language. One of the signs of approach towards a classic style is a development towards greater complexity of sentence and period structure. Such development is apparent in the single work of Shakespeare, when we trace his style from the early to the late plays: we can even say that in his late plays he goes as far in the direction of complexity as is possible within the limits of dramatic verse, which are narrower than those of other kinds. But complexity for its own sake is not a proper goal: its purpose must be, first, the precise expression of finer shades of feeling and thought; second, the introduction of greater refinement and variety of music. When an author appears, in his love of the elaborate structure, to have lost the ability to say anything simply; when his addiction to pattern becomes such that he says things elaborately which should properly be said simply, and thus limits his range of expression, the process of complexity ceases to be quite healthy, and the writer is losing touch with the spoken language. Nevertheless, as verse develops, in the hands of one poet after another, it tends from monotony to variety, from simplicity to complexity; as it declines, it tends towards monotony again, though it may perpetuate the formal structure to which genius gave life and meaning. You will judge for yourselves how far this generalization is applicable to the predecessors and followers of Virgil: we can all see this secondary monotony in the eighteenth-century imitators of Milton—who himself is never monotonous. There comes a time when a new simplicity, even a relative crudity, may be the only alternative. /7

You will have anticipated the conclusion towards

which I have been drawing: that those qualities of the classic which I have so far mentioned—maturity of mind, maturity of manners, maturity of language and perfection of the common style—are most nearly to be illustrated, in English literature, in the eighteenth century; and, in poetry, most in the poetry of Pope. If that were all I had to say on the matter, it would certainly not be new, and it would not be worth saying. That would be merely proposing a choice between two errors at which men have arrived before: one, that the eighteenth century is the finest period of English literature; and the other, that the classical ideal should be wholly discredited. My own opinion is, that we have no classic age, and no classic poet, in English; that when we see why this is so, we have not the slightest reason for regret; but that, nevertheless, we must maintain the classic ideal before our eyes. Because we must maintain it, and because the English genius of language has had other things to do than to realize it, we cannot afford either to reject or to overrate the age of Pope; we cannot see English literature as a whole, or aim rightly in the future, without a critical appreciation of the degree to which the classical qualities are exemplified in the work of Pope: which means that unless we are able to enjoy the work of Pope, we cannot arrive at a full understanding of English poetry. /8

It is fairly obvious that the realization of classical qualities by Pope was obtained at a high price—to the exclusion of some greater potentialities of English verse. Now, to some extent, the sacrifice of some potentialities in order to realize others, is a condition of artistic creation, as it is a condition of life in general. In life the man who refuses to sacrifice anything to gain anything else, ends in mediocrity or failure; though, on the other hand, there is the specialist who has sacrificed too much for too little, or who has been born too completely the specialist to have had anything to sacrifice. But in the English eighteenth century, we have reason for feeling that too much was excluded. There was the mature mind: but it was a narrow one. English society and English letters were not provincial, in the sense that they were not isolated from, and not lingering behind, the best European society and letters. Yet the age itself was, in a manner of speaking, a provincial age. When one thinks of a Shakespeare, a Jeremy Taylor, a Milton, in England—of a Racine, a Molière, a Pascal, in France—in the seventeenth century, one is inclined to say that the eighteenth century had perfected its formal garden, only by restricting the area under cultivation. We feel that if the classic is really a worthy ideal, it must be capable of exhibiting an amplitude, a catholicity, to which the eighteenth century cannot lay claim; qualities which are present in some great authors, like Chaucer, who cannot be regarded in my sense as classics of English literature; and which are fully present in the mediaeval mind of Dante. For in the Divine Comedy, if anywhere, we find the classic in a modern European language. In the eighteenth century, we are oppressed by the limited range of sensibility, and especially in the scale of religious feeling. It is not that, in England at least, the poetry is not Christian. It is not even that the poets were not devout Christians; for a pattern of orthodoxy of principle, and sincere piety of feeling, you may look long before you find a poet more genuine than Samuel Johnson. Yet there are evidences of a deeper religious sensibility in the poetry of Shakespeare, whose belief and practice can be only a matter of conjecture. And this restriction of religious sensibility itself produces a kind of provinciality (though we must add that in this sense the nineteenth century was more provincial still): the provinciality which indicates the disintegration of Christendom, the decay of a common belief and a common culture. It would seem then, that our eighteenth century, in spite of its classical achievement—an achievement, I believe, which still has great importance as an example for the future—was lacking some condition which makes the creation of a true classic possible. What this condition is, we must return to Virgil to discover. /9

I should like first to rehearse the characteristics which I have already attributed to the classic, with special application to Virgil, to his language, his civilization, and the particular moment in the history of that language and civilization at which he arrived. Maturity of mind: this needs history, and the consciousness of history. Consciousness of history cannot be fully awake, except where there is other history than the history of the poet's own people: we need this in order to see our own place in history. There must be the knowledge of the history of at least one other highly civilized people, and of a people whose civilization is sufficiently cognate to have influenced and entered into our own. This is a consciousness which the Romans had, and which the Greeks, however much more highly we may estimate their achievement—and indeed, we may respect it all the more on this account—could not possess. It was a consciousness, certainly, which Virgil himself did much to develop. From the beginning, Virgil, like his contemporaries and immediate predecessors, was constantly adapting and using the discoveries, traditions and inventions of Greek poetry: to make use of a foreign literature in this way marks a further stage of civilization beyond making use only of the earlier stages of one's own—though I think we can say that no poet has ever shown a finer sense of proportion than Virgil, in the uses he made of Greek and of earlier Latin poetry. It is this development of one literature, or one civilization, in relation to another, which gives a peculiar significance to the subject of Virgil's epic. In Homer, the conflict between the Greeks and the Trojans is hardly larger in scope than a feud between one Greek city-state and a coalition of other city-states: behind the story of Aeneas is the consciousness of a more radical distinction, a distinction which is at the same time a statement of *relatedness*, between two great cultures, and, finally, of their reconciliation under an all-embracing destiny. /10

Virgil's maturity of mind, and the maturity of his age, are exhibited in this awareness of history. With maturity of mind I have associated maturity of manners and absence of provinciality. I suppose that, to a modern European suddenly precipitated into the past, the social behaviour of the Romans and the Athenians would seem indifferently coarse, barbarous and offensive. But if the poet can portray something superior to contemporary practice, it is not in the way of anticipating some later, and quite different code of behaviour, but by an insight into what the conduct of his own people at his own time might be, at its best. House parties of the wealthy, in Edwardian England, were not exactly what we read of in the pages of Henry James: but Mr. James's society was an idealization, of a kind, of *that* society, and not an anticipation of any other. I think that we are conscious, in Virgil more than in any other Latin poet—for Catullus and Propertius seem ruffians, and Horace somewhat plebeian, by comparison—of a refinement of manner, springing from a delicate sensibility, and particularly in that test of manners, private and public conduct between the sexes. It is not for me, in a gathering of people, all of whom may be better scholars than I, to review the story of Aeneas and Dido. But I have always thought the meeting of Aeneas with the shade of Dido, in Book VI, not only one of the most poignant, but one of the most civilized passages in poetry. It is complex in meaning and economical in expression, for it not only tells us about the attitude of Dido—still more important is what it tells us about the attitude of Aeneas. Dido's behaviour appears almost as a projection of Aeneas' own conscience: this, we feel, is the way in which Aeneas' conscience would *expect* Dido to behave to him. The point, it seems to me, is not that Dido is unforgiving—though it is important that, instead of railing at him, she merely snubs him—perhaps the most telling snub in all poetry: what matters most is, that Aeneas does not forgive himself—and this, significantly, in spite of the fact of which he is well aware, that all that he has done has been in compliance with destiny, or in consequence of the machinations of gods who are themselves, we feel, only instruments of a greater inscrutable power. Here, what I chose as an instance of civilized manners, proceeds to testify to civilized consciousness and conscience: but all of the levels at which we may consider a particular episode, belong to one whole. It will be observed, finally, that the behaviour of Virgil's characters (I might except Turnus, the man without a destiny) never appears to be according to some purely local or tribal code of manners: it is in its time, both Roman and European. Virgil certainly, on the plane of manners, is not provincial. /11

To attempt to demonstrate the maturity of language and style of Virgil is, for the present occasion, a superfluous task: many of you could perform it better than I, and I think that we should all be in accord. But it is worth repeating that Virgil's style would not have been possible without a literature behind him, and without his having a very intimate knowledge of this literature: so that he was, in a sense, re-writing Latin poetry—as when he borrows a phrase or a device from a predecessor and improves upon it. He was a learned author, all of whose learning was relevant to his task; and he had, for his use, just enough literature behind him and not too much. As for maturity of style, I do not think that any poet has ever developed a greater command of the complex structure, both of sense and sound, without losing the resource of direct, brief and startling simplicity when the occasion required it. On this I need not dilate: but I think it is worth while to say a word more about the *common style*, because this is something which we cannot perfectly illustrate from English poetry, and to which we are apt to pay less than deference. In modern European literature, the closest approximations to the ideal of a common style, are probably to be found in Dante and Racine; the nearest we have to it in English poetry is Pope, and Pope's is a common style which, in comparison, is of a very narrow range. A common style is one which makes us exclaim, not "this is a man of genius using the language" but "this realizes the genius of the language." We do not say this when we read Pope, because we are too conscious of all the resources of the English speech upon which Pope does not draw; we can at most say "this realizes the genius of the English language of a particular epoch." We do not say this when we read Shakespeare or Milton, because we are always conscious of the greatness of the man, and of the miracles that *he* is performing with the language; we come nearer perhaps with Chaucer—but that Chaucer is using a different, from our point of view a cruder, speech. And Shakespeare and Milton, as later history shows, left open many possibilities of other uses of English in poetry: whereas, after Virgil, it is truer to say that no great development was possible, until the Latin language became something different. /12

At this point I should like to return to a question which I have already suggested: the question whether the achievement of a classic, in the sense in which I have been using the term throughout, is, for the people and the language of its origin, altogether an unmixed blessing—even though it is unquestionably a ground for pride. To have this question raised in one's mind, it is almost enough simply to have contemplated Latin poetry after Virgil, to have considered the extent to which later poets lived and worked under the shadow of his greatness: so that we praise or dispraise them, according to standards which he set—admiring them, sometimes, for discovering some variation which was new, or even for merely rearranging patterns of words so as to give a pleasing faint reminder of the remote original. But English poetry, and French poetry also, may be considered fortunate in this: that the greatest poets have exhausted only particular areas. We cannot say that, since the age of Shakespeare, and respectively since the time of Racine, there has been any really first-rate poetic drama in England or in France; since Milton, we have had no great epic poem, though there have been great long poems. It is true that every supreme poet, classic or not, tends to exhaust the ground he cultivates, so that it must, after yielding a diminishing crop, finally be left in fallow for some generations. /13

Here it may be objected that the effect on a literature which I am imputing to the classic, results not from the classic character of that work, but simply from its greatness: for I have denied to Shakespeare and to Milton the title of classics, in the sense in which I am employing the term throughout, and yet have admitted that no supremely great poetry of the same kind has been written since. That every great work of poetry tends to make impossible the production of equally great works of the same kind is indisputable. The reason may be stated partly in terms of conscious purpose: no first-rate poet would attempt to do again, what has already been done as well as it can be done in his language. It is only after the language—its cadence, still more than vocabulary and syntax—has, with time and social change, sufficiently altered, that another dramatic poet as great as Shakespeare, or another epic poet as great as Milton, can become possible. Not only every great poet, but every genuine, though lesser poet, fulfills once for all some possibility of the language, and so leaves one possibility less for his successors. The vein that he has exhausted may be a very small one; or may represent some major form of poetry, the epic or dramatic. But what the great poet has exhausted is merely one form, and not the whole language. When the great poet is also a great classic poet, he exhausts, not a form only, but the language of his time; and the language of his time, as used by him, will be the language in its perfection. So that it is not the poet alone of whom we have to take account, but the language in which he writes: it is not merely that a classic poet exhausts the language, but that an exhaustible language is the kind which may produce a classic poet. /14

We may be inclined to ask, then, whether we are not fortunate in possessing a language which, instead of having produced a classic, can boast a rich variety in the past, and the possibility of further novelty in the future? Now while we are *inside* a literature, while we speak the same language, and have fundamentally the same culture as that which produced the literature of the past, we want to maintain two things: a pride in what our literature has already accomplished, and a belief in what it may still accomplish in the future. If we cease to believe in the future, the past would cease to be fully *our* past: it would become the past of a dead civilization. And this consideration must operate with particular cogency upon the minds of those who are engaged in the attempt to add to the store of English literature. There is no classic in English: therefore, any living poet can say, there is still hope that I—and those after me, for no one can face with equanimity, once he understands what is implied, the thought of being the *last* poet—may be able to write something which will be worth preserving. But from the aspect of eternity, such interest in the future has no meaning: when two languages are both dead languages, we cannot say that one is greater, because of the number and variety of its poets, or the other because its genius is more completely expressed in the work of one poet. What I wish to affirm, at one and the same time, is this: that, because English is a living language and the language in which we live, we may be glad that it has never completely realized itself in the work of one classic poet; but that, on the other hand, the classic criterion is of vital importance to us. We need it in order to judge our individual poets, though we refuse to judge our literature as a whole in comparison with one which has produced a classic. Whether a literature does culminate in a classic, is a matter of fortune. It is largely, I suspect, a question of the degree of fusion of the elements within that language; so that the Latin languages can approximate more closely to the classic, not simply because they are Latin, but because they are more homogeneous than English, and therefore tend more naturally towards the *common style*: whereas English, being the most various of great languages in its constituents, tends to variety rather than perfection, needs a longer time to realize its potency, and still contains, perhaps, more unexplored possibilities. It has, perhaps, the greatest capacity for changing and yet remaining itself. /15

I am now approaching the distinction between the relative and the absolute classic, the distinction between the literature which can be called classic in relation to its own language, and that which is classic in relation to a number of other languages. But first I wish to record one more characteristic of the classic, beyond those I have enumerated, which will help to establish this distinction, and to mark the difference between such a classic as Pope and such a classic as Virgil. It is convenient to recapitulate certain assertions which I made earlier. /16

I suggested, at the beginning, that a frequent, if not universal feature of the maturing of individuals may be a process of selection (not altogether conscious), of the development of some potentialities to the exclusion of others; and that a similarity may be found in the development of language and literature. If this is so, we should expect to find that in a minor classic literature, such as our own of the late seventeenth and the eighteenth century, the elements excluded, to arrive at maturity, will be more numerous or more serious; and that satisfaction in the result, will always be qualified by our awareness of the possibilities of the language, revealed in the work of earlier authors, which have been ignored. The classic age of English literature is not representative of the total genius of the race: as I have intimated, we cannot say that that genius is wholly realized in any one period—with the result that we can still, by referring to one or another period of the past, envisage possibilities for the future. The English language is one which offers wide scope for legitimate divergencies of style; it seems to be such that no one age, and certainly no one writer, can establish a norm. The French language has seemed to be much more closely tethered to a normal style; yet, even in French, though the language appeared to have established itself, once for all, in the seventeenth century, there is an *esprit gaulois*, an element of richness present in Rabelais and in Villon, the awareness of which may qualify our judgment of the *wholeness* of Racine or Molière, for we may feel that it is not only unrepresented but unreconciled. We may come to the conclusion, then, that the perfect classic must be one in which the whole genius of a people will be latent, if not all revealed; and that it can only appear in a language such that its whole genius can be present at once. We must accordingly add, to our list of characteristics of the classic, that of *comprehensiveness*. The classic must, within its formal limitations, express the maximum possible of the whole range of feeling which represents the character of the people who speak that language. It will represent this at its best, and it will also have the widest appeal: among the people to which it belongs, it will find its response among all classes and conditions of men. /17

When a work of literature has, beyond this comprehensiveness in relation to its own language, an equal significance in relation to a number of foreign literatures, we may say that it has also *universality*. We may for instance speak justly enough of the poetry of Goethe as constituting a classic, because of the place which it occupies in its own language and literature. Yet, because of its partiality, of the impermanence of some of its content, and the germanism of the sensibility; because Goethe appears, to a foreign eye, limited by his age, by his language, and by his culture, so that he is unrepresentative of the whole European tradition, and, like our own nineteenth-century authors, a little provincial, we cannot call him a *universal* classic. He is a universal author, in the sense that he is an author with whose works every European ought to be acquainted: but that is a different thing. Nor, on one count or another, can we expect to find the proximate approach to the classic in *any* modern language. It is necessary to go to the two dead languages: it is important that they are dead, because through their death we have come into our inheritance—the fact that they are dead would in itself give them no value, apart from the fact that all the peoples of Europe are their beneficiaries. And of all the great poets of Greece and Rome, I think that it is to Virgil that we owe the most for our standard of the classic: which, I will repeat, is not the same thing as pretending that he is the greatest, or the one to whom we are in every way the most indebted—it is of a particular debt that I speak. His comprehensiveness, his peculiar kind of comprehensiveness, is due to the unique position in our history of the Roman Empire and the Latin language: a position which may be said to conform to its *destiny.* This sense of destiny comes to consciousness in the *Aeneid.* Aeneas is himself, from first to last, a "man in fate," a man who is neither an adventurer nor a schemer, neither a vagabond nor a careerist, a man fulfilling his destiny, not under compulsion or arbitrary decree, and certainly from no stimulus to glory, but by surrendering his will to a higher power behind the gods who would thwart or direct him. He would have preferred to stop in Troy, but he becomes an exile, and something greater and more significant than any exile; he is exiled for a purpose greater than he can know, but which he recognizes; and he is not, in a human sense, a happy or successful man. But he is the symbol of Rome; and, as Aeneas is to Rome, so is ancient Rome to Europe. Thus Virgil acquires the centrality of the unique classic; he is at the centre of European civilization, in a position which no other poet can share or usurp. The Roman Empire and the Latin language were not any empire and any language, but an empire and a language with a unique destiny in relation to ourselves, and the poet in whom that Empire and that language came to consciousness and expression is a poet of unique destiny. /18

If Virgil is thus the consciousness of Rome and the supreme voice of her language, he must have a significance for us which cannot be expressed wholly in terms of literary appreciation and criticism. Yet, adhering to the problems of literature, or to the terms of literature in dealing with life, we may be allowed to imply more than we state. The value of Virgil to us, in literary terms, is in providing us with a criterion. We may, as I have said, have reasons to rejoice that this criterion is provided by a poet writing in a different language from our own: but that is not a reason for rejecting the criterion. To preserve the classical standard, and to measure every individual work of literature by it, is to see that, while our literature as a whole may contain everything, every single work in it may be defective in something. This may be a necessary defect, a defect without which some quality present would be lacking: but we must see it as a defect, at the same time that we see it as a necessity. In the absence of this standard of which I speak, a standard we cannot keep clearly before us if we rely on our own literature alone, we tend, first to admire works of genius for the wrong reasons—as we extol Blake for his *philosophy,* and Hopkins for his *style*: and from this we proceed to greater error, to giving the second rate equal rank with the first rate. In short, without the constant application of the classical measure, which we owe to Virgil more than to any other one poet, we tend to become provincial. /19

By "provincial" I mean here something more than I find in the dictionary definitions. I mean more, for instance, than "wanting the culture or polish of the capital," though, certainly, Virgil was of the Capital, to a degree which makes any later poet of equal stature look a little provincial; and I mean more than "narrow in thought, in culture, in creed"—a slippery definition this, for, from a modern liberal point of view, Dante was "narrow in thought, in culture, in creed," yet it may be the Broad Churchman, rather than the Narrow Churchman, who is the more provincial. I mean also a distortion of values, the exclusion of some, the exaggeration of others, which springs, not from lack of wide geographical perambulation, but from applying standards acquired within a limited area to the whole of human experience; which confounds the contingent with the essential, the ephemeral with the permanent. In our age, when men seem more than ever prone to confuse wisdom with knowledge, and knowledge with information, and to try to solve problems of life in terms of engineering, there is coming into existence a new kind of provincialism which perhaps deserves a new name. It is a provincialism, not of space, but of time; one for which history is merely the chronicle of human devices which have served their turn and been scrapped, one for which the world is the property solely of the living, a property in which the dead hold no shares. The menace of this kind of provincialism is, that we can all, all the peoples on the globe, be provincials together; and those who are not content to be provincials, can only become hermits. If this kind of provincialism led to greater tolerance, in the sense of forbearance, there might be more to be said for it; but it seems more likely to lead to our becoming indifferent, in matters where we ought to maintain a distinctive dogma or standard, and to our becoming intolerant, in matters which might be left to local or personal preference. We may have as many varieties of religion as we like, provided we all send our children to the same schools. But my concern here is only with the corrective to provincialism in literature. We need to remind ourselves that, as Europe is a whole (and still, in its progressive mutilation and disfigurement, the organism out of which any greater world harmony must develop), so European literature is a whole, the several members of which cannot flourish, if the same blood-stream does not circulate throughout the whole body. The blood-stream of European literature is Latin and Greek—not as two systems of circulation, but one, for it is through Rome that our parentage in Greece must be traced. What common measure of excellence have we in literature, among our several languages, which is not the classical measure? What mutual intelligibility can we hope to preserve, except in our common heritage of thought and feeling in those two languages, for the understanding of which, no European people is in any position of advantage over any other? No modern language could aspire to the universality of Latin, even though it came to be spoken by millions more than ever spoke Latin, and even though it came to be the universal means of communication between peoples of all tongues and cultures. No modern language can hope to produce a classic, in the sense in which I have called Virgil a classic. Our classic, the classic of all Europe, is Virgil. /20

In our several literatures, we have much wealth of which to boast, to which Latin has nothing to compare; but each literature has its greatness, not in isolation, but because of its place in a larger pattern, a pattern set in Rome. I have spoken of the new seriousness—*gravity* I might say—the new insight into history, illustrated by the dedication of Aeneas to Rome, to a future far beyond his living achievement. *His* reward was hardly more than a narrow beachhead and a political marriage in a weary middle age: his youth interred, its shadow moving with the shades the other side of Cumae. And so, I said, one envisages the destiny of ancient Rome. So we may think of Roman literature: at first sight, a literature of limited scope, with a poor muster of great names, yet universal as no other literature can be; a literature unconsciously sacrificing, in compliance to its destiny in Europe, the opulence and variety of later tongues, to produce, for us, the classic. It is sufficient that this standard should have been established once for all; the task does not have to be done again. But the maintenance of the standard is the price of our freedom, the defense of freedom against chaos. We may remind ourselves of this obligation, by our annual observance of piety towards the great ghost who guided Dante's pilgrimage: who, as it was his function to lead Dante towards a vision he could never himself enjoy, led Europe towards the Christian culture which he could never know; and who, speaking his final words in the new Italian speech, said in farewell

il temporal foco e l'eterno veduto hai, figlio, e sei venuto in parte dov' io per me più oltre non discerno.

Son, the temporal fire and the eternal, hast thou seen, and art come to a place where I, of myself, discern no further. /21

The speech

1. This is obviously a lecture that was read from a carefully prepared manuscript. How has Eliot tried to make it possible for his audience to follow his argument without undue difficulty? What common ground could he have counted on? If he were lecturing to your class, would he have the same common ground?
2. Trace carefully the organization of the lecture. What are the main headings? Does the speech follow any of the *patterns of organization* suggested in the Glossary?
3. An understanding of the lecture depends upon an understanding of certain key terms. What does Eliot mean by *maturity? Comprehensiveness? Universality?* Does he define each of them explicitly? If so, cite the definitions. If not, show how the context makes the meanings clear.
4. What is gained by approaching the definition of *classic* negatively as Eliot does in paragraphs 2 and 3? Why is such an approach especially useful with a term such as *classic?*
5. What kinds of maturity does Eliot believe a classic should have? Why does Eliot believe that no English classic possesses all of these kinds of maturity? On the other hand, why does he believe Virgil's great poem possesses them?
6. What does Eliot mean by *provinciality?* How is it opposed to maturity? How does provinciality affect literature? How can provinciality in literature be overcome? In speaking?
7. Do you agree with Eliot's belief that we are provincial when we try to solve our problems in terms of engineering? Do you find other criticisms of our age in the lecture? If so, what? How would you sum up Eliot's attitude toward our time?
8. Comment on the style of Eliot's lecture: its level of abstraction, its choice of words, its use of figures of speech, its sentence structure, its conciseness, its use of repetition and recapitulation, its level of learning.
9. In what ways, if any, do you think this lecture might profitably be altered in order to be appropriate for a reading rather than a listening audience? In what specific respects does a lecture like this, designed for a

select and learned audience, vary from a speech meant for a heterogeneous audience?

10. The central idea of the lecture is presumably the answer to the question asked in the title. What is Mr. Eliot's answer?

For further study and discussion

1. What demands do you make of a literary classic? In what ways do your demands differ from those of Eliot? Give several examples of what you consider to be literary classics and defend your selections.
2. What are the unique resources of the English language? What advantages do you feel that English as a language has over Latin, disregarding the fact that one is alive and the other dead? What disadvantages?
3. In what respect can Shakespeare be said to be mature? Comprehensive? Universal? In what respects the opposite of these?
4. What modern poet most deserves in your opinion to be called mature, comprehensive, and universal? Defend your choice.
5. What effect, if any, do you find the character of an age has upon the literary style of that age? Can it be said that we have a common style today?
6. What do you consider to be the main functions of literature? Which of the literary forms—poetry, prose fiction, drama—best fulfills these functions today?
7. What are the chief functions of literary criticism? Can literary criticism when well written properly be called literature?
8. When can a speech properly be called literature? What speeches are generally considered great literature, and why are they?
9. What criteria do you employ in reading a short story to determine whether the story is a good one? Do you find that you employ all of these criteria consciously and deliberately? Can you defend all of the criteria you employ as being relevant and fair?
10. Do you make the same demands of a classic in painting or music that you make of a classic in literature? Account for any differences you observe.

Suggestions for further reading

David Daiches, ***Critical Approaches to Literature*** (Englewood Cliffs, N.J., 1956)

————, ***A Study of Literature*** (Ithaca, 1948)

E. A. Fitzpatrick, ***Great Books: Panacea, or What?*** (Milwaukee, 1952)

Harold Gardiner, ed., ***The Great Books: A Christian Appraisal*** (New York, 1949-1953)

Gilbert Highet, ***Talents and Geniuses*** (New York, 1957)

Robert Maynard Hutchins, ***Great Books, the Foundation of Liberal Education*** (New York, 1955)

Herbert E. Read, ***The Nature of Literature*** (New York, 1956)

Rene Wellek and Austin Warren, ***Theory of Literature*** (New York, 1949)

In defense of abstract art

HERBERT READ

Sir Herbert Read (1893-), who has been described as "one of the most important of living critics," comes from a long line of Yorkshire farmers. He was educated at a boarding school and at the University of Leeds. During World War I he was captain of the Yorkshire Regiment and received the Distinguished Service Order and the Military Cross.

From 1922 to 1931 he was an Assistant Keeper at the Victoria and Albert Museum and from 1931 to 1933 a professor of fine arts at the University of Edinburgh. He has been a director of Routledge and Kegan Paul, Ltd., Publishers, President of the Institute of Contemporary Arts, London, and of the Society for Education in Art. In 1953-1954 he was Charles Eliot Norton Professor of Poetry at Harvard University and in 1954 A. W. Mellon Lecturer in Fine Arts, Washington, D.C.

His extensive publications include: *English Prose Style* (1928), *The Meaning of Art* (1931), *Form in Modern Poetry* (1932), *In Defense of Shelley* (1936), *Art and Society* (1937), *Education Through Art* (1943), *The Philosophy of Modern Art* (1952), *The True Voice of Feeling* (1953), *Icon and Idea* (1955), *The Art of Sculpture* (1956), *The Tenth Muse* (1957), and *A Concise History of Modern Painting* (1959).

Sir Herbert, who has shown particular interest in the theory and practice of his contemporaries, is a vigorous defender of the theoretical foundation of modern art. His views have been the source of controversy, particularly his belief that the arts can be "progressive." It is his opinion, as he says in the last sentence of this essay, that "Abstract art is perhaps more distant than any art of the past; it is perhaps also more beautiful."

In addition to the three paintings reproduced here, the following works were included in the original publication of this essay: "Night, Day and Transformation," by Wojciech Dlugosz; "Narcissus," by Jan Kotik; "Suprematist Composition," by Kasimir Malevich; "Spiral Theme," by Naum Gabo; "Composition," by Joan Miro.

Although this work was originally an essay, it is included here partly because it is a provocative discussion of abstract art and partly because it provides material for an interesting review of the likenesses and differences between speeches and essays.

Herbert Read, "In Defense of Abstract Art," *New York Times Magazine*, April 17, 1960, pp. 32, 40, 45, 48. By permission of the author.

It is exactly half a century since Wassily Kandinsky painted the first abstract picture. During that time the abstract movement has continued to grow, until now non-abstract, or representational, painters are the ones in a minority—at least, among painters of the younger generation. And yet the abstract artists (we must remember that sculptors as well as painters are involved) have not carried a majority of the public with them. /1

Perhaps the gap between the *avant-garde* and the main body of educated taste is always wide, but surely never before has it been as wide as it is today. In spite of the high esteem which abstract art enjoys among collectors, and the fantastic prices paid for it in the salesrooms, the man in the street remains bewildered, sometimes angry, often indifferent. He has an obstinate feeling that his leg is being pulled, that the abstract artist cannot really expect to be taken seriously, that the whole business is a racket of some kind. /2

What are the main charges brought against the abstract movement? Five are set out below, and I shall do my best to answer them one by one. /3

(1) *It fails to communicate any meaning, representing only the artist talking to himself. As Francis Henry Taylor has said, "unless participation is allowed the spectator [a painting] becomes a hopeless riddle and ceases to be a work of art at all."* /4

C. K. Ogden and I. A. Richards wrote a famous book called "The Meaning of Meaning," dealing with problems of language and logic. A similar problem exists in the plastic arts. What is the "meaning" of a painting or a piece of sculpture? /5

Only the most simple people would suggest that the meaning of the picture is the story it tells—that a work of art should be the description of a scene or the narration of an event. Tolstoy, who was not a simple person, asserted that the value of the work of art lies in its truth, and Ruskin, though he had a different conception of the truth, argued in much the same way. /6

The Socialist realists of Russia today adopt this same argument. Art for them, as for Tolstoy and Ruskin, is a means of communicating a message of some kind—about social conditions, about natural phenomena, about human relations—and, as Francis

Jackson Pollock—"Number 1," 1948. (Collection, The Museum of Modern Art, New York.)

Henry Taylor implied in his statement, what should be communicated by the work of art is understanding. /7

At this point we encounter a philosophical problem. Is understanding a rational process, the kind of discourse that should be confined to logical statements; or is it possibly an irrational process, the kind of discourse we can carry on only by the use of symbols? /8

The defender of abstract art believes that art is a form of symbolic discourse, and that, even when it is representational, its message is conveyed by form and color rather than by the imitation of the things we see. He points out that other arts, such as music and architecture, do not necessarily imitate anything in nature, but communicate by abstract arrangements of sounds, intervals, proportions and rhythms. There is no reason why the arrangements of lines and colors on a canvas, or of mass and volume in a piece of sculpture, should not be abstract in the same way. /9

It is merely a convention, of limited historical significance, to maintain that the visual arts should communicate their meaning by imitating the arbitrary forms that nature has evolved. Music might just as logically be confined to the imitation of bird songs or thunder; architecture, to the imitation of caves and mountains. /10

The abstract work of art may be a riddle, but it is not hopeless nor is it meaningless: it is a symbol which may stand for the artist's deepest emotions and intuitions, and in which the spectator may find his own emotions and intuitions defined and illuminated. /11

(2) *There are no standards of imagery or technique. Anyone—even a child—can paint an abstract painting. Mere doodling may be offered as abstract art. Thus, it becomes impossible to tell a good abstract painting from a bad one.* /12

What is a standard of imagery? Presumably, the visual images given in our perception of the external world. Again a philosophical problem is involved, for there is no standard image of the external world. /13

The image of the external world which we have at any moment is a convention, and varies from age to age. This is evident enough from the history of art—each period has its own method of constructing an image of the external world; there is little in common between an image of the Byzantine period and an image of the classical Renaissance. /14

The image of man, as the recent exhibition at the Museum of Modern Art showed, varies not only

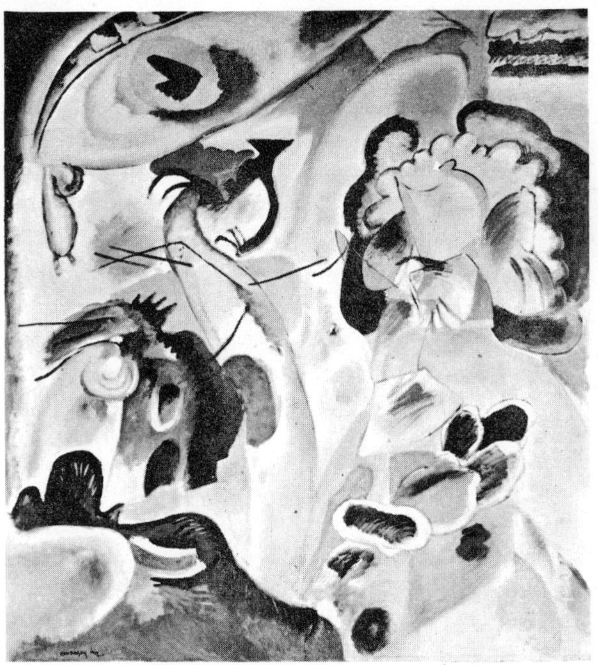

Wassily Kandinsky—"Improvisation 29," 1912. (Courtesy of Philadelphia Museum of Art, The Louise and Walter Arensberg Collection.)

from age to age but also from artist to artist. What is a standard image of man? The Chinese have one image; the Greeks had another. Some religions create an image of the ideal man; others, such as the Mohammedan, forbid the representation of such an ideal (for only God is perfect, and it would be pre-

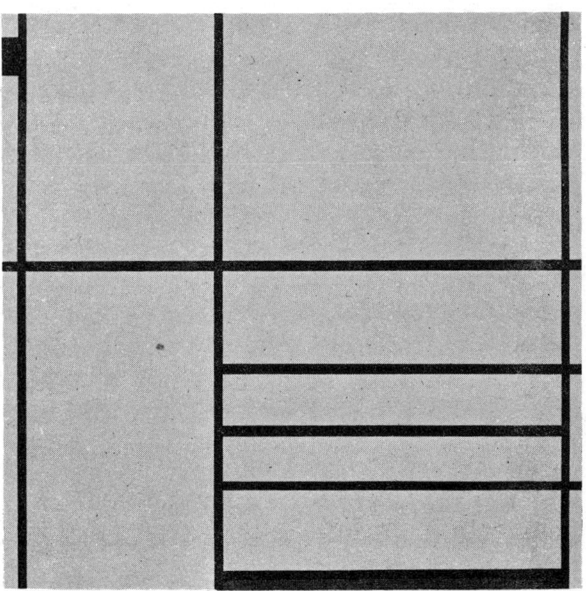

Piet Mondrian—"Composition in White, Black and Red," 1936. (Collection, The Museum of Modern Art, New York.)

sumptuous of man to consider himself capable of representing such perfection). /15

One kind of abstract artist, like the Islamic artist, believes there is an ideal of perfection, but that it is impersonal: that is to say, a question of quantitative harmony—the rhythmical succession of lines, the balance of areas, the harmonious unity of colors, the organic articulation of space. Another kind of abstract artist seeks an image that may, or may not, have such concrete quantities, but is essentially expressive of emotion, or has some inexplicable magical quality. /16

There are shapes that appeal to us for no rational reason—the graining of wood, the eroded pebbles in a stream, cloud formations, sunsets, blots of ink, flotsam from the sea. The Chinese and Japanese take great, irregular pieces of rock and erect them in their gardens because they have a strange animistic power or charm. Form is as mysterious as life itself. The artist is a man who reveals the mystery of form. /17

Even the child as it scribbles can do this. An American teacher, Rhoda Kellogg of the Golden Gate Nursery School in San Francisco, has classified children's scribbles and revealed their symbolic significance. A comparison of abstract art with children's scribbles does not make abstract art ridiculous; on the contrary, it connects it organically with the beginnings of all visual symbols. /18

As for technique, much as this may baffle the critic of abstract art, I would say that the standard is the same as in representational art. It is a question of the artist's skill in using his tools and his materials to their best advantage. There are badly painted abstract pictures just as there are badly painted representational pictures; and there are well painted pictures of each kind. Even spontaneity, which is characteristic of abstract expressionist art, is also found in representational art—in Tiepolo or Magnasco, in the impressionists and the expressionists. /19

In abstract art and in representational art, the standards are the same. There is only good art and bad art. /20

Coherent composition, sensibility to color harmonies, rhythmic movement and significant imagery —abstract art possesses all the essentially esthetic qualities that have been present in the art of the past. David Jones, an English painter who is not abstract, has made this point in his book "Epoch and Artist": /21

"Those of us whose work no one, I imagine, would call 'abstract' know, nevertheless, that it is an abstract quality, however hidden or devious, which determines the real worth of any work." /22

(3) *It represents novelty for novelty's sake. There is a primary concern with being "different" that leads to mere sensationalism. There is a difference between a movement and a cult.* /23

It is true that modern art of all kinds, including poetry and music, has been deliberately concerned to "make it new." At the most general and perhaps profoundest level, this is a reflection of our historical situation. We live in a revolutionary period, and the changes in art are but a reflection of the changes in society. But the position is more paradoxical than this generalization implies, for often the most revolutionary societies—those of Russia and China—have been the most conservative in their arts. /24

This, I believe, has been due to the fact that a revolutionary dictatorship has little understanding of the conditions in which art flourishes. As a result, many of the best artists in these countries (Stravinsky, Kandinsky, Chagall), escaped to become leaders of the modern movement elsewhere. /25

More direct causes for the novelty of modern art are to be found in the scientific and technical discoveries of our time. The invention of photography and the moving picture had a profound effect on the art of painting. So did technical advances in speed, the new dimensions of space given by the airplane, the new world of form revealed by the microscope. Form itself was established as a guiding principle in nature, in the universe, and form inevitably (and perhaps unconsciously) became the preoccupation of the artist. /26

It would be absurd to complain of novelty for novelty's sake in science; it is equally absurd to complain of it in art. Art has merely kept in step with a changing world, and the more art has changed the more it has remained the same thing: the symbolic representation of reality. /27

The suggestion that such an activity constitutes a "cult" is far from the truth. There have been cults in the past—the Pre-Raphaelite Brotherhood was one—and in our own time the surrealist movement had some of the characteristics of a cult—rigid rules, manifestoes of aims, organs of propaganda, etc. /28

Abstract art, by contrast, is one of the most nearly universal movements in the history of art. It is practiced in every country in the world apart from Russia and China (even Communist countries like Poland, Czechoslovakia and Yugoslavia have active movements). Abstract art can accommodate all varieties of human temperament and expression, from the severe classicism of Mondrian to the wild romanticism of a de Kooning. /29

(4) *It is mere decoration, no more profound than a pattern for wallpaper or draperies. Does not the abstract artist work first toward the effect of his canvas on a museum wall (witness the enormous size of abstract-expressionist canvases) rather than toward the intensification of experience?* /30

Ruskin once said that all great art was essentially decorative. The great compositions of Titian, Michelangelo and Rubens are "decorative." In the same manner, the paintings of Kandinsky, Mondrian, Nicholson or Pollock are decorative. If the abstract artist "works first toward the effect of his canvas on the wall," he is doing exactly what Titian, Michelangelo and Rubens did. /31

What are exceptional in the history of painting are the small "cabinet" pictures which are popular with bourgeois collectors. The modern painter wishes to be emancipated from this convention of the past century or two, and to return to the "grand manner" of the great painters of the past. He may not be wise to limit his market in this way, but he is demanding the full scale of his medium. We do not expect architects to restrict themselves to the building of cottages, or musicians to the composition of songs. /32

It is true that some abstract compositions are empty, but that is because they are poor compositions, not because they are abstract. "Intensification of experience" is not a question of size, but of the effectiveness of the symbols used. Any Gothic cathedral will serve as an illustration of intense grandeur; and, in its over-all effect, of abstract spatial expression. /33

(5) *It is devoid of human emotion. It has no philosophical foundation, no concern with basic and permanent values, as great art has always had.* /34

No art could have deeper philosophical foundations. Books like Worringer's "Abstraction and Empathy," Kandinsky's "Art of Spiritual Harmony," Mondrian's "Plastic Art," the writings of Gabo, Malevich, Klee—all these constitute a wealth of speculation on the principles of art without rival in history. All these writings are concerned with "basic and permanent values," and such values are human values. /35

Nevertheless, the charge that abstract art is "devoid of human emotion" has some force if by human emotion is meant the day-to-day feelings of joy and sorrow, hope and despair, which are our normal experiences. If the purpose of art were to "express" such feelings, to embody them in realistic pictures, in music or in drama, then art would be identical with life: a transcript, a report, a reflection. If the artist did no more than this he might be a good journalist or a good photographer, but he would not be venerated as we venerate Michelangelo or Rembrandt. /36

The purpose of the artist is not to represent emotion, but to transcend it. There are two aphorisms of Georges Braque's which describe the true function of emotion in art: "Emotion is neither added nor imitated: it is the seed, and art is the blossom." And "I love the rule that corrects emotion; I love the emotion that corrects the rule." /37

Art is a dialectical process: the resolution of contradictions and ambiguities. A work of art is removed from mundane strife; it is an object of disinterested contemplation. /38

"Distance," said Simone Weil, "is the soul of the beautiful: beauty, a fruit which we look at without trying to seize it." Abstract art is perhaps more distant than any art of the past; it is perhaps also more beautiful. /39

The essay

1. What is Read's purpose in answering what he calls the main charges against modern art? What is gained by this negative approach? Would his position have been stronger had he simply ignored the criticisms of modern art?
2. What methods does he use in answering the charges?
3. Is the analogy with music and architecture in paragraphs 9 and 10 a sound one in your opinion? A convincing one? Why not an analogy with poetry?
4. What are the criteria for measuring the modern artist's excellence? Are these criteria essentially different from those used to establish the excellence of conventional art? Develop your answers with examples.
5. What according to Read are the historical causes for abstract art? Do you agree with Read that it is not a cult? Explain your answer.
6. What does Read mean when he says that abstract art is "perhaps more distant than any art of the past"? Why does he consider this a good thing?
7. Could this article be delivered as a speech to your class just as it is? If not, what changes would you make? Explain them in detail. Especially explain what pictures or slides you might want and how you would use them.
8. How would you handle this material in a speech presented to your public speaking class if you were to ignore the charges against modern art and simply argue positively for it. What material might you want to add? Outline such a speech.

9. How would you handle this material if you were using it in an introductory lecture on abstract art in a required college course on art? In an elective course on modern art? In a graduate course on abstract painting?

For further study and discussion

1. How do you define abstract art? Name three artists whose works fit your definition and indicate what they have in common and how they differ.
2. What do you consider to be the basic appeals of abstract art? How do these appeals differ from those of conventional or representational art?
3. In what sense is abstract art properly decoration? Why, then, is it being attacked for being decoration?
4. What do you think abstract painting has in common with architecture? With sculpture? With music? With poetry? With rug and drapery design? How does it differ in function and effect from each of these?
5. What aspects of our age are clearly represented in abstract art? What aspects are not so clearly represented?
6. What philosophy or philosophies of life might logically give rise to abstract art?
7. How would you defend art against the charge that it is not practical?
8. What is the ultimate function, as you see it, of art?

Suggestions for further reading

George Biddle, ***The Yes and No of Contemporary Art*** (Cambridge, Mass., 1957)
Rudi Blesh, ***Modern Art USA*** (New York, 1956)
Katherine S. Dreier, Naum Gabo, and James J. Sweeney, ***Three Lectures on Modern Art*** (New York, 1950)
Paul Klee, ***On Modern Art*** (London, 1948)
Wyndham Lewis, ***The Demon of Progress in the Arts*** (Chicago, 1955)
Pieter C. Mondriaan, ***Plastic Art and Pure Plastic Art and Other Essays*** (New York, 1945)
Wilhelm Worringer, ***Abstraction and Empathy*** (New York, 1953)

The world of jazz

LEONARD BERNSTEIN

It is difficult to classify Leonard Bernstein (1918-   ), for to label him as pre-eminent in one field would be to offend those who revere him for his performance in others. He has been conductor, composer, pianist, teacher, author, and television lecturer. Serious students of music are acquainted with him through his compositions in the classical mode. Devotees of the musical stage know him as the man who wrote the scores for such Broadway hits as *On the Town, Wonderful Town, Candide,* and *West Side Story.* For some time Bernstein has been well known as a conductor, both here and abroad, but in his latest role as television performer he has gained even greater fame. Perhaps it would be simplest and most descriptive to call him "New York's Mr. Music."

In his book, *The Joy of Music* (1959), Leonard Bernstein has published several of the *Omnibus* scripts which endeared him to his viewers. In "The World of Jazz," which was first presented October 16, 1955, readers can see something of the vivacity of the man who has educated and entertained huge television audiences. Bernstein's performances are full of vitality and abundant nervous energy. No matter what subject he is dealing with, he has never lost the ability to be both engrossed in the work and yet naïvely amazed at its composition.

The following speech ably demonstrates Bernstein's ability to explain a difficult topic by reducing it to terms that can be readily grasped even by the uninitiated. In its unity, organization, movement, use of examples, language, and good humor, this speech bears study as a masterpiece of exposition.

JAZZ BAND:

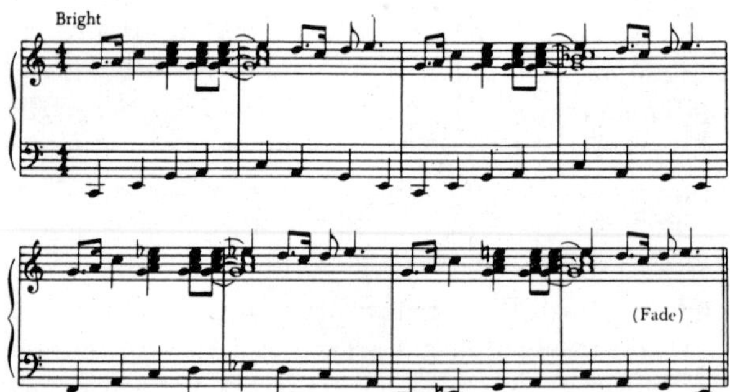

LEONARD BERNSTEIN:

Now, anyone hearing this music, anyone on any civilized part of this earth, east or west, pole to pole, would immediately say: That is jazz. We are going to try to investigate jazz, not through the usual historical approach which has become all too familiar, but through approaching the music itself. We are going to examine the musical "innards" of jazz to find out once and for all what it is that sets it apart from all other music. /1

Jazz is a very big word; it covers a multitude of sounds, all the way from the earliest Blues to Dixieland bands, to Charleston bands, to Swing bands, to Boogie-Woogie, to crazy Bop, to cool Bop, to Mambo—and much more.[1] It is all jazz, and I love it because it is an original kind of emotional expression, in that it is never wholly sad or wholly happy. Even the Blues has a robustness and hard-boiled quality that never lets it become sticky-sentimental, no matter how self-pitying the words are. /2

BLUES SINGER:

"*EMPTY BED BLUES*"[2]
by J. C. Johnson

And, on the other hand, the gayest, wildest jazz always seems to have some hint of pain in it. Listen to this trumpet, and see what I mean:

TRUMPET:

"*OLE MISS*"[3]
by W. C. Handy

That is what intrigues me about jazz; it is unique, a form of expression all its own. /3

I love it also for its humor. It really plays with notes. We always speak of "playing" music: we play Brahms or we play Bach—a term perhaps more properly applied to tennis. But jazz is real play. It "fools around" with notes, so to speak, and has fun with them. It is, therefore, entertainment in the truest sense. /4

But I find I have to defend jazz to those who say it is low-class. As a matter of fact, all music has low-class origins, since it comes from folk music, which is necessarily earthy. After all, Haydn minuets are only a refinement of simple, rustic German dances, and so are Beethoven scherzos. An aria from a Verdi opera can often be traced back to the simplest Neapolitan fisherman. Besides, there has always been a certain shadow of indignity around music, particularly around the players of music. /5

I suppose it is due to the fact that historically *players* of music seem to lack the dignity of *composers* of music. But this is especially true of jazz, which is almost completely a player's art, depending as it does on improvisation rather than on composition. But this also means that the player of jazz is

---

[1] For those who wish to follow examples of the foregoing terms, these recordings are recommended:
Leadbelly: "Good Morning Blues," in *Take This Hammer,* Vol. 1, 10" Folkways, FA 2004
King Oliver, Jelly-Roll Morton, etc.: "Back o' Town," 12" Riverside 12-130
Red Nichols, Dorsey Bros.: "Charleston," in *Jazz of the Roaring Twenties,* 12" Riverside 12-801
Benny Goodman: 1938 *Carnegie Hall Jazz Concert,* 2 12" Col. OSL-160
Meade Lux Lewis, Albert Ammons, etc.: *Giants of Boogie-Woogie,* 12" Riverside 12-106
Charlie Parker: *The Immortal Charlie Parker,* 12" Savoy 12001
Lee Konitz: *Lee Konitz with Warne Marsh,* 12" Atlantic 1217
Perez Prado: *Mambo Mania,* 12" Victor LPM-1075

himself the real composer, which gives him a creative, and therefore *more* dignified, status. /6

Then there are those who argue that jazz is loud. But so are Sousa marches, and we don't hear complaints about them. Besides, it's not always loud. It is very often extremely delicate, in fact. Perhaps this objection stems from the irremediable situation of what is after all a kind of brass band playing in a room too small for it. But that is not the fault of jazz itself. /7

However, the main argument against jazz has always been that it is not art. I think it *is* art, and a very special art. And before we can argue about whether it is or not, we must know *what* it is; and so I propose to share with you some of the things I know and love about jazz. /8

Let's take that Blues we heard before and find out what it's made of:

JAZZ BAND:

Now what are the elements that make that jazz? /9

First of all there is the element of melody. Western music in general is based, melodically speaking, on scales, like the major scale you all practiced as kids:

L. B. PLAYS PIANO:

But there is a special one for jazz, which is a variation of that regular major scale. /10

In jazz, this scale gets modified three different times. The third note gets lowered from this:

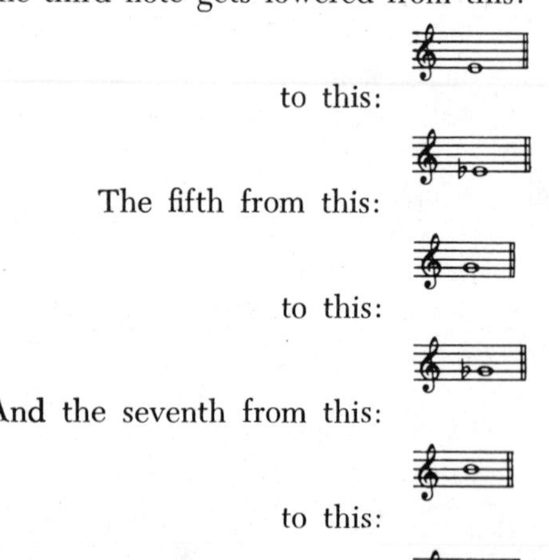

to this:

The fifth from this:

to this:

And the seventh from this:

to this:

Those three changed notes are called "blue notes."[4]

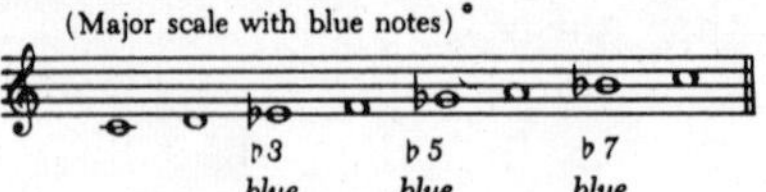

So instead of a phrase which would ordinarily go something like this:

which is not particularly jazzy—we would get, using blue notes, this phrase:

—which begins to show a jazz quality. /11

But this so-called "jazz scale" is used only melodically. In the harmony underneath we still use our old unflatted notes, and that causes dissonances to happen between that tune and the chords:

L. B. PLAYS PIANO:

---

[4] Actually, these blue notes are most commonly used in terms of the descending scale:

Leonard Bernstein. (© Roy Stevens.)

But these very dissonances have a true jazz sound. For example, jazz pianists are always using these two dissonant notes together:

—and there is a reason for it. They are really searching for a note that isn't there at all, but one which lies somewhere between the two notes—between this:

and this:

—and the note is called a quarter-tone. /12

The quarter-tone comes straight from Africa, which is the cradle of jazz and where quarter-tones are everyday stuff. We can produce one on a wind instrument or a stringed instrument or with the voice, but on the piano we have to approximate it by playing together the two notes on each side of it:

The real note is somewhere in there, in that crack between them. /13

Let's see if I can sing you that quarter-tone, if you will forgive my horrid voice. Here is an African Swahili tune I once heard. The last note of it is a quarter-tone:

L. B. SINGS:

Sounds as if I'm singing terribly out of tune, but actually I am singing a real note in another musical language. In jazz it is right at home. /14

L. B. PLAYS PIANO:

Now, just to show you how important these so-called "blue notes" are to jazz, let's hear that same Blues played without them, using only the plain white notes of the scale:

CLARINET:

There is something missing, isn't there? It just isn't jazz. /15

But even more important than melody in jazz is the element of rhythm. Rhythm is the first thing you associate with the word *jazz*, after all. There are two aspects to this point. The first is the beat. This is what you hear when the drummer's foot is beating the drum:

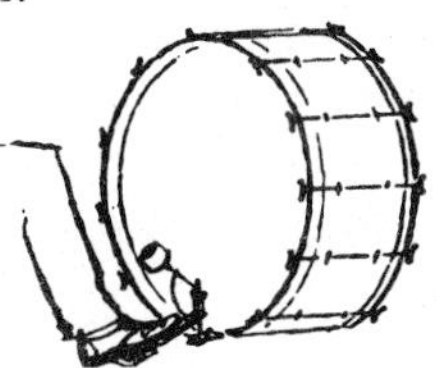

or when the bass player is plucking his bass:

or even when the pianist is kicking the pedal with his foot:

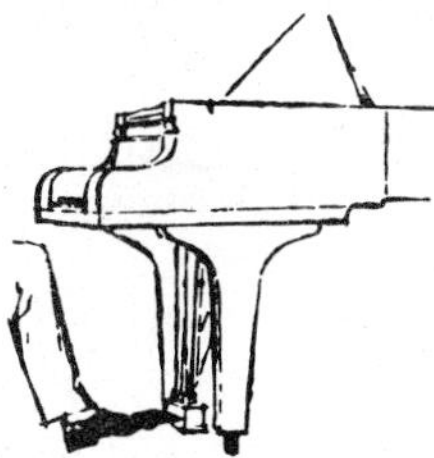

All this is elementary. The beats go on from beginning to end of a number, two or four of them to a measure, never changing in tempo or in meter. This is the heartbeat, so to speak, of jazz. /16

But more involved, and more interesting, is the rhythm going on *over* the beat—rhythmic figures which depend on something called "syncopation," a word you have certainly heard but maybe were never quite sure of. A good way to understand syncopation might be to think of a heartbeat that goes along steadily and, at a moment of shock, misses a beat. It is that much of a physical reaction. /17

Technically, syncopation means either the removal of an accent where you expect one, or the placing of an accent where you least expect one. In either case, there is the element of surprise and shock. The body responds to this shock, either by compensating for the missing accent or by reacting to the unexpected one. /18

Now where do we expect accents? Always on the first beat of a bar, on the downbeat. If there are two beats in a bar, *one* is going to be strong, *two* is going to be weak—exactly as in marching: *right,* left, *right,* left. Even if there are four beats in a bar, it is still like marching. Although we all have only two legs, the sergeant still counts out in four: *hup,* 2, 3, 4, *hup,* 2, 3, 4. There is always that natural accent on *one*. Take it away, and there is a simple syncopation:

L. B. GASPS DURING MISSING FIRST BEAT:

(*!*) 2, 3, 4 (*!*) 2, 3, 4 etc.

You see that that missing accent on the first beat evokes a body response. /19

Now, the other way to make syncopation is exactly the reverse: put an accent on a weak beat, the second or the fourth, where it doesn't belong. Like this:

One, *TWO*, three, *FOUR*
One, *TWO*, three, *FOUR*

This is what we all do, listening to jazz, when we clap our hands or snap our fingers on the offbeat. /20

Those are the basic facts of syncopation; and now we can understand its subtler aspects. Between one beat and another there lie shorter and even weaker beats; and when these get accents the shock is correspondingly greater, since the weaker the beat you accentuate, the greater the surprise. Let's take eight of those fast beats in a bar: 1 2 3 4 5 6 7 8. The normal accents would fall on one and five: **1!** 2 3 4 **5!** 6 7 8. Now, instead, let's put a big accent on a real weak one, the fourth:

1 2 3 **4!** 5 6 7 8

(Drum takes up from count, then claves, trumpet, etc.)

As you see, we get a pure rhumba rhythm. /21

Of course, the strongest syncopation of all would obviously be obtained by doing both things at once: putting an accent on a weak beat and taking away the accent from the strong. So now we will do this double operation: put a wallop on the weak fourth, and remove the strong fifth beat entirely; and we get:

1 2 3 **4!** – 6 7 8

(Various percussion instruments take it up)
It begins to sound like the Congo, doesn't it? /22

TRUMPET ADDS MELODY:

Now that you've heard what syncopation is like, let's see what that same Blues we heard before would sound like without it. I think you'll miss that essential element, the very life of jazz:

PLAYED "SQUARE" BY SAX, NO VIBRATO:

Sounds "square," doesn't it? /23

Well, that takes care of two very important elements: melody and rhythm. But jazz could not be jazz without its special tonal colors, the actual sound values you hear. These colors are many, but they mostly stem from the quality of the Negro singing voice. For instance, when Louis Armstrong plays his trumpet, he is only doing another version of his own voice. Listen to an Armstrong record, like "I Can't Give You Anything but Love," and compare the trumpet solo with the vocal solo. You can't miss the fact that they're by the same fellow.[5] But the Negro voice has engendered other imitations. The saxophone is in itself a kind of imitation of it—breathy, a little hoarse, with a vibrato, or tremor, in it. /24

(Here a saxophone plays a passage first with and then without vibrato)

Then there are all the different growls and rasps we get by putting mutes on the horns. Here, for example, is a trumpet with a cup mute:

(The sounds of these instruments are heard while they are being shown)

[5] Louis Armstrong: "I Can't Give You Anything but Love," *Armstrong Favorites,* Columbia.

and a wah-wah mute:

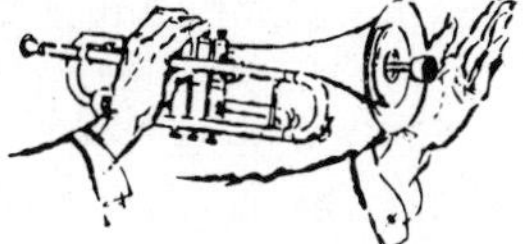

And a trombone with a plunger mute:

There are other tonal colors that derive from Afro-Cuban sources: Bongo drums:

maracas:

the Cuban cowbell:

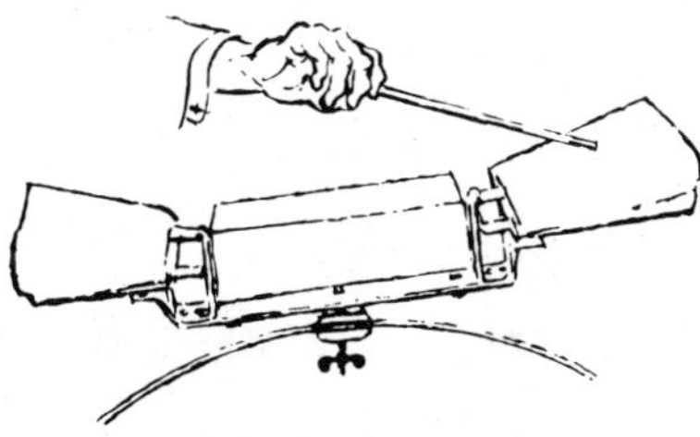

and all the others. /25

Then there are the colors that have an Oriental flavor: the vibraphone:

the various cymbals:

and so on. /26

These special colorations make their contribution to the total quality of jazz. You have certainly all heard jazz tunes played "straight" by non-jazz orchestras and wondered what was missing. There certainly is something missing—the coloration. /27

There is one more jazz element which may surprise some of you who think jazz is not an art. I refer to form. Did you know, for example, that the Blues is a classical form? Most people use the word *Blues* to mean any song that is "blue" or torchy or lowdown or breast-beating—like "Stormy Weather," for example. But "Stormy Weather" is not a Blues, and neither is "Moanin' Low," nor "The Man I Love," or even "The Birth of the Blues." They are all popular songs. /28

The Blues is basically a strict poetic form combined with music. It is based on a rhymed couplet, with the first line repeated. For example, Billie Holiday sings:

"*My man don't love me, treats me awful mean;*[6]
Oh, he's the lowest man I've ever seen."

But when she sings it, she repeats the first line—so it goes:

"*My man don't love me, treats me awful mean;*
I said, *my man don't love me, treats me awful mean;*
Oh, he's the lowest man I've ever seen."

That is one stanza of Blues. A full Blues is nothing more than a succession of such stanzas for as long as the singer wishes. /29

Did you notice that the Blues couplet is, of all things, in iambic pentameter?

"*My man/don't love/me, treats/me aw/ful mean*"

This is about as classic as one can get. It means that you can take any rhymed couplet in iambic pentameter—from Shakespeare, for example—and make a perfect *Macbeth* Blues:

[6] "Fine and Mellow" by Billie Holiday.

"I will not be afraid of death and bane,
Till Birnam forest come to Dunsinane."

It makes a lovely Blues:

L. B. SINGS:

Bright
VOICE
I will not be a - fraid of death or bane— I said I
will not be a - fraid of death or bane— Till
Bir - nam fo - rest come— to Dun - si - nane—

Now if you've noticed, each of these three lines got four bars apiece, making it all a twelve-bar stanza. But the voice itself sang only about half of each four-bar line, and the rest is supposed to be filled up by the accompaniment. This filling-up is called a "break." And here in the break we have the origin of the instrument imitating the voice, the very soil in which jazz grows. Perhaps the essential sound of jazz is Louis Armstrong improvising the breaks in a Blues sung by Bessie Smith. From this kind of voice imitation all instrumental improvising has since developed.[7] /30

Did you notice the instrument that has been accompanying our singers today? It is a harmonium, that wheezy little excuse for an organ which we all associate with hymn tunes. But far from being out of place in the Blues, this instrument is especially appropriate, since the chords in the Blues must always be exactly the same three chords we all know from hymn tunes:

L. B. PLAYS ON HARMONIUM:

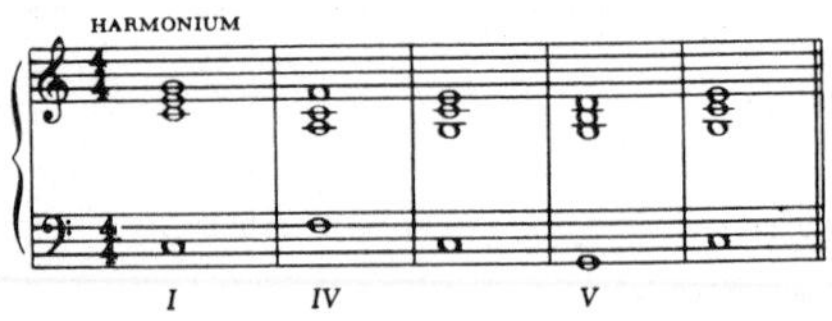
HARMONIUM
I
IV
V

These chords must always remain in a strict classical pattern, pure and simple. Try to vary them, and the Blues quality flies out the window. /31

Well, there you have it: melody, rhythm, tone color, form, harmony. In each department there are special features that make *jazz,* instead of just music. Let's now put them all together, and hear a full-blown, all-out happy Blues. Oh, did you know that Blues could be happy? Just listen.

(Jazz Band plays a Blues arrangement of "King Porter Stomp," Dixieland style)

[7] Bessie Smith and Louis Armstrong: "Reckless Blues," *The Bessie Smith Story,* Vol. I, Columbia LP ML 4807.

By this time I've probably given you the impression that jazz is nothing but Blues. Not at all. I've used the Blues to investigate jazz only because it embodies the various elements of jazz in so clear and pure a way. But the rest of jazz is concerned with applying these same elements to something called the popular song. The popular song, too, is a form; and it has certain strict patterns. Popular songs are in either two-part or three-part form. By far the most numerous are in the three-part. You all know this form, of course, from hearing it so much. It is as simple as pie. Anyone can write one. /32

Take "Sweet Sue," for instance. All you need is the first eight bars, really—which in the trade are called the front strain:

L. B. PLAYS PIANO:

Now the song is practically written, since the whole thing will be only thirty-two bars long—four groups of eight bars apiece. The second eight is the same exactly as the first:

Sixteen bars, and we're already half finished. Now the next eight bars, which are called the release, or bridge, or just simply "the middle part," must be different music. But it doesn't matter if it's very good or not, since most people don't remember it too well anyway:

And then the same old front strain all over again:

and it's finished. Thirty-two bars, and a classic forever. Easy, isn't it? /33

But "Sweet Sue" is still not jazz. A popular song doesn't become jazz until it is improvised on, and there you have the real core of all jazz: improvisation. Remember, I said that jazz was a player's art rather than a composer's. Well, this is the key to the whole problem. It is the player who, by improvising, makes jazz. He uses the popular song as a kind of dummy to hang his notes on. He dresses it up in his own way, and it comes out an original. So the pop tune, in acquiring a new dress, changes its personality completely, like many people who behave one way in blue jeans and a wholly different way in dinner clothes. Some of you may object to this dressing-up. You say, "Let me hear the melody, not all this embroidery." But until you accept this principal of improvisation, you will never accept or understand jazz itself. /34

What does improvising mean? It means that you take a tune, keep it in mind with its harmony and all, and then, as they used to say, just "go to town," or make it up as you go along. You go to town by adding ornaments and figurations, or by making real old-fashioned variations just as Mozart and Beethoven did. Let me show you a little of how Mozart did it, and then you may understand how Erroll Garner does it. Mozart took a well-known nursery rhyme, which he knew as *"Ah, Vous Dirai-je Maman,"* and which we know as "Twinkle, Twinkle Little Star" or as a way of singing the alphabet:

L. B. PLAYS PIANO AND SINGS:

Now Mozart makes a series of variations. One of them begins:

Then another:

Another:

And another:

They are all different pieces, yet they are all in one way or another that same original tune. /35

The jazz musician does exactly the same thing. There are infinite possible versions of "Sweet Sue," for example. The clarinet might improvise one chorus of it this way:

CLARINET:

Now he could have done that in any number of ways; and if I asked him to do it again tomorrow morning, it would come out a whole other piece. But it would still be "Sweet Sue," and it would still be jazz. /36

Now we come to the most exciting part of jazz, for me at any rate: simultaneous improvising. This happens when two or more musicians improvise on the same tune at the same time. Neither one knows exactly what the other is going to do; but they listen to each other, and pick up phrases from each other, and sort of talk together. What ties them together is the chords, the harmony, of "Sweet Sue." Over this harmony, they play two different melodic lines at the same time, which, in musical terms, makes a kind of accidental counterpoint. This is the germ of what is called the "jam session." Now the trumpet is going to join with the clarinet in a double improvisation on "Sweet Sue." See if you can distinguish the two melodic lines:

TRUMPET AND CLARINET:

You see how exciting this can be? This business of improvising together gave rise to the style called Dixieland, which is constantly having a big revival. One of the most exhilarating sounds in all music is that of a Dixieland band blaring out its final chorus, all stops out, with everyone improvising together.[8] /37

But jazz is not all improvization, not by a long shot. Much of it gets written down, and then it is called an arrangement. The great days of the arrangements were the Thirties, when big, startling swing arrangements were showing off the virtuosity of the great bands—like Casa Loma, Benny Goodman, Artie Shaw, the Dorsey brothers, and so on. Now jazz is hard to write down. There is no way of notating exactly those quarter-tones we talked about, nor the various smears and growls and subtle intonations. Even the rhythms can only be approximated in notation, so that much of the jazz quality is left to the instincts of the player who is reading the music. Still, it does work, because the instincts of these players are so deep and genuine. /38

Let's listen to a good, solid swing arrangement of a chorus of "Sweet Sue" as we might have heard it back in 1938.[9] /39

Now remember, this arrangement was for dancing. In 1938 we were all dancing; and that brings up the most important point of all. Nobody seems to dance to jazz very much any more, except for mambo lovers, and they are limited to those who are athletic enough to do it. What has happened to dancing? We used to have a new dance practically every month: the Lindy Hop, the Shag, the Peabody, the Big Apple, Boogie, Susie-Q. Now we have only dances you have to take lessons to do. /40

What does this mean? Simply that the emphasis is on listening, these days, instead of on singing and dancing. This change had to happen. For one thing, the tremendous development of the recording industry has taught us to listen in a way we never did before. But even more significant, with the advent of more complicated swing and jazz like Boogie-Woogie and Bop, our interest has shifted to the music itself and to the virtuosity of its performance. That is, we are interested in what notes are being played, how well, how fast, and with what originality. You can't listen to Bop intelligently and dance too, murmuring sweet nothings into your partner's ear. You have to listen as hard as you can to hear what's happening. /41

So in a way, jazz has begun to be a kind of chamber music, an advanced sophisticated art mainly for listening, full of influences of Bartók and Stravinsky, and very, very serious. Let's listen for a moment to this kind of arrangement of our old friend "Sweet Sue."

L. B. PLAYS VERY COOL ARRANGEMENT OF "SWEET SUE":[10]

[8] Bix Beiderbecke: "Sweet Sue," *The Bix Beiderbecke Story*, Vol. 3, Columbia LP ML 4813.

[9] Benny Goodman: "Sweet Sue," *This Is Benny Goodman*, Victor LP M 1239.

[10] Arrangement by Danny Hurd; reproduced by special permission.

Whether you call this kind of weird piece "cool" or "crazy" or "futuristic" or "modernistic" or whatever the fact is that it is bordering on serious concert music. The arrangement begins to be a *composition.* Take away the beat, and you might not even know it's jazz at all. It would be just a concert piece. And why is it jazz? Because it is played by jazz men, on jazz instruments, and because it has its roots in the soil of jazz and not of Bach. /42

I think the key word to all this is the word *cool.* It means what it implies. Jazz used to advertise itself as "hot"; now the heat is off. The jazz player has become a highly serious person. He may even be an intellectual. He tends to wear Ivy League clothes, have a crew cut, or wear horn-rimmed glasses. He may have studied music at a conservatory or a university. This was unthinkable in the old days. Our new jazz man plays more quietly, with greater concentration on musical values, on tone quality, technique. He knows Bartók and Stravinsky, and his music shows it. He tends to avoid big, flashy endings. The music just stops when it is over. /43

As he has become cool, so have his listeners. They don't dance; they listen respectfully, as if to chamber music, and applaud politely at the end. At jazz night clubs all over the world you find audiences who do not necessarily have a drink in their hands and who do not beat out the rhythm and carry on as we did when I was a boy. It is all rather cool and surprisingly controlled, considering that jazz is essentially an emotional experience. /44

Where does this lead us in our investigation? To some pretty startling conclusions. There are those who conclude from all this that here, in the new jazz, is the real beginning of serious American music, that at last the American composer has his own expression. Of course when they say this they are intimating that all American symphonic works up to now are nothing but personalized imitations of the European symphonic tradition from Mozart to Mahler. Sometimes, I must say, I think they have a point. At any rate, we can be sure of one thing: that the line between serious music and jazz grows less and less clear. We have serious composers writing in the jazz idiom, and we have jazz musicians becoming serious composers. Perhaps we've stumbled on a theory. /45

But theory or no theory, jazz goes on finding new paths, sometimes reviving old styles, but, in either case, looking for freshness. In any art that is really vital and searching, splits are bound to develop; arguments arise and factions form. Just as in painting the non-objectivists are at sword's point with the representationalists, and in poetry the imagists declaim against the surrealists, so in jazz music we have a major battle between the traditionalists and the progressives. /46

These latter are the ones who are trying hardest to get away from the patterns of half a century, experimenting with new sonorities, using note relationships that are not common to the old jazz, and, in general, trying to keep jazz alive and interesting by broadening its scope. Jazz is a fresh, vital art in the present tense, with a solid past and an exciting future. /47

The telecast

1. What is Bernstein's specific purpose in this telecast? Quote the sentence that best states it. Does everything in the telecast relate directly to this central purpose?
2. What is gained by enumerating at the beginning several of the charges against jazz? Does Bernstein successfully refute all of these charges in the course of the talk? Which does he refute most successfully? Why?
3. What according to Bernstein are the main elements of jazz? In your own words describe each element.
4. What is the distinguishing difference between popular music and jazz? How is jazz like chamber music?
5. What are Bernstein's main conclusions about jazz? Is each successfully prepared for in the telecast itself? If so, show how.
6. Clearly this is an expository speech. Indicate what the essentials of such a speech are and how they are exemplified here.
7. What terms does he define in the course of the talk? Discuss his methods of definition.
8. Discuss Bernstein's use of musical passages in detail. What would the telecast lose if they were deleted? How does he get variety in them? Are there any points without musical illustration that you think should have them?
9. Comment on Bernstein's style: lengths and kinds of sentences, choice of words, use of technical talk, concreteness, humor, and so on. Would you call the style colloquial?
10. Thousands of viewers have come to believe that Bernstein has been the clearest expositor of music to appear on radio or television. How do you account for this high reputation he enjoys?

For further study and discussion

1. What briefly are the origins of jazz?
2. What varieties of jazz do you know? Define each and illustrate it with a recording.

3. Why should jazz have become respectable in the last twenty years?
4. Do you consider listening to jazz more of an intellectual experience than an emotional one? Develop your answer in detail. If possible, use recordings to support your points.
5. How can jazz be at once sad and humorous? Illustrate your points with recordings.
6. What do you consider to be essential in the training of a good jazz player?
7. Imitate Bernstein's explanation of "Sweet Sue" but use another song.
8. Draw as many comparisons as you can between jazz and chamber music, jazz and sonatas, jazz and symphonies.
9. In what respects do you consider jazz an expression of our age?
10. Do you agree that jazz is the only really original American contribution to music? To all the arts? Explain your answer in detail.

Suggestions for further reading

Louis Armstrong, ***Satchmo*** (New York, 1954)
Rudi Blesh, ***Shining Trumpets*** (New York, 1958)
Leonard G. Feather, ***The Book of Jazz*** (New York, 1957)
W. C. Handy, ***Father of the Blues*** (New York, 1941)
John F. Mehegan, ***Jazz Improvisation*** (New York, 1959)
Milton Mezzrow and Bernard Wolfe, ***Really the Blues*** (New York, 1946)
Nat Shapiro and Nat Hentoff, eds., ***Hear Me Talkin' to Ya*** (New York, 1955)
Marshall Stearns, ***The Story of Jazz*** (New York, 1956)

Home decoration

OSCAR WILDE

Oscar Wilde (1854-1900) was born in Dublin, the son of Sir William Wilde, an Irish surgeon. He attended Trinity College in Dublin and then in 1874 went to Magdalen College, Oxford, where he received the Newdigate Prize for English Verse. Influenced at an early age by the esthetic philosophy of Walter Pater, he became probably the best known of the Victorian esthetes.

Much of Wilde's reputation as a wit is based upon his habit of frequently treating the serious aspects of life lightly and the light aspects of life seriously. He is supposed to have said that he put all his genius into his life and only his talent into his writings. Some of his best known works include *The Happy Prince and Other Tales,* a collection of fairy stories; *The Ballad of Reading Gaol* and *De Profundis,* poems; *The Picture of Dorian Gray,* a novel; and *The Importance of Being Earnest* and *Lady Windermere's Fan,* plays.

Wilde achieved fame as a speaker, partly because his manner of refined speech, his flowing hair, and his style of dress assured him of ample, although often derisive, newspaper coverage. His most famous and best covered lecture tour brought him to the United States under the aegis of D'Oyly Carte, of Gilbert and Sullivan fame, in 1882. One of his most celebrated costumes consisted of formal tail coat, knee breeches, silk hose, and silver-buckled shoes. Usually he had a lily in his lapel, but at times he carried a sunflower, which eventually became the symbol of the esthete.

Throughout his tour Wilde encountered a great deal of hostility from the press. Few newspaper reporters cared for his languid manner and seeming disinterestedness in his speech. Pointed references to his protruding teeth, large nose, and sallow complexion were frequent, and the cartoonists of the day indulged their fancy to the fullest in drawing him.

The speech "House Decoration" was announced as a lecture on "The Practical Application of the Principles of the Aesthetic Theory to Exterior and Interior Decoration, With Observations upon Dress and Personal Ornaments." The earliest known date for this speech is May 11, 1882. It took thirty minutes to deliver and is one that he frequently gave on his American tour. Apparently it was fairly popular, since in New Orleans, for example, 1000 persons turned out to hear it.[1]

In my last lecture I gave you something of the history of Art in England. I sought to trace the influence of the French Revolution upon its development. I said something of the song of Keats and the school of the pre-Raphaelites. But I do not want to shelter the movement, which I have called the English Renaissance, under any palladium however noble, or any name however revered. The roots of it have, indeed, to be sought for in things that have

From *Essays and Lectures by Oscar Wilde,* Methuen & Company Ltd., 5th ed., 1920, pp. 159-171.

[1] For information about Wilde's lectures in this country, the best source is Lloyd Lewis and Henry Justin Smith, *Oscar Wilde Discovers America* (New York, 1936).

long passed away, and not, as some suppose, in the fancy of a few young men—although I am not altogether sure that there is anything much better than the fancy of a few young men. /1

When I appeared before you on a previous occasion, I had seen nothing of American art save the Doric columns and Corinthian chimney-pots visible on your Broadway and Fifth Avenue. Since then, I have been through your country to some fifty or sixty different cities, I think. I find that what your people need is not so much high imaginative art but that which hallows the vessels of everyday use. I suppose that the poet will sing and the artist will paint regardless whether the world praises or blames. He has his own world and is independent of his fellowmen. But the handicraftsman is dependent on your pleasure and opinion. He needs your encouragement and he must have beautiful surroundings. Your people love art but do not sufficiently honour the handicraftsman. Of course, those millionaires who can pillage Europe for their pleasure need have no care to encourage such; but I speak for those whose desire for beautiful things is larger than their means. I find that one great trouble all over is that your workmen are not given to noble designs. You cannot be indifferent to this, because Art is not something which you can take or leave. It is a necessity of human life. /2

And what is the meaning of this beautiful decoration which we call art? In the first place, it means value to the workman and it means the pleasure which he must necessarily take in making a beautiful thing. The mark of all good art is not that the thing done is done exactly or finely, for machinery may do as much, but that it is worked out with the head and the workman's heart. I cannot impress the point too frequently that beautiful and rational designs are necessary in all work. I did not imagine, until I went into some of your simpler cities, that there was so much bad work done. I found, where I went, bad wall-papers horribly designed, and coloured carpets, and that old offender the horse-hair sofa, whose stolid look of indifference is always so depressing. I found meaningless chandeliers and machine-made furniture, generally of rosewood, which creaked dismally under the weight of the ubiquitous interviewer. I came across the small iron stove which they always persist in decorating with machine-made ornaments, and which is as great a bore as a wet day or any other particularly dreadful institution. When the unusual extravagance was indulged in, it was garnished with two funeral urns. /3

It must always be remembered that what is well and carefully made by an honest workman, after a rational design, increases in beauty and value as the years go on. The old furniture brought over by the Pilgrims, two hundred years ago, which I saw in New England, is just as good and as beautiful today as it was when it first came here. Now, what you must do is to bring artists and handicraftsmen together. Handicraftsmen cannot live, certainly cannot thrive, without such companionship. Separate these two and you rob art of all spiritual motive. /4

Having done this, you must place your workman in the midst of beautiful surroundings. The artist is not dependent on the visible and the tangible. He has his visions and his dreams to feed on. But the workman must see lovely forms as he goes to his work in the morning and returns at eventide. And, in connection with this, I want to assure you that noble and beautiful designs are never the result of idle fancy or purposeless day-dreaming. They come only as the accumulation of habits of long and delightful observation. And yet such things may not be taught. Right ideas concerning them can certainly be obtained only by those who have been accustomed to rooms that are beautiful and colours that are satisfying. /5

Perhaps one of the most difficult things for us to do is to choose a notable and joyous dress for men. There would be more joy in life if we were to accustom ourselves to use all the beautiful colours we can in fashioning our own clothes. The dress of the future, I think, will use drapery to a great extent and will abound with joyous colour. At present we have lost all nobility of dress and, in doing so, have almost annihilated the modern sculptor. And, in looking around at the figures which adorn our parks, one could almost wish that we had completely killed the noble art. To see the frock-coat of the drawing-room done in bronze, or the double waistcoat perpetuated in marble, adds a new horror to death. But indeed, in looking through the history of costume, seeking an answer to the questions we have propounded, there is little that is either beautiful or appropriate. One of the earliest forms is the Greek drapery which is exquisite for young girls. And then, I think we may be pardoned a little enthusiasm over the dress of the time of Charles I., so beautiful indeed, that in spite of its invention being with the Cavaliers it was copied by the Puritans. And the dress for the children of that time must not be passed over. It was a very golden age of the little ones. I do not think that they have ever looked so lovely as they do in the pictures of that time. The dress of the last century in England is also peculiarly gracious and graceful. There is nothing bizarre or strange about it, but it is full of harmony and beauty. In these days, when we have suffered dreadfully from the incursions of the modern milliner, we hear ladies boast that they do not wear a dress more than once. In the old days, when the dresses were decorated with beautiful designs and worked with exquisite embroidery, ladies rather took a pride in bringing out the garment and wearing it many times and handing it down to their daughters—a process that would, I think, be quite appreciated by a modern husband when called upon to settle his wife's bills. /6

And how shall men dress? Men say that they do not particularly care how they dress, and that it is little matter. I am bound to reply that I do not think that you do. In all my journeys through the country, the only well-dressed men that I saw—and in saying this I earnestly deprecate the polished indignation of your Fifth Avenue dandies—were the Western miners. Their wide-brimmed hats, which shaded their faces from the sun and protected them from the rain, and the cloak, which is by far the most beautiful piece of drapery ever invented, may well be dwelt on with admiration. Their high boots, too, were sensible and practical. They wore only what was comfortable, and therefore beautiful. As I looked at them I could not help thinking with regret of the time when these picturesque miners would have made their fortunes and would go East to assume again all the abominations of modern fashionable attire. Indeed, so concerned was I that I made some of them promise that when they again appeared in the more crowded scenes of Eastern civilisation they would still continue to wear their lovely costume. But I do not believe they will. /7

Now, what America wants to-day is a school of rational art. Bad art is a great deal worse than no art at all. You must show your workmen specimens of good work so that they come to know what is simple and true and beautiful. To that end I would have you have a museum attached to these schools —not one of those dreadful modern institutions where there is a stuffed and very dusty giraffe, and a case or two of fossils, but a place where there are gathered examples of art decoration from various periods and countries. Such a place is the South Kensington Museum in London, whereon we build greater hopes for the future than on any other one thing. There I go every Saturday night, when the museum is open later than usual, to see the handicraftsman, the wood-worker, the glass-blower and the worker in metals. And it is here that the man of refinement and culture comes face to face with the workman who ministers to his joy. He comes to know more of the nobility of the workman, and the workman, feeling the appreciation, comes to know more of the nobility of his work. /8

You have too many white walls. More colour is wanted. You should have such men as Whistler among you to teach you the beauty and joy of colour. Take Mr. Whistler's "Symphony in White," which you no doubt have imagined to be something quite bizarre. It is nothing of the sort. Think of a cool grey sky flecked here and there with white clouds, a grey ocean and three wonderfully beautiful figures robed in white, leaning over the water and dropping white flowers from their fingers. Here is no extensive intellectual scheme to trouble you, and no metaphysics of which we have had quite enough in art. But if the simple and unaided colour strike the right key-note, the whole conception is made clear. I regard Mr. Whistler's famous Peacock Room as the finest thing in colour and art decoration which the world has known since Correggio painted that wonderful room in Italy where the little children are dancing on the walls. Mr. Whistler finished another room just before I came away—a breakfast room in blue and yellow. The ceiling was a light blue, the cabinet-work and the furniture were of a yellow wood, the curtains at the windows were white and worked in yellow, and when the table was set for breakfast with dainty blue china nothing can be conceived at once so simple and so joyous. /9

The fault which I have observed in most of your rooms is that there is apparent no definite scheme of colour. Everything is not attuned to a key-note as it should be. The apartments are crowded with pretty things which have no relation to one another. Again, your artists must decorate what is more simply useful. In your art schools I found no attempt to decorate such things as the vessels for water. I know of nothing uglier than the ordinary jug or pitcher. A museum could be filled with the different kinds of water vessels which are used in hot countries. Yet we continue to submit to the depressing jug with the handle all on one side. I do not see the wisdom of decorating dinner-plates with sunsets and soup-plates with moon-light scenes. I do not think it adds anything to the pleasure of the canvas-back duck to take it out of such glories. Besides, we do not want a soup-plate whose bottom seems to vanish in the distance. One feels neither safe nor comfortable under such conditions. In fact, I did not find in the art schools of the country that the difference was explained between decorative and imaginative art. /10

The conditions of art should be simple. A great deal more depends upon the heart than upon the head. Appreciation of art is not secured by any elaborate scheme of learning. Art requires a good healthy atmosphere. The motives for art are still around about us as they were round about the ancients. And the subjects are also easily found by the earnest sculptor and the painter. Nothing is more picturesque and graceful than a man at work. The artist who goes to the children's playground, watches them at their sport and sees the boy stoop to tie his shoe, will find the same themes that engaged the attention of the ancient Greeks, and such observation and the illustrations which follow will do much to correct that foolish impression that mental and physical beauty are always divorced. /11

To you, more than perhaps to any other country, has Nature been generous in furnishing material for art workers to work in. You have marble quarries where the stone is more beautiful in colour than any the Greeks ever had for their beautiful work, and yet day after day I am confronted with the great building of some stupid man who has used the beautiful material as if it were not precious almost beyond speech. Marble should not be used save by noble workmen. There is nothing which gave me a greater sense of barrenness in travelling through the country than the entire absence of wood carving on your houses. Wood carving is the simplest of the decorative arts. In Switzerland the little barefooted boy beautifies the porch of his father's house with examples of skill in this direction. Why should not American boys do a great deal more and better than Swiss boys? /12

There is nothing to my mind more coarse in conception and more vulgar in execution than modern jewellery. This is something that can easily be corrected. Something better should be made out of the beautiful gold which is stored up in your mountain hollows and strewn along your river beds. When I was in Leadville and reflected that all the shining silver that I saw coming from the mines would be made into ugly dollars, it made me sad. It should be made into something more permanent. The golden gates at Florence are as beautiful to-day as when Michael Angelo saw them. /13

We should see more of the workman than we do. We should not be content to have the salesman stand between us—the salesman who knows nothing of what he is selling save that he is charging a great deal too much for it. And watching the workman will teach that most important lesson—the nobility of all rational workmanship. /14

I said in my last lecture that art would create a new brotherhood among men by furnishing a universal language. I said that under its beneficent influences war might pass away. Thinking this, what place can I ascribe to art in our education? If children grow up among all fair and lovely things, they will grow to love beauty and detest ugliness before they know the reason why. If you go into a house where everything is coarse, you find things chipped and broken and unsightly. Nobody exercises any care. If everything is dainty and delicate, gentleness and refinement of manner are unconsciously acquired. When I was in San Francisco I used to visit the Chinese Quarter frequently. There I used to watch a great hulking Chinese workman at his task of digging, and used to see him every day drink his tea from a little cup as delicate in texture as the petal of a flower, whereas in all the grand hotels of the land, where thousands of dollars have been lavished on great gilt mirrors and gaudy columns, I have been given my coffee or my chocolate in cups an inch and a quarter thick. I think I have deserved something nicer. /15

The art systems of the past have been devised by philosophers who looked upon human beings as obstructions. They have tried to educate boys' minds before they had any. How much better it would be in these early years to teach children to use their hands in the rational service of mankind. I would have a workshop attached to every school, and one hour a day given up to the teaching of simple decorative arts. It would be a golden hour to the children. And you would soon raise up a race of handicraftsmen who would transform the face of your country. I have seen only one such school in the United States, and this was in Philadelphia and was founded by my friend Mr. Leyland. I stopped there yesterday and have brought some of the work here this afternoon to show you. Here are two disks of beaten brass: the designs on them are beautiful, the workmanship is simple, and the entire result is satisfactory. The work was done by a little boy twelve years old. This is a wooden bowl decorated by a little girl of thirteen. The design is lovely and the colouring delicate and pretty. Here you see a piece of beautiful wood carving accomplished by a little boy of nine. In such work as this, children learn sincerity in art. They learn to abhor the liar in art—the man who paints wood to look like iron, or iron to look like stone. It is a practical school of morals. No better way is there to learn to love Nature than to understand Art. It dignifies every flower of the field. And, the boy who sees the thing of beauty which a bird on the wing becomes when transferred to wood or canvas will probably not throw the customary stone. What we want is something spiritual added to life. Nothing is so ignoble that Art cannot sanctify it. /16

The speech

1. Does Wilde make much attempt to show why he should be listened to on this subject? Why might he not have had to do so?
2. What is Wilde's attitude toward his American audience? Cite particular passages that make this attitude clear. What does he assume about the interests and values of the audience? In short, what is the tone of the speech?
3. What assumptions about art are basic to Wilde's lecture?
4. What does Wilde want in men's and women's dress? Would he be more pleased, do you suppose, with our dress today? Explain your answer.
5. How does the paragraph about museums fit into the main argument? What kind of museums does he want? Do we have any of this type today?
6. What complaints are common to Wilde's criticism of American rooms, furniture, pottery, and jewelry? Put several of these complaints into syllogistic form. Would you say he might be better pleased with what he would find in America today?
7. Do you find any use of exaggeration for satirical effect? Of irony? Of ridicule? Would you call the speech as a whole satirical?
8. Develop in detail Wilde's argument in the last paragraph that art is both moral and spiritual.
9. Comment on Wilde's choice of words. What words used frequently by Wilde are not ordinarily employed by American males? Would a typical American audience today find his choice of words irritating?
10. Are Wilde and Read in essential agreement on the nature and function of art? Explain your answer.

For further study and discussion

1. How do you account for the fact that often our more expensive china, furniture, etc., tend to be simple whereas the less expensive tend to be more highly ornamented? Why should we have to pay for simplicity?
2. What would Wilde say about American automobiles? Which ones do you think he would particularly like? Dislike? What would be the bases of his judgments?
3. Is the American workingman becoming more of an individual craftsman or less of one? What are the advantages of the tendency you discern? The disadvantages?
4. Do you believe that form to be beautiful must be functional? Give examples of what you consider to be functional and nonfunctional forms in furniture and appliances.
5. What makes wallpaper beautiful? Linoleum? Carpeting? Painted walls? Pictures? Do you use the same criteria judging all of these? If so, what are they?
6. What do you think the functions of a museum should be? Which one have you enjoyed most and why?
7. Do you believe the English are still as disdainful as Wilde of American art and decoration? Give the evidence on which your opinion is based.
8. Do you feel that learning is unnecessary for an appreciation of natural beauty? Of house decoration? Of painting and sculpture? Of architecture? Does it help?
9. Are good abstract art and attractive home decoration the result of the application of the same principles? Defend your answer with illustrations.
10. Does advertising affect our judgment of beauty in contemporary craftsmanship? If so, how? Are the results hopeful or dispiriting? Develop your answer with illustrations.

Suggestions for further reading

Jakob von Falke, ***Art in the House*** (Boston, 1879)
Paul Frankl, ***New Dimensions*** (New York, 1928)
Harriet Goldstein, ***Art in Everyday Life*** (New York, 1954)
Maitland E. Graves, ***The Art of Color and Design*** (New York, 1951)
William Morris, ***Architecture, Industry, and Wealth*** (London, 1902)
Richard J. Neutra, ***Survival Through Design*** (New York, 1954)
Denman W. Ross, ***A Theory of Pure Design*** (Boston, 1907)
Russell Sturgis, ***The Interdependence of the Arts of Design*** (Chicago, 1905)
Frank Lloyd Wright, ***The Natural House*** (New York, 1954)

Wanted: A Marshall Plan for the arts in America

REBECCA LYNCH

Rebecca Lynch, who composed and delivered "Wanted: A Marshall Plan for the Arts in America," has played the

---

Reprinted by permission of Miss Lynch from a copy of her speech supplied by Professor Wilbur E. Gilman, Chairman of the Department of Speech at Queens College, Flushing, N. Y.

violin professionally for the past sixteen years, supplying background music for motion pictures and television and "occasionally being seen on the medium." According to Miss Lynch, who is at present a student at Queens College, Flushing, Long Island, she returned to college to major in music education in order to qualify herself to teach in the public school system. Her speech was prepared for a regular class assignment in the basic public speaking course.

Do you realize that by contrast with the billions of dollars our federal government spends on its defense policy it does not contribute a penny toward the support of the arts? The irony of this situation strikes one if he is aware of the fact that it has been through the Marshall Plan that some European countries have been able to continue their policy of subsidization of the serious arts in spite of their economic adversity. Our financial aid is not specifically earmarked for particular institutions. Since the national budgets of European countries provide for opera houses and musical organizations, we have in effect contributed to their upkeep. /1

I suppose that serious music will never achieve the indispensability in America that it has in European countries, and it seems curious that our values are at such variance with those of our cousins across the ocean. I say cousins because most Americans are Europeans either by birth or by inheritance. Perhaps Europeans are aware of the need of nurturing the arts because the history of the arts is inseparable from the history of their land. /2

Originally, the great patrons of the arts were the czars, popes, emperors, and kings. The palace and the cathedral were the marketplaces of culture. Bach and Haydn are salient examples of musicians who developed under these circumstances. Bach held a series of positions in churches for which he constantly wrote new works. Haydn spent thirty years of his professional career in the service of the Esterhazy family. Not only did he have constant commissions for new works, but he had the private Esterhazy orchestra at his disposal at all times. This fact meant that he could experiment with new musical ideas, hear them immediately, and then either reject them or incorporate them into his style. In addition to their innate talents, Bach and Haydn had economic security, motivation, and the intellectual climate in which to work. /3

With the breakdown of the aristocratic way of life the patronage system ceased. Europeans, proud of their heritage, saw to it that the talented members of their populace were provided with the opportunity to develop and to perform. Today every European country sets aside an impressive amount of its treasury for music and would find it as unthinkable to discontinue this policy as to discontinue setting aside funds for public health and education. /4

To cite just one country as an illustration of what the results of government subsidization can be, let us look at Switzerland. This country, which is one half of one per cent the area of the United States, has one hundred repertory theatres which present nightly performances eleven months of the year. Opera and symphony orchestras are found in most cities. The prices for admission are comparable to the cost of a movie ticket. Thousands of singers and instrumentalists are employed. New works are constantly created and performed. /5

By contrast, only twice in history has the budget of the American government included cultural expenditures of any appreciable size, and both times objectives other than the advancement of culture were in view. The first occasion was during the depression of the thirties when the projects of the WPA included art, writing, the theatre, and music. The purpose of the projects was to preclude starvation. When the depression ended so did the projects. The second occasion of the government subvention was at the advent of the Cold War when the competition of men's minds was begun. In 1954 the Arts, Foundations and Commissions Subcommittee of the House, Education, and Welfare Committee, after hearings in which federal aid for the fine arts had been urged by numerous witnesses, declined to recommend any of the proposed bills because, "we do not believe this is a proper area for the expenditure of federal funds." By contrast with this tight-fistedness, the same Congress made provisions for a five million dollar emergency fund for the use of the President "to meet extraordinary and unusual circumstances arising in the international affairs of the government" with the understanding that part would be used to expand the overseas itineraries of American performing artists. That is how "Porgy and Bess" was enabled to follow its Moscow run with appearances in Yugoslavia, Greece, Israel, Egypt and Spain. That is how the New York Philharmonic played in Peru, how New York City and San Francisco ballet groups were scheduled for Asia. /6

Let us take a look at the picture in America where serious music is concerned. The arts are developed on a local basis. Local funds, local tastes, and local leadership dictate the tempo. Private patronage largely sustains the arts. But in the first place, the cost of operating institutions has gone up. And in the second place, it is no longer possible for individuals to amass fortunes to a degree that they can contribute enough for serious music to exist and maintain a high level. Do you have any idea what the average yearly income for a member of a major symphony orchestra is? It is $1800. The seasons are short and in between seasons unemployment is widespread. In many cities where the symphony cannot afford to pay their musicians enough they persuade local businesses and education systems to make places and give jobs to musicians. The result of this situation is that there is an increasing shortage of string players. Where the possibility of making a livelihood is so slight fewer students have the incentive to study seriously with the intention of making music a career. /7

The problem of the musician is not his alone. It is everybody's concern. The survival of the musician and the survival of culture in a free world are linked. James C. Petrillo, former head of the American Federation of Musicians, sees slow death for music at the professional level in American cities of a population of 300,000 and under. I should like to close with a quotation of his which sums up the picture of music in America. Mr. Petrillo states, "Subsidy is not a pretty word in our language, but I can find no other word, no other means, to answer our immediate needs." /8

For discussion

1. Aside from the title is there any place where the speaker explicitly tells what she wants? Is the central idea nevertheless clear? If so, tell how it becomes clear.
2. What organization is followed here? Would it be correct to say that this is a truncated problem-solution organization? Explain your reply.
3. What is gained by approaching the subject historically?
4. Would the speech have been stronger had Miss Lynch provided a glimpse of the accomplishments of the arts in America under the WPA?
5. Do you have any evidence to refute any of Miss Lynch's contentions?
6. What basis does the speaker have in the last paragraph for saying that "survival of the musician and the survival of culture in a free world are linked"? What meaning or meanings of "culture" are implied? Does the argument collapse if this point is unacceptable?
7. Do you see any ways in which Miss Lynch's speech could be improved?

3/ SCIENCE

Science and society

HAROLD C. UREY

Harold C. Urey's speech on the intellectual aspects of science was delivered at the 100th Anniversary Academic Convocation of The Cooper Union for the Advancement of Science and Art in New York City on November 2, 1959.

Urey, a Nobel Prize winner in 1934 (for discovery of deuterium, or heavy hydrogen), and a professor of chemistry at the University of California, Berkeley, chose an appropriate subject for a speech to be delivered at the Cooper Union. Edwin S. Burdell, director of the Cooper Union, has said in the *Encyclopedia Americana* that the institution is devoted to "instruction in the application of Science and Art to the practical business of life," and that the guiding policy of the institution is "the educational philosophy of Scientific Humanism, a curricular synthesis of science, art, and the humanities."

Of the difficulties of talking to a general audience on a specialized subject, Urey has written: "In order to make a good scientific speech it is necessary to speak loud enough so the person in the back row can hear, and not do as some people do—talk to a little group in the front row. It is necessary to remember that if the subject is complicated and intricate, the complicated and intricate details are known to specialists in the field, in which case they do not need to hear them again; if these details are unknown to others, then they cannot possibly learn them in a few minutes. Hence, again it is useless to include such things. Beyond this, it is always necessary to speak slowly and clearly, and have something to say in which one has interested one's self and which may be of interest to the audience."[1] In making scientific information accessible to a wide audience, Urey is pursuing the basic purpose of the Cooper Union. It is with the crucial problem of applying the complexities of modern scientific investigation to social needs that Urey is concerned.

One approach to understanding and evaluating this speech will be to investigate how extensively Urey's views are compatible with the scientific humanism of the Cooper Union and its desires to promote a "synthesis of science, art and the humanities" and to sponsor instruction in "the application of Science" to "the practical business of life."

During the years of this century and particularly since the end of World War II, it has become evident to the people of civilized countries that the practical applications of scientific knowledge are of immense importance in our modern society. To those of us who have been interested as professionals in science and engineering, this fact has been recognized even earlier than it has by the non-specialist in these fields. In fact, these practical applications of science come close to dominating all considerations of government and economics of our own country and those of Europe and Asia. Also, the purely intellectual aspects of science are beginning to dominate our ideas in philosophical and religious matters. /1

It may be well to recall to ourselves certain immense developments of this century particularly. At the turn of the century, the steam engine, the railroad, telegraph and telephone represented the outstanding technical achievements of the nineteenth century, and they were very great achievements indeed. In all countries of the world where these developments occurred, one of the most ancient and disgraceful institutions disappeared never to return, namely, that of slavery. It is well to remember that these developments, and particularly that of inanimate power, abolished this hard labor of unfortunate human beings which had supported all the luxury of the ancient and medieval civilizations. But the closing years of the old century or the beginning years of the new witnessed the beginnings of the development of the internal combustion engine, wireless telegraphy, the aeroplane, and the discovery of radioactivity which led inevitably to the development of atomic energy. These developments have given the modern technical countries a degree of luxury beyond the most fanciful dreams of the preceding

Harold C. Urey, "Science and Society," *Vital Speeches of the Day*, Vol. XXVI, December 15, 1959, pp. 141-144. By permission of the author and The Cooper Union for the Advancement of Science and Art.

[1] Letter to the editors, June 15, 1960.

centuries. The steady developments of biology and their application to agriculture have produced such an abundance of food that in this country this abundance has produced economic embarrassment. /2

The most effective way of illustrating these general statements is by means of the statistics relating to the use of mechanical power and the use of steel, since these are general measures of activities of the kind being considered. /3

The use of fossil fuels in this country increased by a factor of 8 between 1900 and 1955. Coal was the principal source of energy in 1900. In 1955, petroleum and natural gas contributed 67% of the total energy, while coal supplied only 30%. Electrical power increased from negligible amounts in 1900 to about 500 watts per person. This is not large but nevertheless about 6 per cent of our total energy is in this flexible form, enabling us to do such neat and convenient things as light our houses, run the many small convenient machines, operate our communication systems, etc. This growth of the use of power emphasizes the physical basis of our industrial transformations. The increased use of steel and other metals and of many other substitutes emphasizes the same point in another way. /4

Such statistics may be necessary as a means of impressing the younger generation present in this room but are quite unnecessary for those of my age. I remember easily events and conditions of the last 60 years. These years span the time between the horse and buggy age and that of 55,000,000 private automobiles; also, the time between Marconi's primitive experiments and television in the many homes of the U.S.; also the time when the 20th Century Limited was the magnificent train through the local town of my boyhood and its virtual discontinuance because of the competition of aeroplanes. I have some nostalgia for the old days. What could be so thrilling as a ride with grandfather in a sleigh behind a matched team of blacks on a clear night with stars above and white snow around, with me and grandpa nestled warm and cozy beneath a buffalo robe? My own children have never known this luxury at all. Today we read about these things or see them in the Currier and Ives prints. /5

The great changes in our everyday mode of life that have resulted from these developments have been so rapid that it is difficult to visualize them. Sixty years ago, people were often born in a house and lived in that house as children, took over the place from their parents, and were taken care of by their children in their old age and died in that same house. Various deviations from this situation existed, of course, since the population of this country has increased rapidly, but during the course of one generation a very cohesive family development existed and this has been even more true of some other countries. Since 1900, the situation has changed markedly. At the present time, my own children and those of my near relatives and of my friends and acquaintances live far from their parents and scattered over the entire United States and sometimes abroad as well. This fundamental change has come about because of the rapid means of transportation and communication and our dependence on modern industrial developments for our livelihood. /6

Also, our mutual dependence on other sections of the community has greatly increased. Today even farmers do not grow their own food or even essential parts of it, and this was definitely not the case 60 years ago. We do not do any of our own carpentry or other building. Our plumbing facilities and electrical requirements are beyond our capacities to install or repair. I studied in grade and high school by the light of a kerosene lamp and the only place which uses these at the present time so far as my experience goes is Sequoia National Park. /7

What was once a society of rather small, closely knit communities in the rural and small town regions of the United States has been replaced by a roving population where blood relatives know each other only slightly and see each other only a few times a year in many cases. This has come about because of the rapid means of transport and the demands of industrial employment, or because of wanderlust made easy by these means. These few simple illustrations point up a very great social change in our country and other parts of the world within two generations. These changes could not have occurred without the help of applied sciences. /8

The methods of making war have changed greatly in these 60 years. In 1900, General Bacterium and his hordes probably claimed more lives of soldiers than did the weapons of human enemies. Today this is not true, but the expense of preparation for war and the stupendously greater expense of actual war have both greatly increased during these years. Wars and the curious psychology of politicians have produced a fantastic national debt in the United States. The physical cost in machines and weapons was met during the war by greater effort on the part of the populations of the world and by reduced standards of living. Only the paper value as debts plagues us since then. However, all these things are finally the result of the applications of science to another phase of human activity. /9

These activities have had profound effects upon government activities and undoubtedly we have not learned how to adjust our governments to them. A few illustrations show how these industrial developments have increased government activities. Not only have government budgets increased because of the decreasing value of the dollar, but they have increased in proportion to the total income of countries. /10

Automobiles require vast expenditures for roads and police. Aeroplanes require airfields, air navigation facilities and government regulation. Radio and television must be regulated by the community. In my opinion, this is done better in the United Kingdom than in the U.S.A. (Parenthetically, I do not like advertising.) Electric power requires public regulations and the practical requirement of monopoly leads to price control. (Again, more control is needed in order to do something about those ugly power poles which have not been improved in the last 60 years. Odd, isn't it, that street lighting can be supplied from underground, but private power cannot? I speak feelingly. The view of the Pacific Ocean from my house is through a maze of power lines.) Railroads long ago required public regulation in the U.S. or public ownership in Europe. Large manufacturing facilities and the necessary large labor organizations require government control because of the great financial interests of the public. The mobility of the population leads to additional social security needs and additional police problems. This feature affects our moral and religious problems. Large and effective weapons have completely changed our international problems in the last 60 years. /11

I wish to state as my firm belief that the enormous growth of government activities since 1900 is due in large measure to the importance of applied science in this age, and to predict that this growth will continue to a very substantial degree in the future. Probably all of us deplore this situation, but only a return to the general conditions of 1900 or possibly 1859 by us and the rest of the world could correct the trend. In a certain sense, applied science is forcing various phases of socialism upon the modern world in the sense that its successful activities require more community interference in our activities. /12

Those who discuss these problems often mention the exponential character of the increase in all these things, i.e., the factor by which they have increased since 1900 is about the same as that by which they increased between 1840 and 1900. But there is a difference. Somewhere in this century some saturation must occur. There are only so many waking hours in which to use gadgets, to listen to radios, to drive cars or space machines, etc. Also, surely we have now reached the limit of our use of war in human disputes. This country has in some ways marked certain approximate limits with respect to some of these activities. /13

To those of us who spend our lives working on scientific problems, science is a great intellectual adventure of such interest that nothing else we ever do can compare with it. We are attempting to understand the order of a physical universe, vast in extent in space and time, and most complicated and beautiful in its details. In this vast universe we find living things of which we ourselves are a part and these living things, constituting in bulk only a minute fraction of the whole, are yet some of the most amazing and most fascinating parts of the whole. The ideas developed in these studies are changing the entire philosophy of men, their entire view as to their place in this universe. The applications of science are purely incidental to these intellectual studies and we believe that these purely intellectual aspects will modify the lives of man more than will all the applications of science to the material welfare of men. /14

It is well to mention some of the more important intellectual developments of the past centuries: /15

1) The structure of the solar system as developed by Copernicus was one of the first intellectual achievements that modified men's ideas profoundly. The earth was no longer the center of the universe and established institutions at the time realized this and attempted to extinguish this idea. The victory has gone to science without question. /16

2) The proposal of biological evolution, a century old this year, again modified the ideas of men regarding themselves and their place in nature. This idea was again opposed by established institutions. The victory has gone to scientific thought overwhelmingly. /17

3) Geology has established the history of the earth and today we know much about its age, namely some 3 billion years for the oldest rocks and about 4.5 billion years for the meteorites. These facts have greatly increased our concepts of time and the intricate details of the history of the earth and universe. /18

4) The nineteenth century witnessed the discovery and development of our ideas regarding electricity, magnetism, the properties of light and the fundamental laws of thermodynamics. These ideas laid the basis for much of our exact knowledge in

physics and chemistry, and their application to practical affairs has given us our important sources of energy during this century. /19

5) During this century we have learned much in regard to the structure of the universe, its extent to vast distances, its possible origin and details of evolution, its possible age. These ideas have not been opposed and this signifies an acceptance by a large section of the community. /20

6) Other scientific ideas have not been so controversial because they did not contradict established thought, as they were not capable of being observed without the aid of complex apparatus. Today after two centuries we know much about the chemical and physical properties and structure of matter. This is of great intellectual success. It has resulted from the work of many minds of varying capacities. This knowledge made a very important contribution to man's physical existence and also to his effectiveness in waging war. /21

7) During this century we have learned much about the mechanisms of living things. Among these one of the most fascinating has been the problem of heredity. Today the actual details of these mechanisms are being elucidated so that we begin to understand the actual punch card system by which hereditary characteristics are carried from one generation to the next. /22

8) At the close of the nineteenth century and the beginning of the twentieth century, the quantum theory and the relativity theory were discovered. They have profoundly influenced all physical thought during the years since. They deal with concepts not easily observed and they are the result of most careful and penetrating analysis. With their aid we have come to understand much about the structure of matter. In fact, we understand the origin of all chemical phenomena in principle from these developments even though the immense detailed complexity largely can be described only by direct observation. /23

9) During the years of this century and especially during the last 20 years, we have learned much in regard to the nuclei of atoms. This is one of the most magnificent intellectual accomplishments of all history. It leads to an understanding of the evolution of stars, the origin of the elements and the vast supplies of energy required for these processes. It influences our lives mostly through its practical applications. Its revolutionary conclusions on the intellectual side are accepted today without question. One wonders how they would have been received a century ago! /24

10) During recent years another great intellectual scientific advance is in the making. Out of the rockets which bombarded England, that stubborn stalwart of freedom, and the possibility of launching atomic bombs from great distances has come the possibility and, indeed, the fact of space exploration. Radiation belts about the earth have been explored and we now know that the moon has no magnetic field and that it has a "peculiarly low" level of radioactivity in its surface. Why do we investigate these things? The great fundamental driving force of the human intellect is curiosity, but it is a very sophisticated curiosity that drives us to investigate these things. Thus the radiation belts are due to the high energy particles moving in the neighborhood of the earth as they are trapped by the earth's magnetic field, and we are interested in these very energetic particles, where they originate, and how they acquired their high energies. Also, a study of the moon's surface tells us much about its past history, and thus of the history of the earth and solar system, and thus of the development of the stars generally. During the coming years, space exploration will proceed at an increased pace. Eventually we may prove that life does exist or has existed on Mars and Venus. /25

These ideas and many others have fascinated active scientists during all the time which they have been developed. But they are modifying the most fundamental ideas of people also. /26

By religion most scientists are sceptics, that is, they do not subscribe to the dogmas of Christianity, Judaism, or any other religion. They mostly regard the supernatural aspects of these religions in the same light as they do those of the religions of ancient Egypt, Greece and Rome. On the moral side, they are mostly close followers of the precepts of Christianity and Judaism. It seems to me that these attitudes have resulted from their scientific studies. This is true of myself. It is my opinion that these attitudes have already spread to the general population to some extent and that this will occur to an even greater degree in the future. To many, these are unpleasant statements, but I believe they are facts and progress is not made by sweeping facts under the rug. /27

Science is not a substitute for religion. It very often imposes a condition represented by the word "must." We cannot do things which do not conform to the requirements of natural laws and facts. But science never imposes a condition represented by the word "ought." There is no requirement imposed by science that certain types of human behavior are morally right and others are morally wrong. Scientists live by the morals taught to them directly or indirectly by the great religions practiced in the countries where they reside. /28

Also, science gives us no purpose in living beyond having a pleasant existence in one way or another. Scientists themselves are inspired by the magnificent things which they study. But science does not give the ordinary man whose daily life is often drab and anything but sublime any objective that gives him a feeling of dignity. Such feelings are so necessary if he is to rise above the disappointments and temptations of life and if he is to do the best of which he is capable. One of the great needs of this age is a great prophet who can accept the facts of science and at the same time can give inspiration to fill this great void. I do not believe that current evangelists so popular from time to time have made any contribution to this fundamental problem. /29

It may be that the view expressed here is unduly pessimistic. Probably at all times in the past some fraction of the population was frankly sceptical, another most thoughtfully devout, and the great mass mostly unconcerned and mostly uncritically thoughtless and conforming and possibly this will continue into the future. Certainly, certain situations relative to these problems have been anything but ideal at certain historical periods of the past. But may it not be that the rapid rise of juvenile delinquency in recent years is due to the lack of the feeling given by the word "ought" imposed by the community, by parents, or by teachers, and may it not be that this in turn is due to its absence from science which is coming to dominate the thinking of this age? /30

These things could all become much simpler if the clock were turned back one century. This cannot be done and most of us do not wish for this at all. What some people desire is that it be turned back on some phases and not on others. We wish for low cost government, but wish for new roads for that new Detroit monstrosity and a new airport able to handle those new jets. We wish for a decreased state budget in California, but also demand a new irrigation ditch. We wish for a lower military appropriation, but at the same time worry about falling behind in the missile race. We wish for a return to the old philosophical security, but are fascinated by the new ideas brought forth by science. /31

We cannot turn the clock back. We must face our social, philosophical, and governmental problems in each age. They present a great challenge to us and surely we will solve our problems again in this scientific age. I hope that the solutions may be better than were some such solutions of past problems. /32

The speech

1. What is the central idea of this speech? Basically, is the speech expository or argumentative? Defend your answer.
2. In what ways does the speaker establish his authority to speak on the subject? Quote specific passages where he does this.
3. Since Urey's main interest here is obviously in the intellectual aspects of science, what is the purpose of the first part of the speech where he discusses the practical applications of science?
4. What are the chief effects on society of the practical application of science? Of the intellectual developments in science? Compare the two sets of results in their implications for human happiness.
5. Do you believe that the speech supports the conclusion that "surely we will solve our problems again in this scientific age"? Give the reasons for your answer.
6. Since Urey's audience at the Cooper Union would know all of the ten "important intellectual developments of the past centuries," what is gained by listing them?
7. How completely do you feel the speaker has covered the relation between science and society? Can you think of any major effects science has had upon our society that are not mentioned here?
8. What different kinds of support does Urey employ? Which kind do you think is most effectively used? Why?
9. What devices does he use to keep the attention of the audience?
10. Characterize the style in detail. Especially, show why it is or is not appropriate to the subject and audience.

For further study and discussion

1. In what ways did technical achievements help to eliminate slavery?
2. Are they likely to help us eliminate our present racial discord?
3. Do you feel that your family is less cohesive than your father's family was? Than his father's was?
4. How does our mutual dependence liberate us? In what ways does it make living more precarious?
5. Show by a careful cause and effect sequence how applied science can result in big government.
6. Do you think we have reached the saturation point in gadgets and luxury items? Explain your answer.
7. Which intellectual developments of the past century do you consider the most influential in shaping man's thought and life?
8. How do you account for man's "sophisticated curiosity"?

9. Is it progress to discard the dogmas of religion? Develop your answer in considerable detail.
10. What do you believe are the chief limitations of science?
11. What do you think would be the nature of the teaching of a prophet who bases his arguments and exhortations upon scientific truth?
12. How can science serve to improve our moral conduct?

Suggestions for further reading

Lyman Bryson, ***Science and Freedom*** (New York, 1947)
Vannevar Bush, ***Endless Horizons*** (Washington, D.C., 1946)
I. Bernard Cohen, ***Science, Servant of Man*** (Boston, 1948)
Albert Einstein, ***The World as I See It*** (New York, 1949)
Aldous Huxley, ***Science, Liberty, and Peace*** (New York, 1946)
William L. Laurence, ***Men and Atoms*** (New York, 1959)
Bertrand Russell, ***The Scientific Outlook*** (New York, 1931)
Edward Teller and Albert L. Latter, ***Our Nuclear Future*** (New York, 1958)
George P. Thomson, ***The Foreseeable Future*** (Cambridge, Eng., 1955)

Science, technology, and world development

HARRISON BROWN

This speech by Harrison Brown, professor of geochemistry at the California Institute of Technology, was delivered in Austria in 1958 at the third Pugwash conference, which was attended by some eighty scientists, including twenty from the United States and ten from the U.S.S.R.

The Pugwash conferences resulted "from a spontaneous movement among scientists of different countries, seeking international exchange of ideas on problems arising from the impact of science on human affairs."[1] They were originally undertaken to examine the perils resulting from the development of weapons of mass destruction, but the third conference was more extensive in scope than the earlier meetings. In addition to the dangers posed by modern weapons, the scientists discussed political problems of the arms race; science, technology, and education in the scientific age; international exchange and cooperation in science; and the responsibility of the scientists.

The public statement (called the Vienna Declaration) which was issued at the end of the conference "calls upon scientists not merely to serve willingly as experts for their governments, but to assume on their own initiative a pioneering role in the education of public opinion and political leadership to the facts of the atomic age. . . ."[2]

It is, of course, in the context of this international meeting of scientists, with its broad concern for the relationship between science and the improvement of man's condition, that Brown's speech must be read. Additional information and the official statement of the Pugwash conference may be found in *Science*, 128:1071-73, in the *Bulletin of the Atomic Scientists*, 14:338-44, and in F. L. Wormald's *The Pugwash Experiment; an Essay in Liberal Education* (Washington, D.C.: Association of American Colleges, 1958).

The most obvious threat to the survival of civilization today is nuclear war between the present world powers. This is also the most immediate threat, but in the long run it is not necessarily the most serious one. In the decades ahead we are going to be faced by a sequence of problems of great complexity, all of which will demand solution and which must be anticipated if they are to be solved. Most of the problems are directly related to the changes which are taking place in the world as a result of the upsurge of science and technology. Solution of the problems will necessitate the concerted and intensive application of science and technology on an unprecedented scale. /1

Most of the difficulties confronting us today stem from the fact that we are living in the middle of an enormous revolution which is characterized primarily by rapid technological change. Never before in history has society changed as rapidly as it is changing today. The closest parallel to our modern situation occurred about 7,000 years ago when our primitive food-gathering ancestors learned that they could cultivate edible plants and that they could domesticate animals. With the emergence of these new techniques more than 500 persons could be supported in areas where previously only one could be supported. /2

Harrison Brown, "Science, Technology, and World Development," *Bulletin of the Atomic Scientists*, December 14, 1958, pp. 409-412. Reprinted by permission of the *Bulletin of the Atomic Scientists*.

[1] *Bulletin of the Atomic Scientists*, XIV (November 1958), p. 338.

[2] Ibid., p. 340.

During the past 300 years, man has attained a remarkable degree of control over his environment. Through the achievement of a partial understanding of how nature operates, he has learned how to grow more crops on a given piece of land; he has learned a great deal about disease and how to control it; he has learned how to harness the energy of fossil fuels; he has learned how to transport himself, his ideas, and his goods rapidly. /3

One result of these innovations has been to accelerate the spread of agriculture over the world. A second result has been to shift man in many parts of the world from a predominantly rural existence within the framework of an agricultural economy to a predominantly urban existence within the framework of an industrial economy. A third result has been to stimulate increasing individual demands for material possessions. A fourth result has been to stimulate an unprecedented rate of increase of human population. /4

During the last three centuries, we have seen the emergence of industrial-scientific civilization in England, and we have seen it spread throughout Western Europe. In the last 150 years, we have seen industrialization cross the Atlantic and spread over North America. In the last sixty years, we have seen industrialization cross the Pacific to Japan. In the last thirty-five years, we have seen it spread to the USSR. Today, we can observe it spreading to Australia and to parts of Africa. We can hear rumblings of impending industrialization in India, China, southeast Asia, and South America. /5

In the absence of a world catastrophe, this spread of industrialization to the rest of the world is inevitable, in the same sense that the spread of agriculture throughout the world was inevitable, once agriculture was invented. It seems unlikely that industrialized and unindustrialized nations can coexist indefinitely any more than the agricultural and food-gathering cultures of the past were able to coexist indefinitely. /6

In addition, it seems clear that the further spread of industrialization necessarily must take place within a framework that differs considerably from the framework within which industrialization has thus far spread throughout the Western world. One of the primary reasons for this is that the ratios of people to available land, and of people to readily available resources, are much larger now than they were then. /7

Industrial civilization consists today of a vast interlocking network of mines, factories, and transportation systems. It feeds on huge quantities of raw materials such as ores of iron, copper, and aluminum, phosphate rock, sulfur, and water. Huge quantities of energy in the form of fuels such as coal, natural gas, and petroleum are necessary for its functioning. /8

As per capita demands for goods continue to grow, as population increases, and as industrialization spreads to other regions of the world, the demands for raw materials will surge upwards. Each decade we must produce more metals than were produced the decade before, we must produce more fertilizers, insecticides, machines, and medicines. Correspondingly, we must consume more ores, more coal, more petroleum, and we must tap new sources of energy. /9

In terms of the changes which are being brought about by the spread of industrial civilization, we are much closer to the beginning of the revolution in which we now find ourselves than we are to its end. The problems which will confront us will increase in complexity as time goes by. /10

Today we are confronted by diminishing grades of raw materials in many areas of industrial activity. For example, only a few decades ago copper ores were being mined that contained 5 per cent copper. Today our average copper ore contains only 0.6 per cent of the metal. Undoubtedly in the years ahead we shall be mining ores that contain even smaller concentrations of the element. From the point of view of technology, this is something well within the realm of technological feasibility—but at a price. In order to extract copper from ores of still lower grade, we must pour more technology into the system; we must move and process larger quantities of ore per unit of production; we must use more machines and consume more energy. In short, extraction of metals from lower grades of ore requires using more steel and other metals, and consuming more energy. /11

No matter how we look at the situation, we must conclude that consumption of energy and raw materials, even in the presently industrialized societies, must continue to increase with time. When we couple this with the fact that per capita demands for goods are still increasing, population is increasing, and industrialization is spreading, it seems inevitable that world-wide demands for raw materials in the years ahead will pale those of today into insignificance. /12

As the changes take place it will be necessary for nations to obtain their raw materials from progressively leaner ores. In order to do this, it will be necessary to put more technology into the system, and to consume larger quantities of energy per unit of production. /13

So long as there is an ample supply of energy, we shall be able to process extremely low-grade substances in order to obtain the raw materials we need. As grades move downward, increasing emphasis will be placed on the isolation of by-products and co-products, and eventually we may reach the time when as many as twenty to thirty products are obtained from the single operation of "mining" ordinary rock. As grade goes down, energy costs per unit of output will of course go up, but given adequate energy, industry can be fed for a very long time from the leanest of substances. /14

Fortunately, nature has placed at our disposal huge reservoirs of energy. We know that, if necessary, the sun's rays can be harnessed directly to produce mechanical power. We know that useful power can be produced from uranium and thorium, and we know that sufficient quantities of these substances are available in the earth's minerals and rocks to keep a world civilization operating at a high level of productivity for many millennia. We know that it is possible to generate eventually thermonuclear power in almost infinite quantities. We know that in some regions of the world there are large quantities of coal and petroleum that have not yet been tapped. It seems clear that given the trained manpower, imagination, and the collaborative research, man has at his disposal ample supplies of energy. /15

In the years ahead we can expect that competition between nations for the earth's resources will become increasingly keen. But resource depletion will eventually become the great leveler of nations, and most of the major industrial areas of the world will eventually find it easier to gain their sustenance by applying science and technology to the task of processing domestic, low-grade substances than to look abroad. /16

The depletion of resources will make it more and more difficult for the less developed areas of the world to obtain the materials they need for their own industrialization. Increasing difficulty of importation will necessitate the application of an ever greater amount of technology to their own industrialization problems. Indeed, it seems likely that we are approaching the interesting situation in which the less developed and more impoverished an area is, the higher is the level of technology required to achieve and maintain an adequate standard of living. For these reasons, the industrialization of the unindustrialized part of the world will become more difficult with each passing year. /17

The industrial-scientific revolution has had profound effects upon human populations. World population jumped from about 500 million persons in 1650 to about 2,700 million persons in 1958. Even more significant is the fact that the *rate* of increase of population is increasing rapidly as well. /18

Some of the reasons for this accelerating population growth are clear. Scientific methods of agriculture make it possible to obtain higher crop yields. Modern transportation systems have virtually eliminated large-scale famine in most regions of the world by making it possible to transport food quickly from one region to another. Techniques of immunization and sanitation have eliminated a variety of epidemic and endemic diseases. Widespread use of insecticides such as DDT have greatly decreased the incidence of malaria in many regions and have eliminated a variety of other insect-borne diseases. Infant mortality and childhood diseases have been greatly decreased so that increasing numbers of persons survive to reproduce. /19

How far will this upsurge in population carry us? It is, of course, impossible to predict but we can obtain some idea by examining past patterns of behavior. /20

Throughout the greater part of human history human numbers have tended to increase up to the limits imposed by the food supply. There is little reason to suppose that this situation is not true today. /21

The availability of techniques of contraception has, of course, resulted in a lowering of birth rates in the industrial world, and the birth rates themselves are now sensitive to fluctuating economic conditions. But although we see about us these variations in rates of growth, the number of human beings inhabiting the earth appears to be moving inexorably upward. It is obvious that this increase cannot continue indefinitely. But at what point will population cease to grow? /22

In the absence of a major catastrophe there does not appear to be the slightest possibility that world population will level off much below 7 billion persons. As industrialization spreads throughout the world and if our ability to produce food is indeed the population-determining factor, the number of human beings might eventually exceed even that high figure. Ten billion persons could be supported but with extreme crowding and using the most elaborate of technologies. A much greater number is difficult to imagine. /23

It is clear that at some point in time population growth must stop. When growth ceases, it will either be within the framework of high birth rates balanced by equally high death rates, or by low death rates balanced by equally low birth rates. The outcome will be determined by the efforts which are placed upon these problems in the years which lie immediately ahead. /24

The slow rate at which food production can be increased within the framework of our existing abilities aggravates the situation still further. It is possible to grow enough food on the earth's surface to support the growing population of the world for the next fifty years—and this merely by doing more intensively things we already know how to do. In principle, too, it is possible, through extending our agriculture by procedures which we now regard as uneconomical, to produce sufficient food to support the growing population through perhaps the next century. But, unfortunately, although there is no barrier in principle to feeding a far larger number of persons than now exist in the world, the fact remains that it is difficult to increase the amount of food produced each year as rapidly as the number of people is likely to increase. Thus, unless it is possible in some way to slow down birth rates or to speed up production rates, we are faced with the prospect of watching industrialization spread to areas where people are hungry today and will remain hungry for a long time. /25

One important aspect of the dangers which confront us is concerned with the understandable impatience of people to improve their lot. The process of industrialization is a slow one when viewed in terms of the length of a human lifetime. A doubling time of between five and ten years for industrial production represents a very rapid rate of growth. Yet even under conditions of such rapid development a considerable span of time is required for the average individual to notice much improvement in his life. One reason for this is that the products of industry at first must be diverted largely to the creation of new industry. Machines must be built which can be used to produce other machines. In economic terms, there must be "savings," the creation of capital, with the result that the consumer's lot is not rapidly improved. The delay in the arrival of visible economic benefits to the average person can lead, particularly in the growing cities, to discontent and violence. /26

Thus, it seems likely that, in the absence of our bringing something new into the picture, the process of industrialization in the underdeveloped areas of the world will be characterized more by increasing numbers of people, by poverty and deprivation, than by a rapid improvement in the standards of living. /27

The vast network of mines, factories, and communication systems, upon which the industrialized part of the world has become dependent, is extremely sensitive to disruption. So interdependent are the components of the network that the sudden failure of but a relatively small section of it could result in a breakdown of the entire system. It is for this reason that machine civilization is probably far more vulnerable to disruption from nuclear attack than most persons suspect. For example, not many well-placed hydrogen bombs would be required to destroy the productive capacities of the larger world powers. Indeed it is quite possible that far more persons would die in the chaotic aftermath of a nuclear war as a result of the breakdown of the industrial network than would be killed directly by explosions. /28

As industrialization spreads, the world as a whole will become more vulnerable in this respect. At the same time as the years pass by, increasing numbers of nations will find themselves in a position to wage large-scale nuclear war. Hand in hand with industrialization goes the power of manufacturing the tools of war, including nuclear armaments. Thus, it would appear that the likelihood of disruption will increase steadily in the future—at least in the absence of some semblance of international order. /29

If industrial civilization were destroyed on a world-wide basis, there would be a very real question as to whether it could ever be started again. Our own civilization was made possible by an abundance of ores and other resources which could be easily tapped. As we have seen, these resources are disappearing and will one day vanish. As long as we maintain a high level of technology and an intact industrial network we can keep going for an indefinitely long period of time. But if there were a catastrophe, the technological requirements of getting started again might prove to be impossible to surmount. We are indeed approaching a "point of no return"—a point in time beyond which the machines of the world must continue to function, or industrial civilization will perish, possibly never to reappear. /30

The problems which face us in the years ahead are indeed both numerous and grave, but, theoretically at least, it seems likely that they can be solved by the proper application of our intelligence. For example, some of the dangers which confront us can be relieved by strengthening the international institutions which are designed to prevent war, such as the United Nations and its subsidiary organizations. Others can be minimized by concerted effort on the part of the present industrialized countries to enable the inevitable industrial transition of the underdeveloped areas to be made with minimum difficulty. This can be done in part by the transfer of machines and goods and in part by technical assistance. It can be promoted also by the development of new techniques in industry, agriculture, education, and birth control—techniques which have thus far not yet been developed in the industrialized areas because they have not been needed, but which would be of great value to developing countries. /31

It is in these areas that scientists and engineers can make contributions of considerable importance, first by creating an awareness among the world's people concerning the gravity of the dangers which lie ahead, and second by establishing collaborative programs aimed at anticipating and solving the problems we must face. /32

There are a number of approaches which might be used to encourage this collaboration. I believe that one of the more useful approaches would be establishing an International Institute of World Development, which would be staffed by physical, biological, and social scientists, and engineers. The Institute would be financed jointly by the participating nations and its services would be made available to all nations which are faced by development problems. /33

One can conceive of a variety of problems which might be studied profitably in such an institute. Generally speaking, these would be problems which are not at present receiving adequate attention in those areas of the world which are already industrialized, because they are not critical problems in those areas and, similarly, although these problems are of the greatest importance to the unindustrialized areas, they are receiving insufficient attention there because of the lack of adequate technical manpower and facilities. /34

A part of the effort in such an institute might be devoted to devising techniques of fertility control which might be applicable in specific unindustrialized areas, and studies of ways and means of spreading knowledge of these techniques. New methods of producing and preserving food might be devised. Other efforts might be placed on problems of solar energy utilization, the application of nuclear energy, the development of pumps and engines for special purposes, the reclamation of sea water, and special mining and metallurgical operations. Attention could be given to speeding up education in unindustralized areas. Techniques of construction, transportation, and communication might be studied. /35

I believe that given a broad international base, such an institute could aid materially in world development, and although its operations would be expensive, the cost would be trivial when compared with the gains to be achieved. And, perhaps even more important, it could provide a precedent for broad international technological collaboration on a large scale in which science and technology are mobilized for constructive uses. /36

The speech

1. What is Brown's specific purpose here? Would you label it expository or argumentative? Defend your choice.
2. What pattern of organization do you find in the speech? Show each of the main divisions of the organization. Is the organization especially well suited to the speaker's purpose?
3. Brown does not suggest to his audience how the proposal for an International Institute of World Development can be implemented. Is this a weakness in the speech? Explain your answer.
4. Plot on paper the cause and result sequence that emerges from this speech.
5. Brown does not resort to anecdotes, humor, novelty, or other such devices to gain and keep the attention of his audience. Do you feel that he should have done so?
6. In what sense can it be said that there is an emotional appeal in this speech?
7. This is a rather short speech for treating so vast a problem. Is there too little support for the main propositions? In answering this, keep the audience in mind.
8. Tell how you would deliver a speech such as this.
9. Analyze the style, giving special attention to transitions, sentence structure, and diction. For what kinds of subjects would a style like this not be appropriate? Compare Brown's style with that of Urey.
10. Does Brown's description of the problem lead you to believe that his proposed solutions will be adequate?
11. In what way can it be said that Brown's speech is an extension of one aspect of Urey's?

For further study and discussion

1. In what ways do we have firm control over our physical environment? In what respects do we still lack control?
2. Why should the spread of industrialization to Asia and Africa seem inevitable?
3. Has the United States already seriously depleted one or more of its resources? Support your answer with as many facts as you have time to pull together.

4. Will the depletion of resources encourage or discourage war? Explain your view on this in detail.
5. What differences has the population explosion already made in the United States?
6. What new means of feeding the world's growing population could conceivably be developed in the next one hundred years?
7. Do you agree that industrial civilization as we know it could not be re-established if the present one were wiped out?
8. What obvious difficulties will face any organization attempting to work out and put into effect a plan for world development?
9. Do you feel that the future of our civilization rests primarily in the hands of the scientists and engineers? Explain your answer.
10. Discover what you can about the theories of Thomas R. Malthus (1766-1834), and compare them with the ideas of Harrison Brown.

Suggestions for further reading

John D. Bernal, ***The Social Function of Science*** (London, 1939)
Farrington Daniels and T. M. Smith, ***The Challenge of Our Times*** (Minneapolis, 1953)
Julian Huxley, ***Science and Social Needs*** (New York, 1935)
Frank Pirone, ***Thinking Ahead of Communism*** (Brentwood, N. Y., 1954)
Reflections on Our Age (New York, 1949). Lectures given at the opening session of UNESCO at the Sorbonne University of Paris.
Don K. Price, ***Government and Science*** (New York, 1954)
James Stockley, ***Science Remakes Our World*** (New York, 1946)

Science and spiritual values

JAMES B. CONANT

James B. Conant's recent study of high schools in the United States is known to all those who are interested in modern education. His career in education includes teaching chemistry at Harvard University, being chairman of Harvard's department of chemistry, and finally, serving as president of Harvard from 1933 to 1953.

After retiring from Harvard, Conant served as United States High Commissioner to Germany (1953-1955) and Ambassador Extraordinary and Plenipotentiary to the Federal Republic of Germany (1955-1957). His study of United States high schools was made in 1957-1958, under a grant from the Carnegie Foundation.

In addition to specialized studies in chemistry, Conant's published works include: *On Understanding Science* (1947), *Science and Common Sense* (1951), *Education and Liberty* (1953), *The Citadel of Learning* (1956), *Germany and Freedom* (1958), *The Child, the Parent, and the State* (1959). His work as scientist, writer and lecturer, educator, and public servant shows the scope of his achievement.

This lecture, given to a Columbia University audience in 1952, concluded a series of four lectures, the title of which was "Modern Science and Modern Man." Conant's explanation at the beginning of the first lecture indicates the general context of the series:

"When I was honored by the invitation to be the Bampton lecturer for 1952, President Eisenhower, then of Columbia, expressed on behalf of the committee the hope that I would undertake to provide 'some understanding of the significance of recent developments in the physical sciences.' On my inquiring as to the nature of the audience, I was assured that professional philosophers and scientists would be conspicuous by their absence. My exposition, if not aimed at the proverbial man-on-the-street, was to be directed to the equally proverbial college graduate—the hypothetical individual whom college presidents welcome each commencement to the fellowship of educated men. Being thus assured that I was not expected either to give an appraisal of the impact of physics on metaphysics or a technical account of the inner workings of the atom, I gratefully accepted the privilege of being a guest lecturer at Columbia University."

Conant's statement of the purpose of the four lectures will be useful in examining the following speech:

"I propose to examine the cultural significance of what has been going on in science since, say, 1935. And by 'cultural' I have in mind the whole social pattern of Western civilization. I have in mind far more than the modes of production, distribution, and communication; I wish to include in my survey the impact of modern science on the philosophic presuppositions of the average enlightened citizen of a modern democracy—on his ambitions, his hopes, his fears, his outlook on the world. So in a sense I shall relate physics to philosophy, but only by handling both subjects in a general fashion and viewing each from the point of view of a deeply troubled modern man."[1]

[1] Quotations are from the published lectures: *Modern Science and Modern Man* (New York, 1952), pp. 3-5.

In my last lecture I explored the false antithesis between science and value judgments. Let me continue this exploration by examining the impact of science on one type of conduct that is associated with a moral judgment shared in common by many different cultural groups. A recurring phenomenon in history is the attempt of individuals to mitigate the physical suffering of others. In the Judaic-Christian tradition such attempts have been given a high status; they have been portrayed as examples of a conduct to be emulated. So much so that out of a hundred people picked at random here in New York, I would wager at least ninety would assert that helping the sick and suffering was "good" and that indifference or cruelty was "bad." Furthermore, a large majority would have demonstrated by their actions their adherence to this value judgment. The reasons for the judgment would cover a wide range, but whether expressed in dogmatic religious terms or related only to broad philosophic ideas, almost all of these come within the scope of what I am going to call "the realm of spiritual values." In one way or another it is implied or explicitly stated that an unselfish act is a good act; that quite apart from the social consequences to the individual performing the act, lending a hand to a sufferer is something a person ought to do. /1

Whatever may be the basis for our belief in the imperative, "Help the suffering," this precept can be an effective guide for conduct only insofar as one has power to alleviate such suffering. It need hardly be pointed out that the advance of the medical sciences has made possible the mitigation of many types of human misery to a degree undreamt of a few centuries ago. The present status of medicine and public health is the result of the efforts of thousands of scientists over the last three hundred years. Admittedly, many of these men were not motivated in the least by their concern with suffering humanity. Indeed, some were totally unaware of the fact that their work would throw light on the problems of the physician. On the other hand, in the last hundred years a great many investigators have been prompted by their desire to improve the ancient art of healing; not only physicians but chemists and biologists as well. /2

A conscious effort on the part of many investigators to control disease, to prolong life, and to alleviate pain has yielded results of a most dramatic nature. I should like to point out that the conduct of almost every individual who participated in this advance of science and progress in the art of healing was determined by a set of value judgments. These judgments were closely connected with the exhortation, "One ought to help the suffering." The conduct of doctors, we all know, is regulated by a set of ethical principles which in themselves are based on value judgments. What I am here emphasizing is the degree to which a judgment of value has determined the investigation of scientists or those seeking by empirical means to improve an art. Once again I make the point that those who say that science and value judgments are in separate compartments have failed to examine the nature of scientific undertakings and the motivation of many scientists. /3

Considering how much is now published about technical achievements in the way of atomic bombs, poison gas, even the possibility of bacteriological and radiological warfare, it is well to stop a moment and recognize what an army of men and women is now employed in helping sufferers by means of tools provided by modern science. This is something quite different from providing additional creature comforts, raising the standard of living, increasing the pleasures of either the mind or the flesh. Much of what our modern industrial civilization produces for the consumer can be branded as materialistic—the invention of the devil, some ascetic Christian fundamentalists would say. But strengthening the hand of the Good Samaritan is an entirely different matter. This consequence of science needs to be underlined. If loving your neighbor as yourself is the epitome of a religious outlook, it can only have meaning as a policy to the extent that one is able to help the neighbor when he or she is in pain or trouble. /4

As to relieving physical pain, there can be no doubt of the effectiveness of the advance of science. Whether a hundred years from now a similar statement will be possible about emotional and mental suffering, no one can say. The hope that this may be the case is surely one of the factors spurring on the efforts of those who study the behavior of human beings. Once again a value judgment is seen at work. /5

The whole idea that the practical arts can be improved by other than empirical procedures is relatively new, as I pointed out in my first lecture. As a firm conviction on the part of a number of influential citizens, this idea is a product of the seventeenth century. That the arts thus improved included the healing arts was inherent in the dreams of the proponents of the new experimental philosophy of that time; making these dreams come true has taken much longer than many of them imagined. On the other hand, all sorts of powers have been made available for transforming nature, for transportation, and for communication that could not have been imagined three hundred years ago. From the Renaissance on, there was an increasing stream of opinion in Christian countries to the effect that some of the sufferings of the human race could be relieved by human action. Utopias were depicted where not only did milk and honey flow, but disease was cured, pain removed. That the alleviation of physical distress would be not only desirable but also in the spirit of the Christian religion, only a few doubted. Those who did would be likely to turn to the Book of Job. /6

The problem of evil as set forth in the Book of Job is not the problem of evil conduct on the part of humans but the problem of why good men suffer grievous calamities. The problem is recurring; what one of us has not felt its bruising impact within the year? Of the answers given by Job's comforters, none suggested that some evils of the flesh could be overcome by human action. Yet this in essence seems to me the eighteenth century's rationalistic answer to Job's laments. It was an answer that ever since has been echoed by ardent supporters of the work of scientists. Forty years ago it was widely accepted by what are now called "liberal" Christians; in the last twenty years, doubts as to its validity have been expressed by certain Protestant leaders as well as Catholics. The liberal tradition, it is constantly asserted today, has been forced "by the wry advance of world events to adjust its large principles to the hard reality of things as they are." Of the world events, Hitler, Stalin, and the explosion of the atomic bomb are usually cited as examples. /7

If I read the Book of Job correctly, its lesson is a denial of the assumption that the universe is explicable in human terms; it is a corrective to the presumption of human beings in applying their standards of value to the cosmos. The Lord rebukes Job's three comforters for their attempt to persuade the sufferer that he must have sinned by arguing that otherwise he would not have been afflicted. The universe is not constructed along the lines of an automatic machine distributing rewards and punishments—at least not in this world of mortals. As to a future life, the Book of Job reflects the Judaic as contrasted to the Christian position; the New Testament answer to the problem of evil is largely absent in the Old Testament. And as to the exact meaning of that answer, Christians have been debating for nearly two thousand years. /8

Salvation by good works as opposed to salvation by faith, I shall not discuss. Rather I wish to stay within the setting of the Book of Job. The writer presents two answers, it seems to me, to the question of why men and women of the purest character may suffer the most hideous afflictions. The first is essentially that the universe is inexplicable. With almost a stoic resignation, Job accepts this fact and ceases to lament. This is the philosophic answer; the other is the spiritual one; it may be expressed in Job's own words. After the Lord had answered him out of the whirlwind, Job said, "I have heard of thee by the hearing of the ear; but now mine eye seeth thee. Wherefore I abhor myself, and repent in dust and ashes." /9

Taken literally, this passage means something very specific in theological terms to an orthodox Jew or fundamentalist Christian. Taken symbolically, it has deep spiritual meaning for those who interpret broadly the Judaic-Christian literature. I shall so regard it. Indeed, to those who ask, "What do you mean by the term 'spiritual values'?" I would reply by reference to this episode in the Book of Job. /10

To explain further what I have in mind, let me give one example of an evaluation that seems to me significant. People have undergone a spiritual enrichment as a consequence of their sufferings, I would say, if they have become less rebellious in their attitude towards the universe, less frightened of the future, more sympathetic towards other people; on the other hand, those who have become more embittered, more apprehensive, more hostile have suffered a spiritual deterioration. Such changes are only partially indicated by the verbal formulations of the individual in question; the state of a person's spirit is indicated far more by actions than by formal statements of a philosophy of life. Judgments of the type I have just mentioned seem to me to have meaning and to be concerned with a value we may well call spiritual. /11

The twofold answer of the Book of Job stands in sharp contradiction to the belligerent optimism of a typical nineteenth-century materialist. For such a person there was only one explanation of Job's afflictions—ignorance. Disease could be conquered if scientists kept at work and people were sensible enough to follow their advice; so, many an intelligent person maintained as early as the 1800's. And as a bit of prophecy, I submit, fewer statements by optimists have ever been more right. This needs to be emphasized in these days when prophets of gloom are so readily listened to on all sides. We have been triumphantly successful in our efforts to right the scales of apparent injustice in this vale of tears, at least as regards the ills of the flesh; and it was this type of affliction—Satan's touching "his bone and his flesh"—which finally moved Job to question God's justice. /12

But it is one thing to make great progress in curing or preventing disease and another to say that *all* the afflictions of man can be overcome by human intelligence. Yet this almost became the creed of those who, throughout the nineteenth century and well into this, proclaimed the coming salvation of man on this earth by the good works known as science! This outlook on the world has become embodied—one might almost say enshrined—in the set of doctrines known as dialectical materialism. One version of these doctrines is the official philosophy of the Kremlin and all those who obey its injunctions and slavishly follow its moods. Another version is, I believe, the accepted philosophy of the Communists of Yugoslavia; in less belligerent and doctrinaire form, the Russian version is accepted by some non-Communist Marxists in English-speaking countries. But in all its forms, it breathes that spirit of the mid-nineteenth century, which was carrying forward the rationalistic optimism of the eighteenth. /13

To the doctrinaire dialectical materialist, the Book of Job is worse than nonsense—it is an opiate of the people. His answer to the problem of all evil, to calamities of all sorts, is essentially as follows: Through science all evils may be overcome. By "science" he means science based on the doctrine of dialectical materialism, the laws that govern not only inanimate nature but the development of society as well. Of these laws, the recognition of the triad—thesis, antithesis, synthesis—as illustrated by the equation, heat plus ice equals water, is usually given prominence in popular expositions. /14

I do not propose to discuss the grim political consequences of accepting the Soviet interpretation of dialectical materialism. Philosophically the whole doctrine seems to me utter nonsense. It presents in the most dogmatic and extravagant form the optimism of those scientists who are interested in translating their discoveries into practical effects. It is a creed suited in a crude way to the scientist turned inventor, for it glorifies his role; more than that, it denies that the scientist ever was anything more than an inventor or ever could be. Indeed, this point of view has been widely publicized by some non-Marxists who to my mind have unwittingly swallowed a bit of the Communist bait! /15

I have purposely placed before you a false dichotomy—the Book of Job taken literally or dialectical materialism. I have already suggested, I hope, my own predilection; I would not repudiate the nineteenth-century optimism about the continued improvement, with the aid of science, of all the practical arts (including the art of human relations). I would not, however, subscribe to any "in principle" argument about what science can accomplish. I would be certain that for the next century, under the best conditions, the areas of uncertainty and empiricism[1] would remain enormous. As to the Book of Job, I would subscribe to the answer that the universe is essentially inexplicable and I would interpret Job's vision symbolically, using this as one entrance to the whole area of inquiry that can be designated as the universe of spiritual values. /16

Before proceeding further with an exposition of my own ideas about the relation of the realm of spiritual values to the universes of inquiry wherein, as practical men and scientists, human beings daily operate, let me remind you that many scientists interpret modern physics in a different light. To them, not only does the universe have a structure of which modern physical theory provides at least an approximate picture (though a very difficult one to explain, they must admit), but the history of this universe is also of significance. Here there is a cleavage among those who take seriously the map-maker analogy of my previous lectures. Some would adhere to a naturalistic evolutionary philosophy not too unlike that of certain nineteenth-century materialists. Others see in the new physics, and above all in the most recent cosmology, evidence for some form of theism quite compatible with the Judaic-Christian tradition. /17

I quote two recent authors to illustrate the latter trend in modern thought. Sir Edmund Whittaker in his *Space and Spirit*, written in 1946, expresses the opinion that "the achievement of mathematical physics is precisely this, that it has constructed a scheme of the universe which is trustworthy (that is, predictions based on it are always verified by experience), and which can be carried backward . . . to a time before the emergence of any sentient creature." After stating that "the line of descent of the modern physicist is to be traced not from the humanists of the Renaissance, but from the schoolmen of the

[1] The philosophically minded reader is reminded that I am using the word "empiricism" as defined on p. 23; see also p. 26. [On page 23, Conant says: "(And I am giving this quotation to define my use of the word 'empirical.') 'By this is meant the observation of facts apart from the principles which explain them, and which give the mind an intelligent mastery over them.' " On page 26, Conant states: "What is often defined as the scientific method is nothing more or less than an approximate description of a well-ordered, systematized empirical inquiry. Now, systematized or well-ordered, empirical inquiries are one element in the advance of science; the other element is the use of new concepts, new conceptual schemes that serve as working hypotheses on a grand scale."—*[Editor's note]*

twelfth and thirteenth centuries," he concludes his review of the theories of the universe and the arguments for the existence of God as follows: /18

"It cannot be denied, however, that natural theology is not an altogether straightforward matter to the inquirer who has been trained in the ways of modern science. The aim of the present work has been to indicate—for the consideration of theologians who are not men of science—what the obstacles are, and to show—for the consideration of the scientific inquirer—that they are less formidable than has sometimes been supposed, and moreover, that the deeper understanding of the nature of the material universe . . . has opened up new prospects and possibilities to the advocate of belief in God."[2] /19

Pascual Jordan in his *Physics of the Twentieth Century*, published in 1944, gives a clear exposition of those new ideas to which I referred briefly in my second lecture. He does not seek to escape the difficulties inherent in the altered picture; for example, he writes, "From a really modern standpoint the older idea of the atom must be regarded as just as much disproven as confirmed, since the corpuscular concept considers only one side of the picture, neglecting the other complementary side. If the quantum theory strips the atom of its clear tangible qualities and leaves only a framework of mathematical formulae for its characterization, our theory of knowledge attitude is confirmed again—physical research aims not to disclose a 'real existence' of things from 'behind' the appearance world, but rather to develop thought systems for the control of the appearance world." In spite of this and similar expressions which seem to place Jordan on the side of those who regard scientific theories as policies rather than creeds, his account of the modern ideas of cosmology is as definite as that of a geographer about a thoroughly explored island, for he writes: "It might well have been expected that the great sun were a much older inhabitant of the universe than the small earth expelled from it; but as we see, that is not the case at all. [He is referring to the data from radioactivity as to the age of the earth.] No less remarkable are the result of age determinations on meteors which likewise become possible through radioactivity investigations. . . . If we summarize our knowledge up to the present, we must say that we have found no body the age of which was shown to be higher than ten billion years. . . . Let us look back into the past; the world diameter, growing with the velocity of light, was formerly smaller than it is now; if we mentally pursue the development of the universe farther and farther back, we come to a point where everything is at an end, or rather, everything is at the beginning . . . ten billion years ago . . . the initially small universe arose from an original explosion." He concludes his book as follows: /20

"It is remarkable that modern natural research gives rise to knowledge and ideas which drive our feelings in such different directions from those of natural research from the times of Lamettrie to Haeckel. It is doubtless very justifiable for the author of a modern book on the mathematical theories of relativity and cosmology to pronounce at the conclusion that our scientific research on the future and past of the universe need not be influenced by human desires and hopes or by theological theories of creation. It is also characteristic that the state of development of our science suddenly makes such warnings necessary again. /21

"But when we pay just recognition to this warning, when we don't allow any motivation for our scientific research other than the inexorable striving after the knowledge of truth, who would hinder us *afterwards* from once dreaming about the results achieved? /22

"And certainly this picture of the universe as exploding fireworks which went off ten billion years ago invites us to consider the remarkable question of Miguel de Unamuno, whether the whole world—and we with it—be not possibly only a dream of God; whether prayer and ritual perhaps be nothing but attempts to make HIM more drowsy, so that HE does not awaken and stop our dreaming."[3] /23

I have referred to these two writers in order to do justice to one significant trend in the recent interpretations of the relation of modern science to the predicament of modern man. Time does not permit me to review the neo-Thomistic approach to the same subject; nor consider to what extent a faith in the ability of modern science to give a clear description of the structure and history of the universe will conflict with faith in the evidence presented in the New Testament, which, if taken literally, requires belief in lapses in the validity of the laws of the conservation of mass and energy. I have seen no attempt by fundamentalists, who might welcome the new cosmological theories as evidence for a creation and a creator, to handle the problem of the empty tomb in terms of any scientific conceptual scheme. /24

[2] *Space and Spirit* (Chicago: Henry Regnery Co., copyright 1948), pp. 128-29. Reprinted with permission of the publishers.

[3] Pascual Jordan, *Physics of the Twentieth Century* (New York: Philosophical Library, Inc., 1944). Reprinted with permission of the publishers.

My own inclinations lie in a totally different direction. Scientific theories are guides to the action of scientists which gradually become part of our common-sense ideas about the material universe. They have little or no bearing on the age-old problem of good and evil. I would attach meaning to Job's vision, but a symbolic meaning. Inquiries into the nature of this meaning would be inquiries about what I have called spiritual values. /25

The dialectical materialists and also some agnostics would question whether the universe of inquiry I have just postulated is more than a name for a mythology. They would relate all ethical behavior to the welfare of society or to an individual's adaptation to human relationships. Some sort of materialistic World Hypothesis would provide a unifying principle; there would be no place for any theistic interpretation. Almost certainly these people would maintain that advances in the social and biological sciences could eventually result in the final substitution of value judgments based on science for those now accepted as part of our Judaic-Christian tradition, that it would be possible some day for psychiatry, social psychology, biology, and anthropology to occupy this whole area of inquiry. Yet they would hardly challenge the statement that a vast number of value judgments today contain elements that have no connection with science. The question then appears to come down to this: Can those value judgments that do not now involve scientific concepts be replaced in principle by those that have originated in scientific investigations? /26

I have referred more than once in these lectures to this "in principle" argument and expressed my suspicion of it. To me, its use indicates an attempt by someone who is constructing a new hypothesis to overreach himself. I doubt if the employment of this type of argument has advanced the physical sciences, though it has often inflated the ego of some scientists. I doubt its applicability to the wider topic that I am attempting to explore; there is nothing to be gained by asserting that in principle all our common-sense ideas about the universe and human behavior, all our ethical principles, and our moral convictions could be replaced by "concepts growing out of experiment and observation." Even in the restricted area of the physical sciences there are huge spots where empiricism alone is the guide for the conduct of scientists as scientists. One can argue that for the sake of his morale a scientific investigator must believe that in principle all these spots can be eliminated. Possibly this may be true, but I doubt it. All that an ardent scientist has to believe is that the lowering of the degree of empiricism can go on indefinitely, not infinitely; as a cautious investigator he should be wary of unnecessary and unwise extrapolations. /27

As to the unifying, materialistic World Hypothesis, my doubt stems from its manifest inadequacy. As a conceptual scheme attempting to account for everything in the whole universe, it seems to me unsatisfactory because it is incomplete. It fails to provide for the altruistic and idealistic side of human nature. It fails to accommodate what I regard as highly significant facts, not facts of science but facts of human history. These are the unselfish ways in which human beings often act with compassion, love, friendliness, self-sacrifice, the desire to mitigate human suffering. In short, it is the problem of "good," not "evil," that requires some other formulation of human personality than that provided by the usual naturalistic moralist. On the other hand, the formulations that attempt to include spiritual values, modern physics, biology, and cosmology within one total consistent scheme attempt, to my mind, far too much. Whether the unifying principle can be a dualism of matter and spirit, mechanism, formism, or some form of idealism, the whole attempt seems to me to be in the wrong direction. My preference would be for more adequate exploration of special limited areas of experience; one of these would include those experiences which can be ordered in terms of a system of spiritual values. /28

Each of these restricted areas of exploration I venture to designate a universe of inquiry. I do so only to underline my objection to those who insist on using the "in principle" argument to relate concepts in one set of inquiries to those used in another. Such insistence is, of course, almost second nature for those who regard a scientific theory as a creed or a map of at least a portion of the universe. But for those who regard scientific concepts and conceptual schemes as policies and guides for action, the need for an "in principle" consistency between inquiries in different areas disappears. If two policies in two areas (universes of inquiry, to use my phrase) can actually be brought into conflict as guides to action, then an observational or experimental test between them becomes possible. The conflict generates, so to speak, a series of limited working hypotheses, a chain of reasoning that finally eventuates in a hypothesis so restricted that a fairly clean-cut yes or no answer can be obtained. But if attempts to bring the two policies into conflict fail, as in the case of the corpuscular and wave theories of light, then one may say that the two theories are so dissimilar as to constitute incompatible universes of inquiry. In the case of physics, the possibility of this dissimilarity was denied for years by those who clung to the "in principle" type of argumentation. /29

How many universes of inquiry can be conveniently recognized today I would not care to state. For practical purposes two or more may be telescoped and treated as one by means of suitable postulates and sets of rules. In a sense, a unitary theory can be constructed to handle the dissimilarities of two universes of inquiry. This is what has occurred in modern physics, according to my reading of recent scientific history. When the highly limited working hypotheses in each area can be formulated quantitatively, then, by the use of mathematical reasoning, the unitary theory can be so stated as to be a very useful policy—so useful, in fact, that if its origins are not carefully traced, one can easily be deceived into thinking it represents a consistent map of one section of the universe. /30

Within the general field of the natural sciences, I suggest that those inquiries that involve the assumption of the uniformity of nature over long periods of time constitute a special universe of inquiry (or perhaps a group of such universes). To what degree the concepts used in paleontology, for example, must be in principle entirely consistent or compatible with those employed in biochemistry is for me an open question. Such questions arise, for example, whenever cosmologists, biologists, and chemists discuss the origin of life. Many of the so-called theories of the origin of life are not scientific theories at all in the sense of being guides to action. They are merely speculative ideas which no one now knows how to connect with new experiments or observations. On this point, by the way, the general public is apt to be much confused. People fail to distinguish between a new theory about the origin of life (or the origin of granite or of petroleum), which is merely one more speculative idea, and a theory from which flow new consequences that can be tested. Speculation in the field of cosmogony is not to be disparaged, but the wide publicity given to each new flight of fancy tends to confuse the general public and encourage credulity. /31

The point of view I have presented regards scientific theories as restricted policies, not parts of a unified cosmic creed. I am well aware that it can be attacked in the name of man as a rational being. It can be labeled defeatist, obscurantist,[4] or just a lazy man's way out of embarrassing difficulties. The adherents of a religious creed which sets forth in detail the origin, nature and destiny of man are almost sure to repudiate any view of the universe that is as provisional and fragmentary as the one I am suggesting. Materialistic atheists, interestingly enough, react in much the same fashion. Indeed, as witnesses for my defense I might call representative proponents of various unitary systems, including systems expressed in theological terms, and by cross-questioning show the diversity of their arguments. There would be no agreement among them, that much is clear. Another witness might be, of course, a modern physicist confronted with the ghost of his professional grandfather. On the consequences of such a confrontation I need not elaborate, for I have already pointed out that as regards particles and waves, the present picture would be regarded by the nineteenth-century physicists as the juxtaposition of two theories so dissimilar as to be in principle incompatible. /32

A view of the universe that rejects the necessity for a unified World Hypothesis consistent in principle throughout is not defeatist as regards the advance of science. For if one regards scientific theories as guides to investigations, each theory is continuously open to testing by experiment and observation. Such a view leads to suspicion of all assumptions carried over from one area of investigation to another. It represents a skeptical approach to all arguments divorced from actual observation or experimentation. It places the burden of proof on those who claim that *all* of a given set of concepts are, in practice as well as in principle, in the same universe of inquiry. There is nothing in such an outlook to discourage attempts to bring different scientific theories into close relation. On the contrary, since the compatibility of two theories can only be determined by the consequences of an apparent conflict and never can be assumed, the emphasis is on observation and experiment rather than on speculative thinking or abstract reasoning. /33

"The man of action has to believe, the inquirer has to doubt; the scientific investigator is both." This statement of Charles S. Peirce will serve to direct attention to the two fold purpose that many of our general ideas must fulfill. At least some of the concepts and conceptual schemes with which we as scientific investigators work must have a provisional status.

---

[4] I doubt if believers in astrology, bizarre interpretations of astronomy, or modern necromancy will find any comfort in these lectures. A basically skeptical outlook, even if it denies the ability of science to provide a map of the structure of the universe, can hardly provide a platform for the superstitious. The extension of common-sense ideas by domesticated scientific concepts provides the framework of the modern world. The burden of proof is heavy on one who claims to have found a new effect contradicting accumulated practical experience.

They are working hypotheses on a grand scale, to use the terminology of a previous lecture. On the other hand, even in scientific investigations, some of the ideas that originated in the early advance of science must be regarded as having a more durable status. They must, that is, if progress is to be made. If a scientist attempted, every time he entered his laboratory, to retrace the steps in the development of the scientific theories he takes for granted, he would go mad. /34

When the scientist steps out of his laboratory and takes part in activities other than research, as a man of action he has to believe. The philosopher, whose profession it is to doubt, is under the same compulsion. All of us as sane individuals accept without a flicker of doubt a mass of concepts whose origin is obscure because they have been part of each of us as long as we can remember. As children, at least, we never doubted the reality of a three-dimensional world or the existence of other people. In other words, our degree of attachment to a certain set of ideas is so high as to constitute a belief. The reality of other people, of a solid world with a past and future, and of the partial uniformity of nature are thus matters of common-sense faith. Our degree of conviction as to the correctness of this faith is so great that I do not think anyone can question it in the sense that one questions the existence of a neutrino or even the germ theory of disease. To entertain the solipsist doctrine is not possible in the sense that it is possible for a beginner to consider the pros and cons of the caloric theory of heat. /35

Scientists have a degree of attachment to some scientific theories almost as great as that which all of us have for the concepts of a real world of rocks and trees and people. There is obviously no clear-cut line. Faith in the validity of the principles of physics and chemistry over billions of years and in the reality of a cosmic history is essential for an astronomer, a geologist, or a paleontologist. This is completely unnecessary and often lacking in a microbiologist or a nuclear physicist, to choose only two examples of scientists who are investigating immediate occurrences. An organic chemist's belief in the reality of atoms arranged in three-dimensional patterns in a molecule is usually almost as great as his belief in the existence of other people. But his predecessors of the nineteenth century held the same views to be highly provisional, it may be noted. And lest any one be tempted to generalize from this instance and say that the history of all science has been from provisional belief to faith, I would remind you of the discarded theories of phlogiston, the caloric fluid, the luminiferous ether, and the idea that the electron could be exactly located within a molecule. /36

As a man of action, each of us must not only manipulate a world of inanimate nature full of all sorts of plants and animals (including pathogenic bacteria), but also accommodate ourselves to other people. We must have not only common-sense concepts about a real world, but also some general principles about those entities we believe to be other personalities. We must deal as best we can with what William James has called "the whole paradoxical physico-moral-spiritual Fatness." Only as an inquirer, philosophical or scientific, can a man "single out some skinny fragment" of this Fatness. /37

For many people in the Western world the concepts that are particularly relevant to human intercourse are religious doctrines. For some, these are provisional beliefs; for others, ideas to which the degree of attachment is extremely high. This is particularly true for those who have grown up in an orthodox form of Christianity or have undergone a conversion of the type described by William James in his *Varieties of Religious Experience*. The parallel with the common-sense belief that other people exist and with the geologists' belief in a geologic past can hardly be denied. Therefore, I am not inclined to quarrel with those who say that a faith in the reality of the God of Calvin, or the God of Catholicism, or the Jehovah of Orthodox Judaism is the same sort of faith as faith in a real external world. But I would question the correctness of considering a belief in God which carries no consequences for the believer as parallel to a belief in the reality of other people which clearly carries some meaning for everyone, except perhaps the sole inhabitant of a desert isle. /38

Those people who have a high degree of attachment to the beliefs that are orthodox within a certain religion may well be said to have a firm conviction that their theology is not only right but also real. Others may have different degrees of faith in regard to various parts of the total doctrine. But in general, all those who adhere even loosely to a formal religious creed will wish to substitute the word "religious" for "spiritual" wherever I have used the term in this lecture. They would probably not agree that there is any separate universe of inquiry embracing religious values, for their theology would involve a unitary World Hypothesis; but as to the reality of what I have called the realm of spiritual values, they would have no doubt. /39

My concluding remarks will be addressed not to those whose theology is so certain as to be comparable with a belief in the reality of an external world. Nor will they be addressed to those whose picture of the universe leaves no room for spiritual values. Neither the Christian who interprets the Bible literally rather than symbolically nor the materialist will find any sense in what follows. But for the others I should like to suggest that in regard to many phenomena, we require, as men of action, at least provisional beliefs. These phenomena are open to scientific investigation, but until the degree of empiricism has been greatly lowered, we must operate with rules of conduct that are *not* based on science. This being so, I doubt if we can escape some attempt to put these rules into a conceptual scheme, however hazy. The evidence for the scheme is not affected one way or another by findings of the scientist, whether he be a physical scientist or social scientist. The evidence is based on personal experience and its prolongation by history. It is in the category of naive common-sense assumptions about a world of objects and persons. In the background of most people's thoughts there appears to be a World Hypothesis to portions of which, at least, they have a high degree of attachment. Just as I doubt our ability to think ourselves into the state of solipsism, so too I doubt the ability of most people to escape from some elements of a conceptual scheme which is keyed to human conduct, to moral principles or ethical rules, and to value judgments. Statements by an individual to the contrary are of little value as evidence against my generalization. We all know that actions speak far louder than words, and modern psychiatry has drawn attention to the number of mentally sick persons who seem to have difficulty in making decisions because of a conflict between their guides to action. /40

Among the common-sense ideas from which we cannot escape, even if we would, is our belief in the reality of other people. This conviction is the starting point for one set of ideas that are involved in making moral value judgments. We are convinced that except for minor differences, our close relatives are essentially like ourselves; they seem close duplicates in regard to what we call physical actions, thoughts, and feelings. We step both literally and figuratively on other people's toes; we hurt their feelings. This we know, because we have toes on which we can ourselves step and feelings that can be hurt. The attachment to this conviction about the close relation of ourselves to others is for most people extremely high and in origin similar to the other common-sense beliefs. It may be modified by sophistication, weakened by some types of argumentation, strengthened by some experiences. A test of the degree of attachment is suggested by the behavior of the Indian guide I mentioned in my last lecture. He vomited when he saw someone else do something that would have caused him to vomit himself. The phenomenon of nausea at the sight of human suffering is by no means rare. Such physical behavior is real testimony to the strength of the attachment of an individual to a point of view. The pain and distress of other people become to some degree our pain and distress. And except for mentally sick people, avoidance of personal pain and distress is as basic a postulate as acceptance of a three-dimensional world. /41

What are the minimal commitments required by a modern man to construct his philosophy of life if he be neither a religious dogmatist nor a materialistic atheist? What is the minimum number of postulates required to bring into some system the deeply imbedded assumptions about human conduct? These are questions which can hardly be answered except in terms of each individual's total experience. For if I am right, each person will have a different degree of attachment to those ideas which have been part of the Judaic-Christian tradition for generations. His rational construction of a conceptual scheme involving human beings will attempt to accommodate the presuppositions on which he really acts. Of these, his assumption of his close relation to other people, his almost physical identification with them, seems likely to be so basic as to be an essential element in a concordant scheme. For him to act as though cruelty were good in itself is no less difficult than to act as though cannibalism were good. If this be so, then a number of consequences follow that seem to lead back to the realm of spiritual values to which I have so often referred in this lecture. Time permits me to name but two. /42

The postulation of a sharp cleavage between animal behavior and human conduct seems essential in order to give meaning to the ideas expressed in terms of any system of spiritual evaluations. A further assumption following close on the first is that, as a minimum, the possibility may exist that our intentions and our overt actions have a relation to some large pattern of events. These would seem the minimal commitments for a modern man in the Judaic-Christian tradition who seeks to develop a philosophy of life without "jumping the fence" into the materialistic camp. /43

I am concerned here with the minimal commitments we seem to be driven to accept as practical men, not scientists. I am suggesting that these are imbedded in a man's total personality, much as are his beliefs in a real world, and that there is a minimal content of his ideas about what one ought and ought not to do not dissimilar to his ideas about what one ought or ought not to eat. This search is by definition a highly individual undertaking, and the results are not as uniform as those gained in the search for premises in the common-sense world of objects and other people. The results are more like the ingrained dietary beliefs to which I have already referred in these lectures. However, for people with a common cultural background, I think the basic postulates are more uniform in motivation than a verbal analysis might reveal. At all events, it seems to me worth while to attempt to formulate the minimal assumptions along the lines I have just suggested. That they represent far too small a commitment to satisfy most believing Christians, I readily admit. Yet the assumptions necessary to give meaning to the words "a universe of spiritual values" can be regarded as a common denominator among all religious faiths. /44

In this search for the minimal commitments, modern science can be of little or no service to modern man. Nevertheless, the benefits that flow from scientific investigations are by no means all material. Quite apart from what has been done to strengthen the hand of the Good Samaritan, science creates an atmosphere that encourages those who believe that man is not merely a social animal. The history of the last three hundred years is a record of accomplishment in the manipulation of ideas; it is a story of the flowering of the creative powers of the human mind. In the present period of reaction, in the shadow of fusion and fission bombs, we do well to stress this aspect of modern times. To have constructed a great fabric of new concepts and conceptual schemes arising from experiment and observation and fruitful beyond measure of new experiments is no small achievement. Like the Parthenon and the cathedrals of the Middle Ages, the scientific theories of the nineteenth and twentieth centuries stand as witnesses to what the human spirit can accomplish. With humility we recognize the vast oceans of our ignorance where empiricism alone can be our guide; yet we can set no limits to the future expansion of the "empire of the mind." A continued reduction in the degree of empiricism in our undertakings is both possible and of deep significance—this, in a few words, is the message that modern science brings to modern man. /45

The speech

1. What is the specific purpose of this lecture?
2. What does Conant mean by the terms *science* and *spiritual values*? How does he make his meaning clear? How does he feel each depends upon the other?
3. What two extreme interpretations of the Book of Job does Conant describe? Show how his own position lies between these two extremes. Comment upon the effectiveness of this kind of exposition. Does it result in argument that is largely implicit but nevertheless effective?
4. What does Conant mean by "World Hypothesis"? By "in principle" type of argumentation? What is his attitude toward each?
5. With examples of your own choosing, build up Conant's argument that the scientist must be both a believer and a doubter.
6. Trace the argument of the speech carefully. If possible, work it out graphically showing extreme and mean positions.
7. Does the conclusion involve what properly can be called an *action step*? (See Glossary.) If so, what action is called for? If not, what does the conclusion involve?
8. Characterize Conant's style.

For further study and discussion

1. Do you find that the scientists you know or have read are profoundly interested in spiritual values?
2. How do the dialectical materialists make use of science? Evaluate their use of it.
3. Has science given support to Christian beliefs and doctrines? If so, how?
4. Would you say that most modern scientists believe in God? In immortality? Cite examples to prove your point.
5. Why cannot Conant be called a religious dogmatist? A materialistic atheist? What label, if any, does seem appropriate for him? If you cannot think of an appropriate label, describe his religious position.
6. What do you find most provocative about the lecture for your own thinking? Give reasons for your choice.
7. How do you label yourself: an orthodox Christian? An orthodox Jew? A materialist? A skeptic? What? Justify the label you choose. If no label fits, tell why.
8. What conditions must obtain for personal immortality to be a reality?
9. Read the Book of Job. How do *you* interpret the story?
10. Read Archibald MacLeish's *JB*, a play based on the story of Job. What is MacLeish's interpretation of Job's suffering? Which of the interpretations put forth by Conant does MacLeish's most closely resemble?

11. Do you feel that science will ultimately, assuming that the race persists, fill in all the gaps in our information and understanding? Why or why not?
12. What minimum commitments have you made in constructing your philosophy of life? Explain each of them.

Suggestions for further reading

P. W. Bridgman, ***The Way Things Are*** (Cambridge, Mass., 1959)
Arthur H. Compton, ***The Human Meaning of Science*** (Chapel Hill, N.C., 1940)
Julian Huxley, ***Religion Without Revelation*** (New York, 1957)
Pascual Jordan, ***Physics in the Twentieth Century*** (New York, 1944)
Charles E. Raven, ***Science and the Christian Man*** (London, 1952)
———, ***Science, Medicine, and Morals*** (New York, 1959)
Bertrand Russell, ***The Will to Doubt*** (New York, 1958)
Edmund Whittaker, ***Space and Spirit*** (Chicago, 1948)

Mingled blood

RALPH ZIMMERMANN

"Mingled Blood" was composed and delivered by Ralph Zimmermann when he was a senior at Wisconsin State College, Eau Claire, Wisconsin. He presented the speech in the 1955 annual contests of the Interstate Oratorical Association, winning first place in the men's final contest. The following year, in March 1956, Zimmermann then a student at the School of Law, University of Wisconsin, died. The oration was published by the Interstate Oratorical Association, and the 1956 edition of *Winning Orations of the Interstate Oratorical Association* was dedicated to Mr. Zimmermann's memory.

The oration was also printed by The National Hemophilia Foundation, 175 Fifth Avenue, New York City. A prefatory note to this pamphlet states: "Ralph Zimmermann was one of the hemophiliacs who joined the Foundation in its earliest stages. The Foundation was able to furnish him with some help at the time he needed his first braces. We take pride in the fact that one of 'our boys' overcame so many obstacles to prove himself a credit to his family, his college and the Foundation. The oration speaks for itself and is, as many will recognize, a typical personal experience."

A concluding note in the pamphlet says: "The author wishes to express his gratitude to Miss Grace Walsh, Chairman of the Forensic Department at Wisconsin State College at Eau Claire. Her understanding of the problem and her aid and encouragement were primary factors in making this oration a reality."

I am a hemophiliac. To many of you, that word signifies little or nothing. A few may pause a moment and then remember that it has something to do with bleeding. Probably none of you can appreciate the gigantic impact of what those words mean to me. /1

What is this thing called hemophilia? Webster defines it as "a tendency, usually hereditary, to profuse bleeding even from slight wounds." Dr. Armand J. Quick, Professor of Biochemistry at Marquette University and recognized world authority on this topic, defines it as "a prothrombin consumption time of 8 to 13 seconds." Normal time is 15 seconds. Now do you know what hemophilia is? /2

It is by no means a 20th century phenomenon. Ancient writings reveal the Jewish rabbis upon the death of first born sons from bleeding after circumcision, allowed the parents to dispense with this ceremony for any more sons. Family laws of ancient Egypt did not permit a woman to bear any more children if the first born should die of severe bleeding from a minor wound. How odd it seems to link the pyramids of the 4th dynasty with prothrombin consumption of 1955. /3

Hemophilia has had significant influence on the pages of history. Victoria, the queen of an empire on which the sun never set, was a transmitter of this dread ailment. Through her daughter, Alice, it was passed to the Russian royal family and Czarevitch Alexis, heir apparent to the throne of Nicholas II. Alexis, the hemophilic heir apparent, was so crippled by his ailment that the Bolshevik revolters had to carry him bodily to the cellar to execute him. And through Victoria's daughter, Beatrice, it was carried to the sons of the Spanish monarch, Alfonso XIII. While this good queen ruled her empire with an iron hand and unknowingly transmitted this mysterious affliction, my forebears, peasants of southern Germany, worked their fields, gave birth to their children, and buried their dead sons. Hemophilia shows no respect for class lines. It cares not whether your blood be red or blue. /4

For hemophilia is a hereditary disease. It afflicts only males, but paradoxically is transmitted only by females. The sons of a victim are not hemophiliacs, and do not pass it on. However, all of the daughters are transmitters. Of the transmitter daughter's children, half of the girls may be transmitters like their mother, and half of the sons may be hemophiliacs. Thus the net spreads out and on. Theoretically, it follows strict Mendelian principles. But because it is a recessive characteristic, it may lie dormant for generation after generation. As far back as my ancestral line can be traced, there is no evidence of hemophilia until my older brother Herbert and me. The same is true of 50 per cent of America's bleeders. /5

And there are many of us. Medical authorities estimate that there are some 20,000-40,000 hemophiliacs of all types in the United States. Clinically we divide into three groups: classic hemophilia AHG, and two other less common types of hemophilia, PTC and PTA. I am a classic hemophiliac—the real McCoy. /6

What does it really mean to be a hemophiliac? The first indication comes in early childhood when a small scratch may bleed for hours. By the time the hemophiliac reaches school age, he begins to suffer from internal bleeding into muscles, joints, the stomach, the kidneys. This latter type is far more serious, for external wounds can usually be stopped in minutes with topical thromboplastin or a pressure bandage. But internal bleeding can be checked only by changes in the blood by means of transfusion or plasma injections. If internal bleeding into a muscle or joint goes unchecked repeatedly, muscle contraction and bone deformity inevitably result. My crooked left arm, the built-up heel on my right shoe, and the full length brace on my left leg offer mute but undeniable testimony to that fact. Vocal evidence you hear; weak tongue muscles are likely to produce defective L and R sounds. /7

Childhood and early adolescence are the danger periods of a hemophiliac's life. As recently as November, 1950, *The Science Digest* reported that 85 per cent of all hemophiliacs die during that period. While the figure is exaggerated, it tends to indicate this salient point: if society can keep a hemophiliac alive until after adolescence, society has saved a member. During those years, society is given a responsibility it too often refuses to accept. /8

You might ask—but what can I do? What do you expect of me? The answer lies in the title of this oration: mingled blood. For all that boy needs is blood, blood, and more blood. Blood for transfusions, blood for fresh frozen plasma, blood for serum fractions. Not Red Cross Bank Blood, for stored blood loses its clot-producing factors. But fresh blood directly from you to him in a matter of hours. Your blood, dark and thick, rich with all the complex protein fractions that make for coagulation—mingled with the thin, weak, and deficient liquid that flows in his veins. Blood directly from you to the medical researcher for transformation into fresh frozen plasma or antihemophilic globulin. During those years, his very life is flowing in your veins. No synthetic substitute has been found—only fresh blood and its derivatives. /9

Because medical science had not advanced far enough, and fresh blood not given often enough, my memories of childhood and adolescence are memories of pain and heartbreak. I remember missing school for weeks and months at a stretch—of being very proud because I attended school once for four whole weeks without missing a single day. I remember the three long years when I couldn't even walk because repeated hemorrhages had twisted my ankles and knees to pretzel-like forms. I remember being pulled to school in a wagon while other boys rode their bikes, and being pushed to my table. I remember sitting in the dark empty classroom by myself during recess while the others went out in the sun to run and to play. And I remember the first terrible day at the big high school when I came on crutches and built-up shoes carrying my books in a sack around my neck. /10

But what I remember most of all is the pain. Medical authorities agree that a hemophilic joint hemorrhage is one of the most excruciating pains known to mankind. To concentrate a large amount of blood into a small compact area causes a pressure that words can never hope to describe. And how well I remember the endless pounding, squeezing pain. When you seemingly drown in your own perspiration, when your teeth ache from incessant clenching, when your tongue floats in your mouth and bombs explode back of your eyeballs; when darkness and light fuse into one hue of gray; when day becomes night and night becomes day—time stands still—and all that matters is that ugly pain. The scars of pain are not easily erased. /11

Once a hemophiliac successfully passes through the dangerous period, his need for blood steadily decreases and his health improves. The nightmare of youth is gradually hidden behind a protective curtain of objectivity that is seldom raised. In contrast to my childhood days, I can look back on more than three years of college with joy and a sense of achievement. I've had some good breaks. I've been in debate and forensics for four years and had a variety of satisfying experiences. I've been lucky in politics. My constituents, the student body at our college, elected me President of Student Government. Like so many other American youths, I've worked my way through college as a clerk in a hardware store. On warm weekends, while not a Ben Hogan at golf, I have shot an 82. And back home, a girl wears my wedding band. /12

For today, except for periodic transfusions, my life is as normal as anyone else's, and my aims and ambitions are the same as anyone else's. But now, a different type of social relationship needs to be found. Because a hemophiliac is so totally dependent on society during his early years and because his very existence is sometimes then precarious, society now tends to lag in recognizing the change. It sometimes fails to realize that this hemophiliac's life is no longer in serious question and that now his right to aspire to any new height should not be frowned on by a society still vividly remembering the past. Now, he seeks neither pity nor privilege. He wishes to be regarded not as a hemophiliac but rather a human being to be evaluated like any human being. /13

I cannot change that part of my life which is past. I cannot change my hemophilia. Therefore, I must ask you to help those hemophiliacs that need help. For I remember too well my older brother Herbert, so shattered in adolescence by hemophilia, that his tombstone reads like a blessing: "May 10, 1927–April 6, 1950, Thy Will be Done." And I ask you to help hemophiliacs because one day my grandson may need your blood. But I also must ask you to recognize a hemophiliac for what he is today; to realize that past is prologue, that weakness sometimes begets strength; that man sometimes conquers. And so I pray: /14

"God give me the courage to accept the things that I cannot change; the power to change the things which I can; and the wisdom always to know the difference between the two." /15

For discussion

1. How does Zimmermann catch his listeners' attention immediately? And by what means does he hold it throughout?
2. Outline the speech, and characterize its pattern of organization.
3. What is gained by the historical sketch?
4. Note the careful transitions between paragraphs. Make a list of the various transitional devices used.
5. What senses are appealed to here? Describe carefully the effect that sensory or concrete details have that generalizations do not have, and account for this difference in effect.
6. What part of the speech is most moving for you, and why?
7. Describe carefully the nature of the proof used here. How does it differ, if it does, from the proof employed in most of the other speeches you have read in this volume?
8. Assuming that it was well delivered, why would a speech like this be even more moving when heard than when read? Tell in detail how you think it should be delivered.
9. Compare the style of this speech with the style of your own speeches. Is there anything you can learn from a style like this?

4 / THE MEDIA OF MASS COMMUNICATION

The man with the muck-rake

THEODORE ROOSEVELT

Theodore Roosevelt, twenty-sixth President of the United States, was born in New York City in 1858, graduated from Harvard College in 1880, and began a remarkably vigorous public life by winning election to the New York State Assembly in 1882. His rise in the councils of the Republican party was at first slow, for he associated himself with the reform wing of the organization. The Spanish-American War gave him opportunity to attract truly national attention, first as Assistant Secretary of the Navy and then as lieutenant colonel and leader of the famous cavalry group known as "Roosevelt's Rough Riders." Nomination and election to major public offices quickly followed. In November 1898 he was elected governor of New York; in 1900 he was nominated and elected Vice President of the United States on the Republican ticket headed by William McKinley. Upon McKinley's death in September 1901, Roosevelt succeeded to the Presidency. He was elected to the same office in 1904, retired in 1909, but re-entered politics in 1912 to seek the Presidency again, this time as the candidate of the Progressive party. The Democratic candidate, Woodrow Wilson, won the election of 1912, and Theodore Roosevelt withdrew from active public life. He died in 1919. During his busy political career he had also found time to engage in ranching, to establish some reputation as a naturalist, and to write extensively.

On the speaker's platform as elsewhere Roosevelt was energetic and enthusiastic. He "incessantly extolled some gospel, and in a manner distinctly homiletical."[1] "The Man with the Muck-Rake," of all his many addresses, was the speech "most attuned to the times and having the greatest impact on the culture of the period."[2] Its subject was an important one in 1906, and the address was eagerly awaited for several reasons. In March 1906 Roosevelt had given an informal, unreported speech on journalistic responsibility to the Washington Gridiron Club, an association of newspaper men. The press understood that the President would later make a formal address on the same subject. When his son-in-law, Nicholas Longworth, told a Chicago audience on April 5 that journalistic attacks on public men had reached hysterical proportions, the public assumed Roosevelt's own attack on the press would be strong indeed. At least some journalists were uneasy. The editor of *Collier's Weekly,* one of the leading "muckraking" magazines, was moved to defend himself and his profession in advance of Roosevelt's speech. "Slight and necessary exaggerations" were inevitable "when any good work like this goes on," he told the Phillips Exeter alumni in New York on April 10.

The so-called muckrakers were journalists and publishers who had discovered that detailed exposures of malpractice in government and business sometimes contributed to reform and almost always built newspaper and magazine circulation. Some who made exposure their chief occupation aimed at producing legitimate historical studies: Ida Tarbell had bared the monopolistic and exploitive practices of the Standard Oil Trust with this hope in view. Some muckrakers were lifelong social and political reformers: Lincoln Steffens, Gustavus Meyers, Upton Sinclair. Others were simply sensationalists who had found a market for cynicism and innuendo. "What was new in muckraking . . . was neither its ideas nor its existence, but its reach—its nationwide character and its capacity to draw nationwide attention, the presence of mass muckraking media with national circulation and huge resources for research that went into exposure."[3] It was not the fact of muckraking but its intensity and pervasiveness that caused President Roosevelt to make it the subject of a major address.

Roosevelt chose as the occasion for his speech the ceremony at which the cornerstone was laid for a new House of Representatives Office Building in Washington. Here, on April 14, 1906, he undertook to define the responsibilities of critics using a mass medium of communication. Whether by accident or design, he incidentally dropped the hint that he favored federal income and inheritance taxes, and this small portion of the speech received more public attention than what he said about journalism. Whether he intended this immediate effect, we do not know. Four days after the speech the great San Francisco

[1] Richard Murphy, "Theodore Roosevelt," in Marie K. Hochmuth, ed., *History and Criticism of American Public Address* (New York, 1955), Vol. III, p. 347.

[2] Ibid., p. 359.

[3] Richard Hofstader, *The Age of Reform* (New York, 1956), p. 186.

earthquake drove discussion of muckraking and income taxes from the press of the country; hence the immediate results of the speech are almost impossible to assess. Sensational muckraking did decline somewhat in the months that followed the speech, and the address has been read and reread in the years since its delivery. At least Roosevelt brought the dignity of his office to bear in behalf of fairness in the management of the media of mass communication. Because he dealt with a persistent problem of free societies, most of what he said is as relevant to our day as to his own.

Over a century ago Washington laid the corner-stone of the Capitol in what was then little more than a tract of wooded wilderness here beside the Potomac. We now find it necessary to provide by great additional buildings for the business of the Government. This growth in the need for the housing of the Government is but a proof and example of the way in which the Nation has grown and the sphere of action of the National Government has grown. We now administer the affairs of a Nation in which the extraordinary growth of population has been outstripped by the growth of wealth and the growth in complex interests. The natural problems that face us to-day are not such as they were in Washington's time, but the underlying facts of human nature are the same now as they were then. Under altered external form we war with the same tendencies toward evil that were evident in Washington's time, and are helped by the same tendencies for good. It is about some of these that I wish to say a word to-day. /1

In Bunyan's "Pilgrim's Progress" you may recall the description of the Man with the Muck-rake, the man who could look no way but downward, with the muck-rake in his hand; who was offered a celestial crown for his muck-rake, but who would neither look up nor regard the crown he was offered, but continued to rake to himself the filth of the floor.* /2

In "Pilgrim's Progress" the Man with the Muck-rake is set forth as the example of him whose vision is fixed on carnal instead of on spiritual things. Yet he also typifies the man who in this life consistently refuses to see aught that is lofty, and fixes his eyes with solemn intentness only on that which is vile and debasing. Now, it is very necessary that we should not flinch from seeing what is vile and debasing. There is filth on the floor, and it must be scraped up with the muck-rake; and there are times and places where this service is the most needed of all the services that can be performed. But the man who never does anything else, who never thinks or speaks or writes save of his feats with the muck-rake, speedily becomes, not a help to society, not an incitement to good, but one of the most potent forces for evil. /3

There are, in the body politic, economic, and social, many and grave evils, and there is urgent necessity for the sternest war upon them. There should be relentless exposure of and attack upon every evil man, whether politician or business man, every evil practice, whether in politics, in business, or in social life. I hail as a benefactor every writer or speaker, every man who, on the platform, or in book, magazine, or newspaper, with merciless severity makes such attack, provided always that he in his turn remembers that the attack is of use only if it is absolutely truthful. The liar is no whit better than the thief, and if his mendacity takes the form of slander, he may be worse than most thieves. It puts a premium upon knavery untruthfully to attack an honest man, or even with hysterical exaggeration to assail a bad man with untruth. An epidemic of indiscriminate assault upon character does no good, but very great harm. The soul of every scoundrel is gladdened whenever an honest man is assailed, or even when a scoundrel is untruthfully assailed. /4

Now, it is easy to twist out of shape what I have just said, easy to affect to misunderstand it, and, if it is slurred over in repetition, not difficult really to misunderstand it. Some persons are sincerely incapable of understanding that to denounce mud-slinging does not mean the indorsement of whitewashing; and both the interested individuals who need whitewashing, and those others who practice mud-slinging, like to encourage such confusion of ideas. One of the chief counts against those who make indiscriminate assault upon men in business or men in public life is that they invite a reaction which is sure to tell powerfully in favor of the unscrupulous scoundrel who really ought to be attacked, who ought to be exposed, who ought, if possible, to be put in the penitentiary. If Aristides* is praised overmuch as just, people get tired of hearing it; and overcensure of the unjust finally and from similar reasons results in their favor. /5

*See the Second Part of John Bunyan's famous allegory, *The Pilgrim's Progress*. Roosevelt preserved much of Bunyan's language in his paraphrases of the original description. *(Editor's note)*

*Athenian statesman and general, also called Aristides the Just. *(Editor's note)*

Any excess is almost sure to invite a reaction; and, unfortunately, the reaction, instead of taking the form of punishment of those guilty of the excess, is very apt to take the form either of punishment of the unoffending or of giving immunity, and even strength, to offenders. The effort to make financial or political profit out of the destruction of character can only result in public calamity. Gross and reckless assaults on character, whether on the stump or in newspaper, magazine, or book, create a morbid and vicious public sentiment, and at the same time act as a profound deterrent to able men of normal sensitiveness and tend to prevent them from entering the public service at any price. As an instance in point, I may mention that one serious difficulty encountered in getting the right type of men to dig the Panama Canal* is the certainty that they will be exposed, both without, and, I am sorry to say, sometimes, within, Congress, to utterly reckless assaults on their character and capacity. /6

At the risk of repetition let me say again that my plea is, not for immunity to but for the most unsparing exposure of the politician who betrays his trust, of the big business man who makes or spends his fortune in illegitimate or corrupt ways. There should be a resolute effort to hunt every such man out of the position he has disgraced. Expose the crime, and hunt down the criminal; but remember that even in the case of crime, if it is attacked in sensational, lurid, and untruthful fashion, the attack may do more damage to the public mind than the crime itself. It is because I feel that there should be no rest in the endless war against the forces of evil that I ask that the war be conducted with sanity as well as with resolution. The men with the muck-rakes are often indispensable to the well-being of society; but only if they know when to stop raking the muck, and to look upward to the celestial crown above them, to the crown of worthy endeavor. There are beautiful things above and round about them; and if they gradually grow to feel that the whole world is nothing but muck, their power of usefulness is gone. If the whole picture is painted black, there remains no hue whereby to single out the rascals for distinction from their fellows. Such painting finally induces a kind of moral color-blindness; and people affected by it come to the conclusion that no man is really black, and no man really white, but that all are gray. In other words, they believe neither in the truth of the attack, nor in the honesty of the man who is attacked; they grow as suspicious of the accusation as of the offense; it becomes well-nigh hopeless to stir them either to wrath against wrongdoing or to enthusiasm for what is right; and such a mental attitude in the public gives hope to every knave, and is the despair of honest men. /7

To assail the great and admitted evils of our political and industrial life with such crude and sweeping generalizations as to include decent men in the general condemnation means the searing of the public conscience. There results a general attitude either of cynical belief in and indifference to public corruption or else of a distrustful inability to discriminate between the good and the bad. Either attitude is fraught with untold damage to the country as a whole. The fool who has not sense to discriminate between what is good and what is bad is well-nigh as dangerous as the man who does discriminate and yet chooses the bad. There is nothing more distressing to every good patriot, to every good American, than the hard, scoffing spirit which treats the allegation of dishonesty in a public man as a cause for laughter. Such laughter is worse than the crackling of thorns under a pot,* for it denotes not merely the vacant mind, but the heart in which high emotions have been choked before they could grow to fruition. /8

There is any amount of good in the world, and there never was a time when loftier and more disinterested work for the betterment of mankind was being done than now. The forces that tend for evil are great and terrible but the forces of truth and love and courage and honesty and generosity and sympathy are also stronger than ever before. It is a foolish and timid, no less than a wicked thing, to blink the fact that the forces of evil are strong, but it is even worse to fail to take into account the strength of the forces that tell for good. Hysterical sensationalism is the very poorest weapon wherewith to fight for lasting righteousness. The men who, with stern sobriety and truth, assail the many evils of our time, whether in the public press, or in magazines, or in books, are the leaders and allies of all engaged in the work for social and political betterment. But if they give good reason for distrust of what they say, if they chill the ardor of those who demand truth as a primary virtue, they thereby betray the good cause, and play into the hands of the

*In 1906 construction of the Panama Canal was an exciting and problematical enterprise. Disease control was a paramount problem, and almost seven years of work lay ahead. *(Editor's note)*

*"It is better to hear the rebuke of the wise than for a man to hear the song of fools. For as the crackling of thorns under a pot, so is the laughter of the fool: this is also vanity." (Ecclesiastes 7:5-6) The allusion hinges on the fact that thorns burn up too quickly to provide much useful heat. *(Editor's note)*

very men against whom they are nominally at war. /9

In his "Ecclesiastical Polity" that fine old Elizabethan divine, Bishop Hooker,* wrote:

"He that goeth about to persuade a multitude that they are not so well governed as they ought to be shall never want attentive and favorable hearers, because they know the manifold defects whereunto every kind of regimen is subject; but the secret lets and difficulties, which in public proceedings are innumerable and inevitable, they have not ordinarily the judgment to consider." /10

This truth should be kept constantly in mind by every free people desiring to preserve the sanity and poise indispensable to the permanent success of self-government. Yet, on the other hand, it is vital not to permit this spirit of sanity and self-command to degenerate into mere mental stagnation. Bad though a state of hysterical excitement is, and evil though the results are which come from the violent oscillations such excitement invariably produces, yet a sodden acquiescence in evil is even worse. At this moment we are passing through a period of great unrest—social, political, and industrial unrest. It is of the utmost importance for our future that this should prove to be not the unrest of mere rebelliousness against life, of mere dissatisfaction with the inevitable inequality of conditions, but the unrest of a resolute and eager ambition to secure the betterment of the individual and the Nation. So far as this movement of agitation throughout the country takes the form of a fierce discontent with evil, of a determination to punish the authors of evil, whether in industry or politics, the feeling is to be heartily welcomed as a sign of healthy life. /11

If, on the other hand, it turns into a mere crusade of appetite against appetite, a contest between the brutal greed of the "have-nots" and the brutal greed of the "haves," then it has no significance for good, but only for evil. If it seeks to establish a line of cleavage, not along the line which divides good men from bad, but along that other line, running at right angles thereto, which divides those who are well off from those who are less well off, then it will be fraught with immeasurable harm to the body politic. /12

We can no more and no less afford to condone evil in the man of capital than evil in the man of no capital. The wealthy man who exults because there is a failure of justice in the effort to bring some trust magnate to an account for his misdeeds is as bad as, and no worse than, the so-called labor leader who clamorously strives to excite a foul class feeling on behalf of some other labor leader who is implicated in murder. One attitude is as bad as the other and no worse; in each case the accused is entitled to exact justice; and in neither case is there need of action by others which can be construed into an expression of sympathy for crime. There is nothing more anti-social in a democratic republic like ours than such vicious class-consciousness. The multi-millionaires who band together to prevent the enactment of proper laws for the supervision of the use of wealth, or to assail those who resolutely enforce such laws, or to exercise a hidden influence upon the political destinies of parties or individuals in their own personal interest, are a menace to the whole community; and a menace at least as great is offered by those laboring men who band together to defy the law, and by their openly used influence to coerce law-upholding public officials. The apologists for either class of offenders are themselves enemies of good citizenship; and incidentally they are also, to a peculiar degree, the enemies of every honest-dealing corporation and every law-abiding labor union. /13

It is a prime necessity that if the present unrest is to result in permanent good the emotion shall be translated into action, and that the action shall be marked by honesty, sanity, and self-restraint. There is mighty little good in a mere spasm of reform. The reform that counts is that which comes through steady, continuous growth; violent emotionalism leads to exhaustion. /14

It is important to this people to grapple with the problems connected with the amassing of enormous fortunes, and the use of those fortunes, both corporate and individual, in business. We should discriminate in the sharpest way between fortunes well won and fortunes ill won; between those gained as an incident to performing great services to the community as a whole, and those gained in evil fashion by keeping just within the limits of mere law-honesty. Of course no matter of charity in spending such fortunes in any way compensates for misconduct in making them. As a matter of personal conviction, and without pretending to discuss the details or formulate the system, I feel that we shall ultimately have to consider the adoption of some such scheme as that of a progressive tax on all fortunes, beyond a certain amount, either given in life or devised or bequeathed upon death to any individual—a tax so

*Richard Hooker (1554?-1600), an English theologian. The work to which Roosevelt refers is *The Laws of Ecclesiastical Polity*. (Editor's note)

framed as to put it out of the power of the owner of one of these enormous fortunes to hand on more than a certain amount to any one individual; the tax, of course, to be imposed by the National and not the State Government. Such taxation should, of course, be aimed merely at the inheritance or transmission in their entirety of those fortunes swollen beyond all healthy limits.* /15

Again, the National Government must in some form exercise supervision over corporations engaged in inter-State business—and all large corporations are engaged in inter-State business,—whether by license or otherwise, so as to permit us to deal with the far-reaching evils of over-capitalization. This year we are making a beginning in the direction of serious effort to settle some of these economic problems by the railway rate legislation. Such legislation, if so framed, as I am sure it will be, as to secure definite and tangible results, will amount to something of itself; and it will amount to a great deal more in so far as it is taken as a first step in the direction of a policy of superintendence and control over corporate wealth engaged in inter-State commerce, this superintendence and control not to be exercised in a spirit of malevolence toward the men who have created the secure definite and tangible results, will amount to some wealth, but with the firm purpose both to do justice to them and to see that they in their turn do justice to the public at large. /16

The first requisite in the public servants who are to deal in this shape with corporations, whether as legislators or as executives, is honesty. This honesty can be no respecter of persons. There can be no such thing as unilateral honesty. The danger is not really from corrupt corporations: it springs from the corruption itself, whether exercised for or against corporations. /17

The eighth commandment reads, "Thou shalt not steal." It does not read, "Thou shalt not steal from the rich man." It does not read, "Thou shalt not steal from the poor man." It reads simply and plainly, "Thou shalt not steal." No good whatever will come from that warped and mock morality which denounces the misdeeds of men of wealth and forgets the misdeeds practiced at their expense; which denounces bribery, but blinds itself to blackmail; which foams with rage if a corporation secures favors by improper methods, and merely leers with hideous mirth if the corporation is itself wronged. The only public servant who can be trusted honestly to protect the rights of the public against the misdeeds of a corporation is that public man who will just as surely protect the corporation itself from wrongful aggression. If a public man is willing to yield to popular clamor and do wrong to the men of wealth or to rich corporations, it may be set down as certain that if the opportunity comes he will secretly and furtively do wrong to the public in the interest of a corporation. /18

But, in addition to honesty, we need sanity. No honesty will make a public man useful if that man is timid or foolish, if he is a hot-headed zealot or an impracticable visionary. As we strive for reform we find that it is not at all merely the case of a long uphill pull. On the contrary, there is almost as much of breeching work as of collar work; to depend only on traces means that there will soon be a runaway and an upset. The men of wealth who to-day are trying to prevent the regulation and control of their business in the interest of the public by the proper Government authorities will not succeed, in my judgment, in checking the progress of the movement. But if they did succeed they would find that they had sown the wind and would surely reap the whirlwind, for they would ultimately provoke the violent excesses which accompany a reform coming by convulsion instead of by steady and natural growth. /19

On the other hand, the wild preachers of unrest and discontent, the wild agitators against the entire existing order, the men who act crookedly, whether because of sinister design or from mere puzzleheadedness, the men who preach destruction without proposing any substitute for what they intend to destroy, or who propose a substitute which would be far worse than the existing evils—all these men are the most dangerous opponents of real reform. If they get their way, they will lead the people into a deeper pit than any into which they could fall under the present system. If they fail to get their way, they will still do incalculable harm by provoking the kind of reaction which, in its revolt against the senseless evil of their teaching, would enthrone more securely than ever the very evils which their misguided followers believe they are attacking. /20

More important than aught else is the development of the broadcast sympathy of man for man. The welfare of the wage-worker, the welfare of the tiller of the soil—upon this depends the welfare of the entire country; their good is not to be sought in pulling down others; but their good must be the prime object of all our statesmanship. /21

Materially we must strive to secure a broader economic opportunity for all men, so that each shall

*It was what Roosevelt said in the latter part of this paragraph and his implied threat of interstate commerce regulations in the following paragraph which were headlined and heatedly discussed immediately after Roosevelt's address. *(Editor's note)*

have a better chance to show the stuff of which he is made. Spiritually and ethically we must strive to bring about clean living and right thinking. We appreciate that the things of the body are important; but we appreciate also that the things of the soul are immeasurably more important. The foundation stone of national life is, and ever must be, the high individual character of the average citizen. /22

The speech

1. What *pattern of organization* (see Glossary) did Roosevelt use in developing the body of his speech?
2. It has been said that Roosevelt relied surprisingly little on fact or specific information to support the main headings and subheadings of his speeches. Is that true of this speech? What kinds of supporting material are used?
3. One way to test the generalization that Roosevelt "incessantly extolled some gospel" would be to discover whether the supporting materials he used in this speech are like those you would expect to find in a sermon or inspirational speech. Are they? Illustrate.
4. It has been said of Roosevelt's speeches that: "They are essayish in that they are spun around the mood that was upon him whether of moral righteousness, patriotism, or preparedness." How accurately does this description suit "The Man with the Muck-Rake"?
5. Theodore Roosevelt was widely admired for his ability to use colorful and memorable metaphors or labels to express abstract ideas. What terms, other than "muckraker," can you find in his address?
6. It has been said that Roosevelt's management of sentences, phrases, and words, rather than his management of reasoning and logical arrangement, gave strength to his speaking. Is this true of "The Man with the Muck-Rake"? Support your answer.
7. What portion of the speech do you consider to be the conclusion? Does it fulfill the functions of a good conclusion for this speech and speaker?
8. Theodore Roosevelt was reputed to have formulated his public statements with care. Identify several points in this speech where great pains seem to have been taken to avoid vagueness and possible misunderstanding.
9. What reasons, other than impulse or poor planning, might have led Roosevelt to include his controversial reference to income and inheritance taxes in a speech ostensibly about journalism?

For further study and discussion

1. Robert M. Hutchins, as Chairman of the Fund for the Republic, proposed in 1955 that an independent Commission on the Freedom of the Pres lished "to appraise and report annuall formance of the press" in the United Stat felt such a Commission could bring pressure on to devote more attention to "enlightening the p about current events." Would such an agency be useful today? How might it improve modern journalistic practices?
2. Explore *McClure's* magazine for January 1903 or some of the other muckraking magazines such as *Pearson's* or *Collier's Weekly* in the period just prior to Roosevelt's speech. Do you find his criticisms of these publications accurate and just?
3. Should government license and regulate newspapers and magazines (as Roosevelt tentatively suggested) in the manner by which radio and television are licensed and regulated? Why have we never regulated the press but always regulated broadcasting?
4. Do we need stronger libel laws or other legislation to protect individuals against unfounded criticisms published through our mass media of communication?
5. Explore Great Britain's legislation covering the reporting of criminal cases. Is their system or ours the wiser? Why?
6. What is a responsible journalist's duty? To report facts without interpretation? To interpret the news with a view to enlightening the public? To function as a political or social critic?
7. Is there any evidence that highly publicized legislative and journalistic investigations are discouraging qualified persons from serving in government today?
8. Do you think business receives fair treatment in the press today? Labor? Government officials?
9. Some have said that the federal regulation of railways, inaugurated under Theodore Roosevelt, has outlived its usefulness. What support or refutation can you find for this view?
10. What advances, if any, have we made since 1906 toward establishing truly equal justice before the law for rich and poor alike?

Suggestions for further reading

Silas Bent, ***Newspaper Crusaders; A Neglected Study*** (New York, 1939)

Edwin Emery and Henry Ladd Smith, ***The Press and America*** (New York, 1954)

Theodore E. Kruglak, ***The Foreign Correspondents*** (New York, 1956)

Frank L. Mott, ***American Journalism,*** rev. ed. (New York, 1950)

Arthur E. Rowse, ***Slanted News*** (Boston, 1957)

Harry M. Scoble, ***Press and Politics*** (Boston, 1957)

Frederick S. Siebert, Theodore Peterson, and Wilbur Schramm, ***Four Theories of the Press*** (Urbana, 1956)

Leon Svirsky, ed., ***Your Newspaper; Blueprint for a Better Press*** (New York, 1947)

[illegible]*al bankruptcy*

[illegible] MAURICE N. EISENDRATH

The F[illegible]s Commission was established by Congress in 1934 as an independent agency of the federal government, authorized to regulate the services of commercial and noncommercial radio broadcasting. As television broadcasting developed, its operations also came within the jurisdiction of the FCC. The Commission is composed of seven members appointed by the President of the United States with the consent of the Senate and is responsible to the President.

The year 1959 was filled with difficulties and embarrassments for both the broadcasting industry and the Federal Communications Commission. Revelations that some of the most popular televised quiz programs had been "fixed" came not from the Commission but from the highly publicized confessions and accusations by quiz program participants and from investigations conducted by District Attorney Frank Hogan of New York. Additional evidence of malpractice was uncovered by the House Committee on Legislative Oversights. The Federal Communications Commission was, naturally, charged with neglecting its duties, but its chairman, John Doerfer, insisted that the Commission's monitoring of radio and television programs would be a dangerous step toward censorship and governmental control of the communications industry. Finally, the Commission was further embarrassed when District Attorney Hogan and the Federal Trade Commission uncovered evidence that a number of radio and television disk jockeys were in the pay of recording companies.

Acting under these pressures, the Federal Communications Commission late in 1959 began a detailed survey of television practices and opened a series of public hearings to explore expert and lay opinion on proper regulatory policies for the radio-television industry. It was during these hearings that Rabbi Eisendrath appeared before the Commission to present the statement printed below. He was one of a number of religious leaders invited to offer their views.

On the day Rabbi Eisendrath appeared, the Commission also heard Ralph Renick of station WTVJ-TV, Miami, speak against hasty regulatory action which, if born of excitement about the recent scandals, might curtail news programing. On the same day the Commission received a statement from Dr. Reinhold Niebuhr, who criticized sponsors' interference in television programing, and heard Rev. Dr. Stanley I. Stuber of Kansas City ask for stronger regulation of radio and television.

Ultimately, Chairman Doerfer resigned from the Federal Communications Commission, and Frederick W. Ford succeeded him in the chairmanship. In May 1960 Chairman Ford asked Congress to appropriate $300,000 to finance a program of constant FCC monitoring of radio-television broadcasting. How much the Commission was influenced to change its policy by the statements of persons such as Rabbi Eisendrath is not publicly known.

Maurice Nathan Eisendrath was born in Chicago in 1902. He received his A.B. from the University of Cincinnati in 1925, became a rabbi in 1926, and was awarded the D.D. by Hebrew Union College, Cincinnati, in 1945. He served as Rabbi at the Virginia Street Temple, Charleston, West Virginia, from 1926 to 1929 and at the Holy Blossom Temple, Toronto, Ontario, from 1929 to 1943. In 1943 Rabbi Eisendrath became Director of the Union of American Hebrew Congregations, Cincinnati, and since 1946 has been president of this organization. He has been active in Jewish and other religious educational organizations throughout his adult life.

When Rabbi Eisendrath presented his statement to the Federal Communications Commission, his audience was the Commission, members of its staff, representatives of the press, and others who attended the public hearing in Washington, D.C., on December 15, 1959.

Mr. Chairman, ladies and gentlemen of the Commission. My name is Rabbi Maurice N. Eisendrath. I am the President of the Union of American Hebrew Congregations, the parent body of Reform Judaism in the United States, embracing nearly 600 Reform Jewish synagogues with a total combined membership of approximately a million persons. In my remarks here today, I do not presume to speak in behalf of the members of our temples. I speak as an individual, although I will strive to reflect the concerns and anxieties which have been expressed to me increasingly by rabbis and other Jewish leaders in all parts of the United States. Neither will I presume to speak as an expert on television and on the many specialized, technical questions which fall within the purview of the FCC. I am a rabbi, a religious teacher, and I will seek to bring to bear the insights and the ethical ideals

"Statement of Rabbi Eisendrath at Hearings of Federal Communications Commission," *Congressional Record*, 86th Congress, 2nd Session, Appendix A292-A294, Vol. 106, No. 5, January 13, 1960. By permission of the author.

of the Judaeo-Christian heritage which ostensibly, at least, underlie our American way of life. /1

Permit me to express to you my profound appreciation for this opportunity to present my views to this important body. I take it that you have not invited religious leaders in order to put a sermonic froth on these hearings. I am confident that you would prefer—and my own definition of religion demands—a frank, unvarnished analysis of the situation as I see it and an equally frank set of proposals for what in my judgment must be done to rectify the wrongs which command our attention today. What follows then is not expert testimony but the soul-searching of a deeply troubled American who is anguished, as millions of Americans are anguished, by what we are becoming, and whither we are drifting. /2

In a sense it is fortunate that the television scandals have broken out. The quiz shows opened a Pandora's box in our national life and jolted a slumbering, complacent public into at least temporary attention. The question is: Where is the Hope that is supposed to emerge from that legendary box at the end? Needless to say, these much-publicized quiz scandals, and now the disc jockey investigations, "are mere symptoms, mere signals of a moral sickness which has pervaded the bloodstream of our national life." The Hebrew prophet Hosea, thousands of years ago, excoriated his contemporaries with words which are burning in their relevance to our nation in its self-indulgent sleekness, depicting so prophetically and literally the plight of TV today. /3

"Hear the word of the Lord,
For the Lord has a grievance against the people of the land.
There is no fidelity,
Only false swearing and lying, murder, stealing, and adultery.
Bloodshed follows bloodshed—
Therefore the land mourns and all that dwell in it languishes." /4

Where does responsibility lie for this slackness of spirit, this deterioration of the moral fabric which plagues so much of our land? *We cannot isolate television and make it the scapegoat for all our national ills.* We must all confess our complicity, our silence, our indifference to the truth that throughout our contemporary society men in high places and low mock at ethical standards and lie and cheat and steal in great things and small—on income tax returns, at Congressional hearings and in political campaigns, as well as amid the councils of nations. /5

We talk of God, but the American people now worship at pagan idols of money, success, status and comfort. We exalt individualism, but we have allowed individualism to be converted into a mean and narrow doctrine of the "survival of the slickest," "me first and the devil take the hindmost." We have prostituted the doctrine of "love thy neighbor as thyself" into the commandment "caveat emptor" ("let the buyer beware"). And implicit is the assumption "my neighbor is a dope." /6

What has happened to us? It seems to me that we have lost that sense of national purpose which, alone, can bind all Americans together through the ties of mutual responsibility. What are these national purposes today? Our greatest present goals seem negative in character—to stop the Communists, to beat them to the moon, to launch a bigger and better missile, to balance the budget. Is this the vision worthy of so historically and potentially great a nation? We seem somehow to have lost our sense of positive, dynamic mission in the world—the mission of changing the world in the direction of God's Kingdom, of eliminating poverty and sickness and racism, of translating our religious principles into broad-visioned action throughout the earth, here and abroad; we have grown flabby, unwilling to make sacrifices, afraid of discipline, weary of the demands of a frightening and swiftly changing world. And so we lower our sights and our TV sets virtually scream at us the priorities of material comfort and private gain. And the only sin in securing all these mundane goals seems to be not lying, or deceiving, or demolishing a competitor, or defrauding the public—the only sin is in getting caught. /7

Frankly, I am less concerned about the scandals *in* television than I am with the fact that American television itself *is* a national scandal. The moral lapses of Charles Van Doren* and others like him are of minor significance compared to the moral bankruptcy of American television itself. With some noteworthy exceptions here and there, I submit that television has not been a formidable, positive force for good in American life. Too often, when the balance sheet is struck, it has been a veritable invincible factor in the widespread exploitation of crime and violence. It has glamorized patterns of

*Charles Van Doren, member of a well-known literary family and a university instructor, had been one of the most successful "contestants" on a quiz program later discovered to have been dishonest. He quickly became the symbol of all pretenders to great knowledge who had won fame on "rigged" programs. (*Editor's note*)

behavior which are anti-social. It has contributed to the cheapening of human life and the desensitization of the American people. It has pandered to the lowest and meanest tastes and emotions of the public. It has encouraged the American people to squander our leisure in a sodden, bleary-eyed stupor and to wallow in sticky sentimentality, sadism, callous cynicism, in violence, vileness, and vice. Again, with an admitted minimum of notable and noble exceptions—notable primarily because they have been so exceptional—it has exalted the shoddy and has beamed its message at the moron. Above all, at a time when America faces the gravest, most crucial and decisive ideological contest with a resourceful opponent, our mass media have failed to project the highest aspirations and ideals of the democratic spirit—the ideals which alone distinguish us from the totalitarian foe. /8

If this is a severe indictment—and it is—it is not as I have already inferred, because I am unaware of the many fine efforts of high creative quality and the religious programs of significance which have appeared from time to time on each of the major networks. But I contend that the over-arching evils I have recited are due to the absence of a standard which has yet to be set on the national level—a standard to which the aspiring might repair. Consider commercial television as it is presently practiced in the U.S. The concern of the advertising agency and the sponsor is not thus to lift the moral and cultural standards of the public. Rather, in selling a product which, because it is not much different from the product of some competitor, no hawking, huckstering, hard-sell representation—or misrepresentation—is spurned to sell one's wares through exaggeration, fantastic claims and counter-claims, through downright deception and flagrant denigration of another's product. So long as advertisers are the kings, cutting up, like so many apple pies, the airwaves which the American people have extended on public franchise to the television networks and stations, just so long will television cater to the lowest common denominator, and fill the screen with banalities which bespeak a contempt for the intelligence and integrity of the American public. /9

What can be done? I do not know any easy answers, but I would like to propose the following for your earnest consideration:

(1) In 1951, as you know, a bill was introduced in Congress to create a national citizens' advisory board for radio and television, to be appointed by the President, to serve as a watchdog and to issue annual reports for the guidance of the President, the Congress, the FCC, and the public. Such a board, it seems to me, is urgently needed, not so much to ferret out specific abuses but to make a comprehensive survey examining the entire broadcasting system in this country. Further, it should aim at raising the cultural and educational levels of both television and radio. Its goal should be to make our broadcasting system a better vehicle of public interest than is presently the case. /10

(2) In any such survey as I have recommended above, I would plead for a bold willingness to abandon the old and to confront the new. For example, prior to my coming to the Union of American Hebrew Congregations in 1943, I served for some fifteen years as rabbi in Toronto, Canada. During that decade-and-a-half, I derived much intellectual nourishment, as well as solid entertainment, through the programs made possible by both the Canadian Broadcasting Corporation and the private Canadian stations. While to suggest the establishment here of such a counterpart of the Canadian Broadcasting Corporation or of similar vehicles established by our sister democracies in Great Britain, France, and elsewhere would seem to some to be too drastic a departure from existing patterns, we dare not freeze our minds against the possibility that a United States government-sponsored network might well be created in America to supplement our existing networks and to provide, as a public service, educational and cultural programming freed from the blight of commercials and the trauma of Trendex ratings. Shall the Voice of America be heard in every land but our own? Programs of quality are beamed throughout the world but, God forfend, we would call down upon our heads the shrieks of "creeping socialism" were we to target our own programs to our own people. We do not need to be propagandized into acceptance of our own way of life. But in creative terms, do we not deserve one network at least that we can call our own? Perhaps what the American people need is not just a choice between tweedledee and tweedle-dum on Channels 2, 4, or 7 or 9, but a genuine and meaningful choice made possible by the creative competition—or shall we say constructive supplementation—of a government network. /11

Of course, it will be necessary to study this possibility in all its many-faceted complexities, and it may turn out to be unfeasible or even unwise. I do not know. But I do feel strongly that we must be more adventurous in our planning and vaster in our vision than we have been thus far. Divested of all vested interest, we should consider seriously *all* means, including public subsidies, pay-as-you-go television—any and all proposals which might make good-quality programs consistently available to the public, by *night* as well as by day. May I say parenthetically I deem government subsidies to playwrights, poets, and producers as valid as to pigs. /12

(3) And, lastly, I would like to submit, with all due deference, that the Federal Communications Commission has started late to discharge the high responsibility entrusted to it by the United States Congress. It seems to me that the FCC has not been nearly vigorous enough in exerting the substantial powers already vested in it. At the very least, the FCC should make broadcasters responsible for what they broadcast and no longer permit them to hand over control to sponsors, producers, and advertising agencies. The FCC should insist that networks sell their programs on their merit and not, as is presently done, through forcing purchase of an entire block of programs in order to secure the one they want. The FCC should enforce the rules and standards set down in its own codes and regulations and should compel stations and networks to allocate their time to public service, religious programming, and other worthwhile facets of American life. And if the codes cannot effect these things, then let us strengthen them. Charles Van Doren has been pilloried and discharged for what happened on television. Many disc jockeys are now being burned in the oil of witch-hunting publicity. But has the FCC refused to renew the licenses of television stations which by sins of omission, if not commission, by negligence if not by complicity, have been at least equally culpable; stations which have been guilty of breach of contract by slipping 4 or 5 commercials into a single station break, which have filled the screen with bang-bang, pistol-packing, shoot-em-up Westerns? And might I ask further, has a single cent of advertising been refused from those, who wittingly or unwittingly, have perverted public idols and disillusioned a whole generation of youngsters, youngsters perverted not so much by Van Doren nor by payola-plagued disc jockeys, as by this whole miasma of what Walter Lippmann recently and rightly called the "prostitution of merchandising" which is dispatching our youth on to the skiddy road to juvenile delinquency? Regulation is not a panacea. But surely some stronger federal regulation is now urgently required to save television from itself, to restore the public interest and to redeem American morality and morale. I congratulate you, ladies and gentlemen, that moves are now being made in this direction. /13

At the risk of abusing your gracious invitation to testify, I must confess, however, that I was not impressed with the statement that the FCC must avoid control of television programming because that would mean censorship and that would interfere with the constitutional protections of free speech. I, too, despise censorship, and I do not believe that those religious organizations which advocate censorship are serving us well. Yet, the truth is that we already have censorship in television—harsh, rigorous, and destructive. It is the censorship of the dollar, unchecked by the public interest. It is the censorship of super-cautiousness and timidity which, because of this dollar dictatorship, stifles most controversial social ideas. We must be as troubled about what does *not* appear on the screen as about what does. Just last week it was revealed that Playhouse 90 had cancelled a dramatic program about the Warsaw Ghetto because the sponsor felt the subject was too depressing. In this same manner the whole question of Negro rights and race relations has been virtually blacked out in our national dramatic programs for fear of offending one geographical section in our country. It is the censorship of blandness which has sullied over the sharp and rebellious spirit which was once the quintessence of American genius. It is the censorship of vested commercial interests whose motif is: thou shalt not offend a single viewer, because even the lowliest and the dullest can buy our toothpaste or our deodorant. /14

(4) In utter frankness, and in the spirit of indignation which I believe is shared by millions of Americans of all faiths, I have been sharply critical —of the networks, the advertisers, and the Federal Communications Commission. In fairness, I must not exclude myself from this indictment. Religious organizations must share in the general blame and guilt. Religious bodies have contented themselves too long with a negative and carping role, too often giving aid and comfort to those who believe censorship is the only solution. We have not sufficiently encouraged the good and creative programming of some brave producers. We have not been imaginative enough nor sufficiently generous with our admittedly limited funds in our own radio and television programming. We have not come forward with our own constructive ideas

and suggestions about what should be done. We have not transcended what divides us to unite in beaming our common spiritual values to those who hunger for moral guidance. It should be a part of our high calling as religionists, of all faiths, to summon the moral stamina which will help the American people to put its own house in order—and to make the television screen worthy of a place of honor and dignity in that house. /15

In this task of making our broadcasting system and the magic of our mass media worthy of the best in ourselves, we—all of us—have work to do. Clucking over the salacious scandals and savoring the details of the onrushing drama of muck-raking—these are human tendencies. But there is a great work that waits to be done. An ancient rabbi once said: "It is not incumbent upon us to complete the task. But neither are we free to desist from it." /16

I thank you most sincerely for this opportunity to speak on matters which have long concerned and disturbed me and my co-religionists, as well as my fellows of all faiths. /17

The speech

1. Suppose Rabbi Eisendrath were to discuss this subject in his synagogue. What changes, if any, would he have to make in his introduction? What features of the present introduction were dictated by the circumstance that the audience was a federal commission?
2. Has Eisendrath established a need for a change in the operating and regulating of television broadcasting? If so, by what methods of persuasion has he established it? Remember that the speech was made during an investigation of admitted deceptions in television programs.
3. Is the following statement an example of fresh, lively expression: "The quiz shows opened a Pandora's box in our national life and jolted a slumbering, complacent public into at least temporary attention"? How does one distinguish original, lively language from cliché-ridden language? Find examples of both in this speech.
4. It is said that in every speech one end or general purpose must dominate if the speech is to be unified. What is the general purpose of this speech? To evoke feeling? To induce action? To inquire? Is the speech predominantly forensic or deliberative? Which of these two kinds of speech was more appropriate to the occasion?
5. Does the inclusiveness of Eisendrath's indictment of television affect his credibility as a witness before the Commission? In what ways, if at all, would you have modified paragraphs 3 through 9 if you had been preparing this testimony for the Commission?
6. Assuming the speaker wanted the Commission that comprised his audience to adopt the policies he recommended, should he have been more conciliatory in paragraphs 13 and 14? Could he have established common ground with his audience here? What effect does his concession in paragraph 15 have upon his persuasiveness?
7. In several respects the structure of this speech follows a *motivated sequence* (see Glossary). To what extent does it follow this standard pattern of organization? To what extent does the body of the speech conform to the "disease-remedy" pattern?
8. After reading many speeches that criticized the television industry, the editors selected this speech as one that covered the subject with originality and liveliness. At what points do you think it achieves these qualities and at what points does it fall short of them?

For further study and discussion

1. Eisendrath says that the insights and ethical ideals of the Judaeo-Christian heritage only "ostensibly . . . underlie our American way of life." Do you think there are good reasons for his indirect suggestion that this tradition does not *actually* underlie our way of life?
2. What period of American history would you choose as a better model of moral and social wisdom than our own era?
3. How should a television station or network decide what to select or reject in programing? Should it rely on audience reaction polls? On advertisers' suggestions? On educational potentialities? On profit prospects?
4. What is the "code of good practice" of the National Association of Broadcasters? What does it require of a station or network? Is the code enforced? If so, how? If not, why not?
5. Hutchins' proposal for a citizens' advisory commission on freedom of the press (see question 1, p. 107) is very much like Eisendrath's proposal for a committee on television practices. Do you think such commissions are a practical, new way of elevating the standards of our media of mass communication? Do they exist in any other countries? With what effects?
6. How does the Canadian Broadcasting Corporation operate? The British Broadcasting Corporation? What relation is there between these corporations and their national governments? What is their relation to commercial broadcasting in Canada and Great Britain? Do you agree with Eisendrath that we ought to have a similar government-sponsored network?

7. What are the procedures used by audience-survey services such as Trendex? Are they equally reliable? Do these services and their reports have a bad influence on radio and television programing?
8. What plans have been devised for establishing "pay-TV" in this country? Explore the Bartlesville, Oklahoma, "pay-TV" experiment or some other. What were the results?
9. How is a typical, new, commercial program for television born, tried out, sponsored, and accepted or rejected for a place on the program schedule of a major television network? Is there anything in this process that is inimical to high artistic quality in programs finally accepted?
10. Make an hour-by-hour log of all television programs that can be seen in your area. To what extent does it support or refute Eisendrath's thesis that television in the United States is "morally bankrupt"?

Suggestions for further reading

Philippe Bauchard, ***The Child Audience*** (Paris, UNESCO, 1954)

George A. Codding, Jr., ***Broadcasting Without Barriers*** (Paris, UNESCO, 1959)

William Y. Elliott, ed., ***Television's Impact on American Culture*** (East Lansing, 1956)

Hilde T. Himmelweit, ***Television and the Child*** (New York, 1958)

Burton Paulu, ***British Broadcasting: Radio and Television in the United Kingdom*** (Minneapolis, 1956)

Charles A. Siepman, ***TV and Our School Crisis*** (New York, 1958)

Moppet manipulation

NANCY JEANNE MYERS

"Moppet Manipulation" is a speech prepared and delivered by Nancy Jeanne Myers of Otterbein College, Westerville, Ohio. It is an expression of her reaction to mass media conditions that held the anxious attention of many Americans as the decade of the 1950's ended. A number of books, reviews, and other studies offered unflattering analyses of the attitudes being inculcated by these media. Two of the most famous works of this kind were David Riesman's *The Lonely Crowd* (1950) and Vance Packard's *The Hidden Persuaders* (1957). In her address Miss Myers indicates her indebtedness to these authors, but it should also be remembered that the same best-selling and widely discussed books had done much to create among audiences a receptive attitude toward further discussion of the character of television programing.

Indeed, in the spring of 1959, when Miss Myers prepared the speech that follows, there were few adults or adolescents unaware of real or alleged malpractices by television producers and performers. Whoever chose to speak about what television was doing to the American mind and character could, in this period, expect that almost any audience would receive the speech with a lively interest and, probably, much active concern.

Miss Myers' address was prepared for delivery at the Women's State Original Oratory competition at Wittenberg College, Springfield, Ohio, in February 1959. Subsequently, it was presented to the national Pi Kappa Delta Convention, to the student body at Otterbein College, and to several service club audiences in Ohio. Because of its special timeliness it was at once a "contest speech" and one with immediate meaning for general audiences. In this it differed from "The Haven of the Defeated" (pp. 160-164) and "The Inner City—Our Shame" (pp. 246-250), though the latter speeches were no less significant in content than "Moppet Manipulation."

Much can be learned about audience adaptation—its possibilities and difficulties—by studying how each of these three student speakers adapted his or her appeal for action to the peculiar requirements of the subject, judged against the events of the day and the audience's preexisting attitudes and concerns. Miss Myers could appeal to her audience for direct action because events had already aroused anxieties about her subject; moreover, most listeners in any audience she addressed were already, or soon would be, involved in rearing and teaching children. Karos and Dinwoodie had not these advantages.

Although only a sophomore at Otterbein College when she composed and delivered "Moppet Manipulation," Miss Myers was already an experienced speaker. In 1957 she had been a member of a national ... ionship high school debate team, and in her firs... he was awarded first place in the Oh... temporaneous Speaking Contest. S... participant in college dramatic pr...

Picture for a moment the ... tered among the various u...

Reprinted by permission of Miss Myers from a copy of her speech provided by Professor James A. Grissinger, Chairman of the Speech Department of Otterbein College, Westerville, Ohio.

are the toys which amuse the room's owner during his hours of play. Two decades ago these objects would have been production-imitating equipment such as toy trucks and steam shovels, miniature printing presses and sewing machines, and Lincoln logs. Stop and think for a minute. What objects dominate the scene of our children's play area today? We would notice a definite increase in the range of the child's toys. They now include a whole new field of objects modeled after the service trades: toy Bell telephones, Sohio service stations, Revlon make-up kits, Toni dolls, and Roy Rogers voice recorders. David Riesman, a prominent psychologist, in his book, *The Lonely Crowd,* says this is a visible indication of the changing American emphasis on consumption. Formerly the nation's youth were trained for production and creation; today the mass media are training young minds in a different line. Today our moppets are being trained for the future positions of skilled consumers. No doubt some of you remember the famous "cheese-glut" of the mid-fifties. Senator Alexander Wiley of Wisconsin made a statement during this time that has been used resourcefully by the modern advertising agencies. He said, "Our problem is not too much cheese produced, but rather too little cheese consumed." This has become the contemporary American ideology. /1

This ideology is not confined to adults as you might expect. Today it is the youth of America who are bearing the brunt of the advertiser's campaign—a campaign designed to so condition our reflexes that we subconsciously prescribe to a certain brand or brands . . . "Be sociable, be smart, be up to date with Pepsi!", "Wheaties—breakfast of Champions!", "Wonder bread builds strong bodies twelve ways!", "Kleenex pops up like a jack-in-the-box!" The American Marketing Association has said that it need not worry now about obtaining funds to penetrate the youth market, that its problem is instead the determining of the way in which they can most effectively penetrate it with lasting impression. After all, as an ad appearing in a TV manufacturer's trade journal once exclaimed, "Where else on earth is brand consciousness so firmly fixed as in the minds of four-year-old tots?" The Association has also pointed out, with some exultation by the admen, that today most children can, and do, memorize long strings of beer and other commercials even be[illegible]re they learn to sing the "Star-Spangled Banner" [illegible]y the Lord's Prayer. Are these the ideals we [illegible] in our moppets' minds? /2

[illegible]nt statement of the liberties taken by [illegible]ubconscious direction of children's minds appeared in an edition of *Printer's Ink* several years ago. The following appeal was made to merchandisers and advertisers by a firm specializing in supplying such educational materials as manuals, room decorations and wall charts. It ran: "Eager minds can be molded to want your products. In the grade schools of America there are twenty-three million boys and girls. These children eat food, wear out clothes, use soap. They are consumers today and will be the buyers of tomorrow. Here is a vast market for your goods. Sell these children on your brand name and they will insist that their parents buy no other. Many far-sighted advertisers are cashing in today—and building for tomorrow by molding eager minds. . . ." through material supplied to teachers. /3

Is this the future toward which we wish to look? Will we be complacent enough to allow our children's minds to be conditioned in such a way? What can we do to dispel the growing characterization of America's youth as "consumer-trainees"? /4

You may question whether or not this control of children's minds by industry actually is a problem facing America at the present time. In other words, "What's wrong with it? The worst that can happen is that we'll end up with pantries full of breakfast cereal we don't need. In the field of commerce children are considered fair game and legitimate prey." Yet in the fields of religion or politics, manipulation of children's minds would result in a storm of parental protest and a rash of congressional investigations. Can we be sure that the manipulation of our children's minds will end with merely the field of commerce? Especially when the other institutions recognize the success of depth or motivational research in this area. Already we can find evidences of motivational techniques being used by church and service groups and state and federal governments. Do we not adjust the dials on our TV set when the picture becomes distorted? What can we do to combat this threat to America's future before it too spreads and distorts our focus? /5

There are, as you have noticed, two major areas through which this "depth research" is attempting to etch itself in the children's subconscious—education, or the classroom, and TV. From this "mind-engraving" the admen desire two things: first, that the conditioning will result in ten million who, as adults, will be trained to buy a certain brand of product just as Alaskan huskies are trained to advance when they hear the word, "Mush." The other thing the admen want is that parents' consumption will shift and increase because of their children's submission to the siren song of the solicitor. /6

Certainly our first and major consideration should be as parents, for as parents we are affected not only by irrational demands for certain products, but also by the knowledge that minds are being molded without the knowledge of their owners. The first thing we must do as parents is keep a firm hand on the dial of the TV set. Too many parents are too satisfied with the golden moments of relaxation stolen during the time the kiddies are absorbed in the messages of the "electronic wonder"—too satisfied to be concerned with what their children are watching. It has been said that while children cannot be turned off, the set can. By keeping one eye on the TV screen and one hand on the dial of the set, we can prevent much of what is objectionable in depth research from reaching our impressionable "trainees." Second, because we will not always be able to stop the advertisers at their outlet, we should insist that our children have rational bases for requests for certain brands and particular products. In this way we can thwart the efforts of the TV commercials aimed at "impulse buying" at supermarkets and well-stocked grocery shelves. And third, we must as parents accept the "ruling relationship" that is ours in the modern family. Social research reports have shown that "to children, adults are a ruling class against which they cannot successfully revolt." We would do well to be what our children think we are. Let's put our proverbial feet down when it will do the most good. When Junior reaches for that new cereal package because he has seen the man on TV demonstrate the plastic space gun inside, and the kitchen pantry is already overflowing with buys of just such motivation, let's say "No!" and stick to it. It is easy to say "Yes" to a child's demands. The strength is needed when a time to deny his wishes approaches. /7

In this way we neutralize one of the two opportunities used to etch admen's images into America's youth—TV. What about the other—the classroom? What can we do there? /8

Well, first, as teachers, which many of us are or intend to be, we can select carefully the educational materials we use in our classrooms, minimizing "brands for brands' sake." This could be a major way of reducing the unconscious impression brand names make on pupils from wall decorations and materials. Then, secondly, and most important, we can include logic as a part of our curriculum. Logic is not restricted to the college professor's use as a classroom subject. Dr. Frances Horwich, "principal" of TV's "Ding Dong School," in her intimate conversation with the eager tots viewing her program advised them to insist that their mothers select the "right" bottle of vitamins the next time they went to the store. Teachers can turn this kind of experience into a fascinating logic lesson. It could be done simply by discussing kinds of pills and arriving at a rational decision about which kind was best. Such questions as: Can we tell which is best by the color? By the size? By how many are in a bottle? could eliminate the conditioning of impulses to buy a pill just because "Miss Frances" said so! Indeed, as instructors we are responsible and can do something about the distorting effect of consumerism. /9

If, then, we as parents and teachers have partially succeeded in tuning out the interference of moppet manipulators, can we not use another channel also—that of the consumer? /10

We all know that merchandisers offer inducements to encourage children to lead their parents into a salesroom. Vance Packard reminds us in his book, *The Hidden Persuaders,* how General Electric offers a sixty piece circus, a magic-ray gun, and a space helmet to children who bring their parents into dealers' stores to witness demonstrations of new GE refrigerators. Sylvania offers a Space Ranger kit complete with disintegrator, flying saucer, and space telephone to children who manage to deliver parents to the salesroom. And Nash offers a toy service station. We can "turn off" this method by refusing to be "conned" into buying, or even examining, unnecessary products. Also we, as consumers, have perhaps the loudest voice of all when we make our disapproval of such techniques known to manufacturers, advertisers, and broadcast media who are interested always in maintaining a contented public. Listening councils, P.T.A., and community groups, plus individual efforts can have considerable effect on the way in which advertising dollars are spent. /11

Just as we can turn the TV screen on and off, change its focus and its brightness, we as parents, teachers and consumers have controls that can turn on and off and change the focus or brightness of the distorting and potentially subversive efforts of the admen employing depth research. By using these controls, we can provide the child in that playroom with hours of contented play—play with telephones, not Bell telephones—make-up kits, not Revlon products—and dolls, not Toni dolls. We can watch his future being molded by rational thinking . . . not by those who would be "moppet manipulators." /12

The speech

1. Review *appeal, attitude, motivation,* and *suggestion* in the Glossary, and then describe as precisely as possi-

ble the persuasive potentials of Miss Myers' choice of a title for her speech.

2. Like Karos' "The Haven of the Defeated" (pp. 160-164) and Dinwoodie's "The Inner City—Our Shame" (pp. 246-250), this speech was delivered in a public speaking contest. Compare Miss Myers' attempts to adapt to the active interests of her student-faculty audience with similar attempts by Karos and Dinwoodie. Which speaker succeeds best in breaking through the contest situation to genuinely involve the listeners in the problem discussed? What are the reasons for your answer?
3. David Riesman, Senator Alexander Wiley, and Vance Packard are cited as authorities in this speech. Does the speaker adequately qualify each as an authority? Which of these authorities probably has the greatest prestige and therefore lends the most suggestive support to Miss Myers' arguments?
4. What emotions and drives does Miss Myers rely on to insure that her listeners will take unfavorable views of the advertising methods she describes?
5. From paragraph 7 to the end of this speech "we" are pictured as being engaged in a kind of competition with "admen." What attention factors and interest value does this add to the speech?
6. Miss Myers' speech conforms rather closely to the pattern of organization called the "motivated sequence." Identify the five steps of the sequence in this speech.
7. "Moppet Manipulation" is a persuasive speech. Does it aim at changing attitudes, opinions, or emotions, or all three? Identify several points at which the speaker is clearly trying to effect these kinds of changes.
8. An analogy provides the framework for the conclusion of this speech (paragraph 12). Is the analogy used as argument or figurative illustration? How, if at all, does this analogy contribute to variety in the speech?

For further study and discussion

1. Most adults identify commodities by specific trade names or their derivatives: coke, kleenex, etc. Is this undesirable? Why? Is it more undesirable that children should do so? Why? Why not?
2. What criteria do you suggest for distinguishing improper from proper advertising addressed to children or adolescents? Should advertising addressed to these groups be prohibited?
3. Senator Wiley's "explanation" of the cheese surplus has been applied to most farm surpluses. Do you think federal and state departments of agriculture should continue to spend tax money to promote wider use of eggs, milk, corn, cotton, and like products? Does Miss Myers' implied criticism of "consumerism" properly apply in such circumstances?
4. What is your opinion of "built-in obsolescence"—building products to wear out earlier than necessary or changing models to render older but usable products less appealing? Does our competitive economy require such practices in order to prosper?
5. Make a survey of advertising addressed to children. Is Miss Myers right in implying that most such advertising encourages children to prefer one product over another for illogical reasons? If so, is this more nearly true when children are addressed than when adults are addressed?
6. Many corporations and industrial organizations offer so-called educational services and teaching aids for use in the classroom. Study some of these services and materials. Are they objectionable? How does one decide when "moppet manipulation" is involved and when it is not?
7. Miss Myers assumes that the young actually believe and imitate what they see and hear via the media of mass communications. Is this really true? To what extent and under what circumstances? Is there scientific evidence on the point?
8. It has been alleged that there is as much cruelty, horror, and dishonesty in a typical fairy tale taken from *Grimm's Fairy Tales* as in the most violent children's fare on television. Is this true? If so, should it make any difference in our opinion of television programs for children?
9. Would action by parents' groups, PTA groups, and others seeking to force changes in television advertising be open to charges of "pressure-group" censorship such as Preminger levels at the Legion of Decency (see "Movies and Censorship," pp. 121-128, pars. 27, 29, and 63)?

Remarks on government regulation of broadcasting

FRANK STANTON

In choosing to honor Frank Stanton, President of the Columbia Broadcasting System, the *Printers' Ink* Gold Medal Award Jury for 1959 paid tribute to the man and declared its confidence in the broadcasting industry. Stanton became the twenty-eighth recipient of this high honor for achievement in advertising when he accepted the award at a special luncheon on February 18, 1960. The Advertising Gold Medal Award was established by Edward Bok in 1924.

The occasion for Stanton's speech was itself an answer to current attacks on the media of mass communication. The act of honoring Stanton was a part of that answer. Henry M. Schachte, Chairman of the Award Jury, emphasized this in his presentation speech, saying, "More than anything else, Frank Stanton has become the deeply respected spokesman for his industry." At another point Schachte said, "While we are, according to tradition, recognizing the entire career of the man we here salute, our jury's action was taken *after* most of the debate, the testimony, the allegations, and the confusions about the current and past deportment of broadcasting." Thus neither Stanton's speech nor the temper of his audience can be fully understood unless one remembers that the advertising and broadcasting industries were here reacting to the intensive criticism directed at them during 1959. (Rabbi Eisendrath's "The Moral Bankruptcy of Television," pp. 108-113, was a part of this criticism.) Stanton had previously responded to these attacks, a fact specifically noted in Schachte's presentation; now, Stanton's colleagues had gathered to applaud his efforts and to give him a new occasion to defend his industry and theirs.

Frank Stanton was born in Muskegon, Michigan, in 1908. He received his M.A. and Ph.D. in psychology from Ohio State University. Upon completing his graduate study he joined the research department of the Columbia Broadcasting System and since 1946 has been President of CBS. He is Chairman of the Center for Advanced Study in the Behavioral Sciences and serves on the directorial boards of a variety of professional and educational agencies. Throughout his career he has maintained a special interest in radio-TV and newspaper journalism.

A luncheon audience of about 1300 heard Stanton's speech on government regulation of broadcasting. They were chiefly businessmen connected with advertising, publishing, broadcasting, and philanthropic agencies. The meeting was held in the Grand Ballroom of the Waldorf-Astoria Hotel, New York City. Robert T. Lund, publisher of *Printers' Ink*, presided and the Gold Medal Award was presented to Stanton by Henry M. Schachte, executive vice-president of Lever Brothers, Inc.

I am most grateful for this award—the more so because it comes at a time when broadcasting is the object of less than universal admiration. Selecting me for a place in the long line of recipients of the Gold Medal Award falls, I am afraid, somewhat short of wisdom. But it certainly speaks well for the jury's courage. /1

The fact is that anyone in broadcasting is rather easily moved by honors these days. We have become somewhat more expert in the acceptance and usage of censure. This expertise we acquired the hard way—by direct exposure. I have even begun to take an interest—thus far academic, for the most part—in epithets. Let me quote you some: "Base . . . servile . . . venal . . . polluted the foundations of society . . . the most ignorant, mercenary, and vulgar automatons that ever were moved by the continually rusting wires of sordid mercantile avarice. . . ." /2

However familiar these denunciations may seem to you, they were not taken from a column of television criticism, a seminar on mass communications, or a Washington hearing. They are not even a concomitant of the age of advertising. They were used on March 4, 1799, to describe the state of the press in the United States. And they were used, not by an outsider, but by John Ward Fenno, editor of the leading newspaper of the day, and presumably an expert. /3

I bring all this up nearly two centuries afterwards for, I think, very good reason. I do not do it necessarily to remind you that the older media have also had their troubles—reassuring as the contemplation of that fact might be to me at the moment. The real point is that the editor of an outstanding newspaper made this scathing indictment of his own field a year after the United States had undertaken, in the Sedition Act of 1798, the only statutory venture in our history aimed at the direct control of a medium of expression. Nor was Fenno alone in his opinion. Another editor the same year accused the press of "mawkishness, dreariness, and gross folly. . . ." /4

After four editors were jailed under the Sedition Act for criticizing the Government, the law was abandoned—killed off by public opinion. But the notion of getting a more responsible medium of expression by legislative action has persisted throughout our history. Every time that any vehicle of expression, any medium of communication, any institution of culture or education has widespread public attention concentrated on a weakness or a failure or even a dilemma, there are always demands that "There ought to be a law." /5

The road to Utopia by Government regulation looks invitingly easy. And it *is* easy. /6

The easiest way for us in television to duck responsibility for the tough business of planning balanced programing is to default and say to the Government, "*You* tell us what to do, and we'll do it." /7

The easiest way is to let some government agency fix the percentage of the day's programing that will be hard news, the percentage that will be serious drama, the percentage that will be classical music and the percentage that will be westerns. The easiest way is to sidetrack competition altogether—every network doing exactly what the Government prescribes and not *one* risky whit more. The easiest way is to dump into the lap of Government the most challenging problem of television—the achievement of that elusive, arduous, perplexing objective of a democracy: meeting the will of the majority and at the same time accommodating the rights and interests of minorities. Government prescription is the easiest way. But it's also the irresponsible way. It promises imaginary short-term gains at the price of real long-term loss. It is a way full of delusions, traps and unending enmeshments. It is based on fallacies almost inevitable in any attempt to short-cut normal growth in any areas of expression. And in the end it leads, not up to Utopia, but to weakness and timidity. /8

Sometimes from surprising quarters usually dedicated in freedom and ordinarily keenly sensitive to any government intrusion into expression in America, the argument is advanced that, because there is a technical limit on the number of television channels available, the Government should be empowered to regulate what is broadcast on those channels. This is unrealistic as well as a shortsighted view. The Government is no more competent to dictate the contents of a medium that has technical limitations on the number of its outlets than it is to dictate to those that have economic limitations. /9

Once the Government tells three television stations in a city what they must broadcast, how long does anybody suppose it would be before the Government also tells the only newspaper in town what it must print? Most metropolitan centers in the United States have more competing television stations than competing mass circulation dailies. Indeed, today there are only 12 metropolitan centers with three or more dailies; there are four times that many cities with three or more television stations. It would be as logical to seek constitutional reforms to impose government standards on newspapers because their number is limited by economics, as to regulate programing on television stations because their number is limited by the spectrum. It is not at all helpful that those who would regulate television programing protest that they would concern themselves only with cultural and entertainment material and leave the news alone. What sort of arbitrary definition—and whose?—is to determine what is informational, what is cultural, and what is entertaining? Last night the "Circle Theatre" presented a dramatic exposition of the city of Pittsburgh's noteworthy method of dealing with juvenile delinquency. Was this primarily entertainment? Was it sociology? Or was it news? Not only would such distinctions be impossibly difficult, they are very apt to be contradictory in some cases and almost wholly overlapping in others. /10

No thoughtful observer wants to restrict the application of the tenets of a free press to what some agency in Washington defines as news. If the principle is once established that the Government has the right to supervise everything else in communications or expression, I don't think it would make any difference whether we got what was clinically tested as news or not. To have freedom merely to report events in your own way, to cover those you want to, and to omit others, to edit—essential as such freedom is—is only the beginning of a free press. For isolated events are merely fragments of experience reflecting the national character. The formative powers are rooted deep in other areas of expression—a fact that Professor William Ernest Hocking established, in fine and perceptive phrasing, in his *Freedom of the Press: A Framework of Principle:* /11

"Neither the value nor the duty of expression is limited to its more purposeful aspects. Speech and press may be trivial, casual, emotional, amusing, imaginative, speculative, whimsical, foolish; all utterance serves a social end—to report to fellow-beings mutual presence and interest, the play of mood, the vagaries of taste, the groping for principle, the barometric flux of belief and disbelief, hope and fear, love and hate, and thus to shape attitudes . . . there is a common duty to protect the whole range of this freedom, as a right of social existence." /12

Advocates of government control of television programing have also spoken in such gentle terms as "guidelines." We ought not to be misled by these. I would be as repelled by a newspaper "guided" by Government as one controlled by it. If the guidance has no element of force in it, it would have no significance. If it does have force, it is merely a euphemism for government control. There is not such thing as "a little" government control. Any control at all is repugnant to all our values and a damper on creativity and the stimulation of freely competing expression. A society that sees one more Indian bite the dust on television is far safer than a society that sees one iota of its freedom of expression given up to its Government. /13

I am familiar with the hypothesis that we could evolve some kind of responsible commission, made up of eminent altruistic citizens appointed by the Government to review and report on television periodically. But unless they had punitive powers, what would it mean? Television is already reviewed regularly by some of the most articulate people in the American press. Great and powerful publications, moreover, frequently editorialize on what we have done that we ought not have done and what we have left undone that we ought to have done. They examine not only the substance of our programing but also our policies, our trends, our economics, our personnel and even our private deliberations. There is nothing left for a commission to review. /14

Suppose, on the other hand, the hypothetical commission is given real teeth to enforce its standards. Then we are in the dilemma that dependence on benevolent despots always involves. There is no way to tell whether they will remain benevolent or whether their successors will be benevolent at all. Walter Lippmann spelled this out very plainly in *The Good Society*, in his discussion of the flaw in "planning" social improvements: /15

"Not only is it impossible for the people to control the plan, but what is more, the planners must control the people. . . . By a kind of tragic irony, the search for security and a rational society, if it seeks salvation through political authority, ends in the most irrational form of government imaginable—in the dictatorship of casual oligarchs. . . . The reformers who are staking their hopes on good despots, because they are so eager to plan the future, leave unplanned that on which all their hopes depend: . . . the selection of the despots who are to make society so rational and so secure has to be left to the insecurity of irrational chance." /16

This whole theory of benevolent censorship—anticipatory or by way of review—is mischievous doctrine. There is no conceivable way that it can be limited in degree or in nature. Control of what goes out over the air waves is no more justified than control of what is distributed by the postal system. The Second Class mailing privilege—as vital to many publications as the air waves to broadcasters—should not be withheld from any magazine because it will not submit its editorial contents to review by a commission. Newspapers should not be required to yield control of editorials and features to a commission because economic facts preclude an unlimited number of papers in the community. /17

Regulation is just the wrong, the precipitous, the penny-wise, pound-foolish way of seeking improvement. /18

The truth of the matter is that the road to Utopia is hard and rocky and uncharted. No one is satisfied with television when he considers the unlimited potentialities of the medium. Each of us looks at it from the little window framed by his own values and concerns—and knows that it could be better. But the thoughtful man knows also that improvement will come hard and slow after many a false start, after many years of trial and error, and, above all, by facing realities rather than attempting to evade them. /19

I cannot share the defeatist view that, if the Government does not take the improvement of television programing under its control, there will be no improvement at all. There is nothing in our national experience to support this view. The fact of the matter is that any worthwhile improvement must have a deeper and sounder foundation than Government policing. It seems to me that such a foundation consists in the stake that all of us in this country have in a vigorous, freely competing, unrestricted television medium. /20

At this particular moment in history, all of us—whatever our individual interests—have one overriding common interest: that in this rapidly moving age of conflict, the democratic process does not go down—a lumbering anachronism, the victim of totalitarian swiftness and directness. In this decisive battle, the immediacy, the speed and impact of television can be decisive factors in informing the American people during crises and creating a prompt feedback of the sense and purpose of the people to the Government. It is both a lesson of history and ordinary common sense that this function cannot be carried out except in an atmosphere of freedom. /21

All of us here also have a special stake in a free television because we are all devoted to a free and expanding economy. The stimulative effect of television on that economy has been tremendous. None of us can afford to let it stagnate and fall short of its highest capacities; if we do, its strength as a medium will so deteriorate that it won't be worth saving. /22

All of us recognize that, because of the unique characteristics of the medium and the speed of its growth, the problems facing television are complex and, in some respects, unprecedented. The major part of the burden in solving these problems must rest with the broadcaster. We have fully acknowledged this responsibility and intend to discharge it. But we cannot, and should not, withdraw from the world of which we are a part and make command decisions. A trust in a democratic society is given, not in a context of isolated authority, but on the assumption that one will have constant reference to the values and objectives of his fellow citizens. /23

We may be slow in perceiving these. We may be in need of a better, surer way of determining them. But we are aware of them, and we mean to respect them. For television will begin to reach toward its Utopia only when it has full confidence that it is realizing in one way or another the values and objectives of all the people. This means not just always "catering" to the majority, but also taking into account and respecting intellectual and esthetic minorities. /24

The quest for Utopia always falls short of achievement. But it is the quest itself that is important—not the illusion that we will ever achieve perfection. I hope that in our quest we will not be lured into shortcuts that turn out to be dead ends or seek remedies more devastating than the ills they are supposed to cure. I am for undertaking the quest the hard way, the responsible way, the enduring way. /25

If I may take away one meaning from this highly flattering occasion, it is the conviction that I am not alone. /26

The speech

1. What are the probable persuasive functions of Stanton's quotation from John Ward Fenno and the comments on the Sedition Act given in paragraphs 2 through 5?
2. In paragraphs 9 through 11 the speaker seeks to refute the argument that regulation of broadcasting is peculiarly necessary and justifiable. What forms of reasoning and evidence does he use here? How reliable are they, logically? In making these evaluations, remember that absolute reliability is seldom attainable in rhetorical reasoning.
3. Ordinarily one example is an insufficient proof of an argumentative point unless the audience already believes the point or unless one is refuting an absolute generalization that can be destroyed by identifying a single exception to it. How effective is Stanton's "Circle Theatre" example (paragraph 10) likely to be with his audience?
4. Stanton argues that any regulation of radio-TV programing must lead to censorship. To what extent does he establish a credible causal relationship here? Could the argument be made stronger? How? Do you think it needs to be strengthened for his audience?
5. What special, motivational advantages does the speaker gain by his repeated use of analogies and examples that involve the newspaper business?
6. This speech can be considered a general rebuttal against the positions taken by people who agree with Rabbi Eisendrath ("The Moral Bankruptcy of Television," pp. 108-113). Review *rebuttal* and *refutation* in the Glossary, and then identify as many standard methods of such argument as you can find in Stanton's speech.
7. Would Stanton's audience assign him the burden of proving that self-regulation will succeed in the broadcasting industry? Would you? Does he sufficiently discharge that burden to satisfy you? If so, how? If not, why?
8. Suppose Stanton had delivered these remarks to the Federal Communications Commission as Rabbi Eisendrath did. Would Stanton's ethos before the Commission be significantly different from what it was before the award luncheon audience? Why?
9. What common ground is established with the luncheon audience in paragraph 20? What is the "special stake" referred to? Would this have been an equally good common-ground argument if the audience had been 1300 college students instead of 1300 business executives? Why or why not?
10. Does the conclusion of this speech accomplish what a good conclusion should? If redesigned, could it have achieved more with this audience? How or why not?

For further study and discussion

1. Is there evidence that broadcasters are now exercising their responsibilities with the greater wisdom Stanton promised?
2. Do you think the steady decline in the number of daily newspapers, especially in metropolitan centers, is a cause for concern? Why or why not?
3. What evidence is there, if any, that advertisers exercise more censorship over radio-TV programing than over editorial policies of newspapers and periodicals?
4. What truth is there in the allegation that we have a one-party press in the United States?
5. For many years public opinion polls have shown that Americans have more confidence in radio-TV news reporting than in newspaper reporting. Do you think this high regard for radio-TV is justified? Why or why not?

6. The famous physicist and Nobel prize winner, P. W. Bridgman, has written, "It seems to me that society tries to formally control, by means of laws, too many sorts of things. Popular sentiment has ways of getting results which are effective and more flexible . . . . " (*The Way Things Are* [Cambridge, 1959], p. 307.) Do you think this applies to regulation of public information agencies? Why or why not?
7. What is the history and present value of the Second Class mailing privilege in our postal system? Do publishers use it responsibly? Does it contribute to the improvement of public knowledge and taste as originally intended?
8. Why was the Sedition Act passed in 1798? What was the effect?
9. Explore the career of Edward Bok. What were his contributions to journalism? Are his ideals of citizenship and professional success applicable today?

Suggestions for further reading

Leo Bogart, ***The Age of Television*** (New York, 1956)

Mary Crozier, ***Broadcasting*** (London, 1958)

Charles A. Siepmann, ***Radio, Television and Society*** (New York, 1950)

Gilbert V. Seldes, ***The Public Arts*** (New York, 1956)

United States Congress, House Committee on Interstate and Foreign Commerce, ***Political Broadcasts: Equal Time,*** Hearings before the Committee, 86th Cong., 1st Sess. on HR 5389 and other bills . . . . June 29, 30 and July 1, 1959 (Washington, U.S. Govt. Printing Office, 1959)

Movies and censorship

CBS "SMALL WORLD" TELECAST

Small World is a unique discussion program produced by Edward R. Murrow and Fred W. Friendly and broadcast over the Columbia Broadcasting System Television Network. From various parts of the world the "Small World" broadcasts bring together, electronically, outstanding personalities for half-hour discussions of significant issues.

The four participants in the *Small World* telecast, "Movies and Censorship," of April 10, 1960, were separated from each other by thousands of miles, as indicated in the transcript below; but the effect of the production was, for the viewer, very nearly that of seeing a face-to-face discussion. The program's director and engineers followed the discussion closely, broadcasting the image of each speaker as he or she began a contribution or when the remarks of one participant seemed to be making a strong impression on another. The conversation was spontaneous and unrehearsed, though there had been preliminary planning. Those who saw and heard the program could hear all participants at all times.

Each of the three guests on the program had first-hand knowledge of the subject being considered. Monsignor John J. McClafferty was born in New York City in 1906. He attended Xavier High School, received his A.B. from Cathedral College in 1927, attended St. Joseph's Seminary, was awarded his A.M. by the Catholic University in 1932 and a diploma by the New York School of Social Work in 1936. He was ordained a priest of the Roman Catholic Church in 1930, appointed Monsignor in 1943, and Domestic Prelate in 1953. Father McClafferty has had a special interest in education and in social work throughout his career. From 1936 to 1947 he was Executive Secretary of the National Legion of Decency; during part of the same period he was a consultant for the National Church of the Air, Columbia Broadcasting System. He has also been an adviser to other religious and educational programs. At present he is at the Catholic University of America, Washington, D.C., where he was Dean of the National Catholic School of Social Service from 1947 to 1955 and is now Assistant to the Rector.

Deborah Kerr is a highly successful actress. She was born at Helensburgh, Scotland, in 1921 and attended the Helensburgh schools and Northumberland House School in Bristol, England. She began her film career by appearing in the British motion picture *Major Barbara* in 1940. After considerable success in the cinema and on the stage in England, she came to the United States in 1947. Among the later films in which she has appeared are: *From Here to Eternity, Tea and Sympathy, The King and I, Bonjour Tristesse,* and *The Journey.* As she indicates in the discussion, Miss Kerr has from time to time found reason to protest against certain forms of film censorship.

Otto Preminger is an outspoken, eminently successful producer-director of motion pictures and stage plays. He was born in Vienna, Austria, in 1906, and he holds the LL.D. from the University of Vienna. He began his career as producer-director at the Max Reinhardt Theatre der Josefstadt in Vienna but came to the United States in 1935. In New York he directed several major stage productions, among them *Margin for Error* and *Outward Bound.* In recent years Preminger has been primarily engaged in producing and directing motion pictures and has been outstandingly successful, both artistically and commercially.

Some of his pictures have been universally praised while others have been the sources of controversy and even litigation. Among the more famous of his many films are: *Fallen Angel, Forever Amber, Whirlpool, The Moon Is Blue, Carmen Jones, Saint Joan, Anatomy of a Murder,* and *Bonjour Tristesse.*

The text of "Movies and Censorship" that follows is from a typescript of the broadcast, supplied by the Columbia Broadcasting System. It is an accurate rendering-in-print of actual, spontaneous conversation. It can, therefore, be studied as an unedited representation of the language used by educated, articulate persons engaged in serious discussion. The organizational and stylistic qualities found here can be compared and contrasted with similar qualities found in transcripts of formal discussion, public speaking, or the various forms of written discourse. And, since the oral styles of the three major participants in this discussion are very different, these differences may themselves be the objects of profitable study.

ANNOUNCER: *Small World* is a four way trans-oceanic conversation filmed and edited by Murrow and Friendly. /1

DEBORAH KERR: This is Deborah Kerr, speaking from Klosters in Switzerland. /2

OTTO PREMINGER: This is Otto Preminger in Rome. /3

JOHN J. MC CLAFFERTY: This is Father McClafferty at the Catholic University of America, Washington, D.C. /4

EDWARD R. MURROW: This is *Small World,* and this is Ed Murrow in Hong Kong. /5

COMMERCIAL

MURROW: Good evening. Today on *Small World:* "Movies and Censorship"—or perhaps I should say "classification." From Washington, Monsignor John J. McClafferty, of the Catholic University of America, former head of the Legion of Decency. Monsignor, may I present that very fine actress, Miss Deborah Kerr. We all remember her in *Tea and Sympathy* and *From Here to Eternity*—two movies that are perhaps bench marks in the continuing controversy as to what the general audience should and should not see. Miss Kerr is in Klosters, Switzerland, tonight. Deborah, how's the snow? /6

KERR: Lovely, thank you. I understand from the skiers, it's great. /7

MC CLAFFERTY: How do you do, Miss Kerr. /8

KERR: How do you do, Monsignor. /9

MURROW: Our third guest ought really to be in Israel tonight, because he is filming *Exodus* there, but he's flown to Rome because the circuits from there are a little more reliable. Otto Preminger, produced *Anatomy of a Murder* and *The Moon Is Blue.* Both of these pictures brought him into very considerable controversy with the Legion of Decency and other organizations. Mr. Preminger, I'm delighted that three people of such differing views have agreed to appear on *Small World* and disagree agreeably about the subject of censorship and movies. /10

PREMINGER: I am happy to be here and I can add to the conversation about the weather. The weather in Haifa, Tel Aviv, and in Rome, today, is delightful and very warm. /11

MURROW: Well, since we are going to talk about censorship or classification,* I suggest we begin by trying to define it. /12

PREMINGER: I think that censorship is an evil institution, where the State or other authorities try to impose their will on people who otherwise should enjoy the free expression of a medium of communication. I think that censorship is the first step in totalitarian government, regardless of whether the government is from the right or from the left, and therefore, I call it evil. When we speak about censorship today, we speak mainly about pre-censorship. It is a submission of some work or expression that we want to put into communication (like books, newspapers, or a speech on radio or a motion picture)—to submit it before we show it to the public, for permission to be shown. /13

MC CLAFFERTY: Yes. I gather, then, that Mr. Preminger, you make a distinction between censorship in respect to prior restraint and censorship in respect to post restraint. /14

PREMINGER: Naturally, I think that the laws of the United States give the police, in every State, the right, if somebody shows something obscene—whether it is in a magazine, in a book, or on the screen—to confiscate it, and to start criminal procedure. /15

KERR: It's not done enough then—is it? /16

PREMINGER: Huh? /17

KERR: That's not done enough. I'm always astounded at how many obscene magazines there are. /18

---

*As used here this term refers to the practice of classifying and publicly announcing the kind of audience for which a film is intended. See also paragraph 48. (*Editor's note*)

PREMINGER: Well, I am there with you as far as magazines are concerned, because I have suffered, personally, probably as much as you, Deborah, but I must say that the freedom of the press is probably worthwhile taking a little abuse, personally. /19

KERR: Yes, I agree with you there, but it's so difficult this whole business of censorship. Isn't it? I feel like the Libran* that I am, on the scales between you, Otto, and you, Monsignor, in that I always see both sides of the question, and . . . /20

PREMINGER: Well, I don't think it's really so difficult, because, at least in the United States, the Supreme Court has very often, in almost all cases, expressed, as far as the movies go, the opinion that pre-censorship is illegal, and whenever the Supreme Court was asked, it has declared censorship unconstitutional. /21

MC CLAFFERTY: I think I would differ with you with regard to that, because as far as I know, the Supreme Court has not definitively determined, up to the present time, with regard to the constitutionality, per se . . . /22

PREMINGER: That is true—because the Supreme Court . . . /23

MC CLAFFERTY: . . . of censorship. /24

PREMINGER: . . . tries to avoid making laws. But you must admit, Monsignor, that in no case has a Censorship Board won in front of the United States Supreme Court, at least not since 1923, since the Supreme Court has made it clear that motion pictures are a means of communication. /25

MC CLAFFERTY: In a ruling of the Supreme Court, fairly recently, in *Kingsley vs. Brown*, that Court held that prior restraint should be considered in the case of the particular analysis of each film, and in the case of *Roth* and in the case of *Alberts*, the Supreme Court has undertaken to define rather precisely what obscene is, in terms of a regulation or a control with regard to the exhibition of films. /26

PREMINGER: There is, of course, in the United States, another unofficial censorship. There are private groups which I may call pressure groups, which have never been very successful with books, magazines or newspapers, but have been very successful with the motion pictures during the last thirty years, telling them what they may and may not show on the screen. I don't want to seem or sound like a crusader, and I would like to keep the perspective of good humor in this, but I made a small comedy called *The Moon Is Blue*, and both the Code Administration in Hollywood and the Legion of Decency declared that this cannot be shown on the screens of the United States. In the United States there was a great, great, tremendous publicity campaign against the picture, and I was told by many people the picture would never be shown. /27

MC CLAFFERTY: May I make . . . /28

PREMINGER: So I played the picture anyway, and the picture was a very big success all over the world, and particularly in the United States, in spite of being banned by both the Motion Picture Code Administration in Hollywood and the Legion of Decency, and I really don't think that anybody's character has been corrupted by seeing this rather harmless little comedy.* /29

MC CLAFFERTY: We have to enter at this point a discussion of fundamental moral values, and also make a consideration of the nature of the film as a medium of entertainment in terms of theme and thesis, but before entering into that . . . /30

PREMINGER: But films are not a medium of entertainment. They are mediums of communication. /31

MC CLAFFERTY: That it is. /32

PREMINGER: In fact, the theatre is the same medium or a very similar medium, and why did nobody object to people seeing the same comedy in the theatre, and why should it be sinful to see it in the movies? /33

KERR: Isn't it because there are so many more people involved? /34

MC CLAFFERTY: Yes, definitely. /35

PREMINGER: Why shouldn't the people—this is a, a very—I am surprised, Deborah, this is a rather, a rather snobbish and rather reactionary point of view. /36

KERR: No, No. /37

PREMINGER: Why shouldn't many people see the same thing as a few? /38

KERR: Well, I don't mean many people. I think there are more children involved. /39

MC CLAFFERTY: Yes, and adolescents. /40

KERR: And I am with you entirely, Otto. I have suf-

---

*From Libra, the seventh sign of the zodiac. Miss Kerr was born on September 30, a date that falls under the sign of Libra, a balance or pair of scales. *(Editor's note)*

*This film and Rossellini's *The Miracle* were among the most controversial pictures shown in the United States during the 1950's. Recent history of film censorship is virtually epitomized in the record of local, state, and federal decisions concerning *The Moon Is Blue*, *The Miracle*, and the French film *La Ronde*. *(Editor's note)*

fered myself, from a very lovely play—it was *Tea and Sympathy*—being censored as far as the movie is concerned, and consequently being ruined as a movie, and yet its message that it carried was one of great, great compassion and tenderness, and really a message for the world, put through perhaps rather startling means. So, I am with you on that, but I have to say that I do see both sides of the question. I can see that in a mass medium, which television is, and movies are, I think you have got to have some form of control. Should I say control rather than censorship? /41

PREMINGER: But, darling, who should control it? /42

MC CLAFFERTY: Now, a State, and this is true, historically, has the right of self-protection and self-preservation. It must exercise certain kinds of responsible controls, whether it be in the field of public safety; whether it be in the field of public morals. But in the United States, with our cherished tradition, and thanks be to God for this tradition, the tradition of freedom, the central issue is the right balance between freedom and restraint. /43

PREMINGER: Well, there is no . . . /44

MC CLAFFERTY: Now, this freedom must be a responsibly exercised freedom with due cognizance taken of the social and moral welfare of the community; with due cognizance taken of the impressionable young people who view films, whose lifes' habits and attitudes are being formed and shaped. For their own welfare and for society's well-being, these considerations should counsel us to be socially and morally responsible in this exercise of one of the most precious freedoms that we have. /45

PREMINGER: Monsignor, your speech would have converted me if it had been necessary. I agree with you in everything you said, but it does not touch the real, practical problem that we are trying to discuss here. /46

KERR: No, I don't think so either. /47

PREMINGER: Censorship becomes in almost all cases —or I would say in all cases—a political question and a political football, and that is the danger. Now, I must say that I, personally, think that no grown-up man or woman should be told what they can see. There is another question that Deborah has brought up before about children. Now, strangely enough, as much as I am against any kind of censorship, particularly private censorship by pressure groups, I am very much for self-classification of pictures, and wherever I can, I classify my own pictures and ask the exhibitors to, in their publicity, have a warning to parents . . . /48

KERR: Yes, well . . . /49

PREMINGER: . . . because I feel that parents should have a right to bring up their children in their own way, and if they don't want them to see pictures of some kind, they shouldn't see them. /50

KERR: But think about—think—there are too many parents that don't seem to have enough control over their children to stop them going to these pictures. /51

PREMINGER: But this cannot be helped by motion picture producers. /52

KERR: This is—this is the—this is the trouble, isn't it? /53

PREMINGER: I mean, there must be somebody else helping these parents. You cannot blame everything on—on motion pictures. If parents cannot control their children, then the motion picture censorship certainly won't help it, because there are many, many other areas where these children probably will be sinning and doing very bad things, regardless of motion pictures. /54

KERR: Yes, I agree. After all, we can—we can censor ourselves. We don't have to buy a newspaper if we find its policy offensive to us. /55

PREMINGER: That's right. /56

KERR: And we could just as well, you know, not go into the cinema if we don't like the subject. /57

MURROW: Excuse me. I am afraid I must censor all of us for one moment while we hear from Olin Mathieson. /58

COMMERCIAL

ANNOUNCER: *Small World* continues with Deborah Kerr, Otto Preminger, Monsignor John J. McClafferty, and Ed Murrow. /59

MC CLAFFERTY: I like very much, Miss Kerr, what you say about the individual having a responsibility to choose well and to not choose that which he may deem to be morally harmful to himself. I think that you can conceive of these ways of control in a series of expanding concentric circles. The first control, of course, is the control by the individual, according to the light of his conscience, and according to the information which he has at hand about the particular film in question. Then, of course, there is the area of parental control and the area of the counsel of voluntary associations. I don't term such counsel "censorship" or "pressure." /60

PREMINGER: No. I agree with you, as long as the Legion of Decency would tell only their members what to see and what not to see, I would never object to it. /61

MC CLAFFERTY: The Legion of De . . . /62

PREMINGER: But when the Legion of Decency threatens the theatres with boycott if they play certain pictures, then I think they go beyond what should be permissible. /63

MC CLAFFERTY: Yes. The Legion of Decency counsels its own members and, exercising its right of free association and free expression and free communication, makes known to its followers what its moral estimate of a given film is, but again, may I backtrack in the discussion, to something—or rather two things that you said, Mr. Preminger? First of all, you indicated that you felt you had a right to produce and exhibit whatever you wished. I do not think that that is an absolute right. I think that that is a right that must be exercised in a morally and socially responsible way in the light of the commonweal. /64

PREMINGER: That's right, but I must be the sole judge of what is morally responsible. /65

MC CLAFFERTY: Yes. And secondly, you said that each adult has the right to see what he wishes. Again, I do not think that that is an absolute right. I think that that is a right which must be exercised intelligently, prudently and wisely by the individual. /66

PREMINGER: But Monsignor, why should the censor's character not be corrupted when he sees these things, in order to tell people not to see them? And why should any other adult be corrupted when he sees them? /67

MC CLAFFERTY: Well, I . . . /68

PREMINGER: What makes the censor so special? /69

MC CLAFFERTY: I do not wish to be put into any position of advocating or sustaining, necessarily, official censorship. My own personal opinion is this (and I want to make it clear that I am not speaking for any group of any organization when I say it)—my own personal opinion would be against federal censorship of motion pictures. I would like to . . . /70

PREMINGER: I am all for that. /71

KERR: Otto, I am dying to ask you something. /72

PREMINGER: Yes? /73

KERR: About—you know, one has often thought, "Right, abolish censorship!" What happens if you abolish censorship? /74

PREMINGER: But we don't have censorship in the United States, Deborah. /75

KERR: No. What I was going to say, Otto, what I really wanted to ask you about was this, which has always bothered me. Were—it's all to do with censorship. If you have no censorship, or even if you have it in a very strict form, how can you—how can we . . . You are a sincere person. When you make your films, you do it with sincerity and you do it with taste, and I think taste is probably the keynote of this whole thing. I mean, anything, any message, can be given and point made if it's done with taste, but we are so wide open in our medium, and certainly in television, it seems to me, or perhaps less at the moment, I don't know, to the unscrupulous, half-talented person who sees in the making of a movie a great deal of money. /76

PREMINGER: Deborah, may I say that I personally believe in the good taste of the great masses? I have never heard of anybody becoming rich because he sold dirty books or dirty postcards, and I don't think anybody has ever become rich by making really dirty or obscene motion pictures. /77

KERR: Well, not rich—shall we say done rather well. /78

MURROW: Monsignor McClafferty, is it admissible that any group should attempt to control or influence what those who are not members to that group should see or hear? /79

MC CLAFFERTY: Well, it would be my thought that the voluntary group, exercising its right of free comment and moral evaluation, ought to communicate that moral evaluation to those who follow it, and communicate it likewise to the media of communication, so that that opinion may be communicated to the public at large. /80

PREMINGER: I must say that I would not object to it at all. /81

MC CLAFFERTY: I just wanted to make this point: I do not think that voluntary groups would wish to exercise coercive methods, but rather that they would wish to exercise persuasive methods. /82

PREMINGER: May I repeat my question which you did not answer, Monsignor, before? Then why does then the Legion of Decency, when it condemns a picture, also threaten the theatres that play it with boycott for their next pictures? Do you think this is right? /83

MC CLAFFERTY: First of all, I am not here as the spokesman of the Legion. /84

PREMINGER: No, but—but you are familiar with the practices of the Legion. /85

MC CLAFFERTY: I want to clarify the position in

which I express myself. I express myself as an individual. /86

PREMINGER: I realize this, but I still, for information, would like to ask you this question—what your personal opinion about it is. /87

MC CLAFFERTY: The Legion does not go, according to my recollection of its operation, to a motion picture company and make demands that this or that be done, or that this or that not be done. /88

PREMINGER: But it's my own picture, *The Moon Is Blue*. Here both—both Archbishops of New York and Philadelphia published letters in the newspapers, threatening theatres which played the picture to be boycotted by the members of the Legion of Decency—also for future exhibitions which by themselves were not condemned. /89

MC CLAFFERTY: The action of the Legion, under the leadership of such spiritual leaders that you mention, was in furtherance of the pastoral Ministry of the Church, namely, the spiritual well-being of those who are members of the Church, and those and others who follow the Legion classifications. I do not know of any central policy of the national office of the Legion which imposes any boycott or abstention for a period of time. There may be efforts on the local level for such supplementary action, but that is within the discretion and within the freedom of those subsidiary local efforts, because the national office of the . . . /90

PREMINGER: Do you, personally, approve of such actions? /91

MC CLAFFERTY: . . . Legion would give to those local efforts the freedom which all of us would like to see observed in all of the sectors of society, namely, a responsibly used freedom. /92

PREMINGER: Do you, personally, Monsignor, approve of such actions? /93

MC CLAFFERTY: Well, I don't explicitly understand what you mean by "such actions." You mean boycott? /94

PREMINGER: Yes. /95

MC CLAFFERTY: I, personally, would prefer that such voluntary associations utilize persuasive and interpretative methods rather than coercive methods, but it may be that the judgment of prudent men on the . . . /96

PREMINGER: I am very glad to hear that. /97

MC CLAFFERTY: . . . on the local level—that they have high responsibilities and the highest within a given territory, to see to it that their people are protected morally and spiritually, and that the people not be roadblocked in their progress towards spiritual perfection—roadblocked by any such thing as a film that might be immoral or obscene. /98

PREMINGER: You agree, though, that this should only be done to members, by members, of a certain group, and should not extend to people who do not belong to the same creed, the same Legion, or the same group of people? /99

MC CLAFFERTY: Well, we must remember this—that just as the Code is based upon generally accepted moral standards, so too, the work of the Legion, generally, is based upon the fundamental Ten Commandments which should guide our relations to our neighbor in terms of rights and duties, and our relation to God in terms of our rights and duties. I believe, Mr. Preminger, that a great majority of the pictures which have been deemed worthy of receiving a so-called Oscar, have been rated in the "A" category by the Legion of Decency. I think this is a tribute not only to the good judgment of the Legion, but also to the good judgment of the audience, in having such a coincidence of opinion with respect to films that are judged to be worthwhile and outstanding. /100

PREMINGER: I want to state here, that neither Greta Garbo nor Ernest Lubitsch, nor Chaplin ever received an Oscar, and these certainly are three geniuses of the motion picture business. /101

KERR: Hear! Hear! /102

PREMINGER: Does anyone disagree? /103

KERR: No—not me! /104

PREMINGER: I think a producer has a right to make social comments, and it still can be very entertaining. As, for instance, recently, a picture *On the Beach* has proved—which made considerable social comments and still seems to be doing very, very well at the box office—and I do feel that pictures can be controversial and attack certain principles that might be very dear to certain segments of the population, without really insulting those segments of the population, if they are done in good taste and with the right feeling for drama. /105

MC CLAFFERTY: There is also the hazard, I believe, that when certain subject materials are shown on the screen, certain impressionable and perhaps unstable audience members may be tempted toward an experimental adoption of such a way of life . . . /106

KERR: Yes. /107

MC CLAFFERTY: . . . or toward an experimental use of such a way of life. /108

PREMINGER: But that is always true. We live in a very hazardous world. /109

KERR: That's why I would do away with horror films. I think they are much worse . . . /110

MC CLAFFERTY: Yes. /111

KERR: . . . all the dreadful tortures they practice and horrible things they do to people—ugh! /112

MC CLAFFERTY: When the Senate was investigating juvenile delinquency, a number of clinical experts testified, and in their opinion, there was a likely connection, a presumed connection between the amount and character of violence and horror on the screen, and the rising tide of juvenile delinquency, and I believe that this rising tide of juvenile delinquency is one of the reasons why there has been some resurgence of opinion and pressure within the population for some forms of control on the mass media of communication. /113

KERR: Yes. /114

MURROW: I'm sorry. Monsignor McClafferty, Miss Deborah Kerr, Mr. Otto Preminger, thank you all very much, indeed. Next week's guests in just a moment. /115

COMMERCIAL

ANNOUNCER: Next week on *Small World,* Professor Harold Urey of the University of California; Dr. Wernher von Braun of the National Aeronautics and Space Administration; and John Davy, Scientific Correspondent of the London Observer, discuss the problems of space and why should man want to get to the moon. /116
Tonight's conversation between Deborah Kerr, Otto Preminger and Monsignor John J. McClafferty was recorded and filmed simultaneously in Klosters, Switzerland; Rome; and Washington, D.C. Again, next week, Olin Mathieson brings you *Small World.* /117

The telecast

1. This discussion follows the *reflective* pattern of organization in some but not all respects (see Glossary). Which phases of reflection have the participants neglected? With what results for their listeners?
2. Evaluate the ways in which McClafferty and Preminger handle evidence in paragraphs 21 through 26. Which speaker has the better evidence? Which handles it more persuasively? Why?
3. In paragraph 27 Preminger seems to propose a change in what he calls "unofficial censorship." Does he thus assume the burden of proof on this point for the rest of the discussion? If so, does he effectively discharge that burden during the discussion?
4. Mr. Preminger and Miss Kerr contend that Monsignor McClafferty has missed "the practical problem we're trying to discuss here" (paragraphs 46-47). Can you identify that problem? What could have been done to make it easier for listeners to be sure of what these speakers meant?
5. Speeches, whether long or short, are most easily understood if they have central ideas, are related to their settings by introductions of some sort, and are concluded in a way that reminds the listener of the point that has been made. Using these criteria, evaluate the structure of the "speeches" that form paragraphs 13, 27-29, 41, 43-45, and 90-92.
6. This program evolved into a kind of debate between Monsignor McClafferty and Mr. Preminger, with comment and questions from Miss Kerr. In the remarks of the two "debaters" identify examples of each of the following methods of argument: dilemma, refutation, rebuttal.
7. Review the topic of *implication* in the Glossary. Is there any ground for thinking that in this discussion there is too much argument by implication and too little direct statement of propositions? If so, what are the principles and the evidence on which such a judgment is to be made?
8. The transcript of this discussion accurately represents an "animated conversation as carried on among educated persons" (see *conversational quality,* Glossary). Identify three or four passages having the directness, spontaneity, and informality a good public speaker might well copy. Identify three or four passages that illustrate uncertainty in language and organization that public speakers in more formal circumstances should avoid even while aiming at conversational quality.
9. What principles of formal speechmaking, if any, do *not* apply to informal, discussional speaking of the kind represented by this transcript?
10. Had you been the moderator of this program, would you have intervened in the discussion more often than Murrow did? If so, where and for what purpose?

For further study and discussion

1. Trace the history of F. Hugh Herbert's play *The Moon Is Blue* as a theatrical and then as a film production, or trace the court battles leading to the United States Supreme Court's decision on censorship of *The Miracle* by New York State. Can you draw any conclusions from these records as to whether censorship of motion pictures is desirable or legal?
2. Professor Fred B. Millett said in a speech entitled "The Vigilantes," "That the censorship of literature is usual-

ly self-defeating is so obvious as hardly to need explication. The very fact that a censor openly designates a work as dubious . . . is enough to draw the attention . . . of the public to a work that might otherwise have gone unnoticed." Do you agree or disagree? On what evidence? If Millett was right, is Preminger's practice of warning parents concerning some pictures equally self-defeating?

3. What is the Motion Picture Producers' Code? What is its history and how does the Code Administration work? Has it significantly affected the quality of motion pictures?
4. What is the Legion of Decency? What are its objectives and how does it work? What have been the results of its efforts?
5. Do you agree with Miss Kerr and Monsignor McClafferty that the standards of acceptability cannot be the same for the legitimate theater and for movies and television? Why?
6. What taboos other than those concerning sex are observed in television and motion picture production? Is there any clear evidence that the taboos of these industries directly affect the creation of original and significant works?
7. Explore the history of federal action through antitrust suits aimed at breaking the connection between the agencies producing films and those distributing them. What was the reason for these suits? What have been the results?
8. What significance have these films in the history of cinematic art: *The Great Train Robbery, Birth of a Nation, Intolerance, Nanook of the North, The Covered Wagon, The Jazz Singer*? What technical advances or creative ideas made each of these films a "landmark"?
9. How has the advent of television affected the organization and economy of the motion picture industry? How did the development of the motion picture industry affect the legitimate theater?
10. Assume that Preminger is right in saying that a good film is not an entertainment but a "communication." What was being communicated in the most impressive motion picture you have recently seen?

Suggestions for further reading

Harold C. Gardiner, ***The Catholic Viewpoint on Censorship*** (Garden City, N.Y., 1958)

William E. Hocking, ***Freedom of the Press*** (Chicago, 1947)

Ruth A. Inglis, ***Freedom of the Movies*** (Chicago, 1947)

Walter Kerr, ***Criticism and Censorship*** (Milwaukee, 1956)

Richard McKeon, Robert K. Merton, and Walter Gellhorn, ***The Freedom to Read*** (New York, 1957)

Alexander Meiklejohn, ***Political Freedom*** (New York, 1960)

Elmer E. Smead, ***Freedom of Speech by Radio and Television*** (Washington, D.C., 1959)

5 / SOCIAL PROBLEMS

The philosophy of social justice through social action

FRANKLIN D. ROOSEVELT

In June 1932 when the Democratic and Republican parties met one after the other in Chicago's Coliseum to nominate their candidates for president in the approaching election, the country was in the depths of the Great Depression. Falling steadily since the stock market crash of October 1929, railroad and industrial stocks stood at less than 20 percent of their former value. Factory payrolls had been cut in half. Government reports recorded 85,000 business failures, with total liabilities amounting to some 4.5 billion dollars. Five thousand banks were closed; private construction had practically ceased; annual corporate income was down from 11 billion dollars to 2; wages from 55 billion to 33; gross national income from 85 billion to an estimated 37. Worst of all, 11.5 million men and women were unemployed, and thousands more were losing their jobs daily. Bread lines, tar-paper shack villages, and street corner apple sellers became common sights in the cities; farmers poured milk on the ground and burned grain and produce in protest against sinking agricultural prices.

Believing that the roots of the depression lay in international economic and political causes over which the United States had no control and convinced that the economic policies of the current administration were sound, the Republicans reaffirmed their faith in the incumbent President, Herbert Hoover, by nominating him for a second term. The Democrats, after eliminating such other prominent contenders as Alfred E. Smith and Albert Ritchie, on the fourth ballot nominated Franklin D. Roosevelt (1882-1945), then governor of New York.

From the beginning, the campaign of 1932, centering on the issues of recovery, relief, and the repeal of the Eighteenth Amendment, was a dramatic one. Upon learning of his nomination, Roosevelt broke precedent by flying from Albany to Chicago to deliver a stirring speech to the convention delegates. During the campaign Roosevelt traveled more than twenty-five thousand miles, visiting thirty-seven states and delivering twenty major addresses and sixty-seven briefer speeches, in addition to making almost a thousand rear-platform appearances as his campaign train moved about the country.

The speech that follows marked the close of Roosevelt's western tour of September 12 through October 3. On this tour he had made major addresses at Topeka, Sioux City, Seattle, Portland, and San Francisco, dealing with such subjects as agriculture, the tariff, public utilities, and his philosophy of government. Coming to Detroit on Sunday, October 2, for the final appearance of his trip, Roosevelt chose to deal with a subject he had not specifically treated in any of these other speeches—that of social justice through social action. It may well be that he deliberately selected Detroit as the place most suitable for an exposition of his ideas on this subject. Certainly this industrial city was one of the economic sore spots of the nation, with many thousands of its citizens unemployed and many more inadequately fed and housed.

Roosevelt's day in Detroit followed the typical campaign pattern. It began with a parade from the railroad station to the Statler Hotel, where he was guest of honor at a luncheon and informal reception. And following this speech, which was delivered at the Naval Armory, there was a second parade as the cavalcade of official cars moved back to Roosevelt's hotel. In the evening the newspaper correspondents who had accompanied Roosevelt on his trip gave him a farewell dinner.

The Detroit *News* reported that the streets were thronged with friendly and enthusiastic crowds that "waved and shouted words of welcome and cheer" as Roosevelt passed by on his way to the Naval Armory. The Armory itself was packed with an audience of more than six thousand persons, while outside there were four or five thousand more who had been unable to find seats. So dense was this crowd around the building that Rabbi Leo Framm, who had been scheduled to deliver the invocation, was unable to make his way through it, and Father Charles Coughlin of radio fame was pressed into service as a substitute. Mayor Frank Murphy introduced Roosevelt in glowing phrases, describing him as "a great spiritual figure in the political life of our country."

Considered historically, Roosevelt's speech on this occasion is notable as one of the first systematic statements of the social philosophy of the New Deal—the social philosophy that in the following decade was to revolutionize the American way of life and give rise to one of the bitterest and most prolonged disputes in our political history. The speech is interesting rhetorically as an example of Roosevelt's unusual resourcefulness as a campaign orator. Attempting to remove the discussion from the arena of partisan politics by identifying it with "fundamentals that antedate parties," he skillfully adapted his remarks to a Sunday afternoon audience and at the same time gained strong moral support for his views by showing they were no more advanced than the views held by the leaders of the major religious faiths. Moreover, he took advantage of his achievements as a New York legislator and as governor of that state to enhance his own prestige, and within the framework of an essentially philosophical and professedly nonpolitical address he still was able to direct telling jabs at his opponents.

The Detroit audience was warm and friendly, and the speech was enthusiastically received, being interrupted at many points by prolonged applause, laughter, and cheers. According to a reporter for the New York *Times*, the statement which drew the loudest ovation was Roosevelt's declaration that when all other methods had failed the federal government must see to the well-being of its citizens. This response to what was then a new and revolutionary doctrine becomes all the more significant when we realize that in 1932 Roosevelt himself was still relatively unknown outside of New York and that public reaction to his policies as governor had been mixed.

All accounts agree that although Roosevelt was at the close of an arduous three-week campaign trip, he looked tanned and fit, except for dark circles under his eyes, as he arose to speak. His voice was clear and fresh, and his articulation, as always, was sure and precise. Because of the crippled condition in which he had been left many years before by polio, he stood in one spot while speaking, his hands grasping the sides of the high reading desk on which his manuscript lay. Although he used few arm gestures, his typical head and shoulder movements and mobile facial expression helped to communicate his ideas forcibly.

The text of the speech as presented here was established by LeRoy Cowperthwaite and represents a synthesis of the official stenographic report with the "reading copy" used by Roosevelt in delivery.[1] A transcription of the speech preserved in the National Archives was apparently made either before or after its actual delivery since no applause or background noise is present.

My old friend Mayor Murphy, my old friend Governor Comstock, (*Applause*) and you—many of you—my old friends of Detroit and of Michigan: (*Applause*) /1

I have had a wonderful reception today, and I am awfully glad to be back in Detroit, and I am especially glad to be once more the guest of the Navy. (*Applause*) There is only one fly in the ointment, and I might just as well be perfectly frank with you—I would much rather be cruising the Great Lakes on the U.S.S. DuBuque. (*Laughter, applause*) /2

You know today is Sunday, and I am afraid that some of you people today in Detroit have been talking politics. (*Laughter*) Well I am not going to. My friends, I want to talk to you about Government. Well, that is a very different thing. (*Laughter, applause*) And I am not going to refer to parties at all. /3

But, I am going to refer to some of the fundamentals that antedate parties, and antedate republics and empires, fundamentals that are as old as mankind itself. They are fundamentals that have been expressed in philosophies, for I don't know how many thousands of years, in every part of the world. And today, in our boasted modern civilization, we are facing just exactly the same problem, just exactly the same conflict between two schools of philosophy that they faced in the earliest days of America, and indeed the earliest days of the world. One of them—one of these old philosophies—is the philosophy of those who would "let things alone," and the other is the philosophy that strives for something new—something that the human race has never attained yet, but something which I believe the human race can and will attain—social justice, through social action. (*Prolonged applause*) /4

Now the philosophy of "letting things alone" has resulted in the days of the cave man, and in the days of the automobile—has resulted in the jungle law of the survival of the so-called fittest. But this philosophy of social action results in the protection of humanity and the fitting of as many human beings as possible into the scheme of surviving. And in that first philosophy of "letting things alone" I am sorry to say that there are a lot of people in my community back home—which is a little village—and in the farming districts of the Nation and in the great cities of the country, such as yours—we can fit a great many splendid people into that category, splendid people who keep saying, not only to themselves and to their friends, but to the community as a

[1] Lowery LeRoy Cowperthwaite, "A Criticism of the Speaking of Franklin D. Roosevelt in the Presidential Campaign of 1932" (Unpublished Ph.D. thesis, State University of Iowa, 1950), 2 vols., I, 8-9; II, Preface and 558-567.

whole, "Why shouldn't we 'let things alone'? In the first place they are not as bad as they are painted, and in the second place they will cure themselves. Time is a great healer." An easy philosophy! The kind of philosophy, my friends, that was expressed the other day by a Cabinet officer of the United States of America,* when he is reported to have said, "Our children are apt to profit rather than suffer from what is going on." (*Applause*) /5

While he was saying that, another branch of your Government and mine, the United States Public Health Service, which believes in my kind of philosophy, I think—telling the truth—said this: "Over six million of our public school children do not have enough to eat. Many of them are fainting at their desks. They are a prey to disease. Their future health is menaced." (*Applause*) /6

What school do you believe in? /7

And in the same way, there are two theories of prosperity and of well-being: The first theory is that if we make the rich richer, somehow they will let a part of their prosperity trickle through to the rest of us. (*Applause*) The second theory—and I suppose this goes back to the days of Noah—I won't say Adam and Eve, because they had a less complicated situation—(*Laughter and applause*) but, at least, back in the days of the flood—there was the second theory that if we make the average of mankind comfortable and secure, their prosperity will rise upward, just as yeast rises up, through the ranks. (*Applause*) /8

Now, my friends, the philosophy of social justice that I am going to talk about this Sabbath day, the philosophy of social justice through social action, calls definitely, plainly, for the reduction of poverty. And what do we mean when we talk about the reduction of poverty? We mean I think the reduction of the causes of poverty. When we have an epidemic of disease in this land in these modern days, what do we do? We turn to find out in the first instance the sources from which the disease has come; and when we have found those sources, those causes of the disease, we turn the energy of our attack upon them. /9

We have got beyond the point in modern civilization of merely trying to fight an epidemic of disease by taking care of the victims after they are stricken. We do that; but we do more. We seek to prevent it; and the attack on poverty is not very unlike the attack on disease. We are seeking the causes and when we have found them, we must turn our attack upon them. What are the causes? What are the causes that destroy human beings, driving millions of them to destruction? Well, there are a good many of them and there are a good many of us who are alive today who have seen tremendous steps taken toward the eradication of those causes. /10

For instance, ill health: You and I know what has been accomplished by community effort, state effort, and the efforts and association of individual men and women toward the bettering of the health of humanity. /11

We have spent vast sums upon research. We have established a wholly new science, the science of public health; and we are carrying what we call today "instruction in health" into the most remote corners of our cities and our country districts. Well, the result is what? It is two-fold: First an economic saving. It has been money which has been returned to the community a thousand times over. You and I know that a sick person—a man, woman or child, who has to be taken care of—not only takes the individual who is sick out of active participation and useful citizenship, but takes somebody else, too. And so, from the purely dollars and cents point of view that we Americans are so fond of thinking about, public health has paid for itself. /12

And what have we done along other lines for the prevention of some causes of poverty? /13

I go back twenty-two years to a day when, in my State of New York, we tried to pass in the Legislature what we called a Workmen's Compensation Act, knowing, as we did, that there were thousands of men and women who every year were seriously injured in industrial accidents of one kind or another, who became a burden on their community, who were unable to work, unable to get adequate medical care—and a lot of us youngsters in the Legislature in those days were called radicals. We were called Socialists—they didn't know the word Bolshevik in those days, but if they had known that, we would have been called that, too. (*Applause*) And we put through a Workmen's Compensation Act, and the courts, as some courts do, thinking in terms of the Seventeenth Century, declared it to be unconstitutional. So we had to go about amending the Constitution, and the following year we got a Workmen's Compensation Act. /14

What has it done? We were not the first state to have it. One of the earliest States, by the way, was New Jersey, which, the year before the action in the

*Secretary of the Interior Wilbur. *(Editor's note)*

State of New York, passed a Workmen's Compensation Act at the bidding of that great humanitarian Governor, Woodrow Wilson. (*Prolonged applause*) But the result has been that almost every State of the Union has eliminated that cause of poverty among the masses of the people. /15

Take another form of poverty in the old days. Not so long ago, you and I know, there were families in attics—in every part of the Nation—in country districts and in city districts—hundreds and thousands of crippled children who could get no adequate care, crippled children who were lost to the community and who were a burden on the community. And so we have, in these past twenty or thirty years, gradually provided means for restoring crippled children to useful citizenship; and it has all been a factor in going after and solving one of the causes of poverty and disease. /16

And then in these later years, we have been wondering about old people; and we have come to the conclusion in this modern civilization that the theory and the idea of carting old people off to the county poorhouse is not perhaps the best thing after all. (*Applause*) /17

I will tell you what sold me on old age pension insurance—old age pensions. Not so long ago—about ten years—I received a great shock. I had been away from my home town of Hyde Park during the winter time and when I came back I found that a tragedy had occurred. One of my farm neighbors, who had been a splendid old fellow—Supervisor of his town, Highway Commissioner of his town—one of the best of our citizens. And before I had left, around Christmas time, I had seen the old man, who was eighty-nine, and I had seen his old brother, who was eighty-seven, and had seen his other brother, who was eighty-five, and I had seen his "kid" sister, who was eighty-three. /18

And they were living on a farm; I knew it was mortgaged. I knew it was mortgaged to the hilt; but I assumed that everything was all right, for they still had a couple of cows and a few chickens. But when I came back in the spring, I found that in the heavy winter that followed there had been a heavy fall of snow, and one of the old brothers had fallen down on his way out to the barn to milk the cow, and had perished in the snow drift, and the town authorities had come along and they had taken the two old men and they had put them into the county poorhouse, and they had taken the old lady and had sent her down, for want of a better place, to the insane asylum, although she was not insane, she was just old. /19

That sold me on the idea of trying to keep homes intact for old people. (*Applause*) /20

And then in another respect modern science has been good to us. It is not so very long ago that a young person, or an old person, who had anything the trouble with their mentality—they were put into what was called an asylum and not long before that they used to call it a "madhouse." Even when I was a boy, the States of the Nation used to provide asylums. And when anybody was not entirely complete mentally—when anyone was a mental defective as we call them today, in any shape, manner or form,—he used to be carted off to the asylum and they would always stay there until he came out to go to the graveyard. /21

Today that is not true. Medical science today is now doing two things: first, that the young people, the young people who are not mentally deficient but who require special mental training, and when schools allow them to remain in most cases in the bosom of their own families, we are applying special treatment and special education to them so that, instead of becoming a burden when they grow up, they are going to be useful citizens. (*Applause*) /22

And then, on the other side of it, there are the older people, the people who do have to go to hospitals for mental troubles—and the other day, just before I left Albany, I got a report from my State Department that showed that instead of the old-fashioned system by which the rule was observed of "once in, always in," this past year in the State of New York we had sent back to their families 23 per cent of all those in our hospitals for mental cases, sent them back cured to their families. (*Applause*) /23

Now, these are some of the causes, the causes that have destroyed in past ages countless thousands of our fellow human beings. They are the causes that we must attack if we are to make the future safer for humanity. We can go on taking care of the handicapped and the crippled and the sick and the feeble-minded and the unemployed; but common sense and humanity call on us to turn our back definitely on these destroyers. Poverty resulting from these destroyers is largely preventable, but, my friends, poverty, if it is to be prevented, requires a broad program of social justice. (*Applause*) /24

We cannot go back, we cannot go back to the old prisons, the old systems of mere punishment under which when a man came out of prison he was not fitted to live in our community alongside of us. We cannot go back to the old system of asylums. We cannot go back to the old lack of hospitals, the lack of public health. We cannot go back to the sweatshops of America. We cannot go back to children working in factories. (*Applause*) Those days are gone. (*Applause*) /25

And there are a lot of new steps to take. It is not a question of just not going back. It is a question also of not standing still. (*Applause*) /26

For instance, the problem in the long run, and I am not talking about the emergency of this year, but the problem of unemployment in the long run can be and shall be solved by the human race. (*Applause*) Some leaders have wisely declared for a system of unemployment insurance throughout this broad land of ours; and we are going to come to it. (*Applause*) /27

But I do not believe the Secretary of the Interior [Wilbur] would be for it. (*Laughter and applause*) He would say that great good is coming to this country because of the present situation. (*Laughter*) Yes, the followers of the philosophy of "let alone"—these people have been decrying all of these measures of social welfare. What do they call them? They call them "paternalistic." All right, if they are paternalistic, I am a father. (*Laughter and applause*) /28

They maintain that these laws interfere with individualism, forgetful of the fact that the causes of poverty in the main are beyond the control of any one individual, any czar, either a czar of politics or a czar of industry. (*Applause*) And the followers of the philosophy of "social action for the prevention of poverty" maintain that if we set up a system of justice we shall have small need for the exercise of mere philanthropy. Justice, after all, first is the goal we seek. We believe that when justice has been done individualism will have a greater security to devote the best that individualism itself can give. In other words, my friends, our long-range objective is not a dole, but a job. (*Applause*) /29

At the same time, we have in this Nation—and I know you have in Detroit, because Frank Murphy has talked to me of it many times in the past year or two—widespread suffering which all of us in the city and country alike have got to do everything we can to tide over. All agree that the first responsibility for the prevention of poverty and the alleviation of distress and the care of its victims rests upon the locality, the individuals, the organizations and the Government. First of all, perhaps, upon the private agencies of philanthropy, just as far as we can drag it out of them, secondly, the other social organizations, and last, but not least, the Church. And yet all agree that to leave to the locality the entire burden would result in placing the heaviest proportion of the burden in most cases upon those who are the least able to bear it. In other words, the communities that have the most difficult problem, like Detroit, would be the communities that would have to bear the heaviest burdens. /30

And so the State steps in to equalize the burden by providing for a large portion of the care of the victims of the poverty and by providing assistance and guidance for local communities. /31

Above and beyond that the national Government has a responsibility. (*Applause*) /32

I would like to enlarge on that a lot, but that would be politics, and I cannot. (*Applause*) My friends, the ideal of social justice of which I have spoken—an ideal that years ago might have been thought over-advanced—is now accepted by the moral leadership of all of the great religious groups of the country. Radical? Yes, and I will show you how radical it is. I am going to cite three examples of what the churches say, the radical churches of America—Protestant, Catholic and Jewish. (*Applause*) /33

And first I will read to you from the Sunday sermon, the Labor Sermon sent out this year by the Federal Council of Churches of Christ in America, representing a very large proportion of the Protestants in our country. /34

Hear how radical they are: They say: /35

"The thing that matters in any industrial system is what it does actually to human beings. . . . /36

"It is not denied that many persons of wealth are rendering great service to society. It is only suggested that the wealthy are overpaid in sharp contrast with the underpaid masses of the people. The concentration of wealth carries with it a dangerous concentration of power. It leads to conflict and violence. To suppress the symptoms of this inherent conflict while leaving the fundamental causes of it untouched is neither sound statesmanship nor Christian good-will. /37

"It is becoming more and more clear that the principles of our religion and the findings of social sciences point in the same direction. Economists now call attention to the fact that the present distribution of wealth and income, which is unbrotherly in the light of Christian ethics, is also unscientific in that it does not furnish purchasing power to the masses to balance consumption and production in our machine age." (*Applause*) /38

And now I am going to read you another great declaration and I wonder how many people will call it radical. It is just as radical as I am. (*Applause*)

It is a declaration from one of the greatest forces of conservatism in the world, the Catholic Church. And it is a quotation, my friends, from the scholarly encyclical letter issued last year by the Pope, one of the greatest documents of modern times, and the letter says this: /39

"It is patent in our days that not alone is wealth accumulated, but immense power and despotic economic domination are concentrated in the hands of a few, and that those few are frequently not the owners but only the trustees and directors of invested funds which they administer at their good pleasure. . . . /40

"This accumulation of power, the characteristic note of the modern economic order, is a natural result of limitless free competition, which permits the survival of those only who are the strongest, which often means those who fight most relentlessly, who pay least heed to the dictates of conscience. (*Applause*) /41

"This concentration of power has led to a threefold struggle for domination: First, there is the struggle for dictatorship in the economic sphere itself; then the fierce battle to acquire control of the Government, so that its resources and authority may be abused in the economic struggle, and finally, the clash between the Governments themselves." /42

And finally, I would read to you from another great statement, a statement from Rabbi Edward L. Israel, Chairman of the Social Justice Commission of the Central Conference of American Rabbis. (*Applause*) Here is what he says: /43

"We talk of the stabilization of business. What we need is the stabilization of human justice and happiness and the permanent employment of economic policies which will enable us to preserve the essential human values of life amid all the changing aspects of the economic order. We must have a revamping of the entire method of approach to these problems of the economic order. We need a new type of social conscience that will give us the courage to act. . . . /44

"We so easily forget. Once the cry of so-called prosperity is heard in the land, we all become so stampeded by the spirit of the god Mammon, that we cannot serve the dictates of social conscience. . . . We are here to serve notice that the economic order is the invention of man; and that it cannot dominate certain eternal principles of justice and of God." (*Applause*) /45

And so, my friends, I feel a little as if I had been preaching a sermon. I feel a little as if I had been talking too much of some of the fundamentals, and yet those fundamentals enter into your life and my life every day. More, perhaps, than we can realize. If we realized that far more, it would result throughout this country in a greater activity, a greater interest on the part of the individual men and women who make up our Nation, in some of the problems which cannot be solved in the long run without the help of everybody. /46

We need leadership, of course. We need leadership of people who are honest in their thinking and honest in their doing. We need leadership if it is straight thinking—that is, unselfish; but in the last analysis we have got to have the help of the men and women all the way from the top to the bottom, especially of men and women who believe in the school of philosophy which is not content to leave things as they are. /47

And so, in these days of difficulty, we Americans everywhere must and shall choose the path of social justice—the only path that will lead us to a permanent bettering of our civilization, the path that our children must tread and their children must tread, the path of faith, the path of hope and the path of love towards our fellow man. (*Prolonged applause*) /48

The speech

1. What use does Roosevelt make of contrast in the opening passages of the speech? Is this an effective means of introducing and developing his theme? Why or why not?
2. How does Roosevelt's reference to his activities as a member of the New York legislature help to enhance his prestige with his listeners? How does this reference help to support the central idea of his speech?
3. Form a general estimate of Roosevelt's style. What are its dominant characteristics? What are its strengths? Its weaknesses? Is it suitable to the subject matter of the speech? To the audience and occasion? What part, if any, does it play in furthering his purpose? What, in particular, do you think of the phrase "social justice through social action"? Does it accurately epitomize the philosophy Roosevelt is attempting to present? What suggestive or persuasive power does it have?
4. What references does Roosevelt make to local conditions in Detroit? Would more such references have helped or hindered him in achieving his purpose?
5. What end is served by introducing the quotations from church leaders? Do you think it was a good idea to re-

peat these verbatim, or should Roosevelt have restated them in his own words? Was Roosevelt wise to save these quotations for near the close of his speech, or would it have been better to introduce them earlier?

6. How well does Roosevelt's address conform to our general notion of a campaign speech? What specific marks of a campaign speech are present? What things that you might expect to find in the average campaign speech are missing?
7. Comment on the structure or organization of the speech as a whole. Is it clear? Coherent? Do the important ideas and arguments receive proper emphasis? Are the rules of correct subordination observed? Would the speech outline easily?
8. Evaluate the anecdote Roosevelt uses to explain why he is "sold" on old age insurance. How clearly and strikingly is it presented? How well does it actually prove the need for a system of government-supported old age pensions?
9. How does Roosevelt turn to his advantage the charge that his proposals are "paternalistic"?
10. Trace the reasoning process by which Roosevelt arrives at the conclusion that the federal government "has a responsibility" in "the alleviation of poverty and distress." What are his premises? What inferences does he draw from them? Granted his premises, does he reason from them clearly and cogently?

For further study and discussion

1. What are some of the ways in which Roosevelt's philosophy of "social justice through social action" was implemented during his years in the White House and since? What were the principal criticisms of these implementing measures? To what extent do you think these criticisms were justified?
2. Compare the "two theories of prosperity and of well-being" Roosevelt mentions—the one which holds that "if we make the rich richer, somehow they will let a part of their prosperity trickle through to the rest of us," and the other which says that "if we make the average of mankind comfortable and secure, their prosperity will rise upward, just as yeast rises up, through the ranks." Point to some of the evidence that might be cited to support each view. Which, if either, would present-day economic theory accept as true? Must the alternative be as sharp as Roosevelt pictures it? Within limits, could both processes operate simultaneously?
3. Evaluate Roosevelt's argument that fighting poverty is like fighting disease and should be gone about in the same way. Can we isolate and control the causes of poverty? Is the prevention of poverty possible in the same sense and to the same extent that the prevention of disease is?
4. To what extent can any individual nation fight poverty and distress by a program of social action or by any other program? Aren't all of the nations of the world so bound together economically that the prosperity and well-being of each is directly dependent upon the prosperity and well-being of all?
5. Do you agree with Roosevelt "that the causes of poverty in the main are beyond the control of any one individual"?
6. Is it always true that the concentration of wealth carries with it the concentration of power? If so, is this necessarily bad? Are people who are successful economically also likely to be successful in running the affairs of a community or a nation?
7. Roosevelt strongly disagrees with the notion that sometimes people may actually benefit from adversity. What do you think?
8. Has the United States government gone as far as the governments of certain other democracies in trying to insure the social and economic well-being of its citizens? How are these attempts working out in other countries?
9. Should the government have the right to remove foodstuffs from the market if there is a possibility that they might be poisonous—as it did with cranberries just before Thanksgiving in 1959? Should it issue public warnings about the possible connection between cigarette smoking and lung cancer?
10. Admitting that a certain measure of governmental regulation is inevitable in the modern world, how can we yet preserve our individual rights and freedoms?

Suggestions for further reading

Sheldon Glueck, ed., ***The Welfare State and the National Welfare,*** A Symposium on Some of the Threatening Tendencies of Our Times (Cambridge, Mass., 1952). Contains statements by Bernard Baruch, John Foster Dulles, Dwight D. Eisenhower, Herbert Hoover, and others.

Robert Edwards Lane, ***The Regulation of Businessmen; Social Conditions of Government Economic Control,*** Yale Studies in Political Science, Vol. I (New Haven, 1954)

Herbert L. Marx, comp., ***The Welfare State,*** The Reference Shelf, Vol. XXII, No. 4 (New York, 1950)

Arthur M. Schlesinger, Jr., ***The Age of Roosevelt*** (Boston, 1957-). Vol. I, ***The Crisis of the Old Order;*** Vol. II, ***The Coming of the New Deal;*** Vol. III, ***The Politics of Upheaval.***

Dixon Wecter, ***The Age of the Great Depression, 1929-1941*** (New York, 1948)

Recordings

Rendezvous with Destiny. NBC Documentary Recording (New York: Linguaphone Institute, 1946). Selections from more than twenty of Roosevelt's speeches, from the First Inaugural, March 4, 1933, to the Report to Congress on the Crimea Conference, March 1, 1945.

The Voice of F. D. R. (1932-1945), the Presidential Years (Decca Gold Label). Special narration by Quentin Reynolds.

Crime and criminals

CLARENCE DARROW

Clarence Darrow (1857-1938) is perhaps the most famous trial lawyer America has produced. He is best remembered today for his dramatic defenses of the McNamara brothers (1911), of Loeb and Leopold (1924), and for his jousts with William Jennings Bryan in the Scopes "evolution" trial at Dayton, Tennessee (1925). During a legal career of more than half a century, however, he appeared in hundreds of cases, in nearly all of which he was fantastically successful, and in most of which his unusual speaking ability contributed in a major way.

In addition to his work as a lawyer, Darrow was an active platform speaker. He lectured extensively throughout the country and engaged in numerous public debates with some of the leading men of his day—among them T. V. Smith, Will Durant, John Haynes Holmes, Albert Edward Wiggam, and George B. Foster.

Not only as a speaker but as a prolific writer of books and articles, Darrow habitually expressed views which on the surface seemed to be at wide variance with majority opinion but in reality often represented the suppressed attitudes and desires of his listeners. This, perhaps more than any other single factor, accounts for the remarkably persuasive power of his discourses and explains the success of his highly unorthodox methods. He attacked big business, capital punishment, religious fundamentalism, prohibition, and the doctrine of free will, marking himself as a social maverick and winning such titles as "attorney for the damned," "the big minority man," and "the friendly enemy."

The speech presented here represents Darrow's unusual views concerning the causes and cures of crime. It was delivered in as bizarre a situation as can be imagined. In 1902, when Darrow was forty-five years old and had already gained wide recognition as a criminal lawyer, the warden of the Cook County jail in Chicago invited him to address the inmates. Eager to propagate his unusual views where they might have some effect, Darrow accepted the invitation and delivered the following lecture to the prisoners.

Aside from the ideas expressed, the speech is interesting as an example of skillful audience adaptation. The language is uniformly clear and simple; examples are numerous and appropriate; and the many thrusts of wit and humor are used to good effect. Moreover, the address is organized in such a way that its central purpose stands out clearly and is strongly reinforced by repetition and restatement.

How well the speech was received by the majority of the inmates, we can only conjecture. One prisoner when asked for his reaction is reported to have shaken his head and declared the ideas altogether "too radical." When reports of what Darrow had said were circulated among his friends, they were much distressed and argued that his theories, even though they might contain some measure of truth, should not have been presented to criminals in a jail.[1]

Darrow responded to this criticism by having the lecture printed at his own expense, affixing to it this introductory paragraph: "Realizing the force of the suggestion that the truth should not be spoken to all people, I have caused these remarks to be printed on rather good paper and in a somewhat expensive form. In this way the truth does not become cheap and vulgar, and is only placed before those whose intelligence and affluence will prevent their being influenced by it." As Arthur Weinberg reports, the pamphlet sold for five cents.

That Darrow was entirely sincere in developing the basic doctrines presented in this lecture is evident, for although he never repeated them again in quite so striking a form, they reappear in a number of his later writings, notably in *Crime, Its Causes and Treatment* (1922) and *The Story of My Life* (1932). Moreover, he reported with obvious pride that although his opinions might change from time to time, he never said in any speech, article, or book anything he did not earnestly believe.[2]

Darrow's delivery was as unorthodox as his ideas. Violating nearly all textbook precepts, he was careless in dress and grooming and for many of his lectures and debates made little or no preparation. He slouched and shuffled and lounged upon the speaker's stand, his head down and his left hand deep in coat or trouser pocket. His voice was low-pitched and unvaried, falling now and again into a monotonous drone. He drawled his words and generally spoke softly, although at times he could crack out a sentence like a whip. His vocal quality was husky and harsh. Yet, withal, Darrow held the attention and interest of his audiences as few speakers have done, and he drove home his ideas with an emotional force that was often overpowering. At the conclusion of his plea in the Loeb-Leopold case, for example, many of his spectators were in tears. As T. V. Smith, his opponent in many debates, summed it up, "He was at his prime a great speaker, not because he had much strategy about it, but be-

From *Address to Prisoners in Cook County Jail*, by Clarence Darrow, 3rd reprint, Charles H. Kerr and Company, Chicago, 1913.

[1]Arthur Weinberg, ed., *Attorney for the Damned* (New York, 1957), p. 15.

[2]Clarence Darrow, *The Story of My Life*, (New York, 1932), p. 281.

cause he was a massive man with good glands, a fine heart, and mind enough to give priority to his heart and glands. His speech was impressive because he himself was impressive. We shall not soon see his full like again."[3]

If I looked at jails and crimes and prisoners in the way the ordinary person does, I should not speak on this subject to you. The reason I talk to you on the question of crime, its cause and cure, is because I really do not in the least believe in crime. There is no such thing as a crime as the word is generally understood. I do not believe there is any sort of distinction between the real moral condition of the people in and out of jail. One is just as good as the other. The people here can no more help being here than the people outside can avoid being outside. I do not believe that people are in jail because they deserve to be. They are in jail simply because they can not avoid it on account of circumstances which are entirely beyond their control and for which they are in no way responsible. /1

I suppose a great many people on the outside would say I was doing you harm if they should hear what I say to you this afternoon, but you can not be hurt a great deal anyway, so it will not matter. Good people outside would say that I was really teaching you things that were calculated to injure society, but it's worth while now and then to hear something different from what you ordinarily get from preachers and the like. These will tell you that you should be good and then you get rich and be happy. Of course we know that people do not get rich by being good, and that is the reason why so many of you people try to get rich some other way, only you do not understand how to do it quite as well as the fellow outside. /2

There are people who think that everything in this world is an accident. But really there is no such thing as an accident. A great many folks admit that many of the people in jail ought to be there, and many who are outside ought to be in. I think none of them ought to be here. There ought to be no jails, and if it were not for the fact that the people on the outside are so grasping and heartless in their dealings with the people on the inside, there would be no such institution as jails. /3

I do not want you to believe that I think all you people here are angels. I do not think that. You are people of all kinds, all of you doing the best you can, and that is evidently not very well—you are people of all kinds and conditions and under all circumstances. In one sense everybody is equally good and equally bad. We all do the best we can under the circumstances. But as to the exact things for which you are sent here, some of you are guilty and did the particular act because you needed the money. Some of you did it because you are in the habit of doing it, and some of you because you are born to it, and it comes to be as natural as it does, for instance, for me to be good. /4

Most of you probably have nothing against me, and most of you would treat me the same as any other person would; probably better than some of the people on the outside would treat me, because you think I believe in you and they know I do not believe in them. While you would not have the least thing against me in the world you might pick my pockets. I do not think all of you would, but I think some of you would. You would not have anything against me, but that's your profession, a few of you. Some of the rest of you, if my doors were unlocked, might come in if you saw anything you wanted—not out of any malice to me, but because that is your trade. There is no doubt there are quite a number of people in this jail who would pick my pockets. And still I know this, that when I get outside pretty nearly everybody picks my pocket. There may be some of you who would hold up a man on the street, if you did not happen to have something else to do, and needed the money; but when I want to light my house or my office the gas company holds me up. They charge me one dollar for something that is worth twenty-five cents, and still all these people are good people; they are pillars of society and support the churches, and they are respectable. /5

When I ride on the street cars, I am held up—I pay five cents for a ride that is worth two and a half cents, simply because a body of men have bribed the city council and the legislature, so that all the rest of us have to pay tribute to them. /6

If I do not want to fall into the clutches of the gas trust and choose to burn oil instead of gas, then good Mr. Rockefeller holds me up, and he uses a certain portion of his money to build universities and support churches which are engaged in telling us how to be good. /7

Some of you are here for obtaining property under false pretenses—yet I pick up a great Sunday paper and read the advertisements of a merchant prince—

---

[3]T. V. Smith to John Buckley Roberts, Urbana, Illinois, March 12, 1941, in John Buckley Roberts, "The Speech Philosophy of Clarence Darrow" (Unpublished master's thesis, State University of Iowa, 1941), p. 168.

"Shirt waists for 39 cents, marked down from 3.00." /8

When I read the advertisements in the paper I see they are all lies. When I want to get out and find a place to stand anywhere on the face of the earth, I find that it has all been taken up long ago before I came here, and before you came here, and somebody says, "Get off, swim into the lake, fly into the air; go anywhere, but get off." That is because these people have the police and they have the jails and the judges and the lawyers and the soldiers and all the rest of them to take care of the earth and drive everybody off that comes in their way. /9

A great many people will tell you that all this is true, but that it does not excuse you. These facts do not excuse some fellow who reaches into my pocket and takes out a five dollar bill; the fact that the gas company bribes the members of the legislature from year to year, and fixes the law, so that all you people are compelled to be "fleeced" whenever you deal with them; the fact that the street car companies and the gas companies have control of the streets and the fact that the landlords own all the earth, they say, has nothing to do with you. /10

Let us see whether there is any connection between the crimes of the respectable classes and your presence in the jail. Many of you people are in jail because you have really committed burglary. Many of you, because you have stolen something: in the meaning of the law, you have taken some other person's property. Some of you have entered a store and carried off a pair of shoes because you did not have the price. Possibly some of you have committed murder. I can not tell what all of you did. There are a great many people here who have done some of these things who really do not know themselves why they did them. I think I know why you did them—every one of you; you did these things because you were bound to do them. It looked to you at the time as if you had a chance to do them or not, as you saw fit, but still after all you had no choice. There may be people here who had some money in their pockets and who still went out and got some more money in a way society forbids. Now you may not yourselves see exactly why it was you did this thing, but if you look at the question deeply enough and carefully enough you would see that there were circumstances that drove you to do exactly the thing which you did. You could not help it any more than we outside can help taking the positions that we take. The reformers who tell you to be good and you will be happy, and the people on the outside who have property to protect—they think that the only way to do it is by building jails and locking you up in cells on week-days and praying for you Sundays. /11

I think that all of this has nothing whatever to do with right conduct. I think it is very easily seen what has to do with right conduct. Some so-called criminals—and I will use this word because it is handy, it means nothing to me—I speak of the criminals who get caught as distinguished from the criminals who catch them—some of these so-called criminals are in jail for the first offenses, but nine-tenths of you are in jail because you did not have a good lawyer and of course you did not have a good lawyer because you did not have enough money to pay a good lawyer. There is no very great danger of a rich man going to jail. /12

Some of you may be here for the first time. If we would open the doors and let you out, and leave the laws as they are to-day, some of you would be back to-morrow. This is about as good a place as you can get anyway. There are many people here who are so in the habit of coming that they would not know where else to go. There are people who are born with the tendency to break into jail every chance they get, and they can not avoid it. You can not figure out your life and see why it was, but still there is a reason for it, and if we were all wise and knew all the facts we could figure it out. /13

In the first place, there are a good many more people who go to jail in the winter time than in summer. Why is this? Is it because people are more wicked in winter? No, it is because the coal trust begins to get in its grip in the winter. A few gentlemen take possession of the coal, and unless the people will pay \$7 or \$8 a ton for something that is worth \$3, they will have to freeze. Then there is nothing to do but to break into jail, and so there are many more in jail in the winter than in summer. It costs more for gas in the winter because the nights are longer, and people go to jail to save gas bills. The jails are electric lighted. You may not know it, but these economic laws are working all the time, whether we know it or do not know it. /14

There are more people go to jail in hard times than in good times—few people comparatively go to jail except when they are hard up. They go to jail because they have no other place to go. They may not know why, but it is true all the same. People are not more wicked in hard times. That is not the reason. The fact is true all over the world that in hard times more people go to jail than in good times, and in winter more people go to jail than in summer. Of course it is pretty hard times for people who go to jail at any time. The people who go to jail are almost always poor people—people who have no other place to live first and last. When times are hard then you find large numbers of people who go to jail who would not otherwise be in jail. /15

Long ago, Mr. Buckle, who was a great philosopher and historian, collected facts and he showed that the number of people who are arrested increased just as the price of food increased. When they put up the price of gas ten cents a thousand I do not know who will go to jail, but I do know that a certain number of people will go. When the meat combine raises the price of beef I do not know who is going to jail, but I know that a large number of people are bound to go. Whenever the Standard Oil Company raises the price of oil, I know that a certain number of girls who are seamstresses, and who work after night long hours for somebody else, will be compelled to go out on the streets and ply another trade, and I know that Mr. Rockefeller and his associates are responsible and not the poor girls in the jails. /16

First and last, people are sent to jail because they are poor. Sometimes, as I say, you may not need money at the particular time, but you wish to have thrifty forehanded habits, and do not always wait until you are in absolute want. Some of you people are perhaps plying the trade, the profession, which is called burglary. No man in his right senses will go into a strange house in the dead of night and prowl around with a dark lantern through unfamiliar rooms and take chances of his life if he has plenty of the good things of the world in his own home. You would not take any such chances as that. If a man had clothes in his clothes-press and beefsteak in his pantry, and money in the bank, he would not navigate around nights in houses where he knows nothing about the premises whatever. It always requires experience and education for this profession, and people who fit themselves for it are no more to blame than I am for being a lawyer. A man would not hold up another man on the street if he had plenty of money in his own pocket. He might do it if he had one dollar or two dollars, but he wouldn't if he had as much money as Mr. Rockefeller has. Mr. Rockefeller has a great deal better hold-up game than that. /17

The more that is taken from the poor by the rich, who have the chance to take it, the more poor people there are who are compelled to resort to these means for a livelihood. They may not understand it, they may not think so at once, but after all they are driven into that line of employment. /18

There is a bill before the legislature of this State to punish kidnaping children, with death. We have wise members of the Legislature. They know the gas trust when they see it and they always see it,—they can furnish light enough to be seen, and this Legislature thinks it is going to stop kidnaping children by making a law punishing kidnapers of children with death. I don't believe in kidnaping children, but the Legislature is all wrong. Kidnaping children is not a crime, it is a profession. It has been developed with the times. It has been developed with our modern industrial conditions. There are many ways of making money—many new ways that our ancestors knew nothing about. Our ancestors knew nothing about a billion dollar trust; and here comes some poor fellow who has no other trade and he discovers the profession of kidnaping children. /19

This crime is born, not because people are bad; people don't kidnap other people's children because they want the children or because they are devilish, but because they see a chance to get some money out of it. You cannot cure this crime by passing a law punishing by death kidnapers of children. There is one way to cure it. There is one way to cure all the offenses, and that is to give the people a chance to live. There is no other way, and there never was any other way since the world began, and the world is so blind and stupid that it will not see. If every man and woman and child in the world had a chance to make a decent, fair, honest living, there would be no jails, and no lawyers and no courts. There might be some persons here or there with some peculiar formation of their brain, like Rockefeller, who would do these things simply to be doing them; but they would be very, very few, and those should be sent to a hospital and treated, and not sent to jail; and they would entirely disappear in the second generation, or at least in the third generation. /20

I am not talking pure theory. I will just give you two or three illustrations. /21

The English people once punished criminals by sending them away. They would load them on a ship and export them to Australia. England was owned by lords and nobles and rich people. They owned the whole earth over there, and the other people had to stay in the streets. They could not get a decent living. They used to take their criminals and send them to Australia—I mean the class of criminals who got caught. When these criminals got over there, and nobody else had come, they had the whole continent to run over, and so they could raise sheep and furnish their own meat, which is easier than stealing it; these criminals then became decent, respectable people because they had a chance to live. They did not commit any crimes. They were just like the English people who sent them there, only better. And in the second generation the descendants of those criminals were as good and respectable a class of people as there were on the face of the earth, and then they began building churches and jails themselves. /22

A portion of this country was settled in the same way, landing prisoners down on the southern coast; but when they got here and had a whole continent to run over and plenty of chances to make a living, they became respectable citizens, making their own living just like any other citizen in the world; but finally these descendants of the English aristocracy, who sent the people over to Australia, found out they were getting rich, and so they went over to get possession of the earth as they always do, and they organized land syndicates and got control of the land and ores, and then they had just as many criminals in Australia as they did in England. It was not because the world had grown bad; it was because the earth had been taken away from the people. /23

Some of you people have lived in the country. It's prettier than it is here. And if you have ever lived on a farm you understand that if you put a lot of cattle in a field, when the pasture is short they will jump over the fence; but put them in a good field where there is plenty of pasture, and they will be law-abiding cattle to the end of time. The human animal is just like the rest of the animals, only a little more so. The same thing that governs in the one governs in the other. /24

Everybody makes his living along the lines of least resistance. A wise man who comes into a country early sees a great undeveloped land. For instance, our rich men twenty-five years ago saw that Chicago was small and knew a lot of people would come here and settle, and they readily saw that if they had all the land around here it would be worth a good deal, so they grabbed the land. You cannot be a landlord because somebody has got it all. You must find some other calling. In England and Ireland and Scotland less than five per cent own all the land there is, and the people are bound to stay there on any kind of terms the landlords give. They must live the best they can, so they develop all these various professions—burglary, picking pockets and the like. /25

Again, people find all sorts of ways of getting rich. These are diseases like everything else. You look at people getting rich, organizing trusts, and making a million dollars, and somebody gets the disease and he starts out. He catches it just as a man catches the mumps or the measles; he is not to blame, it is in the air. You will find men speculating beyond their means, because the mania of money-getting is taking possession of them. It is simply a disease; nothing more, nothing less. You can not avoid catching it; but the fellows who have control of the earth have the advantage of you. See what the law is; when these men get control of things, they make the laws. They do not make the laws to protect anybody; courts are not instruments of justice; when your case gets into court it will make little difference whether you are guilty or innocent; but it's better if you have a smart lawyer. And you can not have a smart lawyer unless you have money. First and last it's a question of money. Those men who own the earth make the laws to protect what they have. They fix up a sort of fence or pen around what they have, and they fix the law so the fellow on the outside can not get in. The laws are really organized for the protection of the men who rule the world. They were never organized or enforced to do justice. We have no system for doing justice, not the slightest in the world. /26

Let me illustrate: Take the poorest person in this room. If the community had provided a system of doing justice the poorest person in this room would have as good a lawyer as the richest, would he not? When you went into court you would have just as long a trial, and just as fair a trial as the richest person in Chicago. Your case would not be tried in fifteen or twenty minutes, whereas it would take fifteen days to get through with a rich man's case. /27

Then if you were rich and were beaten, your case would be taken to the Appellate Court. A poor man can not take his case to the Appellate Court; he has not the price; and then to the Supreme Court, and if he were beaten there he might perhaps go to the United States Supreme Court. And he might die of old age before he got into jail. If you are poor, it's a quick job. You are almost known to be guilty, else you would not be there. Why should any one be in the criminal court if he were not guilty? He would not be there if he could be anywhere else. The officials have no time to look after all these cases. The people who are on the outside, who are running banks and building churches and making jails, they have no time to examine 600 or 700 prisoners each year to see whether they are guilty or innocent. If the courts were organized to promote justice the people would elect somebody to defend all these criminals, somebody as smart as the prosecutor—and give him as many detectives and as many assistants to help, and pay as much money to defend you as to prosecute you. We have a very able man for State's Attorney, and he has many assistants, detectives and policemen without end, and judges to hear the cases—everything handy. /28

Most of all our criminal code consists in offenses against property. People are sent to jail because they have committed a crime against property. It is of very little consequence whether one hundred people more or less go to jail who ought not to go—you must protect property, because in this world property is of more importance than anything else. /29

How is it done? These people who have property fix it so they can protect what they have. When somebody commits a crime it does not follow that he had done something that is morally wrong. The man on the outside who has committed no crime may have done something. For instance: to take all the coal in the United States and raise the price two dollars or three dollars when there is no need of it, and thus kill thousands of babies and send thousands of people to the poorhouse and tens of thousands to jail, as is done every year in the United States,—this is a greater crime than all the people in our jails ever committed, but the law does not punish it. Why? Because the fellows who control the earth make the laws. If you and I had the making of the laws, the first thing we would do would be to punish the fellow who gets control of the earth. Nature put this coal in the ground for me as well as for them and nature made the prairies up here to raise wheat for me as well as for them, and then the great railroad companies came along and fenced it up. /30

Most of all the crimes for which we are punished are property crimes. There are a few personal crimes, like murder—but they are very few. The crimes committed are mostly those against property. If this punishment is right the criminals must have a lot of property. How much money is there in this crowd? And yet you are all here for crimes against property. The people up and down the Lake Shore have not committed crime, still they have so much property they don't know what to do with it. It is perfectly plain why those people have not committed crimes against property; they make the laws and therefore do not need to break them. And in order for you to get some property you are obliged to break the rules of the game. I don't know but what some of you may have had a very nice chance to get rich by carrying the hod for one dollar a day, twelve hours. Instead of taking that nice, easy profession, you are a burglar. If you had been given a chance to be a banker you would rather follow that. Some of you may have had a chance to work as a switchman on a railroad where you know, according to statistics, that you can not live and keep all your limbs more than seven years, and you can get fifty dollars or seventy-five dollars a month for taking your lives in your hands, and instead of taking that lucrative position you choose to be a sneak thief, or something like that. Some of you made that sort of choice. I don't know which I would take if I was reduced to this choice. I have an easier choice. /31

I will guarantee to take from this jail, or any jail in the world, five hundred men who have been the worst criminals and law-breakers who ever got into jail, and I will go down to our lowest streets and take five hundred of the most abandoned prostitutes, and go out somewhere where there is plenty of land, and will give them a chance to make a living, and they will be as good people as the average in the community. /32

There is a remedy for the sort of condition we see here. The world never finds it out, or when it does find it out it does not enforce it. You may pass a law punishing every person with death for burglary, and it will make no difference. Men will commit it just the same. In England there was a time when one hundred different offenses were punishable with death, and it made no difference. The English people strangely found out that so fast as they repealed the severe penalties and so fast as they did away with punishing men by death, crime decreased instead of increased; that the smaller the penalty the fewer the crimes. /33

Hanging men in our county jails does not prevent murder. It makes murderers. /34

And this has been the history of the world. It's easy to see how to do away with what we call crime. It is not so easy to do it. I will tell you how to do it. It can be done by giving the people a chance to live—by destroying special privileges. So long as big criminals can get the coal fields, so long as the big criminals have control of the city council and get the public streets for street cars and gas rights, this is bound to send thousands of poor people to jail. So long as men are allowed to monopolize all the earth, and compel others to live on such terms as these men see fit to make, then you are bound to get into jail. /35

The only way in the world to abolish crime and criminals is to abolish the big ones and the little ones together. Make fair conditions of life. Give men a chance to live. Abolish the right of private ownership of land, abolish monopoly, make the world partners in production, partners in the good things of life. Nobody would steal if he could get something of his own some easier way. Nobody will commit burglary when he has a house full. No girl will go out on the streets when she has a comfortable place at home. The man who owns a sweatshop or a department store may not be to blame himself for the condition of his girls, but when he pays them five dollars, three dollars, and two dollars a week, I wonder where he thinks they will get the rest of their money to live. The only way to cure these conditions is by equality. There should be no jails. They do not accomplish what they pretend to accomplish. If you would wipe them out there would be no more criminals than now. They terrorize nobody. They are a blot upon any civilization, and a jail is an evidence of the lack of charity of the people on the outside who make the jails and fill them with the victims of their greed. /36

The speech

1. Describe as fully and as accurately as you can the nature of the speaking situation Darrow faced. Estimate the probable attitude of the audience toward him and his subject. Point out at least four specific ways in which—through his choice of ideas, organization, and language—Darrow attempted to adapt his speech to this attitude.
2. What is the central idea of Darrow's speech? Where is it first explicitly stated? How many times and in what ways is it reiterated? What advantage is gained by these repetitions? Might it have been better to state the central idea earlier in the speech? Give reasons for your answer.
3. Where in the speech do you find instances of humor? How do these aid Darrow in achieving his purpose?
4. Would you regard this speech as primarily persuasive or expository? As primarily a logical argument or an emotional harangue? As primarily a refutation of generally received beliefs or a constructive development of the speaker's own ideas and convictions?
5. Does the speech move toward a discernible climax? If so, at what point does the climax occur?
6. Do you think that Darrow's strong attacks on "preachers," the gas and oil trusts, Rockefeller, etc., are essential to the achieving of his purpose? Do they sometimes pass the bounds of good taste and responsible statement?
7. In what specific way does Darrow use language to try to create the impression that people outside of jail are just as bad as those who are in jail?
8. Find in the speech at least three statements which seem to you to stand as completely unsupported assertions. Find two places at which, in your opinion, an example would have helped to clarify Darrow's meaning.
9. Where does the conclusion of the speech begin? What method does Darrow use in developing his conclusion?
10. If you had to cut this speech by six or seven paragraphs in order to fit it within a restricted time limit, which paragraphs would you eliminate? Why?

For further study and discussion

1. Does the ordinary person today look "at jails and crimes and prisoners" in the same way that Darrow says the ordinary person looked at them in 1902? If so, why have these views remained stable? If not, what has happened to change them?
2. If you were called upon to present additional arguments in favor of Darrow's position, what would they be? If you were called upon to refute his position, how would you proceed?
3. What are some of the leading theories today concerning the causes of crime and its cures? How do these compare with Darrow's views?
4. Do you think it wise or unwise to present to the inmates of a jail or prison the views Darrow expressed in this speech?
5. What do you think Darrow means by these statements? "In one sense everybody is equally good and equally bad. We all do the best we can under the circumstances."
6. If someone were to point out to Darrow that many present-day juvenile delinquents come from wealthy homes, what do you think his answer would be?
7. When Darrow implies that "pretty nearly everybody" outside of jail would pick his pockets if there were an opportunity, he is taking a decidedly pessimistic view of his fellow men. Is such a view justified? Why or why not?
8. Should the purpose of a prison sentence be to punish a man or to attempt to rehabilitate him?
9. How do the crime rates of the major countries correlate with the severity of their penal codes? In what states in our country is capital punishment outlawed? Do they have more or fewer murders than states with capital punishment?
10. In what ways may the practices and policies of our law enforcement agencies sometimes tend to foster rather than prevent crimes?

Suggestions for further reading

Aristotle, "The Causes of Wrongdoing," ***The Rhetoric,*** Book I, Chapters 10-14. The most readily accessible—and also perhaps the best—translations of ***The Rhetoric*** are those by Lane Cooper (New York, 1932) and Rhys Roberts (New York, 1954).

Harry Elmer Barnes and Negley K. Teeters, ***New Horizons in Criminology,*** 3rd ed. (Englewood Cliffs, N.J., 1959)
George Bernard Shaw, ***Crime of Imprisonment*** (New York, 1946)
Gresham M. Sykes, ***Crime and Society*** (New York, 1956)
Arthur Weinberg, ed., ***Attorney for the Damned*** (New York, 1957). A collection of Darrow's courtroom and platform speeches, including his debate with Judge Alfred Terry, "Is Capital Punishment Necessary?" his summation in the Loeb-Leopold trial, and his summation and examination of William Jennings Bryan in the Scopes case.

Segregation: two points of view

On May 17, 1954, in a unanimous decision, the Supreme Court of the United States ruled that racial segregation in public schools was unconstitutional. Reversing the historic "separate but equal" doctrine handed down in the case of *Plessy v. Ferguson* in 1896, the Court declared that in the field of public education "separate . . . facilities are inherently unequal."

This opinion, striking at the school systems of seventeen states in which racial segregation was compulsory and of four in which it was permitted, immediately called forth a flood of controversy. Although varied in emphasis and detail, this controversy for the most part centered on two issues: (1) Did the decision of the Supreme Court violate the traditional doctrine of states rights by injecting the federal power into an area forbidden it by the Constitution? (2) What would be the immediate and long-term consequences of so radical a reordering of a social system that for more than three centuries had determined the Southern way of life?

The following speeches reflect the concern which spokesmen on both sides felt for these issues. Expressing the predominant Southern white reaction is an address by James F. Byrnes. Born in Charleston, South Carolina, on May 2, 1879, Byrnes served his native state in the House of Representatives from 1911 to 1925 and in the Senate from 1931 to 1941. In June 1941 he was appointed a justice of the Supreme Court, but he resigned on October 3, 1942, to become Director of Economic Stabilization and later Director of War Mobilization in the wartime administrations of President Franklin D. Roosevelt. From July 1945 to January 1947 he was Secretary of State in the Truman cabinet and played a prominent role in shaping the peace settlement at the close of World War II. Between 1951 and 1955 he served as governor of South Carolina.

Byrnes' speech was delivered at the annual meeting and Lincoln Day dinner of the Illinois State Bar Association, held at Peoria on February 9, 1957. Still fresh in his listeners' minds was the mob violence that had occurred during the preceding fall and early winter in the little town of Clinton, Tennessee, when a school board directive ordered the all-white high school integrated. The still more explosive Little Rock situation, in which federal troops were eventually called out, did not occur until some six months later.[1]

As a Southerner speaking in the North at a Lincoln Day dinner and to an audience composed almost entirely of lawyers, Byrnes undoubtedly faced an audience skeptical of, if not hostile to, the point of view he was presenting. In studying the address, therefore, look particularly for ways in which he may have sought to conciliate the audience and to adapt his remarks to their attitudes and convictions. Note also the skillful manner in which he combines an extensive use of evidence with the ethical appeal of his own prestige as a former Supreme Court justice and respected Southern governor to help establish his contentions.

The second of these two speeches, which represents the pro-integration position, was delivered over station WXEX-TV, Richmond, Virginia, on Sunday, January 25, 1959, at 7:30 p.m., by Oliver W. Hill, chairman of the Legal Committee of the Virginia State Conference of NAACP (National Association for the Advancement of Colored People) Branches. Mr. Hill, a member of the firm of Hill, Martin, and Olphin, is also a practicing Richmond attorney. As Hill indicates in the opening paragraphs, his speech is intended both as a general refutation of the segregationists' arguments and as a specific answer to a radio and television address delivered five days earlier by the governor of Virginia, J. Lindsey Almond.

Governor Almond's speech and Mr. Hill's answer came at the height of a Virginia school crisis that had been developing since the preceding September. In that month, acting under authority given him by the state legislature, Governor Almond closed six white public schools in the city of Norfolk, to which seventeen Negro students had been assigned by order of a district federal court. In addition, he closed schools in the cities of Charlottesville and Front Royal. All told, about thirteen thousand students were affected.

Despite various attempts to force their reopening, these

[1]For a week-by-week account of developments at Clinton and Little Rock, see *Facts on File,* September 1 to December 31, 1956, and September 1 to December 31, 1957.

schools remained closed during the fall and early winter months of 1958; some of the students attended hastily improvised private schools, and others attempted to carry on their studies at home. Then on January 19, 1959, in two decisions delivered within the space of an hour and a half, the Supreme Court of Virginia in Richmond and a district federal court in Norfolk struck decisive blows at this suspended state of affairs.

By a majority of 5 to 2, the state supreme court declared that the so-called "massive resistance" laws, which the Virginia legislature had passed in an effort to delay or prevent school integration, violated Section 129 of the state constitution of 1902, requiring the maintenance of a system of "efficient free public schools." The three-man district federal court sitting in Norfolk unanimously declared that the law which gave the governor authority to close schools threatened by integration violated the "due process" and "equal protection" clauses of the Fourteenth Amendment. In addition, it warned against "evasive tactics." The effect of both decisions was to negate all laws passed to stop integration and to return the control of the schools to the local communities.[2]

Under the circumstances, it is understandable why feelings on both sides ran high. In his address Almond had declared in impassioned language his continued opposition to school desegregation and his determination to fight it with all of the resources at his command. Although adopting a more subdued tone and presenting a carefully developed rebuttal of the segregationists' leading arguments, Hill also used many motivational appeals and emotionally toned references to history and tradition to help support his views.

The South respects the written Constitution

JAMES F. BYRNES

Long ago thoughtful people of the South realized that Abraham Lincoln was correct in his opposition to slavery. /1

For the indefensible traffic in human beings many people were responsible. Traders from Spain and France, as well as from Great Britain, encouraged the African chiefs to sell their people into slavery. Later, New England traders brought thousands of slaves to our shores. /2

Southerners who bought and worked African slaves shared the guilt of the slave traders. Certainly, I would make no defense of slavery. God never made a man wise enough or good enough to own another human being. /3

Most Southerners now believe that had Lincoln lived, the South would not have been subjected to the oppressions of the reconstruction period which aroused more resentment than the sufferings of the war. /4

They believe, too, that Lincoln would have appreciated that the heroic fight of Confederate soldiers, the vast majority of whom owned no slaves, was due, not to the desire to perpetuate slavery, but to their belief that under the Constitution of the United States it was the right of each State to regulate its own internal affairs. /5

They feared that if the right of a State to control its internal affairs in one instance was denied, the Federal Government would soon make further encroachments upon local governments. /6

The people of the South respect the written Constitution of the United States. Heretofore they have had great respect for the Supreme Court because they have regarded that Court as the defender of the Constitution. They have relied upon the Court for protection against either the Executive or the Congress, acting in violation of the Constitution. /7

When we speak of the law of the land we refer to the United States Constitution which, according to article 4, "shall be the supreme law of the land." /8

We regard the Constitution as a statement of principles by which all departments of government are bound, the liberties of the people assured and that it can be altered only in the manner provided in the instrument. /9

In the early days of the Republic, the people were vigilant in protecting their liberties. /10

But in time, the people became busy and indifferent. Gradually in the courts there was developed the doctrine of judicial review, but it was founded on the principle that acts of government contrary to the Constitution were void. /11

All of us will agree, as Chief Justice Marshall stated in the Marbury-Madison case, "The Constitution is either a superior paramount law, unchangeable by ordinary means, or it is on a level with ordinary legislative acts and, like other acts, is alterable when the legislature shall please to alter it." /12

If the latter be true, a written Constitution is an absurdity. It is equally clear that if the Constitution

---

[2]The complete texts of both decisions may be found in the New York *Times* for January 20, 1959.

James F. Byrnes, "The South Respects the Written Constitution," *Vital Speeches of the Day*, Vol. XXIII, March 15, 1957, pp. 331-325. By permission of the author.

is the superior paramount law, it cannot be altered whenever the Supreme Court wishes to alter it. That would be an absurdity. /13

If the Supreme Court can alter the Constitution by its decisions, then five men—a majority of the Court—can make the Court a constitution maker instead of a constitution defender. /14

Throughout our history, Presidents of the United States from Washington to Franklin D. Roosevelt have warned against the Court attempting to usurp such power. /15

Time and again the Court itself has declared that it had no power to amend the Constitution. Now it is agreed by students of the law that the Court, while still admitting its lack of power to amend, is exercising new powers without the public realizing that the powers are new. /16

The trend is well illustrated by the school case. /17

In 1952 a 3-judge court presided over by Hon. John J. Parker, senior judge of the fourth circuit, in a case from Clarendon County, S. C., held that the segregation statutes of South Carolina did not violate the 14th amendment. Lawyers for the National Association for the Advancement of Colored People appealed to the Supreme Court. /18

Some months after the case was first argued, the Court asked for further argument. Because the 14th amendment makes no reference to schools, the Court requested counsel to direct their arguments to the question "What evidence is there that the Congress which submitted and the State legislatures and conventions which ratified the 14th amendment, contemplated or did not contemplate, understood or did not understand, that it would abolish segregation in public schools." /19

The attorneys general of all States interested in the issue, were invited to file briefs. Many of them responded. Among other things it was shown that about the time the amendment was submitted Members of the Congress proposed that in the Constitution and in statutes, segregated schools should be prohibited. The proposals were rejected. /20

The legislative history so conclusively demonstrated that the prohibition of segregated schools was not contemplated either by the framers of the 14th amendment or by the States in ratifying it, that the Supreme Court could not assert otherwise. The most it could declare, in an effort to justify its decision, was that the legislative history was inconclusive. /21

When the 14th amendment did not mention schools and the Court decided the legislative history was inconclusive, the Court should have declared, as it did only 11 months ago, in March 1956, in the case of *Ullman v. U.S.* (350 U.S. 427), that "nothing new can be put into the Constitution except through the amendatory process." /22

The Court should have upheld the Constitution its members are sworn to uphold. It should have upheld the doctrine of separate but equal facilities which had been sustained by the Supreme Court in 8 different cases since 1896. /23

Instead, the Court declared, "We cannot turn the clock back to 1868 when the amendment was adopted, or to 1896 when *Plessy v. Ferguson* was written." Then why did the Court ask counsel to file briefs as to the intent of the Congress in 1868? And why did the Court ask counsel to argue whether the Court was bound by its previous decisions such as *Plessy v. Ferguson*? /24

If the Court could not turn the clock back to consider the intent of the drafters of the 14th amendment in 1868, what chance is there of the Court turning the clock back to 1778 when the Constitution was drafted? /25

If age so outmodes the eternal truths of the Constitution, what chance would the Ten Commandments have with the present Court? /26

The doctrine of *stare decisis** is not sacred but when a case involves an interpretation of the Constitution and that interpretation is sustained by the Court's decisions over a period of 60 years, we should be able to rely upon it as the law. /27

Plessy v. Ferguson was not the only case precedent. There were seven others. When the Court included such great Justices as Taft, Holmes, Brandeis, and Stone, it declared, in *Gong Lum v. Rice* (275 U.S. 78), that segregation in public schools had been "many times decided to be within the constitutional power of the State legislatures to settle without interference of the Federal courts under the Federal Constitution." /28

In another case, Chief Justice Hughes said the question could "no longer be considered an open one." /29

Relying on the decisions of the Court, while Governor, I urged the issuance of bonds and the levying of a sales tax to build schools under the segregated system. Of the first $75 million we allotted 70 percent to Negro schools, even though Negro students constituted only 39 percent of the total enrollment. /30

The Supreme Court could not cite a single legal

---

*Literally, to stand by decided matters. *(Editor's note)*

precedent in support of its segregation decision. It cited only the writings of a group of psychologists, several of whom had been declared by the House of Representatives Un-American Activities Committee and by the Department of Justice to be subversive. /31

A law-abiding citizen may ask, If a decision is not based upon law, is that decision law? /32

If the Court can disregard the process for amendment of the Constitution and add a prohibition as to segregated schools, why can it not add prohibitions on other subjects, destructive of the rights and liberties of the people? /33

If the Constitution is whatever the Supreme Court says it is, instead of taking an oath to defend the Constitution, citizens should be required to swear to uphold and defend the decisions of the Supreme Court. /34

After the Court adopted the school amendment to the Constitution, it had a further hearing to determine how the new 14th amendment should be enforced. Let us look at the 14th amendment itself. /35

The 5th section of the 14th amendment reads: "The Congress shall have the power to enforce by appropriate legislation the provisions of this article." /36

In the case of *Fay v. The People of the State of New York* (332 U.S. 261) decided 10 years ago, the Supreme Court indicated in the absence of congressional authority, it had no power to enforce the 14th amendment. /37

That case involved alleged racial discrimination against Negroes serving as jurors. The Court called attention to an act of Congress specifically prohibiting such discrimination, by which it was controlled. Referring to the 5th section of the 14th amendment, the Court said: /38

"It is not said the judicial power of the General Government shall extend to enforcing the prohibitions and to protecting the rights and immunities guaranteed. It is not said that branch of the Government shall be authorized to declare void any action of a State in violation of the prohibitions. It is the power of Congress which has been enlarged. Congress is authorized to enforce the prohibitions by appropriate legislation." /39

Clearly, then, when the Court added to the 14th amendment the prohibition against segregation in public schools, that prohibition, like all other prohibitions of the amendment, could be enforced only by congressional legislation. /40

Instead of legislating to prohibit it, Congress for 75 years specifically appropriated for segregated schools in the District of Columbia. /41

And in recent years in appropriating for the school-lunch program, Congress, by implication, approved segregated schools by providing that if a State maintained separate schools for races, funds should not be paid unless they were equitably distributed between the segregated schools. /42

But the Court that was unwilling to leave the amendment of the Constitution to the Congress and the States, as provided in that instrument, likewise was unwilling to leave to the Congress the enforcement of the new 14th amendment. /43

It substituted the courts for the Congress. That means the power of injunction. The power of injunction is a dangerous power, often abused. /44

Where Congress, in precise language, applicable to all citizens, would define what constitutes a crime, and the punishment therefor, already it is apparent that the judge-made laws will radically differ in the different jurisdictions. /45

In July 1955, the Honorable John J. Parker, senior judge of the fourth circuit, speaking for the three-judge court having jurisdiction of the South Carolina segregation case, said that the Supreme Court "has not decided that the States must mix persons of different races in the schools or must require them to attend schools, or must deprive them of the right of choosing the school they attend. What is decided, and all that it has decided, is that a State may not deny to any person, on account of race, the right to attend any schools that it maintains. . . . The Constitution, in other words, does not require integration. It merely forbids discrimination." /46

That court held voluntary segregation possible. However, in Tennessee a United States district judge took a different view. He issued an order on January 4, 1956, which according to him, "requires adoption by school authorities of Anderson County of a program of integration that will expeditiously permit the enrollment of Negroes of high-school grades to the high school of that county." /47

Later that district judge enjoined certain parties who were named, and all others who may be acting in counsel with them from interfering with what the judge called the integration order or from picketing Clinton High School, either by words or acts or otherwise. /48

Subsequent events demonstrate the chaos that will result from these judge-made laws. In Clinton, Tennessee, troops and tanks were ordered to a school, but disorders continued, in and out of the school. When the soldiers withdrew, the Attorney General of the United States ordered an investigation by the Federal Bureau of Investigation of violations of the court order. /49

In December a white minister who had no connection with the school, voluntarily accompanied certain colored students to the school. After he left and while passing some citizens on the street in front of the police station, he was struck in the face by a man who claimed the minister shoved him. The minister was not seriously hurt. /50

By order of the court, the man who struck the minister, along with about 12 other persons including another minister and a woman, who were on the sidewalk where the fight took place, were charged with criminal contempt for violating the injunction order. Released under heavy bond, they were to have a hearing on January 28 but the hearing was postponed. /51

The people of many States await with interest the result of that hearing. They are anxious to know: /52

First, whether the district judge instead of enjoining discrimination against individuals, had the power to issue an order requiring adoption of an integration program. /53

Second, whether striking a citizen who has no connection with the public schools, at a point some distance from the school building, constitutes an interference with the court's integration order. /54

Third—heretofore it has been thought that where an act was alleged to violate an order of injunction and at the same time violate the criminal law of the United States, or any State, the defendant was entitled to trial by a jury. The people want to know if this has been repealed by the court. /55

Fourth—whether the presence of citizens at a place on the street, where an assault and battery is committed upon a person not connected with the school or its students, constitutes an interference with the court's integration order, justifying punishment by a judge with or without a jury trial. /56

The President was quoted as saying in response to a question at a recent press conference, that the problem at Clinton was now in the hands of the local courts and local officials. If correctly quoted, the President was misinformed. The citizens have been arrested by order of the United States district judge and the school children have been threatened with the secret police of the United States who were sent to the scene by the United States Attorney General. /57

The only local official in the picture is the prosecuting attorney of the county who was so thoroughly frightened that he told the assembled children of the school that if they were guilty of misconduct they would be reported to the FBI and "uncalled-for provocations will be dealt with swiftly and harshly." /58

If school children who engage in a fist fight or other disorderly conduct at school are not to be punished by school authorities, a juvenile court, or other State tribunal, but are to be arrested by the FBI and without trial by jury, are to be sentenced by a United States district judge for violation of an injunction, I fear the consequences in districts where the races are evenly divided. /59

In the Tennessee school of 804 pupils, only 14 are Negroes. In the school district in South Carolina where there originated the case decided by the Supreme Court, the school population is 2,900 Negroes and 290 white students. There are many such districts in the South and they present a far more serious problem than the situation in Clinton. /60

In Tennessee a man was sentenced by the district judge to imprisonment for 1 year and a fine of $10,000 for making a speech which the judge regarded as inciting people to violation of the injunction and to acts of violence. That individual was not a citizen of Tennessee or any Southern State. /61

The facts of the case I do not know. But law-abiding Southerners do not encourage or condone acts of violence. If a white man from a Northern State comes South and does incite white people to violence, he should be regarded with the same disfavor as the professional agitator from the North who comes to incite our colored neighbors to acts of violence. In our midst, we have trouble makers in both races. They need no assistance from other States. /62

The Southern people know the United States Government has the military power to enforce the orders of its courts. They say, however, that the Supreme Court which ordered this experiment in sociology must enforce it. It cannot expect the States to voluntarily enforce a decision they regard as having no basis in the Constitution or any statute. /63

When they are criticized by some of the metropolitan press, they recall that only a few decades ago the Constitution was lawfully amended in the manner provided in that instrument and prohibition laws were enacted. Unquestionably, that was the law of the land. Many of the present critics of the South strongly urged the nullification of the prohibition laws. They made it fashionable to carry whiskey flasks and boasted of distilling gin in bathtubs. They did not cease fighting for nullification until the 18th amendment was repealed. /64

The Supreme Court did not create the people of the United States. The people created the Supreme Court. And the people gave to Congress in article 4 of the Constitution, the specific power to regulate the appellate jurisdiction of that court. /65

Congress should exercise that power. It should deny to the Supreme Court the power to invalidate the provisions of a State constitution affecting public schools or affecting the security of the State or the United States Government. /66

In view of the judicial threat to take out of the Constitution, through the injunctive process, the guarantee of trial of all crimes by a jury, Congress by legislation should protect the people against judicial abuse of the power of injunction. /67

Heretofore when a man has been charged with a felony and has pleaded "not guilty," he has said he would be tried "By God and my country." We must make certain that a man charged with committing a crime, as well as violating a judicial order, is not forced to plead that he will be tried—not by God or his country—but by a United States district judge. /68

One could not discuss this segregation decision without admitting that entirely apart from the legal phases, there is a fundamental objection by the people of the South to the social experiment of the Supreme Court. /69

They fear the purpose of many of those advocating integration in schools is to break down social barriers in the period of adolescence and ultimately bring about intermarriage of the races. They are opposed to this and they are determined to resist in every legal way the efforts to mix the races in the schools. This is not petty prejudice. It is a serious problem of race relations. /70

Pride of race has been responsible for the grouping of people along ethnic lines throughout the world. Race preservation is the explanation of the political unrest and race tension in South Africa. /71

Pride of race as well as loyalty to religion contributes to the conflict between Jews and Arabs in the Middle East, which today threatens the peace of the world. Jews do not marry Arabs. Several Arab governments will not even allow a Jew to enter those countries. /72

It was a realization of the wisdom of segregating races that prompted 46 governments, including the United States, to agree in the Geneva Convention of 1929 that "belligerents shall, so far as possible, avoid assembling in a single camp prisoners of different races or nationalities." /73

In the United States, pride of race is not confined to the South. Today in 23 States, intermarriage of the races is prohibited by law. The degree of race tension in various States and communities is dependent upon the percentage of Negro population. /74

In the mountainous areas of the South there are few Negroes and little tension. There are other areas where the races are more evenly divided. There the race problem is acute and is the principal topic of conversation among all classes of people. /75

Similarly in northern States in the rural areas there is little tension while in the great cities of New York, Detroit, Washington, and Chicago, there is increasing tension. /76

It is useless for men to argue whether the racial instinct is right or wrong—it exists. It is nothing new. /77

Thomas Jefferson, the patron saint of the Democratic Party, when he was nearly 80 years of age, said "Nothing is more certainly written in the book of fate than that these people are to be free; nor is it less certain that the two races, equally free, cannot live in the same government. Nature, habit, opinion, have drawn indelible lines of distinction between them." /78

Abraham Lincoln, who signed the Emancipation Proclamation, and has been regarded as the patron saint of the Republican Party, said in his joint debate with Douglas, at Charleston, Ill., on September 18, 1858, "I will say then that I am not, nor ever have been, in favor of bringing about in any way the social and political equality of the white and black races; that I am not, nor ever have been in favor of making voters or jurors of Negroes, nor of qualifying them to hold office nor to intermarry with white people; and I will say, in addition to this, that there is a physical difference between the white and black races which I believe will forever forbid the two races living together on terms of social and political equality." /79

Lincoln further said, "Whether this feeling accords with justice and sound judgment is not the sole question, if indeed it is any part of it. Universal feeling, whether well or ill founded, cannot be safely disregarded." (Vol. 4, *Writings of Abraham Lincoln,* edited by Arthur Brooks Lapsley.) /80

The prophesies of these two statesmen were made a century ago. In the early days, following the war, the people of other sections showed no great interest in educating the recently freed slaves. The problem of helping him educationally and economically was left to the impoverished people of the South. They so generously did what they thought was right, now they can boast that since the days of reconstruction the Negro in the South has made greater progress than he has made in any country of the world. /81

I am proud of their progress in South Carolina. They are in all the professions. Some few are engaged in banking, hundreds in insurance, and real estate. They are engaged in merchandising, farming, and in the skilled trades. They own radio stations. More than 18,000 own their own farms. Others manage farms. Thousands own their homes which are equipped with television and electrical refrigeration. /82

With a Negro population of approximately 800,000 Negroes, about 140,000 own automobiles. /83

I am confident the number of automobiles owned by Negroes in South Carolina is greater than the number of automobiles privately owned in Russia with its population of 200 million. /84

As a result of the educational program which I sponsored while Governor, there is at least one Negro high school in every school district. Because these schools are new, in most instances, they are better than the high schools for white pupils. /85

In the state we have 7,500 Negro schoolteachers. In New York City with a larger Negro population, less than 5 percent of the regular teachers are Negroes. /86

For the State of Illinois with a Negro population of approximately 700,000, I do not have the figures, but I am certain the number of Negro teachers is not one-half the 7,500 in South Carolina. /87

Proud as I am of this progress, I am even prouder that in the last 25 years there has been a vastly improved relation between the races. /88

Because this is true, the decision of the Supreme Court was a tragedy. It has undone all that men of good will in both races had accomplished in improving race relations. Instead of improving, the situation is worsening. Now we fear for the future. /89

In the cities, where Negro homes are concentrated, schools were built near their homes. Students are assigned to the schools nearest their homes. If, however, a district judge insists on disregarding State assignments laws and orders the mixing of the races in the schools, I fear the American people will have as serious a problem in the Southeast as we now have in the Mideast. /90

In several States laws have been enacted providing that "if by order of any court, State or Federal, a student is assigned to a school different from that to which he is assigned by school officials, all appropriations for the school to which that student is assigned and all appropriations for the school from which he comes, shall immediately cease." /91

Counsel for the National Association for the Advancement of Colored People predict the Supreme Court will declare these laws unconstitutional. I do not think so, but in view of the segregation decision, I would not bet on what the Court would do. /92

However, I predict that if the Court shall declare unconstitutional all State statutes having in its opinion the effect of continuing segregation, then with great regret, many States will discontinue public schools. /93

In anticipation of this last resort, provisions in State constitutions requiring appropriations for public schools have been repealed by the voters. Private schools will be preferred to integrated schools. /94

Of one thing I am confident, should the Supreme Court cause the closing of public schools, leaders of the white race in the South will see to it that the innocent Negro children receive an education. They must not be permitted to suffer because of the well-intentioned but misguided efforts of overzealous do-gooders. /95

In South Carolina a similar law was passed as to recreation parks. There are parks for both races. When a suit was brought by several Negroes to be admitted to a park set aside for white people, the legislature passed a law closing that park. A United States district judge recently held the question of discrimination was moot because the park was closed. /96

The people do not feel as keenly about integration in parks as in schools. Recreation is desirable, but education is essential. However, law officers believed that with the existing tension, integration in parks where there are cabins for lodging and swimming pools, was dangerous. /97

Governors of several States have announced they will not follow the Tennessee example and call out the National Guard to escort Negro children to white schools. They take the position, taken by the Governor of Texas, that under the police powers, it is the duty of a Governor to quell disorders, not to cause them. /98

In its decision, the Supreme Court said that segregation would retard the development of Negro children. It did not comment upon the effect integration would have upon the development of white children. We believe the presence of troops and tanks, and the secret police, at a school will do great psychological harm to children—white and colored. Instead of thinking of mathematical problems, they will think of race problems. /99

The people of the South are not an alien people. They are loyal Americans. Whatever may have been the differences between the North and South 100 years ago, in the Spanish-American War southerners proved their devotion to the United States. In World War I and again in World War II they demonstrated their patriotism and their courage on the battlefields of the world. /100

Today they are overwhelmed by this problem of race which was inherited by them more than a century ago. Through the years that cross has borne heavily upon them. /101

Now they earnestly appeal to you for understanding, as they pray that their burdens may be lessened, if not lifted. /102

The case against segregated schools

OLIVER W. HILL

Ladies and Gentlemen:

On behalf of the Virginia State Conference of NAACP Branches, myself and many other vocal and nonvocal opponents of racial segregation, I thank the management of TV Station WXEX for affording me this opportunity to express some of our views in opposition to those expressed by Governor Almond on last Tuesday night, January 20, 1959, in which he attempted to justify and seek support for the continued denial by the State of Virginia of the constitutional rights of Negro school children to a non-segregated public school education. /1

It is impossible in the generous but brief amount of time allocated, to point out all of the fallacies in the position of the segregationists and, therefore, I will direct my efforts to two or three points. /2

One of the arguments advanced by Governor Almond, and generally asserted by supporters of racial segregation in public schools, is that the United States Supreme Court in its 1954 decision in the School Segregation Cases usurped the function of the state and unlawfully interfered with its operation of its public schools. This is the states rights argument and implicit in this argument is the erroneous idea that the foundation of American democracy rests upon the doctrine of states rights. /3

A careful consideration of the political history of the United States and of Virginia will clearly demonstrate the fallacies of this argument. /4

The underlying philosophy of the American way of life is not states rights, but rather is as expressed in the Declaration of Independence:

> "We hold these truths to be self-evident, that all men are created equal, that they are endowed by their Creator with certain unalienable Rights, that among these are Life, Liberty and the pursuit of Happiness."

The equality mentioned is not natural equality, because obviously all men are not equally endowed with health, strength, or intelligence, but merely means that all persons are entitled to equal treatment under the law. /5

When the Constitution was adopted, the right of the individual to life, liberty, and the pursuit of happiness was safeguarded through the first eight amendments and future contingencies were safeguarded through the 10th Amendment. Admittedly, in Virginia only a small minority conceived these rights as being applicable to its Negro residents, and at that time the leaders in Virginia thought that these rights could best be secured through the aegis of the state government. But in the orderly evolution of the underlying principle of the right of the individual to life, liberty, and the pursuit of happiness, under a form of government whose economy was principally supported by a capitalist system of free enterprise, it was not long before irreconcilable conflict had arisen between this principle and the South's peculiar institution of slavery. /6

Irrespective of where you or I would place the responsibility for the starting of the war, the hard, cold fact remains that this conflict was resolved by force of arms in a war which some historians think should more properly be designated as the "Second American Revolutionary War." It was out of this conflict that arose the second phase in the establishment in the United States of the right of the individual to life, liberty, and the pursuit of happiness. /7

As an aftermath of this war and the grave issues involved, the 13th, 14th and 15th Amendments to the Constitution of the United States were adopted. The 13th Amendment terminated the legality of human slavery. The 15th Amendment extended suffrage to Negroes upon the same terms and conditions extended to white persons. /8

But the most important changes—changes of which the segregationists of Virginia seem not to be aware—are those contained in the 14th Amendment. Firstly, the reduction in the sovereignty of all of the

Oliver W. Hill, "Reply to Broadcast Address to the People of the State," *Crisis*, March 1959. By permission of the author.

States of the Union by the transfer of the primary obligation of allegiance of all citizens from the state in which they reside to the federal government; secondly, the extension of the protection of the Bill of Rights to all black Americans, whether formerly free or slave; and, thirdly, the prohibition of the denial of these rights by action of the states. /9

Thus, it is manifest that the force and effect of the 10th Amendment as originally adopted has been considerably altered by the adoption of the 14th Amendment directly limiting the sovereignty of the states. /10

From time immemorial, certainly in this country, the obligation of allegiance to our government carries with it the correlative duty on the part of the government to protect its citizens. From the early 1870's right down to the School Segregation Cases, the United States Supreme Court has acted to protect the rights of individuals and corporations against actions of the various states asserted under the provisions of the 14th Amendment. Why, then, is it suddenly in the school cases a usurpation of states rights to protect rights guaranteed by the Constitution of the United States? /11

The segregationists complain that in 1896 the United States Supreme Court decided that racial segregation did not violate the provisions of the 14th Amendment in the case of *Plessy vs. Ferguson.* But, for some unexplained reason, they ignore the fact that in the Plessy case—which, incidentally, involved segregation on street cars—the United States Supreme Court arbitrarily determined that racial segregation did not violate the rights of the Negro as guaranteed by the 14th Amendment. No evidence was introduced in the case on this question. In the *Gong Lum* case, in 1928, neither the detrimental effects of segregation nor the right of the state to make racial classifications was an issue, because the little Chinese girl conceded the right of the state to make racial classifications. /12

But in the School Segregation Cases, for the first time concrete evidence was presented to the Court which overwhelmingly preponderated over any evidence to the contrary that racial segregation was in fact detrimental to Negroes. /13

Faced with this history and these facts, there was no logical or just conclusion that the United States Supreme Court could reach other than to hold racial segregation in public schools unconstitutional. The Constitution does not guarantee any right to any racial solidarity or to the protection or preservation of any race. Its guarantees go to the right of the individual to life, liberty, and the pursuit of happiness. /14

It is impossible for me to conceive how any objective observer can logically contend that the action of the Supreme Court violated any right of the state. The contention that the fact that the Court had once passed on the question and was thereafter foreclosed from correcting a demonstrated error is as illogical as would be the contention of a motorist who, when charged with driving down the highway in a careless and reckless manner at ninety miles an hour, declared that the officers arresting him were out of order because peace officers had been observing him driving in this manner for the past quarter of a century and none of them had so charged him before. /15

The contention is made that racial segregation in public schools must be maintained in order to preserve a way of life to which Virginians have been accustomed. I certainly make no pretense that the elimination of racial segregation will not change the way of life in many Virginia communities—as a matter of fact, such a change is necessary and is being forced daily by the evolution of American constitutional principles—however, that anything worth preserving of the so-called southern traditions will be detrimentally affected by the elimination of racial segregation is emphatically denied. /16

What will be eliminated will be the need for white citizens to degrade themselves by acting in a manner unbecoming a human being in their contacts with persons of African ancestry. All essential qualities based upon honesty, integrity and the Christian ethics will not only be preserved, but strengthened; that is, for example, the necessity for denying a patient treatment at a hospital, a traveler food and lodging, a spectator the right to sit in accordance with his individual preferences at places of public amusement and entertainment, the right of a man to secure employment, the right of a person to exercise his personal preferences in the selection of his residence—these and similar denials currently practiced against Negro citizens in our segregated communities would be changed. /17

It is a matter of common observation that in the communities wherein the rights of black persons to exercise their constitutional rights to life, liberty and the pursuit of happiness are recognized and safeguarded, that the rights of white persons are equally as well protected. But I can point out to you hundreds of individual instances in Virginia wherein the totalitarian concept of racial segregation not only deprives the Negro of his constitutional rights, but similarly deprives the white persons of their rights. One clear-cut illustration commonly known is the denial to white people who oppose massive resistance of their right to freedom of expression because of their fear of social, economical or political reprisals. There are even rumors of reprisals against the Justices of the Supreme Court of Appeals of Virginia for exercising their honest judgment and declaring the massive resistance laws unconstitutional. /18

One of the biggest excuses for the maintenance of racial segregation is that a vast cultural difference exists between Negroes and white persons residing in Virginia. I submit that in any community in which such cultural lags exist, these lags are caused, preserved and fostered by segregation and not because of any racial differences. /19

We must recognize that the American heritage of virtually all Negroes residing in Virginia extends back within a range of 150 to 340 years. The Negro is an integral part of the fiber of America, ante-dating the landing at Plymouth Rock, and he has participated in every movement for the development and preservation of the right of the individual to life, liberty and the pursuit of happiness. His blood was shed on Boston Commons when Virginians were still debating whether they were going to be American patriots or remain loyal to the King of England. Negro blood, sweat, tears and laughter have contributed to every facet of American life. /20

In every area of activity where given a full opportunity, the Negro measures up to other Americans. Thus it is apparent that where cultural lags exist, they are created by the evils inherent in segregation. It is also significant that in the areas where segregation is the most strictly enforced, you will find the greatest cultural lag. /21

In order to emphasize the so-called cultural lag, statistics on illegitimacy, venereal disease, and such are constantly cited. I would be the last to deny that illegitimacy constitutes a grave social problem which should be corrected at the earliest possible moment. But I submit that the first step in eradicating this evil is the elimination of racial segregation—its breeding place—just as the first step in eradicating malaria was to dry up the swamps and destroy the breeding places of the malaria bearing mosquito. /22

I also call your attention to the fact, though, that while I recognize illegitimacy as a grave social problem, I deny the basic conclusion for which these statistics are generally paraded—that is, morality of persons of Negro ancestry is lower than that of persons who have no ascertainable Negro ancestry. /23

When you are going to equate sexual morality, you not only have to consider illegitimacy statistics, but, I submit, you have to consider the million dollar abortion rings; the large amount of money spent on prophylactics and contraceptives used for illicit sexual relations; the number of sophisticates who enter hospitals under fictitious names and give birth to their childen as married women, thereby avoiding the illegitimacy statistics, and in many instances financing such hospitalization by supplying material for the billion dollar black market adoption ring which exists in this country; to say nothing of the legalized prostitution which masquerades under the guise of marriage with speedy and frequent divorces. /24

Segregationists contend that non-segregated schools will destroy the purity of the white race. I doubt the purity of the white race, but I see no more reason why non-segregated schools should cause the destruction of the white race any more than freedom of religion has tended to destroy Catholicism, Judaism or Protestantism. /25

Typical of segregationists' arguments, Governor Almond made a sweeping statement charging that sadism, sex, immorality, and juvenile pregnancy infest the desegregated schools of the District of Columbia and elsewhere. But immediately this charge was convincingly and forthrightly denied in a joint statement issued by Messrs. Walter N. Tobriner, Chairman of the Board of Education, and Carol F. Hansen, Superintendent of Schools, of the District of Columbia, in which, among other things, they say: /26

"It condemns the many for the misfortunes and the deviations of the few. It implies that conditions relative to the morality among some children are peculiar to Washington and cannot be found in other cities as well, whether segregated or integrated. /27

"It subjects to profound indignity and unprovoked assault a public school system that is dedicated to the educational improvement of all children in accordance with the highest ideals of democracy." /28

Anyone truly concerned about "The Truth About Desegregation in Washington's Schools" should read the series of articles under that title by Erwin Kroll, published in *The Washington Post and Times Herald* from December 22 through December 28, 1958, and now reprinted in pamphlet form. /29

There is one other half-truth currently being circulated in Virginia to the effect that all lines of communication between the races are broken down. The truth is that Negroes are as willing to work cooperatively toward the solution of the problems of desegregation now as they were five or even ten years ago. The only severance in the lines of communication exists at the end resting among the white people and can easily be reunited once the white people of this state decide to work constructively upon the problems, real and fancied, incident to the elimination of racial segregation. /30

The question is not whether you believe in racial segregation, for racial segregation is crumbling—not merely because the Negro wants it eliminated, but because it is incompatible with the fundamental concept of the right of the individual to life, liberty and the pursuit of happiness. The only question, my friends, is whether you will continue to follow the false doctrine of evasion, resistance and defiance of the law and the principles of American democracy and suffer the change from segregation to desegregation amid the turmoil and tension of another lost cause, or whether you will repudiate the actions of your politicians and work cooperatively to bring the transition to pass with a minimum of emotional impact. /31

The speeches

1. Compare the ways in which Mr. Byrnes and Mr. Hill employ supporting material. Who employs the greater variety of forms or types of support? Does the supporting material in the two speeches seem to you to be of equal worth and cogency, or is one speech superior to the other in this respect?
2. Find in each of the two speeches three instances of appeal to history or tradition, two strictly logical arguments, and three or four emotional appeals.
3. Trace the reasoning by which Hill arrives at the conclusion that "the force and effect of the 10th Amendment as originally adopted has been considerably altered by the adoption of the 14th Amendment." Would you characterize this reasoning as inductive? As deductive? As based primarily upon explanation and interpretation of historical facts?
4. Why does it suit Hill's purpose particularly well to refer to the War Between the States as the "Second American Revolution"?
5. As explained in the Glossary, *turning the tables* is a method of refutation in which a speaker admits his opponent's premise but draws a contrary conclusion from it. Can you find one or more examples of turning the tables in Hill's speech?
6. How well do you think Byrnes adapted his remarks to his audience, as described in the headnote? What particular methods and techniques did he use in his opening paragraphs to win a hearing and build good will? What methods did he use later in the speech?
7. Again considering the nature of his audience and remembering his own distinction as a lawyer and judge, do you think Byrnes was wise to deal with the constitutional argument first and the social or moral argument second, or should this order have been reversed? What general rules and principles should govern the ordering of arguments in a speech situation of the sort Byrnes faced?
8. Evaluate the unity and coherence of Byrnes' speech as a whole and of each of his major contentions or arguments. Does he always hold closely to the subject under discussion, or does he sometimes wander and introduce a variety of ideas and proofs under a single head? Would the speech outline easily?
9. To what extent does Hill's speech refute specific arguments advanced by Byrnes? In your opinion, how effectively does it do so?
10. Compare the two speeches as to style. Which gives evidences that it may have been written out and read from manuscript? Which seems to be more extemporaneous in tone and expression? Defend your choice by pointing to specific words and passages.

For further study and discussion

1. Review thoroughly what the Constitution of the United States has to say about the distribution of powers between the federal government and the states. Be sure that you examine all pertinent clauses and amendments.
2. Investigate some of the court decisions mentioned by Byrnes and Hill, as well as any others that might be relevant. What, specifically, did the court hold in each instance? What issues were involved? What effect, if any, did each decision have on later ones? On the immediate course of events?
3. It is sometimes argued that Congress should be given the power to reverse decisions of the Supreme Court. Do you think this would be a good idea? Defend your answer.
4. Review the history and present state of school desegregation in the South. Which states are now entirely integrated? Which have only token integration? Are there any states in which the schools are still completely segregated? Can you explain why these differences exist?
5. How has school integration worked out where it has been tried? Base your answer upon a comprehensive study of all the available facts, and be sure to consider the claims and arguments advanced by the opponents of desegregation as well as by its proponents.
6. Investigate the history and present state of racial integration in the South outside the schoolroom—on

public transportation, in hotels and restaurants, in employment practices, in the election of colored men and women to public offices, etc.

7. What countries besides the United States have had or still have serious problems of race relations to solve? What may we learn from their experience?
8. Where in the United States outside the South are we confronted with problems in race relations and the integration of minority groups? Are we solving these problems successfully?
9. What effect do you think the increased industrialization and urbanization of the South is likely to have on relations between the races? Explain your answer.
10. What is the present situation regarding integration in institutions of higher learning in the South? What may we learn from experience in this area?

Suggestions for further reading

Harry S. Ashmore, **An Epitaph for Dixie** (New York, 1958)

Ruth Benedict, **Race: Science and Politics,** rev. ed. (New York, 1943)

Hodding Carter, **The South Strikes Back** (New York, 1959)

Brooks Hays, **A Southern Moderate Speaks** (Chapel Hill, N.C., 1959)

George Bernard de Huszar, comp., **Anatomy of Racial Intolerance.** The Reference Shelf, Vol. XVIII, No. 5 (New York, 1946)

George Eaton Simpson and J. Milton Yinger, **Racial and Cultural Minorities: An Analysis of Prejudice and Discrimination,** rev. ed. (New York, 1958)

The American family

ROBERT J. HAVIGHURST

In recent decades sociologists, social workers, religious leaders, and educators as well as thoughtful parents, have become increasingly concerned about the state of health of the oldest and most fundamental of all social institutions—the family. Throughout the Western world there are signs that the family is disintegrating. The home, once the source of enduring values and satisfactions, is now for many persons little more than a combination lunch counter, dormitory, and waiting room—a place to eat and sleep and await in listless boredom the pleasures of the theater, stadium, or country club. With divorce rates steadily mounting, more and more families are breaking up, thus giving rise to economic problems and emotional tensions among adults and contributing to maladjustment and delinquency among children.

What are the causes of this apparent breakdown of family life? How can we rehabilitate the family and adapt it to new times and circumstances? Why is it imperative that we do so? Among the many students who have given attention to these problems, one of the most thoughtful and articulate is Robert J. Havighurst.

Although he has for many years been professor of education at the University of Chicago, Havighurst was trained as a scientist. He received his bachelor's degree from Ohio Wesleyan in 1921 and his Ph.D. in chemistry from Ohio State in 1924. After two years as a National Research Council Fellow at Harvard, he became assistant professor of chemistry at Miami University at Oxford, Ohio, and subsequently assistant professor of physics at the University of Wisconsin. In 1932 Havighurst returned to Ohio State as associate professor of science education and in 1934 became Assistant Director for General Education of the General Education Board of the Rockefeller Foundation. From 1937 to 1941 he served as director of this board.

Upon coming to Chicago in 1941, Havighurst became associated with the University's Committee on Human Development and from 1947 to 1950 served as its chairman. His many books and articles reflect his interest in the work of this committee. Among his books are *Development Tasks and Education* (1948) and *Human Development and Education* (1953). He is coauthor of such volumes as *Father of the Man* (1947), *Adolescent Character and Personality* (1949), *Personal Adjustment in Old Age* (1949), and *Community Youth Development Program* (1952). His articles have appeared in *School and Society, Survey, Annals of the American Academy of Political and Social Science,* and *Elementary School Journal.*

The following speech was delivered to some two thousand delegates attending the twenty-fifth annual Conference of the National Congress of Parents and Teachers held at Cleveland, May 24-26, 1948. It is noteworthy not only for the provocative nature of its content but also for the clarity and attractiveness with which the ideas are expressed. Casting his remarks into a general problem-solution pattern, Havighurst distinguishes sharply between the "essential" and merely "accidental" functions of the family and lays out in a systematic fashion the three or four most basic "needs" which the modern family must satisfy. Aspects of the speech particularly worthy of study are the vivid word portraits of the home of fifty years ago as contrasted with the home of today; the skillful use of rhetorical questions as transitions; and the clarity with which the leading ideas are made to stand out from their supporting material.

Robert J. Havighurst, "The American Family," *Vital Speeches of the Day,* Vol. XIV, July 1, 1948, pp. 565-568. By permission of the author.

Havighurst's speech was only one of many given during the three-day conference. Other speakers included Leonard W. Mayo, vice president of Western Reserve University, and Raymond Walsh, professor of economics at Columbia.

A shorter and somewhat revised version of this speech appeared as an article in the September 1948 issue of *The National Parent-Teacher*. The student interested in exploring some of the differences between oral and written discourse will find it profitable to compare that article with this speech, to see how Havighurst adapted his ideas for the printed medium.

Can people like ourselves *do* anything about the family? Or is the destiny of the family as an institution determined by the blind working of social forces, over which we have no power? /1

The family stands eternal and impregnable in human history, like the rock of Gibraltar, and yet the family is also vulnerable and evanescent. It has a "here today, gone tomorrow" aspect. The lifetime of an individual family is seldom more than fifty years, reckoning from its beginning in marriage to its ending with the death of the people who married. The family consists literally of *what we do* as family members. Every man and woman who marry and start a family take the destiny of the family in their hands. The family is the fleeting product of their passions, needs, habits and aspirations. The family is as old as human life on this planet and as young as this afternoon, when John and Jane got married. /2

I doubt that the family has changed more than other social institutions during the past fifty years. Schools have changed just as much, and government and industry and business and the church. The bare words, "we live in a changing society" hardly do justice to the process which has almost turned our society upside down and inside out within the lifetime of the older of us. /3

Consider what has happened to the home, the stage on which the drama of family life is played. What was the home like, fifty years ago? There was the parlor, always cold and clean and quiet, with an organ which was pumped with the feet, a hard horsehair sofa, and a photographic album. The sitting room was more cheerful, with its baseburner standing in the middle of the room on a metal sheet to protect the carpet, the coals glowing red-hot through the isinglass windows of the stove, the stove pipe going straight up through the ceiling to lend a little warmth to the bedroom above; the coal scuttle beside the stove, half full of coal, and garnished with nutshells and apple cores. On the library table a big kerosene lamp shedding a yellow glow, and the latest copies of *Harper's Bazaar* and the *Youth's Companion*. Beside the table a big rocking chair, in which mother rocked the baby to sleep, singing lullabies. And I almost forgot to mention the brick sewn up in a piece of carpet, and used as a doorstop. /4

In the kitchen there was the range, with a fire burning briskly, and the oven door open to warm the room on a cold morning, while oatmeal cooked in the double boiler and eggs and bacon sizzled in the frying pan. At the sink was the cistern pump for rain water, and beside it stood the pail of drinking water, with a long-handled dipper. Down in the cellar was the vegetable room with a bin of potatoes and a sack of turnips and a barrel of apples. /5

Let us not omit from this picture the icy-cold bedroom, with the wash-water frozen in the washbowl on the washstand on winter mornings; the Saturday-night bath ritual in the washtub in the kitchen; the souring milk and the running butter during hot summer days, and the dread of typhoid fever always threatening to break into epidemic proportions. /6

Would we trade the old home for the modern one, with thermostatically-controlled heat coming through radiators at the turn of a valve, light at the turn of a button, clean white kitchen equipment, electric refrigeration, and electrical cleaning equipment which makes unnecessary "beating the rugs" until one gets blisters on the hands and knees? /7

Whether we approve of modern gadgets completely or not, we will take most of them and enjoy them. They are results of man's unquenchable thirst for knowledge, which produces a technology that changes the conditions of life and sets in motion great social forces which change the social landscape as irresistibly as the glacier, creeping down from the north in the ancient days, changed the physical landscape. /8

Social change has changed the home, and it has also changed the family which lives in the home. Social change will continue to change the home, and it will continue to change the family. No matter how firmly wedded we are to yesterday's conception of the good family life, we shall have to come to terms with today's conception, and we must expect a new conception to arise tomorrow. /9

But here we must ask ourselves the question whether the family of tomorrow is to be created blindly by the blind forces of social change, or to be fashioned by men and women who can partially control their fate. Is the destiny of the family outside of man's control like the coming of an ice age? We know that some time, a few thousand or a few million years hence, the earth's axis may tip, or some other cosmic process may occur which will bring another ice age on this continent. The winters will gradually grow longer. The sun will seem to lose its heat and will shine wanly from the south during the short winter days, unable to melt the snow and ice that lock the land and water in rigid embrace. Slowly but relentlessly an ice sheet will form in Canada and move south, a few feet or a few inches in a year. This glacier will surmount and grind into debris the cities and farms and all the handiwork of men. As the glacier reaches the Great Lakes, the cities of Buffalo and Cleveland and Toledo and Detroit and Chicago will become uninhabitable. Industry and business will move south, and so will most of the people, leaving only a few hardy souls to turn Eskimo and hack out a living from the frozen wilderness at the edge of the advancing ice. /10

This physical event, when and if it comes, will be irresistible. Even atomic energy will not avail against it. It lies outside of man's control. /11

But the forces of social change are not like the blind forces of physical change. Social change is man-made, and can be man-controlled. Men can foresee consequences and can modify their institutions so as to preserve old values and gain new ones. /12

The problem, then, of the family is the problem of controlling social forces and modifying institutional forms so as to achieve values which the family has given in the past or may give in the future. /13

The great difficulty of this problem can be estimated from a look at the recent vicissitudes of the American family since World War I. /14

First, immediately after World War I, there were the mad and riotous 1920's. This was the age of the flapper, when divorce rates first commenced their alarming rise; when the movie and the automobile drew people out of their homes, and the front porch lost its function in the American home. /15

Then came the gloomy thirties, when the economic base of the family crumbled. People could not afford to marry. People could not afford to have children. The birth rate dropped to its lowest point in America's history in 1933. Families were held together, like the old Fords, with baling wire provided by the W.P.A. /16

Just when it seemed that we might climb out of the Great Depression, there came the anxious forties, when young men and women married and then the men went off to war. When children were born to hundreds of thousands of women without the supporting presence of a father. When young mothers had to move in with their parents, and families of war industry workers lived in trailers. /17

And finally comes the frustrating and pressing present—a postwar period of confusion of purposes and of doubt as to our ability to recreate a stable and peaceful society on a world scale. This is an age in which we see clearly our social weakness, but seem impotent to do anything about it. We can describe our social ills with a wealth of statistics. It is an age of great understanding and little will power. /18

To see what the needs of the American family are in this situation, it would be well to make a distinction between the essential functions of the family and its accidental functions. The essential functions are the things the family does for human life and happiness which no other institution can do nearly as well. The accidental functions are things the family has done or is doing which are useful, but can be done as well or better by other social institutions. /19

One accidental function of the family is to create economic goods. Jacob, the father of the Children of Israel, had a family consisting of his wives and concubines, his children and their children, and his slaves. This family was a self-contained economic unit. It produced nearly all of the goods and services that it consumed. The present-day farmer's family continues to perform a vestige of this function. To a limited extent, the entire family works and produces. Before the industrial revolution in England, the weaver's cottage was a factory, and his family made cloth for sale. But nowadays, modern society has found more efficient ways of producing goods than the family unit could achieve. /20

A second accidental function of the family is the collection and preservation of property. In some societies, marriages are arranged so as to combine lands and herds and other holdings. The family members are reared and trained to preserve and increase their property, whether it consist of land, or animals, or ships, or banking houses. But modern societies have found other and probably better institutions, such as the corporation, for this function. /21

A third accidental function of the family is government. In simpler societies, the family, or a group of families, makes rules of conduct, settles disputes among the members, and generally carries on the functions which we assign to government in our society. /22

Religious worship is another accidental function of the family. Jacob, the father of the Children of

Israel, was the priest of his family. He spoke with God, and he taught his family how to get along with God and the supernatural. We have family worship in many of our homes today, with the head of the family teaching religion to the children. But the church has been invented as an institution with the essential function of religious worship, and the family's responsibility has become secondary in this respect. /23

Other accidental functions of the family are health care, and education in the narrow, formal sense. Special institutions have been created and assigned these responsibilities as their essential functions. /24

What, then, are the essential functions of the family? There are three, or possibly four of them. /25

The first essential task of the family is the rearing of children. No society has found a successful substitute for the family to do this job. Plato imagined what he thought would be a better way, but no one seems to have taken him seriously. Soviet Russia experimented with other institutions during the first crucial years after the revolution of 1917, when the Communist Party decided to wean children away from the political beliefs of their reactionary parents. But as soon as that crisis was past, the Soviet family was entrusted with the principal responsibility for child-rearing. /26

The reason that this is an essential task of the family lies in the young child's need for an abundance of personal and personalized care. The mere feeding and caring for the child's physical comfort are not enough. The infant does not develop into a happy human being unless he has the loving attention of one or more older persons. So far, at any rate, human experience has not discovered any large-scale substitute for the family in rearing the child so that he feels good about himself and so that he feels trusting of others. /27

The second essential function of the family is to provide companionship for men and women. Although life may be full of friendships of man with man and woman with woman and of man with woman outside of the family, none of these relationships equals in satisfaction and importance to the individual the companionship of husband and wife, cemented by the most intimate and most satisfying of all relations. /28

A third essential function of the family is the provision of emotional security for its members. This is closely related to both of the ones previously mentioned, but it applies to all members of the family and to all ages. Home, the seat of the family, is a refuge in time of trouble or weariness. The hurt child runs home, and so does the unsuccessful young man or woman who has been defeated in the first attempt to be independent. Home is the place where you are always welcome, where you can go without being invited, and where you do not have to earn a welcome. In a world where one has to build psychological defenses for his insecurity and be constantly on his guard for eight or twelve hours a day, the family provides the one place where he can relax and "be himself." /29

A possible fourth essential function of the family is housekeeping—the task of providing food and shelter for its members. There is some disagreement as to whether this function is essential, although it is well nigh universal. It has been called into question in our own society because of its economic inefficiency. Some two-thirds of the adult women of our society are housekeeping, doing work which could be done by a fraction of their number if we had multifamily housing and feeding arrangements. With modern efficiency, the work of buying and preparing food, cleaning house, and washing clothes could be done much more cheaply and probably on a better material standard than under the present family system, where it is done by housewives. /30

But if this function of housekeeping were to be taken over by another institution, what would happen to the other essential functions of the family? Wives would spend increasing amounts of time outside the home and away from the rest of the family. Would the functions of child-rearing and of providing emotional security be threatened by removing the wife from the home for several hours a day and by the disappearance of the family dinner table? /31

With these three and possibly four essential functions of the family in mind, we may ask what are the needs of the American family. Taking account of the possible effects of present social trends on our life, what should we do to keep the family intact and to make it more able to perform its essential functions? /32

There are several needs of the family which can be met by educating the individual better. I am convinced that there is a need for education for marriage and child-rearing. This is perhaps the most difficult kind of education to give. It involves the teaching of attitudes as well as facts. It deals with the most intimate problems of sex and courtship. One of my male students recently told a class that he had given up his interest in a certain girl when he found that her blood was Rh-negative and consequently she might have difficulty in bearing his children.

Such knowledge is important, and we can make good use of it. But it is only a minor part of education for marriage. This kind of education is more an art than a science, though it can be improved by scientific study. It should be provided in school and college, whenever the "teachable moment" comes. But the most teachable moments for education for marriage and child-rearing come when people are out of school—about to be married, having their first child, having the first child go to school, having the first child reach adolescence, having the last child leave the home. And so the task of education for marriage and child-rearing is essentially a task for adult education. /33

Another need is for education for acceptance of responsibility for having children. With the rapid and continuing spread of birth control knowledge and practices, a significant section of our population now have too few children to reproduce their numbers. In general, the people who do not reproduce their numbers are in the upper-middle and upper socio-economic levels.* If the universities of Princeton, Yale, and Harvard, and the colleges of Wellesley, Smith, and Vassar were to limit their enrollment to children of former students, and if all such children were to attend these institutions, their enrollment would drop to one-half the present size in fifty years, and to a quarter of the present size in a hundred years. That is, enrollments would drop unless these universities did something about educating their students to have more children. But why single out the blue-ribbon colleges for such special attention? If all higher educational institutions were to limit enrollment to children of former college students, their enrollments would decrease almost as rapidly. And I do not make an exception of the Catholic colleges. /34

The low birth rate in the upper social groups has certain advantages to our society. It leaves vacant places among the more desirable positions, which can be taken by the upward-moving children of working-class parents, and thus it tends to preserve democratic fluidity in our social structure. But birth control practices are spreading, and will probably spread further, bringing our population to a standstill in another generation or two. Perhaps we shall then have sufficient population for an efficient and productive economy. Perhaps we shall have too large a population, as some economists argue. But I think no one could argue for the desirability of a rapid decrease of population, led by the very people who are in the best economic position to have and to rear children. /35

Reasons for our better-educated people having few children are not hard to find. They want to give their children the benefits of an expensive education. In addition they want to live—themselves and their children—at a high economic standard. They want to have a busy and active life outside of the home. All these argue against having many children. In addition, some of them may not trust the future enough to desire to bring children into this world to face it. I hope there are not many such. /36

Anyway, I venture to say that although a two-child family may be fashionable, it is socially unhealthy. /37

The need for individual acceptance of responsibility for having children is matched by a need for social measures to assist parents who have large families. Such measures as government-paid family allowances in addition to a basic salary paid by the employer, and substantial income tax exemptions for children should be developed in this country, as, indeed, they have been in England. Social assistance should be devised to assist two classes of people. /38

Those who have few children now, but can do a good job of child-rearing, should be encouraged to have more children. And those with very large families should be assisted to do a better job of providing for the health and education of their children. I think there would be no danger of overpopulating the land by these means. The toil and pain and responsibility of bearing and rearing children is in itself a deterrent to over-large families when birth control is understood. /39

There is also a need for closer relations between middle-aged people and their ageing parents. In other words, the American concept of the family should be that of a three-generation instead of a two-generation family. If the family exists for the sake of human happiness, as it largely does, grandparents are family-members, too, and deserve companionship and emotional security from the family. /40

Middle-aged people of middle economic status are accustomed to feeling responsible for their children, but not for their parents, yet ageing people become less and less self-sufficient, and more and more subject to loss of the things that have meant most in their lives. If their families will not help them, they often become depressed and lonely. The number of people over sixty-five will double in the next thirty

*In a recent letter (March 6, 1960) Havighurst pointed out that here the speech is now dated, since there has been a substantial increase in the birth rate of the upper and middle social groups in the United States since 1948. *(Editor's note)*

years, which means that the number of three- and four-generation families will increase greatly. There will be an inordinate increase of misery in our society if the middle-aged group does not learn to take more responsibility for the happiness of their parents. This does not necessarily mean that they should take their ageing parents into their own homes. Sometimes this would be undesirable. But it does mean that we must study and learn more about the problems of personal adjustment in old age and then put what we learn into practice. /41

These, then, are some of the needs of the American family if it is to perform its essential functions for the advance of the common good in our society. /42

Family life is the source of the greatest human happiness. This happiness is the simplest and least costly kind, and it cannot be purchased with money. But it can be increased if we do two things: if we recognize and uphold the essential values of family life and if we get and keep control of the process of social change so as to make it give us what is needed to make family life perform its essential functions. The future of the family is in our hands, and with it the health and happiness of our people. /43

The speech

1. What two methods are used at the outset of the speech to catch attention and arouse interest in the subject? Evaluate their appropriateness and estimate their probable effectiveness.
2. Comment on the way in which Havighurst masses specific details to create contrasting pictures of the home as it was fifty years ago and as it is today.
3. In what way does this contrast help lay the groundwork for the central idea of the speech? What is that idea? Where is it first stated? Does it express the substance of the speech fully and accurately?
4. Comment on the amount of concrete, as distinguished from abstract, material in the first ten or twelve paragraphs of the speech. What are some of the forms this concrete material takes?
5. Is the summarizing sketch of the period between World War I and the close of World War II sufficiently detailed to make the speaker's point clear and convincing? Why or why not?
6. Was Havighurst wise to deal with the "accidental" functions of the family before treating its "essential" functions, or would the reverse order have been desirable? Why?
7. Consider the "needs" of the family as Havighurst describes them. How closely are these "needs" correlated with his discussion of the family's "essential functions"? If all of the "needs" were met, would the family be satisfactorily performing all of its "essential functions" in society?
8. Do you think the conclusion of the speech is sufficient in length and scope to summarize the main ideas and to reinforce them adequately? Or is it too abrupt and insufficiently related to the leading ideas developed in the body?
9. How would you evaluate the number of major ideas presented during the course of the speech? Too few to make most efficient use of the time available? Too numerous to be explained adequately and remembered easily? Just right for the time available and for a subject of this scope and complexity?
10. How would you evaluate the quality of the major ideas? Fresh or hackneyed? Sound or unsound? Significant or trivial? Objective or prejudiced?

For further study and discussion

1. Do you think that television has a desirable or an undesirable effect on modern family life? How about the automobile? The movies?
2. Are young people today adequately prepared psychologically and emotionally to assume the responsibilities of marriage? If not, should courses in preparation for marriage be required of all high school and college students?
3. To what extent are the schools taking over functions that might better be performed by the family? How about the churches? Boys' clubs? Community recreation programs?
4. Do small families really have all the evils Havighurst implies?
5. In what respects is the family of today doing a better job than the family of a century ago? A poorer job?
6. How does the modern American family compare with families in other countries in respect to size, stability, organization, distribution of responsibilities and functions, etc.?
7. Is divorce too easy today? If so, would it help to have uniform marriage and divorce laws in all of our states?
8. How does the increasing tendency for wives and mothers to work affect family life? In what ways has the increase in life span affected the family and added to its problems?
9. How can marriage counseling services, marital adjustment clinics, and similar agencies be extended and rendered more effective? Should they be provided by the government or financed privately? Would more and better child guidance clinics help? Could adult education in general do more to rehabilitate the family?

10. What is the relationship between the apparent disintegration of family life and the rising rates of juvenile delinquency, adult crime, and alcoholism? Are children from unhappy families more prone to divorce and marital maladjustments in later life? What are some of the effects that broken homes often have on children?

Suggestions for further reading

Ruth Shonle Cavan, ***American Marriage: A Way of Life*** (New York, 1959)

Evelyn Mills Duvall, ***Family Development*** (New York, 1957)

Paul G. Glick, ***American Families,*** A Volume in the Census Monograph Series, (New York, 1957)

Sister Frances Jerome Woods, C.D.P., ***The American Family System*** (New York, 1959)

See also the current files of ***The American Journal of Sociology*** (published bimonthly by the University of Chicago Press) and ***Marriage and Family Living*** (journal of the National Council of Family Relations)

The haven of the defeated

PETER A. KAROS

In June 1890, in response to an invitation issued by the University of Michigan, delegates from the University of Wisconsin, Northwestern University, and Oberlin College assembled at Ann Arbor to organize the Northern Oratorical League, one of the oldest and most distinguished of the many associations designed to promote extracurricular speaking activities among college students. Since the first annual contest at the University of Michigan in 1891, the League has varied considerably in membership. Today the League consists of six schools: Iowa, Michigan, Minnesota, Northwestern, Western Reserve, and Wisconsin.

In 1901 the Honorable Frank O. Lowden, later United States congressman and governor of Illinois and in 1920 a leading contender for the Republican nomination for the Presidency, endowed the League with a sizable sum of money. The interest from this endowment has since been used to provide cash prizes for the first, second, and third place winners in the annual speaking competition. These prizes are still known by their original name the "Lowden testimonials."

Being named to represent one's school in a Northern Oratorical League contest is among the highest honors that can come to a student speaker. The list of participants who later achieved distinction in public life or the professions is impressive. In 1913 Paul Blanshard, author and sociologist, represented the University of Michigan with a speech entitled "Christianity and the Social Order." In 1923 Senator Wayne Morse, then a student at the University of Wisconsin, spoke on "The Supreme Court and the People." In 1927 Harold Stassen, representing the University of Minnesota, discussed "National Will or International Good Will?"

The speech that follows won second place in the League's competition for 1950 and was delivered by Peter A. Karos, a student at the University of Minnesota. It is included here because of the unusual nature of its subject matter and because it provides a good example of a so-called "personal involvement" speech—a speech rooted in the first-hand experience of the speaker. In addition to its clear organization and rapidly moving style, this speech is notable for the vivid descriptive passages in which Karos depicts skid row and its inhabitants and for the skillful fashion in which he relates his subject to his listeners, arousing their sympathy as well as their interest in the problems of the men he describes. Structurally, the speech illustrates the disease-remedy or problem-solution pattern of organization.

While reading "The Haven of the Defeated," keep in mind the severely restricted time limits to which Karos was confined by the contest situation and the fact that the speech was written out and memorized. Even within these limitations, Karos' address provides a good example of how interesting and impressive a short student speech may be when the speaker selects a subject which he knows well and about which he has deep convictions.

How many of you have a nickel for a cup of coffee? When you stop to consider, five cents is really a very small amount. Yet I have known many men who had to beg for a cup of coffee, men who have degenerated to one of the lowest possible strata of life, a life spent on skid rows such as Washington Avenue in Minneapolis. To these rejected people skid row is both a physical and mental condition; physical, in that they are down and out. They have skidded to the depths of the pit. Mental, in that it's a continuous state of mind that forces them to consider themselves as shameful outcasts. /1

From *Winning Orations of the Northern Oratorical League, 1945-1950,* The Northwestern Press, Minneapolis. By permission of the Northern Oratorical League.

These havens of defeat constitute a major disgrace to our country, and a disgrace to every city which has them. The men inhabiting these jungles are living—if you call it that—in momentous fear, in terrible remorse, in a hell on earth. They're more than failures, for they have hit the rock bottom of despair after attempting to climb up again and again. /2

I sense this evening that your relationship towards them may be different from mine. Most of you have probably visited skid row areas. Outwardly you express sympathy for these men, but somehow I can't help believing that inwardly you are experiencing a deep sense of satisfaction at being superior to those human derelicts. My relationship was once like yours. Now it's different because as a restaurant owner on skid row I made many acquaintances with these so-called "bums." Although I've now sold the restaurant I still visit them from time to time. /3

If the majority of our respected citizens continue secretly to view them with scorn and contempt, then these sorrowful jungles will always remain in our cities. If I'm able to change your attitude to one of sympathy and understanding—then we have taken the first step towards eliminating these ghettos and raising these former exiles to a respectable level in life. /4

Let me take you behind the scenes on skid row. Many of you have expressed dissatisfaction with the boredom and daily routine of your lives. But as we move down skid row I wish you would constantly compare the occasional unhappiness of your lives to the constantly deplorable and frustrating conditions under which this forsaken population must exist. /5

First let's see where they live. A typical example is the Anchor Hotel on lower Nicollet Avenue in Minneapolis. This "hotel" has over 100 dingy, airless, and gloomy rooms on one floor, rooms which are separated only by thin plywood. The walls extend six or eight feet towards the ceiling of the large room. Each cubicle is covered across the top by chicken wire, and contains a bunk-like bed, a battered dresser, and perhaps a crate box for a chair. That's all. Fourteen windows provide ventilation for these one hundred rooms. The stench which exists, particularly in the summer time, is nauseating and repugnant. It doesn't sound very pleasant, does it? /6

Next, let's see what they do in their spare time. You and I have many social outlets. But what about these men—because of the conditions in which they find themselves they have long ago lost their families and friends. Having no responsibility except existing, and no friends or families to visit, they have large amounts of free time. They can read or they can go to a cheap show, but the main attraction is the ample number of saloons accessible to them. There they can go and drink their dime beers, or perhaps one of their "pink ladies"—canned heat strained through a rag to eliminate impurities. /7

We have seen where they live and how they spend their days. I'd like to introduce you to some of the people who frequent these saloons. Actually in most cases their alcoholism is an effect rather than a cause—the causes including homosexuality, physical deformities, marital difficulties, and business disappointments; in short, all things of our complex society which produce frustration and result in social misfits. Remember, I'm not speaking of freaks of nature, because, you see, they're human beings the same as you and I. They, too, have been endowed with a heart, a body, and a soul. /8

Meet Sam Running. Sam is one of a large family which was unable to meet the financial strain brought about by the depression. As a result, his education was interrupted and he was forced to seek employment. Resentment and loneliness started his drinking. He worked in garages and became an accomplished body and fender man. Any employer would be glad to hire Sam—but Sam is a "deehorn." That is, he drinks anything with alcohol in it—anything from vanilla extract to bay rum. When sober, Sam is quiet, clean and respectable. However, when drunk a transformation occurs; a transformation which I cannot fully describe. He's then troublesome, dirty and repulsive. /9

Next, shake the hand of William Nelson. I met Bill when he washed dishes for me. Bill is a man who has had three years of college. He's intelligent, a good-looking man, and has a most pleasing personality. He was a conscientious worker. I could never quite figure out why Bill was on skid row. I soon got my answer. One day I was talking with a friend of Bill's. It seems that Bill had been a successful merchant in a small Minnesota town. However, because of general economic conditions his business failed. Shortly thereafter his wife became ill and required expensive medical treatment which Bill couldn't provide. Possibly because of the lack of medical treatment—she died. This dual misfortune caused Bill to withdraw to the irresponsible life of the bowery. I wonder how many of us here tonight could have met this test. /10

Now I would like you to meet Alfred "Buck" Jones. Buck is forty-three years old, married, has two children, and ran away from his faithless wife. I've known Buck, who is a machinist, for several years, and Buck is a person who attempts to give the impression he's enjoying the life of a derelict on Washington Avenue. But he's not. Oftentimes Buck would become serious and say, "Pete, whatever you do, don't ever start drinking. Look at me." After one of his periodic sprees Buck would come in and borrow fifty cents "to straighten out." I would place the half dollar on the counter, but his hands trembled so that he would be unable to pick it up. Then he would once more repeat his sincere advice. "Don't ever start drinking—look at me." /11

Yes—I could go on giving you many more examples of men like Sam, Bill, and Buck. I merely wanted to suggest that many men on skid row have the ability and capacity to become productive human beings. But without human help, their hopeless conviction that "once on skid row, always on skid row" will be more deeply rooted within them. I'm not attempting to make rash generalizations or excuses for them, and maintain that every man on the bowery can be rehabilitated to a useful citizen, because I don't believe that's true. But there are many men who, with the proper guidance and support, can be made good citizens. /12

Before we can attack this problem intelligently it's necessary to determine why these ports of loneliness harbor thousands of people. Skid row inhabitants seem to fall into two general categories: Those with dormant productivity and those unable to produce. /13

The first class includes ex-criminals, people with physical deformities, and fugitives from their former lives. Why is it that these particular types are universally found on skid rows? Because nearly all business men refuse to employ former convicts; because we shun people with physical deformities; because people, like those of us here tonight, shut these derelicts out of our lives, our minds, our consciences, and put them into association only with their own kind. /14

In the second class, those of sub-marginal incomes, we find people who are unable to produce. They are old-age pensioners and those on relief. The responsibility for their welfare lies with the federal and state governments. Relief or pension payments are simply below the minimum standards for decent living. Would you care to try living on a salary of forty dollars a month? /15

We must now ask—what can we do about the problem? Before anything constructive can be done we must conquer our ignorance concerning skid rows as we have regarding prisons and mental hospitals. Doing this will provide the foundation upon which the rest of the structure can be built. /16

Let's look and see what changes have occurred in prisons and mental hospitals. In the former, the men in prisons are no longer simply confined to cells. On the contrary, they have farms on which they work cooperatively, they have a form of government, they practice vocations in which they can become skilled. They're taking active parts in group activities. They're being prepared to assume a place in society. /17

In mental hospitals strait jackets and confinement are being eliminated. Patients are permitted hobbies, they're given responsibilities, discussion groups are encouraged. Institutions are attempting to change futile hopelessness to anticipation of the future. /18

As a people we have learned slowly and painfully, but we have learned, that men in prison cells cannot be returned to good citizenship by being shut off from human associations and productive work. We have learned that men in mental hospitals cannot be returned to good health in confinement and segregation. We must learn the similar truth that men on skid row can be returned to society only if that society opens the doors for them for useful work and healthy association with other men. /19

Civic projects must be undertaken in skid rows. Business men must hire people from the bowery to help them feel they can live as other people do. This can be done! Brown and Bigelow, a large corporation in Minneapolis, has successfully employed several hundred ex-criminals. /20

Well established churches must change their attitudes concerning skid rows and organizations like the Salvation Army. How would a dignified congregation react if a bowery bum came to church? How many churches have tried to aid the Salvation Army, a sincerely purposeful, religious organization that has successfully changed lives of skid row people? /21

Let's assume an enlightened public attitude and eager cooperation by various civic organizations. Specifically, what could be done? /22

First: Establish a farm in the state for the derelicts. As it is today, a person attempting to reform hasn't a place to go where he can stay away from the temptation of "slipping." /23

Second: The state or city can erect some new, sanitary, and livable rooming houses. By so doing, we will be helping to restore the dignity and respect which a human being is entitled to have. /24

Third: Establish a vocational guidance center, staffed with trained psychologists and sociologists, who can analyze the downfall of the people on the bowery and help them readjust to life. /25

If the feeling of the American public remains unchanged—and in our democracy this means our personal attitudes—skid rows will always be a discredit to our communities. /26

Let's give these fallen men an opportunity to live as human beings, an opportunity to serve useful ends in society, and possibly, an opportunity to help someone else. /27

The speech

1. Evaluate Karos' introduction. Is it well calculated to arouse interest in his subject? Does it have a sufficient amount of concrete material? Does it give a clear indication of what the speech is to be about? Does it move the listener easily and rapidly into a consideration of the subject, or does it bog him down in unnecessary or irrelevant details? Is it closely related to the body of the speech by means of a clear and smooth transition?
2. What specific steps does Karos take early in the speech to counteract any unfavorable attitudes his listeners may have toward his subject and to win a sympathetic hearing for his point of view? What means does he use at various points throughout the speech to relate his subject to his listeners and to arouse their sympathy?
3. In which paragraph is the central idea or specific purpose of the speech stated? Is it stated clearly, concisely, and accurately?
4. How successful would you say Karos is in describing skid row for us—in actually enabling us to see the street and its inhabitants? What specific methods and techniques does he employ in developing this description?
5. What do you think of Karos' plan of introducing Sam, Bill, and Buck to us as if we were actually meeting them face to face? Do you think this device is appropriate and effective, or is it excessively dramatic—too obviously a rhetorical trick or technique?
6. How would you evaluate the analogy which Karos draws between the reforms he would like to see for skid row and the reforms made in our prisons and mental hospitals? What specific point is he trying to prove? How successful is he in proving it?
7. Would you say that Karos adequately substantiates his contention that ex-convicts make good employees?
8. Consider the three-point program Karos sets forth for solving the problem of the skid row derelicts? Is it sufficiently clear and specific? Does he prove to your satisfaction that it would work—that if put into effect it would help solve the problem? Does he give adequate consideration to various objections that might be raised against it?
9. Is the style of the speech always as natural and conversational as one might wish? If you answer no, rewrite several passages to show how they might be improved in this respect.
10. Would you say that Karos has used a "summary" conclusion, an "appeal" conclusion, or that he has combined the two types? Defend your answer.

For further study and discussion

1. Mr. Karos seems to imply that, except for the crippled and mentally deficient, most of the men on skid row are there through no fault of their own, but because fate has dealt with them unkindly. Do you agree with this, or is it perhaps too sympathetic a view? What about the thousands of persons who have surmounted adversities and personal tragedies without losing their ambition and self-respect?
2. What do you think of the proposal that "new, sanitary, and livable rooming houses" be built for skid row inhabitants at municipal expense? Is the rehabilitation of these men a public responsibility or should it be carried on primarily by private social and religious agencies? What are the policies of some of our major cities in this respect?
3. Have the pressures and tensions of modern industrial society significantly increased the number of persons who are unable to compete successfully? Are there more "defeated" individuals today than there were fifty or a hundred years ago? Didn't ancient Rome, medieval Paris, and every other great city of every age always have a large number of "rabble" living on the edge of respectability?
4. What are the latest and most authoritative facts concerning chronic alcoholism? Would most authorities agree with Karos that it is "an effect rather than a cause" of man's downfall? Is alcoholism regarded as primarily a physical or a mental disease. What forms of treatment are thought best? How successful are they?
5. Do you think that men like Sam Running, William Nelson, and Alfred "Buck" Jones could be rehabilitated? Why? If you believe they could be, outline what you would consider to be an ideal rehabilitation program. Be as specific as you can, and stand ready to explain and defend your proposals.
6. Why do you suppose that although men of the type Karos describes are constantly in trouble with the law for drunkenness, vagrancy, and petty crimes, they do not often commit such major crimes as armed robbery or murder?

7. Are the "beatniks" only "skid rowers" in another form? What particular social and economic forces have contributed to the creation of the so-called "beat generation"?
8. Do social workers, ministers, and policemen who have worked with "skid rowers" believe most of them can be rehabilitated? What would they probably think of Karos' proposals?
9. Are there any facts available concerning the employability of ex-convicts? Do they make good employees? Are many companies hiring them successfully? What about the employability of the physically handicapped?
10. What, in general, are the churches doing to help skid row inhabitants? Should they be doing more? If so, how and what?

Suggestions for further reading

Alton L. Blakeslee, ***Alcoholism, A Sickness That Can Be Beaten,*** Public Affairs Pamphlet No. 118 (New York, 1952)

Earl Jerome Ellison, "The Shame of Skid Row," ***Saturday Evening Post,*** December 20, 1952, pp. 13-15, 48-51.

Hyman Feldman, "What Can We Do About Skid Row?" ***Today's Health,*** XXXV (December 1957), 18-21.

Sara Harris, ***Skid Row, U.S.A.*** (Garden City, New York, 1956)

J. M. Jellinek, ed., ***Alcohol Addiction and Chronic Alcoholism,*** Research Council on Problems of Alcohol (New Haven, 1942)

6 / ETHICS AND MORALS

The irrepressible issues of the 60s

ADOLF A. BERLE, JR.

E. D. Canham in the *Christian Science Monitor* (May 23, 1957) described Adolf A. Berle, Jr., as a "uniquely experienced and informed American . . . . the best and rarest kind of intellectual . . . . part lawyer, part philosopher, part diplomat, part economist."

Berle was born in Boston, Massachusetts, in 1895 and attended Harvard University, where he received his A.B. in 1913 and his M.A. and LL.B. in 1916. After graduation he practiced law in New York City, and in 1927 he became a professor at Columbia University Law School, a position he still holds. In addition, he is a member of the Graduate Faculty of Political Science at Columbia.

His extensive career in public service includes serving as a member of President Roosevelt's "brain trust" during the early 1930's and as Assistant Secretary of State for Latin American affairs from 1938 to 1944. In 1945 he was appointed United States Ambassador to Brazil. He has also been the United States delegate to various conferences, among them the Inter-American Peace Conference in Buenos Aires and Pan-American Conferences in Lima and Havana.

Besides his competence in Latin American affairs, Berle has considerable knowledge of the American economy. He has contributed much to our understanding of the position of the large corporation in American society in such books as *The Modern Corporation and Private Property* (1939), *The Twentieth Century Capitalist Revolution* (1954), and *Power Without Property* (1959).

Because of his training and experience, Berle is particularly well qualified to discuss his subject, "The Irrepressible Issues of the 60s." The address was delivered in Chicago on March 6, 1960, to the opening general session of the Fifteenth National Conference on Higher Education, sponsored by the Association for Higher Education.

Adolf A. Berle, Jr., "The Irrepressible Issues of the 60s." *Vital Speeches of the Day*, Vol. XXVI, May 15, 1960, pp. 450-452. By permission of the author.

Educators and teachers are today facing a severe trial. They are no longer accorded the protection of an ivory tower. Results are expected from them. If, in the next few years, the United States encounters trouble or disaster, at home or abroad, educators are likely to be held partly, perhaps even primarily, responsible. /1

Quite plainly, we are approaching the end of an era. In the savage, implacable world drawing nearer to America every hour, new demands are made on our human resources. The added freight alone of a population which will increase by one hundred millions or so in the next generation, would give strain enough. We shall also be under bitter attack from other civilizations. Briefly, we have a single choice: renaissance or regression. The first means triumph, and the attainment of a splendid, new plateau. The other means defeat, with unknown consequences. A perilous share of the burden in making the choice and achieving the renaissance rests on the institutions of higher education. /2

College presidents and classroom professors are not used to being treated like politicians. Insensibly almost, they have moved from staff headquarters to the firing line. They are likely to occupy that position for a good while. So we had best get used to it, understand what is wanted of us, take inventory of our own resources, and prepare to meet some very precise demands. /3

My belief is that the United States will have reverses, possibly serious ones, in the next few years. In part these will be ascribed to the failures of the government. Secondarily, it will be charged, that the universities of the country, as its intellectual general staff, failed to prepare the country to take the necessary preventive measures. But at the same time, universities will be expected to supply the ideas, the analysis, the measures and even the men to meet any current emergency in almost any field. /4

Specifically, I think: /5

First. Within the next two or three years there will be an economic recession. I cannot forecast its proportion. It could come as soon as late summer 1960. It seems certain before, say, mid-1963. /6

Second. In foreign affairs there will be turbulence. This could come any time. The Summit Conference this spring will not be a love-feast. It may well prove the most dangerous crisis since World War II. As one result the United States will be compelled either to lead or to follow in a reconstruction of the world economic system, or at any rate of a big regional economic system. /7

Third. Either separately or in connection with both these events, there will be an American moral crisis. Included in it will be a demand that Americans generally stop their self-indulgence, develop a far higher degree of personal conscientiousness, accept great engagements toward common effort looking towards a better civilization both here and in other parts of the earth. There will be insistence on a new era of intense personal responsibility, resting on every man, woman and child, in every expression of life. /8

It is not possible to suggest the particular incidents which will spark any of these crises. Conditions are such that any of a number of things might happen, triggering an explosion in national life or international affairs. A tiny local incident illustrates. We have just rediscovered the old institution of private bribery now known as "payola." This has already crystallized a general question: How honest—or how crooked—is our system of mass communication? Have our advertising media become a moral menace? Where and why did the motivations go wrong? Is there a connection between cheating in school, misreporting on income tax returns and corruption in commercial and public life? Inevitably it will be asked, where have parents, teachers, professors, schools and colleges been all this time? None of this is fanciful, and you all know it. The Association of Higher Education is meeting some of these questions now. /9

A second, more striking evil may shortly come up. This is the notion, now tolerated in some quarters, of commercially "planned" or "designed" obsolescence. This means manufacturing machines, appliances, cars or other products so designed that after a limited length of time they will go to pieces, wear out, become obsolete, or otherwise unusable. Obsolescence can be hastened by other methods, for example, marketing propaganda, or failure to provide maintenance service. The purpose, of course, is to force consumers to buy the product oftener than necessary, each time, of course, at a profit to the manufacturer. At best the result is organized waste. At worst it falls uncomfortably close to sabotage or cheating. The resulting moral reproach easily becomes applied to innocent as well as guilty corporations and business organizations whose operations are the country's supply line. The results could be profound. The profit motive is a useful economic incentive toward getting things done. But if this sort of thing can be included in the commercial value system, the danger is obvious. The question will arise, where were the men trained who accepted this perversion of values? /10

Simultaneously, there has recently been a sudden discovery that a number of countries are doing a better job of education than seems to be true here. In some cases, other systems produced better quality of top brains in research and administration. In other cases, greater quantity in technical training was achieved. /11

At the top of the scale, it is apparent we are not training enough scientists. In technical fields, we are not training enough engineers. Despite severe limitation of medical education and the high standing accorded it, the number of students seeking to enter medical schools is beginning to drop off, although we need more doctors. It so happens that in these, and other fields, students have to be willing to do hard, disciplined and exact work. Somehow they have been diverted. Education and training, or at least its rewards, it was thought, could be effortlessly acquired, without the grueling labor involved in mastering any subject, or the dedication needed to push out into new ground. We are discovering that America is entering a period of great national stress and of unlimited international rivalry, without adequate resources of trained and responsible men at all levels. That discovery has already led to an uproar, directed at educational institutions all the way from top to bottom. It has not died down. /12

Each successive realization that the quality of American life and American intellectual effort must be far tougher, far better disciplined and far more productive will bring more criticism of our educational system, from parents to graduate faculties. The only question is how long it must last before something really gets done. At the moment, we are still listening to the old siren songs. Possibly we can find a cheap and easy way out by television teaching. Perhaps shifting administrative patterns will be enough. Possibly raising teachers' salaries all along the line will change the picture. Maybe personal purpose can be instilled by mass media, and paid for by complaisant advertisers. And so forth. Everyone knows the list of panaceas, from capsule textbooks (sold at a profit) to high-minded basketball teams, or adult education in painless installments. Devices run all the way from true-false examinations marked by clerks to centralized psychological testing. /13

I am not attacking any of these things as such. Probably some can learn something by television. Perhaps true-false testing can contribute something to evaluation of a student's character and work. I like sports, though I regret that only a tiny fraction of students get a chance to engage in them. But none of this can possibly do much toward development of individual character, dedicated to putting something into our civilization, and not merely toward getting the most out of it. Nor will it replace the limitless influence of parents and teachers who devote their efforts to the personal development of their children and students. Machines and mechanics do not make values. Honor and truth are not products of aptitude adjustment. Purpose cannot be inspired by IBM machines. Love and devotion are not synthetic forms of address: they are lambent flames. The aggregate of all the results will be the nation that is America, entrusted in its youth to teachers and scholars, whom we must serve. But of this comes national purpose, and international success or failure in the greatest era history has yet recorded. What this shall be, and how produced, is the crucial problem in every walk of life. /14

The issues we have to meet in the next few years all arise, I think, out of this central problem. Let us confront it, squarely, without fear and without favor. It splits into several divisions. The first is far and away the greatest and deepest for it is essentially philosophical. The second is social, and fixes the direction of current politics. The third raises problems of technique and organization—the level at which most of us have to work. /15

In the first and deepest issue, universities and American intellectuals have, I am clear, been running away from the greatest and most constant of all human issues. This is, quite simply, whether life has an enduring significance, or whether it is an anarchy of chance, meaning nothing. Properly, this should have been the concern of the Departments of Philosophy in our universities. Yet so far as I recall, the last great study of eternal values in the United States was published by Hugo Muensterberg of Harvard—who died in 1916. Nor have historians and social scientists filled the gap, though some of them have tackled fragments of it. England's Toynbee has had the courage to make the attempt to make a philosophy of history, whether one agrees with it or not. Sociologists describe—and commonly let it go at that. Economists set out the result of human wants. None of these have dealt with the primary question of values. /16

As a student of the American business and financial machine, I know that without an accepted system of values as base the economic system simply cannot be sound. We can play, as our statisticians must do, that production of plastic balloons is no less "productivity" than building cathedrals or developing first-rate housing. But we all know better. We can, and our figures do, classify the ten billions a year Americans spend on liquor as of equal value to the ten billions they spend on education. But we know that the comparison is discreditable. We know that taxes paid for necessary work, from roads to schools, are a way of buying something infinitely important, and we know the same amount of money spent privately on luxuries or diversion takes lesser rank of importance. Yet we are content to let go, without challenge, the idea that taxes are a form of robbery—while inflated installment charges collected by finance companies for anything from mink coats to summer vacations on pay-later plans can be considered sound bargains. The best brains in the country, which I still think are represented in our universities, must be saying with bluntness what things are first and first rate, and what are secondary and second rate, and what are discreditable, and due to be discarded. Bluntly, universities everywhere ought to concern themselves with a moral order. In academic lingo this is called a value system. /17

The second group of issues necessarily relates to politics and social organization. Obviously, these cannot be met unless there is general consensus on values. /18

Here I think the unsung American public at this moment is far ahead of its politicians, even ahead of the public expressions of its teachers and college presidents. /19

Most Americans realize that the greatest values come not from personal pleasure or profit, but from contributions made to the community, the country, and the progress of humanity. They know quite well that education comes ahead of transient luxuries. They know that the running gear of business is justified not by its profit, but because it meets human needs. Profit is essential, but secondary. They know there is more to a job than the paycheck, essential as the paycheck is, but that a paycheck without a real job is a form of poorhouse. So they want a system providing stable employment. They also want the jobs to mean active participation in civilization and in life. They want an economics that does not accept slums as a necessary condition of housing. They want business that does not organize waste at consumers' expense, and they understand quite well that "planned obsolescence" is either cheating or waste, or both. In other words, they want an organization of affairs that realizes instead of violates their value system. /20

All this adds up to two things. It means that the United States must produce more. Also, that she must plan or guide her economy. /21

I know the gust of abuse that comes from saying this. Classical economists talk about the road to serfdom—but they don't live in New York's Harlem or in Chicago's Cicero. Chambers of Commerce mouth old clichés about free enterprise. But they do not induce their members to make ice chests that will last, or prevent mass medium advertising from peddling class-symbols instead of well-made products, or show us how slums will be cleared. Social advice from these quarters will be more impressive when they are doing the job better. /22

Planning a democratic economy at bottom, is a straightforward matter. It means providing a place where certain decisions can be made. The decisions settle what activities are most important, what are less important, what are nonessential, and what can be let go. This is the economic expression of the value system we have been talking about. High on this list comes health, education, scientific research. Close behind transportation and communications, staple commodities like food, basic materials like steel, copper, oil. Then, adequate housing, heavy consumers goods, and then the soft goods. I am not trying to make a list: make your own. The community will decide what it wants, under the guidance of the best thinking available to it. /23

Many of these needs are adequately met. Many are not. The job of the planner is to steer enough of the goods and services produced in this country towards meeting the list in order of their importance. /24

Are we doing this now? We have, for example, quite recently committed many tens of billions of government money to building roads. This helps motor cars and motor travel. Did we need this more than we needed a program of education and health—which we are told we cannot afford? On the private side we commit more than twelve billions to buying motor cars. Should not an equivalent sum be steered into slum clearance? If we want both slum clearance and twelve billions worth of motor cars, should we not increase our productivity and put some of it where there is real need? /25

This places new burdens on our economists, and our social scientists. It puts new obligations on businessmen. A good beginning would be abandonment of the style racket in cars and household appliances which organize waste rather than provide honest service. Politicians will have to meet the issue in the coming campaign. Elected officials will have to deal with it when in office. /26

The issue of guiding the economy so that it will increasingly realize an honorable, effective and civilized value system is dimly understood by everyone. It awaits the solid academic and political work that will make it real. /27

One touch of economic emergency will explode all this into a set of immediate, fighting political issues. Then, politics becomes rough and personal. The system comes under fire—but the attacks are leveled against the men in positions of power, and responsibility and influence, for sins of commission and of omission, often unjustly; at this stage personal scapegoats are sought and found. So it was in 1930, and so it can easily be again. /28

I hold it the task of the universities, guardians of our intellectual dynamo, to give definition, form and intellectual leadership in developing the new social concepts and the new measures we obviously need. /29

The last level—providing technique and personnel is in some ways as profound as the philosophical problem. Through our school system every effective American must pass. From it are supplied, at every level, from top to bottom, the men and women whose individual efforts and whose combined opinion give direction to American national purpose. Out of the school system come the men who think and study and write, who push the world into new fields, intellectual and spiritual. From it also come the captains, the lieutenants, the engineers, the maintenance crews and the operating crews. They supply the men who must plan and direct the campaigns and conduct the continuous operations of life, civilian and, if necessary, military; and the men whose devotion and responsibility carry out the design to success. As international affairs become more complex, they are likely to have to pilot America towards the emerging stages of regional organization, and in the farther future, perhaps, towards a higher degree of world organization. Their combined resources of character and of capacity, from the children coming out of grammar school to the Doctors of Philosophy attacking great problems in social or physical science, will determine what happens. The educational system, in conjunction with their parents, will determine what they are. /30

We are fortunate in having a country and a system technically and physically able to produce material goods enough for everyone, beyond the dreams of our grandfathers. Do we also have spiritual and intellectual resources capable of mobilizing this enormous heritage? We are at long last learning that this cannot and will not be decently done by Madison Avenue, or smart sales campaigns, or political quackery. Clearly appeals to not-so-enlightened self-interest, excesses based on opinion polls do not assist. We know that the rat race for status-symbols is a pathetic humbug propagated by hucksters for personal gain. From our education we are entitled to have a product of graduates who know this, and who cannot be fooled into false values by the monkey-business of public relations counsel. /31

All this means a value system. It means teachers who teach according to that system. It means a public life carried on in that system. It requires men who would rather not be in office than get office by false promises, or by promising to support measures they believe are unsound, or who, once in office, want merely to coast from election to election. It means judging statements with fearless honesty. It means social engineers at all levels, from the village council to Washington, who act with the integrity of trustees for their community. It means lawyers (by trade I am a lawyer) who use their technique to secure justice and honorable arrangements, instead of peddling influence. /32

The speech

1. What is Berle's specific purpose in this speech? Where is it best stated?
2. In what ways is the speech adapted to the particular audience? How would you change it if you were asked to deliver it to a meeting of the National Association of Manufacturers? A Congressional committee? Your speech class?
3. Outline the speech. What *pattern of organization* described in the Glossary does it follow most closely? Attack or defend the use of this pattern.
4. What do the crises listed in paragraphs 6-8 have to do with the speech as a whole? Do they indicate a need? Represent points to be developed? Or what? Does such prophesying get the speech off to a shaky start?
5. Attack or defend the order of issues stated in paragraph 15 and developed in the subsequent paragraphs. Be as specific as you can in showing what is lost and/or gained by this order.
6. What is meant by the expression "value system" in the last paragraph? What do you gather Berle thinks is wrong with our present value system? To whom would he have us look for improvement in the system? For Berle, what presumably is a desirable value system?
7. Would you say that Berle is arguing in this speech for a planned economy and against private enterprise? Develop your answer in detail.
8. Characterize Berle's style. In doing so, compare it with the style of at least one other speech in this section, "Ethics and Morals." Do you think this speech would have been an easy one to listen to? Defend your answer.
9. Thinking over Berle's speech as a whole, would you say that he has persuaded you of the need for higher ethical standards in American life? Has he indicated convincingly the ways in which we can meet this need? In answering each question, list specifically the various forms of *proof* that Berle used (see Glossary).

For further study and discussion

1. Do you feel that a falling off in personal and national morality is at the heart of our national and international crises? Develop your answer in detail.
2. Do you find evidence of moral irresponsibility in student speeches and essays? Consider not only so obvious a matter as plagiarism but also such things as factual inaccuracy, exaggeration, false categorical generalizations, and undue coloring in details and choice of words.
3. What is "planned obsolescence"? Have you found examples of it in commodities you own? Do you think industrialists should be free to make their products the way they want to make them? Is this the "American way"?
4. What is popularly meant by the expression "Madison Avenue"? What means does Madison Avenue use to mold American thought? How effective are these means? What are the values commonly attributed to Madison Avenue?
5. In what precise ways are American colleges and universities responsible for American attitudes and values? Develop your answer in detail.
6. Do you think we can make any substantial change in our value system without more federal planning and control? Would you be willing to accept more control from Washington if it resulted in more money for education, housing, conservation, and the like?
7. Do you feel that your college lectures and discussions have failed to face up to the central issue—whether life has any enduring significance? Do you believe that the college classroom is a place where such an issue should be faced? Explain your position.
8. If you were to decide to adopt a value system in which

material things play a less dominant role than they now play for you, what precisely would you do? Spell out your answer in detail.

Suggestions for further reading

America and the Intellectuals, a Symposium (New York, 1953)
Donald C. Blaisdell, **American Democracy under Pressure** (New York, 1957)
Denis Brogan, **American Themes** (London, 1948)
Morris R. Cohen, **American Thought** (Chicago, 1954)
Ralph E. Flanders, **Letter to a Generation** (Boston, 1956)
Robert L. Heilbroner, **The Future as History** (New York, 1960)
Adlai E. Stevenson, **What I Think** (New York, 1956)
P. G. Wodehouse, **America, I Like You** (New York, 1956)

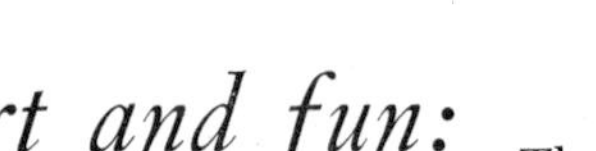

Comfort and fun: morality in a nice society

DANIEL LERNER

Daniel Lerner (1917-), a social scientist, has taught at various schools in the United States and France. During World War II he served in Europe with the U.S. Army in the Psychological Warfare Division and during that period received the Bronze Star and the Purple Heart.

A member of numerous learned societies, Lerner has received from France the *Palmes Academique* and has been designated *Officier d'Academie*. At present he is Ford Professor of International Communication in the department of economics and senior research associate of the Center for International Studies at the Massachusetts Institute of Technology. He is the author of *Sykewar: Psychological Warfare Against Germany* (1949); *Propaganda in War and Crisis* (1951); *The Policy Sciences*, with H. D. Lasswell (1951); *The Nazi Elite* (1951); *France Defeats E.D.C.*, with Raymond Aron (1957); *The Passing of Traditional Society in the Middle East* (1958).

This speech was originally delivered from notes and then written in its present form. Lerner wrote that his talk was given in January 1958 to the Faculty Seminar of The Institute for Social and Religious Studies, a group of people from universities, foundations, business, and public affairs who met for several years under the chairmanship of the late Lyman Bryson to discuss questions of ethical and responsible behavior in the contemporary world.

Normally, Mr. Lerner went on to say, he speaks only to groups with a high degree of interest and at least semi-professional competence in current world affairs. Such speaking occasions have ranged over recent years from a small selected panel of high government officials at the International Affairs Seminar (sponsored by the American Friends Service Committee) to an audience of several hundred colonels at the Air War College and Army War College. According to Mr. Lerner, "For such groups, the rule to follow is very simple: since these are meat-and-potatoes people, I try to deliver a nutritious and satisfying main dish, and go light on the trimmings."

In the following speech Mr. Lerner said he tried to show "that as a society we are not doing nearly so bad as some of our critics would have us believe."[1]

The living generation of Americans has quietly acquired a new human right—the right to be constantly entertained—which is conferred upon us by the mass media and underwritten by the business structure of radio, movies, picture magazines, digests, book clubs and, surpassing all others, television. This is a quiet right because it has not yet figured in any ideological manifestoes. The Atlantic Charter, the Four Freedoms, and the Declaration of the United Nations are all equally silent upon the right to be continuously entertained. But this does not impede the rapid spread of this particular right, which is quietly working the largest sort of transformation possible in the affairs of any society—by altering the levels of desire, the categories of contentment, and the criteria of judgment among its citizens. /1

Some of the symptoms of this transformation have been widely noted and just as widely attacked. Few among our intellectual spokesmen have many kind words to say for the mass media. Their impact, while widely discussed, is rarely studied, usually deplored and not too well understood. Juvenile delinquency has been attributed to movies and comics. Television, in its brief career, has already been found guilty of the New Illiteracy. A terribly stern justice has given public floggings to the "other-directed organization man in the gray flannel suit." /2

[1]Letter to the editors, June 16, 1960.

But these summary judgments may be too hasty. They may relieve the anguish of those who respect the old austerities by overlooking the virtues that others find in the new conveniences. In reading the rash of morality plays about executives and suburbanites coinciding with the work of David Riesman, Erich Fromm, William Holly Whyte, I am reminded of the carol "God Rest You Merry, Gentlemen!" There it is suggested that "to save us all from Satan's power" we must heed the "tidings of comfort and joy." Those who struggle so mightily with the diabolical mass media sometimes fail to notice their tidings of comfort and fun. /3

There is no room for dogma in such matters, but there is much room for inquiry. Is the "other-directed" man really the "other-respecting" man? Is the "organization man" really the "organized man"? There has been a change in America's psychic weather, no doubt, but perhaps the change is not so joyless as some suppose. What we need, paraphrasing Spinoza, is neither to weep nor to laugh—but to understand. /4

In the transformation of American morality, now well advanced, the mass media are both index and agent. Every facet of each person's and each family's daily round is touched in some way, and it is the whole "style of life" that needs study. An apt phrase that has been proposed is "fun morality." Under the dispensation of fun morality, the old key proposition about "being good" is transformed into "having a good time." There is little doubt that Americans today are more deferential than their ancestors were, or any other living people are, toward the virtues and values of having a good time. /5

This small shift in vocabulary represents a large shift in American practices and perspectives. Perhaps basic is the drive to transform the notion that ours is an "economy of abundance" from a fine phrase to an everyday reality. There is nothing new to American ideology in the high valuation placed upon widespread sharing of wealth. Jefferson based the stability of democratic society upon possession, by a substantial majority, of a real stake in its economic life. Herbert Hoover, or his aides, popularized the phrase "two chickens in every pot." The new thing is that this desire for a wide sharing of wealth has, in the present American generation, come closer to realization than ever before in history. There is only slight exaggeration in the propaganda put out by the New York Stock Exchange that we are a "nation of investors" and "every man a shareholder." Celebrating this state of affairs is the new direction that the American social conscience appears to have taken. /6

In the early days of the New Deal, America's social conscience was heavily preoccupied with the survival of "one third of the nation." Since that time, with employment and income running at all-time highs, the social conscience has shifted to assuring every man's *comfort.* The objective is to create conditions under which nearly all can be "haves"—and in which "have-nots" do not become an "internalized proletariat," as Toynbee claims to be the historic rule. The public welfare now is looked after by public and private organizations, and this requires organization men. /7

The theory that every man has a right to comfortable conditions of life is the economic counterpart of the theory that every man has the right to be continuously entertained. Comfort and fun go together. This leads to a quite different perspective than that which has governed most societies in the past. We appear to be, as a nation, committed to the lifeways of *non*adversity. The Spencerian gloss on the Darwinian doctrine has lost its claim to credence. We no longer believe that life needs to be a struggle in which only the fittest survive. On the contrary, we seem to have become convinced that life can be relatively pleasant for all and that all may survive at a rather high level of contentment. /8

This, right or wrong, is a revolutionary new idea in the world. It directs effort toward creating those conditions of life which enable people to "take things easy." The old puritan ethic (or perhaps, more exactly, simply "Protestant"), with its emphasis on effort, ambition, achievement, struggle and success, has yielded to a whole new array of words expressing the new conception of right conduct and the good life. The shift is from "getting on" to "getting along." The emphasis is on "being nice." /9

Naturally, the puritan ethic dies hard. For the past three centuries it governed conceptions of right conduct in much of the Western world—and particularly in those countries which made the greatest technological and industrial progress. It had come to seem, indeed, the only possible view of morality. To those of us still committed to an ethic of effort and achievement, the new "fun morality" seems a form of moral degeneracy. We are concerned about "conformism." We attack the "adjusted man" as a mere unthinking Babbitt. We inflict heavy verbal scars upon the "organization man," who represents a model of success other than that on which most of us were raised. /10

But the attack on fun morality is perhaps itself less thoughtful and less virtuous than we imagine. Associated with fun morality are many practices which those who don't love Lucy and disdain Elvis would *not* like to see abandoned. Would those who scorn "consumer mentality" also prefer less real consumption? It is quite possible that we cannot have our kind of society without some version of fun morality. I do not say that this *is* so. I say only that there are plausible reasons for thinking it may be so. The hypothesis merits more consideration than it has been given. The burden of responsibility for acquiring knowledge, not manufacturing stereotypes, falls most heavily on precisely those of us who suspect the symptoms of a popular culture without wishing to undermine a consumer's economy and a representative democracy. /11

How did this new American mixture come about? The crucial word in the dramatic transformation of American lifeways is "mobility." This nation of immigrants was founded upon the mobility of the individual. Such mobility became possible in the New World only when the Old World had achieved conditions of life which unbound men from their native heath. Once ordinary men found themselves free to move from their ancestral soil, they began to move in huge numbers from farms to flats and from fields to factories. As the physical means for transporting people improved, they began to move overseas in growing numbers. America was the goal of many millions. This bore little resemblance to the migrant or crusading hordes of earlier centuries, driven by war and famine. This was movement by individuals, each having made a personal choice to seek elsewhere his own version of a better life. /12

Physical mobility of this type induced ideas of *social mobility* previously unknown in the Old World. Stirred by new desires, these new Americans voiced new demands. Each wanted his own stake in the new society and his own say in how it was to be organized. So there came to prevail in this country ideas of equal opportunity and democratic governance which would have been "unseemly" in the Old World. Perhaps no single institution so clearly expressed this new spirit as the victory of free public education for all who wanted it. This certified the idea that every man was entitled to a fair chance at winning for himself a good life by his own efforts and merits. Thus developed a new kind of participant society—a secular and rational society based on equal rights for each individual. Along with it, through the generations, developed a new style of personality. /13

A mobile society has to be rational, for the calculus of choice shapes individual behavior and conditions its rewards. People come to see social arrangements as manipulable rather than ordained, and to gauge their own prospects in terms of achievement rather than heritage. The test of merit is skill, not birth. Ways of thinking and acting are instruments of intention, not articles of faith; they succeed or fail by the test of what they accomplish, not what they worship. So whereas traditional men tended to reject innovation by saying "It has never been thus," modern Americans were more likely to ask only "Does it work?" and try the new way without further ado. /14

The psychic gap between these two postures is vast. It took long interweaving of ways of doing with ways of thinking before men could work out a style of living daily with change that *felt* consistent and seamless. Mobile society required a mobile personality, a self-system so adaptive to change that rearrangement is its permanent mode. It required the experience of psychic mobility through many generations to evolve participant institutions which, to ordinary men, felt "normal." /15

The mobile person shows a high capacity for identifying himself with new and strange aspects of the environment. He is capable of handling unfamiliar demands upon himself outside his habitual experience. The capacity for psychic mobility tends to enlarge a man's identity in two ways: *projection* facilitates identification by assigning to others certain preferred attributes of the self (others are "incorporated" because they are "like me"); *introjection* enlarges identity by attributing to the self certain desirable attributes of the object (others are incorporated because "I" am like them, or would like to be like them). We use the term "empathy" as shorthand for these techniques of enlarging a man's "self-system." In ordinary parlance, empathy is the capacity to see oneself in the other fellow's situation. This capacity leads us to put a high value on negotiation, mediation, compromise—on "getting along." /16

Empathy is the psychic instrument which enables newly mobile persons to act effectively in the world we live in. This is why the mobile personality is not to be regarded as mere psychic aberration or moral degeneration, but as a social phenomenon with a history. Our concern must be with the large historical movement (which started in the West and is now becoming apparent elsewhere)—a movement in which a strong capacity for empathy is the distinctive psychic component. And it is useful to study the way in which the person who possesses this quality to a high degree tends to become also the cash customer, the radio listener, the voter and the "nice person." /17

This emphasis upon empathy is dominant only in modern society—which is distinctively industrial, urban, literate and participant. (A society is participant if most people in it go through school, read newspapers, receive cash payments in jobs they are free to change, buy goods in a free market, vote in free elections, and express opinions on many matters which are not their business.) Any society develops a predominant personal style which people find most appropriate for daily life; the "style" of modern society is distinctive for its capacity to rearrange the "self-system" on short notice. /18

This is the style partially characterized by David Riesman as "other-directed." But the term "other-direction" has acquired, among our self-abnegating intelligentsia, a negative moral charge. The term "empathy" more nearly does justice to the elements of skill and the positive social functions of other-direction. Empathy enables people to respond efficiently to strange and varied stimuli; in so doing it enlarges the self-system of ordinary people. By enabling them to "see" the other fellow's situation more readily, empathy provides the psychological underpinning for the participant lifeways of modern society. The latent statistical assertion involved here is this: in modern society *more* individuals exhibit a *high* empathic capacity than in any previous society. In brief, there has been a *net increase in human imaginativeness,* as construed, in modern society (whether the society be favorably interpreted as "participant," or unfavorably as "conformist"). /19

To identify psychic mobility with the proposition that there has been an increase in empathy—that more people now command a greater skill at imagining themselves in strange situations than did people in any previous historical epoch—is to assign a large function to popular culture, notably elementary education and mass media. The technical history of the popular arts illuminates their function as an empathy multiplier. A generation before Columbus sailed to the New World, Gutenberg set up his printing press. Press, radio, film and television today climax the evolution thus set into motion. The mass media opened to mankind the infinite *vicarious* universe. Many more millions of persons in the world were to be affected directly, and perhaps more profoundly, by the communication media than by the transportation agencies. For the vicarious universe not only involves more people; it involves them in a different order of psychic experience. /20

Vicarious experience requires other skills and stimulates other psychic mechanisms from those used in travel. Travel involves direct personal exposure to a complex natural environment, whereas mediated experience explores mainly the simplified settings contrived by those who have prepared the "experience." Thus, while the traveler is apt to become bewildered by the profusion of strange sights and sounds, the radio listener or movie viewer is likely to be enjoying a composed and orchestrated version of some new reality. He has the benefit of more facile perception of the new experience as a "whole," with the concomitant advantage (which is sometimes illusory) of facile comprehension. /21

On the other hand, the reader-listener-viewer loses the traveler's pragmatic advantage of being physically present in the strange environment, of having to make responsive action toward the stimuli it presents. The passive receiver of mediated communications finds his response to new stimuli necessarily confined to his own interior. Thus, while the stimuli he receives are usually less complex, the demands of exclusively interior response are often much more strenuous. The inhibition of overt response is a learned behavior and a difficult one. It was common, in the early days of movies, for persons strained beyond endurance to throw themselves or some objects at the screen to stop the villain from strangling the heroine. Even our sophisticated youngsters today will sometimes, at an agonizing moment in the television show, hide their faces. /22

The point is that mediated experience simplifies *perception* (what we "see") while greatly complicating *response* (what we "do"). In this way the media have helped to shape the modern, highly responsive self-system, ready to rearrange itself on short notice from a variety of cues. As history's great teacher of the skills of empathy, the mass media have multiplied psychic mobility among men in the West. (This is not to be construed as genial endorsement of current media operations, which too often tend to routinize, not stimulate, imagination.) /23

This capacity to empathize, to see ourselves in the other fellow's situation, is essential to our "nice person" morality. Its spread has made America a society in which most people can "take things easy"—can make it a rule of life to "get along with everybody." It underlies the national distrust of odd-balls, eight-balls and screwballs. It has made "puritanism" a pejorative word and "straitlaced" not less so. It leads to suspicion of a person who is "too ambitious," who "tries too hard" to overcome an obstacle instead of simply "sweating it out." The course of life in a nice society is "give and take"; the rule is "live and let live." /24

Popular attitudes of this sort can be painful for intellectuals and others who still live by (or at least believe they do) the old puritan ethic as compared with, in Holly Whyte's phrase, a "social ethic." But it may well be that the older ethic is obsolescent, not merely because the newer morality is more comfortable for most people but, possibly, because it is genuinely superior as a guide to life in an abundant society. Some clues to the newness of American lifeways are furnished by the attitudes toward America expressed in other countries. There is, for example, the attack launched from the highly "sophisticated" culture of contemporary France. /25

Because American intellectuals have borrowed ideas from France over the past three centuries, they have seen no reason to change their ways during the past three decades. Many postwar slogans deprecating American conformism and vulgarity have spread from France over much of the world, and even into our own country. These slogans have been more repeated than scrutinized. For some years there was much talk about American "bathtub culture"; but this left wide open the question of whether greater morality necessarily attaches to a population with a significantly higher proportion of microbes. There was also a period of talk about "Coca-Cola culture"; but this did not explore the question of whether a people is more virtuous because even more heavily alcoholic than we are. It is not without interest that Coca-Cola, in fact, spread rapidly through France, as all over the world, and remains, so far as I know, the only drink which can be bought by people almost anywhere for the equivalent of a nickel (except, of course, in the heavily protected French beverage market). /26

Much of this fancy talk about American vulgarization of taste and standardization of mind stems from a potent distrust, among French intellectuals, of our extraordinarily developed "popular culture." The fear of the mass media seems to me a *class* attitude of the least admirable variety. In its simplest form, this may be only the fear of technological unemployment: the mass media require skills quite different from those usually found among the traditional intelligentsia. On a somewhat more complex level, the French intelligentsia defends certain standards constructed largely by itself over past centuries and attacks everything which appears to threaten the institutional arrangements by which those standards are maintained. These standards express traditional and class aesthetic preferences, but often they parade as ethical judgments and are delivered in a high moral tone. A fine case study could be made of the "TV snob," usually a person with some pretentions to intellectuality, and nowhere more numerous than among the French intelligentsia. It is not irrelevant that artistic life in France has failed to flourish under the continued prevalence of this attitude. I refer here not only to the failure of the French intelligentsia to develop new creative lines in the modern arts of the mass media, but even the drying up of the old French creative spirit in the traditional arts. /27

This is not to be construed as a counterattack on French anti-Americanism. My own Francophilia lies too deep to be uprooted by the current show of petulance among a people who gave our modern world its great Cartesian myth of rationality. It is no easy thing to "speak for" a great power which has been diminished, a lovely culture which has been bypassed; and French intellectuals today have a tough assignment. But one who shares their heritage has a right to expect, a duty to demand, better of them than the defensive negativism they have been producing. In any case, the slogans created and diffused by an ambivalent intelligentsia ought to be scrutinized and evaluated before they are merely repeated by Americans. For there is a point underlying French petulance that goes deeper than French—or American—parochialism. It is a point on which may turn the future of Western civilization. /28

The great dialogue of the Western tradition has been "the dialogue of Self with Self"—in a word, conscience. If it is agreed that the dialogue has taken a new turn in modern times, has become a "dialogue of Self with Others," what does this mean for the future of Western civilization? Can *social* conscience—responsibility to others—adequately perform the functions historically assigned to individual conscience, which was responsible only to God or to the God-within-oneself? /29

The question is too important for a glib solution. It is all too easy to settle such problems by facile, derogatory references to hell fixation or stargazing. There are many people, less concerned with damnation or salvation than with the prospects for a decent future on this earth, who want reasonable answers, not easy quips. /30

The question has been posed, but even the few serious efforts to deal with it base their judgment on untested assumptions. It is not at all clear that Riesman's "other-directed" man is incapable of "autonomy" (as Riesman himself, if not his acolytes, has pointed out). It is even less clear why Whyte's "organization man" should not be taken as a highly moral man in a new sense—as an approximation of a model for the rational fusion of individual with social conscience. Of the treatises by Sloan Wilson, Vance Packard and A. C. Spectorsky, one must say that suburbia merits better than clever travesties lacking wit or insight. /31

Suburbia is, in parochial terms, the fulfillment of

the American Dream for the full range of "middle" classes of our society. Its concern with nice houses and cars, with the competition between school and TV for the education of its children, with community relations and civic activities—all these occur on a quasi-educated level of discourse that makes an easy mark for the American intelligentsia. But American suburbia, in global terms, may be the functional equivalent of what most peoples of the world seem, nowadays, to want. For suburbia may be the highest reach of civilized life that has yet been represented as within the grasp of common humanity. /32

A few years ago I visited a walled village of Iran, whose daily life-ways antedate the Christian era. There, among peasants in rags, a uniquely enterprising soul had just returned from the distant market town, where he had sold his crop for cash. Overstimulated by the sight of a city, he had spent his first cash on a battery radio, baubles for his wife, a ready-made suit for himself (the first in his village), and a calendar for their mud hut. The calendar now decorating their wall (it had been reproduced by a Teheran bank) portrayed the American Family—Dad, Mom, Junior and Sister—on the lawn in front of their ranch house with a station wagon parked in the driveway. O bright dream of suburbia! /33

Item: In suburbia *everybody has cash—or credit!* Decisions as to the desirable ratio to be maintained between cash and credit elicit real ingenuity in family conclaves. In traditional society there is no cash; in "modern" France there is no credit; in "modern" Russia there is no choice. Only in America is the great dialogue between present pleasure and future felicity thrown open for discussion and decision by the generality of individuals and families. "You pays your money and you takes your choice"—there resonates, in uncultivated but understandable tones, the American music of humanity. /34

Item: In suburbia *everybody has opinions!* As a student of the Middle East, I first learned what a giant step this was from the stoic, isolate silence of the constricted peasant in traditional society. Only in the lowest reaches of America's slums is there still any question as to whether people ought to have opinions. In the climactic scene of *Sweet Thursday*, John Steinbeck relates how the madam of a whorehouse prepares one of her hustlers, not really made for the business, to go out into the world of respectability. The first rule is to keep her mouth shut:

"Next thing is opinions. You and me is always busting out with opinions. Hell, Suzy, we ain't got no opinions! We just say stuff we heard or seen in the movies. We're scared we'll miss something, like running for a bus. That's the second rule: lay off opinions because you ain't really got any."

But in suburbia everybody has opinions, however acquired, and his right to them is beyond challenge. As a social psychologist somewhat wearied by the theories of my trade, I have sat through hours of P.T.A. meetings, bemused by the easy familiarity of my neighbors with the views of Doctors Spock, Gesell, Dewey and Freud. It is not necessary to be impressed by the technical skill displayed in handling these ideas in order to be overwhelmed by their extraordinary diffusion among a population which, not so many years ago, got their ideas on these matters mainly from Mother. /35

If all this sounds too much like a paean, I want to make it clear that the praise is for what freedom has accomplished in America until now. What may follow is another matter. Arnold Toynbee assures us that the passing of the Judaeo-Christian tradition spells the end of the West. That admirable Jesuit Father La Farge suggests that the new secularized dialogue of Self with Others can only sustain an afterglow" of the scintillant Western epoch. But how do they know? Toynbee, by a series of brilliantly executed tautologies which mainly recapitulate his own characterological preferences; Father La Farge, with his broader tolerance, by his wish that humanity shall not sin against itself. These are fine, decent, intelligent men. So are David Riesman and Holly Whyte. They care for men and worry for their humanity. But I am not sure that any of them has knowledge surpassing his own anxieties. /36

Nor have I. My exhortation is no counsel of unbounded optimism. But it does advise against selling short, in a time of crisis, the good portfolio of stocks that we hold. I think we can weather the storm of a clamorous world population wanting our dividends while they do not share our calculations, risks, investments. I think we can do so by sharing our dividends with others while they learn how to calculate risks, by sharing our know-how about getting on while getting along. I think that man's responsibility to others may produce a superior civilization even to that which evolved under the aegis of man's responsibility to himself—that reshaping the great dialogue as Self with Others can have a happy outcome for common humanity. I think that the mass media may be the principal instrument whereby men around the world can swiftly acquire the human skills needed to cope with their accelerating hopes and dreams. I think; but who, as yet, knows? /37

The speech

1. How do Lerner's opening remarks set the stage for his talk?
2. What was Lerner's audience like? What kind of background could he assume they had?
3. Prepare a précis of the speech that will bring out the main points and show their relation.
4. What pattern of organization is employed in this talk?
5. List at least five familiar phrases to which Lerner has given a new twist. What is the rhetorical effect of this device?
6. Comment on Lerner's use of irony. Who or what is treated ironically? Does this ironic treatment prepare you for the central idea stated in the conclusion? Does the title prepare you for the content and tone of the conclusion?
7. What is Lerner's scale of values? What, for example, does he prize most highly in American life? Least highly?
8. What precisely is the rhetorical effect of the speech on you? Does it confirm your present thought? Change it? Not affect it?

For further study and discussion

1. Do you agree that our society prizes comfort and fun above all? Expand your answer with illustrations.
2. Explain the seeming paradox in the phrase "fun morality." Demonstrate to what extent the phrase can be applied to American life.
3. What is the basis for contemporary criticism of business executives, ad men, and suburbanites by such writers as Riesman, Fromm, Packard, and Whyte? Is the criticism primarily on moral grounds?
4. To what extent do you believe the puritan ethic is dying out? Develop your answer with as many facts and examples as you can assemble.
5. How long do you think our physical mobility will continue to increase? Cite supporting evidence.
6. Do you believe social mobility is still on the increase? Explain your answer.
7. Do you agree that we have a "Coca-Cola culture"? Before answering this question, tell what the term means to you.
8. Do you agree that everyone in suburbia has opinions? If so, what are the implications as you see them?
9. Does the shift from man's responsibility to himself to man's responsibility to others imply for you a decline in moral standards? Explore the question in detail. (For the most direct statement in this book of man's responsibility to himself, read Emerson's "The American Scholar," pp. 36-46.)
10. What are the best things that can be said of contemporary American society? The worst things?

Suggestions for further reading

Ruth Anshen, ed., ***Moral Principles of Action*** (New York, 1952)
Erich Fromm, ***Man for Himself*** (New York, 1947)
————, ***The Sane Society*** (New York, 1955)
John H. Hallowell, ***The Moral Foundation of Democracy*** (Chicago, 1954)
Arnold H. M. Lunn, ***Enigma; A Study of Moral Rearmament*** (London, 1957)
Reinhold Niebuhr, ***Moral Man and Immoral Society*** (New York, 1932)
Harold Prichard, ***Moral Obligation*** (Oxford, 1949)
David Riesman, ***Individualism Reconsidered, and Other Essays*** (Chicago, 1954)
Arnold Toynbee, ***A Study of History,*** an abridgment of Vols. 1-10 by D. C. Somervell (New York, 1946-1957)
William H. Whyte, ***The Organization Man*** (New York, 1956)

The three parts of morality

C. S. LEWIS

C. S. Lewis, the British novelist, was born in Belfast, Ireland, in 1898 and entered Oxford in 1918. After serving in the First World War, Lewis became a lecturer at University College, Oxford, and in 1925 a fellow and tutor at Magdalen College, where he still lectures on English literature. Lewis has been described as a shy, sensitive, scholarly man who likes "sitting up till the small hours in someone's college rooms talking nonsense, poetry, theology, and metaphysics over beer, tea, and pipes."

Lewis has written a number of novels, including *Out of the Silent Planet* (1938) and the famous *Screwtape Letters* (1942), of which C. E. M. Joad said: "Mr. Lewis possesses the rare gift of being able to make righteousness readable."

In 1942 Lewis gave several talks over the British Broadcasting Corporation system which were subsequently published in 1943 as *Christian Behavior* and later anthologized in *Mere Christianity*. In his talks Lewis concerned himself with morality in relations between man and man, in the things inside each man, and in relations between man and the power that made him. Two talks are reprinted here: "The Three Parts of Morality" and "Social Morality."

Lewis' talks were widely discussed at the time of their delivery. In the *New Republic* (April 24, 1944) British correspondent Alistair Cooke, commenting on the reception of Lewis' speeches, said: "From the way the talks were received in Britain and from the eagerness of American networks to have Mr. Lewis shed light on our own dark continent, it may be assumed that the personal values of several million Britons and Americans stand in imminent danger of the befuddlement at which Mr. Lewis is so transparently adroit." In contrast, F. J. Moore, writing in *Christian Century* (January 26, 1944), insisted that "Mr. Lewis' special characteristics in thought and style are exhibited at their best in the discussion of ethical questions." A careful study of the following speeches should help you decide whose judgment—Joad's and Moore's or Cooke's—seems most just.

There is a story about a schoolboy who was asked what he thought God was like. He replied that, as far as he could make out, God was "The sort of person who is always snooping round to see if anyone is enjoying himself and then trying to stop it." And I am afraid that is the sort of idea that the word Morality raises in a good many people's minds: something that interferes, something that stops you having a good time. In reality, moral rules are directions for running the human machine. Every moral rule is there to prevent a breakdown, or a strain, or a friction, in the running of that machine. That is why these rules at first seem to be constantly interfering with our natural inclinations. When you are being taught how to use any machine, the instructor keeps on saying, "No, don't do it like that," because, of course, there are all sorts of things that look all right and seem to you the natural way of treating the machine, but do not really work. /1

Some people prefer to talk about moral "ideals" rather than moral rules and about moral "idealism" rather than moral obedience. Now it is, of course, quite true that moral perfection is an "ideal" in the sense that we cannot achieve it. In that sense every kind of perfection is, for us humans, an ideal; we cannot succeed in being perfect car drivers or perfect tennis players or in drawing perfectly straight lines. But there is another sense in which it is very misleading to call moral perfection an ideal. When a man says that a certain woman, or house, or ship, or garden is "his ideal" he does not mean (unless he is rather a fool) that everyone else ought to have the same ideal. In such matters we are entitled to have different tastes and, therefore, different ideals. But it is dangerous to describe a man who tries very hard to keep the moral law as a "man of high ideals," because this might lead you to think that moral perfection was a private taste of his own and that the rest of us were not called on to share it. This would be a disastrous mistake. Perfect behaviour may be as unattainable as perfect gear-changing when we drive; but it is a necessary ideal prescribed for all men by the very nature of the human machine just as perfect gear-changing is an ideal prescribed for all drivers by the very nature of cars. And it would be even more dangerous to think of oneself as a person "of high ideals" because one is trying to tell no lies at all (instead of only a few lies) or never to commit adultery (instead of committing it only seldom) or not to be a bully (instead of being only a moderate bully). It might lead you to become a prig and to think you were rather a special person who deserved to be congratulated on his "idealism." In reality you might just as well expect to be congratulated because, whenever you do a sum, you try to get it quite right. To be sure, perfect arithmetic is "an ideal"; you will certainly make some mistakes in some calculations. But there is nothing very fine about trying to be quite accurate at each step in each sum. It would be idiotic not to try; for every mistake is going to cause you trouble later on. In the same way every moral failure is going to cause trouble, probably to others and certainly to yourself. By talking about rules and obedience instead of "ideals" and "idealism" we help to remind ourselves of these facts. /2

Now let us go a step further. There are two ways in which the human machine goes wrong. One is when human individuals drift apart from one another, or else collide with one another and do one another damage, by cheating or bullying. The other is when things go wrong inside the individual—when the different parts of him (his different faculties and desires and so on) either drift apart or interfere with one another. You can get the idea plain if you think of us as a fleet of ships sailing in formation. The voyage will be a success only, in the first place, if the ships do not collide and get in one another's way; and, secondly, if each ship is seaworthy and has her engines in good order. As a matter of fact, you cannot have either of these two things without the other. If the ships keep on having collisions they will not remain seaworthy very long. On the other hand, if their steering gears are out of order they will not be able to avoid collisions. Or, if you like, think of humanity as a band playing a tune. To get a good result, you need two things. Each player's individual instrument must be in tune and also each must come in at the right moment so as to combine with all the others. /3

But there is one thing we have not yet taken into account. We have not asked where the fleet is trying to get to, or what piece of music the band is trying to play. The instruments might be all in tune and might all come in at the right moment, but even so the performance would not be a success if they had been engaged to provide dance music and actually played nothing but Dead Marches. And however well the fleet sailed, its voyage would be a failure if it were meant to reach New York and actually arrived at Calcutta. /4

Morality, then, seems to be concerned with three things. Firstly, with fair play and harmony between individuals. Secondly, with what might be called tidying up or harmonising the things inside each individual. Thirdly, with the general purpose of human life as a whole: what man was made for: what course the whole fleet ought to be on: what tune the conductor of the band wants it to play. /5

You may have noticed that modern people are nearly always thinking about the first thing and forgetting the other two. When people say in the newspapers that we are striving for Christian moral standards, they usually mean that we are striving for kindness and fair play between nations, and classes, and individuals; that is, they are thinking only of the first thing. When a man says about something he wants to do, "It can't be wrong because it doesn't do anyone else any harm," he is thinking only of the first thing. He is thinking it does not matter what his ship is like inside provided that he does not run into the next ship. And it is quite natural, when we start thinking about morality, to begin with the first thing, with social relations. For one thing, the results of bad morality in that sphere are so obvious and press on us every day: war and poverty and graft and lies and shoddy work. And also, as long as you stick to the first thing, there is very little disagreement about morality. Almost all people at all times have agreed (in theory) that human beings ought to be honest and kind and helpful to one another. But though it is natural to begin with all that, if our thinking about morality stops there, we might just as well not have thought at all. Unless we go on to the second thing—the tidying up inside each human being—we are only deceiving ourselves. /6

What is the good of telling the ships how to steer so as to avoid collisions if, in fact, they are such crazy old tubs that they cannot be steered at all? What is the good of drawing up, on paper, rules for social behaviour, if we know that, in fact, our greed, cowardice, ill temper, and self-conceit are going to prevent us from keeping them? I do not mean for a moment that we ought not to think, and think hard, about improvements in our social and economic system. What I do mean is that all that thinking will be mere moonshine unless we realise that nothing but the courage and unselfishness of individuals is ever going to make any system work properly. It is easy enough to remove the particular kinds of graft or bullying that go on under the present system: but as long as men are twisters or bullies they will find some new way of carrying on the old game under the new system. You cannot make men good by law: and without good men you cannot have a good society. That is why we must go on to think of the second thing: of morality inside the individual. /7

But I do not think we can stop there either. We are now getting to the point at which different beliefs about the universe lead to different behaviour. And it would seem, at first sight, very sensible to stop before we got there, and just carry on with those parts of morality that all sensible people agree about. But can we? Remember that religion involves a series of statements about facts, which must be either true or false. If they are true, one set of conclusions will follow about the right sailing of the human fleet: if they are false, quite a different set. For example, let us go back to the man who says that a thing cannot be wrong unless it hurts some other human being. He quite understands that he must not damage the other ships in the convoy, but he honestly thinks that what he does to his own ship is simply his own business. But does it not make a great difference whether his ship is his own property or not? Does it not make a great difference whether I am, so to speak, the landlord of my own mind and body, or only a tenant, responsible to the real landlord? If somebody else made me, for his own purposes, then I shall have a lot of duties which I should not have if I simply belonged to myself. /8

Again, Christianity asserts that every individual human being is going to live for ever, and this must be either true or false. Now there are a good many things which would not be worth bothering about if I were going to live only seventy years, but which I had better bother about very seriously if I am going to live for ever. Perhaps my bad temper or my jealousy are gradually getting worse—so gradually that the increase in seventy years will not be very noticeable. But it might be absolute hell in a million years: in fact, if Christianity is true, Hell is the precisely correct technical term for what it would be. And immortality makes this other difference, which, by the by, has a connection with the difference between totalitarianism and democracy. If individuals live only seventy years, then a state, or a nation, or a civilisation, which may last for a thousand years, is more important than an individual. But if Christianity is true, then the individual is not only more important but incomparably more important, for he is everlasting and the life of a state or a civilisation, compared with his, is only a moment. /9

It seems, then, that if we are to think about morality, we must think of all three departments: relations between man and man: things inside each man: and relations between man and the power that made him. We can all co-operate in the first one. Disagreements begin with the second and become serious with the third. It is in dealing with the third that the main differences between Christian and non-Christian morality come out. For the rest of this book I am going to assume the Christian point of view, and look at the whole picture as it will be if Christianity is true. /10

The speech

1. What is the specific purpose here? How does this talk set the context for the subsequent talks?
2. What assumptions does the speaker make? For instance, does he assume we have freedom of will? That life is purposeful? That the soul is immortal?
3. Show in detail whether the argument is primarily deductive or inductive.
4. Evaluate the analogy of the ships, commenting especially on its aptness and its rhetorical effectiveness.
5. Comment on the style. Do you find it especially adapted to radio speaking? What special demands, if any, does radio presentation make on a speaker, and how are they different from the requirements of television presentation?

For further study and discussion

1. Define *morality*. How does it differ from *ethics*? From *religion*?
2. In your opinion is one a Christian by living according to the Golden Rule?
3. How do one's beliefs about the nature of the universe affect his moral standards? Develop your answer with examples.
4. Evaluate the college students you know, using Lewis' "three parts of morality" as your criteria.

Suggestions for further reading

Crane Brinton, ***A History of Western Morals*** (New York, 1959)
Matthew, "The Sermon on the Mount"
Plato, ***Phaedo***
George N. Shuster, ***Education and Moral Wisdom*** (New York, 1960)

Social morality

C. S. LEWIS

The first thing to get clear about Christian morality between man and man is that in this department Christ did not come to preach any brand new morality. The Golden Rule of the New Testament (Do as you would be done by) is a summing up of what everyone, at bottom, had always known to be right. Really great moral teachers never do introduce new moralities: it is quacks and cranks who do that. As Dr. Johnson said, "People need to be reminded more often than they need to be instructed." The real job of every moral teacher is to keep on bringing us back, time after time, to the old simple principles which we are all so anxious not to see; like bringing a horse back and back to the fence it has refused to jump or bringing a child back and back to the bit in its lesson that it wants to shirk. /1

The second thing to get clear is that Christianity has not, and does not profess to have, a detailed political programme for applying "Do as you would be done by" to a particular society at a particular moment. It could not have. It is meant for all men at all times and the particular programme which suited one place or time would not suit another. And, anyhow, that is not how Christianity works. When it tells you to feed the hungry it does not give you lessons in cookery. When it tells you to read the Scriptures it does not give you lessons in Hebrew and Greek, or even in English grammar. It was never intended to replace or supersede the ordinary human arts and sciences: it is rather a director which will set them all to the right jobs, and a source of energy which will give them all new life, if only they will put themselves at its disposal. /2

People say, "The Church ought to give us a lead." That is true if they mean it in the right way, but false if they mean it in the wrong way. By the Church they ought to mean the whole body of practising Christians. And when they say that the Church should give us a lead, they ought to mean that some Christians—those who happen to have the right talents—should be economists and statesmen, and that all economists and statesmen should be Christians, and that their whole efforts in politics and economics should be directed to putting "Do as you would be done by" into action. If that happened, and if we others were really ready to take it, then we should find the Christian solution for our own social problems pretty quickly. But, of course, when they ask for a lead from the Church most people mean they want the clergy to put out a political programme. That is silly. The clergy are those particular people within the whole Church who have been specially trained and set aside to look after what concerns us as creatures who are going to live for ever: and we are asking them to do a quite different job for which they have not been trained. The job is really on us, on the laymen. The application of Christian principles, say, to trade unionism or education, must come from Christian trade unionists and Christian schoolmasters: just as Christian literature comes from Christian novelists and dramatists—not from the bench of bishops getting together and trying to write plays and novels in their spare time. /3

All the same, the New Testament, without going into details, gives us a pretty clear hint of what a fully Christian society would be like. Perhaps it gives us more than we can take. It tells us that there are to be no passengers or parasites: if man does not work, he ought not to eat. Every one is to work with his own hands, and what is more, every one's work is to produce something good: there will be no manufacture of silly luxuries and then of sillier advertisements to persuade us to buy them. And there is to be no "swank" or "side," no putting on airs. To that extent a Christian society would be what we now call Leftist. On the other hand, it is always insisting on obedience —obedience (and outward marks of respect) from all of us to properly appointed magistrates, from children to parents, and (I am afraid this is going to be very unpopular) from wives to husbands. Thirdly, it is to be a cheerful society: full of singing and rejoicing, and regarding worry or anxiety as wrong. Courtesy is one of the Christian virtues; and the New Testament hates what it calls "busybodies." /4

If there were such a society in existence and you or I visited it, I think we should come away with a curious impression. We should feel that its economic life was very socialistic and, in that sense, "advanced," but that its family life and its code of manners were rather old-fashioned—perhaps even ceremonious and aristocratic. Each of us would like some bits of it, but I am afraid very few of us would like the whole thing. That is just what one would expect if Christianity is the total plan for the human machine. We have all departed from that total plan in different ways, and each of us wants to make out that his own modification of the original plan is the plan itself. You will find this again and again about anything that is really Christian: every one is attracted by bits of it and wants to pick out those bits and leave the rest. That is why we do not get much further: and that is why people who are fighting for quite opposite things can both say they are fighting for Christianity. /5

Now another point. There is one bit of advice given to us by the ancient heathen Greeks, and by the Jews in the Old Testament, and by the great Christian teachers of the Middle Ages, which the modern economic system has completely disobeyed. All these people told us not to lend money at interest: and lending money at interest—what we call investment —is the basis of our whole system. Now it may not absolutely follow that we are wrong. Some people say that when Moses and Aristotle and the Christians agreed in forbidding interest (or "usury" as they called it), they could not foresee the joint stock company, and were only thinking of the private moneylender, and that, therefore, we need not bother about what they said. That is a question I cannot decide on. I am not an economist and I simply do not know whether the investment system is responsible for the state we are in or not. This is where we want the Christian economist. But I should not have been honest if I had not told you that three great civilisations had agreed (or so it seems at first sight) in condemning the very thing on which we have based our whole life. /6

One more point and I am done. In the passage where the New Testament says that every one must work, it gives as a reason "in order that he may have something to give to those in need." Charity—giving to the poor—is an essential part of Christian morality: in the frightening parable of the sheep and the goats it seems to be the point on which everything turns.

Some people nowadays say that charity ought to be unnecessary and that instead of giving to the poor we ought to be producing a society in which there were no poor to give to. They may be quite right in saying that we ought to produce that kind of society. But if anyone thinks that, as a consequence, you can stop giving in the meantime, then he has parted company with all Christian morality. I do not believe one can settle how much we ought to give. I am afraid the only safe rule is to give more than we can spare. In other words, if our expenditure on comforts, luxuries, amusements, etc., is up to the standard common among those with the same income as our own, we are probably giving away too little. If our charities do not at all pinch or hamper us, I should say they are too small. There ought to be things we should like to do and cannot do because our charitable expenditure excludes them. I am speaking now of "charities" in the common way. Particular cases of distress among your own relatives, friends, neighbours or employees, which God, as it were, forces upon your notice, may demand much more: even to the crippling and endangering of your own position. For many of us the great obstacle to charity lies not in our luxurious living or desire for more money, but in our fear—fear of insecurity. This must often be recognised as a temptation. Sometimes our pride also hinders our charity; we are tempted to spend more than we ought on the showy forms of generosity (tipping, hospitality) and less than we ought on those who really need our help. /7

And now, before I end, I am going to venture on a guess as to how this section has affected any who have read it. My guess is that there are some Leftist people among them who are very angry that it has not gone further in that direction, and some people of an opposite sort who are angry because they think it has gone much too far. If so, that brings us right up against the real snag in all this drawing up of blueprints for a Christian society. Most of us are not really approaching the subject in order to find out what Christianity says: we are approaching it in the hope of finding support from Christianity for the views of our own party. We are looking for an ally where we are offered either a Master or—a Judge. I am just the same. There are bits in this section that I wanted to leave out. And that is why nothing whatever is going to come of such talks unless we go a much longer way round. A Christian society is not going to arrive until most of us really want it: and we are not going to want it until we become fully Christian. I may repeat "Do as you would be done by" till I am black in the face, but I cannot really carry it out till I love my neighbour as myself: and I cannot learn to love my neighbour as myself till I learn to love God: and I cannot learn to love God except by learning to obey Him. And so, as I warned you, we are driven on to something more inward—driven on from social matters to religious matters. For the longest way round is the shortest way home. /8

The speech

1. What does Lewis mean by "social morality"? What is its basic principle?
2. If Christian morality is simply a reassertion of old simple principles, where and when *did* these principles originate? Does Lewis make this clear? If so, how? Is it important that he should clearly point out the origins of these principles to accomplish his purpose?
3. Does Lewis believe reform should begin with the individual or with a change in the social structure? Cite passages to substantiate your answer.
4. What is the pattern of organization in this talk? Can the talk be easily outlined? If so, show that it can.
5. Show whether Lewis allows for varying standards of morality or whether he assumes a kind of absolute morality. To motivate a radio audience toward belief, would one of these assumptions about morality be a more compelling basis for argument than the other? Why?

For further study and discussion

1. Describe in some detail what you think a Christian Utopia might be.
2. How closely do our accepted principles of good business correspond to Christian morality? Give examples to support your contentions.
3. Is Christianity primarily socialistic in its implications? If so, why are so many American Christians antagonistic to the ideas of socialism?
4. Why do children almost always consider their parents "old-fashioned" about morals?

Suggestions for further reading

Edward Bellamy, ***Looking Backward*** (Boston, 1888)

Edward D. Eddy, Jr., and others, ***The College Influence on Student Character*** (Washington, D.C., 1959)

William Dean Howells, ***A Traveler from Altruria*** (New York,

Erich A. Walter, ed., ***Religion and the State University*** 1958)

Frederic R. White, ***Famous Utopias of the Ren*** 1946). More, Rabelais, Montaigne, Bacon, Ca

"*What is truth?*"

PAUL TILLICH

Paul Tillich, one of the most distinguished contemporary Protestant theologians and religious philosophers, was born in August 1886 in the Prussian province of Brandenburg. His father was a minister of the Prussian Territorial Church (Lutheran). After attending the Friedrich Wilhelm Gymnasium in Berlin, Tillich matriculated in the theological faculties of Berlin, Tübingen, and Halle, receiving his doctorate of philosophy in Breslau in 1911.

After the First World War, in which he served as a chaplain, Tillich held professorships in various German universities until 1932, when he was dismissed from the University of Frankfurt-am-Main by Adolf Hitler. Then, through the influence of Reinhold Niebuhr, he became a professor of philosophical theology at Union Theological Seminary, a nondenominational theological graduate school in New York City. When he retired from the Seminary in 1954, he accepted an appointment as University Professor at Harvard, where he continues the lecturing, teaching, and writing which have made him such a powerful intellectual force in Europe and America.

Tillich's philosophy is based upon his concept of the opposition of the essential and the existential in life and man's estrangement from the essential. Before the Fall, man was "essential being"; but exercising his freedom, he became estranged from the Ultimate, and his life became chaotic and meaningless. Sin is not transgression, but separation. The problem is how "existential being"—man as he exists on the earth—can be united with "essential being"—man as he previously existed. The answer lies in Tillich's conception of the New Being, uniting in his person both the existential and the essential. Jesus, as the Christ in which essential "Godmanhood" appears, conquers the gulf between God and man. God becomes manifest as Love, overcoming estrangement, transforming and illuminating the h... situation.

The f... n is an important expression of these ... in 1949 to the students and faculty ... minary.

... *and dwelt among us, full* ... *For the law was given through Moses; grace and truth came through Jesus Christ.* John 1:14, 17. /1

Why do you not understand what I say? . . . you are of your father the devil. . . . He was a murderer from the beginning, and has nothing to do with truth, because there is no truth in him. When he lies, he speaks according to his own nature, for he is a liar and the father of lies. John 8:43, 44. /2

Pilate said to him, "So you are a king?" Jesus answered, "You say that I am a king. For this I was born, and for this I have come into the world, to bear witness to the truth. Every one who is of the truth hears my voice." Pilate said to him, "What is truth?" John 18:37, 38. /3

Jesus said to him, "I am the way, and the truth, and the life." John 14:6. /4

He who does what is true, comes to the light. John 3:21. /5

And I will pray the Father, and he will give you . . . the Spirit of truth, whom the world cannot receive, because it neither sees him nor knows him; you know him, for he dwells with you, and will be in you. John 14:16, 17. /6

When the Spirit of truth comes, he will guide you into all the truth. John 16:13. /7

Let us love one another; for love is of God, and he who loves is born of God and knows God. He who does not love does not know God; for God is love. I John 4:7, 8. /8

Jesus then said to the Jews who had believed in Him, "If you continue in my word, you are truly my disciples, and you will know the truth, and the truth will make you free." John 8:31, 32. /9

In the above passages there are words in which Jesus speaks about truth. Another of these words shall be the center of our meditation, the word in which He combines truth and freedom: "The truth will make you free." /10

The question of truth is universally human; but like everything human it was first manifest on a special place in a special group. It was the Greek mind in which the passionate search for truth was most conspicuous; and it was the Greek world in which, and to which, the Gospel of John was written. The words, here said by Jesus, are, according to ancient custom, put into His mouth by the evangelist who wanted to show the answer of Christianity to the central question of the Hellenic mind: the question of

---

truth. The answer is given also to us, for we, too, ask the question of truth. And some of us ask it as passionately, and sometimes as desperately, as the Greeks did. /11

It is often at an early age that we are moved by the desire for truth. When I, myself, as a fifteen-year-old boy received the words of our text as the motto for my future life from the confirming minister, who happened to be my father, I felt that this was just what I was looking for; and I remember that I was not alone in my group with this longing for truth. But I also observed, in myself and in others, that the early passion for truth is due to be lost in the adolescent and adult years of our lives. How does this happen? /12

The truth the child first receives is imposed upon him by adults, predominantly by his parents. This cannot be otherwise; and he cannot help accepting it. The passion for truth is silenced by answers which have the weight of undisputed authority, be it that of the mother or the father, or an older friend, or a gang, or the representatives of a social pattern. But sooner or later the child revolts against the truth given to him. He denies the authorities either all together, or one in the name of the other. He uses the teachers against the parents, the gang against the teachers, a friend against the gang, society against the friend. /13

This revolt is as unavoidable as was his early dependence on authority. The authorities gave him something to live on, the revolt makes him responsible for the truth he accepts or rejects. /14

But whether in obedience or in revolt, the time comes when a new way to truth is opened to us, especially to those in academic surroundings: The way of scholarly work. Eagerly we take it. It seems so safe, so successful, so independent of both authority and willfulness. It liberates from prejudices and superstitions; it makes us humble and honest. Where else, besides in scholarly work, should we look for truth? There are many in our period, young and old, primitive and sophisticated, practical and scientific, who accept this answer without hesitation. For them scholarly truth is truth altogether. Poetry may give beauty, but it certainly does not give truth. Ethics may help us to a good life, but it cannot help us to truth. Religion may produce deep emotions, but it should not claim to have truth. Only science gives us truth. It gives us new insights into the way nature works, into the texture of human history, into the hidden things of the human mind. It gives a feeling of joy, inferior to no other joy. He who has experienced this transition from darkness, or dimness, to the sharp light of knowledge will always praise scientific truth and understanding and say with some great medieval theologians, that the principles through which we know our world are the eternal divine light in our souls. And yet, when we ask those who have finished their studies in our colleges and universities whether they have found there a truth which is relevant to their lives they will answer with hesitation. Some will say that they have lost what they had of relevant truth; others will say that they don't care for such a truth because life goes on from day to day without it. Others will tell you of a person, a book, an event outside their studies which gave them the feeling of a truth that matters. But they all will agree that it is not the scholarly work which can give truth relevant for our life. /15

Where else, then, can we get it? "Nowhere," Pilate answers in his talk with Jesus. "What is truth?" he asks, expressing in these three words his own and his contemporaries' despair of truth, expressing also the despair of truth in millions of our contemporaries, in schools and studios, in business and professions. In all of us, open or hidden, admitted or repressed, the despair of truth is a permanent threat. We are children of our period as Pilate was. Both are periods of disintegration, of a world-wide loss of values and meanings. Nobody can separate himself completely from this reality, and nobody should even try. Let me do something unusual from a Christian standpoint, namely, to express praise of Pilate—not the unjust judge, but the cynic and sceptic; and of all those amongst us in whom Pilate's question is alive. For in the depth of every serious doubt and every despair of truth, the passion for truth is still at work. Don't give in too quickly to those who want to alleviate your anxiety about truth. Don't be seduced into a truth which is not really your truth, even if the seducer is your church, or your party, or your parental tradition. Go with Pilate, if you cannot go with Jesus; but go in seriousness with him! /16

Twofold are the temptations to evade the burden of asking for the truth that matters. The one is the way of those who claim to have the truth and the other is the way of those who do not care for the truth. The first ones are called "the Jews" in our gospel. They point to their tradition which goes back to Abraham. Abraham is their father; so they have all truth, and do not need to be worried by the question which they encounter in Jesus. Many among us, Christians and secularists, are "Jews" in the sense of the Fourth Gospel. They point to *their* tradition which goes back to the Church Fathers, or to the popes, or to the Reformers, or to the makers of the American Constitution. Their church or their nation is their mother, so they have all truth and do not need to worry about the question of truth. Would Jesus tell them, perhaps, what He told the Jews—that even if the church or the nation is their mother, they carry with them the heritage of the father of untruth; that the truth they have is not the truth which makes free? Certainly there is no freedom where there is self-complacency about the truth of one's own beliefs. There is no freedom where there is ignorant and fanatical rejection of foreign ideas and ways of life. There is no freedom but demonic bondage where one's own truth is called the ultimate truth. For this is an attempt to be like God, an attempt which is made in the name of God. /17

There is the second way of avoiding the question of truth—the way of not caring for it, of indifference. It is the way of the majority of the people today, as well as at the time of Jesus. Life, they say to themselves, is a mixture of truth, half-truth and falsehood. It is quite possible to live with this mixture, to muddle through most of the difficulties of life without asking the question of a truth that matters ultimately. There may be boundary situations, a tragic event, a deep spiritual fall, death. But as long as they are far removed, the question of truth can also stay far away. Hence, the common attitude—a little bit of Pilate's scepticism, especially in things which it is not dangerous today to doubt, as, for instance, God and the Christ; and a little bit of the Jew's dogmatism, especially in things which one is requested to accept today, as, for instance, an economic or political way of life. In other words, some scepticism and some dogmatism, and a shrewd method of balancing them liberate one from the burden of asking the question of ultimate truth. /18

But those of us who dare to face the question of truth may listen to what the Fourth Gospel says about it. The first thing which strikes us is that the truth of which Jesus speaks is not a doctrine but a reality, namely, He Himself: "I *am* the truth." This is a profound transformation of the ordinary meaning of truth. For us, statements are true or false; people may *have* truth or not; but how can they *be* truth, even *the* truth? The truth of which the Fourth Gospel speaks is a true reality—that reality which does not deceive us if we accept it and live with it. If Jesus says, "I am the truth," he indicates that in Him the true, the genuine, the ultimate reality is present; or, in other words, that God is present, unveiled, undistorted, in His infinite depth, in His unapproachable mystery. Jesus is not the truth because His teachings are true. But His teachings are true because they express the truth which He Himself is. He is more than His words. And He is more than any word said about Him. The truth which makes us free is neither the teaching of Jesus nor the teaching about Jesus. Those who have called the teaching of Jesus "the truth" have subjected the people to a servitude under the law. And most people like to live under a law. They want to be told what to think and what not to think. And they accept Jesus as the infallible teacher and giver of a new law. But even the words of Jesus, if taken as a law, are not the truth which makes us free. And they should not be used as such by our scholars and preachers and religious teachers. They should not be used as a collection of infallible prescriptions for life and thought. They *point* to the truth, but they are not a law of truth. Nor are the doctrines about Him the truth that liberates. I say this to you as somebody who all his life has worked for a true expression of the truth which is the Christ. But the more one works, the more one realizes that our expressions, including everything we have learned from our teachers and from the teaching of the Church in all generations, is not the truth that makes us free. The Church very early forgot the word of our Gospel that He *is* the truth; and claimed that her doctrines about Him are the truth. But these doctrines, however necessary and good they were, proved to be not the truth that liberates. Soon they became tools of suppression, of servitude under authorities; they became means to prevent the honest search for truth—weapons to split the souls of people between loyalty to the Church and sincerity to truth. And in this way they gave deadly weapons to those who attacked the Church and its doctrines in the name of truth. Not everybody feels this conflict. There are masses of people who feel safe under doctrinal laws. They are safe, but it is the safety of him who has not yet found his spiritual freedom, who has not yet found his true self. It is the dignity and the danger of Protestantism that it exposes its adherents to the insecurity of asking the question of truth for themselves and that it throws them into the freedom and responsibility of personal decisions, of the right to choose between the ways of the sceptics, and those who are orthodox, of the indifferent masses, and Him who *is* the truth that liberates. For this is the greatness of Protestantism: that it points beyond the teachings of Jesus and beyond the doctrines of the Church to the being of Him whose being is the truth. /19

How do we reach this truth? "By doing it," is the answer of the Fourth Gospel. This does not mean being obedient to the commandments, accepting them and fulfilling them. Doing the truth means living out of the reality which is *He* who is the truth, making His being the being of ourselves and of our world. And again, we ask, "How can this happen?" "By remaining in Him" is the answer of the Fourth Gospel, *i.e.*, by participating in His being. "Abide in me and I in you," he says. The truth which liberates is the truth in which we participate, which is a part of us and we a part of it. True discipleship is participation. If the real, the ultimate, the divine reality which is His being becomes our being we are in the truth that matters. /20

And a third time we ask, "How can this happen?" There is an answer to this question in our Gospel which may deeply shock us: "Every one who is of the truth hears my voice." Being "of the truth" means, coming from the true, the ultimate reality, being determined in one's being by the divine ground of all being, by that reality which is present in the Christ. If we have part in it, we recognize it wherever it appears; we recognize it as it appears in its fullness in the Christ. But, some may ask in despair: "If we have *no* part in it, if we are *not* of the truth, are we then forever excluded from it? Must we accept a life without truth, a life in error and meaninglessness? Who tells me that *I* am of the truth, that *I* have a chance to reach it?" Nobody can tell you; but there is one criterion: If you *seriously* ask the question, "Am I of the truth?" you *are* of the truth. If you do not ask it seriously, you do not really want, and you do not deserve, and you cannot get, an answer! He who asks seriously the question of the truth that liberates, is already on his way to liberation. He may still be in the bondage of dogmatic self-assurance but he has begun to be free from it. He may still be in the bondage of cynical despair, but he has already started to emerge from it. He may still be in the bondage of unconcern about the truth that matters, but his unconcern is already shaken. These all are of the truth and on their road to the truth. /21

On this road you will meet the liberating truth in many forms except in one form: you never will meet it in the form of propositions which you can learn or write down and take home. But you may encounter it in one sentence of a book or of a conversation or of a lecture, or even of a sermon. This sentence is not the truth, but it may open you up for the truth and it may liberate you from the bondage to opinions and prejudices and conventions. Suddenly, true reality appears like the brightness of lightening in a formerly dark place. Or, slowly, true reality appears like a landscape when the fog becomes thinner and thinner and finally disappears. New darknesses, new fogs will fall upon you; but you have experienced, at least once, the truth and the freedom given by the truth. Or you may be grasped by the truth in an encounter with a piece of nature—its beauty and its transitoriness; or in an encounter with a human being in friendship and estrangement, in love, in difference and hate; or in an encounter with yourself in a sudden insight into the hidden strivings of your soul, in disgust and even hatred of yourself, in reconciliation with and acceptance of yourself. In these encounters you may meet the true reality—the truth which liberates from illusions and false authorities, from enslaving anxieties, desires and hostilities, from a wrong self-rejection and a wrong self-affirmation. /22

And it may even happen that you are grasped by the picture and power of Him who is truth. There is no law that this must happen. Many at all times and in all places have encountered the true reality which is in Him without knowing His name—as He Himself said. They were of the truth and they recognized the truth, although they had never seen Him who is the truth. And those who have seen Him, the Christians in all generations, have no guarantee that they participate in the truth which He is. Maybe they were not of the truth. Those, however, who are of the truth and who have encountered Him who is the truth have one precious thing beyond the others: They have the point from which to judge all truth they encounter anywhere. They look at a life which never lost the communion with the divine ground of all life, and they look at a life which never lost the union of love with all beings. /23

And this leads to the last word which the man who has written the Gospel and the Letters of John has to say about truth: that the truth which liberates is the power of love, for God is love. The father of the lie binds us to himself by binding us to ourselves—or to that in us which is not our true self. Love liberates from the father of the lie because it liberates us from our false self to our true self—to that self which is grounded in true reality. Therefore, distrust every claim for truth where you do not see truth united with love; and be certain that you are of the truth and that the truth has taken hold of you only when love has taken hold of you and has started to make you free from yourselves.

The speech

1. What do the Biblical selections at the beginning of the sermon have in common? What use is made of them in the sermon?
2. What is the general purpose ordinarily of a sermon? Does this one share this general purpose? What is the specific purpose of this sermon?

3. What is scientific truth as Tillich uses the term? What methods has he used to define or clarify his meaning? What does he feel are its strengths and weaknesses? What proofs does he use to support his views on this point?
4. What is meant by "Go with Pilate, if you cannot go with Jesus; but go in seriousness with him!"?
5. What, according to Tillich, are the two ways of avoiding the question of truth? What does Tillich gain in the sermon by mentioning these before tackling the problem of facing up to truth?
6. What arguments would Tillich use, or does he use, in showing that those who believe in Jesus are not placing themselves in intellectual bondage?
7. Put into your own words the distinction Tillich makes between seeing truth in Jesus and seeing it in the doctrines about Jesus. Why does he insist upon the former? Show in detail how his whole argument hinges upon this distinction.
8. What is truth as Tillich uses the term? How may it or may it not be grasped? Is Tillich suggesting that the best way to apprehend truth is through a mystical experience?
9. Describe the organization of the sermon. Comment especially on the nature and value of the introduction and the conclusion.
10. Discuss the style, noting especially the word choice and sentence structure. Despite the fact that the subject is highly abstract, does the style help to hold your attention? If so, why? Would you say that the style of this sermon is livelier or duller than the style of most sermons you have heard? Defend your answer with specific references.
11. Would you say that the argument here is primarily deductive? If so, what are the basic premises? If not, what is the evidence upon which the inductive reasoning is based?
12. Why would you expect to find little humor here? Answer this by reference to the nature of *humor* (see Glossary).

For further study and discussion

1. In what respects have you revolted from "truth" you once accepted on authority? What were the reasons for the revolt? Were the reasons always relevant ones? Comment.
2. What is your belief about the nature of Jesus? Can you determine the origins of this belief?
3. Do you think there are different kinds of truth (e.g., religious truth, scientific truth, historical truth) or that truth is a term that should be reserved for only what is absolute and eternal?
4. What is similar about our age and that of Jesus? Why should both ages breed skepticism?
5. Would you say that we live primarily by myth rather than truth (e.g., myths about ourselves, our friends, our country, etc.)? Develop your answer in detail.
6. What is the relation of education to truth—in theory and in practice?
7. How can you explain the belief that has been widely held through the ages that truth is beauty? That truth is goodness? That truth is love?
8. Is the object of all art and literature, as well as religion, truth? Describe whatever differences you see between the aims of art and religion.
9. Why do so many people not want to face up to the truth in the sense of the known facts? Explore this by discussing both the nature of man and the nature of truth. What truth have you been unwilling to confront frankly and openly?
10. In what sense can the truth "set you free"?

Suggestions for further reading

Barrows Dunham, ***Man Against Myth*** (Boston, 1947)
David Greenwood, ***Truth and Meaning*** (New York, 1957)
William James, ***The Meaning of Truth*** (New York, 1909)
Martin C. Johnson, ***Science and the Meanings of Truth*** (London, 1946)
David Starr Jordan, ***The Stability of Truth*** (New York, 1911)
Reinhold Niebuhr, ***Faith and History*** (New York, 1949)
Bertrand Russell, ***An Inquiry into Meaning and Truth*** (New York, 1940)
Albert Schweitzer, ***The Quest of the Historical Jesus*** (London, 1954)
Paul Tillich, ***The Shaking of the Foundations*** (New York, 1948)

7/ BUSINESS AND INDUSTRY

The value of self-criticism for business and labor

ERWIN D. CANHAM

More than ever before in its history the business community recognizes the need for self-criticism and for self-regulation. Recalling the "trust busting" activities of an earlier era and the governmental controls imposed during the 1930's, most businessmen realize that to avoid additional interference by the government, and to win public confidence in their products, the conduct of their businesses must be above reproach. The rapidity with which the major broadcasting chains moved to suspend suspect quiz shows provides dramatic evidence of this concern.

Among the organizations devoted to raising the standards of business ethics and interpreting the aims and policies of business to government and the general public, one of the most important and influential is the Chamber of Commerce of the United States. Founded in 1912, the Chamber has more than twenty-five thousand members and a staff of eight hundred. It is a federation representing all segments of business and industry, with special committees and departments devoted to agriculture, construction and civic development, domestic distribution, education, foreign commerce, insurance, labor relations and manufacture, natural resources, taxation and finance, transportation, and communication.

On November 12, 1959, speaking as national president of the Chamber of Commerce, Erwin D. Canham, editor of the *Christian Science Monitor,* delivered the following address to the National Association of Real Estate Boards meeting in Toronto, Canada. Reviewing changes in the public's attitude toward business since the closing decades of the last century, he undertook to show that much of the criticism directed against business had been unjustified. In closing, he called for a new sense of moral responsibility on the part of businessmen and urged that they take an active part in public affairs "from the precinct on up."

Born in Auburn, Maine, in 1904, Canham was graduated from Bates College and attended Oxford University as a Rhodes Scholar, where he earned both B.A. and M.A. degrees. Since 1925 Canham has been on the staff of the *Christian Science Monitor,* serving in various foreign posts, as head of the Washington Bureau, as news editor and managing editor, and since 1945 as editor. He is a past president of the American Society of Newspaper Editors, has been an alternate delegate to the General Assembly of the United Nations, and has served on UNESCO. Among his books are *The World at Mid-Century* (1951) and *New Frontiers of Freedom* (1954).

As a student debater at Bates College, Canham was elected to Delta Sigma Rho, national honorary forensics society. "My 'philosophy of effective speaking,' " he writes, "is that a speaker must think what he is saying if he is to communicate it effectively. Thus I believe in sparing use of manuscript, and frequent departure from text to avoid the curse of mere reading, and to achieve some measure of thinking."[1]

This morning, I would like to talk to you for a little while about the value of self-criticism. Or, you could call it self-appraisal—self-analysis—or—the proposition of letting your conscience back you into a corner —and trying to defend yourself against the questions which your own conscience might ask. /1

What I have to say applies specifically to business in the United States, although I hope that our Canadian friends, colleagues and associates will not find the subject entirely alien to their interests. /2

Mark Twain once observed that "The public is the only critic whose opinion is worth anything at all." I am sure that Mr. Clemens undoubtedly had in mind the opinion of the public with reference to the creative arts, such as public opinion with respect to novel and fiction stories, but I believe his epigram can logically be translated much more freely. /3

Erwin D. Canham, "The Value of Self-Criticism for Business and Labor," *Vital Speeches of the Day,* Vol. XXVI, December 15, 1959, pp. 147-150. By permission of the author.

[1] Letter to the editors, March 10, 1960.

For example, the business community in the United States, in general, ardently desires the good opinion of the public. I am sure the same wish applies in Canada. Most business men today work hard at winning public approval. There are few corporations without a vice president in charge of public relations. There is hardly a company of any size at all without at least one man devoting the bulk of his time to the task of creating and maintaining good will for the business. /4

We maintain local, state and national associations which—in effect—are the public relations departments of entire industries. Your association is an example. Your association undoubtedly deals with legislation affecting the real estate business. You also discuss other common problems. You exchange ideas. But at one and the same time, your association endeavors to present and portray the real estate business in a favorable light. /5

That is all to the good. /6

For another example, we might cite the Chamber of Commerce of the United States. /7

Our National Chamber is primarily a policy-making organization, but it is also a vast public relations institution working in behalf of all types of free, competitive enterprise. /8

I believe it can be said with authority that American business today—taken as a whole—enjoys the respect and confidence of the public majority. That is because business—in the main—has demonstrated a sense of economic morality. Business has a conscience. It has a powerful sense of responsibility to the general well-being. /9

The typical business man may not put it into so many words—indeed, he would probably blush to so define himself—but I believe it to be true that he regards himself somewhat in the light of a steward for our competitive, enterprise system. /10

As a result of all this, the views of business are not only cordially entertained by the Congress, but are frequently invited. At the same time, business receives no favors from government which are not in keeping with the broad, general interest. What is more important, it is not asking for special favors. /11

This is the way things should be. We have today the kind of relationship with the public and with government which the business man must maintain and must consistently work to improve. Like friendships, good public relations must be kept in a constant state of repair. /12

Sometimes, the best way to plan ahead is to look back. /13

Let us do that for a few minutes. /14

It was just 30 years ago this month that the American people were looking around for a villain. They were in trouble, and they wanted a scape-goat. /15

On October 29, 1929—the top-heavy structure of stock prices had collapsed. It was almost as though a 50-story building had been erected on a foundation of slithery mud. /16

Almost overnight, a chimera of national thinking was irretrievably buried. A few thoughtful persons had recognized that economic trouble had been building up for some years, but it took the Wall Street crash to make it common knowledge that the great boom of the 1920's was all over. /17

As of today, we know that no group of men or no special pattern of activity can be pointed out and identified as the primary cause of the depression in the 1930's. Even if he had the power, no man would be the instigator of an industrial and financial cataclysm which would involve himself and everybody else. We now realize that no one was especially to blame for the depression, but that everyone was to blame. /18

It is hardly an exaggeration to say that there had been a junior-grade South Sea Bubble in many, many towns and cities. We were buying stocks with money we did not have at values which had no semblance of reality. And we were eagerly mopping up the worthless bonds of bankrupt foreign nations. /19

In general, our metropolitan population was so busy living it up, it paid scant attention to the fact that the farm belt had been in the grip of a major depression for almost a decade. Some of us who are old enough to remember that era can recall how city people brushed off the farmer's complaints on the grounds that farmers are always griping. /20

But the trouble on the farm was very real, and we must remember that agriculture was a somewhat more important factor in our economic equation in the 1920's than it is today. /21

In two years—from 1920 through 1922—three hundred thousand farmers lost their land through mortgage foreclosure. The farmer was then earning less than three per cent on his investment, while he was paying five, six and seven per cent in interest charges. /22

The farm was a center of infection—far from the only one, of course, but still a center. The infection was slow to spread, but spread it did, and when the urban bubble broke, the collapse was complete—from farm to factory and all the way in between. /23

So the American people began hunting for a villain. And there is one thing we can always be sure about: when the American people begin hunting for a villain they do not come home empty-handed. /24

Actually, they found two villains. One was the national administration then in power, but the villain which the public chose to adorn with the biggest pair of horns was business—and especially big business—which included—by popular selection—Wall Street at one end and the Minneapolis and Chicago grain pits at the other. /25

In 1933, when a new national administration and a new Congress took over, business received the biggest public beating ever administered to any segment of the American economy. /26

Some of the new laws were good. Some were not so bad, and others were very bad indeed. /27

And in their application, the innocent suffered along with the guilty. /28

But who cared? The public wanted business whipped, and whipped it was. And business remained in the public dog house until the industrial mobilization for World War II came along and gave everybody something new to think about. /29

I am sure that you have run across—as I have—people who will argue that business never had any kind of conscience—never had a sense of economic morality—and never gave two whoops what the public thought of it until it was chosen Public Villain No. 1 at the outset of the depression. Or, they may put it another way and say that business was forced to hit the sawdust trail and accept a shotgun conversion. /30

I would not deny that business learned some valuable lessons under the lash of public censure. Adversity has a habit of bringing out the true character and mettle of men, and business, after all, is only a term which defines an economic segment composed of very human people. /31

If we read our economic history in the light of human nature, we find that business in bygone years did not do many things which it automatically does today in the interests of good public relations, because the public was quite happy with the way things were. /32

Here, of course, I am speaking generally. There were periods of hostility toward certain elements in business long before the depression of the 1930's. Around the turn of the century, for example, it was popular to "bust the trusts." This was virtually a national slogan. But there were not many trusts to be busted, and public opinion did not identify the corner bank or the local grain elevator or even the manufacturer with the so-called trusts. /33

In the main, we find that throughout most of the 19th century and the early years of the 20th, the public majority never regarded business—as a community—or as an institution—as an enemy of the people. /34

Indeed, for a long period of time, the public seemed to have a special affection for the worse elements in business. There was even a profound admiration for the most hard-bitten—and the most ruthless entrepreneurs. /35

You need not take my word for it. I refer you to the newspapers, magazines, the fiction stories and even the jokes which were produced when the so-called robber barons and free-booters of industry were riding rough-shod, high, wide and handsome. /36

Now—I am compelled to say that perhaps we owe a certain debt to those free-booters and robber barons. It is entirely possible that it took men of iron-will and ruthless determination to carve a continental empire out of a gaunt wolf preserve—and west of the eastern mountains, that is about all our continent offered as a prospectus in the 19th century. /37

But I am deviating. My point is that the so-called robber barons and free-booters were often considered in their day as great constructive geniuses, and they were held up as models of deportment to poor but ambitious boys. /38

It sometimes happened that a slippery operator would be sued by an indignant victim. Naturally, a considerable fanfare would ensue. /39

But at the same time, John Q. Public would sagely wag his collective head and declare that "They can sue him all they like, but he will wriggle out of it." /40

In those days, the art of wriggling out of something seems to have been greatly esteemed—even by the victims of a swindle. Apparently the victims hoped someday to duplicate the accomplishment. /41

Recently, I ran across an anecdote of that bygone period which may serve to illustrate the admiration for trickiness and clever dealings. /42

It seems that one of our middle-sized cities was having a construction boom, and the local landscape was polka-dotted with piles of lumber. Street lighting was poor, and the police force undermanned, so considerable pilfering took place under cover of darkness. It was no trouble at all to walk away with a few choice planks or two by fours. /43

There was also a labor shortage, and night watchmen were hard to get. One bright young builder told his colleagues that he had a watchman on his payroll who would be glad to make regular rounds of all the lumber piles. He argued that pilfering would be curbed if it became known that an armed guard might show up at almost any time. /44

All he asked was two dollars a week to help defray his watchman's wages. And about a hundred builders took him up on the deal—at $2.00 a week. /45

One day, our enterprising young man told a group of friends about his arrangement, and according to the anecdote, the following conversation ensued: /46

"Do you mean to say that about 100 other builders are each paying you two dollars a week? What kind of wages do you pay your watchman?" /47

Our clever friend then pulled his punch line: /48

"Why," he said, "that's the big joke. I don't have a watchman. They just think I have." /49

From all I can gather out of old files, the story was widely circulated and was considered a regular side-splitter in circa 1880. /50

At about the same time, there was a man who was amassing the beginnings of a fortune as a cattle drover. I won't mention his name, because it happens to belong to an institution which he endowed in later years. /51

He bought small lots of cattle from farmers and drove them to market in great herds. The animals were sold by weight. /52

Just before they neared the market, the drover fed the cattle salt, and then he gave them all the water they could hold. As you know, a gallon of water weighs about eight pounds. If you put three or four gallons in a cow, you have got something extra when it comes to selling her. /53

In later years, the drover told this story on himself, and it was repeated from person to person. It did him no harm at all. To the contrary, he was looked upon as a man of astuteness and distinction. He was also considered a worthy character because every Sunday, without fail, he passed the collection plate in church and was known to speak highly of religion. /54

Religion, he said, had its place, but its place was in church and in the home and not in business. He appears to have been rigidly faithful to his own philosophy. He was violently opposed to the transaction of any business on Sunday, and after services he spent the rest of the day reading pious works. /55

In retrospect, I think we can safely say that the latter part of the 19th century in particular was a gaudy era in the life of this country. The making of money was greatly admired, no matter how made. /56

But I do think it is a fact that for every goldbrick peddler, for every employer who flagrantly exploited his employees and for every ruthless robber baron—big or small—there were many thousands of business men who believed in justice in the warehouse and the counting house as firmly as they believed in justice in the courthouse. One can only suppose that they drifted along in the sublime belief that because of their innocence, no one would ever point a damning finger at their operations. /57

The rude jolt of the 1930's was based on the alleged sins of business in the 1920's, even though such terms as robber baron, free-booter and malefactor of great wealth were resurrected. If any of you real estate people would like to know what sins you were supposed to have committed in the 1920's, I suggest you reread "Babbitt," by the late Sinclair Lewis, the story of a man described by the author as one who was "highly nimble in the art of selling real estate for more than it was worth." /58

I am not going to defend all of the practices of business in the 1920's, but I believe that, in the main, the sins of business were largely sins of omission—and not sins of commission. /59

They were all too quiet about their own contributions to the national well-being in the midst of a sensation-loving era. Few people knew that many, many concerns, on their volition, had put in effect what we now call fringe benefits. They had set up retirement income plans. /60

Without any prompting except introspection, they had contrived devices to give employees a sense of participation. /61

Some of our larger corporations gave their employees a chance to acquire stock at actual values —not inflated values. /62

And there were safety measures in effect before any unions ever thought of them. /63

It was not at all unusual for business men to recognize the value of adequate pay scales. Just at random, the other day, I plucked a sentence from an address delivered by an executive of one of our biggest electric companies in April, 1929—six months before the market crash. (Note: This was F. W. Willard, Western Electric.) /64

This speaker said that "high wages for competent operators of the best kind of tools by the best kind of methods are the sure road to the lowest costs and consequently the highest profits." /65

This comment does not stand alone in the public comment by business leaders in the 1920's and in previous years. /66

Why, then, did business find it so difficult to turn away the wrath of the public in the 1930's? /67

Well, first, I would say that it came as a surprise to a majority of the business community. In their attempts to defend themselves, they found themselves either stuttering in confusion, or they fell back on truculence. /68

They had not learned how to speak out for themselves. /69

Neither had they fully grasped the opportunities for good will contained in efficient, well-staffed, well-supported voluntary organizations of their own design. /70

In particular, they had not learned the value of self-criticism. /71

They had not learned how to police themselves. /72

There was, of course, a great deal of talk about the value of good service to the customer, and—in fact—many of the products manufactured in the 1920's were almost the equal of many products of today's output. I suppose I am thinking particularly in terms of the typewriter. Because that is my own working tool. The machines produced in the interlude between the two World Wars were really wonderful. /73

On the other hand, automobile tires produced in those same years were not so good. It was not so many years ago that a driver expected to have a flat tire on the average of every 20 or 40 miles. We have come a long way since then. Of course, I am mentioning only two products—an old product that was good—a new product which is better. There could be hundreds of other examples—mostly in favor of the latest developments. /74

Still another sin of omission on the part of business, before lightning hit it in the 1930's, was that business had not learned to bargain collectively with labor. And there was no prevailing idea that labor was going to achieve its present power, wealth and status. Business had not learned to live with labor. /75

Perhaps I could sum it all up by saying that business—business men—did not seem to know how to assume leadership in community affairs or in the total community of the nation. /76

In many respects, it is all very different as of now, but I cannot avoid thinking about the perils of complacency. At this moment, I have a feeling that it is a part of wisdom to be introspective, self-searching—and self-critical. /77

I am sure you would all agree that self-righteousness is the emotional equivalent of a geographical area which abounds in the traps of quick-sand. /78

In our agreements with labor today, we expect the worker to give an honest day's work in return for honest pay. By the same token, the business man has an obligation to provide a serviceable, durable, quality product. He is expected to see that his guarantee means something. /79

For example— /80

A year's warranty of free service on a household convenience probably ought to be enough. That is, if we were all coldly logical. But few of us are coldly logical. After the first year of free service is expended, the buyer is apt to build up resentment against a concern which sold him a product in constant need of expensive repair after the warranty year is over. /81

Today, the business man encourages credit buying—and in many cases he asks a carrying charge. I am sure that in most cases, those charges are equitable. On the other hand, if they are excessive, the public will soon catch on. Somebody once said that we should never overestimate public information, and never underestimate public intelligence. /82

Again, by the same token, I think it would be generally agreed that the real estate man is expected to see that settlement services and fees are all really necessary. Nor is it too much to expect that he and others in the housing field will occasionally take a hard and honest look at the federal subsidy problem. In that direction, lies good business citizenship. /83

Currently, in the United States, television quiz shows have been caught with their answers showing. The honesty of advertising is being questioned. Congressional committees are turning some hard looks at such popular commodities as weight-reducing pills. We are reading about complaints against the practices of used car dealers. New centers of infection of the anti-business virus may be slowly building up. /84

In saying all this, I am actually only quoting what has been in the news for the past few months. And so long as man bites dog is the basic rule of news, I am sure that only a small minority in every enterprise I have mentioned has been guilty of infraction against today's business conception of economic morality. /85

I do feel, however, that business must strive to be beyond reproach—for its own sake. That would apply to the quality of the product. It would apply to service charges. It would apply to advertising. /86

It also is essential that we augment the good beginnings we have made in exercising national leadership. We cannot be smug about the fact that labor is now in about the same kind of public dog house to which business was relegated in the 1930's. Labor has not been very original. Right now, labor has a priority on the mourners' bench. It is sitting where business sat about 30 years ago. /87

But we have no reason to gloat because labor has failed to exercise self-criticism—which is exactly what has happened to it. Because that is what happened to us. /88

We cannot sit aloof from politics. It is not enough to send a contribution to the party of our choice. The business man today should be in politics from the precinct on up. He ought to have his heart in it, but if he is asked to be a legman and a doorbell-ringer, he ought to be glad to do that too. /89

Our task then, is to strengthen our own moral sense. We can do that by exemplifying it. We can strive for decency, honor and integrity in our own acceptance and fulfilment of our life and professional responsibilities. Remembering that our whole society depends upon the validity and dignity of individual man, we can live and act like men who believe in the values of their lives and their society. We can help build an invincible society, even though today we are tragically far from that goal. I believe we know what it is we have to do. /90

The speech

1. Which of the methods named in the Glossary does Canham employ in his *introduction*? Would you say that this method was both appropriate and effective? If you had been delivering the speech, would you have used a different type of introduction? Why or why not?
2. Although speaking to an audience made up in part of Canadians, Canham says that his remarks will apply specifically "to business in the United States." Do you think he was wise to limit his subject in this way or should he have attempted to include in his discussion a more direct appraisal of the problems of Canadian businessmen? In answering, remember his position as President of the United States Chamber of Commerce.
3. How would you classify the speech as to type or purpose? As a speech to inform? To persuade? To stimulate? As a "good will" speech on behalf of business and such organizations as the Chamber of Commerce?
4. Do you think that Canham's "look back" at the history of American business since the turn of the century is unnecessarily long and rambling, or was it necessary to survey past events in such detail in order to bring out the central idea of the speech: that businessmen must have a sense of public responsibility?
5. Scattered throughout Canham's speech are many metaphors, similes, epigrams, and the like. What contribution, if any, do you think these make to the general effectiveness of the speech? Identify and characterize several of these figures of speech. Are they on the whole fresh or trite, vivid or commonplace?
6. Do you think Canham is sufficiently specific when discussing the "contributions" industry made "to the national well-being" during the 1920's? Should he have named some of the companies that granted "fringe benefits," introduced safety devices, adjusted pay scales, etc., or does the quotation from F. W. Willard adequately substantiate his contention?
7. At many points throughout the speech Canham employs reiteration and restatement—sometimes of a single phrase, sometimes of a sentence, sometimes of an entire idea. Search out several of these instances of restatement and evaluate the contributions they make toward clarifying and supporting the speaker's ideas.
8. Remembering that Canham was speaking to a group of real estate dealers, how well would you say he adapted his speech to the audience? Suppose he were asked to address a group of labor leaders on the same subject. Should he deliver practically the same speech or make fundamental changes in approach and organization? What if his audience were composed entirely of college professors? Of farmers?
9. Evaluate the unity and coherence of Canham's speech. Do the ideas hold together well? Are his arguments aimed at a single clearly defined purpose, or are there some unnecessary side excursions and irrelevancies?
10. If you had to characterize the style of the speech would you call it lively or dull? Conversational or oratorical? Forceful or weak? Impressive or commonplace? Fast moving or ponderous? Clear or confusing? Justify your answer.

For further study and discussion

1. Would you agree with Canham's assertion that "business—in the main—has demonstrated a sense of economic morality"? Defend your answer by pointing to specific facts and instances.
2. Do you think that most of the reforms Canham mentions were brought about as a result of self-criticism on the part of business or were they forced on business by governmental regulations and controls?
3. Are our present controls on business good or bad? Should they be extended or relaxed?
4. What geographical, historical, or economic factors may account for the high status accorded the successful businessman during the closing decades of the nineteenth century?
5. If, as Canham suggests, the "ruthless entrepreneur" is no longer the American folk hero, who has taken his place? The laboring man? The professional man? The scientist? The modern corporation executive? Why?
6. What do leading economists regard as the principal causes of the depression of the 1930's? Would they

agree with Canham that the farm was an important "center of infection"? Might they be more inclined than he is to center the blame on unwise business expansion and speculation in stocks?

7. What is the relative status of doctors, lawyers, businessmen, and college professors in Russia? In England? In France? Is it the same as in the United States or different? If different, which system do you think measures the worth of a man's contribution to society most realistically?
8. Is moneymaking less admired in our society today than it was sixty or seventy years ago?
9. Would you agree with Canham that labor has now taken over the role of scapegoat which was once held by business? If so, would you say that perhaps people always demand a scapegoat upon which to blame their economic and social ills?
10. Work out an ideal code of conduct and fair dealing to which you believe business should adhere.

Suggestions for further reading

Howard R. Bowen, ***Social Responsibilities of the Businessman*** (New York, 1953)

Joel B. Dirlam and Alfred E. Kahn, ***Fair Competition: The Law and Economics of Antitrust Policy*** (Ithaca, N. Y., 1954)

Matthew Josephson, ***The Robber Barons: The Great American Capitalists*** (New York, 1934)

Harold Koontz and Richard W. Gable, ***Public Control of Economic Enterprise*** (New York, 1956)

Allan Nevins, ***Ford: The Times, the Man and the Company*** (New York, 1954)

Andreas G. Papandreou and John T. Wheeler, ***Competition and Its Regulation*** (New York, 1954)

The greatest invention of them all

HENRY B. DU PONT

Established in 1824, The Franklin Institute of Pennsylvania is the oldest private foundation in the United States devoted to the study and encouragement of applied science and the mechanic arts. In its Philadelphia home the Institute houses a museum with extensive permanent and temporary exhibits and a large scientific library known throughout the world for its collection of patent literature. In addition, it publishes an influential journal, awards medals and prizes for outstanding achievements in the fields of engineering and applied science, underwrites numerous research projects, and sponsors an annual series of some twenty symposia and lectures which are open to the general public.

One of the more important of the public lectures held at the Institute each year is named in honor of Edward G. Budd, president of the Budd Company of Philadelphia, manufacturers of railroad cars, automobile bodies, and stamped metal products. In 1959 the Budd lecturer was Henry B. du Pont, a vice president of the E. I. du Pont de Nemours Company of Wilmington, Delaware.

Du Pont, a great-great-grandson of E. I. du Pont de Nemours, founder of the company, was trained as a mechanical and aeronautical engineer, having attended the Massachusetts Institute of Technology for three years following his graduation from Yale in 1920. He worked in the engineering department of General Motors prior to joining the Du Pont Company as assistant treasurer in 1928. The following year he was transferred to engineering work and has since been prominently associated with engineering research and development. Since 1939 he has been a Du Pont vice president and member of the Executive Committee.

Actively interested in the problems of engineering education, Du Pont has spoken extensively before educators' groups on this subject, with particular emphasis on the role of the liberal arts in preparing for careers in industrial technology. The lecture included here falls into the general category of a "good will" speech. That is, Du Pont's purpose is not primarily to inform or persuade, but rather to lead his listeners to a fuller appreciation of the role of the modern industrial corporation in promoting technological advancement. This purpose is achieved by contrasting the work of the large industrial laboratories of today with the sporadic and isolated efforts of the inventors and scientists of a century and a half ago. Moreover, as part of this contrast we are given a highly informative account of early American inventors—especially those who lived in the Philadelphia area. The style of the lecture is clear and attractive; the illustrations are numerous and well chosen; and the organization is interesting as an example of indirect or implicative development. Judged from a rhetorical point of view, Du Pont's effort does credit to himself as an engineer-business executive as well as to The Franklin Institute and the Budd Lecture Foundation.

There is, I suppose, no more appropriate place than The Franklin Institute for a discussion of technology. The Philadelphia Story is rich in technological history, for much of it was enacted—at least in its early stages—within a relatively short distance of this room. /1

I am thinking not only of Dr. Franklin's work. His contributions would be remarkable anywhere, any time. I am thinking, as well, of the astonishing number of other scientists and inventors who worked in or near Philadelphia in the early days of the country. /2

There was the naturalist John Bartram and, a little later, John Audubon, whose interest in ornithology began while he was living in Mill Grove, near Mount Carmel. There was Benjamin Rush, the physician. There was David Rittenhouse with his planetarium, and Owen Biddle with his telescope at Cape Henlopen. There was John Fitch, a transplanted Connecticut Yankee, puffing along the Schuylkill and the Delaware in a fire-breathing contraption called a steamboat. A few miles downstream, on Brandywine Creek, there was Oliver Evans who built a flour mill which operated almost without human attention. Among his neighbors was E. I. du Pont, recently arrived from France, who went into the powder business at the urging of Jefferson and made important contributions to the manufacture of explosives then badly needed to clear the forest lands, build the roads and defend the nation. /3

There was Thomas Paine, remembered as the pamphleteer of the Revolution, but due equal honors for his engineering contributions. One of Paine's more imaginative schemes was an engine driven by a continuous series of tiny gunpowder explosions, actually a sort of internal combustion engine. Unfortunately, the "Internal Explosion Engine" did not work out. I say "unfortunately" because the Du Pont Company was mighty close to bankruptcy for many of its early years, and a large-scale development in this field would have created a welcome new market. However, let us not criticize Citizen Paine for his mistakes. He also developed the iron bridge and had some worthy thoughts about planing machines, cranes, and carriage-wheel construction. /4

The list of Philadelphia contributors could be extended indefinitely, for in the eighteenth and nineteenth centuries, this small sector of the American geography was the home of dozens who were instrumental to the progress of technology. /5

It could be argued that "technology" is not the word to use for the scientific contributions of a Franklin or a Bartram, so let me define my terms. Technology is much more than engineering. It is much more than invention, much more than the nuts and bolts, as is sometimes said. Technology, as I see it, is the sum total of man's work in developing the tools and techniques which lend leverage to human effort. Whether a man be a research scientist, or engineer, or an "inspired tinkerer" as some were called, he contributes to and is an integral part of the technology which has shaped this nation. /6

America in 1800, despite its vast potential wealth, was one of the poorest of the have-not nations, although few nations of that day were well off. The natural resources which we know today were undeveloped and many of them were unsuspected. In 1800, standards of living even for the well-to-do were crude, and for the mass of the population, they approached the hand-to-mouth level. Farming occupied the attention of more than 90 per cent of the population, and the primitive equipment used would have been recognized by any farmer from the time of Julius Caesar. Manufacture had hardly reached a level where it deserved the title "industry." In 1814, in a report prepared for the United States Senate, a Philadelphian named Tench Coxe estimated that the output of manufacturing in the United States came to a value of something less than $175 million a year. That meant an average of $35 worth of manufactured goods for each man, woman, and child in the population, hardly an impressive amount. /7

The real poverty of the nation, however, lay in the inadequacy of its human resources to meet growing needs. Tench Coxe was among those who saw that technology held bold possibilities of enriching the nation, and he pleaded for the development of labor-saving machines to lift human burdens and increase output. Men simply could not be spared from the fields. Manpower was so scarce that in a textile mill, for example, Mr. Coxe said that not more than one employee in eight could be an adult male; the rest of the work had to be done by women and children. Before we send Mr. Coxe to the pillory for suggestions which would shock us today, let me add that no less noble a man than Jefferson shared these views. Coxe was simply stating facts. Men were needed to raise food and could not be spared for manufacture. /8

In such a restricted economy, there was obviously little money and little time to expend in research and development. The men whose enthusiasm carried them into science or engineering did so, for the most part, on their own initiative just as we today might take music lessons or write poetry. But, for the necessities of life, they had to turn to other fields. Some of the most significant work done in America came about as a result of the two-job practice we would now describe as "moonlighting." /9

Samuel Morse, for example, was a portrait painter by day and a scientist by night. John Fitch sold maps as he traveled the Eastern Seaboard looking for someone, anyone, to invest in his fire-breathing boat. Eli Whitney earned his living as a school master before he earned a nickel from his inventions. /10

Joseph Henry, another part-time scientist, deplored the fact that his experiments had to be confined to the summer months when the school in which he taught was closed. /11

Oliver Evans got along by operating a store and an iron foundry, and Paine, who first had plied his trade as a staymaker, later eked out a living by his writing and political work. /12

Few scientists were as well situated as Franklin whose early successes in publishing enabled him to live amid comforts while indulging his interest in such diverse subjects as the Gulf Stream, electricity, and bifocal spectacles. Most were obliged to expend so much of their energies to earning a livelihood that their most memorable achievements were made on borrowed time. The strain told. Fitch died poor, by his own hand, broken by years of frustration and want. Elias Howe, while enduring hunger and privation, was worn out by toil and died at the age of 48. /13

To add to the difficulties of these early technologists, poor communication led to frequent duplication of effort, with the result that many things were invented several times by different people who were ignorant of each other's work. When Eli Whitney set up his factory to make guns with interchangeable parts, he spent a large amount of time working out machine tools which already had been developed, or at least anticipated, in other countries. He had no way of knowing that they even existed. Fitch worked for years on a double-acting steam engine, apparently ignorant of the fact that James Watt and Matthew Boulton had already solved many of the problems he faced. Oliver Evans started from scratch, and had no access to technical books, although many had been written in the fields in which he worked. Henry worked for six years on magnetism and electric currents before discovering that Faraday, an ocean away, was doing the same research. /14

Inevitably, when two or more men brought forth the same discovery at approximately the same time, there were conflicting patent claims. This produced some of the stormiest and most extended legal battles in history. No doubt, it provided amusement for many interested spectators. But it was costly national fun because it dissipated the creative energies of men who could not easily be replaced or duplicated. Genius is too rare a commodity to be squandered lavishly or used inefficiently. /15

Looking back to the conditions of the eighteenth and nineteenth centuries, it should cause little wonder that technical progress came slowly. The marvel is that anything was accomplished at all, and our respect and admiration for the talents and persistence of the men involved grows as we come to appreciate their handicaps. They earned every tribute we pay them. I cannot help but wonder how different our history might have been if these extraordinary minds had been unleashed for full-time experiment and invention. /16

If we were asked to construct a list of the technological developments most fundamental to America's progress, it would be difficult indeed to single out any group upon which we could present a clear case. The nominations most meaningful would be those representative of broad application, spanning all categories of human need. /17

For, the most notable thing about the technical development of America is that its industrial revolution was not confined mainly to manufacturing, as was the case in Europe. Instead, American technical development was spread broadly across the entire economic and scientific field. The growth of our industrial technology was accompanied by parallel gains in agriculture, in communications, and in transportation. There was no single stream of technological advance. Instead, America's progress resulted from the converging of many streams, uniting to produce a flood-tide of inventive achievement. In this great creative outpouring, it is difficult to identify any small group of inventions which would be judged outstanding in importance. /18

Everyone has his own list of "greatest inventions," and every invention has, I suppose, its partisans. My own list has three virtues to commend it. First, it is brief; second, most of my selections are simple; and third, it is based not on scientific pre-eminence, but on the universal importance to our economic revolution. /19

I would include, for example, the steel plow. A humble device, perhaps—John Deere simply hammered it out of an old circular saw blade. But it speeded the work of the farmer and was the predecessor of a host of other labor-saving farm equipment—the reaper, the binder, the tractor, the combine. Some might argue that these were more significant and, in a way, they would be right. But the important thing about the steel plow is that it was the first in a long line of major advances which lifted man from the subsistence level of agriculture, thus freeing increasing numbers of people for other occupations. Improved farm tools, supplemented by insecticides, weed killers, fertilizers, and better planting and irrigation techniques, have multiplied the efficiency of the farmer by a factor of 25. /20

Second, I include Oliver Evans' wonderful flour mill, the precursor of automatic control. In terms of scientific merits, it was a modest accomplishment. But it showed the world how a whole series of production operations could be linked together, driven by machinery, and tended by one or two men. All of the technologists who followed Evans, and the millions of consumers who use mass-produced goods, are eternally indebted to this extraordinary man. /21

The steam locomotive, of course, put power on wheels and gave man a wholly new mobility of special significance in a nation spanning such great distances. The locomotive was not unique to America, and it was more a compendium than an invention, but it should not be ruled out on that score. After all, no nation can claim many major inventions which are all its own, created without outside help. Technology is a cumulative force. To credit all of the people who made the locomotive possible, we would have to track down the inventors of the lever, the wheel, and the inclined plane, not to mention the steam engine and similarly modern developments. Incidentally, some of the most important contributions to railroad development came from this area. George Westinghouse, the inventor of the air brake, was a Pennsylvanian by adoption if not by birth. Matthias Baldwin, the locomotive builder and one of the men who helped found The Franklin Institute, was a Philadelphian. John Edgar Thompson, who did as much as any man to build the Pennsylvania Railroad, was born and raised in Delaware County. In the hands of men like these, the railroad reached a high level of development in the United States and, with the vast distances of the continent falling beneath its iron wheels, the locomotive counts more heavily in our history than many inventions we like to think of as 100 per cent home grown. /22

Fourth on the list is the telegraph which presaged the telephone and did more to speed communication than any device since the printing press and movable type. /23

I have mentioned here four basic inventions covering each of the major fields. There is a fifth which pertains to all. I think in any list of inventions, we should include this one which, strictly speaking, is not an invention at all, but a legal fiction. Yet it seems to me to equal in importance any specific invention in history. This is the development of the modern corporation. /24

The industrial corporation, as we know it today, is a creature of technology just as certainly as the flying machine or the cotton gin, and it has proved the most effective device for extending technology which man has ever known. Its contributions have been unique. /25

For the modern industrial establishment is the agency which made the pursuit of technology a full-time job, and not for a few men, but for hundreds of thousands. Industry employs today more than 550,000 scientists and engineers, a majority of the nation's technical work force. Such figures amaze few today. But, in contrast to the struggling little band of amateurs of the early days, it is a vast army. /26

Development of the industrial organization as we now recognize it came too late to aid the earlier inventors. In some ways, the "corporate" form of organization dates from medieval times, but it was not until the twentieth century that the corporation came into wide usage as the structural form of large-scale organization. In this century, it has changed the world. It has provided a focal point for the development of technology, taking it out of the sideline class and making it a full-time profession. The corporation has brought to the support of technology an extraordinary number and variety of services and resources. In our own company, as an example, we have about 2,400 technically trained employees in research and development, assisted by more than 3,500 specialists and technicians. We spent $90 million last year to underwrite their work. /27

All the facilities which can be mustered are employed to assist the research worker and make his effort more productive. No longer does he work in ignorance of what others are doing: Today, few developments throughout the world escape notice, for there is a constant interchange of information, and scientists have major reference publications at their fingertips. Our own technical libraries stock over 800 different periodicals, and we have one divisional group whose sole function is to keep track of research discoveries elsewhere and pass on pertinent information. Whether new ideas originate in our own laboratories or elsewhere, they are eagerly studied and their applicability is appraised quickly. If one man's experience is insufficient to evaluate the work, another's frequently will prove to be, offering, as it does, a different background and perspective. /28

What is true in Du Pont is true in many other companies today. Large corporations consolidate information from many disciplines of science and engineering and bring to scientific development a breadth of vision extending far beyond any one man's capacities. The individual scientist is stimulated and encouraged. His discoveries no longer are left to languish on the laboratory shelf while their creator goes out to search for a sponsor. /29

In addition, the development of the modern corporation has created the national resources which support technology in many other types of institutions. The research efforts of universities, private foundations, and government laboratories contribute importantly to the advancement of American science and engineering, but these institutions could not exist were it not for the wealth generated by American industry. /30

The size of the institutions furthering technology has become an important element in our progress. With its engineering and production resources, the modern industrial organization can direct large groups of technologists—people skilled in many areas of science—to projects no one individual technologist could undertake. For example, it is possible to produce penicillin in a one-man laboratory in quantities sufficient to save a few lives. Produced in major pharmaceutical plants, penicillin has saved the lives of millions. I remember from my early interest in flying that a number of enterprising individuals built airplanes in backyard garages. Perhaps some still do. They would be the first to admit, however, that their efforts, in scale or in volume, are not quite comparable to the accomplishments of North American or Boeing. /31

Some of my colleagues at Du Pont, given a few days' notice and a small set of laboratory apparatus, could formulate a kind of nylon and spin a bobbin or two of yarn. But, to supply a national market, this would be like trying to feed an army with the grain you could raise in a flower pot. Moreover, the factor of size also has an important value to national defense. During World War II, for example, the Government asked Du Pont to build the atomic materials plant at Hanford, Washington. More recently, we were asked to undertake the construction of the Savannah River hydrogen-materials plant. These were perhaps the most ambitious engineering projects in history; they could not have been completed without the services of a large institution employing thousands of specialists in dozens of fields. /32

Quite obviously, all of the technological efforts of companies like Du Pont are not of this magnitude. And, obviously, not all of the technological jobs required for the nation's advancement require large institutions. Some of the most significant accomplishments have come, and will continue to come, from smaller organizations. In technology, as in other facets of American life, there is a need for business units of every size. Small firms supply companies like Du Pont with tools, materials, and special services which are basic to large-scale research and production efforts. At the same time, the small are important customers of the large, buying products which only the large firms can produce in a volume sufficient to meet national needs. Very often, the small firm makes its contribution to technology and finds its route to commercial success by developing and marketing a product created in the research laboratories of a large company. Thus, small and large business units work as a team to expand America's technology, with each contributing its special talents. /33

Four years ago, the Swiss economist, William Rappard, set down his views on the causes of America's prosperity. Most important of all, he wrote, were the application of science to production, the "passion" for efficiency in industry, mass production to bring large quantities of goods to people at low cost, and the spirit of competition. It is worth noting that the development of large industrial units is a factor in each of Professor Rappard's considerations. These organizations, consolidating many talents, have provided to technology and the technologist a whole new dimension of performance and potential. They have elevated the horizons of science and engineering, and they have literally extended man's reach into the boundless areas of outer space. /34

When the history of our era is written, the birth and development of the modern corporation must be recorded as a vital factor in our technological progress. Indeed, the corporation may well prove to be the greatest invention of them all. /35

The speech

1. Evaluate the appropriateness of the subject Du Pont chose to discuss. Was it well adapted to the audience and occasion, as you understand these from the headnote? Was it well adapted to the speaker himself?
2. Would you rate Du Pont's review of early American

inventions and inventors as highly interesting, moderately interesting, or dull and boring? If you consider it interesting, explain the various elements of subject matter, style, and organization which you believe made it so. If you consider it uninteresting, suggest several ways in which its interest value might have been enhanced.

3. Would you agree that the central idea of the speech is that the corporation is perhaps the greatest of all inventions? If so, can you justify the great amount of time Du Pont spends reviewing the history of technology and describing early inventions? Does this contribute to the achieving of his purpose, or is it extraneous material? Where is the central idea of the speech first stated? Should it have been made evident earlier?
4. Evaluate Du Pont's definition of "technology." Does it make his meaning clear? Does it do so quickly and economically or only at the expense of a long and involved explanation? Which of the standard methods of definition are employed?
5. How closely and smoothly do the major ideas of the speech fit together? Do they grow out of one another naturally and easily? Do they form a coherent pattern of thought progression? Are they tied together by easy and unobtrusive transitions? Defend your answer.
6. In calling a corporation an "invention," Du Pont is using the word "invention" in a figurative sense—that is, in other than its generally accepted meaning. What do you think of this figurative use of the word? Does it help clarify the central idea of the speech? Does it help make that idea more striking and memorable? Can you think of any serious objections to this usage?
7. Are you willing to accept the statement in the headnote that this is essentially a "good will" speech? What is a "good will" speech? How does it differ in purpose from a speech to inform or persuade? What are some of its leading traits and characteristics?
8. Do you feel that Du Pont refers to his own company too frequently when recounting the contributions industry has made to technology, or does he give sufficient credit to other companies and fields of endeavor?
9. Where would you say the conclusion of the speech begins? Which of the usual methods of developing a conclusion is employed? How would you rate the conclusion as to appropriateness and general effectiveness?
10. Basing your answer upon internal evidence drawn from the speech itself, would you say that Du Pont knew his subject well and had thought about it long and carefully, or do you get the impression that he did some hasty research a couple of days before speaking? Point to specific evidences and signs within the speech that support your answer.

For further study and discussion

1. Report at some length on one of the early American scientists or inventors mentioned by Du Pont or on one of the "battles" produced by conflicting patent claims.
2. Report on the research program carried on by one of our major corporations—Bell Telephone, General Electric, etc. How has this program contributed to technological progress? Has it resulted in better and cheaper products? Has it aided our defense effort?
3. Is communication among scientists today as full and free as it should be? Can American and Russian scientists exchange information without restriction? Should they be allowed to do so?
4. To what extent are most corporations primarily interested in applied, as distinguished from pure or basic, research? How has this affected their research programs?
5. If you were a research scientist, would you want to work in an industrial laboratory? Why or why not?
6. Is the day of the lone-wolf inventor working in a garage or backyard workshop past? Will all of the major technological advances of the future probably come from the mass research efforts of large laboratories?
7. Do you think Du Pont tends to undervalue the role played by universities, government, and private foundations in sponsoring significant research?
8. Give some actual examples of how "small and large business units work as a team" in promoting technological progress.
9. Would you agree with Rappard's analysis of the principal causes of American prosperity? Does he give sufficient credit to our rich natural resources and climate?
10. In view of the emphasis which industry places upon research, should the corporation executive be a trained engineer or scientist? If not, how can he keep himself informed of what his research men are doing and decide questions of policy that affect them?

Suggestions for further reading

Roger Burlingame, ***Machines That Built America*** (New York, 1953)

David Dietz, ***Harvest of Research: The Story of the Goodyear Chemical Division*** (Akron, Ohio, 1955)

Maurice Holland and others, ***Management's Stake in Research*** (New York, 1958)

Philip R. Marvin, ***Top Management and Research*** (Dayton, Ohio, 1953)

Lewis Mumford, ***Technics and Civilization*** (New York, 1934)

James B. Quinn, ***Yardsticks for Industrial Research; The Evolution of Research and Development Output*** (New York, 1959)

Charles Singer, E. J. Holmyard, A. R. Hall and others, eds., ***A History of Technology,*** 5 vols. (Oxford, 1954-1958). See especially Vol. IV, ***The Industrial Revolution,*** and Vol. V, ***The Late Nineteenth Century.***

Administered prices

On August 17, 1957, in the face of continued inflation and the growing threat of a business recession, the Executive Committee of the AFL-CIO[1] United Auto Workers made public a dramatic proposal. The "Big Three" of the automobile industry—General Motors, Ford, and Chrysler—were asked to reduce the cost of their 1958 models on the average of $100 a car instead of advancing prices as rumored. In return, the union would "give full consideration to the effect of such reduction" in framing the wage demands to be advanced when negotiations for a new contract got under way the following April.

This proposal was made in the form of a letter from Walter Reuther, president of the 1,300,000 man union, and addressed to Harlow Curtice, president of General Motors; L. L. Colbert, president of Chrysler; and Henry Ford II. Such reductions, declared the UAW, would "be an effective beginning in stopping and reversing the inflationary trend." As was immediately apparent to everyone, the proposal in effect was also a sharp criticism of what the union alleged to be "administered" automobile prices—prices set by considerations other than the traditional factors of cost of production and the laws of supply and demand.

In letters dated August 22, 23, and 24, respectively, Curtice, Colbert, and Ford unanimously rejected the Reuther proposal, declaring that the UAW should have no voice in determining the pricing policies followed by management. If the union actually was concerned with striking a blow against inflation, said Curtice, it could better do this by agreeing to extend the existing contract for another two-year period. Colbert and Ford countered with the suggestion that the workers "take an immediate and sizable wage cut, which the companies would then 'take into consideration' in pricing their 1958 automobiles." Nor, despite direct requests from the union, would either President Eisenhower or Secretary of Labor Mitchell comment on the issues involved. Such comment on their part, they announced, would not only be inappropriate but would constitute an unwarranted interference in the normal processes of collective bargaining.

With this original proposal rejected, Reuther and the UAW Executive Committee startled the nation on January 13, 1958, with a second and even more dramatic suggestion. After allowing the auto makers a 10 percent profit on "net capital" plus a 50 percent division of excess profits, all remaining earnings, Reuther recommended, should be split three ways—one half going to stockholders and executives, one fourth to employees, and one fourth to car buyers in the form of "a year-end rebate." Such a distribution of the "upper layer" of "the fantastic" profits earned by the automobile producers would, the union said, act as an effective counter against the threatened recession by giving the sagging economy "a massive injection of consumer purchasing power."

Again rejection by the auto makers was prompt and emphatic. General Motors' Curtice denounced the plan as "a radical scheme . . . foreign to the concepts of the American free enterprise system." Chrysler's Colbert called it an attempt "to fight inflation . . . by new inflationary demands." Ernest R. Breech, Ford chairman, said it would increase "the tremendous and unprecedented . . . monopoly power" already wielded by the union. President George Romney of American Motors thought it threatened the economic strength and progress of the entire nation.

Approximately two weeks after this second exchange of letters between Reuther and the auto makers, the Senate's Subcommittee on Antitrust and Monopoly, headed by Senator Estes Kefauver of Tennessee, opened an inquiry into "administered" prices in the automobile industry. On January 28 and 29 Reuther appeared before this committee to state the position of the union and to give testimony. He was followed by Curtice on January 30 and 31; Theodore O. Yntema, vice president, finance, Ford Motor Company, February 4 and 5; Colbert, February 6; and Romney, February 7 and 10. Selected portions of the testimony given by Reuther and Curtice at these hearings are reproduced here.

According to the New York *Times*, "Mr. Reuther appeared at the packed hearing room with a 110-page prepared statement, a seven-page supplement, twenty-nine tables and seven pages of corrections for the prepared material. . . ." The statement itself, however, was entered into the record without being read, and Reuther testified extemporaneously, using "handwritten notes."[2] Curtice, on the contrary, read his prepared statement prior to answering questions.

Walter Reuther was born at Wheeling, West Virginia, on September 1, 1907. He began as an apprentice tool and die maker at the Wheeling Steel Corporation in 1924. Later he worked for the Briggs Manufacturing Company and General Motors and was a foreman in the Ford plant for two years. He attended Wayne State University but did not receive a degree. In 1935 he organized the United

[1] American Federation of Labor-Congress of Industrial Organizations.

[2] In addition to appearing in *Administered Prices*, this prepared statement, with accompanying charts and tables, may be found in *Price Policy and Public Responsibility*, Publication No. 107P, UAW Publications Department, Solidarity House, Detroit 14, Michigan. 25 cents.

Auto Workers and has been that union's president since 1946. Widely known as an effective and provocative speaker, Reuther was once introduced by Governor G. Mennen Williams of Michigan as "the great spellbinder" of the labor movement.[3]

Harlow Curtice was born at Eaton Rapids, Michigan, August 15, 1893, and attended the Ferris Institute. After working briefly for the Standard Rule Company, Curtice became associated with the AC Sparkplug Division of General Motors in 1914. He was president and general manager of Buick Motor Division, General Motors, 1943-1948; a vice-president, 1948-1952; and acting president and president, 1952-1958.

In reading the statements and testimony that follow keep in mind the special circumstances in which the speakers found themselves. Remember that they were appearing as witnesses at a congressional hearing rather than on the public platform and that their listeners could interrupt them with questions and comments. Remember also that while Reuther acted in the role of critic or accuser, Curtice was on the defensive not only because he was obliged to answer the charges advanced by Reuther but also because the announced purpose of the hearing was to determine whether the auto makers were, indeed, guilty of charging "administered" prices.

Irrelevant and less important sections of the testimony are omitted, the omissions being indicated by ellipses.

WALTER REUTHER

Mr. Chairman, we appreciate very much the opportunity of appearing here, and I appear on behalf of the UAW and the 1½ million members of our organization. /1

We are very much concerned with the impact of the administered price policy of the automotive industry upon the general economic well-being of the Nation. We are very much concerned about the growing and serious imbalance in the American economy, the increase in unemployment, and the forces of recession which have set in in many aspects of the American economy. /2

Our appearance here today, Mr. Chairman, is the culmination of 2½ years of continuous efforts on the part of our organization to get the United States Congress to take a good look at the wage-price-profit equation in the automotive industry and especially on the part of the big three: General Motors, Ford, and Chrysler, who dominate this industry and who represent 97 percent of the production of the passenger-car industry. We believe that the impact of their administered prices, the fact that they can in the exercise of their monopoly position in this industry set aside the laws of supply and demand and rig their prices at a level which we believe short-changes the American consumers, American farmers, and American workers, and that this rigging of prices in the automotive industry since the automotive industry does have a tremendous impact upon the whole economy, is a very important and contributing factor in the creation of the growing imbalance in the American economy, and so we are very happy to appear here. /3

. . . .

Mr. Chairman, the thing that disturbs us is this tremendous loss of production that we are now suffering, and which will even become more serious, almost 4 million unemployed, basic industries operating at 60 percent of capacity. /4

The steel industry operated at 56.6 percent of capacity in the week of January 21. /5

The automotive industry is operating at 60 percent of capacity; other basic industries are operating way below their capacity. /6

We believe that this margin of unemployment, the margin of unused capacity, can represent freedom's margin of survival in a critical period. /7

I wish that the Soviet Union were only using their steel capacity at 56 percent. /8

I wish they had the workers who could make tractors and trucks and combines and earth-moving equipment, I wish they were only working 60 percent; I would feel more sure. /9

But when they are mobilizing every ounce of economic muscle, we are dragging our feet. I think what we need to do is to comprehend more clearly the dimensions of the world challenge, and then find a way to mobilize the capacity of the American economy, both our human and material resources, and use those resources for the development of our maximum economic position so that we can be equal to the challenge in the world. /10

We get in trouble—and I have said many, many times to workers that I have the privilege and responsibility of representing, "You don't really have to be a graduate of Yale or Harvard or the Ivy

[3] *Time*, February 3, 1958, p. 16.
Statement on *Administered Prices*, Hearings Before the Subcommittee on Antitrust and Monopoly of the Committee on the Judiciary, United States Senate, Eighty-fifth Congress, Second Session, Pursuant to S. Res. 57 and S. Res. 231, Part 6, Automobiles, pp. 2175, 2179-2183, 2194, 2225-2227, 2279-2283.

League universities, with a doctor of philosophy degree in economics, to know what is wrong with the American system, why it gets into trouble." /11

It gets into trouble because of the imbalance that develops between expanded productive power and the lag in purchasing power. /12

This is what happened in 1929. Here is a *Fortune* article, which spells this out in very clear terms. /13

It was published in February 1955. It is called "Portrait of an Economy Going to Pot." /14

It has also all sorts of statistical charts to illustrate, and I would just like to read one short paragraph, because what is happening now is exactly what happened then. /15

SENATOR KEFAUVER: We will put that article in the record. /16

MR. REUTHER: Thank you. /17

I just want to read this one short paragraph. It deals with what we were doing with the economic pie, the gross national product in the period before the crash in 1929. /18

Now, history is important only as we can learn lessons from it and avoid the mistakes that gave us difficulties in the past. /19

Here is what *Fortune* magazine says: /20

"How the pie was sliced: Factory productivity, measured as output per man-hour, increased rapidly through the twenties. But hourly factory wages did not keep pace. A rising share of national income in the late 1920's went to upper income groups. Interest, profits, rent rose 14 percent between 1926 and 1929, while wages and salaries rose only 7 percent." /21

What is happening in this period? /22

Well, essentially the same things that brought about the imbalance in 1929 are beginning to create imbalance in 1958. /23

The only essential difference is that in 1958 we have built into the American economy some economic cushions: unemployment insurance, social security; we have got strong unions that can push for their equity in the American economy, and the result is that the negative compounding impact of unemployment, which breeds more unemployment, cannot snowball at the rate that it snowballed in the period of 1929; but the underlying economic causes are the same. /24

You can see what happened to the share of the gross national product that farmers got and wage earners got in the period before 1929, as contrasted with those who were getting dividends and interest and nonwage income, and then parallel that in this period, and you will find that essentially the same thing is taking place. /25

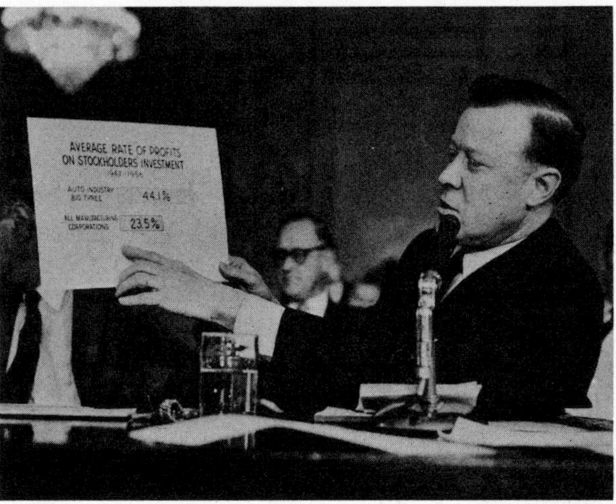

Reuther uses a bar graph in telling the committee the profit average for auto industry stockholders during the years 1947-1956. (Nate Fine Photo)

In other words, we are making the same mistakes now as we made in the period before 1929. Big business, these powerful corporations, by the exercise of monopoly control of vital sectors of our economy, are able to rig prices and set aside the law of supply and demand; and, because of that policy, they are getting a disproportionately large share of the gross national product. /26

If this were just a matter of their being selfish, that would not be too serious. But their taking more than their share means that you siphon out of the economy essential purchasing power, and that creates the imbalance, and it gets you into trouble. /27

Therefore, what we need to do is to find a way by

Listening to Reuther's testimony are Paul Dixon, counsel to the committee; Senator Estes Kefauver, and Senator Alexander Wiley. (Nate Fine Photo)

which we can share the greater abundance made possible by our developing technology, by automation, by the peaceful use of the atom. We must share that with workers, with consumers, with farmers, with stockholders, so that we maintain this dynamic balance that is essential to growth and to the well-being of our whole economy. /28

Everyone reads the papers, and the average citizen of America must be very much confused, because he has been subjected to a continuous barrage of propaganda and counterpropaganda. /29

Big industry says that labor is responsible for the inflationary situation, and labor counteracts by saying that big business is responsible, and if you could solve economic problems with propaganda and name-calling, we would not have any economic problems in America. /30

But, unfortunately, economic problems are stubborn, and they only yield to intelligent, rational economic action, and that is where we have not solved them. /31

We have reams of articles from the newspapers in our office about inflation. /32

Here is a headline: "Inflation Blamed on Wages." /33

Here is another one: "Industrialists Ask End of Pay Rises." /34

Here is another: "Industrialists Attacks High Wages and Says the Only Cure for Inflation Is Recession and Unemployment." /35

We believe that the recession, and the inflation which helped pave the way to the present recession and unemployment, grow out of this serious imbalance in the economy, which is reflected by the fact that huge corporations have gotten tremendous gains; and the consumers have been overcharged, because these corporations operate in industries in which the price is not determined in the market place by the law of supply and demand, but is determined arbitrarily by corporations which have got enough power to set aside the law of supply and determine how much they are going to charge. /36

I would like to show you a chart which, in a simple way, illustrates the source of this growing imbalance. /37

This is the period 1952 to June 1957, which shows — /38

SENATOR LANGER: Mr. Chairman, could we have that marked as "Exhibit 1"? /39

SENATOR KEFAUVER: Without objection, this chart will be marked as an exhibit. Let us identify it as "Reuther exhibit 1." It will be placed in the record. /40

MR. REUTHER: This chart indicates—these are from sources of reliable governmental statistics—that profits after taxes plus depreciation were up 48 percent; interest—and this, again, reflects the tight-money policy, because the bankers had a field day—interest is up 52 percent; dividends are up 38.9 percent, all salary and wages are up 30.2 percent. /41

Now, that— /42

SENATOR KEFAUVER: What period is that from? /43

MR. REUTHER: This from December 1952 to June 1957, so that it comes up to quite recently. This is the most recent information we could get because it is difficult to get the data on the last half of 1957 this early. /44

But it indicates very clearly the growing imbalance that has resulted from a disproportionate share of the gross national product going to the nonwage and nonsalary groups excluding farmers, and this other group, wage and salary earners, getting a disproportionately small share. /45

This second chart indicates— /46

SENATOR WILEY: Mr. Reuther, you mentioned gross national product. Do you mean the national income? /47

MR. REUTHER: Well, the gross national product is the total of the goods and services that we create. It is the value of all the goods and services put together. /48

SENATOR WILEY: I understand that. But when you are talking about the income having gone up that much, there is a difference between income and product of course. /49

MR. REUTHER: That is correct. /50

SENATOR WILEY: And you are talking now in terms of the average in percentage in national income. /51

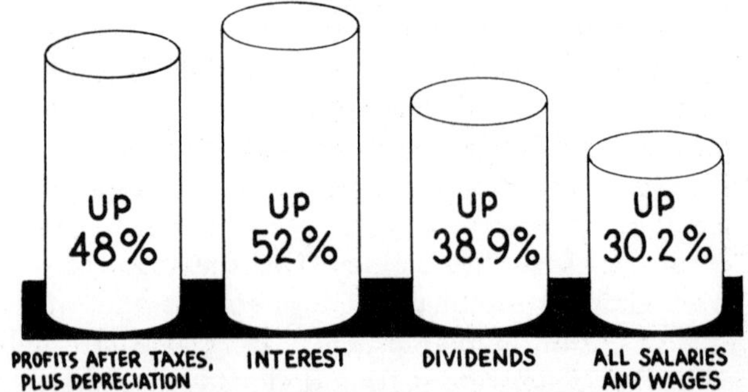

From *Administered Prices*, p. 2181.

MR. REUTHER: That is correct. /52

SENATOR WILEY: Have you the figures showing what the national income is and what the percentage amounts to? /53

MR. REUTHER: I will show you in a moment the relative movement upward of wages and profits and so forth in specific situations and then I think you will get the point that I am trying to make here, which is that the pressure on the price structure did not come from the fact that wage earners had gotten huge increases. /54

The pressure came from the other source, from the nonwage, nonsalary sector of our economy. This chart shows trends in prices and costs per unit in the private nonagricultural economy. /55

SENATOR KEFAUVER: We will mark that chart as "Reuther exhibit 2." /56

MR. REUTHER: This is a copy of the BLS* chart put out by the Department of Labor, and the heavy line here is the movement of prices. That is the price change from 1947 to 1956. You will notice that the line above that, with the little circles, is the nonlabor payments per dollar of real product, and all through this period it was well above the movement of prices. In other words, the income of nonwage and nonsalary groups was higher than the movement of prices. /57

The lower line is the labor payments per dollar of real product, and that line, showing the position of labor, of wages and salaries in relationship to the change in prices was well below the movement excepting this small point here, where it got very close, but never equaled it. /58

So there is no question about it. You cannot exert pressure on the price structure when you are well below the movement of prices, because its keeps moving above you. /59

This is the line that explains the movement upward of the price structure. We have not been pushing it. We have been chasing after the price movement. /60

Yet this does not tell the whole story, because the real killing came not in the economy as a whole, which those figures reflect, but in the group of giant corporations which, as I said before, exercise monopoly control and can arbitrarily determine the price structure unrelated to the supply and demand forces. /61

. . . .

If you take the profit position of General Motors in 1947 before taxes, they made $554 million. In 1955 they made $2,543 million. In 1947 the average wage of a GM worker was $1.44 per hour. In 1955 it was $2.18 per hour, and if wages had gone up from 1947 to 1955 in the same percentage as profits, the wage instead of being $2.18 per hour would have been $6.60 per hour for GM workers. /62

If you take the Ford comparison, you find that in 1947 Ford had a profit of $109 million after taxes, and in 1955 a profit of $968 million before taxes. Wages on the average in Ford in 1947 were $1.44 per hour, the same as GM, and in 1955 they were $2.18 per hour, but if Ford wages had gone up the same as Ford profits from 1947 to 1955, the average Ford worker would have made $12.79 per hour. /63

These are the facts. This is why we believe that these companies are getting a disproportionate share of the fruits of our advancing technology. These fantastic profits clearly reflect that they are getting more than their equity. For every dollar in wage increase during that period they raised prices $5. /64

Our union has been very much concerned about this, not just as wage earners, but as consumers, as American citizens, because we believe that this kind of selfish pricing policy, which takes more and more out of the purchasing power stream that people need, workers and farmers and consumers generally, that if this goes on, unemployment will increase, the idle capacity will get greater and the position of America to meet the challenge in the world and to meet the unfilled needs of people at home will get worse and worse and worse, and we are in trouble. We believe that we are playing for keeps, that we are engaged in a one-game world series. You have got to win the first game because there will be no return matches. The Russians are not going to say "Well, you lost the first game, we will give you a return match." /65

* Bureau of Labor Statistics. *(Editor's note)*

TRENDS IN PRICES AND COSTS PER UNIT IN THE PRIVATE NONAGRICULTURAL ECONOMY

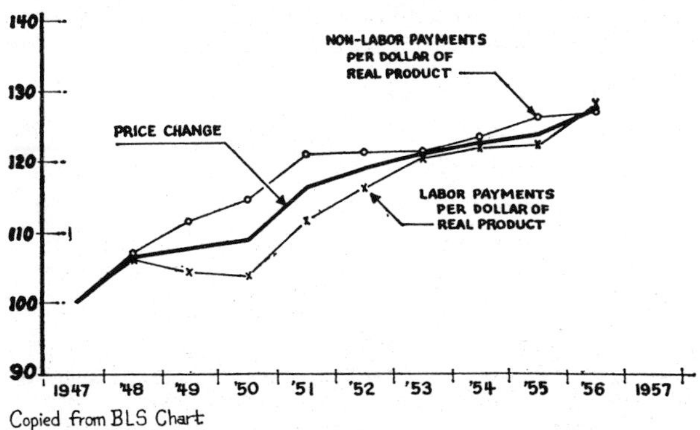

Copied from BLS Chart

From *Administered Prices*, p. 2182.

It is a one-game world series. We had better win the first game because there will be no second game, and we cannot do it if we continue to waste our capacity and our manpower. /66

That is what we are worried about. That is what our membership is worried about. /67

. . . .

SENATOR LANGER: Mr. Reuther, when you were interrupted a few moments ago you stated that you made an offer to the Big Three to reduce the price of their automobiles $100. Then you were interrupted. Would you mind going on with that? /68

I want to know what happened. /69

MR. REUTHER: This is a copy of the original proposal that we made to General Motors, Ford, and Chrysler corporations. We proposed that they cut the price of their 1958 models $100 per car on the average. That would be their contribution toward trying to correct the imbalance in our economy. We, in turn, made a commitment that at the bargaining table we would negotiate within the economic framework of the profit position of the company that flowed out of a cut of $100; but we said that the overall position of the company may not suffer, because if they cut the price of the cars they stimulate sales, so that while they may make a smaller profit per unit, they may make the same total profit out of a larger volume. We pointed out to them the arithmetic of this based upon what happened in 1955 and 1956. /70

These are figures that I think are very significant because they show that volume is the key to getting unit costs down and profits up. /71

Volume is the key to the economic future of the worker, the consumer and the stockholder. /72

In 1956 production in General Motors was down 23 percent below 1955, but profits were down 31.5 percent. /73

So you see the profits dropped much faster than the volume. /74

Ford is even more dramatic. Production of Ford in 1956 was 25.5 percent lower than in 1955, but their profits were 50 percent lower. In Chrysler it is even more dramatic because as their volume goes down, the shrinkage of profits is accelerated, the ratio steps up. /75

Chrysler had 36 percent less production in 1956 as compared to 1955, and their profits dropped 81 percent. /76

So what we have really been saying is this: We said if we can have a full employment-full production economy, and if you can stimulate the achievement of a full production-full consumption economy and start cutting prices, maybe other industries will follow suit and create a more favorable climate. Then we can bring into the market thousands and thousands of new customers and that will stimulate employment and sales. While you make less per car you may wind up making more money in total, because you have a larger volume. /77

So it makes sense from everybody's point of view. /78

Well, they turned this down, Senator Langer. They said we had no business even talking about it. We said we are not saying we want to bargain about prices. We have never asked to bargain about prices. But we do say that we have a responsibility to urge the industry to adopt a responsible pricing policy when an irresponsible pricing policy creates imbalance and mass unemployment and a serious threat of recession. /79

They rejected our proposal. This was last August, I believe. /80

SENATOR KEFAUVER: Is it contained in this pamphlet that you have here? /81

MR. REUTHER: It is. /82

SENATOR KEFAUVER: That is what you have been talking about? /83

MR. REUTHER: That is right; that is our proposal. /84

SENATOR KEFAUVER: Let that be printed as "Reuther exhibit 15." /85

MR. REUTHER: Then we got to the period where we are now, and we are getting close to the bargaining table although we will not be bargaining yet for 2 months—we obviously have to begin to formulate our demands in advance of the day we go to the bargaining table. /86

I sat down with my colleagues in the leadership of our union and I said to them—and they shared my concern—I said that we are in trouble in America, and what we need to do is to try to find a way to make our maximum contribution toward the correcting of the imbalance. Our maximum contribution can be made only if we increase the income of workers at the same time that we reduce the prices of cars so that we can give more people more purchasing power. So we decided to recommend to our convention, and we did so recommend, a two-package approach to our collective bargaining problems. /87

It was very unorthodox, it was unusual but these are unusual times that we live in. We explained this to our members and they adopted this program by better than 90 percent last week. /88

There were over 3,000 delegates, we debated this thing for 3 days and by better than a 90 percent vote they approved this approach. /89

There were some people there who preferred that we make the shorter work week, the 4-day week, our demand. /90

I took the position that in view of the worsening world situation and our increasing world responsibilities, we as the strongest of the free nations needed to assume that this was not a time to fight for more leisure. /91

This was a time to fight for full employment and full utilization of our manpower and our economic resources. /92

The point of view we recommended was supported by better than 90 percent. What did we propose to do at the bargaining table? Here again I want to emphasize this: Theory in collective bargaining is very shortlived. You get to practical things very quickly. You tell the boss what you want and he says "No," and that is the end of the theory and you are right up against the practical aspects of the problem. /93

So we said O. K., what do we do, what can we do in a practical way to meet this problem? /94

We said, let us have a two-package approach. We say that in the minimum package we want only what we know can be paid out of the increased productivity as measured in the total economy, not the auto industry, not the Big Three, but the total economy, that represents, we believe, that measure of economic and social progress to which every wage earner and his family is entitled, based upon the improvement in the whole of our economy, based upon the progress that we all make together. /95

But, we said, while we are willing to take that minimum concession as a downpayment, we do not want to forfeit our full equity because only as we realize our full equity can we make our maximum contribution to the expansion of purchasing power. /96

But if we demand our full equity now, the company can say "Well, this is inflationary," and we cannot disprove it. We can bring up a lot of economic statistics that we think would give us a good case, but we could not positively say we know absolutely that this is not inflationary, because General Motors can say, "Well, something might happen and we might lose money this year," and then it would be inflationary because the company would have to raise its prices. So we said "O. K., we will defer the realization of our full equity until after the customers who buy your cars have paid the price, after you have met all of your basic operating costs, and then after you set aside profits equal to 10 percent on your net capital we then want to share in the excess profits on the following basis: /97

"Fifty percent for the stockholders and the executives; 25 percent in the form of a consumer rebate—we do not make that as a bargaining demand, we are not trying to bargain about prices, we say this as a strong suggestion which we hope you will take; and 25 percent, which is a bargaining demand, to be shared among the workers." /98

In General Motors, that means 500,000 workers who would share in this equity. Now, why do we take this position——. /99

SENATOR KEFAUVER: Mr. Reuther, just on the details, the 10 percent you are talking about is before taxes? /100

MR. REUTHER: That's right. That doesn't mean that we are putting a 10 percent ceiling on earnings. This merely means that is the point that we break in. /101

Now, why did we choose that, Mr. Chairman? /102

SENATOR KEFAUVER: That is approximately 5 percent after taxes? /103

MR. REUTHER: That's right. /104

We chose that figure because that is the basis which General Motors executives and Ford executives, and essentially Chrysler executives, have used to determine at what point they share in the profits, through the executive bonus system. So we just borrowed their arithmetic, and we said that since Mr. Curtice is an employee, a very highly paid employee of General Motors Corporation, and he breaks in at this point to share in the excess profits, we want all of the employees to share, and we will use the same arithmetic that they use themselves. This is not of our creation; this is their creation. We merely borrowed it from them. /105

Looking at the overall increase in productivity in the economy, according to the BLS, for the period from 1940 to 1956 it went up roughly 64 percent. . . . /106

At General Motors, automotive wages in this period went up roughly 27.7 percent; the fringe benefits went up a little bit less than that, and we are actually using this figure—we are shy somewhere between 30 or 32 cents, the amount by which our economic gains have fallen behind the increases in productivity in the whole economy, not General Motors, not Ford, not Chrysler, but in the whole economy. /107

. . . .

I want to say this not as a labor leader but just as a human being, about where we are going in this world. I have a couple of young girls growing up back home, and I am concerned about the world they are going to grow up in. I have been trying to get people to understand a couple of simple ideas that I learned as I pushed around the world. /108

The Communists do not have to convince anybody. I mean, when they decide to expand their steel industry, when they decide to expand some other basic sector of their economy, they do not have to go out and convince the workers they ought to do it that way, and pay for it in lower living standards. /109

The Politburo meets in the Kremlin, and they make a decision, and that is the end of it. /110

In other words, under a system of communism, or any other totalitarian system, they get unity by rigid conformity from the top down. /111

But we, in the free world, have to get unity in diversity. While we think differently about problems, and while we have competing economic equities in sharing the economic pie, we always have to understand that while we have differences, we need to achieve unity in diversity by reconciling the differences within the framework of the values that we have in common. If we do not recognize the differences and get unity in diversity within the framework of these values, then the conflict within destroys the values of all of us. /112

When you sit at the bargaining table this is not an abstract philosophical concept, because values have no meaning unless you can apply them to practical problems. /113

So when labor sits down and management sits down they have to start dealing with these values. They have to understand that all of the basic values are essentially indivisible in character. You cannot have free management without free labor. You cannot have free labor without free management. And neither can be free excepting as they learn to work together to preserve our free society in a free world. /114

It seems to me that if we start from that basic starting point, then we can begin to reconcile the areas of conflict so we can go together and make progress together, preserve our common freedom, and contribute to the preservation of peace and freedom in the whole world. /115

. . . .

We propose, Mr. Chairman, that the way to encourage, the way to facilitate the maximum discharge of voluntary responsibility so that we can minimize the necessity for Government compulsion, is to get the public fully enlightened about the economic problems. /116

I sit down with General Motors Corporation. We have a public relations department, and when we get ready to make a demand we get our public relations department into high gear and we try to get our ideas out to the public. /117

And General Motors has a big public-relations department, with a public-relations budget that runs into many millions of dollars; we do not have that kind of money. Then we have a propaganda contest; and sometimes the contest deteriorates into a name-calling contest; but that does not solve any of the problems and the people of America think, "Well, a plague on both your houses," and they never really get around to knowing the facts. /118

This is why we put forward the proposal we make, which is based upon the concept that Senator O'Mahoney had back in 1948. The Government is not to get into wage-price decisions, not to get into the areas in which voluntary decisions ought to be made by labor and management, but the Government is essentially to provide the mechanism by which the public of America, the people of America in whom the ultimate authority for decision must rest on all basic matters of public policy, can learn the facts. Then we would get to the people not propaganda, not the unions' propaganda or the companies' propaganda or somebody else's propaganda, but get to the people the basic economic facts, so that an enlightened public opinion can exercise moral persuasion upon all the parties who are going to make private economic decisions which bear upon the public welfare. /119

You cannot expect an enlightened public opinion if the only access they have to basic economic data is what they get in the climate of a competing propaganda contest between a big union and a big corporation. /120

We believe that if the Government had an agency that would operate in that way, it need not be trying to put anybody on the spot or trying to be partisan in a labor dispute. Such a governmental agency would concern itself, not with all companies, but with companies whose production represents from 20 to 25 percent of the total product of a given industry. This is only a handful of giant corporations, but it is a small group of giant corporations whose economic power, whose domination of vital sectors of the American economy, is so tremendous that their private economic decisions have broad ramifications upon the well-being of the whole economy and the welfare of all of its people. /121

So what we propose is a very simple thing, not a czar, not a government agency with any power to make a decision about whether a price is 1 penny too high or 1 penny too low, or whether a labor union's demand is 1 penny too high or 1 penny too low but a governmental agency for one simple basic purpose:

to provide a public hearing in this fishbowl I talked about yesterday when a company whose production represents 20 or 25 percent or more wants to raise prices. General Motors, for example, will make 50 percent of the total car production in 1958, so that when they get around to wanting to raise their price, they would have to have a public hearing and tell the people of America why they think they are justified. /122

Now the public agency could not say you cannot do it. But if they did raise prices they would do it knowing that the public knows all the facts—not the propaganda we gave them, not the propaganda the company gave them, but the economic facts as they were developed in a public hearing. /123

Now supposing that General Motors Corporation was acting responsibly on its pricing policy, and supposing they were not short-changing the American consumers as they are, we believe, and we then came in and we were flexing our economic muscles as a union, and we were asking for more than our share made possible out of the advancing technology, and the greater productivity. /124

General Motors could say that would require a price increase and we will not give it to you, and we could have a public hearing where we would have to defend ourselves because we would be the group who were forcing a price increase. /125

And we would then have to stand before the American public. Such a governmental agency would be for the sole purpose of holding public hearings in these exceptional cases where big corporations can get economy out of balance, with no other rights or powers or authority. But we suggest further that in addition to this agency, there be established separate and apart from it, and independent of it, a department or an office of consumer counsel, and the person directing such a department would be the advocate and the champion and the defender of the American consumers. /126

He would be authorized to go before a board and to question companies and to compile data, for the purpose of defending the economic interests of the American consumers, who cannot sit at the bargaining table, who are not invited into General Motors when they are talking about raising prices. We would give the American consumer an advocate who could fight their battles. /127

Why do we think this is the answer? /128

This is neither a proposal that says we ought to just keep drifting where irresponsible private economic decisions get the economy deeper and deeper into recession, where unemployment increases and idle capacity gets more serious and more tragic, nor do we propose to take the other road which is to get the Government in with both feet with price control and wage control. We do not want to travel that road. /129

We do not believe that the answer to the problem of America is for the Government to take over the American economy. /130

We want to preserve the broadest possible areas of our free economic system, but we believe that it has to be made both responsible and responsive to the peoples' need. /131

So we propose a middle course, a course where the Government comes in only as an agency to get the facts before the public, and then the public, knowing the facts, can exert a powerful, constructive, restraining moral influence upon both labor and management at the point they are making private economic decisions in the areas of their activity which have a serious impact upon the well-being of the whole economy. We believe, Mr. Chairman, that the constructive influence of the moral persuasion that would flow out of an enlightened public opinion could be the most decisive factor affecting these decisions which now in many cases are made as the result of the exercise of economic power. They would be tempered by a sense of responsibility, and only thus, we believe, can we get decisions not based upon the persuasion of economic power, but rather upon the persuasion of economic logic. /132

That is why we offer these proposals, Mr. Chairman, because we think they are sound, we think they will work and we think they will make our free enterprise system stronger by making it more responsible and more responsive to the peoples' needs. /133

Now we do not claim that this is a magic formula, that this will cure every problem we have. /134

Democracy must experiment. It must try all kinds of tools. It should not be wedded to any rigid doctrine. It should not say that because we never did something we should never try to do it, because the problems of the future will not be solved in every case by yesterday's tools. /135

What we propose here is an approach to the idea of trying to get the pressure of enlightened public opinion to exert its moral influence at the point of private decision in those sectors of our economy where private decision has such an impact upon the total economy that the private decision either can bring great good or great evil to the whole economy and to the whole people. /136

We make these suggestions not as a back-door approach to socialism, because we are not committed to travel the road to socialism. /137

We think that free enterprise will be strong only if it serves the needs of people, because no economic system has a moral right to exist except as economic activity serves human needs. The more we can gear our free-enterprise system to the basic needs of people, to make it more responsible and more responsive, to that extent we will preserve the system, and we want to preserve it. /138

I would much rather bargain with General Motors with all of their money, with all of their resources, than I would want to bargain with Uncle Sam. At least General Motors cannot call out the troops. Uncle Sam can. So we do not want to travel that road. /139

But we know that the best way of assuring that we do not travel the road in which governmental compulsion becomes the substitute for voluntary economic decision, the best guaranty is not to create the vacuum that government compulsion will fill if we fail to find a way in which free labor and free management together can meet their joint responsibilities to all the people on a voluntary basis without governmental compulsion. /140

HARLOW CURTICE

We appear before you today in response to the invitation extended by you in your letter of November 7 addressed to me. /1

In that letter you stated that one of the purposes of these hearings was "to come to grips with . . . the problem of inflation." /2

We, too, as a corporation and as individuals, are seriously concerned about inflation. It is a destroyer of values. It must be studied and its causes must be removed. /3

Your letter indicated that you were concerned with the fact that "prices thus far announced by the automobile manufacturers for 1958 models . . . have been increased considerably in excess of the amounts directly attributable to the increased price of steel." /4

I propose to show, first, that steel cost increases represented but a small part of our overall cost increases over the past year. /5

I propose to show in some detail that the cost of a composite 1958 car is up $125 over the cost of its 1957 counterpart, whereas the wholesale price increase of this composite car has been only $74. In other words, for every dollar of increase in our known costs, price has increased only 60 cents. /6

I shall also show that this pressure of costs on prices is not an isolated phenomenon of recent origin. /7

Another question raised in your letter was why automobile manufacturers rejected the price reduction proposal made last August by Mr. Walter Reuther, president of the UAW. I shall comment on this and also on the belief expressed by some that wages and prices in a free economy can be fixed by formula. /8

Inasmuch as your letter would seem to question our pricing practices, I feel that it is necessary to review the various factors affecting price. It would be most unfortunate if emphasis on the cost-price relationship—which is the subject of your inquiry—left the impression that cost is the only factor that enters into the pricing of our products. /9

Pricing is like a tripod. It has three legs. In addition to cost, there are the two other legs of market demand and competition. It is no more possible to say that one or another of these factors determines price than it is to assert that one leg rather than either of the other two supports a tripod. /10

The first leg that any manufacturer must consider is the market in which he sells. The market for new automobiles has some unusual aspects that deserve consideration. For one thing, an automobile is an unusual product. To the purchaser it represents a sizable investment. It is also a durable product with an average life expectancy of thirteen years. It has come to be a necessity to millions of users, but, because of its durability, it is a necessity whose replacement can be postponed for a considerable period of time. /11

This means that the car markets of the past and the future can affect the current car market. An owner may prefer the car he purchased last year or the year before to the new cars on display. Or he may decide that next year's car will be more to his liking. /12

Our studies over many years prove conclusively that the size of the new-car market is importantly influenced by the general level of consumer income after taxes. It is also dependent on the willingness of consumers to buy, which is importantly influenced by their confidence in the future. Other products, too, affect the new-car market. The consumer is constantly being confronted with new and attractive products which compete with the automobile for his dollar—such as new homes, household appliances of all kinds, and more expensive vacations, et cetera. /13

Statement on *Administered Prices*, Hearings Before the Subcommittee on Antitrust and Monopoly of the Committee on the Judiciary, United States Senate, Eighty-fifth Congress, Second Session, Pursuant to S. Res. 57 and S. Res. 231, Part 6, Automobiles, pp. 2473-2475, 2477-2478, 2487-2491, 2499-2500.

The used car also is a most important factor to be considered. Used cars constitute about two-thirds of all cars sold in any given year. In other words, two used cars are sold for every new car. Used cars are sold in wholesale auction markets and in thousands of retail establishments under highly competitive conditions. They compete with new cars, and this is particularly true of higher-priced used cars. /14

In view of all this, the conclusion, I believe, is inescapable that establishing a price that will develop a satisfactory market demand for new cars is no easy matter but requires a study of fundamental factors over a long period of time. /15

The second leg of our tripod is the intense competition among new cars for a share of the market. First of all, the manufacturer must price his models from the lowest priced to the most expensive in such a way that the value of each model in relation to the others in his own line will be properly reflected. /16

It might be assumed that the less expensive a model, the larger its sale. This is not necessarily true. New cars that are stripped—that is new cars that are bare of accessories, de luxe trim and optional equipment such as automatic transmissions—do not sell well in the retail market in competition with more fully equipped new cars of the same make offered at higher prices. This trend, which was apparent before World War II, has been an important feature of the postwar market. /17

Secondly, the manufacturer must consider the values offered by competing manufacturers. Of necessity, he must quote closely competitive prices for similar models. /18

It should be emphasized again that competition in the automobile industry is much broader than price. The customer's decision to buy a car is influenced by the availability and quality of service. The annual model change has contributed importantly to the intensification of competition in the area of performance, style appeal, et cetera. A product that the public considers inferior, even though low priced, will not sell. On the other hand, substantially increased product values may make a higher price fully acceptable. /19

The factor of style deserves special emphasis, for style has become increasingly important in determining the share of the market which each manufacturer obtains. It is also the least predictable factor. The customer favors change. He wants his new car not only to look attractive but to look new. On the other hand, he is likely to reject anything that represents a too radical departure from an evolutionary trend. The risk to the manufacturer is obviously great, and a wrong decision can be competitively disastrous. /20

In order to keep the price of the basic new car as low as possible, it has been our practice to offer special equipment on an optional basis. This not only has resulted in greater competition but also has given the buyer a wider variety of choice. He selects only those additional features and improvements that he desires. /21

The fact that an automobile is a complex piece of equipment and ranks second only to the purchase of a house as an item of expenditure has an impact on competition in the industry. The buyer looks hard at the product and at its engineering, styling and special features. He is likely to do a great deal of comparison shopping. /22

As for the last leg of our tripod—cost of production—the individual manufacturer can remain in business only if he is able to keep his unit costs below the price that he can get for his automobile in a highly competitive market. /23

A price that may seem desirable from the cost point of view is not necessarily the price that customers will pay or the price that will prove to be competitive with values offered by other manufacturers. Whatever may be considered theoretically wise must adjust itself to this hard fact, and we can only hope that the price that is finally arrived at will prove profitable as well as competitive. /24

To be specific, let us consider the 1958 cost-price picture. Your comments regarding higher steel costs and their relationship to our prices overlook the fact that steel, while an important element of cost, is only one of many cost items in a car. And during this past year steel has been only one of many items contributing to cost increases. /25

To demonstrate where and how much costs have risen, we have prepared comparison of costs and prices on a unit basis in relation to what we call a composite car. /26

By this term, we mean the average of all passenger car models in our file lines, weighted on the basis of projected sales volume. /27

Total unit costs rose $125 for the 1958 General Motors composite passenger car in the period between the introduction of the 1957 models in the fall of 1956 and the introduction of our 1958 models a year later. However, the average increase in the wholesale price of this 1958 composite car is only $74 over the corresponding price of its 1957 counterpart. /28

. . . .

Thus, 40 percent of our increased costs—about $51 per unit—are not being recovered through price. Another way of saying this is that for every dollar of increase in our known costs, price has risen only 60 cents. /29

I should emphasize at this point that the figure of $125 reflects our cost position at the time the 1958 prices were set. Following our established procedure, our cost data do not make any allowance for possible future increases in labor rates and material prices which may occur during the 1958 model run. By the same token, we did not increase the prices of 1957 models at any time after they were announced in the fall of 1956, even though labor rates and material prices in general were rising throughout the 1957 model run. /30

We felt your committee would be interested to know how the total cost increase of $125 came about, and so we have prepared a detailed analysis. /31

In your letter, Mr. Chairman, you referred to statements by the presidents of certain steel companies who appeared before your committee as witnesses with respect to the effect of car prices of recent increases in the cost of steel. One of these witnesses, on the basis of an assumption of 1¾ tons of steel per car, estimated that the additional cost of steel resulting from the July 1957 price increase of $6 per ton should amount to no more than $8 to $10 per car. /32

These figures, of course, reflected only the July increase in steel prices. Earlier increases totaled about $4 per ton. Thus, steel costs have increased about $10 per ton since our 1957 models were priced in the fall of 1956. And since 1.84 tons of steel were required to build our 1957 model composite car, the increase in costs resulting from the higher price alone amounted to more than $18 per car. /33

In addition, there was a further increase of $9 in the steel cost of the 1958 composite car as a result of added refinements and design changes which increased its size and weight. This brought the total steel cost increase to $27 per car. /34

SENATOR KEFAUVER: Mr. Curtice, would you mind yielding at that point or would you rather finish your statement? /35

MR. CURTICE: No, whichever is your pleasure. /36

SENATOR KEFAUVER: While you are talking about the steel increase, is it not true also that the increase in the cost of steel increases the cost of automobiles more than just the actual amount of steel that goes into the automobile, that it involves a snowballing of cost? You have to use steel in your machinery that you buy, in your buildings that you build, an increased amount for transportation charges, the charges by the railroad as the result of the increased price of steel that they have to use. /37

All around the lot an increase in the price of steel affects your price other than just the actual number of tons or pounds that goes into a composite or a model automobile. /38

MR. CURTICE: That which we can identify directly is what goes into our automobile. /39

SENATOR KEFAUVER: All right, we will come back to that later on, Mr. Curtice. /40

MR. CURTICE: Other material costs, including increased freight costs, showed a net increase of $8, after allowing for lower prices for nonferrous metals in the amount of $9 per car. These costs too were affected by design changes and added refinements. /41

The total increase in all material costs amounted to $35 per unit for the 1958 composite car. /42

Payroll and related employment costs represent the largest single item of cost increase during the past year. They have accounted for an increase in cost of $52, which is 42 percent of the total cost increase of $125 per composite car. /43

These increased costs result from (1) a higher level of wage-salary rates and fringe benefit costs, and (2) additional labor content in the product due to improvements in car design, offset in part by the effect of improvements in manufacturing processes. Increased wage and salary rates and fringe benefit costs account for about $45, or 36 percent of all unit cost increases in the last year. If the increases in wage and salary rates and fringe benefit costs had not occurred, increased payroll costs would have amounted to only $7 per composite car, not $52. /44

Special tools—the tooling which is required to produce a new line of cars—have also been responsible for an increase in unit costs during the past year. The increase in the cost of special tools in 1958 over 1957, which reflects increased labor costs as well as increased complexity of the product, has amounted to about $24 per car. /45

Other items, including local taxes, depreciation, and miscellaneous costs have accounted for increases totaling approximately $14. /46

This brings us to the total cost increase of $125 for our composite car, which compares with our wholesale price increase of $74 per car (chart 2). /47

SENATOR KEFAUVER: Chart 2 will be listed in the record as "General Motors Exhibit 2." /48

. . . .

MR. CURTICE: I believe you will have gathered from my discussion that the prices that enter into costs are largely beyond the control of the manufacturer. For example, the prices we pay for materials are established in the market place. Increases in our

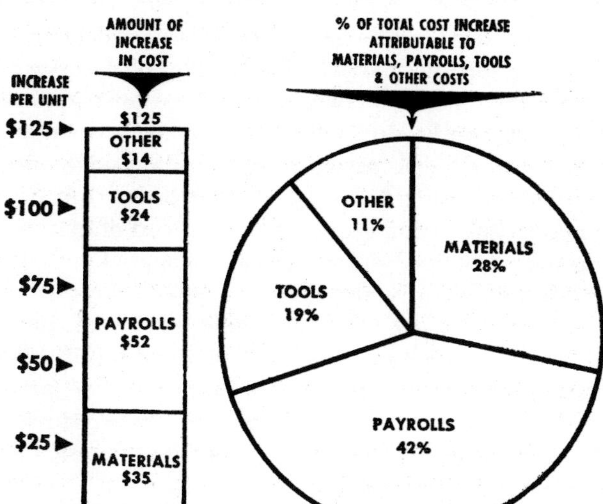

From *Administered Prices*, p. 2479.

material costs are attributable primarily to higher prices of metal products, which make up the bulk of our outside purchases. These higher prices in turn reflect higher labor costs in the metal producing and fabricating industries. /49

Our payroll costs, as I have pointed out, increased 66 percent from 1948 to 1958. This increase was due in part to the added labor costs of the improvements that have to be built into our cars each year to meet competitive market conditions, but primarily to a pronounced upward trend in wage rates and fringe benefits established through collective bargaining with the unions representing our employees. As a matter of fact, substantially all cost increases are the result of an upward trend in wage rate and fringe benefits since most of the cost of any product, raw material, or service represents labor costs. /50

At this point I would like to comment on the use of the word "administered" to characterize prices in the automobile industry. Those who use this word would seem to imply many things. /51

One implication is that the pricing practices of the automobile industry are different from the practices of most industries. Such is not the case. The facts are, of course, that the prices of most manufactured goods sold in this country are set ahead of time and do not change with each individual transaction. /52

Another implication is that prices in the automobile industry are in some way insulated from the forces of competition. Nothing, of course, could be further from the truth. /53

Changes in prices in the automobile industry, as we have shown, are the result of three powerful forces—the nature of the automobile market, competition, and cost of production. /54

Prices of any one manufacturer must be competitive with values offered by other automobile manufacturers and with the values of other products competing for the customer's dollar. I would like to add that just as the operation of these factors closely limits the actions of each producer, so, too, does it make impossible pricing by any arbitrary formula. /55

The invitation to testify at this hearing included reference to Mr. Walter Reuther's proposal last August to the presidents of three automobile companies to the effect that 1958 car prices be reduced "at least $100" per unit. /56

Mr. Reuther's proposal was indeed "vague and indefinite" insofar as what he offered to do was concerned. /57

Further, I think you will agree that in the light of the facts I have given you today, the proposal was completely unrealistic. /58

Mr. Reuther asked that the companies reduce their prices last fall. In return Mr. Reuther offered to give "full consideration" to the effect of the reductions on the corporations' financial position in drafting 1958 wage demands. /59

The point that was apparently missed by many was that, while Mr. Reuther was asking virtually immediate concessions from the companies, he offered no concessions of his own, but merely "consideration" 9 months later when wage negotiations are scheduled and the bulk of the 1958 model run will have been produced. /60

At best his offer can be interpreted only to mean that he might make his 1958 demands somewhat less excessive than UAW publicity has indicated they will be. /61

As I told Mr. Reuther in my reply to his proposal, I found it somewhat difficult to reconcile his professed concern over inflation with his announced 1958 collective-bargaining program. /62

As I have shown here, increased wage costs have been the largest single element in our rising costs. In view of this fact, the proposed reduction of $100 in the price of our cars—without an equivalent reduction in costs—would have been entirely unjustified. /63

I think it is pertinent here to point out that Mr. Reuther's proposal was not new. We heard much the same thing 12 years ago. /64

You may recall the UAW-CIO 119-day strike against General Motors in 1945-46. At that time, too, Mr. Reuther called upon General Motors not only to grant his wage demands but to reduce the price of its Chevrolet car by $100. /65

He demanded that General Motors "open the books" to prove or disprove his theory that wage demands could be settled on the basis of a company's "ability to pay." /66

Yet Mr. Reuther himself subsequently characterized these proposals for what they were. /67

At a press conference held shortly after the settlement of the 119-day strike he said: "Thomas (R. J. Thomas, then president of the UAW-CIO) knows as well as I do that the whole question of producing the books was merely a public-relations job on our part. . . ." /68

And further: ". . . It was used to put the company on the spot so that they would have to talk economics or be over a barrel. . . ." /69

In view of the similarity between the proposal of last August and the historical record, it is obvious that this maneuver was just another "public-relations job." /70

SENATOR KEFAUVER: Mr. Curtice, I think this might be a very good place to bring this up. /71

I do not know if you followed Mr. Reuther's testimony in detail. He said in connection with the matter back in 1945, among other things, that he offered to have some disinterested arbitration group. I think he said that there was one at that time, to see any records, that the union officials did not particularly want to see them, but to let an arbitration committee see the confidential information and keep it confidential, but to make a finding as to whether price reductions could be made and whether wage demands could be met and just what the situation was. /72

That was in 1945. He said that later, after the strike had gone on for a long time, it became a very serious matter not only for the automobile industry but for industries and their employees depending upon the automobile industry. /73

He said that President Truman appointed an arbitration committee composed of the present President's brother, Milton Eisenhower, Lloyd Garrison of New York, and a judge from the circuit court in North Carolina, that they went before the President's Committee—President Truman's Committee—and presented their side, but General Motors refused to come before the Committee or give it any information, and he denies that he wanted any trade secrets, that is, that the union wanted any trade secrets. They just wanted an arbitration committee to have a chance of confidentially examining them. /74

What is your recollection or what do you say about that? /75

MR. CURTICE: I think reading from the statement made public by the UAW-CIO before the fact-finding board—this says: "The union also declared that occasion might arise where it might be necessary for it (the union) to consider whether the company is 'paying the President too much money'—whether the directors, 'who aren't doing anything might be getting too much money'—whether 'the engineers ought to be sweeping the shop up instead of designing their products'—whether 'the managerial personnel has gone to seed.'" /76

SENATOR KEFAUVER: I was asking you specifically about these two committees, one of which was to arbitrate the matter between you and the UAW, and the other was a committee appointed by President Truman, apparently, as to whether his representations were correct. /77

In other words, did you refuse to appear before the President's Fact-finding Committee? /78

MR. CURTICE: He suggested arbitration, which was rejected by the corporation. /79

The Fact-finding Committee to which you have referred, appointed by President Truman, we did appear before that Committee but we did not remain. We did not remain when the matters under discussion or the position taken by the Fact-finding Committee seemed to follow in the direction of ability to pay and open the books. /80

SENATOR KEFAUVER: You mean you did testify before the Committee? /81

MR. CURTICE: We came and appeared before the Committee. We found it necessary to withdraw. /82

SENATOR KEFAUVER: Without giving the Committee any information or testifying? /83

MR. CURTICE: I am informed that before we could testify, President Truman did state that profits and ability to pay were a matter for negotiation. /84

SENATOR KEFAUVER: You mean a matter for consideration? /85

MR. CURTICE: For consideration, for collective bargaining, were matters for collective bargaining. /86

I think you will remember at that time, too— /87

SENATOR KEFAUVER: You mean at that point you withdrew? /88

MR. CURTICE: Yes, that is right. /89

SENATOR KEFAUVER: I do not want to rehash the whole matter, but don't you think he had a right to say they were matters for consideration? /90

If you were a company losing money, you would want that considered; and if you are a company making money, wouldn't you want that considered? /91

MR. CURTICE: We would not negotiate at any time on the basis of ability to pay. /92

SENATOR KEFAUVER: You mean if you were losing money, you would not feel that was important to bring out before a Presidential Committee? /93

MR. CURTICE: I think if we were losing money, I think it would probably be a matter of taking a good look at our management. /94

SENATOR KEFAUVER: Anyway, you withdrew from participation before the committee. /95

I just wanted to get the record straight about what happened. /96

MR. CURTICE: Yes, sir. /97

I think I might— /98

SENATOR KEFAUVER: And never presented any evidence before the Committee? /99

MR. CURTICE: No, sir. /100

I think I might add at that time we were still under price controls, also, and the policy with respect to pricing was changing. /101

As a matter of fact, before the strike occurred, the announced policy of the administration was that cost increases might be recovered in price, not that they could, but that they might be; and, on that basis, according to our interpretation and in relation to the cost-of-living rise which had occurred, we calculated that the 13½ cents would represent a fair estimate, and we made such an offer prior to the time that the union elected to strike. /102

However, their demands at that time were very substantially above that—I think about 35 cents, if my memory is correct—30 percent. They were 30 percent, rather than— /103

SENATOR O'MAHONEY: Mr. Chairman— /104

SENATOR KEFAUVER: Senator O'Mahoney? /105

SENATOR O'MAHONEY: I do not pretend to voice any judgment about the facts in this instance concerning which the chairman of the committee has been interrogating Mr. Curtice; but I am very much interested in the principle upon which you have testified that you acted. /106

In order that it may be clear in my mind, may I ask you the question in this form: /107

Do I understand you correctly that when a fact-finding committee, appointed by the President of the United States, indicated the desire to examine the books of General Motors Corporation, you felt compelled to withdraw? /108

MR. CURTICE: That is correct. /109

SENATOR O'MAHONEY: Then it was your position that you would not exhibit the books— /110

MR. CURTICE: There were other facts also but that was among those other facts. /111

SENATOR O'MAHONEY: Then this was one of the facts, that you felt that you were compelled for your own reasons to decline to disclose to a fact-finding commission, appointed by the President of the United States, the costs that might be exhibited in your books? /112

MR. CURTICE: That is correct. /113

SENATOR O'MAHONEY: Did I understand you also to say that one of the factors in this withdrawal of General Motors was that the decision to withdraw was made when it appeared to you that the discussion was tending toward a determination of the ability of a manufacturer to pay? /114

MR. CURTICE: Well, that was a part of it, yes, sir. /115

SENATOR O'MAHONEY: In other words, it was your feeling, the feeling of management of General Motors, that the ability of a corporation or an employer to pay should not be taken into consideration? /116

MR. CURTICE: Yes, sir. /117

. . . .

SENATOR WILEY: I have refrained from making any suggestions or questioning the witness, but it is almost time to get something to eat. I want to make it clear that I think I sense the situation as it existed back in 1945, but I want to ask a few questions about it. /118

First I understand that at that time, as now, the wages of the automobile men were probably the highest in the Nation among wage earners, is that correct? /119

MR. CURTICE: I believe they were among the highest; yes, sir. /120

SENATOR WILEY: Secondly, that the union at that time wanted an increase of 30 percent? /121

MR. CURTICE: That is correct. /122

SENATOR WILEY: And you people said no to it? /123

Then there was some arbitration board, as it was called, apparently by the President, and at that time you people took the position that it was not an issue—your capability to pay more, and was not to be determined by your books? /124

MR. CURTICE: That is correct. /125

SENATOR WILEY: And that you exercised your right, which was in question then, and which is in question now as to, I presume, similar committees appointed, that those books belong to you personally, belong to your company and are not public property? /126

MR. CURTICE: That is correct. /127

SENATOR WILEY: That being so, I have a number of other questions, but I want to just ask several in relation to that very situation. /128

You have not refused to sit down and seek to arbitrate with labor any time, have you? /129

MR. CURTICE: We have never refused to bargain with the representatives of unions who represent our employees, no, sir. /130

SENATOR WILEY: Yes. /131

You recognize that this committee has no function to interject itself as arbitrator in a situation of collective bargaining, don't you? /132

MR. CURTICE: I would understand it that way; yes, sir. /133

SENATOR WILEY: And you understand that is not our function here today? /134

MR. CURTICE: I thought that it was a matter of price. /135

SENATOR WILEY: What we are authorized to do is find out whether there has been any violation of antitrust or whether there is a monopoly situation. /136

MR. CURTICE: Yes, sir. /137

SENATOR WILEY: That is our function here. /138

And I think that Mr. Reuther understood that very plainly yesterday, and so what happened back in 1945, or what is happening now in relation to collective bargaining is none of this committee's business as I see it, and so, I would like to spend some time in finding out what your position is in relation to the obligation of applying what we call the rules of equity between men, great power, political, economic or what not, and I think you will have a chance to reply to some of my questions after lunch. /139

MR. CURTICE: Very good. /140

SENATOR KEFAUVER: Suppose you finish the rest of your statement and then that will be a very good breaking off point for lunch. /141

MR. CURTICE: All right. /142

In this statement I have endeavored to present — /143

SENATOR KEFAUVER: The committee will please be in order. /144

We will be recessing shortly but our spectators must let us proceed without interruption. /145

MR. CURTICE: In this statement I have endeavored to present the relationship of our costs and prices in the light of conditions as they actually exist. /146

It is clear from a study of the influence of competitive factors on costs and prices that there can be no automatic wage-and-price formula—short of arbitrarily enforced wage and price controls—that can be applied to the problem of inflation. /147

The same economic forces are at work in our industry as in any other industry. The upward pressure of costs in the long run will affect prices, no matter what the industry. /148

With rising costs, prices have to rise or else the automobile industry cannot long continue to supply the cars that the market wants. This is basic in a competitive industry and the automobile industry certainly is competitive. /149

Thank you very much. /150

SENATOR KEFAUVER: Thank you very much, gentlemen. We will stand in recess until 2 o'clock this afternoon. /151

MR. CURTICE: We will be here at your pleasure. /152

The testimony

1. Reuther presented his remarks extemporaneously, while Curtice read from a prepared manuscript. Taking their statements as representative examples of extemporaneous oral and written style, compare them as to word choice, sentence structure, clarity of development, interest value, and the like. Which mode of presentation do you believe was preferable under the given circumstances? Defend your answer.
2. Comment on the visual aids employed by the speakers to illustrate and support their arguments. Were the aids clear and simple? Did each convey only one central idea? Did they present data fairly, or did they distort or mutilate them? Did they help communicate the speakers' ideas more quickly and forcefully than would have been possible by the use of verbal presentation alone?
3. What special problems are introduced into a speaking situation when, as in this case, listeners are free to interrupt a speaker with questions and comments? How well do you think Reuther and Curtice handled the questions put to them? How well did they tie in their answers with their own planned remarks, and get back on the track after an interruption or interchange?
4. In their statements both Reuther and Curtice were obliged to deal with a good deal of theoretical and complex material—the causes of inflation, the relation between wages and prices, factors determining the cost of production, etc. In your judgment, did they succeed in making these complex ideas reasonably clear and comprehensible? If you feel that they did not and that many of their statements and arguments were vague and confusing, how do you think they might have made them more readily understandable? Through additional illustrations or comparisons? Simpler language? Repetition and restatement? Fuller def-

initions of technical terms? Which of the two speakers do you think succeeded better in making difficult ideas clear?

5. How well, in your opinion, does Reuther prove his contention that because the Big Three of the automobile industry produce 97 percent of the cars they can effectively "set aside the laws of supply and demand"? Does Curtice answer this point directly in his testimony? How strong do you think his answer is?
6. To what extent does Reuther use purely logical arguments to support his general position in this controversy? To what extent does he resort to emotional or motivational appeals? What do you think of the balance he strikes between these two modes? Does he use too many motivational appeals?
7. Both speakers cite statistics extensively, but their figures seem to show quite different things and are used to arrive at quite different conclusions. What does this tell you about the nature and dangers of statistics as supporting material? What rules and cautions should be observed when you use statistics in your own speeches?
8. In proving that cost is not "the only factor that enters into the pricing of . . . products," Curtice proceeds largely by the method of explanation. Do you think that explanation provides effective substantiation of this contention? Would it have been better to quote authorities and cite statistics in support of the point? Why or why not? What general conclusions, if any, can you draw concerning the worth of explanation as a means of proof?
9. Would you say that the portions of Curtice's testimony reproduced here constitute a direct or an indirect refutation of Reuther's arguments? Defend your choice.
10. Evaluate the interchanges between Senator O'Mahoney and Mr. Curtice or between Senator Wiley and Mr. Curtice relative to General Motor's refusal to allow a Presidential fact-finding committee to examine the corporation's books. Do the questions press to the heart of the matter at issue? How effectively does Mr. Curtice maintain his position in the face of questions? What do you think of this sort of oral cross-examination as a method for getting at the facts?

For further study and discussion

1. Would most economists and business analysts agree with Reuther's contention that the principal cause of a business recession such as we had in 1958 is an imbalance between productive capacity and purchasing power? What other explanations and theories might be offered?
2. Evaluate Reuther's plan for distributing the "top layer" of profits among workers, customers, and stockholders. Has such a plan ever been tried? If so, with what success? What effect do you think it would have on sales? On stockholders' dividends? On tax revenues?
3. Should Presidential and Congressional fact-finding committees have the right to subpoena the books and records of private corporations?
4. Is management's ability to pay a wage increase a legitimate issue for collective bargaining? Is a corporation's pricing policy a legitimate collective bargaining issue?
5. What responsibilities and obligations do parties engaged in collective bargaining have to the nation as a whole? Are strikes justified?
6. How is the importation of foreign cars affecting the position of the Big Three? What American-made cars are providing strong competition? What do you predict will be the general situation in the automobile industry ten years from now?
7. Do virtual monopolies exist in other major American industries—steel, chemicals, electrical equipment, etc.? If so, are they a good or a bad thing? Should they be permitted or broken up? How do the Sherman Act and other antitrust legislation affect them?
8. How can we best protect the consumer against unfair pricing practices on the part of business?
9. Considering the post-World War II period as a whole, have the wage demands of labor unions been unfair and excessive, or have they been justified by the state of our economy and by advances in productivity? Have prices risen unnecessarily?
10. Are our present collective bargaining procedures a fair and efficient means of settling questions in dispute between labor and management? If not, what alternative method or methods would you recommend?

Suggestions for further reading

Jules Backman, ed., ***Price Practices and Price Policies: Selected Writings*** (New York, 1953)

Edward H. Chamberlin and others, ***Labor Unions and Public Policy*** (Washington, D.C., 1958)

Walter M. Daniels, comp., ***The American Labor Movement,*** The Reference Shelf, Vol. XXX, No. 3 (New York, 1958)

Roscoe Pound, ***Labor Unions and the Concept of Public Service*** (Washington, D.C., 1959)

Wages, Prices, Profits, and Productivity, Background Papers and the Final Report of the Fifteenth American Assembly, Arden House, Harriman Campus of Columbia University, Harriman, New York, April 30-May 3, 1959 (New York, 1959)

For the complete text of Mr. Reuther's price-cutting proposal, see New York ***Times,*** Sunday, August 18, 1957, p. 80; for the complete text of his profit-sharing plan and the answers from General Motors, Ford, and Chrysler, see New York ***Times,*** Tuesday, January 14, 1958, p. 36.

8 / POLITICS

Pericles' funeral speech

This famous address to the people of Athens is a powerful expression of political ideals which were never fully attained in Athens or elsewhere but are striven for today as they were in ancient Greece. The text of what Pericles said in honor of those who had died in war has not come down to us, but the historian, Thucydides, reconstructed the speech as part of his *History of the Peloponnesian War*. Thucydides was a contemporary and a supporter of Pericles, and he probably heard the address when it was delivered. Most historians believe Thucydides was faithful to the spirit and argument of Pericles' "Funeral Speech"; at the very least, it is a speech that a great historian believed would have deeply touched and encouraged an Athenian audience in 431 B.C.

Pericles was born about 495 B.C. and died during the great plague of 429 B.C. He studied with distinguished Athenian teachers of music, science, and philosophy and psychology; they, it is said, freed Pericles "from the superstitions of the multitude whom it was his task to guide." His active political career in Athens began about 470 B.C. By knowledge, restraint, and eloquence he rose to leadership in Athenian politics. The expansion of Athenian naval and commercial influence abroad and the development of culture and tolerance at home were leading objectives of Pericles' policies, and he sought to attain these ends through the support and consent of the Athenian citizens. Although he was not always successful in maintaining popular support, he was indisputably the first citizen of Athens at the time when he delivered his famous "Funeral Speech."

The long series of struggles among the Greek states, which is known as the Peloponnesian War, began in March, 431 B.C. In the winter of that year the Athenians arranged the customary public funeral for all who had died in battle during the year. It was at this funeral that Pericles spoke, under circumstances that Thucydides describes in some detail:

"These funerals are held in the following way: two days before the ceremony the bones of the fallen are brought and put in a tent which has been erected, and people make whatever offerings they wish to their own dead. Then there is a funeral procession in which coffins of cypress wood are carried on wagons. There is one coffin for each tribe, which contains the bones of members of that tribe. One empty bier is decorated and carried in the procession: this is for the missing, whose bodies could not be recovered. Everyone who wishes to, both citizens and foreigners, can join in the procession, and the women who are related to the dead are there to make their laments at the tomb. The bones are laid in the public burial-place, which is in the most beautiful quarter outside the city walls. . . .

"When the bones have been laid in the earth, a man chosen by the city for his intellectual gifts and for his general reputation makes an appropriate speech in praise of the dead, and after the speech all depart. . . . Now, at the burial of those who were the first to fall in the war Pericles, the son of Xanthippus, was chosen to make the speech. When the moment arrived, he came forward from the tomb and, standing on a high platform so that he might be heard by as many people as possible in the crowd, he spoke as follows":

Many of those who have spoken here in the past have praised the institution of this speech at the close of our ceremony. It seemed to them a mark of honour to our soldiers who have fallen in war that a speech should be made over them. I do not agree. These men have shown themselves valiant in action, and it would be enough, I think, for their glories to be proclaimed in action, as you have just seen it done at this funeral organized by the state. Our belief in the courage and manliness of so many should not be hazarded on the goodness or badness of one man's speech. Then it is not easy to speak with a proper sense of balance, when a man's listeners find it difficult to believe in the truth of what one is saying. The man who knows the facts and loves the dead may well think that an oration tells less than what he

From *The Peloponnesian War*, tr. by Rex Warner, Penguin Books Ltd., 1954. By permission of The Bodley Head Ltd.

knows and what he would like to hear: others who do not know so much may feel envy for the dead, and think the orator overpraises them, when he speaks of exploits that are beyond their own capacities. Praise of other people is tolerable only up to a certain point, the point where one still believes that one could do oneself some of the things one is hearing about. Once you get beyond this point, you will find people becoming jealous and incredulous. However, the fact is that this institution was set up and approved by our forefathers, and it is my duty to follow the tradition and do my best to meet the wishes and the expectations of every one of you. /1

I shall begin by speaking about our ancestors, since it is only right and proper on such an occasion to pay them the honour of recalling what they did. In this land of ours there have always been the same people living from generation to generation up till now, and they, by their courage and their virtues, have handed it on to us, a free country. They certainly deserve our praise. Even more so do our fathers deserve it. For to the inheritance they had received they added all the empire we have now, and it was not without blood and toil that they handed it down to us of the present generation. And then we ourselves, assembled here to-day, who are mostly in the prime of life, have, in most directions, added to the power of our empire and have organized our State in such a way that it is perfectly well able to look after itself both in peace and in war. /2

I have no wish to make a long speech on subjects familiar to you all: so I shall say nothing about the warlike deeds by which we acquired our power or the battles in which we or our fathers gallantly resisted our enemies, Greek or foreign. What I want to do is, in the first place, to discuss the spirit in which we faced our trials and also our constitution and the way of life which has made us great. After that I shall speak in praise of the dead, believing that this kind of speech is not inappropriate to the present occasion, and that this whole assembly, of citizens and foreigners, may listen to it with advantage. /3

Let me say that our system of government does not copy the institutions of our neighbours. It is more the case of our being a model to others, than of our imitating anyone else. Our constitution is called a democracy because power is in the hands not of a minority but of the whole people. When it is a question of settling private disputes, everyone is equal before the law; when it is a question of putting one person before another in positions of public responsibility, what counts is not membership of a particular class, but the actual ability which the man possesses. No one, so long as he has it in him to be of service to the state, is kept in political obscurity because of poverty. And, just as our political life is free and open, so is our day-to-day life in our relations with each other. We do not get into a state with our next-door neighbour if he enjoys himself in his own way, nor do we give him the kind of black looks which, though they do no real harm, still do hurt people's feelings. We are free and tolerant in our private lives; but in public affairs we keep to the law. This is because it commands our deep respect. /4

We give our obedience to those whom we put in positions of authority, and we obey the laws themselves, especially those which are for the protection of the oppressed, and those unwritten laws which it is an acknowledged shame to break. /5

And here is another point. When our work is over, we are in a position to enjoy all kinds of recreation for our spirits. There are various kinds of contests and sacrifices regularly throughout the year; in our own homes we find a beauty and a good taste which delight us every day and which drive away our cares. Then the greatness of our city brings it about that all the good things from all over the world flow in to us, so that to us it seems just as natural to enjoy foreign goods as our own local products. /6

Then there is a great difference between us and our opponents, in our attitude towards military security. Here are some examples: Our city is open to the world, and we have no periodical deportations in order to prevent people observing or finding out secrets which might be of military advantage to the enemy. This is because we rely, not on secret weapons, but on our own real courage and loyalty. There is a difference, too, in our educational systems. The Spartans, from their earliest boyhood, are submitted to the most laborious training in courage; we pass our lives without all these restrictions, and yet are just as ready to face the same dangers as they are. Here is a proof of this: When the Spartans invade our land, they do not come by themselves, but bring all their allies with them; whereas we, when we launch an attack abroad, do the job by ourselves, and, though fighting on foreign soil, do not often fail to defeat opponents who are fighting for their own hearths and homes. As a matter of fact none of our enemies has ever yet been confronted with our total strength, because we have to divide our attention between our navy and the many missions on which our troops are sent on land. Yet, if our enemies engage a detachment of our forces and defeat it, they give themselves credit for having thrown back our entire army; or, if they lose, they claim that they were beaten by us in full strength. There are certain advantages, I think, in our way of meeting danger voluntarily, with an easy mind, instead of with a laborious training, with natural rather than with state-induced courage. We do not have to spend our time practising to meet sufferings which are still in the future; and when they are actually upon us we show ourselves just as brave as these others who are always in strict training. This is one point in which, I think, our city deserves to be admired. There are also others: /7

Our love of what is beautiful does not lead to extravagance; our love of the things of the mind does not make us soft. We regard wealth as something to be properly used, rather than as something to boast about. As for poverty, no one need be ashamed to admit it: the real shame is in not taking practical measures to escape from it. Here each individual is interested not only in his own affairs but in the affairs of the state as well: even those who are mostly occupied with their own business are extremely well-informed on general politics—this is a peculiarity of ours: we do not say that a man who takes no interest in politics is a man who minds his own business; we say that he has no business here at all. We Athenians, in our own persons, take our decisions on policy or submit them to proper discussions: for we do not think that there is an incompatibility between words and deeds; the worst thing is to rush into action before the consequences have been properly debated. And this is another point where we differ from other people. We are capable at the same time of taking risks and of estimating them beforehand. Others are brave out of ignorance; and, when they stop to think, they begin to fear. But the man who can most truly be accounted brave is he who best knows the meaning of what is sweet in life and of what is terrible, and then goes out undeterred to meet what is to come. /8

Again, in questions of general good feeling there is a great contrast between us and most other people. We make friends by doing good to others, not by receiving good from them. This makes our friendship all the more reliable, since we want to keep alive the gratitude of those who are in our debt by showing continued goodwill to them: whereas the feelings of one who owes us something lack the same enthusiasm, since he knows that, when he repays our kindness, it will be more like paying back a debt than giving something spontaneously. We are unique in this. When we do kindnesses to others, we do not do them out of any calculations of profit or loss: we do them without afterthought, relying on our free liberality. Taking everything together then, I declare that our city is an education to Greece, and I declare that in my opinion each single one of our citizens, in all the manifold aspects of life, is able to show himself the rightful lord and owner of his own person, and do this, moreover, with exceptional grace and exceptional versatility. And to show that this is no empty boasting for the present occasion, but real tangible fact, you have only to consider the power which our city possesses and which has been won by those very qualities which I have mentioned. Athens, alone of the states we know, comes to her testing time in a greatness that surpasses what was imagined of her. In her case, and in her case alone, no invading enemy is ashamed at being defeated, and no subject can complain of being governed by people unfit for their responsibilities. Mighty indeed are the marks and monuments of our empire which we have left. Future ages will wonder at us, as the present age wonders at us now. We do not need the praises of a Homer, or of anyone else whose words may delight us for the moment, but whose estimation of facts will fall short of what is really true. For our adventurous spirit has forced an entry into every sea and into every land; and everywhere we have left behind us everlasting memorials of good done to our friends or suffering inflicted on our enemies. /9

This, then, is the kind of city for which these men, who could not bear the thought of losing her, nobly fought and nobly died. It is only natural that every one of us who survive them should be willing to undergo hardships in her service. And it was for this reason that I have spoken at such length about our city, because I wanted to make it clear that for us there is more at stake than there is for others who lack our advantages; also I wanted my words of praise for the dead to be set in the bright light of evidence. And now the most important of these words has been spoken. I have sung the praises of our city; but it was the courage and gallantry of these men, and of people like them, which made her splendid. Nor would you find it true in the case of many of the Greeks, as it is true of them, that no words can do more than justice to their deeds. /10

To me it seems that the consummation which has overtaken these men shows us the meaning of manliness in its first revelation and in its final proof. Some of them, no doubt, had their faults; but what we ought to remember first is their gallant conduct against the enemy in defence of their native land. They have blotted out evil with good, and done more service to the commonwealth than they ever did harm in their private lives. No one of these men weakened because he wanted to go on enjoying his wealth: no one put off the awful day in the hope that he might live to escape his poverty and grow rich. More to be desired than such things, they chose to check the enemy's pride. This, to them, was a risk most glorious, and they accepted it, willing to strike down the enemy and relinquish everything else. As for success or failure, they left that in the doubtful hands of Hope, and when the reality of battle was before their faces, they put their trust in their own selves. In the fighting, they thought it more honourable to stand their ground and suffer death than to give in and save their lives. So they fled from the reproaches of men, abiding with life and limb the brunt of battle; and, in a small moment of time, the climax of their lives, a culmination of glory, not of fear, were swept away from us. /11

So and such they were, these men—worthy of their city. We who remain behind may hope to be spared their fate, but must resolve to keep the same daring spirit against the foe. It is not simply a question of estimating the advantages in theory. I could tell you a long story (and you know it as well as I do) about what is to be gained by beating the enemy back. What I would prefer is that you should fix your eyes every day on the greatness of Athens as she really is, and should fall in love with her. When you realize her greatness, then reflect that what made her great was men with a spirit of adventure, men who knew their duty, men who were ashamed to fall below a certain standard. If they ever failed in an enterprise, they made up their minds that at any rate the city should not find their courage lacking to her, and they gave to her the best contribution that they could. They gave her their lives, to her and to all of us, and for their own selves they won praises that never grow old, the most splendid of sepulchres—not the sepulchre in which their bodies are laid, but where their glory remains eternal in men's minds, always there on the right occasion to stir others to speech or to action. For famous men have the whole earth as their memorial: it is not only the inscriptions on their graves in their own country that mark them out; no, in foreign lands also, not in any visible form but in people's hearts, their memory abides and grows. It is for you to try to be like them. Make up your minds that happiness depends on being free, and freedom depends on being courageous. Let there be no relaxation in face of the perils of the war. The people who have most excuse for despising death are not the wretched and unfortunate, who have no hope of doing well for themselves, but those who run the risk of a complete reversal in their lives, and who would feel the difference most intensely, if things went wrong for them. Any intelligent man would find a humiliation caused by his own slackness more painful to bear than death, when death comes to him unperceived, in battle, and in the confidence of his patriotism. /12

For these reasons I shall not commiserate with those parents of the dead, who are present here. Instead I shall try to comfort them. They are well aware that they have grown up in a world where there are many changes and chances. But this is good fortune —for men to end their lives with honour, as these have done, and for you honourably to lament them: their life was set to a measure where death and happiness went hand in hand. I know that it is difficult to convince you of this. When you see other people happy you will often be reminded of what used to make you happy too. One does not feel sad at not having some good thing which is outside one's experience: real grief is felt at the loss of something which one is used to. All the same, those of you who are of the right age must bear up and take comfort in the thought of having more children. In your own homes these new children will prevent you from brooding over those who are no more, and they will be a help to the city, too, both in filling the empty places, and in assuring her security. For it is impossible for a man to put forward fair and honest views about our affairs if he has not, like everyone else, children whose lives may be at stake. As for those of you who are now too old to have children, I would ask you to count as gain the greater part of your life, in which you have been happy, and remember that what remains is not long, and let your hearts be lifted up at the thought of the fair fame of the dead. One's sense of honour is the only thing that does not grow old, and the last pleasure, when one is worn out with age, is not, as the poet said, making money, but having the respect of one's fellow men. /13

As for those of you here who are sons or brothers of the dead, I can see a hard struggle in front of you. Everyone always speaks well of the dead, and, even if you rise to the greatest heights of heroism, it will be a hard thing for you to get the reputation of having come near, let alone equalled, their standard. When one is alive, one is always liable to the jealousy of one's competitors, but when one is out of the way, the honour one receives is sincere and unchallenged. /14

Perhaps I should say a word or two on the duties of women to those among you who are now widowed. I can say all I have to say in a short word of advice. Your great glory is not to be inferior to what God has made you, and the greatest glory of a woman is to be least talked about by men, whether they are praising you or criticizing you. I have now, as the law demanded, said what I had to say. For the time being our offerings to the dead have been made, and for the future their children will be supported at the public expense by the city, until they come of age. This is the crown and prize which she offers, both to the dead and to their children, for the ordeals which they have faced. Where the rewards of valour are the greatest, there you will find also the best and bravest spirits among the people. And now, when you have mourned for your dear ones, you must depart. **/15**

The speech

1. Epideictic or ceremonial speakers usually praise extensively those whom the ceremony honors, but Pericles spends little more than a paragraph for direct praise of the dead. What reasons might he have had for such a neglect of customary practice?
2. Among the standard topics of praise commonly used in ceremonial speeches are: uniqueness deserves praise, moderation deserves praise, bravery deserves praise, to do things for others rather than for one's self deserves praise. Does Pericles use these topics? Where? Does he use others like them?
3. Are there any sections of Pericles' address which, if adapted slightly, could be incorporated in a Memorial Day address in the United States? Which sections, if any?
4. Most funeral orators talk about the dead first and, after that, about the living. Pericles speaks of the living first and last and comments on the dead in a middle section of the speech. Suggest ways in which his specific purpose may have made this arrangement seem desirable.
5. Pericles cites relatively little concrete evidence to prove his statements. Can a speech be great without such evidence? Justify your answer.
6. Thucydides said of Pericles, "Because of his position, his intelligence, and his known integrity, [he] could respect the liberty of the people and at the same time hold them in check." Where, in this speech, do you find Pericles apparently trying to check popular feelings?
7. Do you think Pericles' final statement is an appropriate concluding remark for this occasion? Why or why not?
8. The famous scholar Richard C. Jebb described Pericles' speech as "tranquil, stately . . . but varied by occasional bursts having the character of lofty poetry." What sections of this speech illustrate each of these qualities?
9. The speeches Thucydides included in his history were intended to display the motives and beliefs of the important men of whom he wrote. What Periclean motives and beliefs has he illustrated by including this speech?
10. Among historic speeches Pericles' "Funeral Speech" has been especially admired by the English and the Americans. In the last three hundred years it has been repeatedly translated into English and has continued to be a favorite with successive generations. What are some of the qualities that may have given it this high popularity?

For further study and discussion

1. What are the most important traditions or practices we have inherited from the founders of this country (Puritans, framers of the Constitution, etc.)?
2. How far do we have equality before the law in the sense that Pericles claims it for Athens?
3. Do you think public office is open to all in the United States without regard for class or wealth?
4. How successful was the Athenian democracy as a form of government?
5. What degree of democracy do you think is practicable for a country as large as the United States?
6. Is it for the virtues Pericles enumerates that the modern world honors ancient Athens? If not, why did Athens influence the Western world so deeply?
7. Do you think the United States should become less concerned than it is about military security? Why or why not?
8. What social or spiritual uses have such public ceremonies as weddings, funerals, Independence Day observances, holy days, and the like?
9. Which comes closer to the Periclean ideal, Athens in Pericles' time or the United States at the present time? Why?
10. Woodrow Wilson said, "Loyalty means you ought to be ready to sacrifice every interest that you have and your life itself, if your country calls upon you to do so." Pericles would have agreed with Wilson. Do you? Why or why not?

Suggestions for further reading

Leland Dewitt Baldwin, ***Best Hope of Earth*** (Pittsburgh, 1956)

Dennis Brogan, ***Politics in America*** (New York, 1954)

Stimson Bullitt, ***To Be A Politician*** (Garden City, N.Y., 1959)

Bertrand Russell, ***Human Society in Ethics and Politics*** (New York, 1955)

Graham Wallas, ***Human Nature in Politics*** (London, 1929)

The future of liberalism: a debate

The two discourses that follow were composed and printed as essays. They were addressed to readers of *The Reporter,* a magazine for relatively well educated people who tend to identify themselves as liberals in politics. Each author adapts to the predispositions of this audience. Each rightly assumes that he need not defend the merits of liberalism itself; each derives his supporting materials from the presumed common knowledge and assumptions of *The Reporter's* readers; each tries to adapt to and redirect his readers' somewhat nostalgic approval of the victorious liberalism of the New Deal in the 1930's. In these and other ways the essays of Arthur M. Schlesinger, Jr., and Max Ascoli resemble speeches and serve to illustrate how closely popular, adaptive, personal writing can approach the spoken word in substance and in manner.

These articles were first published in 1956, an election year. The national political conventions had not yet been held, but it was a foregone conclusion that President Eisenhower would be renominated by the Republicans. The chief contenders for the Democratic presidential nomination were Governor Adlai E. Stevenson of Illinois, the Democratic candidate in 1952, and Senator Estes Kefauver of Tennessee. The leadership in both parties, the political record of previous years, and the public opinion polls made it clear that the White House was almost certain to be occupied again by a confirmed "moderate." That Congress would operate under moderate leadership was equally plain. The astute political analyst, Samuel Lubell, had written in 1952 that a "conservative revolution" had taken place in the United States. To liberals this seemed all too true.

In such an atmosphere many liberals wondered how the vigor of the 1930's might be restored to their cause. As the Schlesinger-Ascoli debate shows, they were not entirely agreed on their goals, however. Drawing on his historical studies and his experience in practical politics, Schlesinger undertook to redefine the liberal creed; his essay moved Ascoli, an equally ardent liberal, to reply; hence the debate-in-print.

Arthur M. Schlesinger, Jr., was born in Columbus, Ohio, in 1917. He is the son of the distinguished historian, Arthur M. Schlesinger, Sr., and has, himself, achieved distinction by his studies in American history. He received his A.B. from Harvard College in 1938 and was a member of the Harvard Society of Fellows from 1939 to 1942. During World War II he served in several United States intelligence agencies, and in 1946 he joined the Harvard faculty, where he is now Professor of History. He has been a consultant to various departments of the federal government and was a member of Adlai E. Stevenson's campaign staff in the presidential election contest of 1952. Since writing the essay printed here, he has served in a similar capacity with Adlai Stevenson in 1956 and with John F. Kennedy in 1960.

Schlesinger has received numerous awards for historical research and writing, including the Pulitzer Prize for History in 1946. *The Age of Jackson* and *The Age of Roosevelt* are probably his best known historical studies.

Max Ascoli was born in Ferrara, Italy in 1898. He attended the University of Ferrara where he received his LL.D. in 1920. In 1928 he was awarded his Ph.D. by the University of Rome. After serving as a professor of jurisprudence in Italian universities, he came to the United States in 1931 and was naturalized in 1939.

Since 1933 Ascoli has been a member of the Graduate Faculty of the New School for Social Research in New York City and in 1940 and 1941 served as Dean of that Faculty. He became editor and publisher of *The Reporter* in 1949 and has since continued in these positions. Ascoli is a recognized scholar in political theory as well as a teacher and journalist.

The challenge of abundance

ARTHUR M. SCHLESINGER, JR.

Rarely have the experts differed so sharply about the nature of the American political mood as they do today. I suppose that of living Americans the two men who have shown themselves the most penetrating diagnosticians of the nation's political state of mind have been Harry S. Truman and Samuel Lubell. President Truman's victory over fantastic odds in 1948 establishes him as the most astute professional in the politics of this generation. Mr. Lubell's *Future of American Politics,* published in 1952, remains the most illuminating analysis of the movements of political sentiment in this country written in recent years. Yet President Truman and Mr. Lubell are today in flat disagreement in their reading of the present temper of the country. /1

Arthur M. Schlesinger, Jr., "The Challenge of Abundance," *The Reporter,*. Vol. 14, May 3, 1956, pp. 8-11.

As Mr. Lubell sees it, "The people are in a conservative mood. They don't want 'more' so much as they would like to keep things as they are. Nobody wants war; nobody wants a depression. Few people even want reform. They are content to hold things as they are." Mr. Truman, on the other hand, evidently feels that the people are fed to the point of exasperation with government of the rich, by the rich, for the rich, and that they want more and better New Deals and Fair Deals* in the interests of the worker, the farmer, and the small businessman. /2

Now undoubtedly much of what both Mr. Lubell and Mr. Truman contend is true. There are millions of people in this country who are satisfied with things as they are and see no need for change. And there are millions who are dissatisfied with things as they are and feel that government can do much more to equalize opportunities and benefits. Both groups have existed for a long time—the Republican vote has not fallen under 15 million or the Democratic under 20 million in the last generation—and there is no reason to assume that either has substantially diminished. What is important rather are the 20 or 25 million voters in the middle. How do they feel? Are they perfectly happy with society as it is? Or do their eyes light up and their hearts beat faster when they hear the slogans and appeals of the New Deal and Fair Deal? /3

One is compelled to conclude that for this middle group neither the analysis of Mr. Lubell nor that of President Truman is wholly adequate. It is obvious that these people, most of whom live in tolerable economic circumstances and are not particularly mad at anybody, do not respond very strongly to the rhetoric of the liberalism of the 1930's. But it would seem equally obvious that they are by no means in a condition of unlimited spiritual equability. If there is anything plain about our middle-class society today, it is the evidence on every hand of widespread internal anxiety and discontent. Billy Graham and Senator McCarthy have both been beneficiaries of this tormenting uncertainty;** the so-called religious revival is a significant manifestation of inner unrest; and, indeed, the role of President Eisenhower as a national father image only emphasizes the extent to which many Americans have become today passionate seekers after some form of spiritual reassurance. /4

It thus seems hard to deny that widespread discontent of some kind exists. It seems equally hard to assert that the liberalism of the 1930's has the answer to this discontent. Plainly the problem for the liberalism of the 1950's is to identify the sources of discontent and to develop a program and a philosophy capable of meeting the challenge of a new era. /5

The old brand

The liberalism of this generation was born in the depression. It came of age at a time when social thought was urgently directed toward problems of unemployment, poverty, and want. Liberals were concerned with providing food for the hungry, shelter for the homeless, work for the jobless. The characteristic issues were those involved in refueling the economic machine, raising mass living standards, setting minimum wages, pegging farm prices, refinancing mortgages, vindicating collective bargaining, establishing systems of old-age insurance and social security. The liberals of the 1930's aspired to create a new society characterized by full employment, rising national income, and expanding economic opportunity. /6

Let me call this for a moment "quantitative liberalism." I mean by this that it was a liberalism that thought primarily—and necessarily—in quantitative terms. It had to deal with immediate problems of subsistence and survival. And it had another characteristic too. In dealing with these problems, it had to face the fierce resistance of the business community of the nation—an experience that stamped this liberalism with the conviction that the "special interests" were determined to block or sabotage every advance toward a more decent social order. /7

This liberalism was, in the main, a brilliant success. It overhauled the American economy, equipped it with a set of built-in safety devices and stabilizers, rolled back poverty, instituted a fair measure of social and economic security, and tamed and educated the business community. It laid the foundations for a new age in America. /8

But that new age is now largely upon us. And, ironically, it is the very success of the older liberalism that is the essential cause of its present irrelevance. For the experience of the 1930's gave it the assumption that poverty and reaction were the essential sources of social discontent—an assumption that is in part responsible for the bafflement of many liberals today, when both poverty and reaction have receded from the forefront of our national life. Suppose that the New Dealers of 1936 could have envisaged America twenty years later—a nation with nearly sixty-three million men and women at work, a gross nation-

* The Truman Administration called its reform program the Fair Deal. (*Editor's note*)

** The reference is to Reverend William (Billy) Franklin Graham's evangelistic campaigns in the United States and abroad and to Senator Joseph R. McCarthy's charges that large numbers of Communists had infiltrated governmental services. (*Editor's note*)

al product of 387 billion a year, business progressive and enlightened, trade unions solid and respectable, minimum wages, maximum hours, and farm-price supports written into the law of the land. Transported into so rich and overflowing a society, they might well have supposed that the "more abundant life" had been at last achieved. If people had jobs, and unions, and enough to eat, and prospects for security in case of unemployment or old age—and if all this was accepted by the business community—what more could anyone ask? The dream of plenty seemed to promise a solution for all the problems of life. /9

Today we dwell in the economy of abundance—and our spiritual malaise seems greater than ever before. As a nation, the richer we grow, the more tense, insecure, and unhappy we seem to become. Yet too much of our liberal thought is still mired in the issues, the attitudes, and the rallying cries of the 1930's. It is as if Franklin Roosevelt and his associates, instead of inventing a New Deal of their own, had insisted on repeating the incantations of Woodrow Wilson's New Freedom and Theodore Roosevelt's New Nationalism.* Liberals today must be as alert in identifying the problems of the 1950's as the New Dealers, who were courageous and uninhibited thinkers, were alert in identifying the problems of the 1930's. /10

New strategies for new wars

What is required today is a new liberalism, addressed to the miseries of an age of abundance. I would not mean to suggest by this for a moment that the job of "quantitative liberalism" is finished. There are unhappily still broad areas of poverty in our land. No American can be complacent when approximately four million American families are trying to make ends meet on incomes of less than $2,000 a year. The depressed areas in states like Massachusetts and West Virginia** now threaten to become stagnant industrial slums. There is no excuse for the continued instability in farm income; and, even worse, there remain ugly splotches of grinding rural poverty where farm families live outside the price-support system. Yet, while there is still much to be done in completing the battle against poverty, the central problems of our time are no longer problems of want and privation; and the central sources of discontent are no longer, as they were in the 1930's, economic in character. /11

Liberalism in an age of abundance must begin shifting its emphasis. Instead of the quantitative liberalism of the 1930's, rightly dedicated to the struggle to secure the economic basis of life, we need now a "qualitative liberalism" dedicated to bettering the quality of people's lives and opportunities. Instead of talking as if the necessities of living—a job, a square meal, a suit of clothes, and a roof—were still at stake, we should be able to count that fight won and move on to the more subtle and complicated problem of fighting for individual dignity, identity, and fulfillment in a mass society. The new liberalism implies no repudiation of the old; rather it respects, accepts, and absorbs the triumphs of the New and Fair Deals, regards them as the basis for a new age of social progress, and seeks to move beyond them toward new goals of national development. Nor, should I add, does the distinction between "quantitative" and "qualitative" mean that one form of liberalism requires taxation and spending while the other is cheap and painless. Obviously progress in the "qualitative" area will require government initiative almost as much as the other. Yet a significant difference remains between the two in mood and approach. /12

The issues of 1956 are no longer the issues of 1933—the issues that made the difference between starvation and survival. Depression is dead as an issue, and will remain so until another depression revives it. The question whether trade unions should exist, whether business should be regulated, whether social security should be established—these are no longer issues. Even bigness in business and reaction in the business community, if issues now, take a new form and require a new attack. All these were part of the crisis of the 1930's. Thanks to the liberalism of the 1930's we have surmounted that crisis. /13

The issues of 1956 are those which make the difference between defeat and opportunity, between frustration and fulfillment, in the everyday lives of average persons. They have to do with education, with medical care, with more equal opportunities for minority groups, with the better planning of our cities and our suburbs, with slum clearance and decent housing, with the improvement of life for the sick and the aged, with the freedoms of speech, expression, and conscience, with the bettering of our mass media and the elevation of our popular culture—in short, with the *quality* of civilization to which our nation aspires in an age of ever-increasing abundance and leisure. /14

* "The New Freedom" was one of the slogans Wilson used in the presidential campaign of 1912. In 1913 he published a book with the same title, and the phrase became the "tag" designating the various reforms of his first administration. Theodore Roosevelt's "tag" for his administrations was the "Square Deal," but others sometimes referred to his administrative reorganization of the government as a program of "New Nationalism." *(Editor's note)*

** Massachusetts was depressed by removal of some of its industries to Southern states, and West Virginia by the declining market for coal. *(Editor's note)*

But issues are not enough. There is need too for a new spirit. The liberal program of the 1930's had necessarily to be presented in an atmosphere charged with class tension. The business community of the day was united and ruthless in its opposition to programs of liberal reform—an opposition whose imbecility is demonstrated by the fact that even the business community now back in power has not seriously tried to repeal a single basic New Deal measure. Nor did business behavior in the 1930's constitute a novelty in American history. The dislike of the "economic royalists" in Franklin Roosevelt's day corresponded to Theodore Roosevelt's detestation of the "malefactors of great wealth," to the Populist hatred of the trusts and the millionaires, and to Andrew Jackson's denunciations of "the rich and powerful." Nothing was more traditionally American about the New Deal than its conviction that the business community could not be trusted with undue power. /15

Reformed 'malefactors'

But the business community assumes a more amiable appearance in this age of prosperity. Businessmen plainly have a broader recognition of their social responsibilities than they had twenty-five years ago; and some liberals even think they see in the business world the beginnings of a permanent business conscience. Of course, much the same things were being said about business—and business was saying exactly the same things about itself—at the height of the prosperity of the 1920's. We will know the extent of the change of heart only if economic adversity strikes again. Then we will see whether the business "conscience" will not be, as it was in 1929, the first thing jettisoned by businessmen struggling to keep their heads above water. /16

Still, for the moment, the old anti-business exhortations do not apply in the same way as they did in the 1930's. Where the older liberalism inveighed against business domination per se, the new liberalism must make a subtler point—that is, that government by a single interest is bad, whatever the nature of the interest. And, where the older liberalism rebelled against business rule in the name of the manifestly abused sections of society, the new liberalism can hardly hope to persuade people who do not feel themselves mistreated that they are, in fact, the slaves of an economic tyranny. What the new liberalism must do is again something that is more subtle and perhaps more edifying: It must make the point that our country can grow only if we develop a positive philosophy of the public interest to be asserted against the parochial interests of any special group. /17

It is the rehabilitation of a sense of the public interest that will provide the moral impetus for the new liberalism's legislative program. Here is a nation richer than ever before, and getting even richer every moment, and yet devoting a *decreasing* share of its wealth to the public welfare. Our gross national product rises: our shops overflow with gadgets and gimmicks; consumer goods of ever-increasing ingenuity and luxuriance pour out of our ears. But our schools become more crowded and dilapidated, our teachers more weary and underpaid, our playgrounds more crowded, our cities dirtier, our roads more teeming and filthy, our national parks more unkempt, our law enforcement more overworked and inadequate. And we wonder why, for example, we have a growing problem of juvenile delinquency! /18

While we let the production of consumer goods for the sake of profit achieve a sort of moral priority in our culture, our Federal government is permitted to spend an average of $5 million a year since the war for slum clearance. While private wealth heaps up in our shops and homes, we refuse to undertake adequate programs to improve our schools, our hospitals, our cities, our natural resources, our public domain. While our business leaders, whose first duty is to make money for themselves, demand popular reverence as moral symbols and exemplars, those who serve us all—our public administrators, teachers, foresters, welfare officers, policemen, firemen (all, indeed, except our security officers)—are treated with condescension, when not with contempt. /19

The problem of rehabilitating the public sector of our national life is not financial. If our economic growth continues, and if we maintain taxes at current levels, we will have sizable funds available for public purposes. Each new $10 billion of national income should produce about $3 billion of new revenue. The issue is whether these gains of economic progress should be invested in the welfare of a few or in the general welfare. The Eisenhower Administration last year chose the welfare of the few, which is why the rich received tax reductions when the nation should have received schools, hospitals, and roads.* /20

So long as we refuse to assert the general welfare against the false notion that the unlimited pursuit of profit will guarantee the general welfare, we can expect that, while we privately grow richer, our nation will grow in proportion poorer. While we overstuff

* In 1955 the Eisenhower Administration refused to approve a general tax reduction for individuals or corporations but did recommend lower corporate taxes on income from foreign sources. It is possible, however, that the reference is to the Internal Revenue Act of 1954, a controversial feature of which was the exemption of the first fifty dollars of dividend income from taxation. (*Editor's note*)

ourselves as individuals, we will let the national plant run down. And it is the national plant—health, education, welfare, resources—on which our future so largely depends. /21

How to revive the conception of the general welfare, a conception sufficiently dear to the Founding Fathers that they inscribed it indelibly in the preamble to the Constitution? One thing is clear: that single-interest government is not likely to be the instrument of that revival. Single-interest government inevitably fosters that insidious optical illusion which leads sincere men to mistake their own for the public interest and to contend that what is good for General Motors is necessarily good for the country.* A passion for the *general* welfare is far more likely to emerge from a government that represents the diverse interests of the American community—whose decisions are made not only by representatives of business but by representatives of farmers, workers, professional men, and even, if I may use the word, of intellectuals. /22

The new challenge

Many liberals will agree that there are plenty of things to be done, but will add that we must have a depression before the people will ever again give government a license for reform. But this suggestion is surely one more example of the extent to which liberal thought has become frozen in the mold of the 1930's. Richard Hofstadter has recently developed a distinction between "interest politics"—the clash of material aims and needs among competing blocs—and "status politics"—the clashes arising from status aspirations and discontents. As periods of depression breed interest politics, so periods of prosperity breed status politics; but the dynamics of status politics can lead to reform as well as reaction. Indeed, until the New Deal, nearly every great burst of progressive enthusiasm in American history came in a time of relative prosperity—the age of Jefferson, of Jackson, of the Progressives at the turn of the century. It is the sheerest defeatism to suppose that depression must be the prerequisite to reform. /23

What liberalism requires is a program sharply focused to meet the qualitative discontents of the present age. It requires a spirit that aims not to indict any group in the community as a special obstacle to change but rather to rally men of good will in all groups behind programs designed to improve life in America for all Americans—a spirit that seeks, in other words, not to divide the country and aggravate its tensions, but to unite it around a revitalized sense of the public interest. /24

Above all it needs to commit itself to bringing about a new birth of freedom. In the first instance, this means equal rights for minorities. The great creative proposal of the Truman Administration in the domestic field was the civil-rights program of 1948 (though in time, perhaps, the Brannan farm plan and the Ewing health-insurance plan will receive new recognition).* President Truman perceived that if the coalition forged by depression was breaking up, a new coalition might be brought into being by abundance—a coalition founded not on a common fear of poverty but on a common desire for opportunity. Assurance of equality of opportunity not only for Negroes but for all nationality groups must be an essential ingredient of the new liberalism. /25

And equally important is the issue of civil liberties. Now that the nonsense of the age of McCarthy has begun to clear away, there is a superb opportunity for men of conviction to consolidate the national sense of shame and to restore the Bill of Rights to its central position in our theory of society. The spectacle of the most powerful nation on earth frightening itself to death over Communists in its midst is as disgraceful as the spectacle of the richest country on earth pretending it cannot afford adequate systems of education, medical care, and housing. The United States in the last three years has succeeded in presenting both spectacles to a dismayed world. /26

I have said nothing about foreign affairs. In the immediate future, of course, the issues of peace and war far overshadow problems of justice and polity at home. But it can be said that a truly creative and progressive American foreign policy can only come from a truly creative and progressive America. In a free state, foreign policy can rarely be more effective than the character of the nation that stands behind it. No magic of psychological warfare is likely to persuade the rest of the world that we are different from what we are. /27

We will thus probably require a reawakening of the liberal conscience and the liberal will at home before we can offer positive and compelling alternatives to the world. We cannot convincingly champion freedom before the world so long as we kick freedom

* The allusion is to a statement made by Charles Erwin Wilson, Secretary of Defense, 1953-1957, and former President of General Motors. He had observed that he believed what was good for the country was good for General Motors and vice versa. This corruption of his statement quickly became a catch phrase among his critics. (*Editor's note*)

* Charles F. Brannan, Secretary of Agriculture, 1948-1953, recommended a controversial two-price farm commodity support program; Oscar R. Ewing, Federal Security Agency Administrator, 1947-1952, was an ardent advocate of federal health insurance legislation. (*Editor's note*)

around at home. We cannot convincingly champion equality abroad so long as we practice segregation at home. We cannot convincingly champion opportunity abroad when too many of our own people linger at home in cultural mediocrity and economic want. As we renew a fighting faith against the inequities of our own society, we will generate an enthusiasm that will reverberate across the world—as the New Deal made Franklin Roosevelt a world figure long before Hitler began his war. Nothing would go farther to restore world confidence in American leadership than a display of progressive conviction in our own society. /28

In its fundamentals, the liberal tradition in this nation is as old as the Republic itself. This tradition has been responsible for nearly all the acts of government that have contributed to the growth of freedom and opportunity in America. And its continuing vitality in the days since Jefferson and Jackson has been due to its perennial capacity to define new problems and acknowledge new challenges. /29

The liberalism of this generation has been for some years in the travail of redefinition. It is pointless, as some writers have rather self-righteously done, to dismiss contemporary liberalism as sterile and bankrupt because it hasn't come up with all the new answers overnight. Obviously the process of rethinking takes time, and it cannot be completed until the burden of responsibility gives thought the final instinct for reality. Liberalism seemed sterile and bankrupt in the 1920's, and even in the early years of the depression; but in the end it flowered in the New Deal. /30

Of course it is currently fashionable, among both liberals and conservatives, to patronize the New Deal. Still, if the liberals of our time can do half as well in meeting the problems of this age, they should be more than satisfied. But liberals will never meet the challenge of the 1950's until they realize that it is something essentially different from the challenge of the 1930's. /31

The scarcity of ideas

MAX ASCOLI

Life would be much easier for American liberals these days if Arthur Schlesinger's diagnosis of what's wrong with American liberalism were as sound as it is plausible. /1

Max Ascoli, "The Scarcity of Ideas," *The Reporter*, Vol. 14, May 3, 1956, pp. 12-16.

There is a comfortable, cozy quality in his conception of liberalism. His assumptions, as I understand them, have been with us for so long that they have acquired an aura of near-truth. They can be listed: /2

1. The major obstacle to general welfare and democratic progress is the Business System, which fosters the selfish interests of the few unless, bridled by government, it is made to work in the interests of the many. /3

2. The people best suited to be in charge of bridling, general welfare, improvement, and betterment at large are the liberals. /4

3. The Federal government works in the interests of society as a whole—if enough liberals hold positions of power in it. /5

4. The progressive and bettering job can best be done by government taxing and government spending. /6

There are other assumptions that for a long time have been the stock in trade of American liberalism—first of all the one that in the indivisible interest of nation, government, and individual, progress is ultimately inevitable. But lately the optimistic progressivism of many a liberal has been darkened by some reading of Reinhold Niebuhr. Moreover, the New Deal has made such pragmatists of all liberals that they shun adherence to any general theory—including pragmatism. They tend to shy away from problems that do not lend themselves to quick solutions. This is one reason why they prefer to stick to strictly domestic causes and remedies of our nation's ailments, as Schlesinger shows. /7

There are some other people—liberals and not-so-liberals—who are inclined to think that the widespread restlessness and spiritual malaise of our days is influenced and may even be caused by the precarious state of world affairs. But, if I understand Schlesinger correctly, the issue of war and peace which so overshadows all others "in the immediate future" should not—even in the present—distract us from curing our political and spiritual malaise through increased government spending. It would seem that McCarthy's rise to fame and Billy Graham's immense popularity were determined by inadequate housing projects and other inconveniences that qualitative liberalism can eliminate. /8

Leviathan on parole

Since the Republicans came to power, assumption No. 1 has been temporarily qualified, for this businessmen's Administration,* aside from taking some liberties with natural resources and tinkering with agricultural price supports, has failed to wreck the reforms of the New Deal. Schlesinger has put the Business System on probation: It all depends on how it behaves if and when a depression comes. At present, however, businessmen are in control of the government, in violation of assumptions Nos. 2, 3, and 4. A few liberals say that the greedy old Leviathan is acquiring something like a human soul. But Schlesinger keeps his fingers crossed. /9

The curious thing about this jaundiced view, widespread among American liberals, is that it considers the Business System both irredeemable and indestructible. The way of all business is to be profit-hungry in the interest of the selfish few. As in the Calvinistic concept of human destiny, there is no escape from this original sin. The only thing we can do is to be aware of it and, at times, manage to check it by keeping liberals in positions of governmental power. Our liberals recoil from any dream of ultimate redemption in a socialist heaven or purgatory. /10

This is why they deeply resent—and right they are—being accused of crypto- or creeping socialism. They have no socialist blueprint on hand, no timetable for the verification of a predetermined pattern of history. In fact, it is doubtful that they have much of a concept of history at all. Some may have flirted vaguely with socialist theories in their youth, just as some at present—particularly those who have had an opportunity to become familiar with Big Business—give serious evidence of crypto- or creeping capitalism. /11

By and large, however, all through depression and prosperity, New and Fair Deal, there has been little change in the liberal attitude toward the Business System. It is still considered, actually and potentially, the major obstacle to general welfare. It is to be the object of constant watching and constant nagging. But since it is to stay with us forever, it is to be looked at with gentle, sad, routinized hatred. /12

Private governments

If Schlesinger's article is to some degree representative—as I think it is—the liberal world is an enviably simple one. There is the Business System, there is the individual, and there is the government, which, whenever managed or influenced by liberals, can somehow redress the inequities of the Business System toward the individual. The other large-scale organizations catering to the masses' needs are in general objects either of sympathy or of scant attention. The private, nongovernmental entities that purport to represent the interests of the individual are seldom accused, as business is, of being self-perpetuating and selfish. This is the case with political machines—with the possible exception of Republican ones—as it is with interstate authorities. Other instances are Federally established authorities for power development and flood control of the TVA type. But the most cherished instance is labor. To the American liberal, labor is a prize exhibit of what is public-spirited, innately democratic, and good. /13

In this liberal mythology, labor had a prominent role even before the New Deal actually succeeded in fostering the enrollment of millions of workers into the trade unions. This was one of the major advances of Schlesinger's "quantitative liberalism," and led to the improvement of the workers' lot. But at present, at the time when "qualitative liberalism" should get started, Big Labor controls such a huge hunk of the workers' rights, welfare, and destiny that it may be properly called private government—obviously as fallible and as exposed to the temptations of power as that other private government which goes by the name of Big Business. /14

Yet there is not much evidence that American liberalism is ready or even disposed to tackle the intricacies of private government. There are vast areas of national life where new forms of power have entrenched themselves, unrestrained or inadequately restrained either by the Federal government or by the states. This applies eminently to Big Business, of course, but also to Big Labor, to the Federal and interstate authorities, and to many other public and private agencies, all of which exert sovereign influences on the citizen's life. /15

A man's job, the security of his job, the welfare funds that are to take care of his old age and sickness, his hope of getting adequate lodging, the condition of his neighborhood—all these crucial matters are dependent on decisions made by holders of power who can be forced only with difficulty to give an accounting of their stewardships. Actually, the multiplicity of the centers of power, public and private, territorial or functional, formal or informal, vertical or horizontal, has become so complex and unruly that it is hard to define the few zones where representative democracy still works according to the established principles of limited and responsible authority. Moreover, we have entirely new forms of power that operate with frightening effectiveness not at representing but at molding the people's opinions and habits. /16

* The number of businessmen whom President Eisenhower appointed to the cabinet and other posts in 1953 was a subject of complaint among political liberals. (*Editor's note*)

Feudalism is the proper name for the system, or lack of system, that rules us. Only a very few liberals —Adolf Berle* outstanding among them—are aware of such a state of affairs. Schlesinger too feels something is wrong, but his answer is that more Federal spending is needed, more taxes—and a greater expansion of the Federal bureaucracy. /17

Most of our liberals do not seem to worry about the dangers of an ever-expanding bureaucracy—particularly if it is the one of Big Government. Yet occasionally, some unusually farsighted liberal, like Franklin Roosevelt, has acknowledged how risky it is to expand the system of Federal controls, since the controlling or regulatory agencies may fall into the hands of people who can hardly be called liberals. Indeed, this has been the experience over and over again, following the ebb of a progressive or reforming wave. Our Business System would never have become so resilient and articulate had it not been for the regulatory agencies, which were first established to harness it. Invariably, with the coming to power of a conservative Administration, Big Business has drawn strength from its control of the harnessing equipment. /18

But there is no sign that an allergy toward Big Government has developed among our liberals, if for no other reason than that they were waiting for the next political upheaval that may give them a chance to gain control of Big Government and make it bigger. Usually such a chance comes after a depression. But now Schlesinger tells us that there is no reason why the liberals' reforming skill should be practiced on the government only in the wake of a depression. True, he admits, the liberals haven't done much thinking lately, but, he adds, under the burden of responsibility they will surely think. /19

What price abundance?

The need for sustained, hard thought about how our freedoms can be preserved and invigorated could not be more pressing—a need that is in direct relation to the well-being that an unprecedentedly large number of citizens enjoy and to the multitudinous complexity of the institutions that service them. Each one of these service institutions exacts a price that can hardly be measured in terms of the dollars and cents it charges; each demands allegiance on the part of the citizens. /20

What is, for instance, the real price we pay for the entertainment or the diversions provided at nominal cost or at no cost by the media of mass communication? Are our lives enriched or desiccated by them? What do we actually pay for the gadgets we think we buy at bargain prices—all these things which according to Schlesinger "pour out of our ears"—even when the payment is cash on the barrelhead? What is the cost of goods we acquire with token payments for token ownership? /21

It is the function of government—or at least it should be—to see to it that prices be fair and the ultimate cost to the community not exorbitant. This, however, because of the extraordinary degree to which our economy is based on confidence, and because of the never-ending commitments and relationships the citizens get into or are taken in—this is becoming a function with which government can scarcely keep up. /22

Yet lest we become driven by forces over which we have no measure of control, some order must be made out of this chaos. The powers that rule us and weigh on us—this increasingly cumbersome and increasingly secret government in which all the bureaucracies of government, of business, of labor, of religion, of education, of philanthropy, of entertainment, et cetera, combine to increase their hold on us —must be made limited, representative, and responsible lest our freedom turn out to be a rather ghostly thing. Our individual freedom is frittered away or mortgaged out at such a remorseless pace that at times the symbolic celebration of it in an election booth seems as incongruous as the re-enactment of a medieval pageant. /23

Liberals, incidentally, are supposed to have something to do with freedom. They are not necessarily the seasonal journeymen of Big Government, and liberalism is not supposed to mean the dispensation of government liberalities. Liberals are supposed to be at work whenever and wherever our freedoms are stunted. /24

There can be no more dangerous illusion for liberals than the continued adherence to the notion that the major protagonists of the human comedy are the individual and the government—the official political government which seems to have no other way of establishing its authority over its too many competitors than by getting bigger. Gone are the days when government was the only Leviathan standing in front of the individual, and gone also are the days when it made any remote sense to think that if good men were in control of this one big Leviathan, then there would be no further obstacle to ever-increasing prosperity and freedom. /25

The agenda for American liberalism is as vast as it is compelling. American liberalism must acquire a

* See p. 165. *(Editor's note)*

far greater sophistication toward power and learn how not to hate and not to love it. The liberals' antibusiness demonology is about as outdated as their —alas—frequently platonic love of government. /26

On the agenda of American liberalism a major item should be the delimitation of the various powers and governments now on the loose. We cannot rely optimistically on the hope that they will automatically balance and contain each other. Neither can we assume that the checking, containing job can be the monopoly of the Federal government. Among other reasons, some of these powers—eminently those which provide us with food for our tables and gas for our cars—are international or supranational in scope. /27

If liberty is to survive, the new feudalism which rules us must be replaced by a federal system, in which the economic and occupational powers—like those of business and labor—may become interlocked with the old ones of a political and geographic nature. Practices of diplomacy and administration must be developed that will allow each one of these governments, old and new, to work with responsible independence in its own and the commonwealth's interests. /28

In the sphere of old-fashioned or political government itself there are vast zones that ought to be resettled. Our huge metropolitan areas, for instance, are at the same time ungoverned and subjected to overlapping, wasteful governments. Our regions are not any longer just geographical names but have acquired a powerful economic reality; yet there is no evidence that anything is in the making that can be called regional government, with its own specific, limited authority. Our state governments collect every year more than fifteen billion dollars; yet they manage to operate so quietly that, to all intents and purposes, they have become an instance of semisecret government. /29

The crowded center

Any list of "oughts" and "musts," of reforms and revaluations that are needed, indeed imperative, is bound to be dismissed as entirely theoretical and impractical—egghead stuff. Everybody wants to be a realist these days, including the eggheads, who don't want to have their utterances answered by silence or by yawns. /30

The few items on the liberal agenda that I have hinted at have all to do with governments, public and private. But it will be said there is no use defining the relationship all these governments have among themselves and the impact they exert together on the citizens, since by and large the whole thing works spectacularly well. Our only trouble is abundance. /31

Why should anybody complain that this wondrous system of government we have is not only unwritten and informal but also unknown to those who operate it? What of it? Aren't we prosperous? Isn't the large majority of our people now increasingly conservative and firmly unwilling to have the existing order of things tinkered with by reforms? "Qualitative liberalism" will give not merely to a majority but to the whole citizenry the chance to be conservative. After that, I imagine, we shall sit down contentedly and contemplate the steady growth of our fat. /32

Yet there are still some liberals like myself who think that the fair or fairer distribution of well-being among the citizens should be one but by no means the major concern of liberals. For I believe it is the function of liberals—indeed, it is what entitles them to that name—to keep constant watch over all the agencies that are supposed to serve the individual and, if need be, to overhaul them, seeing to it that the individual is equally provided with the opportunity to play a role in the societies he belongs to and with the right to be left alone by them. /33

But, again, it is said we never had it so good, no other nation on earth ever had it so good. American liberals, so it seems, find no reason to object that our country is ruled by an oligarchy of feudal barons —the barons of government, of politics, of industry, of labor, of philanthropy, and so on. After all, the roster of the leading barons can be read on the letterhead of any nation-wide organization established to further any not-too-controversial, do-goodish cause. Moreover, quite a few of these barons had a liberal future in their pasts. /34

The barons, and the whole nation behind them, are magnificently united in the middle of the road, so huddled around the vital or dead center that, as we can see these days, it takes a considerable effort of partisan public relations to find enough differences between liberal conservatives and conservative liberals to provide the nation with a little electoral excitement and fun. /35

Schlesinger, a practical man, fully acknowledges the conservative, nonradical mood of the country. He agrees with the stated and restated Lubell diagnosis, but he believes that if the Truman technique of 1948 is used again, American conservatism can be brought—for keeps—under liberal management. He brings the spiritual element into the picture for reasons still unclear to me—unless he too is swayed by that revival of all words having to do with the spirit or with religion which is so masterfully managed by our President and Secretary of State.* /36

Schlesinger's article could serve as a succinct program for any Presidential candidate, were it not that his two key words, "qualitative" and "quantitative," are somewhat over the people's heads. Or maybe these two words can be used with equal effectiveness the other way around, since, if I understand Schlesinger correctly, he wants more quantity of the New-Fair Deal quality distributed to more people. /37

Back to Fortress America

Be that as it may, what really stirred me to pick a quarrel with Schlesinger was the offhand way in which he brushed off the impact of international affairs on the fortunes, well-being, and freedom of our country. Maybe what's new and surprising is not the new phase of liberalism he advocates but the rebirth of a virtuous "I-am-unholier-than-thou" isolationism. The idea that before getting messed up in other people's business, we ought to put our own house in order and realize in all its fullness the American dream is an old boiler plate of liberal rhetoric. It has come back into circulation lately, but at no time, because of the conditions prevailing at home and abroad, has it been so dangerous and foolish. /38

In Schlesinger's argument, as I see it, "the issues of peace and war" loom large on the horizon "in the immediate future," but this infatuation should be brought to an early end. According to him, we need qualitative liberalism at home "before" propounding democracy or liberalism abroad. That "before" must mean that Khrushchev and Bulganin** should be invited to take a rest and see to it that Communism is well implanted in their country before propagating it abroad. In fact, for those inclined to think this way, the time should be ripe: If the issue is just one of war and peace, the chances of war seem to have dwindled, while peace is still far off. Why shouldn't we take advantage of such a hiatus to leave wretchedly ungrateful allies to their destiny, and price ourselves out of the world market? /39

Schlesinger is not only skeptical about the role of international affairs in our nation's life now; he makes his skepticism retroactive. A historian of Roosevelt and of the New Deal, he seems to forget that in 1939 there were still ten million unemployed in our labor market. It is quite true, as he puts it, that in 1936 no New Dealer could possibly have envisaged the rich and overflowing society of today. For how could anyone at that time have imagined that our full employment and abundance would be obtained as a by-product of the effort to counteract two extraneous agents—first Adolf Hitler, then Joseph Stalin? /40

The infatuation with peace and war still seems to play some role in keeping our economy in high gear. In this year 1956, of each dollar spent by the government sixty-one cents go to check Communism. Since the end of the war, more than $363 billion has gone for our own and our Allies' protection. Of this tidy sum, I suppose more than a trickle has helped to keep business humming at home. /41

It is rather peculiar to see how Schlesinger is now falling into line with those who ignore the part military expenditure has been playing in energizing the nation's economy. Perhaps isolationism, like middle-of-the-roadism, has spread throughout our prosperous, predominantly middle-class nation. Perhaps isolationism had been only temporarily knocked out by the impact of this national emergency of unlimited duration, just as happens with some of the most evil viruses under the onslaught of antibiotics. /42.

Our system of alliances is in danger of falling apart. But here comes the new twist: Why not accept this trend as irreversible and make the best of it? Even for our defense, it is said, the need for foreign bases has become more than questionable, for we now have intercontinental bombers and soon we shall have intercontinental missiles. David Lawrence in his *U. S. News & World Report* never neglects a chance to show how hopeless is our situation abroad and how mischievous are the Allied leaders. The justifications for the drive back to Fortress America* are many, according to the nature of the various groups, but the drive is unquestionably on. Herbert Hoover can now afford to keep quiet, as he has found a large number of new disciples. /43

It may be somewhat disheartening to find that liberals too are moving gingerly toward Fortress America, but by no means surprising. Intervention in both World Wars—and particularly in the First—was bitterly opposed by large groups of our liberals, and their forebodings have been at least partly

---

* Secretary of State John Foster Dulles, who died May 24, 1959, and President Eisenhower were charged by some with undue moralizing about matters of state. (*Editor's note*)

** Nikolai A. Bulganin was Premier of the U.S.S.R. at this time, and Nikita S. Khrushchev was First Secretary of the Communist Party. In 1956 it was claimed by the Russians that the two men shared equally in the leadership of the country. (*Editor's note*)

* After World War II ex-President Hoover and others recommended a foreign policy that concentrated on defense of the Western Hemisphere, creating what they called a "Fortress America." (*Editor's note*)

vindicated by what happened to them in the aftermath of both wars. /44

After the last war, American liberals did not have very much to contribute to the establishment of a new peace in the world that had become largely dependent on American initiative and means. Not much—aside from a few patented American prescriptions like TVA, trade unions unsoiled by class consciousness, and trust busting. There was also a large export of a curious watered-down Marxism, fervently advocated by internationalists of all political denominations—the firm belief that for any people, under any circumstances, the improvement of living conditions and the march toward democracy are one and the same thing. /45

Now some extraordinarily hard thinking is needed if the new Communist rampage is to be stopped and the network of alliances is to be rewoven around new supranational institutions. It is not surprising, therefore, that there are American liberals who do not relish this prospect and think that there is no use in taking up new troubles when a little bit of hell raising, a new moderate spurt of business baiting, can bring them back into power. Once they were in power, of course, the nation would become further isolated from the rest of the world—isolated not only by its wealth and by its widespread conservatism but also by its liberalism, both quantitative and qualitative. /46

All this would be attractive enough, at least to some, and the prospect of an ever-increasing, evenly distributed prosperity very alluring, were it not for two or three bothersome obstacles. The threat of Soviet Russia is not the greatest of these obstacles. The power, the freedom, even the prosperity of our country are in danger because our system of government—that queer coexistence of governments and baronies—makes for the constantly diminishing freedom of the individual, who is the only bearer of freedom. Everyone who calls himself a liberal should know this. Our nation, far from being the only one afflicted by this unruly, unfree state of affairs, shares it with all the other democracies. /47

The conclusion, at least for liberals, should be that they must enter upon their task of reversing the trend and making freedom operational both at home and abroad—for there is no line of demarcation between home and abroad. /48

Maybe I'm all wrong. Maybe I'm just hearing things, and Schlesinger, who is a realist, has the answer. All that the future of American liberalism needs, for itself and for the world, is that America remain prosperous and free. Schlesinger is paraphrasing Secretary Wilson and, as becomes a scholar, is bringing the Wilsonian principle into a near-universal or at least world-wide context: If liberals regain control of the government, then what's good for America is good for the world. /49

The essays

1. What are the typical differences between an essay and a speech? To what extent do these essays illustrate such differences?
2. Is Ascoli's "The Scarcity of Ideas" more like a speech than Schlesinger's "The Challenge of Abundance"? If so, in what ways and for what reasons?
3. In Schlesinger's article several kinds of definition are used. Identify three.
4. Review *suggestion* in the Glossary. Which of the definitions in Schlesinger's article seem designed to persuade by the "short circuit" of suggestion while at the same time clarifying objective meanings? Of the various kinds of definition, which are most likely to give a speaker the benefit of this double effect and which are least likely to do so?
5. Do you think Schlesinger is trying to win belief through evoking strong attitudes and feelings, or is he simply informing his readers? Support your answer with specific references.
6. Must Schlesinger and Ascoli adapt what they say to an occasion in the manner of a speaker? What generalizations can you make concerning the similarities and differences between speaking and writing in this respect?
7. Paragraph 23 of Schlesinger's essay and paragraphs 1-13 of Ascoli's exemplify the argumentative method called rebuttal. To what extent do they fulfill the requirements for this kind of argument?
8. Is "liberalism," as Schlesinger and Ascoli use the term, a *stereotype* (see Glossary)? Does each writer use it the same way? If not, what meaning does each give it?
9. What is the effect of Ascoli's use of such symbolic terms as "feudalism," "barons," "baronies," "demonology," and others associated with medieval life and with mythology?
10. Evaluate Ascoli's analysis of Schlesinger's arguments (see paragraphs 1-17). Do you think Ascoli has isolated a truly important feature of Schlesinger's case? Are Ascoli's rebuttal and refutation sharply enough focused on the arguments and assumptions isolated by analysis?
11. In part at least both of these essays aim at changing the attitudes of political liberals toward business and government. What are those attitudes? What change

is each writer trying to effect in them? By means of what alternative beliefs, motives, and attitudes?

12. What common ground does Schlesinger try to establish with his readers (see especially paragraphs 11 and 30)? Does Ascoli try to establish the same common ground? If not, how does that fact affect his potential persuasiveness with the readers of *The Reporter*?
13. What part does ethos play in rendering an essay credible? If each of these authors had delivered his composition in person to a convention of political liberals, what difference would there be in the role of ethos as a source of proof?
14. Remembering that both essays were addressed to political liberals, which author's position seems likely to have the greater initial credibility with the audience? Why?
15. How much truth do you think there is in this statement: "With a sprinkling of references to a place and time, either of these essays might easily be mistaken for a transcript of a speech"?

For further study and discussion

1. Who are the "independent voters" in national elections? What makes them independent of partisanship? Do they really decide the outcome of our national elections?
2. Do you think there is a "widespread internal anxiety" in the United States today? If so, what do you think is the cause? Are there any political actions that could remove the cause or causes?
3. Do you agree with Schlesinger that "depression is dead as an issue" in politics? Do you agree that we have surmounted most of the purely economic problems of our society? If so, how did this come about? If not, what important problems still remain to be solved?
4. Explore the history of one of the public welfare enterprises and professions Schlesinger mentions in paragraphs 18 and 19. Does it seem "depressed" in the midst of prosperity? If so, what has made it so? Is political action required? If so, what kind of political action?
5. Schlesinger and Ascoli disagree on whether we must attain perfection at home in civil liberty, education, economic equality, etc., before trying to promote these benefits intensively abroad. What is your opinion? Why?
6. Do you agree with Ascoli that we have "entirely new forms of power that operate with frightening effectiveness . . . at molding the people's opinions and habits"? If so, what is "frightening" about them? If you disagree, what is it that prevents unions, communications networks, corporations, and governmental agencies from exerting dangerous power?
7. What basis, if any, is there for Schlesinger's concession that business is developing a "social conscience" and for Ascoli's claim that the liberals' "antibusiness demonology" is out of date?
8. How do philanthropic foundations affect the conduct and conditions of higher education? Which of their effects are good for the students' interests and which interfere with these interests?
9. In what ways, if any, can governmental agencies and bureaus interfere with fundamental individual freedoms?
10. What basic political differences, if any, divide the Republican and Democratic parties in the United States? Is there justification for the charge that the modern voter's choice is between members of two clubs rather than between advocates of distinct lines of political policy?
11. Schlesinger and Ascoli seem in mild disagreement about the New Deal's success in solving the economic problems of the 1930's. What historical support is there for the position of either writer?
12. How much of the present tax dollar goes for national defense? If defense expenditures were reduced significantly, would the national economy suffer severely? Why or why not?
13. Ascoli and Schlesinger seem to agree that economic well-being, alone, cannot produce political and social well-being. Is their position sound? If so, is our foreign aid policy sound? Should domestic efforts to increase the standard of living at home have first priority in governmental policy?
14. What is the difference between a political "conservative" and a political "liberal"? What were the differences at the time of the French Revolution—in France? In England? In the United States?
15. What influence, if any, has Marxism had on modern liberalism? On modern conservatism?

Suggestions for further reading

William H. Baumer and Donald G. Herzberg, ***Politics Is Your Business*** (New York, 1960)

Hadley Cantril, ***The Politics of Despair*** (New York, 1958)

Henry Steele Commager, ***The American Mind*** (New Haven, 1950)

Richard Hofstadter, ***The Age of Reform*** (New York, 1955)

Sidney Hook, ***Political Power and Personal Freedom*** (New York, 1959)

Valdimer O. Key, ***Politics, Parties, and Pressure Groups,*** 4th ed. (New York, 1958)

Russell Kirk, ***The Conservative Mind*** (Chicago, 1953)

———, ***A Program for Conservatives*** (Chicago, 1954)

Arthur Larson, ***What We Are For*** (New York, 1959)

Samuel Lubell, ***The Future of American Politics,*** 2nd ed., rev. (Garden City, N.Y., 1956)

Changing concepts of public service

WILLIAM O. FARBER

The following address was delivered by William O. Farber to the faculty, students, and friends of the State University of South Dakota on February 19, 1959, as the Seventh Annual College of Arts and Sciences Lecture on Liberal Education. It is a lecture for an educated audience that lacked specialized knowledge concerning public administration. The speaker's view of his subject is for this reason panoramic rather than particular. The possibilities and public consequences of administrative practice, not the technics of administration, are Farber's concern in this speech.

There are few assignments more difficult for a specialist than preparing a popular lecture on the general character of his specialty. This is what was asked of Farber. As you read the address consider some of the rhetorical problems speakers in Farber's situation always have to solve. If he treats his subject comprehensively, he will have many main headings and subheadings. How shall he keep the essential unity of these points before his listeners' minds? What supporting materials will be simple enough to be understood by laymen, yet true to technical fact? Shall he content himself with explaining the general nature of this, his favorite subject? Or shall he also try to make the subject impressive and urgently important?

Farber is head of the Department of Government and director of the Governmental Research Bureau at the State University of South Dakota, Vermillion, South Dakota. He was born at Geneseo, Illinois in 1910, received his B.A. and M.A. from Northwestern University, and in 1935 was awarded his Ph.D. by the University of Wisconsin. Although he has been a college teacher since 1935, he has also served in a variety of governmental capacities: as State Price Officer, Office of Price Administration; member, Regional Loyalty Board, United States Civil Service Commission; director, State Legislative Research Council; and Public Administration Advisor, Seoul National University, Korea. He has also served as a visiting professor at Northwestern University and the University of Wisconsin and has published works dealing with city manager government and with Indian affairs.

From a reprint of Mr. Farber's address published by the College of Arts and Sciences, State University of South Dakota, October 1959. By permission of the author.

On the eastern side of the South Dakota Badlands there is a geologic feature labeled appropriately "The Door." From this entrance, carved long ago by nature's persistent forces, the traveler follows a trail winding past high pagoda-like columns into a maze of oddly shaped rock piles. And if one has the good fortune to take the excursion in early morning or late evening, when the shadows are the longest, the effect is startling and enchanting, substantiating again and again, Frank Lloyd Wright's observation that the Dakota Badlands "have more spiritual quality to impart to the mind of America than anything else in it made by man's God." /1

From "The Door," to guide and safeguard the traveler, yellow stakes have been driven at regular intervals so that the traveler may retrace his journey without fear of being lost. And, if one views the stakes from "The Door" at the start of his journey, they fade into a hazy obscurity and one wonders where the way really goes and what eventually it is like. /2

Just so, tonight, I propose to discuss with you the direction which our public service is taking and appears to be going, and I hope, with some careful focusing and delineation, to point out, as with the aid of a telephoto lens, the difficulties that lie ahead and what needs to be done if our public servants, our formal leaders upon whom our future depends, are to meet the ills and challenges of present as well as yet unopened Pandoran boxes. In short, I propose to present a descriptive analysis of the public service as it is now evolving, and to stress the obligation of the academic world in that development and in the training of responsible leaders. /3

The public service as I consider it here consists of all those persons engaged in the work of our national, state, and local governments and who are employed in government's many and varied activities and functions. Thus defined, public service includes federal, state, and local officials of all ranks and occupations,—governors and judges, mayors and policemen, cabinet members and postmen, school teachers and meteorologists, generals and presidents, county highway commissioners and social workers, city council members and legislators—all who, on the public pay roll, have a special obligation to serve their country. In short I'm talking about those people whom some describe as "those who couldn't find any other job, so they're working for the government." /4

Now public employment is obviously essential to us, because of the services rendered—traffic control, police protection, the construction of highways, the maintenance of public parks, and the like. Significant as these functions are, I would like to suggest that a more vital consequence of public service lies in the extent to which it will enable us to survive in the battles we now face. The competitive struggle with Russia and modified Soviet economic and social systems is only part of this picture. The inability to organize the world to provide employment, to educate it properly, to feed it, to clothe it, to house it, to ease tensions creates far more urgent problems. The importance of the public service lies, as I see it, in this urgency of present world problems and the ability or inability of the United States government through its public service to deal with them successfully. /5

On such an evening as this, one doesn't like to be pessimistic. But I am reminded of the middle-aged lady who, after hearing a discussion of the educational problem, exclaimed, "Oh dear, the critical crisis in education is so full of critical crises." /6

Unfortunately, the dear lady had pointed out the world situation exactly. The critical crisis is full of critical crises. In many areas, the world is sick. A battle is going on that is full of many battles. /7

Let us take stock of the present by considering briefly certain events that have occurred in the past thirty years. I'm referring to obvious things. There is an old Korean saying, "His view of the world is the view of a frog at the bottom of the well." Not only do we often have too limited a view restricted by the sides of the well, but only too often we want to close our eyes to the obvious. /8

The urgency of the present can be shown by reference to three significant recent events: the depression of the thirties, World War II, and the massacres of the Jews in Germany from 1935 to 1941. These tragic events are close enough at hand so that for many of us, only some brief reflection is needed to recall them as sad, to-be-forgotten memories. /9

I do not like to remember 1933, with its hunger and breadlines, its WPA and NYA,* when all the banks were closed and many a person existed only on what he had in his pocket. Somehow, in looking back, it seems impossible that the depression could have happened to a country as wealthy as the United States. With great resources, tremendous productive capacity, and people desiring and needing work, we were as a nation ill-clothed, ill-fed, and ill-housed. Nor do I like to recall the time, when responding to a greeting from Uncle Sam, I found myself picking up cigarette butts in a hot barracks area in Texas, and, along with millions then and thousands since, almost completely bereft of civil rights, at the mercy of the caprice of a Pfc. /10

But most of all, I do not like to review the tragedy of Germany under Hitler, where over six million members of a minority race were put to death by various methods—tragic not alone because of *when* it took place, but because of *where* it took place—in a country known for its religion, its education, its culture. In 1955, I was privileged to be in a small group that asked Toynbee* in London how he accounted for this strange antithesis of civilized conduct. Toynbee responded, "We should never forget: Civilization is at best only a thin veneer, and underneath the man is the brute. It takes very little to remove the veneer." /11

There is no need to elaborate further. The inadequacy of human endeavor when called upon to meet the monumental problems of today is only too clearly evident. And as one surveys the exploding population bomb, the arms race, and the pathetic inability to cope with Berlin, Quemoy, and Panmunjon,** one can find much to worry about. /12

An Italian journalist took me to visit the Roman Forum. It was about eleven o'clock at night, and as one might anticipate, a moon had risen. It was one of those times when one could set his fancies free and one could almost see bold Caesar on the steps of stone across from the temple of the Vestal Virgins and imagine Roman citizens thronging through the narrow ways between the maze of buildings. Here was tangible evidence of what had been the capital of the world, but now was capital no longer. Nations rise and fall; they differ only as to rate. /13

Clearly there is no reason to believe that the United States can occupy its position of pre-eminence forever. There are signs the eclipse has already begun. A word like "co-existence" is a symbol of the distasteful reality. /14

President Eisenhower has observed, "For the first time in history, we have the power to end history." We are challenged not only by the other nations; we are challenged by the weapons we have developed. Certainly, there is little cause at the moment

* Works Progress Administration and National Youth Administration. (*Editor's note*)

* Arnold Joseph Toynbee, historian. (*Editor's note*)

** Korean city in which the United Nations-North Korean armistice was signed July 27, 1953; hence, a symbol of divided Korea. (*Editor's note*)

to be comfortable. The times will come again that will try men's souls. It is in the light of this urgency of the present and the future, when our society, our civilization is in the balance, that this examination of public service is made. /15

This is not the place to review in detail the development of the American public service. Much of this history has not been a proud one. The prestige of government service has been low. Mothers could say, "I didn't raise my boy to be on the public pay roll." The concept of His Majesty's Service has not become The President's Service—and if it had, I doubt if there would be any great struggle for more people to enter it. /16

Today we find some two million persons in national employ and many more, if we include our educational system, in state employ. The numerical rise of civil service employees as well as those in military service has been one of the significant developments of twentieth-century America. For the most part, despite the partial truths of *The Ugly American*, we can be proud of our individual public servants today. I confess, I had not quite realized how proud we should be until I examined the role of Institutes of Public Administration in the Far East. With some exceptions, government in the Far East is carried on as much under as over the table. At least our problem seems to center around electric refrigerators, rugs, and mink coats. /17

But if the individual servant seems properly the object of some admiration, the appropriate yardstick, I feel, is not what he does, but what needs to be done. In short, in the light of the urgent present, the public servant needs to be something more than he has been, if the challenges of the present are to be met. And somehow, the individual competence generally prevalent must be so organized as to minimize the collective incompetence too frequently prevailing. /18

Looking at our public service, certain characteristics seem clear—its increase in size, the growth of field as well as central government service, its developing career aspects, its emphasis on the merit principle and political neutrality as goals. But there are new aspects and needs of the American public service which are apt to be overlooked and which are emerging. And it is these I now wish to call to our attention. /19

First of all, public service has tended to become international. This has occurred in three different ways: first, an actual international public service has come into existence and flourished with the establishment of the League of Nations. This service is far more extensive than most people realize. /20

Secondly, those parts of our own national civil service dealing in international problems have become immeasurably more sizeable and important. In addition to the regular work of the State Department and other departments of the government, commerce and agriculture, for examples, which have important international functions, such specialized agencies as USIS and ICA* are tremendously influential. Indeed the whole technical assistance program is becoming increasingly regarded as one of the great hopes of the world. /21

Toynbee has said that the historian of the future looking back on this period might characterize this century not as a period when the methods of transportation made great advances, not as a time when the ravages of disease were greatly reduced, not as an era when the atom was split, but as the age when man first dared to think that the benefits of civilization might be distributed to all mankind. In line with this thinking, the American Point Four program was initiated, in the words of the President, as "a bold new program for making the benefits of our scientific advances and industrial progress available for the improvement and growth of under-developed areas." /22

Finally, and most important, public service has become international *locally*—in every Main Street in America. The influx of foreign travelers to the United States and their contact with officialdom is important, but an even greater significance is our own treatment of minority groups. I shall never forget the Bank of Korea clerk who was my guide to Kyongju, the Athens of Korea. We had had a wonderful excursion with temple exploration and verbal give and take. He had observed that this was his first opportunity to become really acquainted with an American and he liked the equality of it. "But," he said over the cups, "what about Little Rock?"** /23

Even in remote Kyongju, wherever you may go, the question remains, "But what about Little Rock?" /24

Or, to give another example, a young Korean major in the ROK army invited me to attend the great Yung Nak Presbyterian church in Seoul. It proved to be a thrilling experience. Over 1,500 Koreans were in the audience, and the old hymns were sung with an enthusiasm rare with us these days. After the service, in a Chinese tearoom, as we exchanged

---

* United States Information Service and International Cooperation Administration. *(Editor's note)*

** See the headnote on p. 143. *(Editor's note)*

confidences, expressing some sort of Christian brotherhood, Major Lee quite unexpectedly said, "I've heard the Presbyterians in the north part of the United States quarrel with those in the south. Is it true they are divided? If so, why?" /25

"If so, why?" Yes. "Why?" Our domestic difficulties have a way of boomeranging all the way back to us after spreading doubts around the entire world. /26

The point remains, our attitude, as expressed in law toward our foreign students, toward each other, toward foreign policy, all affect international goals and aspirations. Our public servants administering that law thus become international even though their duties seem ostensibly domestic. /27

I'm well aware that some students of administration would say that the first duty of a public official is to carry out orders, and that he cannot be solicitous of remote effects, when trivial, on international relations. Thus, a leading student of public administration has observed: "If an administrator, each time he is faced with a decision, must perforce evaluate that decision in terms of the whole range of human values, rationality in administration is impossible."[1] What I am thinking about is not so much the actual decision as the manner of making it. Thus, Koreans have asked, "Why don't University department heads in the United States answer letters of inquiry?" Such minute matters have a way of causing impact far beyond their original significance. My first observation then is that from top to bottom the public service has come to have international aspects, and public servants must be trained accordingly. /28

The second observation is that the modern public servant needs to be a humanitarian; he must be tolerant and possess a sympathetic understanding of the culture of other lands. He must have what Harlow Shapley* has called "reverence for humility." The conclusion is commonplace that the transition from nineteenth-century government to twentieth-century government was a shift from the police and defense functions to welfare activities. Thus, government, perhaps of necessity as the power of the voter has grown, has become concerned with people and what becomes of them. /29

Our approach to this in the world setting is cogently stated in President Truman's 1949 inaugural address: "More than half the people of the world are living in conditions approaching misery. Their food is inadequate. They are victims of disease. Their economic life is primitive and stagnant. Their poverty is a handicap and a threat both to them and to more prosperous areas. For the first time in history, humanity possesses the knowledge and the skill to relieve the suffering of these people. . . ." /30

This humanitarian approach does not mean ignoring the law in bestowing governmental largess; it does not mean the winking at legal violations, but it does mean the exercise of administrative discretion where discretion exists to the benefit of mankind, and in a manner designed to promote human dignity. Institutions may be governed in theory and law by regulations designed to insure fairness, hearing, and equal and sympathetic treatment. In practice, as institutions must operate through men, the results may be quite different. /31

I think here of one of the most thought-provoking comments I have ever heard. In the course of investigating the off-reservation Indian problem, the three of us who constituted the research team interviewed an Indian woman, well known for her welfare work. We asked her why the Indian spent so much time in bars, drinking. She hesitated, and then said: "There is more Christianity in the bar than in the church. If the Indian attends church, no one will sit near him, no one will speak to him, no one will shake his hand; in a bar this is not true. Bars are friendly." /32

Thus, just as the rules of the church prescribe friendliness, unless the heart be in it, there is no friendliness; so, too, government can require equality of treatment, but unless the public servant feels that equality none will exist. The power to tear down is a terrible power. And no one has as much opportunity as the teacher to use it. As the scope of government has grown, as discretionary authority has become enlarged, so too the potential humanitarian character of both government and the public servant has increased immeasurably. /33

Let there be no mistaken notion about the extent of discretion in administration these days. Naive is the student who accepts the professor's answer, "I am sorry I cannot give you an 'A' "; or the professor who accepts the department head's statement, "You have not taught long enough to be recommended for promotion"; or the department head who accepts the dean's statement, "Sorry, there is no money left in the budget"; or the dean who accepts the president's statement, "No more out-of-state travel will be permitted this year"; or the president who accepts the governor's statement, "No new building will be recommended by me." To be compelled to accept a negative is simply an indication, for the most part,

---

[1] Herbert A. Simons, *Administrative Behavior* (Macmillan, 1957), p. 13.

* American astronomer. (*Editor's note*)

that one's political resources are insufficient for the occasion. /34

The third characteristic of public service is its multilateral nature. There was a time when we in political science exhibited a certain possessiveness when it came to civil service positions. Government and political science were synonymous, and government employment was political science employment. /35

Professionalization and the rise of technological education laid this pretense to rest. While certain organizational, financial, and personnel problems of civil service were still the primary concern of students of government, the greater problems became those of professional objectives and training. It was, for example, how the health, the highway, and the educational programs attained their goals that counted. /36

But now we have reached a still further stage in this development, when governmental positions in addition to being *multifarious* are *multilateral.* To be the specialist is not enough. The specialist must know something of language and culture, history and government, science and literature, and above all, he must possess the spirit of humanity, a kindly tolerance and humility, a realization that this is a human being's world. /37

All through the public service today one does find to an increasing degree the dedicated doctor, nurse, nutritionist, educator, social worker, economist, meteorologist, engineer, astronomer, aware of this larger role as leader he is called upon to play. I think, for example, of the large number of public servants taking foreign language courses. /38

Therefore, keeping pace with specialization has been the need for the specialist to be mindful of his international and humanitarian obligations, the multilateral or generalist aspects of his work. /39

One final characteristic of the new public service must be considered. The developments previously noted have occurred at a time when the demands that the public service "produce" are greater than ever before. The pragmatic test—"What does it do?" is supplying the answer for much of the world as to which camp a people wishes to be a part of. Can the United States outproduce Russia? Are the people of the United States happier? More moral? More content? "By their fruits ye shall know them" becomes a yardstick that Americans may properly apprehend and a new satellite around the sun becomes a symbol that has significance far beyond its scientific import. /40

From the viewpoint of the public servant, the challenge arises in how to do what policy declares should be done in spite of restrictive rules. Time and again the public servant—whether postal clerk, mayor, county commissioner, state geologist, attorney general, or president—is faced with the frustration of dubious legal sanction. /41

The easy way out is to treat doubtful legal potence as the excuse not to act. This is exactly what the good administrator should not do. "There are no hopeless situations; there are only people hopeless about them." In the public service, no less than in other activities, creativity has an important role to play. /42

Hence, as the final characteristic of the new public service, I would suggest creativity, meaning inventiveness or resourcefulness. The importance of this trait has received increasing attention. Dr. F. S. C. Northrop of Yale University has noted that Socrates regarded the philosopher as a thorn in the flesh, and he observed that nobody is a creative thinker unless continuously he has a thorn in the flesh, that is, unless he is disturbed by something. /43

It has been my experience that public servants have many thorns in the flesh and many, especially those engaged in field work, do something about them, both inside and outside the rules and the regulations. This resultant action is the essence of creativity. In an account of Dr. Arthur H. Compton's* analysis of conditions under which scientists are creative, it is pointed out that he found that each scientist has become conscious of his own "thorn in the flesh." Further, with reference to our own Ernest Lawrence,** Compton observed that Lawrence had more initiative than almost anyone else that he knew, a tremendous energy and a determination to get things done as he wanted them. Compton concluded with this comment: "Here then are the things that I see as I review this group of typical cases. First of all, to my mind, the thing which is the essence of creativity is the *decision* to do something about it when you are irritated. I would agree that irritation is the first step, but the decision to do something about it is the essence of creativity."[2] /44

Now in my own governmental experiences in the Office of Price Administration, both in the field and in Washington, D.C., on the regional loyalty board, with the state legislature, and my contracts with foreign aid agencies, have impressed me not only with the opportunity and the need of public servants to

* American physicist and Nobel Prize winner. (*Editor's note*)

** American physicist and Nobel Prize winner. Reference to "our own" is an allusion to the fact that Dr. Lawrence, a native of South Dakota, was a student at its State University. (*Editor's note*)

[2] Cited in Fred Olson, "Introduction and Summary," *The Nature of Creative Thinking* (Industrial Research Institute, 2nd ed., n.d.), p. 6.

exercise inventiveness, but with the extent to which they actually use it. /45

Illustrations leap up, but the words cannot be put down, for to do so would be to betray illegal albeit humanitarian acts. The tragedy is, especially for our foreign service, that greater discretion has not been officially bestowed upon our public servants. It takes but little imagination to see that what has been called inventiveness is only an aspect, a neglected aspect, of what we more familiarly think of as leadership. /46

So much for the character of our present and incipient modern public servant who thus emerges as now needing to have international, humanitarian, generalist, and inventive or leadership traits. This is what we are getting in the way of a public servant, though in an inadequate way; this is what we need, to a much greater degree. /47

This leads me to the final group of observations. /48

I have tried to stress the urgency of contemporary social problems and the present character of the public service. I should like now to show the relationship of the new public service and the University community. /49

Emerson in his famous Phi Beta Kappa address, "The American Scholar,"* said: "Books are the best of things, well used; abused, among the worst. What is the right use? What is the one end which all means go to effect? They are for nothing but to inspire. I had better never see a book than to be warped by its attraction clean out of my own orbit, and made a satellite instead of a system. The one thing in a world, of value, is the active soul." /50

The urgency of world problems and the type of public servant required to meet these problems make the development of "active souls" imperative. The need is great for men and women whose vision ignores the confines of intellectual disciplines, the harness of the classroom assignment, and the goose-step of fifty-minute periods. We should recruit men of the type of Ulysses, described in the Odyssey: "Many cities did he visit, and many were the nations with whose manners and customs he was acquainted." But the beneficial consequences of mere travel, unaccompanied by knowledge and appreciation of history, language, and culture, and the habit of thinking realistically mean little. Max Weber** in his essay on "Politics as a Vocation," in noting that the age of an individual is not significant, stated: "What is decisive is the trained relentlessness in viewing the realities of life and the ability to face such reality and to measure up to them inwardly." Thus we must cease praising those who build houses by the side of the road to be a friend of man, and encourage the man who is out in the road fighting society's battle. /51

* See pp. 36-45. *(Editor's note)*

** Famous German sociologist. Died 1920. *(Editor's note)*

The function of higher education in times such as these is somehow to provide the meeting ground of theory and realities, to train the public servant broadly and generally, but preserve the relentless instinct to grapple with specific situations. The ivory tower comes into its own as a tower in times such as these. /52

"Comfort without vision is no match for the four horsemen riding in from beyond the hills. . . . Immunity without responsibility, vision without action, means eventual suicide. Human necessity, if no nobler motive, cries out for restoration of the tower, not as a monument to academic irrelevance, but as an indispensable vantage point of vision without which we perish as men. Though no bread may be baked in the tower, no baker is free to bake bread with integrity and peace without the trustworthiness of the tower's primary work and wisdom."[3] /53

I would hope that educators, regarding the ivory tower as part of the battlefield in considering their responsibility to provide public servants, would not lose sight of the need to produce well rounded public servants with an international, humanitarian, multilateral, and inventive orientation. This does not mean extroverts only are needed. Indeed, as Woodrow Wilson noted in his *Leaders of Men*, "a book is often quite as quickening a trumpet as any made of brass and sounded on the field." But it does mean that more and more in urgent times such as these, the stars and mud must be combined. Woodrow Wilson in the work just cited illustrated this point well: /54

"The captain of a Mississippi steamboat had made fast to the shore because of a thick fog lying on the river. The fog lay low and dense upon the surface of the water, but overhead all was clear. A cloudless sky showed a thousand points of starry light. An impatient passenger inquired the cause of the delay. 'We cannot see to steer,' said the captain. 'But all's clear overhead,' suggested the passenger. 'You can see the North Star.' 'Yes,' reflected the officer, 'But we are not going that way.' Politics must follow the actual windings of the channel of the river if it steer by the stars."[4] /55

[3] Glenn A. Olds, "View from the 'Ivory Tower,'" *The Saturday Review*, June 21, 1958, p. 26.

[4] Woodrow Wilson, *Leaders of Men*, ed. by T. H. Motter (Princeton University Press, 1952), pp. 47-48.

I have attempted tonight to present the changing nature of public service in the light of the urgency of present world problems and the place of the universities in these developments. The absorption of these concepts into our way of thinking of the public service as thus described would, I think, do much to improve the position of the United States internationally. /56

I remind you that we have been thinking of the public service broadly as including president, governors, mayors, congressmen, legislators, councilmen, and all federal, state, and local employees, including civil servants, university professors, and school teachers among others. Unless we look on the public servant as partaking and needing to partake to a greater or lesser degree of the developing traits described tonight, we will give the public servant, as a leader, less than his due, at a time when we can ill afford to detract from the dignity and dedication which should belong to him. /57

It takes but little imagination to appreciate that my "changing concepts" are really new *demands* on the public servant in his role as leader—that he be international, humanitarian, generalist, and inventive. And it takes but little more imagination to realize that these are demands which are actually confronting all of us whether public servant or not, if we are to carry the burden of our mission on earth. /58

The peoples of the world are observing critically how, locally, we meet such problems as education, housing, reorganization of government, civil liberties and segregation. If we are concerned about the international situation and sometimes feel that Washington is incompetent, we should not forget that our own failures in meeting local issues have an impact far beyond our national boundaries. /59

Measured against our great natural resources, how adequately do we provide higher education for poor but superior students? How successful have our slum clearance projects been? How satisfactory have been our attempts to safeguard personal liberty and promote human dignity? /60

All American citizens, as well as local and national officials, thus have an important international role to play. The choice between the American and Russian systems will be made by many undecided peoples on the basis of which system, in their opinion, is better able to demonstrate its ability to attain desired human and economic goals. /61

The continuous succession of international crises during the past thirty years emphasizes the urgent need to examine the demands made on our public servants and determine how these demands can best be met. Unless public servants are broadly trained and are recruited for their tolerance, resourcefulness, and understanding of international problems, we can lose to Russia in a race more important than launching satellites into space. /62

As we return to "The Door"—the start of our venture tonight—this final thought: If we continue to think of our own careers, as well as those of public servants, as wholly local, specialized, narrow, and mechanistic, the result will be, I think, disastrous. We need to recognize what the human venture is becoming and needs to become and to train accordingly. We need to appreciate the discretion that is ours, that we all partake of the mission of leadership. As public power, as government continues to grow, as the earth continues to shrink and we must live closer together, these changing concepts, needing and demanding acceptance and appreciation, afford a way to a better and happier world. /63

The speech

1. What is the function of paragraphs 4-15 in the overall plan of this speech? Could the speech have achieved its purpose with these sections omitted?
2. Identify the internal summaries in the speech. Do you think the listeners needed the help of these recapitulations in order to keep the main headings of the speech in mind? Why or why not?
3. Comment on the use of authorities in this speech. Which citations of authority are made more credible by the speaker's remarks about them and which have such prestige that the speaker gains credibility simply by citing them?
4. Does Farber do anything within the speech to make his listeners view him more favorably? Are there any features of the speech that could detract from the listeners' favorable impressions of the speaker?
5. Farber amplifies the humanitarian qualities of the civil servant by definition, authority, assertion, and analogy (see paragraphs 29-33). Identify each form of support in this section and comment on how well it contributes to a clear understanding of the humanitarianism required of the civil servant of modern society.
6. Review the following topics in the Glossary: *conciseness*, *periodic sentences*, *rhythm*, and *style*. What general observations can you make about the oral style of this speech?
7. Farber uses a number of anecdotes as supporting material. How do they make his main headings more believable or understandable? Should any have been longer?

For further study and discussion

1. Farber suggests that the British have a different attitude toward public service than Americans have. What is the difference?
2. Study a curriculum for training administrators or public service personnel: the case study system at the Harvard business school, British Foreign Service selection and training programs, the Brookings Institution seminars in government, or others. Does the program seem likely to produce public servants with the qualifications Farber thinks are needed?
3. What are some recent events that support Farber's proposition that even the local decisions made by American public officials are of national and international importance?
4. Note the series of questions asked in paragraph 60 of this speech. From these questions, compose several topics for speeches and discussions.
5. In view of the "multilateral" nature of modern public service, should all persons appointed to civil service posts requiring college training be also required to have spent a specified period studying the liberal arts?
6. What was the "American Point Four Program"? How did it come to be established? Does it still exist? If so, what is its present character and how successful is it?
7. How do conditions of employment (wages, advancement, tenure, opportunity to make one's own decisions, etc.) in civil service compare with conditions for similar work in private enterprise? Which kind of career seems more inviting to you?
8. How might our methods of nominating candidates for public office be improved? Review some of the plans proposed for changing the Electoral College system. What merits, if any, do you find in these proposed changes?
9. Study the history of the "Authority" as an administrative agency in public service: the Port of New York Authority, Tennessee Valley Authority, various highway and turnpike authorities, etc. How do these agencies function? What is their relation to municipal, state, or national governments?
10. What caused the separation of several Protestant denominations into Northern and Southern branches or associations? Is there any tendency for these church groups to reunite today? Do you think it is important that they should? Has religious leadership become "public service" in Farber's sense too?

Suggestions for further reading

Frederick Lewis Allen, ***The Big Change; America Transforms Itself, 1900-1950*** (New York, 1952)

"American Civilization and Its Leadership Needs, 1960-1990," ***Annals of the American Academy of Political and Social Sciences,*** volume 325 (September 1959)

Robert E. Lane, ***Political Life: Why People Get Involved in Politics*** (Chicago, 1959)

Harold D. Lasswell, ***Politics: Who Gets What, When, How*** (New York, 1958)

Charles E. Merriam, ***Public and Private Government*** (New Haven, 1944)

Robert E. Merriam and Rachel M. Goetz, ***Going Into Politics*** (New York, 1957)

Address to the Russian people

RICHARD M. NIXON

Richard M. Nixon's "Address to the Russian People" was broadcast from a Moscow studio, August 1, 1959, the day before he left the Union of Soviet Socialist Republics. Officially Nixon, who was then Vice President of the United States, had come to the U.S.S.R. to open the American National Exhibition in Moscow; he had also conferred at length with Premier Nikita S. Khrushchev and in the course of his ten-day visit had been to several major cities. His speech on this occasion was delivered in English from a manuscript on which he had worked during much of the day preceding his television appearance. He departed from his text only once—to excuse himself for having preempted the time usually occupied by a popular comedy program. The New York *Herald Tribune* Bureau reported that the speech, including pauses for translation into Russian, took approximately forty-three minutes.

Nixon's speech was telecast over a network of stations covering the Russian capital and seven other cities within a radius of about two hundred miles; it was also filmed and recorded for rebroadcast on television and radio in other parts of Russia, in the United States, and in other countries. The full text of the address was printed in *Izvestia* and in newspapers outside the U.S.S.R. Nixon's immediate audience was, thus, Russian, but his ultimate audience was international. His problems of audience ad-

---

aptation were exceedingly complex for, as James Reston wrote in the New York *Times*, "It was necessary for him to balance his speech and meet sensitive political situations in both this country [U.S.S.R.] and the United States." Reston added, "The general feeling here among Westerners is that he managed to do so with considerable skill."

Nixon has been an exceptionally controversial figure throughout his political career, and the qualities of his speaking have often been at the center of disagreements concerning his personal and political merits. Within hours after his address, Russian radio commentators were charging that he had distorted the truth about American actions by omitting any mention of American air bases encircling the U.S.S.R. and that his analysis of Soviet policies was equally unfair. It was also said that his version of an offer to secure an American National Exhibition ticket for a Muscovite omitted mention that he had offered the Moscow worker money. In Moscow, as at home, Nixon's selection and arrangement of evidence quickly became the objects of both praise and criticism.

It is Nixon's habit to speak from notes, or to prepare his manuscripts from notes, in which topics, rather than logical subdivisions of the subject, form the main headings. His Moscow address reflects this practice in its topical organization. His skillful adaptation to the knowledge and interests of his possibly hostile Russian audience and the directness, concreteness, and simplicity with which he argues his propositions are also characteristic features of Nixon's popular speaking.

Nixon was born in Yorba Linda, California, in 1913, and was educated at Whittier College, California, and at Duke University Law School. Between 1937 and 1942 he practiced law in Whittier and in Washington, D.C. He served in the United States Navy from 1942-1946 and, after his discharge from the Navy, was elected to the House of Representatives from California. In 1950 he was elected to the Senate, and in 1952 and 1956 he was elected Vice President of the United States on the Republican ticket headed by Dwight D. Eisenhower. In 1960 he was narrowly defeated for the presidency by John F. Kennedy.

I first want to express my appreciation to the government of the USSR for giving me an opportunity to speak to the people of this country by radio and television just as Mr. Kozlov and Mr. Mikoyan spoke to the American people on their visits to my country. /1

I realize that nine days is much too brief a time for a visitor to spend in this great country. But in that period I have had the opportunity of having extended and frank discussions with Mr. Khrushchev and other leaders of your government. I have visited Leningrad, Siberia and the Urals and I have had the privilege of meeting thousands of people in all walks of life. /2

What I would like to do tonight is to answer for the millions of people who are listening to this program some of the questions which were asked me over and over again on this trip so that you may get a true picture of the policies of the American government and people. /3

I should like to begin by answering a question which I often heard: What are my impressions of this country and its people? /4

While my visit was brief I did have a chance in addition to visiting this great capital city of Moscow to see the beauty and culture of Leningrad whose brave people won the admiration of the world for their heroic defense of their city during the war; to savor the inspiring pioneer spirit of Novosibirsk; to witness firsthand the thriving productivity of the factory complex of the Urals. I was greatly impressed by the efficient modern equipment of your factories; your magnificent ballets in Leningrad and Novosibirsk; by the competitive drive for progress which is evident on every side. /5

But most of all I was impressed by your people; after all, the greatest asset of a country is not its forests, its factories or its farms but its people. /6

These are some of the characteristics of the Soviet people which I particularly noted on this trip. /7

First, their capacity for hard work, their vitality; their intense desire to improve their lot, to get ahead, is evident everywhere. /8

There was another feature about the Soviet people which I noted that may surprise you and that is in how many respects you are like us Americans. We are similar in our love of humor—we laugh at the same jokes. The people of your frontier East have much the same spirit of what was our frontier West. We have a common love of sports; the name of Vasily Kuznetsov, your great decathlon champion, is known in the United States as well as in the Soviet Union. We are both a hospitable, friendly people. When we meet each other we tend to like each other personally, as so many of our soldiers who met during the last great war can attest. /9

Above all, the American people and the Soviet people are as one in their desire for peace. And our desire for peace is not because either of us is weak. On the contrary, each of us is strong and respects the strength the other possesses. /10

This means that if we are to have peace it must be

a just peace based on mutual respect rather than the peace of surrender or dictation by either side. Putting it bluntly, both of our peoples want peace but both of us also possess great strength and much as we want peace neither of us can or will tolerate being pushed around. /11

That is why I was so surprised at a question that was asked me by a worker on the new scientific center outside of Novosibirsk. My heart went out to him as he told me that he had been wounded in World War II and that his father and mother had been killed by bombs. But then he said, "I don't believe you when you say America is for peace." /12

Nothing he could have said could have astonished or saddened me more. /13

And so to the millions of Soviet people who suffered or lost their loved ones in war, and to all of those in this great country who want peace, I say tonight, if you doubt that the American government and the American people are as dedicated to peace as you are, look at our record, examine our policies and you can reach only one conclusion—only aggressor nations have anything to fear from the United States of America. /14

We have fought in two World Wars and have demanded and received not an acre of territory or a cent in reparations. We enjoy the highest standard of living of any people in the world's history, and there is nothing whatever that we want from any other people in the world except to live in peace and friendship with them. No leader in the world today could be more dedicated to peace than our President. As his brother, who has honored us by making this visit with us, can tell you, President Eisenhower's whole life is proof of the stark but simple truth—that no one hates war more than one who has seen a lot of it. /15

We know as do you that in this age of nuclear weapons it is impossible for either of our nations to launch an attack which would not bring terrible destruction to itself. /16

In this age any leader who is so insane even to think of starting a war should well heed your proverb —"Do not dig a pit for another; you may fall into it yourself." /17

Why then is there any doubt that the American government and people are just as dedicated to peace as the people of the USSR? I think part of the answer is to be found in another question which was often asked of me on this trip and which Mr. Khrushchev, himself, raised in this manner in his speech on July 28 at Dnepropetrovsk. "If you believe in the peaceful intentions of our country, why do you continue the arms race, why do you construct new military bases around our borders?" /18

In answering this question, let me first point out that these bases are not maintained for purposes of attacking you but for purposes of defending ourselves and our allies. /19

Why did we think it was necessary to set up bases? Let us look at the record. We disarmed rapidly after World War II. Then came a series of events which threatened our friends abroad as well as ourselves. The Berlin blockade and the war in Korea are typical of the actions which led the United States and our allies to rearm so that we could defend ourselves against aggression. /20

We must also remember that these events occurred before the 20th Party Congress changed the line to the one Mr. Khrushchev enunciated again in his speech at Dnepropetrovsk—that Communism will now try to achieve its international objectives by peaceful means rather than by force. I could cite statement after statement made by previous leaders of the USSR which advocated and threatened the use of force against non-Communist countries in order to achieve Communist objectives. /21

A striking illustration of why we maintain bases and strong military forces is the fact that one-fourth of the entire production of the USSR goes into armaments. This, in effect, means that every worker in the Soviet Union works one day out of four for armaments. And we in our country are also bearing a heavy burden of armaments. Think what it could mean to both of our countries if we could lift this burden from the backs of our people. /22

Some may ask, why don't we get rid of the bases since the Soviet government declares today that it has only peaceful intentions? The answer is that whenever the fear and suspicion that caused us and our allies to take measures for collective self-defense are removed, the reason for our maintaining bases will be removed. In other words, the only possible solution of this problem lies in mutual rather than unilateral action leading toward disarmament. /23

Another question which was often asked was—why won't the United States agree to stop the tests of atomic weapons? The answer in a nutshell is that the question is not whether we both should enter into an agreement to stop tests but whether that agreement is one which will make sure that the tests actually are stopped. /24

That is why we say that if both sides honestly want to stop tests, we must first agree to set up inspection procedures in both of our countries which will make certain that the agreement is not violated. We believe this position is the only one that gives assurance of accomplishing the objective of stopping tests rather than just signing an agreement to do so. /25

We are encouraged by the fact that at least in this area we are presently engaged in serious negotiations which have made some progress. I know that I express the sentiments of the people of both of our countries when I say that I am hopeful that these negotiations will finally end in agreement. /26

Another question that has often been asked me went something like this: "The United States says it is for peace, but what the world wants are deeds not words, and the United States is short on deeds and long on words." /27

Nothing could be further from the truth. It is possible that many of you listening to me are not aware of the positive programs the United States has proposed which were designed to contribute to peace. Let me tell you about just a few of them and what happened to them: /28

We had a monopoly on the atomic bomb when on June 14, 1946, we submitted the Baruch plan for international control of atomic energy. What happened? It was rejected by the USSR. /29

Under Article 43 of the United Nations Charter, provision was made for the establishment of the United Nations Armed Forces to keep the peace. On June 4, 1947, we made the first of many requests that agreement be reached. What happened? All have been rejected by the USSR. /30

At the Summit Conference in Geneva on July 21, 1955, President Eisenhower made his offer of open skies aerial inspection. What happened? It was rejected by the USSR. /31

On May 1, 1958, the United States offered an Arctic aerial inspection plan to protect both nations from surprise attack. What happened? It was rejected by the USSR. /32

I realize that your government has indicated reasons for its rejection of each of these proposals. I do not list these proposals for the purpose of warming over past history but simply to demonstrate the initiative that our government has taken to reduce tensions and to find peaceful solutions for differences between us. /33

I realize that my answers to these questions indicate that there are some very basic differences between us. But let me emphasize at the same time that the very fact that we have not made as much progress as we would like in the past in settling our differences is the strongest reason for us to redouble our efforts to create better understanding between our two countries; to remove fear, suspicion and misconception where they exist, and thereby, to pave the way for discussions and eventual settlement by agreement of some of the basic conflicts between us. /34

We should both frankly recognize that we have some very real differences; that they are not easily settled: But two men who are friends can settle an argument between them without using their fists and two nations who want to be friends can do so without war. /35

I should like to suggest tonight some practical steps which will contribute to the cause of peace to which we are both dedicated. /36

First there are some positive things we can do which will create better understanding between us. /37

We can start by removing the language barrier. Here is one place where you are ahead of us. I was amazed at the number of people I met on this trip who were studying English. What we need are millions of American students who understand Russian and millions of Soviet students who understand English. /38

Both the exchange of persons and the cultural exchange programs should not only be continued but sharply expanded. The more Americans who visit and get to know first-hand the people of the Soviet Union and the more Soviet citizens who do the same in the United States, the better understanding we shall have. /39

I believe also that visits by officials like the ones Mr. Mikoyan and Mr. Kozlov made to the United States and which I have just concluded can provide the means of frank and full discussion of some of our problems and the development of solutions for them. Consequently, we should explore ways of increasing contacts of this type. /40

Most important of all, we need a much freer exchange of information between our two countries so that misconceptions we may have about you and that you have about us may be removed. I was rather surprised that Mr. Khrushchev should raise a question about the failure of the Western press to report adequately one of his recent statements. I would estimate that at least 100 of Mr. Khrushchev's words are printed in our American press for every one word of President Eisenhower's speeches that are printed in the Soviet press. /41

Perhaps this is an area where the cause of better understanding would be served if we had a more equal exchange. Let us agree that all of Mr. Khrushchev's speeches on foreign policy be printed in the United States and that all of President Eisenhower's speeches on foreign policy be printed in the Soviet Union. /42

Why not go further and set up regular radio and television broadcasts by Mr. Khrushchev to the American people in return for President Eisenhower having the same privilege to talk to the Soviet people? /43

Let us put a stop to the jamming of broadcasts so that the Soviet people may hear broadcasts from our country just as the American people can hear forty hours of broadcasts a day from the Soviet Union. And let us have a freer flow of newspapers and magazines so that the Soviet people can buy American newspapers and magazines here just as we Americans purchased over one and one-half million Soviet publications in last year alone. /44

I recognize that freedom of information can be abused and that neither of us is free from blame in this respect. The press, radio, television and other means of communication such as film studios, have a heavy responsibility for maintaining the spirit of truth and for preventing misinformation. In the final analysis the misrepresentation of facts or distortion of the truth defeats itself. Let me give you an example from an experience that occurred to me on this trip. /45

There was a report in *Pravda* to the effect that on the morning after I arrived in Moscow I tried to give money to a poor Soviet citizen, with the hope that American press photographers might take pictures of the incident and send them around the world. There was not a shred of truth to this story. /46

Here is what actually happened. On an early morning visit to the Danilovsky Market, I had talked to scores of people and received a most friendly welcome. As I was about to leave, several of the people asked me for tickets to the American Exhibition. I told them I did not have any with me, but that I would be glad to buy some tickets for those present who wanted to attend the Exhibition. One of the group explained that it was not a question of their not having money for the tickets, but simply a question of their not being able to obtain them. I told him I would be glad to check into the matter and see if I could get tickets for him. /47

These are the simple facts as far as this incident was concerned, and I can only add that all irresponsible reporters should never forget that in the end the truth always catches up with a lie. /48

Through this greater exchange of information between our two peoples we not only learn from each other and improve our way of life but we reduce the suspicion, the mistrust, and fear and misunderstanding and assure the understanding and friendship which will lead to the peace we all want. That is why, to me, the concept of co-existence is completely inadequate and negative. Co-existence implies that the world must be divided into two hostile camps with a wall of hate and fear between. /49

What we need today is not two worlds but one world where different peoples choose the economic and political systems which they want, but where there is free communication among all the peoples living on this earth. /50

Let us expand the concept of open skies. What the world also needs are open cities, open minds and open hearts. /51

Let us have peaceful competition not only in producing the best factories but in producing better lives for our people. /52

Let us cooperate in our exploration of outer space. As a worker told me in Novosibirsk, let us go to the moon together. /53

Let our aim be not victory over other peoples but the victory of all mankind over hunger, want, misery and disease, wherever it exists in the world. /54

I realize that this era of peaceful competition and even cooperation seems like an impossible dream when we consider the present differences we have between us. But the leaders of our countries can help make this dream come true. So far as the leader of our country is concerned, I can assure you that President Eisenhower has no objective to which he is more dedicated. /55

As far as Mr. Khrushchev is concerned, as I am sure you know, we disagree sharply on political and economic philosophy and on many world problems. But these characteristics are evident to anyone who meets him—He is a self-made man who worked his way up from the bottom; he is an articulate spokesman for the economic system in which he believes; he has immense drive; in sum, he is one of those individuals who, whether you agree with him or disagree with him, is a born leader of men. Because he has these unique qualities and because the decisions he makes will affect not only the 200 million people of the USSR but the 3 billion people on this earth, he carries a tremendous responsibility on his shoulders. /56

I would not be so presumptuous as to try to give him advice on how he should fulfill that responsibility. But could I relate something that I noted on the trip I have just completed? In every factory and on hundreds of billboards I saw this slogan, "Let us work for the victory of Communism." /57

If Mr. Khrushchev means by this slogan working

for a better life for the people within the Soviet Union that is one thing. If, on the other hand, he means the victory of Communism over the United States and other countries, this is a horse of a different color. For we have our own ideas as to what system is best for us. /58

If he devotes his immense energies and talents to building a better life for the people of his own country, Mr. Khrushchev can go down in history as one of the greatest leaders the Soviet people have ever produced. But if he diverts the resources and talents of his people to the objective of promoting the communization of countries outside the Soviet Union, he will only assure that both he and his people will continue to live in an era of fear, suspicion and tension. /59

The Geneva conference is a case in point. It would not be proper for me to comment on the specific proposals that are pending before that conference at this time. But agreements between great powers cannot be reached unless they take into account the views and interests of all parties concerned. I was encouraged to note in my conversations with Mr. Khrushchev that he recognizes this fact and agrees that a successful outcome of this conference could be a great step forward in settling some of the problems I have discussed tonight. /60

I have one final thought to add. Mr. Khrushchev predicted that our grandchildren would live under Communism. He reiterated this to me in our talks last Sunday. /61

Let me say that we do not object to his saying this will happen. We only object if he tries to bring it about. /62

And this is my answer to him. I do not say that your grandchildren will live under capitalism. We prefer our system. But the very essence of our belief is that we do not and will not try to impose our system on anybody else. We believe that you and all other peoples on this earth should have the right to choose the kind of economic or political system which best fits your particular problems without any foreign intervention. /63

As I leave your country, I shall never forget an incident that occurred as I was driving through your beautiful Ural mountains. A group of children on the side of the road threw wild flowers into my car and cried in English the words "friendship," "friendship." Mr. Zhukov told me that the first word children who study English are taught is the word "friendship." There could be no more eloquent expression of the attitude of the Soviet people, an attitude which we share in common with you. /64

Finally, may I express on behalf of my wife and I, and all the members of our party, our deep appreciation for the warm friendship and boundless hospitality we have found everywhere we have gone in the Soviet Union. I pledge to you that in the years to come I shall devote my best efforts to the cause of peace with justice for all the peoples of the world. /65

The speech

1. Nixon says he intends to "answer for the millions of people who are listening . . . some of the questions which were asked me . . . ." Do you think this was his real purpose in speaking? If not, what was his specific purpose?
2. Good introductions should establish common ground between speaker and listeners. By what means does Nixon attempt to do this in his introduction? Where else does he establish such common ground?
3. What are the major divisions of this speech? Are these topics so closely related to one another that to mention the first makes it necessary or natural to discuss the next? Defend your answer.
4. Do you think Nixon used evidence in such a way as to overstate his country's peaceful behavior?
5. What do you think Nixon hoped to accomplish by the passage in which he seems to analyze Khrushchev's probable place in history?
6. What do you think Nixon was trying to suggest to his listeners when he discussed the slogan, "Let us work for the victory of Communism"?
7. A good conclusion ought to restate and vivify the speaker's central idea and re-emphasize his intentions toward his audience. By what means does Nixon try to gain emphasis in his conclusion?
8. One journalist said of this speech, "It may not have convinced them, but at least it gave them pause." In what ways and by what means might the speech raise self-doubts among convinced and loyal Russians?
9. Walter Lippmann called this speech "self-respecting and well directed to the Russians who heard it." What does Nixon do, or avoid doing, that adds to his own dignity as a high public official?
10. Nixon's development of the topic, the United States seeks peace, is predominantly refutational. What justification is there in this section for Lippmann's assertion that the speech was "well directed to the Russians who heard it"?

For further study and discussion

1. Why do you think the United States should or should not stop developing and testing nuclear weapons?

2. If there were an international disarmament agreement, would you be willing to allow Russian and other foreign representatives to travel freely in the United States as inspectors and enforcers of the agreement? Why or why not?
3. What good or harm could arise from regular, uncensored broadcasts by Russians over American networks and by Americans over Russian networks?
4. Why do you agree or disagree with Nixon's statement that millions of young Americans should learn Russian? Should every college student be required to master at least one foreign language? Why or why not?
5. What evidence is there that our newspapers, radio, and television give us a fair understanding of Russia and the Russian people?
6. Do you agree with Nixon that "free communication among all people" is more important than the political or economic systems they choose? Why or why not?
7. What limitations, if any, would you put on the policy that the United States should avoid all interference with other countries no matter what kind of economic or political systems they choose?
8. What reasons are there for believing or disbelieving that the development of missiles will make foreign air bases and troop concentrations unnecessary to American foreign and defense policies?
9. Do you think capitalism will eventually be replaced by socialism in the United States? Justify your opinion.
10. Do you think personal visits by and discussions among high public officials are more likely to advance world peace than traditional diplomacy or negotiations through the United Nations? Why or why not?

Suggestions for further reading

Herbert Agar, **The Price of Power** (Chicago, 1957)

"Asia and Future World Leadership," **Annals of the American Academy of Political and Social Sciences,** volume 318 (July 1958)

Hanson W. Baldwin, **Power and Politics** (Claremont, Cal., 1950)

George E. G. Catlin, **What Does the West Want?** (London, 1957)

Foster Rhea Dulles, **America's Rise to World Power, 1898-1954** (New York, 1955)

Brooks Emeny, **Mainsprings of World Politics** (New York, 1956)

James M. Gavin, **War and Peace in the Space Age** (New York, 1958)

Louis J. Halle, **Choice for Survival** (New York, 1958)

Kenneth Ingram, **History of the Cold War** (London and New York, 1955)

William W. Kaufman, ed., **Military Policy and National Security** (Princeton, 1956)

Grayson Kirk and others, **The Changing Environment of International Relations** (Washington, D.C., 1956)

Edgar Ansel Mowrer, **A Good Time to be Alive** (New York, 1959)

Reinhold Niebuhr, **The World Crisis and American Responsibility** (New York, 1958)

"Resolving the Russian-American Deadlock," **Annals of the American Academy of Political and Social Sciences,** volume 324 (July 1959)

Science and Foreign Policy, pamphlet, Headline series (New York, 1958)

Arnold Wolfers, **Alliance Policy in the Cold War** (Baltimore, 1959)

The inner city—our shame

S. DAVID DINWOODIE

The following speech was delivered by S. David Dinwoodie at the final hearing for the Woodford Prize in Public Speaking at Cornell University in 1958. The Woodford Prize was established at Cornell in 1870 by Stewart Lyndon Woodford and is awarded annually by a faculty committee to the Cornell University senior who presents the best public address in an open competition.

Dinwoodie's speech was delivered in a setting that was relatively informal. He addressed about fifty students and faculty members assembled in one of the lounges of the student union building. Some listeners were seated in lounge chairs along three sides of the room and others sat before the speaker's stand in chairs more formally arranged. Although a prize was at stake, the "contest" features of the occasion were de-emphasized as much as possible. Both speakers and listeners were encouraged to assume that the meeting had been called in order that a group of seniors might address some final remarks to their fellow students and teachers before departing from the university community.

Like Karos' address, "The Haven of the Defeated" (pp. 160-164), Dinwoodie's speech grew out of a deeply moving personal experience. The discourses are alike, also, in that each depicts grave social ills from which urban society suffers, and each does so with art and sincerity.

Although Dinwoodie obviously believes that changes are needed desperately, he does not try to produce a solution for metropolitan overcrowding. Consider, then, whether "The Inner City—Our Shame" is really a message worth hearing for its own sake, or will it, as well as other speeches that offer only a "need step," however moving, inevitably disappoint the audience? Consider, too, whether Dinwoodie's address and Stevenson's "The City—A Cause for Statesmanship" (pp. 250-256) would, if somehow blended, have formed a more complete and compelling case for urban renewal than either speech heard separately.

Dinwoodie holds a B.S. in Industrial and Labor Relations (1958) and an M.A. in English (1960), both from Cornell University.

Last summer I worked with a group of eight-year-old boys in East Harlem, New York, and tonight I want to share with you some of my impressions of that tragic place. /1

Let me begin by telling you of the incident that introduced me to this pathetic area. Of all the new and intriguing experiences that I had last summer none was more profoundly moving than this one. /2

It took place at Bob Vane's apartment. He was one of the boys in my group and I was getting acquainted with his family. The dimly lit apartment was thick with the sickening smells that come from too many people living in too small an area. The three small rooms housed two mothers, their eight copper-colored children—and a dog. As I learned later, no husband lived there permanently, but Bob did have a succession of "uncles" moving in and out with fair regularity. /3

I had been exchanging pleasantries with the mothers and playing and joking with the kids for about only ten minutes, when little Mary, a three-year-old with the kind of arresting beauty that makes you wish you were a poet, boosted herself up onto the sofa where I was sitting, crawled into my lap, planted her feet flat on my legs and stood up bringing her face on a level with mine. She raised her arms and entwined her hands about the back of my neck, gazing into my eyes through long dark lashes with a look that I can describe only as rapt adoration. She stood like that for at least a minute and then, drawing her face close to mine, she kissed me on the cheek. /4

I was overwhelmed—of course—but as I realized only at the end of the summer, after living for two months with many kids who have no permanent fathers, the same thing would happen to any male who gave East Harlem kids his attention and affection. To Mary and the many like her, East Harlem bequeaths a heritage of lovelessness. Such lovelessness is tragic because it warps lives, and as intelligent, sensitive people we can no more ignore the social tragedy of East Harlem than we can ignore the social problems of polio and economic recession. /5

Lovelessness, and a host of other evils, have led social scientists to call East Harlem the Inner City. For it must be distinguished from the rest of New York City and from the rest of our society. The Inner City is alienated and separated; it is walled off from the rest of society by barriers of language, race, religion, and culture. Like an eddy in a great river, East Harlem is swirled around and by-passed by the mainstream of society. It doesn't share the economic and cultural progress of society. It has conditions that work to degrade and defeat its people to an extent that is hard to imagine. /6

My work in the Inner City was an upsetting experience. Before last summer, when I heard or read about the Inner City, I was inclined to ignore the reports—after all, the poor are with us always. But after working in East Harlem's squalor, after living in the midst of its lovelessness, and its racial antagonisms; its dope addiction, and its juvenile delinquency, I can't be passive any longer. The Inner City is maintained at the expense of too many personalities. The Inner City destroys that which makes man great, his creative aspirations! /7

If these were the 1930's when students were hypersensitive to social problems and anxious to correct them, I would make a ringing appeal tonight for recruits to man a great crusade of social reform. If you were a philanthropic organization or a church group, I would ask you to contribute huge donations to the many social agencies working in East Harlem. But this is, after all, 1958, a time of relative peace, prosperity, and progress, when social reform doesn't seem to be a paramount concern of most students. And I'm talking to people whose main concerns are probably to develop personal life philosophies and critical faculties. /8

So, I'm not recruiting a group of reform-minded students to march on New York's City Hall. I am trying to make you aware of the social disgrace of the Inner City, feeling that you—as intelligent, sensitive people—will be moved to some kind of reform action. I don't expect immediate action although that would be desirable. I don't expect noisy radical action although that might help. I do hope for the kind of quiet but dynamic activity that springs from mature adults and citizens who feel responsible for shaping the destiny of their society and who, consequently, devote their energy and talents to that cause. I hope that in the near future—as voters, as teachers, as legislators, lawyers, and doctors—you will work to eliminate the Inner Cities like East Harlem, which can be found in every urban area. Let me tell you about other conditions that make the Inner City intolerable in our society. /9

East Harlem is crowded. On the block where I lived, four thousand people are housed in twenty-seven stinking, rotting tenements. If this people-per-block ratio of East Harlem were applied to the entire country, the nation's population could be put in half of New York City. As a result, East Harlemites are continually jammed, shoved, pushed, and packed together. Naturally, this increases the normal frustrations and tensions of living. Human beings need periods of privacy. We need to be alone once in a while to gain perspective on life. But the people of East Harlem have no place to be alone. And unable to relieve their tensions in solitude, they seek relief in escape—in escapes like liquor, sex, pentacostal religion, and dope. /10

Another result of crowded living conditions is that kids are thrown out onto the streets at a young age. Finding themselves in the asphalt jungle—without the parental protection that most of us of the middle class have known—they soon learn the law of this jungle. They learn to scrap and claw for survival—survival of the fittest—that's their philosophy of life. And if my boys lied, fought, and cheated during my time with them, it was only because they had had to do so all their lives. /11

The crowded living conditions lead to another regrettable characteristic, the school system. East Harlem schools are overcrowded and understaffed. There are forty pupils in classes that, because of the tremendous emotional problems of the kids, should have only five. As a result the schools are mere discipline factories. The harried teachers spend their time trying to maintain order and don't have time or energy to really teach. This situation accounts for the teenagers I met who couldn't read or write. It also helps produce the teenage dope addicts I knew—they were for the most part bright kids, who, attending schools that couldn't challenge their intellects, turned to narcotics to escape the boredom. /12

But the most tragic of all, East Harlem's people are apathetic—they are aimless—they seem unable or afraid to hold a vision of what they might become. I was always amazed by the large number of men who did nothing all day but hang around the stoops. But the lack of inspiration isn't hard to understand, really. Puerto Ricans and Negroes came north even as the Jews had hopefully set out for the promised land. There was opportunity, wealth, and freedom to the north. But what did the Puerto Ricans and Negroes find? When they did get work (which wasn't always), it was as elevator operators, busboys, dishwashers, and sewing machine operators in fly-by-night sweat shops. The small wages they did earn were set upon by racketeering unionists and exploiting landlords. They were forced into ghettos by housing discrimination. But the biggest disappointment was the knowledge—not so much an explicit fact that one could touch, but more a feeling of constant, overwhelming pressure—the knowledge that the rest of society regarded them as second-class citizens. No wonder there is apathy and lack of vision. No wonder huge numbers of men avoid family responsibilities. No wonder they lounge on doorsteps all day and escape into dreamworlds of alcohol, sex, and dope at night. What is a man to do when so many social forces seem bent on destroying his self-respect? /13

The women are lucky. They gain some measure of creative self-realization by having children. And they indulge in this fulfillment with great abandon, knowing that welfare checks will take care of them if transient lovers won't. But what really hurts—what really hurts is to talk to 15 and 16 year old boys, to listen to them spin dreams of long Cadillacs and jobs where they can put their feet up on the desk; and then to see the glow of aspiration slowly fade from their eyes giving way to angry despair as they look at the men lounging about them and realize that this is the true vision of their future. /14

What then are my impressions of East Harlem? I saw the Inner City—an area walled off from the rest of society—an area of lovelessness, racial antagonism, and crowdedness, an area of abominable housing, inadequate educational facilities, escapism, and juvenile delinquency. I saw the Inner City—generating destructive feelings of hatred, fear, prejudice, and apathy. I saw the Inner City—destroying many, many lives. /15

And I saw my impressions brought together most strikingly in the tragic person of Tony. Tony is a 14 year old Negro boy—big for his age and not very bright. He can't read or write. Because of his backwardness, he is not accepted by his own age group and so he seeks companionship with younger boys. Unfortunately, his confused life has led him to make homosexual advances to the younger boys and they of course reject him, too. /16

One cold, drizzly night, I was walking to my apartment when I heard sobs coming from a nearby alley, and I found Tony there huddled against a wall among some garbage cans. I asked him what was wrong and in his convulsive, sobbing answer, I heard the distilled cry of an entire community that is rejected by the rest of society. "I don't know what to do," he cried. "Nobody wants me. Everybody—everything is against me." /17

It is sad when one person is shattered by life. It's

tragic when thousands feel crushed and without hope; the Inner City does this—it crushes and shatters thousands. Its existence is our shame. Its continuance is our shame compounded, and our reaction to this great social problem will be the test of our maturity. An anguished cry breaks into Cornell's comfortable, creative mood tonight. It's the Inner City echoing Tony's pathetic cry—"We don't know what to do. Nobody wants us. Everybody—everything is against us." /18

The speech

1. What is the introduction to this speech? Is the length of the introduction appropriate for the speaker's purpose, occasion, and audience?
2. Does Dinwoodie's explanation of what he expects of his audience occur in about the right place, too early, or too late? Why?
3. The speaker was deeply concerned about his subject, yet his listeners could not alone do much about the problem. In view of this was his plea for present awareness and future action well chosen? Was the plea too remote from the listeners' interests or was it simply realistic? Should he have given this speech to a college audience at all?
4. What could the substance of this speech have achieved if addressed to the ACTION conference that Adlai E. Stevenson spoke to in Newark (see pp. 250-256)? What parts of the speech would Dinwoodie have had to change in adapting to that audience?
5. Much of the persuasion in this speech is achieved through suggestion rather than through argument. To make his suggestion that overcrowding causes escapism logically acceptable, what attitudes and evidence do you have to supply from your own mind as you read paragraph 10? What form or forms of suggestion are used in this paragraph?
6. Review the topic of *proof* in the Glossary. What kinds of proofs does Dinwoodie use to establish that overcrowding leads to juvenile delinquency (see especially paragraph 12)?
7. What is your reaction to the use of the word "kids" in this speech? Is it overused? Should it be used at all? Do the circumstances of the speech make any difference?
8. Do the rather unpleasant qualities in the personality of Tony make you more or less sympathetic toward him? Would it have been more effective for the speaker to have found a different illustration with which to end the speech? Or do Tony's limitations make him an ideal voice for the "Inner City"?
9. Is Dinwoodie's a deliberative, forensic, or epideictic speech? Which of these kinds of speeches is Mr. Stevenson's Newark speech (pp. 250-256)? Will either speech secure specific actions by the audience? If not, were the speeches worth making to these audiences?
10. The force of this speech depends heavily on the speaker's credibility. How many specific points can you find at which what the speaker chooses to say or not to say adds to or detracts from your confidence in him?

For further study and discussion

1. Do you think overcrowding is really the basic cause of the social evils Dinwoodie describes? What about cultural influences?
2. Cardinal Meyer of Chicago says, "It is the [housing] restrictions against the most capable and self-reliant portions of the Negro population which call loudest for remedy." Will second- and third-generation Negroes, Puerto Ricans, and Mexicans be able to move from tenements to better dwellings as their Irish, Italian, or German predecessors have?
3. Has the creation of good, low-income housing had any effects upon family solidarity, quality of education, and individual ambition in cities where such housing programs have been tried?
4. What opportunities do Negroes, Puerto Ricans, Mexicans, and Orientals have to join craft and professional labor unions?
5. What is the governmental relationship between the United States and the Commonwealth of Puerto Rico? What bearing does this relationship have on situations such as Mr. Dinwoodie described?
6. Explore the political career of Vito Marcantonio, Adam Clayton Powell, or William Dawson. To what extent did the "alienation" of the "inner cities" form these political leaders and shape their careers?
7. Representative Powell has said, "The next fight [for civil rights] is in housing and that will come in the next five years. . . . There are a few things I'd like to do . . . for one thing unite the Negroes and the Puerto Ricans." Do you think united political action by such ethnic groups might contribute to the solution of modern urban problems?
8. Make yourself familiar with the activities of the Division of Juvenile Delinquency Services, United States Department of Health, Education, and Welfare. How has it contributed to solving youth problems since its establishment in 1955?
9. Are the urban problems discussed by Stevenson and Dinwoodie peculiarly American? Do they exist in cities of other lands? Are they inevitable features of metropolitan society?

10. Some Congressmen have proposed that federal and state governments should create a National Youth Conservation Corps to provide work on public lands for city youths aged sixteen to twenty-one. Do you think such action is needed? Desirable? Would it be better to increase compulsory requirements for school attendance? Would it be better to modify child labor laws in states where they prevent teen-aged youths from taking full-time employment?

The city—a cause for statesmanship

ADLAI E. STEVENSON

It has been rightly said that "not since William Jennings Bryan won the leadership of the Democratic Party in 1896 with his famous 'Cross of Gold' speech has public address contributed so much to establishing and maintaining a major presidential candidate's national prominence as in the case of Adlai E. Stevenson."[1] There can be little doubt that Stevenson's rise from the middle ranks of party life to national prominence came about largely because of his unique speaking abilities.

Adlai Stevenson was born in Los Angeles, California, in 1900, received his B.A. from Princeton University in 1922, worked briefly as a journalist, and then entered the study of law, receiving a J.D. from Northwestern University in 1926. From 1927 to 1933 he practiced law in Chicago, and from 1933 to the end of World War II he held a variety of governmental positions and practiced law in Washington, D.C. In 1946 and 1947 Stevenson was a delegate to the General Assembly of the United Nations. His rise to national political leadership began with his nomination and election to the governorship of Illinois in 1948. Four years later, and again in 1956, the Democratic party nominated him for the presidency of the United States.

Stevenson's great facility with language—his mastery of witty wordplay, the epigram, and satiric statement—probably derives from his lifelong interest in literature and writing. Whenever possible he writes his own speeches, carefully revises them, and delivers them from manuscript. He professes not to have given much thought to the theory of public address, and he insists that the art of speaking has been difficult for him to learn. He, himself, believes his early experience as a college and professional journalist has significantly affected his practice in speech composition. Of his rhetorical intent Mr. Stevenson has said, "My basic purpose in speaking is to inform."[2]

When Stevenson became widely known as a public speaker, political commentators sometimes alleged that he spoke over the heads of his audiences. Objective analysis shows that his vocabulary is not significantly more difficult than the vocabulary of other political speakers; nor are the topics he treats unfamiliar in political discourse. There is, indeed, no clear evidence that popular audiences have found Stevenson difficult to understand, though his allusions may now and again seem perplexing at a first hearing. It is more probable that Stevenson's unwillingness to make major adaptations to unexpected developments in speaking situations, his commitment to the text of the composition he has so carefully molded, and his editorial tone create in some of his hearers the impression that he is aloof, speaking *to* them rather than *with* them. There can be little question, however, about Stevenson's mastery of words; in this respect he probably excels all American political speakers since Franklin D. Roosevelt.

The speech reprinted here was delivered on May 5, 1959, to an audience of about five hundred business leaders, members of a national group known as ACTION (American Council to Improve Our Neighborhoods) meeting in Newark, New Jersey. The aim of ACTION is to energize public agencies and private enterprises on behalf of urban reconstruction programs. Stevenson was the featured speaker at the Newark conference. In his address he met with consummate skill the audience's desire that its own policies and objectives be rendered urgent and impressive through fresh, exhilarating restatement.

You have assigned me an impressive title—"The American City—A Cause for Statesmanship." I despair, frankly, that any words of mine can satisfy the promise of this title, or that my grasp can equal its reach. /1

As for The American City: I am not expert in its

[1] Russel Windes, Jr., and James A. Robinson, "Public Address in the Career of Adlai E. Stevenson," *Quarterly Journal of Speech*, XLII (1956), p. 225.

[2] Ibid., p. 232.

problems. I confess to not even living in it, but rather as far from it as the logistics of commuting permit.* I know this makes me, in the literature of the subject, a "fugitive from civic responsibility," a form of parasitical growth taking income and culture from the city, and in return only adding to the morning and evening traffic jams. /2

As for Statesmanship: again I pretend no expertise. If certain political adventures of mine—in my youth—may have seemed to involve pretenses of statesmanship, I recognize that issue as having been publicly settled—not once, but twice. /3

Yet surely the first charge upon statesmanship as it applies today to the American city is clear enough. It is the charge upon statesmen responsible for all of the cities of the world. It is that these cities be permitted to survive—that they not become, in a chain of blinding flashes, only smoking, gaping holes in the ground. The point does not bear laboring. But neither may it be forgotten—lest it become the ultimate irony that man's foregathering in the city was to simplify his self-destruction. /4

But survival isn't the only problem we have in common with the rest of the world. Urban renewal and a shortage of housing are universal problems. I was told everywhere from Central Asia to Leningrad that housing is the number-one problem of the Soviet Union. And I have seen the great boom towns in the exploding population areas from Damascus to Manila, and the new central cities that have arisen from the ashes of London, Warsaw, Berlin.** Everywhere on earth the city planners and officials are struggling with the same problems of the decay and death of old centers and the birth and growth of new ones. /5

In distant places, I have, like you, often thought about our fantastic standard of living, and that in spite of blessings that exceed the grasp, even the imagination, of most of the world's people, we in America have still fallen far short of even arresting the spread of blight and decay in our cities. Like you, I have often wondered how we can hope to solve the problems of maintaining our alliances, of meeting the Communist economic and scientific offensive, of extending a helping hand to the peoples now searching for national identity and independence, of standing firm against aggression anywhere, if we can't mobilize our domestic resources to meet the needs of day-to-day work and living. /6

We are not concerned just with the new low-income and minority ghettos in some cities, nor just with real-estate values in the downtown central business districts, nor the bedeviled commuter, nor the costly, growing traffic congestion, nor the general offensiveness of the urban sprawl. The deficiencies in our schools and communal services, like parks, playgrounds, hospitals, and the ugly outcroppings of juvenile violence, are all pleading for attention and are all part of the broader task of revitalization and reinvigoration of the city as a way of life. /7

It is not even a renaissance we seek; rather it is the construction of an entirely new mode of living—poles apart from the Victorian city of old. What we are concerned with is the exciting, exhilarating adventure of constructing economic, financial, social and political tools to build—not a city—but a metropolis. /8

But to return to "statesmanship" in this context—I would define it simply as the marking and the doing of the central thing that needs to be done—finding the right key—and turning it. /9

If there is a key to the answers to the problems which today beset our cities, I am sure I haven't got it. I don't think there is one key. But I think of Pope's line about a key to a drawer wherein lie other keys.* /10

Because, I suppose, many of the best years of my life have been devoted to the problems of government, the drawer I look to is the one marked "government"—government with a small *g* (which suddenly reminds me of Oscar Wilde's remark that nothing produces such pleasing effects as a good platitude). /11

Government with a small *g* does not mean, for me, the agencies of public government as distinguished from those of what we call business or private enterprise. I wish everyone could realize, as you do, how closely the functions of a corporation are related to "governmental" functions when—for example—a great insurance company takes over the clearing of a slum and its replacement with the facilities for decent, twentieth-century living. /12

The problems of the American city will be met when, and not until, we recognize that they are already and inexorably committed to the *joint* trusteeship of private enterprise and public responsibility; that they demand a shoulder-to-shoulder, two-fisted attack; that their solution depends entirely upon an alliance of private and public agencies—with each

* Mr. Stevenson lives in Libertyville, Illinois, somewhat more than thirty miles from the heart of Chicago, where he maintains his legal practice. *(Editor's note)*

** Stevenson had returned from a trip abroad in August 1958. He visited Russia and Central Europe. *(Editor's note)*

* Pope's standard works contain no such references to "keys," "drawers," "lock," or "unlock." See Edwin Abbott, *Concordance to the Works of Alexander Pope*. Stevenson may have in mind a line from Pope's "Translations from Greek and Latin," his "Adaptations of Chaucer," or his "Imitations of English Poets." *(Editor's note)*

respecting its own limitations and the capacities of the other, and with each acting in support of the other. /13

It is equally essential to recognize that the public agencies involved operate at three levels—federal, state and local—and that there is a similar problem of distributing responsibilities among these three, with each being equipped to do its appointed part. /14

America has the resources, the wealth, the raw materials, the intelligence, the technical know-how, the pressing need and the driving desire to solve all the problems which have so far prevented the remaking of the cities. Statesmanship's question here is not *what* to do but *who* is to do it—and how to make an alliance among the agencies involved, as you have evidently done with such spectacular success here in Newark. /15

There is no point in emphasizing at an ACTION conference the stake private enterprise—including every businessman in every city in America—has in the preservation and the strengthening of the urban structure. You, more than any other group, have pointed out that what is good for the American city is good for every businessman who operates there. /16

Part of these returns are direct—in profit on the building projects themselves. But more and more the business community is coming to realize that urban renewal also means more customers coming in the doors, that an equity investment in a slum clearance development project represents philanthropy—at a profit. We are beginning to recognize that not only charity, but investment as well, can best begin at home, *in* homes. /17

I suspect that in the long run the clearing of slums will come less as the result of public concern about the people there being poor people than as a product of the business community's concern about their being poor customers. This isn't cynical. It simply recognizes the fact that it is hard to sustain public concern—except when a school burns down or a rat bites a child—in a problem which neighbors can solve by moving away from it. But businesses can't easily do that. /18

So business, especially big business, has a great opportunity here to make a contribution—and to make a profit. /19

But there are some parts of this job that just cannot be done at a profit, and therefore will not be done privately. The necessary distribution of responsibilities for city saving will not come about as long as influential groups insist that any governmental financial aid, except to guarantee mortgages, is socialist sin—which you are either against in all its manifestations or for, all the way. For that matter we will never get our sights straight as long as influential people persist in the myth that all public spending is bad, all private spending good. I believe it was Justice Holmes who said: "I buy civilization with my taxes." /20

I came across, the other day, a speech I made at a Housing Day Conference in Chicago ten years ago. This line jumped out at me: "The public housing debate is over." That was shortly after, of course, the enactment under the sponsorship of Senators Taft, Wagner and Ellender, of the Housing Act of 1949—providing for the building of 135,000 public housing units a year for six years, or 810,000 in all. /21

But now, ten years later, only half of those 810,000 units have been built, and some of those who denounced Senator Taft as an "old Republican"* have brought in a housing bill providing for no public housing at all. /22

Nobody "likes" public housing. It is a mark of failure, and the nation will welcome and accept the views of those critics of public housing who will develop alternatives which are constructive and realistic. But mere insistence that private enterprise can do the job without public housing is no answer—unless this insistence is backed up with action. We are entitled to say here, with a new meaning, "either put up—or shut up." /23

There is reason for larger satisfaction about the increasing supply of middle-income housing. I saw a few days ago in New Haven the heartening spectacle of a beautiful new city rising from the ashes of ugliness and neglect. We have in Chicago now, as you have in a number of your cities, substantial developments which confirm the willingness and ability of private capital and enterprise to carry the job of reconstruction forward if public funds are available for the preliminary clearing of the old slum areas. /24

I am most encouraged, incidentally, by the reports of success in leasing these new accommodations on "open-occupancy" basis, for any realistic appraisal of the housing problem must take account of the serious danger that subsidized housing will become racially segregated housing and will thereby aggravate a problem as serious as the housing problem itself. /25

Last week a friend of mine who has done a great deal to rebuild Chicago showed me how the private equity investment of $4,725,000 per year for ten years will produce the capital required to completely

* Senator Robert A. Taft and General Dwight D. Eisenhower were competitors for the Republican nomination for President in 1952. Eisenhower's supporters insisted their candidate represented "modern Republicanism" and Senator Taft, the "old Republicans." *(Editor's note)*

rebuild an entire square mile of slums with fine, modern living accommodations which can be rented to low-middle-income families at a fair profit. I was sobered when he added that this proposition assumes a public subsidy to acquire this land and to write it down to use value, and that these costs will run to $8,000,000 per year. Yet this is the kind of cooperative venture, the kind of public-private alliance, which alone can do this job. It appeared, for a while, that there was solid recognition of the degree of aid that would have to come from federal sources to support local urban renewal, in both its private and its public aspects. Of late, there has been considerable doubt cast on both the extent of such aid and its character or continuance. The plain fact is that those who oppose federal aid for urban renewal are actually against urban renewal. For they know full well that many of the possibilities of local revenue have been pre-empted by federal and state taxing bodies, that the largest urban centers are operating under archaic revenue authority with little hope of relief from state legislatures dominated by non-urban lawmakers.* The vast sums urban renewal requires are just not available exclusively from private funds or from the local resources of the overwhelming majority of urban centers. /26

From administrative experience we have learned some lessons the hard way. It is clear now that the administrators of the federal program destroy the effectiveness of local authorities and discourage willing private investors when they keep changing the rules of the game, throwing out projects which were carefully devised to conform to the old rules but which don't meet the new ones. Too many of us here are familiar with the crippling effect in our own cities of arbitrary notices from Washington that all projects are to be scaled down by an arbitrary percentage. Too often the scaled-down project just doesn't make sense. Half a building is not better than none, and it is often the falsest economy to pick at a slum instead of rending a bulldozer all the way through it. /27

It is noteworthy, too, that these pending bills reflect the significance of the conservation principle that a dollar put into preventing urban decay is ten dollars saved in subsequent rebuilding. /28

Such legislation deserves support solely in terms of the human values that are involved. The juvenile delinquency a slum breeds infects a whole city. The tax bill for it—for police regulation, for fire protection, for relief payments—goes to every taxpayer. /29

You and I vote at each election with complacent confidence that democratic capitalism means security and the supplying of life's purposes. But our votes count no more than the votes from slum victims which are not based on that faith. /30

I reread not long ago the story of the twenty-one American soldiers who chose not to return from the Korean Communist prison camp but to stay with those who had captured their minds as well as their bodies. Fifteen of those "21 Who Stayed" came from slums—some in the cities, some in the country. I could only think of Bret Harte's poetic dictum that nobody shoulder a rifle in defense of a boarding house. /31

But, we are being told, we can't afford these things. /32

I would, if it were necessary, say to this that there are emergencies in which you call the doctor without asking the cost, and that cancer in our cities is such a case. When somebody starts talking about the evil of passing a burden of public debt on to the next generation it makes me want to ask if it is better to pass on a burden of slums, of ignorance, of national weakness —and ultimately greater debt. We have a way of saying about reforms and changes that they were "inevitable." But with urban renewal as with everything else—"the mode by which the inevitable comes to pass is effort." /33

But to support a program of full-scale renewal and rebuilding of the cities is not to be soft-hearted (which seems to me no sin); it is also to be hard-headed. I am not a budget buster. But I do believe in America's greatness, and that this greatness can be traced to bold leaders and bold enterprises and the basic notion that money invested properly and adequately will multiply wealth. And every dollar of public funds that goes into slum clearance and urban renewal will be returned to the public coffers in increased revenues. /34

In the face of these great needs which are also great opportunities, I hope we are ready to stop the demagogic political debate which assumes that government and private enterprise are inherently antagonistic. I hope we are now ready to accept, instead, the demanding necessity for a confident alliance of public and private enterprise in meeting the problems of the city. /35

Money is not enough. Indeed the wrong amount of money at the wrong time and in the wrong place may hinder rather than help our efforts to construct the city of the future. We Americans have a penchant for believing that sufficient inputs of energy and dollars can solve any problem. We rush in where angels fear to tread and frequently we profit, but sometimes

* To secure reforms in the revenue authority of cities was one of the official objectives of ACTION. *(Editor's note)*

we learn why the angels, in their greater wisdom, have not joined us and preferred to stay aloft. Urban reconstruction is a case in point. /36

Despite the laudable efforts we have been making to deal with various aspects of the problem in the generation since the New Deal began, does the sum of these parts add up to a meaningful whole? Instead of developing a comprehensive program, are we in danger of creating a patchwork, a conglomeration of temporary and short-sighted solutions to pieces of a problem which cannot be handled piecemeal?* Even in that haven of generalities—a preamble to a federal law—we look in vain for a comprehensive statement of what we are after. /37

What do we want our downtown centers to become? What, in the long run, are the proper uses of the land in the "gray belt"? What kind of transportation system will best meet our needs? How do we want to use the remaining open spaces around our cities—for parks, for wild-life reservations, for industries or for the next wave of developments? /38

We shall have to look to groups like this for responsible, sustained help in finding the answers. But it will have to be left to the citizens of each urban community, acting through their own governments, to settle their own issues. And here we run into another familiar problem of government—the problem of too much government. At the local level the jumble of bureaus, municipalities, counties, commissions, authorities, corporations and officialdom generally has neither a sense of union nor a sense of direction. In most instances even the skeleton of a limp confederation is lacking. /39

At the very root of this problem is also the fact that although we have become a dominantly urban and suburban society, our political thinking and structure is still predominantly country minded. Coming from the country, I have no quarrel with rural people. But the fact is that one hundred million Americans live today in 168 metropolitan areas. This is over 60 percent of our total population. Yet in most legislatures the vote of a small town or rural citizen is worth substantially more than his city cousin's. /40

I know from my years as governor of a divided state how difficult this problem is. There are two sides to it. And yet there is bound to be a change. Local governments must be given the fiscal authority which the discharge of their responsibilities demands. There must be enlargement, in one way or another, of the revenue sources available to them. Gotham won't secede from New York, nor Chicago from Illinois, but this is a serious problem and it is going to take ingenuity—and a willingness to seek out entirely new ways—to meet it. /41

These urban problems have today become metropolitan problems, problems that cross all lines between city and suburbs and between incorporated and unincorporated areas, problems that have no city limits. /42

The plain fact is that the resources on which our urban life depend—land, water and breathable air—are getting scarcer. The decisions about their use, like the decisions about transportation, are hard decisions. Any assumption that the city planners or high level commissions will devise the answers seems to me to go only halfway. For the answers, however wise, won't mean anything unless they are adopted —through the political decision-making process—by those affected by these decisions. /43

I know the difficulties which will be in the way of developing new machinery of decision. The sovereignties and vested interests of established local units and officialdom will be as hard to break down as they are at the national and international levels. The various suburbs which surround our major cities are already developing special ethnic and economic personalities, and this will make it harder and harder for the citizens of one area to be persuaded to submit their interests to a common vote which includes the citizens of another. /44

But I know, too, of the bold, effective way this problem has been met by Toronto. We are all watching eagerly the imaginative inquiry being conducted at Detroit. Other cities have taken the first essential steps toward metropolitan planning and are now looking to the possibilities of limited metropolitan government. /45

If building new instruments seems hopeless, then I must say that I think the other choice is to accept for our cities the fate of eternal worrying at the edges of our urban concerns, of everlasting plucking at ever broadening scabs of blight and decay; while more authority will remain at the higher state and federal levels. /46

A Balkanized metropolis can probably cope, in desperation, with the problems of urban survival. It can make our day-to-day difficulties tolerable. But I doubt if it can ever conceive the great plans, set the great policies, make the great decisions, which are essential if the cities are to be built and rebuilt according to the blueprints of our hopes. /47

I have tried to suggest that the problems of the American city demand the exercise of what is perhaps the most difficult art of democratic government:

* Major, rather than piecemeal, urban renewal was an official ACTION objective. *(Editor's note)*

the effective mobilization of all of the forces which make up the free body politic and the free body economic—not just to make the right decisions, but also to carry them out. /48

There are people in the world today who say that tough public problems are best solved behind closed doors, by dictators or central committees. But in our land we dare not even reach for a goal of human improvement in disregard of human values, human judgments. The central tenet of statesmanship in a democracy is that unless the people understand it and participate in it, no long-term program can endure. /49

The municipality of tomorrow must be renewed in the image of people's hopes and ambitions for a better life. The values to be recreated must have a sound political and economic pedestal, but they must flow from human needs. /50

Thus will we build and rebuild our cities, and in so doing renew and rekindle our faith in ourselves and in the limitless creativeness of free men. /51

The speech

1. Stevenson has sometimes been criticized for treating serious issues with too much humor. Identify the points at which he makes use of humor in this speech. Do you think these usages reflect undue casualness concerning the subject he is discussing?
2. What is the central idea of this speech? Is it an expository or persuasive thesis?
3. What are the main divisions of the body of the speech? What is the pattern of organization?
4. A distinctive feature of Stevenson's style is his use of connotations of a special kind, neither wholly familiar nor truly individual. Review the discussion of *connotation* in the Glossary, and then identify at least four such special connotations used in this speech. Could the occurrence of such usages make some listeners feel Stevenson talked "over their heads"?
5. Stevenson is expert at making epigrams. After reviewing the definition of an *epigram* in the Glossary, identify at least three epigrams in the speech. Do these epigrams reinforce the speaker's points?
6. Do you find any examples of satire in this speech? If so, what reactions were they likely to elicit from the ACTION audience?
7. It has been said that Stevenson's analyses and criticisms are clearer and more precise than his plans and programs. Is this true in this speech? Would plans and programs need to be spelled out in more detail for a popular audience in a political campaign than for the ACTION conference? Why?
8. Are there any passages in the speech that seem more like something you might read in a newspaper than hear from a public platform? If so, what characteristics distinguish those passages from others which you judge to have a clearly *oral* style?
9. Identify some of the points at which Stevenson deliberately tried to strengthen his own ethos before the ACTION audience. Do his references to his "escape" from city dwelling reduce his ethos with this audience?
10. Which of the ends of speaking did Stevenson probably achieve with his audience? To inform? To inspire? To persuade? To inquire?

For further study and discussion

1. What processes of population movement and sociological change produce what Stevenson calls "low-income and minority ghettos"? Are these processes different in northern and southern cities in the United States?
2. Inform yourself concerning a comprehensive urban renewal program in one of our cities—Hartford, Connecticut; Pittsburgh; Baltimore; or some other. How was the program started? How were costs shared? Were living conditions for low-income groups improved?
3. Do you agree with Stevenson and ACTION that only coordinated financing by federal, state, and local governments and by business can solve the planning and reconstruction problems of our major cities? Explain.
4. What is the difference, if any, between the positions of the Republican and Democratic parties on granting and administering federal assistance for slum clearance? If there is a difference, which position do you endorse?
5. What remedies have been proposed for "the jumble of bureaus, municipalities, counties, commissions, authorities, corporations, and officialdom" that constitutes the present government of metropolitan areas? Is the concept of city government, distinct from the government of its suburbs, sound?
6. Is there clear evidence that slums breed juvenile delinquency, or are causes other than housing conditions more important? What do authorities list as the major and the minor causes of juvenile delinquency?
7. What effects have power struggles between rural and urban groups had on the legislation of your state in the last ten years? Have these effects been generally good or bad? In what ways?
8. Is it true that the federal government has pre-empted so many sources of tax money that states and municipalities can no longer finance their proper responsibilities? If so, what should be done about it?
9. What kinds of taxes ought to be levied by federal and state governments in order to finance urban renewal programs?

10. Which do you think is the most critical domestic problem in America today: urban renewal, improvement of education, financing medical care, security for the aged, or highway construction? Support your choice.

Suggestions for further reading

Nels Anderson, ***The Urban Community: A World Perspective*** (New York, 1954)

Sir Maurice Bowra and others, ***Golden Ages of the Great Cities*** (London and New York, 1952)

H. Warren Dunham, ed., ***The City in Mid-Century*** (Detroit, 1957)

Robert L. Marlan, ***Capitol, Courthouse and City Hall*** (Boston, 1960)

"Metropolis in Ferment," ***Annals of the American Academy of Political and Social Sciences,*** volume 314 (November 1957)

Wilfred Owen, ***Cities in the Motor Age*** (New York, 1959)

Inaugural address

JOHN F. KENNEDY

Except in rare circumstances an inaugural address is a ceremonial rather than a persuasive speech. Audiences do not attend the installations of new officers to hear legislative plans debated, laws interpreted, or moral systems compared. They come to observe and to celebrate the assumption of duties they believe are important. Because this is so, inaugural speakers necessarily speak in general rather than specific terms, suggesting rather than contending for the courses of action they hope to further through the authority of their offices.

On January 20, 1961, John F. Kennedy admirably filled these rhetorical obligations in assuming the office of President of the United States. He addressed himself to all the citizens of the country and, indirectly, to all peoples of the civilized world, knowing that his real audience was vastly larger than the several thousands gathered in Washington to hear him. Although he drew upon ideas with which he and his political party had associated themselves during the election contest of 1960, he observed the ceremonial occasion by avoiding any show of partisanship. In campaigning for the presidency he had adopted the theme "New Frontier" and had found much fault with American foreign policy under the preceding Republican administration. Now, in his inaugural speech, he held to the same theme but magnified its least controversial aspects by sketching undoubted opportunities for new ventures in politics and economics and by devoting a greater proportion of time than any other peacetime president to unquestionable challenges in foreign relations.

Kennedy's address received generous praise. Adjectives commonly applied to it were "vigorous," "eloquent," "inspiring." Some commentators said it compared favorably with the great addresses delivered by Lincoln and Franklin D. Roosevelt. Others characterized it as "mood music" but conceded it was an impressive expression of the new president's aspirations and confidence.

As is customary at presidential inaugurals, Kennedy spoke in the open air. The day was unusually cold but clear. A snowstorm had impeded travel in and about Washington during the forty-eight hours preceding the inaugural ceremony, but a satisfactorily impressive audience gathered before the Capitol to hear the address. Millions heard and saw the new president on radio and television.

President Kennedy spoke slowly, in striking contrast to his rapid-fire delivery in impromptu discourse. Sometimes prolonging vowel sounds, sometimes repeating the same pattern of pitch inflections on successive phrases, he emphasized the cadence of his prose. Each major stress in phrasing was further reinforced by a sharp, downward thrust of his right forearm and hand. At points of greatest vocal force he rapped the reading desk sharply with knuckles or fist.

The style of the speech was in keeping with the delivery: again and again balanced and antithetical constructions rendered the language at once economical and rhythmical; direct questions and imperative sentences gave the address a sermonic or hortatory quality; the recurring religious and historical allusions reinforced the solemnity with which the speaker delivered his remarks.

John F. Kennedy was born in Brookline, Massachusetts, in 1917. On graduating from Harvard University with honors in 1940, he entered the Navy. He was severely wounded while serving as a PT boat commander in the Solomon Islands area during World War II. In 1946 he was elected to Congress from Massachusetts and was re-elected in 1948 and 1950. In 1952 he won election to the Senate and was returned for a second term in 1958. He was nominated as the Democratic party's candidate for the presidency in 1960 and defeated Richard M. Nixon (pp. 240-246) in one of the closest presidential elections in American history.

During a period of illness in 1954, Mr. Kennedy began preparation of his now famous book *Profiles in Courage.* It was published in 1955 and became a "best seller" well before the the author's candidacy for the presidency was seriously considered.

My Fellow Citizens: We observe today not a victory of party but a celebration of freedom—symbolizing an end as well as a beginning—signifying renewal as well as change. For I have sworn before you and almighty God the same solemn oath our forebears prescribed nearly a century and three-quarters ago. /1

The world is very different now. For man holds in his mortal hands the power to abolish all forms of human poverty and all forms of human life. And yet the same revolutionary beliefs for which our forebears fought are still at issue around the globe—the belief that the rights of man come not from the generosity of the state but from the hand of God. /2

We dare not forget today that we are the heirs of that first revolution. Let the word go forth from this time and place, to friend and foe alike, that the torch has been passed to a new generation of Americans—born in this century, tempered by war, disciplined by a hard and bitter peace, proud of our ancient heritage—and unwilling to witness or permit the slow undoing of those human rights to which this nation has always been committed, and to which we are committed today at home and around the world. /3

Let every nation know, whether it wishes us well or ill, that we shall pay any price, bear any burden, meet any hardship, support any friend, oppose any foe in order to assure the survival and success of liberty. /4

This much we pledge—and more. /5

To those old allies whose cultural and spiritual origins we share, we pledge the loyalty of faithful friends. United, there is little we cannot do in a host of cooperative ventures. Divided, there is little we can do—for we dare not meet a powerful challenge at odds and split asunder. /6

To those new states whom we welcome to the ranks of the free, we pledge our word that one form of colonial control shall not have passed away merely to be replaced by a far more iron tyranny. We shall not always expect to find them supporting our view. But we shall always hope to find them strongly supporting their own freedom—and to remember that, in the past, those who foolishly sought power by riding the back of the tiger ended up inside. /7

To those peoples in the huts and villages of half the globe struggling to break the bonds of mass misery, we pledge our best efforts to help them help themselves, for whatever period is required—not because the communists may be doing it, not because we seek their votes, but because it is right. If a free society cannot help the many who are poor, it cannot save the few who are rich. /8

To our sister republics south of our border, we offer a special pledge—to convert our good words into good deeds—in a new alliance for progress—to assist free men and free governments in casting off the chains of poverty. But this peaceful revolution of hope cannot become the prey of hostile powers. Let all our neighbors know that we shall join with them to oppose aggression or subversion anywhere in the Americas. And let every other power know that this Hemisphere intends to remain the master of its own house. /9

To that world assembly of sovereign states, the United Nations, our last best hope in an age where the instruments of war have far outpaced the instruments of peace, we renew our pledge of support—to prevent it from becoming merely a forum for invective—to strengthen its shield of the new and the weak—and to enlarge the area in which its writ may run. /10

Finally, to those nations who would make themselves our adversary, we offer not a pledge but a request: that both sides begin anew the quest for peace, before the dark powers of destruction unleashed by science engulf all humanity in planned or accidental self-destruction. /11

We dare not tempt them with weakness. For only when our arms are sufficient beyond doubt can we be certain beyond doubt that they will never be employed. /12

But neither can two great and powerful groups of nations take comfort from our present course—both sides overburdened by the cost of modern weapons, both rightly alarmed by the steady spread of the deadly atom, yet both racing to alter that uncertain balance of terror that stays the hand of mankind's final war. /13

So let us begin anew—remembering on both sides that civility is not a sign of weakness, and sincerity is always subject to proof. Let us never negotiate out of fear. But let us never fear to negotiate. /14

Let both sides explore what problems unite us instead of belaboring those problems which divide us. /15

Let both sides, for the first time, formulate serious and precise proposals for the inspection and control of arms—and bring the absolute power to destroy other nations under the absolute control of all nations. /16

Let both sides join to invoke the wonders of science instead of its terrors. Together let us explore the stars, conquer the deserts, eradicate disease, tap the ocean depths, and encourage the arts and commerce. /17

Let both sides unite to heed in all corners of the earth the command of Isaiah—to "undo the heavy burdens . . . [and] let the oppressed go free." /18

And if a beach-head of cooperation may push back the jungles of suspicion, let both sides join in creating a new endeavor, not a new balance of power, but a new world of law, where the strong are just and the weak secure and the peace preserved. /19

All this will not be finished in the first one hundred days. Nor will it be finished in the first one thousand days, nor in the life of this Administration, nor even perhaps in our lifetime on this planet. But let us begin. /20

In your hands, my fellow citizens, more than mine, will rest the final success or failure of our course. Since this country was founded, each generation of Americans has been summoned to give testimony to its national loyalty. The graves of young Americans who answered the call to service surround the globe. /21

Now the trumpet summons us again—not as a call to bear arms, tho arms we need—not as a call to battle, tho embattled we are—but a call to bear the burden of a long twilight struggle, year in and year out "rejoicing in hope, patient in tribulation"—a struggle against the common enemies of man: tyranny, poverty, disease, and war itself. /22

Can we forge against these enemies a grand and global alliance, North and South, East and West, that can assure a more fruitful life for all mankind? Will you join in that historic effort? /23

In the long history of the world, only a few generations have been granted the role of defending freedom in its hour of maximum danger. I do not shrink from this responsibility—I welcome it. I do not believe that any of us would exchange places with any other people or any other generation. The energy, the faith, and the devotion which we bring to this endeavor will light our country and all who serve it—and the glow from that fire can truly light the world. /24

And so, my fellow Americans: ask not what your country can do for you—ask what you can do for your country. /25

My fellow citizens of the world: ask not what America will do for you, but what together we can do for the freedom of man. /26

Finally, whether you are citizens of America or citizens of the world, ask of us here the same high standards of strength and sacrifice which we ask of you. With a good conscience our only sure reward, with history the final judge of our deeds, let us go forth to lead the land we love, asking His blessing and His help, but knowing that here on earth God's work must truly be our own. /27

The speech

1. A number of critics have remarked that the dominant characteristic of this speech was balance—balance not only in style and organization but also in the policies expressed. What passages seem to confirm this appraisal? Are there any that tend to refute it?
2. Study closely the sequence of ideas in paragraphs 6-11, where President Kennedy speaks first to our allies, second to the newly formed nations of Africa and Asia, third to Latin America, fourth to the United Nations, and finally to those countries "who would make themselves our adversary." What rhetorical and psychological advantages does this sequence have? What disadvantages?
3. To what motive or motives does Kennedy appeal? At what points in the speech are the appeals made? Which of the appeals is strongest? What do you think of his choice of motives?
4. Comment on the introduction of the speech—its length, tone, transition into the body. What effort is made to heal some of the wounds that might have been left by the campaign?
5. The speech is dotted with *epigrams* and *figures of speech* (see Glossary). Find as many as you can. Do they help the speaker communicate his ideas or do they hinder him? Comment on Kennedy's word choice and sentence structure.
6. Before the election some of Kennedy's critics charged he was too young and inexperienced to be president. Can you find in the speech a passage which seems to refute this charge?
7. Except for the paragraph where Kennedy asks "both sides . . . [to] formulate serious and precise proposals for the inspection and control of arms," he speaks in general rather than specific terms. Do you regard the absence of concrete supporting materials as a defect in the speech? Present arguments both pro and con.
8. Study particularly paragraph 23 where Kennedy attempts to drive home his point by using a rhetorical question. Did this device add strength to his argument? If so, why; if not, why not?
9. Some persons believe that at places Kennedy was too idealistic (see, for example, paragraphs 11, 17-19, etc.) and that as a result listeners reacted unfavorably. Do you agree or disagree? Why? Can you find a passage in the speech where this idealism is tempered?
10. Compare this speech with Theodore Roosevelt's "The Man with the Muck-Rake" (pp. 102-107). Does Kennedy

"extol . . . gospel, in a manner distinctly homiletical," as Roosevelt is said to have done? If so, what features of the speech give it this quality? Which are like, and which different from, the features of Roosevelt's address?

For further study and discussion

1. What practical difficulties stand in the way of an international system of arms inspection and control? How might some of these difficulties be effectively removed?
2. In what ways is atomic energy now used for peaceful purposes? How may the nations of the world cooperate to promote developments in this field?
3. What problems have arisen as new independent nations have been formed in Africa and Asia? What policy should the United States follow toward these new nations?
4. Review the present state of our relations with the countries of Latin America. In what respects has our present policy toward them worked well? In what respects has it failed? What recommendations would you make for the future?
5. What problems sometimes strain our relations with our traditional allies—England, France, Canada, etc.? In your opinion, how may these problems be minimized or solved?
6. Do too many people today ask what the government can do for them rather than what they can do for the government?
7. Discuss Kennedy's statement that "the same revolutionary beliefs for which our forebears fought are still at issue around the globe. . . ."
8. What are the advantages and disadvantages of "summit" meetings? Is "personal diplomacy" to be preferred to negotiations carried on through traditional channels?
9. Do you agree with Kennedy that present problems and responsibilities should be welcomed, or would you prefer to "exchange places" with some other people or some other generation?
10. Name some specific ways in which we might go about exploring with other nations "what problems unite us instead of belaboring those problems which divide us"?

Suggestions for further reading

James MacGregor Burns, ***John Kennedy: A Political Profile*** (New York, 1960)

John F. Kennedy, ***Profiles in Courage*** (New York, 1956)

———, ***The Strategy of Peace,*** ed. Allan Nevins (New York, 1960). A collection of speeches delivered by Kennedy in the Senate and elsewhere.

Donald Lloyd Wolfarth, "The Inaugural Addresses of the Presidents of the United States" (Unpublished Doctoral Thesis, University of Minnesota, 1959)

The method of scientific investigation

THOMAS HENRY HUXLEY
(analysis by Walter Blair[1])

Trained as a physician, Thomas Henry Huxley (1825-1895) began his distinctive career as an assistant on an exploring and surveying cruise of the *Rattlesnake*, a vessel in the British navy. The cruise furnished him with exciting new information about marine biology which he wrote up in papers to the Linnaean and Royal societies. Almost immediately the papers made him famous. In 1854 he became Lecturer on Natural History at the Royal School of Mines, and in 1863 he became Fullerian Professor at the Royal Institution and also Hunterian Professor at the Royal College of Surgeons. Thereafter, he held many governmental and university posts; none of them, however, were so demanding that they cut seriously into his research, writing, and lecturing. In 1885 he was elected President of the Royal Society.

Huxley had the happy faculty of being able to speak informatively on his field to laymen as well as to other scientists. His lectures to workingmen in 1860 on the "Relation of Man to the Lower Animals" were models of scientific exposition. And subsequent lectures in which he explained and defended Darwinism to the general public were equally lucid. To this day he remains one of the greatest popularizers of science in the best sense of that term. The speech analyzed here was first delivered in 1866 to an audience of unread workingmen in England. Both as a speech and later as an essay, it has remained one of the finest statements of the method of scientific investigation.

The method of scientific investigation is nothing but the expression of the necessary mode of working of the human mind. It is simply the mode at which all phenomena are reasoned about, rendered precise and exact. There is no more difference, but there is just the same kind of difference, between the mental operations of a man of science and those of an ordinary person, as there is between the operations and methods of a baker or of a butcher weighing out his goods in common scales, and the operation of a chemist in performing a difficult and complex analysis by means of his balance and finely graduated weights. It is not that the action of the scales in the one case, and the balance in the other, differ in the principles of their construction or manner of working; but the beam of one is set on an infinitely finer axis than the other, and of course turns by the addition of a much smaller weight. /1

ANALYSIS: After hearing only the first several sentences, the listener knows what the purpose of the whole lecture is—to explain to a lay audience "the method of scientific investigation." He also learns what the central idea is: that scientific study is a refined brand of common sense, a way of learning truth that every workman in the audience knows. The first paragraph offers proof that this is the central idea by reiterating it. Sentence 1 states it. Sentence 2 repeats it, but avoids monotony by using different words and by emphasizing a concept represented merely by the adjective "necessary" in sentence 1. (It does this by placing the words which paraphrase this one word in the most emphatic part of the sentence—at the end.) Sentences 3 and 4 take up a matter hitherto barely implied—the degree of difference between scientific and ordinary thinking, clarifying the matter by contrasting two common men, the butcher and the baker, with a particular kind of scientist, a chemist. Although the contrast is emphasized, the idea is restated for a second time, since the speaker points out that both workmen and scientists use scales. The listener, as the result of the reiterations, upon concluding the paragraph, has acquired one idea, with a few modifications—that scientists proceed as ordinary men do.

You will understand this better, perhaps, if I give you some familiar example. You have all heard it repeated, I dare say, that men of science work by means of induction and deduction, and that by the help of these operations, they, in a sort of sense, wring from Nature certain other things, which are

[1] Used by permission.

called natural laws, and causes, and that out of these, by some cunning skill of their own, they build up hypotheses and theories. And it is imagined by many, that the operations of the common mind can be by no means compared with these processes, and that they have to be acquired by a sort of special apprenticeship to the craft. To hear all these large words, you would think that the mind of a man of science must be constituted differently from that of his fellow men; but if you will not be frightened by terms, you will discover that you are quite wrong, and that all these terrible apparatus are being used by yourselves every day and every hour of your lives. /2

There is a well-known incident in one of Molière's plays, where the author makes the hero express unbounded delight on being told that he has been talking prose during the whole of his life. In the same way, I trust that you will take comfort, and be delighted with yourselves, on the discovery that you have been acting on the principles of inductive and deductive philosophy during the same period. Probably there is not one here who has not in the course of the day had occasion to set in motion a complex train of reasoning, of the very same kind, though differing of course in degree, as that which a scientific man goes through in tracing the causes of natural phenomena. /3

The second and third paragraphs again restate the idea of the first paragraph and of the speech as a whole. They use new methods, however, and progress toward the next division. The second paragraph is built very differently from the first. Instead of starting with a topic sentence, Huxley holds the whole meaning in suspension. "I [will] give you some familiar example," he says, then, "You have all heard. . . . And it is imagined by many. . . . To hear all these large words, you would think . . . but. . . ." The word "but" is a pivot: only after this is it indicated that what has been heard, imagined, and thought is not so. In other words, this paragraph restates the thesis by setting forth an opposite one and then by denying the antithesis. And the third paragraph restates in still another way—by employing a literary allusion analogically: Prose, he suggests, is to Molière's character as inductive and deductive philosophy is to "you"—a lifelong instrument. Both paragraphs, in addition, forecast later divisions of the speech and thus prepare the listener for them. Paragraph 2 does this unobtrusively when it mentions "induction and deduction . . . hypotheses and theories," since these pairs of items, respectively, will be considered in the next divisions of the speech. Paragraph 3 also forecasts later divisions, once by mentioning "the principles of inductive and deductive philosophy" in the next to last sentence, and once by mentioning "a complex train of reasoning" in the last sentence. The listener has now begun to comprehend the specific nature of the similarity between the scientist and the ordinary man which has been emphasized in these opening paragraphs.

A very trivial circumstance will serve to exemplify this. Suppose you go into a fruiterer's shop, wanting an apple—you take one up, and, on biting, you find it is sour; you look at it, and see that it is hard, and green. You take up another one and that too is hard, green, and sour. The shopman offers you a third; but, before biting it, you examine it, and find that it is hard and green, and you immediately say that you will not have it, as it must be sour, like those that you have already tried. /4

Nothing can be more simple than that, you think; but if you will take the trouble to analyse and trace out into its logical elements what has been done by the mind, you will be greatly surprised. In the first place, you have performed the operation of induction. You found, that, in two experiences, hardness and greenness in apples went together with sourness. It was so in the first case, and it was confirmed by the second. True, it is a very small basis, but still it is enough to make an induction from; you generalize the facts, and you expect to find sourness in apples where you get hardness and greenness. You found upon that a general law, that all hard and green apples are sour; and that, so far as it goes, is a perfect induction. Well, having got your natural law in this way, when you are offered another apple which you find is hard and green, you say, "All hard and green apples are sour; this apple is hard and green, therefore this apple is sour." That train of reasoning is what logicians call a syllogism, and has all its various parts and terms—its major premise, its minor premise, and its conclusion. And, by the help of further reasoning, which, if drawn out, would have to be exhibited in two or three other syllogisms, you arrive at your final determination. "I will not have that apple." So that, you see, you have, in the first place, established a law by induction, and upon that you have founded a deduction, and reasoned out the special conclusion of the particular case. Well now, suppose, having got your law, that at some time afterwards, you are discussing the qualities of apples with a friend: you will say to him, "It is a very curious thing—but I find that all hard and green apples are sour!" Your friend says to you, "But how do you know that?" You at once reply, "Oh, because I have tried them over and over again, and have always found them to be so." Well, if we were talking science instead of common sense, we should call that an experimental verification. And, if still opposed, you go further, and say, "I have heard from the people in Somersetshire and Devonshire, where a large number of apples are grown, that they have observed the same thing. It is also found to be the case in Normandy, and in North America. In short, I find it to be the universal experience of mankind wherever attention has been directed to the subject." Whereupon your friend, unless he is a very unreasonable man, agrees with you, and is convinced that you are quite right in the conclusion you have drawn. He believes, although perhaps he does not know he believes it, that the more extensive verifications are—that the more frequently experiments have been made, and results of the same kind arrived at—that the more varied the conditions under which the same results are attained, the more certain is the ultimate conclusion, and he disputes the question no further. He sees that the experiment has been tried under all sorts of conditions, as to time, place, and people, with the same result; and he says with you, therefore, that the law you have laid down must be a good one, and he must believe it. /5

In science we do the same thing;—the philosopher exercises precisely the same faculties, though in a much more delicate manner. In scientific inquiry it becomes a matter of duty to expose a supposed law to every possible kind of verification, and to take care, moreover, that this is done intentionally, and not left to a mere accident, as in the case of the apples. And in science, as in common life, our confidence in a law is in exact proportion to the absence of variation in the result of our experimental verifications. For instance, if you let go your grasp of an article you may have in your hand, it will immediately fall to the ground. That is a very common verification of one of the best established laws of nature—that of gravitation. The method by which men of science establish the existence of that law is exactly the same as that by which we have established the trivial proposition about the sourness of hard and green apples. But we believe it in such an extensive, thorough, and unhesitating manner because the universal experience of mankind verifies it, and we can verify it ourselves at any time; and that is the strongest possible foundation on which any natural law can rest. /6

Indicating, as it does, that a "trivial circumstance" will now "exemplify" the truth so frequently stated in earlier paragraphs, the opening sentence of paragraph 4 marks off a new division. Paragraph 4 recounts the "circumstance" in the form of a little story with "you" as the leading character; paragraph 5 shows the basic similarity between the mental activity in which "you" engage and that of the scientist; and paragraph 6, which concludes the division, reports that while there is such a similarity, the scientist's activity is more "delicate." In other words, the content of the three closely related paragraphs is a systematic development of the idea expressed in both the last sentence of paragraph 3 and the first sentence in paragraph 6. Note, however, that though Huxley expresses the same idea in both these sentences, he foreshadows the immediate emphasis by manipulating the position of the "though" elements. And a number of additional transitional devices also help to mark off as well as to relate the subdivisions. The word "suppose," for instance, is used twice—each time to introduce a story. In addition, words and phrases such as "in the first place," "having got your natural law in this way," "that train of reasoning," and others, as well as summarizing sentences, are skillfully used to aid the whole movement of the section—a movement from childishly simple illustration to a complex generalization for which the illustration has prepared.

Huxley, by following this procedure, interestingly enlightens the listener. The listener, from the simple story in paragraph 4, learns how the common man effortlessly uses induction and deduction in buying apples, but his understanding has not yet been complicated by his trying to attach labels. In paragraph 5, he learns about the applicability of the terms to the procedures of both the common man and the scientist. Further, by following the generalization in the paragraph, he gets a clear idea of what the terms mean. Then (a) by following another story which exemplifies "experimental verification" and (b) by generalizing with Huxley about this process, the listener acquires an understanding of this new term. By noting comparisons and contrasts as well as specific examples in paragraph 6, the listener becomes acquainted with the essential differences as well as the essential likenesses between common and scientific methods of verification and also learns how the great law of gravitation may be seen to rest upon "the strongest possible foundation." Thus, as a result of the whole orderly and carefully divided presentation in this division, the listener achieves a clear grasp of the meaning.

So much, then, by way of proof that the method of establishing laws in science is exactly the same as that pursued in common life. Let us now turn to another matter (though really it is but another phase of the same question), and that is, the method by which, from the relations of certain phenomena, we prove that some stand in the position of causes toward the others. /7

Paragraph 7, a transitional paragraph, has as its whole purpose marking off the end of a division and announcing a new division. "So much," it says, for this aspect of the subject; "Let us now turn to another matter"—the matter of the proof of cause-effect relationships. Carefully, though, the speaker informs the listener that this other matter "really . . . is but another phase of the same question," thus showing that the divisions are interrelated. The listener therefore knows that he is to shift his attention to a new topic, but that he is to be alert to interrelationships.

I want to put the case clearly before you, and I will therefore show you what I mean by another familiar example. I will suppose that one of you, on coming down in the morning to the parlor of your house, finds that a teapot and some spoons which had been left in the room on the previous evening are gone—the window is open, and you observe the mark of a dirty hand on the windowframe, and perhaps, in addition to that, you notice the impress of a hobnailed shoe on the gravel outside. All these phenomena have struck your attention instantly, and before two seconds have passed, you say, "Oh, somebody has broken open the window, entered the room, and run off with the spoons and the teapot!" That speech is out of your mouth in a moment. And you will probably add, "I know there has; I am quite sure of it!" You mean to say exactly what you know; but in reality you are giving expression to what is, in all essential particulars, an hypothesis. You do not *know* it at all; it is nothing but an hypothesis rapidly framed in your own mind. And it is an hypothesis founded on a long train of inductions and deductions. /8

Section three, which concludes the speech, follows almost exactly the same pattern as does section two—simple story of a commonplace happening (most of paragraph 8); consideration of the reasoning process involved in the illustration (rest of paragraph 8, paragraph 9); simple story of another happening which is the consequence of the one recounted at the start of the division (paragraphs 10 and 11); consideration of the reasoning processes involved in this second happening (paragraphs 12 and 13). It may be worth while to look at paragraph 8 to see how Huxley uses it to prepare the listener for the rest of the speech. The first sentence informs the listener what Huxley is going to do and why he is going to do it. Furthermore, it recalls a pattern which has been used twice before and thereby suggests that it may be followed again. "I will show you what I mean by another familiar example," he says. And in introducing his story, Huxley uses a word heretofore used to introduce stories: "I will suppose. . . ." Again the story is told without incidental comment; but at the end of the paragraph, the mental processes which "you" had in the course of the happenings just set down are labeled: the listener therefore learns that the story showed the working out of a hypothesis. The last sentences repeat this new word twice, thus emphasizing the speaker's new concern. They do more: (a) They show why part 3 of the speech should have been placed last. The hypothesis which the listener has expressed about the burglar, says Huxley, is "founded on a long train of inductions and deductions." Now obviously, if the listener had had to take time out while, at this point, Huxley helped him understand "induction" and "deduction," he would have found the understanding of the speech pretty complicated. As it is, he needs to master only one new term at a time. (b) They show where the speaker will next turn—to another analysis of mental processes, this time the processes which lead to the forming of a hypothesis.

What are those inductions and deductions, and how have you got at this hypothesis? You have observed in the first place, that the window is open; but by a train of reasoning involving many inductions and deductions, you have probably arrived long before at the general law—and a very good one it is—that windows do not open of themselves; and you therefore conclude that something has opened the window. A second general law that you have arrived at in the same way is that teapots and spoons do not go out of a window spontaneously, and you are satisfied that, as they are now not where you left them, they have been removed. In the third place, you look at the marks on the window sill and the shoe marks outside, and you say that in all previous experience the former kind of mark has never been produced by anything else but the hand of a human being; and the same experience shows that no other animal but man at present wears shoes with hobnails in them such as would produce the marks in the gravel. I do not know, even if we could discover any of those "missing links" that are talked about, that they would help us to any other conclusion! At any rate the law which states our present experience is strong enough for my present purpose. You next reach the conclusion that, as these kinds of marks have not been left by any other animals than men, or are liable to be formed in any other way than by a man's hand and shoe, the marks in question have been formed by a man in that way. You have, further, a general law, founded on observation, and experience, and that, too, is, I am sorry to say, a very universal and unimpeachable one—that some men are thieves; and you assume at once from all these premises—and that is what constitutes your hypothesis—that the man who made the marks outside and on the window sill, opened the window, got into the room, and stole your teapot and spoons. You have now arrived at a *vera causa;*—you have assumed a cause which, it is plain, is competent to produce all the phenomena you have observed. You can explain all these phenomena only by the hypothesis of a thief. But that is a hypothetical conclusion, of the justice of which you have no absolute proof at all; it is only rendered highly probable by a series of inductive and deductive reasonings. /9

The opening sentence of paragraph 9 makes clear, more specifically than the sentence just before has, that the speaker will next analyze the inductions and deductions "you" used in getting the hypothesis mentioned in paragraph 8. A series of markings-off ("in the first place"; "a second general law"; "in the third place"; "you next reach"; "you have, further"; and "you have now arrived") set up guideposts which enable the listener to see how reasonings lead to "a general law," how other reasonings result in "another general law," and so on, until the hypothesis is formulated. The listener may wonder why Huxley used the phrase *vera causa* in addressing an audience who would be unlikely to understand it; but the listener will notice that frequent synonyms for "hypothesis" show that the reasoning has led to such a formulation.

I suppose your first action, assuming that you are a man of ordinary common sense, and that you have established this hypothesis to your own satisfaction, will very likely be to go off for the police, and set them on the track of the burglar, with the view to the recovery of your property. But just as you are starting with this object, some person comes in, and on learning what you are about, says "My good friend, you are going on a great deal too fast. How do you know that the man who really made the marks took the spoons? It might have been a monkey that took them, and the man may have merely looked in afterwards." You would probably reply, "Well, that is all very well, but you see it is contrary to all experience of the way teapots and spoons are abstracted; so that, at any rate, your hypothesis is less probable than mine." While you are talking the thing over in this way, another friend arrives, one of that good kind of people that I was talking of a little while ago. And he might say, "Oh, my dear sir, you are certainly going on a great deal too fast. You are most presumptuous. You admit that all these occurrences took place when you were fast asleep, at a time when you could not possibly have known anything about what was taking place. How do you know that the laws of Nature are not suspended during the night? It may be that there has been some kind of supernatural interference in this case." In point of fact, he declares that your hypothesis is one of which you cannot at all demonstrate the truth, and that you are by no means sure that the laws of Nature are the same when you are asleep as when you are awake. /10

Well, now, you cannot at the moment answer that kind of reasoning. You feel that your worthy friend has you somewhat at a disadvantage. You will feel perfectly convinced in your own mind, however, that you are quite right, and you say to him, "My good friend, I can only be guided by the natural probabilities of the case, and if you will be kind enough to stand aside, and permit me to pass, I will go and fetch the police." Well, we will suppose that your journey is successful, and that by good luck you meet with a policeman; that eventually the burglar is found with your property on his person, and the marks correspond to his hand and to his boots. Probably any jury would consider those facts a very good experimental verification of your hypothesis, touching the cause of the abnormal phenomena observed in your parlor, and would act accordingly. /11

The word "suppose" at the start of paragraph 10, as it has before, reintroduces the story element. This piece of narrative, as it is unfolded in this paragraph, has dramatic interest, since it tells about some contentious friends who try to convince "you" that "your" hypothesis is invalid. Here Huxley was mixing in some persuasion—the arguments used by the two callers were quite similar to arguments which some people in Huxley's day were using to discredit hypotheses. When, therefore, in paragraph 11 Huxley indicates that such arguments are not guided by "natural probabilities," he is in reality attacking contemporary opponents of science. And when the listener hears the triumphant vindication of the hypothesis at the end of the paragraph, he learns that these arguments do not vitally affect "your" shrewd guess. Meanwhile the listener has mastered more facts about the nature of a hypothesis, the nature of arguments against it which may be ineffective, and the way it may be verified.

Now, in this suppositious case, I have taken phenomena of a very common kind, in order that you might see what are the different steps in an ordinary process of reasoning, if you will only take the trouble to analyse it carefully. All the operations I have described, you will see, are involved in the mind of any man of sense in leading him to a conclusion as to the course he should take in order to make good a robbery and punish the offender. I say that you are led, in that case, to your conclusion by exactly the same train of reasoning as that which a man of science pursues when he is endeavoring to discover the origin and laws of the most occult phenomena. The process is, and always must be, the same; and precisely the same mode of reasoning was employed by Newton and Laplace in their endeavors to discover and define the causes of the movements of the heavenly bodies, as you, with your own common sense, would employ to detect a burglar. The only difference is, that the nature of the inquiry being more abstruse, every step has to be most carefully watched, so that there may not be a single crack or flaw in your hypothesis. A flaw or crack in many of the hypotheses of daily life may be of little or no moment as affecting the general correctness of the conclusions at which we may arrive; but, in a scientific inquiry, a fallacy, great or small, is always of importance, and is sure to be in the long run constantly productive of mischievous if not fatal results. /12

Do not allow yourselves to be misled by the common notion that an hypothesis is untrustworthy simply because it is an hypothesis. It is often urged, in respect to some scientific conclusion, that, after all, it is only an hypothesis. But what more have we to guide us in nine-tenths of the most important affairs of daily life than hypotheses, and often very ill-based ones? So that in science, where the evidence of an hypothesis is subjected to the most rigid examination, we may rightly pursue the same course. You may have hypotheses, and hypotheses. A man may say, if he likes, that the moon is made of green cheese: that is an hypothesis. But another man, who has devoted a great deal of time and attention to the subject, and availed himself of the most powerful telescope and the results of the observations of others, declares that in his opinion it is probably composed of materials very similar to those of which our own earth is made up: and that is also only an hypothesis. But I need not tell you that there is an enormous difference in the value of the two hypotheses. That one which is based on sound scientific knowledge is sure to have a corresponding value; and that which is mere hasty random guess is likely to have but little value. Every great step in our progress in discovering causes has been made in exactly the same way as that which I have detailed to you. A person observing the occurrence of certain facts and phenomena asks, naturally enough, what process, what kind of operation known to occur in Nature applied to the particular case, will unravel and explain the mystery? Hence you have the scientific hypothesis; and its value will be proportionate to the care and completeness with which its basis has been tested and verified. It is in these matters as in the commonest affairs of practical life: the guess of the fool will be folly, while the guess of the wise man will contain wisdom. In all cases, you see that the value of the result depends on the patience and faithfulness with which the investigator applies to his hypothesis every possible kind of verification. /13

The opening sentences of paragraph 12 inform the listener what Huxley has done so far in this section and why—in terms of clarification—he has done it. The rest of the paragraph clarifies anew—by considering hypotheses rather than inductions and deductions—the main point of the speech, that science uses a refined version of the sort of thinking typical of the man of common sense. First the similarity is stressed, and then (beginning with the words, "The only difference is . . .") Huxley turns to the refinements upon everyday methods which scientists use. Paragraph 13 continues to make the distinction between ordinary hypotheses and scientific ones, chiefly by the use of example and argument. The use of argument in behalf of hypotheses here means, of course, that Huxley is again being an advocate, though now in a somewhat less subtle way than before. And the final paragraph summarizes once more, in a new way, the unifying idea of the speech. Thus, by Huxley's skillful setting forth of facts and ideas in familiar-to-unfamiliar organization, time arrangement, cause-effect arrangement, definition, analogy, comparison, and some persuasion at appropriate points in his speech, his audience has learned about the methods of science.

On the federal Constitution

JONATHAN SMITH

(analysis by Carroll C. Arnold)

On September 17, 1787, the Constitutional Convention of the United States of America heard a reading of the final draft of its proposed Constitution, which the delegates subsequently signed. The Convention then submitted the Constitution to the states, to be debated and approved or disapproved by specially elected state conventions. The approval of nine states was necessary to make the new form of government binding.

Pennsylvania, New Jersey, Connecticut, Georgia, and Delaware ratified the Constitution before the middle of January, the pro-Constitution forces having little difficulty in those conventions. The Massachusetts convention, which convened on January 9, 1788, was different. Historians agree that most of the Massachusetts delegates were opposed to the Constitution or had grave doubts about it when they first came together. Even John Hancock and Samuel Adams were undecided, but the strongest opposition came from farmers and artisans, particularly those from the western part of the state.

On January 24, 1788 (some sources say January 25), a relatively unknown man rose in the Massachusetts convention and made a short speech that still stands as one of the most refreshing and artful to be found in the records of American deliberative argument. What follows is a rhetorical analysis (see "Four Ways of Looking at a Speech," pp. 17-24) of this address. The object of this analysis is to discover what effects this speech probably produced and why.

To discover what probably occurred on January 24, 1788, when a man named Jonathan Smith spoke to some three hundred fifty delegates, we should know something about the man who spoke, the special expectations and purposes that dominated the occasion, the ideas and attitudes the audience had before the speech began, and what the speaker did when he spoke. That we cannot know these things in full detail means that we shall never be able to re-create the event of the speech entirely. How much of the event we can recover with limited information, the analysis that follows will illustrate.

Unfortunately we know little about Jonathan Smith. Were it not for his speech, he would be all but lost to history. He was from Lanesboro, Massachusetts, a tiny village in Berkshire County in the northwest corner of the state. He had fought in the Revolutionary War, entering service as an ensign and leaving as either a captain or a colonel (the records are conflicting on this point). He had held the office of justice of the peace, been a delegate to the convention that framed the Constitution of Massachusetts, and was now the elected delegate from his town to the convention on the federal Constitution. Lanesboro was one of only seven of the twenty-two Berkshire County towns to send pro-Constitution delegates to the convention in Boston. Smith was a farmer, but he may have had other occupations as well. This is all we know of him.

From even so little knowledge some conclusions about Jonathan Smith as a convention speaker are possible:

1. He would get special attention because he came from a part of the state where the Constitution was unpopular, yet he favored it.

2. He could easily establish common ground with some opponents of the Constitution because he was a western farmer.

3. He could probably gain some advantage in advising farmers from the fact that he had had special experience in the military and in government. (Note that in lines 41-44 he uses some of these advantages deliberately.)

So, from what little we know of Jonathan Smith, we can presume that when he rose and began to speak, farmers and perhaps some others found this "plain man" from the "opposition country" worthy of a careful hearing.

But Smith had to fit into a special kind of occasion. He was at a deliberative meeting. The convention was assembled to debate and to vote on a plan that would regulate the future conditions of life in Massachusetts. When its task was finished, the convention would adjourn forever. It had been created for this single purpose. Each Massachusetts town had its delegate or delegates, and all were free to speak their minds on the great subject. Samuel Adams and Fisher Ames might be bigger and more powerful men than a Berkshire County farmer, but on this speaking occasion the farmers and artisans were assured as respectful a hearing as the "learned and moneyed men." We can conclude, then, that a man like Jonathan Smith could speak confidently, with a real hope of influencing the course of events. Such was the occasion; his kind of speaker was not out of place as long as he directed attention to the important action the convention had to take.

What of his audience? No Gallup polls tested the opinions and attitudes of the delegates to the Massachusetts convention, but we can still tell something about their views and anxieties. A good source of information is the speeches they made before Smith spoke. Other sources are their newspapers and the personal records historians have now explored. Such evidence shows that Smith spoke to an audience in which the doubters would finally determine which side would win on the Constitutional question.

Opponents of the Constitution had tried to intensify the following doubts about the Constitution: (a) Congress might become a tyrannical clique; (b) to allow a federal government to set the time for elections and to tax the people might destroy the people's control over the government and over their own property; (c) the powers of Congress to regulate trade, create an army, collect duties, etc., might destroy the rights of states and create a federal tyranny. And the kinds of questions asked by doubters show they were worried about these possibilities and about such other things as whether it was safe to let Senators have terms as long as six years, whether the new government would hide its operations in secrecy, and whether a formal bill of rights was needed to protect the individual citizens against the national government. This kind of evidence, though scanty, tends to show us two most important facts about the audience:

1. The doubters were the people for all persuaders to concentrate on.

2. Since the doubters were fearful of too much government, persuaders would have to show them that there was more to fear from rejecting the Constitution than from ratifying it, that their fears about too much government were groundless.

One other fact about the audience must also be understood. Getting the farmers to support a new, more powerful government was certain to be a more than normally difficult and delicate task. The farmers, or some of them at least, had a record of opposition to strong government, even by the state. Some delegates had been involved in the famous Shays' Rebellion, a violent movement among farmers and artisans in Massachusetts to close the courts by force in order to prevent imprisonment of debtors and foreclosures on mortgaged property. The first threats occurred on September 12 and 13, 1786, at Taunton (Bristol County) and at Concord, both in the eastern part of the state. As Smith indicates in his speech, the violence swiftly spread westward. Berkshire County, in which Smith lived, was caught in the grip of severe anti-government, anti-court, anti-wealth raids in which several persons were killed. In February 1787 a company of rebels fought government troops on one of the Berkshire roads. It was there that the rebels put prisoners between themselves and the militiamen while they reloaded their firearms. With such events in the recent past, farmers and the subject of farmers would have to be handled with great delicacy by any speaker.

With this background concerning Smith, the convention as a speaking occasion, and the audience, we are ready to look at Smith's little composition. Ideally we should examine (a) his arguments and suggestions, (b) their organization, (c) the language he used, and (d) his delivery. About his delivery nothing seems to have come down to us, not even the testimony of any who listened. We cannot, therefore, make a full analysis of the speaking event, but we can at least secure a partial answer to what happened that day if we examine the following things about the text of the speech:

1. We must examine the arguments and suggestions in the speech to:
   a. Identify the kinds of proof used. We can do this by:
      1) Looking for and testing the probabilities of rhetorical syllogisms (deductions and causal relations) that support ideas.
      2) Looking for and testing the probabilities of arguments from example and analogy (inductions) that support ideas.
      3) Looking for statements and assertions that, though not parts of the reasoning, still have influence because of what they suggest to the listeners.
   b. Discover in the reasonings and "proofs" by suggestion:
      1) Whether the audience would think these reasonings and assertions credible, coming from Smith (ethos plus credibility of logic and feeling).
      2) Whether the reasonings and assertions are likely to move the listeners closer to approving the Constitution. The occasion and Smith's general purpose being deliberative, any proofs that move in another direction *may* be irrelevant and confusing, though not necessarily so.
2. We must examine the arrangement of ideas to see:
   a. Whether the main ideas are set forth in a way that listeners could follow easily.
   b. Whether by such means as building climaxes, arranging proofs cumulatively, etc., Smith has gained or lost any potential emphasis for his most important ideas and suggestions.
3. We must examine Smith's style, particularly how his language serves:
   a. To render all ideas clear.
   b. To give an appropriate and consistent reflection of Jonathan Smith, farmer, addressing a democratically elected and conducted meeting in Boston.
      1) Here, we cannot judge with certainty, for his delivery could have much effect on the appropriateness of his utterance.
      2) We must not apply standards of style, grammar, etc., that would not have been applied in 1788.
   c. To render the ideas interesting. (For standards see Glossary: *Activity, Concreteness, Conversational Quality, Figures of Speech, Imagery, Liveliness, Originality, Variety.*)
   d. To supply suggestive proof through connotations of words chosen.

The marginal notes accompanying the text of Jonathan Smith's speech below illustrate the kinds of judgments about the effects of a speech that can be reached by an inquiry of the sort just outlined.

Mr. President. I am a plain man, and get my living by the plough. I am not used to speak in public, but I beg your leave to say a few words to my brother ploughjoggers in this house. I have lived in a part of the country where I have known the worth of good government by the want of it. There was a black cloud that rose in the east last winter and spread out over the west.

[Here Widgery, one of the opponents of the Constitution, interrupted: "Mr. President, I wish to know what the gentleman means by the east." Widgery was from New Gloucester and, like some others, was exceedingly sensitive to any blame thrown on his section (now Maine).]

I mean, sir, the county of Bristol; the cloud rose there, and burst upon us, and produced a dreadful effect. It brought on a state of anarchy, and that led to tyranny. I say it brought anarchy. People that used to live peaceably and were before good neighbors, got distracted, and took up arms against government.

[Here Kingsley interrupted, asking what "the history of last winter" had to do with the Constitution. Several other members, including Samuel Adams, called out that Smith was in order and should "go on in his own way."]

I am going, Mr. President, to show you, my brother farmers, what were the effects of anarchy, that you

ANALYSIS: Emphasizes identification with farmers; doesn't even pretend to address his "betters."

Term of familiarity addressed to fellow farmers.

Ethos: claims qualification to judge what makes for practical happiness.

The metaphor at once suggests Shays' Rebellion but treats the issue euphemistically.

Is Widgery afraid the euphemism might pass without irking listeners who might vote against the Constitution?

Straight answer helps ethos.

Picks up metaphor just where he had left it, thus helping clarity, imagery, activity in his discourse.

Language suggests conflict and danger. So soon after the Revolution, "tyranny" had special, damning connotations. Cause-effect argument forecast.

Explains "anarchy" in concrete terms, adding clarity. If hearers know this is what happened, no proof is needed; so far none is offered.

Smith used no clear introduction and stated no central idea. Kingsley may be confused, or he may be trying to "gag" Smith.

Central idea now clearly stated. A more artful speaker might have stated it earlier to prevent confusion.

may see the reasons why I wish for good government. People, I say, took up arms; and then, if you went to speak to them, you had the musket of death presented to your breast. They would rob you of your property; threaten to burn your houses; oblige you to be on your guard night and day; alarms spread from town to town; families were broken up. The tender mother would cry, "O, my son is among them! What shall I do for my child!" Some were taken captive, children taken out of their schools, and carried away. Then we would hear of an action, and the poor prisoners were set in the front, to be killed by their own friends. How dreadful, how distressing was this! Our distress was so great that we would have been glad to snatch at anything that looked like a government. Had any person, that was able to protect us, come and set up his standard, we should have flocked to it, even if it had been a monarch; and that monarch might have proved a tyrant; so that you see that anarchy leads to tyranny, and better have one tyrant than so many at once.

Now, Mr. President, when I saw this Constitution, I found that it was a cure for these disorders. It was just such a thing as we wanted. I got a copy of it, and read it over and over. I had been a member of the Convention to form our own state Constitution, and had learnt something about the checks and balances

Builds suggestion of active danger, narrating events very concisely. Note the metaphor.

Events narrated gain force from cumulative arrangement.

This attempt to evoke emotion may have seemed less "stagy" in 1788. Such use of direct discourse was common.

Narrative builds to climax: suggestion is that there is little worse than child-stealing . . .

. . . there is one worse thing, after all. But on reaching the climax, Smith does not accuse or blame. To do so would offend some he hopes to persuade.

Emphasizes the *effect*, not blame: lack of good government leads to violence and violence leads to unwise choices (cause-to-effect, cause-to-effect). Hearers will accept if they believe the story as Smith tells it.

"Monarch" had threatening connotations in 1788.

"Tyrant" was even more threatening. Smith repeats those threatening words, then concisely restates the pair of cause-effect arguments he has been proving. Everything since line 5 is neatly unified as an argument, but the vigor of it was achieved through suggestion.

Now it emerges that lines 4-37 were a "need argument." The Constitution is the "remedy."

Ethos: he looked for himself. Note how he stresses his independence in later lines.

Ethos: his special qualifications to judge, modestly expressed.

Many former Revolutionists had strong favorable attitudes toward "checks and balances" as curbs on government.

of power, and I found them all here. I did not go to any lawyer, to ask his opinion; we have no lawyer in our town, and we do well enough without. I formed my own opinion, and was pleased with this Constitution. My honorable old daddy there [points to Amos Singletary who had spoken in opposition to the Constitution just before Smith rose] won't think that I expect to be a Congressman, and swallow up the liberties of the people. I never had any post, nor do I want one. But I don't think the worse of the Constitution because lawyers, and men of learning, and moneyed men, are fond of it. I don't suspect that they want to get into Congress and abuse their power. I am not of such a jealous make. They that are honest men themselves are not apt to suspect other people. I don't know why our constituents have not as good a right to be jealous of us as we seem to be of the Congress; and I think those gentlemen, who are so very suspicious that as soon as a man gets into power he turns rogue, had better look at home.

We are, by this Constitution, allowed to send ten members to Congress. Have we not more than that number fit to go? I dare say, if we pick out ten, we shall have another ten left, and I hope ten times ten; and will not these be a check upon those that go? Will they go to Congress, and abuse their power, and do mischief, when they know they must return and

The opposition had sniped at lawyers in the pro-Constitution forces. Smith dissociates his judgment from lawyers, adding to ethos.

Refutation of opposing arguments begins here but opens with colloquial deference to his older opponent.

Independence and identification with ordinary people suggested.

Opponents had also tried to arouse suspicion of wealthy and college-educated supporters of the Constitution.

Smith uses the ethos he has built up; now he turns it against suspiciousness of opponents.

Rhetorical syllogism (enthymeme) that also suggests an accusation against opponents.

Analogy "turns the tables" on opponents: argument plus suggestion.

Suggests the fault is in the ethos of opponents, not in Constitution.

Refutation (lines 48-63) ends.

Constructive argument resumes: the "remedy" is *safe*.

Rhetorical questions plus an assertion evoke attitudes of pride in selves and predispose listeners favorably toward checks on government.

A rhetorical syllogism is being suggested but not fully stated: whoever is checked will behave; we have a check, so members will behave.

look the other ten in the face, and be called to account for their conduct? Some gentlemen think that our liberty and property are not safe in the hands of moneyed men, and men of learning. I am not of that mind.

Sums up "safety" argument.

Brother farmers, let us suppose a case, now: Suppose you had a farm of 50 acres, and your title was disputed, and there was a farm of 5000 acres joined to you, that belonged to a man of learning, and his title was involved in the same difficulty; would you not be glad to have him for your friend, rather than stand alone in the dispute? Well, the case is the same. These lawyers, these moneyed men, these men of learning, are all embarked in the same cause with us, and we must all swim or sink together. And shall we throw the Constitution overboard because it does not please us alike? Suppose two or three of you had been at pains to break up a piece of rough land, and sow it with wheat; would you let it lie waste because you could not agree what sort of a fence to make? Would it not be better to put up a fence that did not please every one's fancy, rather than not fence it at all, or keep disputing about it until the wild beasts came in and devoured it?

Again addresses his particular audience—farmers.

Analogy: an argument to prove that the *supporters of the Constitution are reliable.* Analogy is as close to farmers' experience as possible.

Mild variation on an old metaphor saves Smith from falling into clichés while clinching "reliability" argument.

Another analogy: to prove Constitution is *desirable.* Smith is moving gently toward an action step, using an experience especially familiar to the western farmers on the frontier. How is suggestion working here?

Some gentlemen say, "Don't be in a hurry; take time to consider"; and "Don't take a leap in the dark." I say, "Take things in time; gather fruit when it is

Action step is reached as conclusion begins. Which proverbs would evoke the more favorable attitudes in farmers?

ripe." There is a time to sow and a time to reap; we sowed our seed when we sent men to the Federal Convention; now is the harvest. Now is the time to reap the fruit of our labor. And if we won't do it now, I am afraid we never shall have another opportunity.

Rhetorical syllogism formed from proverb (lines 97-98), an analogy (lines 98-100), and conclusion (line 100).

Conclusion of the rhetorical syllogism restated, then reinforced by suggestion that need is urgent.

From such a reading of this speech, what new knowledge is unearthed about the event that occurred as Jonathan Smith spoke in Boston in 1788? At least these things can be said:

1. Smith was the right man to make this speech; he could and did, in all reasonable ways, identify himself with that part of his audience he could most probably persuade.

2. Each of Smith's arguments was relevant to the convention's purpose: deciding for or against the Constitution. He never drifted into condemnation or praise for its own sake. His argumentation was efficient.

3. Whether deductions or inductions, his arguments were the kind farmers would most easily understand and readily believe. They did not prove his case scientifically, but they were the kind to establish enough probability to give some doubting listeners reason to endorse the Constitution.

4. His assertions, arguments, and individual words were freighted with suggestion capable of magnifying the dangers of weak government, criticizing opponents of the Constitution as too suspicious and not rational enough to be the best advisers, and calling forth favorable attitudes toward such features of the Constitution as its "checks and balances," its system of responsible representation, its general reasonableness.

5. All the materials of the speech were assembled in a clear, psychologically inviting pattern, except that Smith was somewhat slow to clarify his central idea. In other respects the introduction met most requirements of a satisfactory opening. The body of the speech offered an easy-to-follow and clearly emphasized "disease-remedy" arrangement of ideas, with proper attention to the safety and desirability of the plan the listeners feared unsafe. The conclusion summed up Smith's position in colorful but familiar ways and also constituted an "action step."

6. Of Smith's style we would have to say that though it was colloquial and somewhat rustic, it was never unclear. To those he addressed it seems likely to have appeared entirely appropriate to a "plain man" and hence to make Smith, himself, more credible.

Our conclusion must be that on January 24, 1788, Jonathan Smith was convincing to at least some of the doubting farmers, perhaps even to others. He could scarcely have done more as a speechmaker. Although we do not know whom he convinced, if anyone, we now know that if speechmaking could sway votes in the convention, Smith's speech must have swayed some and so contributed to the final, narrow majority of nineteen by which the Massachusetts convention ratified the Constitution on February 5, 1788.

Address to Congress

DOUGLAS MAC ARTHUR
(analysis by Douglas Ehninger)

At 1:00 A. M. on the morning of April 11, 1951, in the midst of the Korean War, the following statement was released by President Harry S. Truman:

"With deep regret I have concluded that General of the Army Douglas MacArthur is unable to give his wholehearted support to the policies of the United States Government and the United Nations in matters pertaining to his official duties. In view of the specific responsibilities imposed upon me by the Constitution [and] the added responsibility which has been entrusted to me by the United Nations,[1] I have decided that I must make a change of command in the Far East. . . . Full and vigorous debate on matters of national policy is a vital element in the constitutional system of our free democracy. It is fundamental, however, that military commanders must be governed by the policies and directives issued them in the manner provided by our laws and Constitution. . . . General MacArthur's place in history as one of our greatest commanders is fully established. The nation owes him a debt of gratitude. . . . I repeat my regret at the necessity for the action I feel compelled to take in this case."

Twice during the preceding months General MacArthur had been indirectly reprimanded by the White House for expressing views critical of the announced United States and United Nations policy of fighting only a "limited war" in Korea. The immediate cause of his dismissal, however, was in all probability a letter addressed to House Minority Leader Joseph W. Martin. In this letter the General advocated using Chinese Nationalist troops to establish a second front against Red China, pointedly derided the statements of prominent United Nations diplomats, and said in effect that an all-out war in Asia was not only the surest defense against the spread of communism in Europe but also the policy best calculated to save all free nations.

World reaction to MacArthur's dismissal was immediate and sharp. The British House of Commons greeted the announcement with applause. Paris, Rome, The Hague, Stockholm, and New Delhi approved. Most United Nations delegates were obviously pleased. In the United States the press generally supported the President's action on the ground that civilian control of the nation's foreign policy must be insured. Hearst and Scripps-Howard papers, however, were vociferously opposed. Using the strongest language of all, Colonel Robert R. McCormick's Chicago *Tribune* editorialized, "President Truman must be impeached and convicted. . . . He is unfit, morally and mentally, for his high office."

In Congress, where reaction tended to run along partisan lines, there were also demands for the impeachment of the President and of Secretary of State Acheson and Secretary of Defense Marshall as well. From coast to coast the great mass of the American people made their views known by flooding Washington with more than 125,000 telegrams on the two days following the dismissal. As Richard H. Rovere and Arthur M. Schlesinger, Jr., say in their book *The General and the President,* "It is doubtful if there has ever been in this country so violent and spontaneous a discharge of political passion. . . ."[2]

Unmoved by the turmoil, on the evening of April 11, just two and a half hours after issuing his statement, President Truman hastened to address the nation by radio and television. It would be "tragically wrong," he declared, "for us to take the initiative in extending the war."

The General's supporters in Congress also moved swiftly. Following a morning-long policy meeting in which Representative Martin and Senator Robert A. Taft of Ohio played prominent parts, a resolution was introduced that MacArthur be invited to address a joint session of the two houses. After a short delay the resolution was passed, and the invitation issued and accepted.

On April 16, accompanied by his wife and thirteen-year-old son, General MacArthur left Tokyo to return to the United States and to retirement from a military career that had extended over fifty-two years. The trip home has been described as "a series of triumphant send-offs and welcomes."[3] In Tokyo a crowd of 230,000 persons waved farewell as his private plane, the *Bataan,* left the runway; 180,000 greeted the General in Honolulu; and more than 500,000 lined the streets of San Francisco as he passed. In New York, police estimated that MacArthur was seen by 7,500,000 people—nearly twice as many as had greeted President Eisenhower on his return from Europe after World War II. Following the welcoming parade, street cleaners swept up 16,600,000 pounds of paper and ticker tape that had been showered upon him. The previous record was a mere 3,600,000 pounds. On April 26 nearly 4,000,000 Chicagoans greeted MacArthur as a hero.

It was while these homecoming festivities were at their height and while the passions stirred by his dismissal still

---

[1] On July 7, 1950 the United Nations Security Council authorized the United States government to set up a unified military command in Korea. General MacArthur was appointed to this post on July 8.

[2] Richard H. Rovere and Arthur M. Schlesinger, Jr., *The General and the President* (New York, 1951), p. 5.

[3] *Facts on File,* April 20-26, 1951.

boiled that on April 19, 1951, General MacArthur, accompanied by his aid and adviser Major General Courtney Whitney, flew down to Washington from New York to deliver the following address to Congress. Detailed descriptions of the speech and speech occasion were published in the newspapers and news magazines.[4]

At precisely 12:00 noon the House solemnly assembled. At 12:13, as the members "rose and cheered," Mrs. MacArthur entered the gallery. At 12:18 the General's son, accompanied by a group of officers who had served under the General in the Pacific, walked down the aisle and took a seat immediately in front of the rostrum. The members of the Senate appeared in a body at 12:20. Finally, at 12:31 as the blinding beams of a dozen floodlights were suddenly turned on, the seventy-one year old general, relaxed but erect, his "gladitorial features stony," strode into the Chamber escorted by a courtesy committee of Representatives and Senators and by House Doorkeeper William F. Miller. More than six feet tall, he was dressed in dark military slacks and a battle jacket bare of decorations. Only the insignia of his rank as a five-star general was visible on his shoulders. Following a two-minute ovation Speaker Sam Rayburn introduced him with these words: "Members of the Congress, I deem it a high privilege, and I take great pleasure in presenting to you General of the Army Douglas MacArthur."

General MacArthur delivered his address from a prepared manuscript, standing in the place customarily occupied by chiefs of state when they appear before Congress. As all reports agree, from his first words he was in complete control of the speaking situation. Poised and alert, he read slowly and in a low voice—a voice that sometimes rasped and once or twice fell almost to a whisper. Except when turning the pages of his manuscript, the General's hands were anchored firmly to the sides of the lectern. Once he reached for a glass of water, and the tremor with which he had been afflicted since the middle of World War II was discernible.

Even MacArthur's severest critics admitted that his delivery was impressive—his inflections meaningful and precise, his sense of timing superb, and his eye contact with his listeners excellent. The address lasted forty minutes and was interrupted some thirty times by applause. When he had finished speaking the General handed his manuscript to a clerk and walked rapidly out of the Chamber through a "moist" and cheering audience.

Representative Dewey Short, educated at Harvard, Oxford, and Heidelberg, enthusiastically declared, "We saw a great hunk of God in the flesh, and we heard the voice of God." Ex-President Herbert Hoover, hardly less restrained in his comment, saw in MacArthur "a reincarnation of St. Paul into a great General of the Army who came out of the East."

Following the speech MacArthur rode down Pennsylvania Avenue to the Washington Monument under an air cover of jet fighters and bombers flying in formation. In ceremonies held on the Mall he was presented with a silver tea service and the official key to the city while a seventeen-gun salute boomed out. When he left Washington at 8:20 that evening to return to New York, a cheering crowd gathered at the airport.

In addition to the immediate audience packed into the House chamber, it has been estimated that some forty-nine million Americans heard MacArthur's speech over radio and television. This was by all odds the largest audience ever assembled by the mass media up until that time. Ball parks were empty. The Boston marathon which usually attracts a quarter of a million spectators had less than half that number, and most of these were equipped with radios. Work in stores, offices, and factories stopped as men and women everywhere listened. The final paragraph of the address, with its memorable phrase that old soldiers never die but merely fade away immediately became a part of the nation's folklore.

Douglas MacArthur was born January 26, 1880, at Little Rock (Arkansas) Barracks. His father, Lieutenant General Arthur MacArthur, was a Civil War hero and Congressional Medal of Honor winner who later became military governor of the Philippines. Educated at West Texas Military Academy and at West Point, where he earned the highest four-year average ever acquired (98.14), MacArthur first saw active service in the Far East and in the Mexican border action of 1916. When World War I broke out, he organized and led the famous Rainbow Division, composed of National Guard units from throughout the country, becoming at thirty-seven the youngest divisional commander in the American army. Between wars MacArthur served as the youngest commandant in the history of the United States Military Academy and from 1930 to 1935 was Army Chief of Staff. In 1932, under orders from President Hoover, he led troops against the hundreds of World War I veterans who had descended upon Washington to demand a bonus for their military service.

Retiring from the United States Army in 1937 at the age of fifty-seven, MacArthur went to the Philippines to direct the development of the military forces of this newly independent nation. He was recalled to active duty with the American army in July of 1941 and almost immediately was promoted to four-star rank. After escaping from Corregidor in 1942, he led the "island hopping" campaign by which Allied troops gradually regained the areas lost to the Japanese early in the war. In 1945 he presided over the formal Japanese surrender on the battleship *Missouri*. Between the close of World War II and the outbreak of the

[4] See especially the New York *Times* for April 20, 1951, and *Time*, April 30, 1951.

Korean struggle, MacArthur directed the American occupation of Japan. In Korea he was the first commander ever to head a United Nations force composed of troops from a number of nations. His characteristic trademarks, much loved by cartoonists and caricaturists, were a gold-braided military cap and a corncob pipe. These, too, have become a part of America's folklore.

Mr. President, Mr. Speaker, and distinguished members of the Congress: I stand on this rostrum with a sense of deep humility and pride—humility in the wake of those great architects of our history who have stood here before me, pride in the reflection that this home of legislative debate represents human liberty in the purest form yet devised. /1

Here are centered the hopes and aspirations and faiths of the entire human race. /2

I do not stand here as advocate of any partisan cause, for the issues are fundamental and reach quite beyond the realm of partisan considerations. They must be resolved on the highest plane of national interest if our course is to prove sound and our future protected. /3

I trust, therefore, that you will do me the justice of receiving that which I have to say as solely expressing the considered viewpoint of a fellow American. /4

I address you with neither rancor nor bitterness in the fading twilight of life, with but one purpose in mind: To serve my country. /5

ANALYSIS: Paragraphs 1-5 constitute the *introduction* of the speech.

In paragraphs 1 and 2, MacArthur establishes contact with his listeners by referring to the historic place in which his address is being delivered.

In paragraphs 3-5 MacArthur declares himself non-partisan and asks for a fair hearing, thus developing a strong personal or "ethical" appeal.

The issues are global, and so interlocked that to consider the problems of one sector oblivious to those of another is to court disaster for the whole. While Asia is commonly referred to as the gateway to Europe, it is no less true that Europe is the gateway to Asia, and the broad influence of the one can not fail to have its impact upon the other. There are those who claim our strength is inadequate to protect on both fronts, that we cannot divide our effort. I can think of no greater expression of defeatism. /6

If a potential enemy can divide his strength on two fronts, it is for us to counter his effort. The Communist threat is a global one. Its successful advance in one sector threatens the destruction of every other sector. You can not appease or otherwise surrender to communism in Asia without simultaneously undermining our efforts to halt its advance in Europe. /7

The *body* of the speech is composed of paragraphs 6-53. The overall plan of the body of the address is gradually to narrow the listeners' focus of attention, moving from (1) a brief consideration of the general world situation, to (2) a survey of recent social and political changes in Asia, to (3) a statement concerning the "strategic potential" of the Pacific area, and finally to (4) a discussion of the Korean War itself.

In developing his ideas on these subjects MacArthur employs exposition or explanation as his principal form of supporting material and relies almost exclusively upon his own ethical proof to establish the validity of his conclusions.

In paragraphs 6-7, MacArthur gives his analysis of the general world threat posed by communism. This analysis serves as a premise upon which his more specific views concerning the situation in Asia, in the Pacific, and in Korea are based.

Beyond pointing out these general truisms, I shall confine my discussion to the general areas of Asia. /8

Paragraph 8 is a transition, focusing the attention of his listeners upon Asia.

Before one may objectively assess the situation now existing there he must comprehend something of Asia's past and the revolutionary changes which have marked her course up to the present. Long exploited by the so-called colonial powers, with little opportunity to achieve any degree of social justice, individual dignity, or a higher standard of life such as guided our own noble administration in the Philippines, the people of Asia found their opportunity in the war just past to throw off the shackles of colonialism and now see the dawn of new opportunity, and heretofore unfelt dignity, and self-respect of political freedom. /9

Mustering half of the earth's population, and 60 per cent of its natural resources, these peoples are rapidly consolidating a new force, both moral and material, with which to raise the living standard and erect adaptation of the design of modern progress to their own distinct cultural environments. /10

Whether one adheres to the concept of colonialization or not, this is the direction of Asian progress and it may not be stopped. It is a corollary to the shift of the world economic frontiers as the whole epicenter of world affairs rotates toward the area whence it started. /11

In this situation, it becomes vital that our own country orient its policies in consonance with this basic evolutionary condition rather than pursue a course blind to reality that the colonial era is now past and the Asian peoples covet the right to shape their own free destiny. What they seek now is friendly guidance, understanding and support, not imperious direction, the dignity of equality and not the shame of subjugation. /12

Their pre-war standard of life, pitifully low, is infinitely lower now in the devastation left in war's wake. World ideologies play little part in Asian thinking and are little understood. /13

What the people strive for is the opportunity for a little more food in their stomachs, a little better clothing on their backs and a little firmer roof over their heads, and the realization of the normal nationalist urge for political freedom. /14

These political-social conditions have but an indirect bearing upon our own national security, but do form a backdrop to contemporary planning which must be thoughtfully considered if we are to avoid the pitfalls of unrealism. /15

Employing abstract rather than concrete language (except in paragraph 14), MacArthur, in paragraphs 9-15, describes social, economic, and political conditions in Asia.

Of more direct and immediate bearing upon our national security are the changes wrought in the strategic potential of the Pacific Ocean in the course of the past war. /16

Paragraph 16 furnishes a transition, again narrowing the listeners' focus by centering attention on changes wrought in the "strategic potential of the Pacific Ocean in the course of the past war."

Prior thereto the western strategic frontier of the United States lay on the littoral line of the Americas, with an exposed island salient extending out through Hawaii, Midway and Guam to the Philippines. That salient proved not an outpost of strength but an avenue of weakness along which the enemy could and did attack. The Pacific was a potential area of advance for any predatory force intent upon striking at the bordering land areas. /17

All this was changed by our Pacific victory. Our strategic frontier then shifted to embrace the entire Pacific Ocean, which became a vast moat to protect us as long as we hold it. Indeed, it acts as a protective shield for all of the Americas and all free lands of the Pacific Ocean area. We control it to the shores of Asia by a chain of islands extending in an arc from the Aleutians to the Marianas, held by us and our free allies. /18

From this island chain we can dominate with sea and air power every Asiatic port from Vladivostok to Singapore—with sea and air power, every port, as I said, from Vladivostok to Singapore—and prevent any hostile movement into the Pacific. /19

Any predatory attack from Asia must be an amphibious effort. No amphibious force can be successful without control of the sea lanes and the air over those lanes in its avenue of advance. With naval and air supremacy and modest ground elements to defend bases, any major attack from continental Asia toward us or our friends in the Pacific would be doomed to failure. /20

Under such conditions, the Pacific no longer represents menacing avenues of approach for a prospective invader. It assumes, instead, the friendly aspect of a peaceful lake. /21

Proceeding by the method of contrast, MacArthur, in paragraphs 17-21, explains this "strategic potential of the Pacific Ocean."

Our line of defense is a natural one and can be maintained with a minimum of military effort and expense. It envisions no attack against anyone, nor does it provide the bastions essential for offensive operations, but properly maintained, would be an invincible defense against aggression. /22

The holding of this littoral defense line in the western Pacific is entirely dependent upon holding all segments thereof, for any major breach of that line by an unfriendly power would render vulnerable to determined attack every other major segment. This is a military estimate as to which I have yet to find a military leader who will take exception. /23

For that reason, I have strongly recommended in the past, as a matter of military urgency, that under no circumstances must Formosa fall under Communist control. Such an eventuality would at once threaten the freedom of the Philippines and the loss of Japan and might well force our western frontier back to the coast of California, Oregon, and Washington. /24

General Douglas MacArthur addresses the Joint Session of Congress on April 19, 1951.
Seated on the rostrum behind him are Alben Barkley, the Vice President, and Sam Rayburn, the Speaker of the House. (Acme Photo)

In paragraphs 22-24, the defense obligations which this "potential" imposes upon the United States are reviewed.

To understand the changes which now appear upon the Chinese mainland, one must understand the changes in Chinese character and culture over the past 50 years. China up to 50 years ago was completely nonhomogeneous, being compartmented into groups divided against each other. The war-making tendency was almost nonexistent as they still followed the tenets of the Confucian ideal of pacifist culture. /25

At the turn of the century under the regime of Chang Tso-lin efforts toward greater homogeneity produced the start of a nationalist urge. This was further and more successfully developed under the leadership of Chiang Kai-shek, but has been brought to its greatest fruition under the present regime to the point that it has now taken on the character of a united nationalism of increasingly dominant aggressive tendencies. /26

Through the past 50 years the Chinese people have thus become militarized in their concepts and in their ideals. They now constitute excellent soldiers, with competent staffs and commanders. This has produced a new and dominant power in Asia, which, for its own purposes, is allied with Soviet Russia but which in its own concepts and methods has become aggressively imperialistic with a lust for expansion and increased power normal to this type of imperialism. /27

There is little of the ideological concept either one way or another in the Chinese make-up. The standard of living is so low and the capital accumulation has been so thoroughly dissipated by war that the masses are desperate and eager to follow any leadership which seems to promise the alleviation of woeful stringencies. /28

Abruptly and without a unifying transition, MacArthur, in paragraphs 25-28, turns to an explanation of "the changes [which have occurred] in Chinese character and culture over the past 50 years."

I have from the beginning believed that the Chinese Communists' support of the North Koreans was the dominant one. Their interests are of present parallel with those of the Soviet, but I believe that the aggressiveness recently displayed not only in Korea but also in Indo-China and Tibet and pointing potentially toward the south reflects predominantly the same lust for the expansion of power which has animated every would-be conqueror since the beginning of time. /29

Paragraph 29 gives MacArthur's conclusions about the actions and intentions of Red China.

The Japanese people since the war have undergone the greatest reformation recorded in modern history. With a commendable will, eagerness to learn and marked capacity to understand, they have from the ashes left in war's wake erected in Japan an edifice dedicated to the supremacy of individual liberty and personal dignity, and in the ensuing process there has been created a truly representative government committed to the advance of political morality, freedom of economic enterprise, and social justice. /30

Politically, economically, and socially Japan is now abreast of many free nations of the earth and will not again fail the universal trust. That it may be counted upon to wield a profoundly beneficial influence over the course of events in Asia is attested by the magnificent manner in which the Japanese people have met the recent challenge of war, unrest, and confusion surrounding them from the outside and checked communism within their own frontiers without the slightest slackening in their forward progress. /31

I sent all four of our occupation divisions to the Korean battlefront without the slightest qualms as to the effect of the resulting power vacuum upon Japan. The results fully justified my faith. /32

I know of no nation more serene, more orderly and industrious, nor in which richer hopes can be entertained for future constructive service in the advance of the human race. /33

Paragraphs 30-33 give MacArthur's estimate of the situation in Japan, again entered upon without benefit of an explicit transition and, as in the case of all preceding expositions and inferences, advanced with no supporting material except the speaker's own authority.

Of our former ward in the Philippines we can look forward in confidence that the existing unrest will be corrected and a strong and healthy nation will grow in the longer aftermath of the war's terrible destructiveness. We must be patient and understanding and never fail them, as in our hour of need they did not fail us. /34

A Christian nation, the Philippines stands as a mighty bulwark of Christianity in the Far East, and its capacity for high moral leadership in Asia is unlimited. /35

On Formosa the government of the Republic of China has had the opportunity to refute by action much of the malicious gossip which so undermined the strength of its leadership on the Chinese mainland. The Formosan people are receiving a just and enlightened administration with majority representation in the organs of government, and politically, economically, and socially they appear to be advancing along sound and constructive lines. /36

In paragraphs 34-36, the situation in the Philippines and Formosa is sketched in brief and general terms.

With this brief insight into the surrounding areas, I now turn to the Korean conflict. /37

Paragraph 37 provides a transition, the final narrowing of focus to "the Korean conflict" itself.

While I was not consulted prior to the President's decision to intervene in support of the Republic of Korea, that decision, from a military standpoint, proved a sound one. As I say, it proved to be a sound one, as we hurled back the invader and decimated his forces. Our victory was complete, and our objective within reach, when Red China intervened with numerically superior ground forces. /38

This created a new war and an entirely new situation, a situation not contemplated when our forces were committed against the North Korean invaders; a situation which called for new decisions in the diplomatic sphere to permit the realistic adjustment of military strategy. Such decisions have not been forthcoming. /39

Paragraphs 38-39 review our initial successes in Korea and the new and unfavorable situation produced by Red China's intervention.

While no man in his right mind would advocate sending our ground forces into continental China, and such was never given thought, the new situation did urgently demand a drastic revision of strategic planning if our political aim was to defeat this new enemy as we had defeated the old one. /40

Apart from the military need, as I saw it, to neutralize sanctuary protection given the enemy north of the Yalu, I felt that military necessity in the conduct of the war made necessary (1) The intensification of our economic blockade against China; (2) The imposition of a naval blockade against the China coast; (3) Removal of restrictions on air reconnaissance of China's coastal area and of Manchuria; (4)

Removal of restrictions on the forces of the Republic of China on Formosa, with logistical support to contribute to their effective operations against the Chinese mainland. /41

In paragraphs 40-41 the steps which MacArthur regarded as necessary to meet this altered situation are summarized.

For entertaining these views, all professionally designed to support our forces in Korea and to bring hostilities to an end with the least possible delay and at a saving of countless American and Allied lives, I have been severely criticized in lay circles, principally abroad, despite my understanding that from a military standpoint the above views have been fully shared in the past by practically every military leader concerned with the Korean campaign, including our own Joint Chiefs of Staff. /42

I called for reinforcements, but was informed that reinforcements were not available. I made clear that if not permitted to destroy the enemy built-up bases north of the Yalu, if not permitted to utilize the friendly Chinese force of some 600,000 men on Formosa, if not permitted to blockade the China coast to prevent the Chinese Reds from getting succor from without, and if there was to be no hope of major reinforcements, the position of the command from the military standpoint forbade victory. /43

Paragraphs 42-43 tell how MacArthur's views were received, and give his reply to his critics.

We could hold in Korea by constant maneuver and in an area where our supply line advantages were in balance with the supply line disadvantages of the enemy, but we could hope at best for only an indecisive campaign with its terrible and constant attrition upon our forces if the enemy utilized its full military potential. /44

I have constantly called for the new political decisions essential to a solution. /45

Paragraphs 44-45 give MacArthur's general criticism of the policy he was obliged to follow.

Efforts have been made to distort my position. It has been said in effect that I was a warmonger. Nothing could be further from the truth. I know war as few other men now living know it, and nothing to me is more revolting. I have long advocated its complete abolition, as its very destructiveness on both friend and foe has rendered it useless as a means of settling international disputes. /46

Indeed, the second day of September, 1945, just following the surrender of the Japanese nation on the battleship *Missouri*, I formally cautioned as follows:

"Men since the beginning of time have sought peace. Various methods through the ages have been attempted to devise an international process to prevent or settle disputes between nations. From the very start workable methods were found in so far as individual citizens were concerned, but the mechanics of an instrumentality of larger international scope have never been successful. Military alliances, balances of power, leagues of nations, all in turn failed, leaving the only path to be by way of the crucible of war. The utter destructiveness of war now blocks out this alternative. We have had our last chance. If we will not devise some greater and more equitable system, our Armageddon will be at our door. The problem basically is theological and involves a spiritual recrudescence and improvement of human character that will synchronize with our almost matchless advances in science, art, literature and all the material and cultural developments of the past 2,000 years. It must be of the spirit if we are to save the flesh." /47

But once war is forced upon us, there is no other alternative than to apply every available means to bring it to a swift end. War's very object is victory, not prolonged indecision. /48

In war there can be no substitute for victory. /49

In paragraphs 46-49, MacArthur disavows the charge that he is a "warmonger" but reiterates his philosophy that in war "there can be no substitute for victory."

There are some who for varying reasons would appease Red China. They are blind to history's clear lesson, for history teaches with unmistakable emphasis that appeasement but begets new and bloodier wars. It points to no single instance where this end has justified that means, where appeasement has led to more than a sham peace. Like blackmail, it lays the basis for new and successively greater demands until, as in blackmail, violence becomes the only other alternative. Why, my soldiers asked me, surrender military advantages to an enemy in the field? I could not answer. /50

Some may say, to avoid spread of the conflict into an all-out war with China. Others, to avoid Soviet intervention. Neither explanation seems valid, for China is already engaging with the maximum power it can commit, and the Soviet will not necessarily mesh its actions with our moves. Like a cobra, any new enemy will more likely strike whenever it feels that the relativity of military and other potentialities is in its favor on a world-wide basis. /51

In paragraphs 50-51 the view that we should "appease" Red China is refuted, two figurative analogies being used as supporting material.

The tragedy of Korea is further heightened by the fact that its military action was confined to its territorial limits. It condemns that nation, which it is our purpose to save, to suffer the devastating impact of full naval and air bombardment while the enemy's sanctuaries are fully protected from such attack and devastation. /52

Of the nations of the world, Korea alone, up to now, is the sole one which has risked its all against communism. The magnificence of the courage and fortitude of the Korean people defies description. They have chosen to risk death rather than slavery. Their last words to me were: "Don't scuttle the Pacific." /53

MacArthur, in paragraphs 52-53, praises the part Korea has played in the conflict and reports the Korean people's plea to the democracies.

I have just left your fighting sons in Korea. They have done their best there, and I can report to you without reservation that they are splendid in every way. /54

It was my constant effort to preserve them and end this savage conflict honorably and with the least loss of time and a minimum sacrifice of life. Its growing bloodshed has caused me the deepest anguish and anxiety. Those gallant men will remain often in my thoughts and in my prayers always. /55

Paragraphs 54-56 are the *conclusion:*

In paragraphs 54-55, MacArthur, displaying increasingly the emotional tone evident in paragraphs 52-53, praises the "splendid" behavior of our "gallant" men in Korea, and expresses his solicitude for their welfare.

I am closing my 52 years of military service. When I joined the army, even before the turn of the century, it was the fulfillment of all of my boyish hopes and dreams. The world has turned over many times since I took the oath at West Point, and the hopes and dreams have all since vanished, but I still remember the refrain of one of the most popular barracks ballads of that day which proclaimed most proudly that old soldiers never die; they just fade away. And, like the old soldier of that ballad, I now close my military career and just fade away, an old soldier who tried to do his duty as God gave him the light to see that duty. Good-by. /56

Paragraph 56 gives MacArthur's moving personal farewell to military life and to national service.

Suggestions for further reading

John Gunther, ***The Riddle of MacArthur; Japan, Korea, and the Far East*** (New York, 1951)

Richard H. Rovere and Arthur M. Schlesinger, Jr., ***The General and the President*** (New York, 1951)

John W. Spanier, ***The Truman-MacArthur Controversy and the Korean War*** (Cambridge, Mass., 1959)

Charles Andrew Willoughby, ***MacArthur, 1941-1951*** (New York, 1954)

Recordings

MacArthur, Douglas. ***Speech to Congress*** (Washington, April 19, 1951) (C). Capitol, H274. Also (C). Columbia, ML4410. Also (C). Victor, LPM5. Also (C). Mercury, MGMCM.

———. "Speech Aboard USS Missouri" (September 1, 1945) (E: 2 min. 46 secs). ***Those Historic Years.*** Panacoustic, A100.

———. "Formal Japanese Surrender" (Tokyo Bay, September 2, 1945) (C). ***Those Historic Years.*** U. S. Recording, H9485.

———. Fragments in ***I Can Hear It Now,*** Vol. 1. Columbia, MM800. Also in ***Mr. President.*** Victor, LM1753.

General MacArthur's speech: a symposium of critical comment

FREDERICK W. HABERMAN

The forty-nine million Americans who composed the radio, television, and face-to-face audience that heard General Douglas MacArthur's address to the Joint Session of Congress on April 19, 1951, became speech critics overnight. Their criticism had quantity and it had intensity. It ranged from Representative Dewey Short's statement in the *Congressional Record* (April 19, p. 4238): "We saw a great hunk of God in the flesh, and we heard the voice of God" to the opinion that the speech was Satanic in its power to

---

Frederick W. Haberman, "General MacArthur's Speech: A Symposium of Critical Comment," *Quarterly Journal of Speech,* Vol. XXXVII, October 1951, pp. 321-331. By permission of the Speech Association of America and Professor Haberman.

evoke chaos. Like these two examples, much of the criticism was a blend of happy emotionalism and the urge to formulate dicta; but much of it was aesthetic and philosophical. To gather a set of comments on this extraordinary speech and to obtain some samples of contemporary criticism, I invited critics from three groups to contribute to this symposium. The Congressional critics include Joseph W. Martin, Jr., Minority Leader of the House of Representatives; Senator Robert S. Kerr, of Oklahoma; Senator Karl E. Mundt, of South Dakota (formerly Professor of Speech); Senator Hubert H. Humphrey, of Minnesota; Senator Alexander Wiley, of Wisconsin; and Representative Robert J. Corbett, of Pennsylvania (formerly a coach of forensics). The Journalist critics include Richard H. Rovere, contributor to *The New Yorker;* Quincy Howe, School of Journalism and Communications, University of Illinois; and William T. Evjue, editor and publisher of *The Capital Times,* Madison, Wisconsin. Included in the third group—the Academic critics—are W. Norwood Brigance, Wabash College; Herbert A. Wichelns, Cornell University; Wilbur Samuel Howell, Princeton University; Henry L. Ewbank, University of Wisconsin; and A. Craig Baird, State University of Iowa. In my letter of invitation to these critics, I made one suggestion—that the commentary be brief.

I. Congressional critics

JOSEPH W. MARTIN, JR.

In politics, the effectiveness of a speech is measured by its ability to strengthen friendships and win converts. Usually the most effective political speeches contain comprehensive thought, breadth of viewpoint, humor, warmth of words, and emotional impact. All too frequently, political addresses "sound" better than they "read."

The address of General MacArthur to the Joint Meeting of Congress was a masterpiece of content and delivery, possibly the great address of our times, certainly surpassing, in my opinion, the first Roosevelt Inaugural speech in 1933 and the Winston Churchill address to the Joint Session of Congress in 1942. When a speech moves Members of Congress to tears, its impact cannot be denied. In my 27 years in Congress, there has been nothing to equal it.

The MacArthur address not only "sounded" in a masterful fashion, it "reads" even better. Each sentence is freighted with thought; each word is at work. Its logic, its simple directness, its clear-cut statement of the issues, and its orderly exposition make the structure of the speech a model for all to follow.

It was a monumental effort.

ROBERT S. KERR

I listened earnestly and carefully to General MacArthur's speech. I looked for unity. I didn't find it. I watched for an acknowledgment of the necessity to maintain the integrity of civilian control of the military power. It was not there. I searched for language that would give hope of a limited conflict and a purpose to prevent the spread into world-wide conflagration. He did not provide it.

I listened for words which would promote cooperation between this nation and our allies for collective security. Those words were not spoken. I expected him who had been in command of the United Nations forces to acknowledge and report on his stewardship and tell how to strengthen the common front. He did not even mention the United Nations or a single ally.

I hoped he would show the way to promote peace and prevent more or larger war. He was not looking in that direction.

Instead, if I understood him, he sounded a call for an expanded war, a second front for sure, and a third front, if it came. The General spoke sadly, but I was much sadder because I was convinced that his plan would not lead us upward to the goal of peace, but would hurl us downward to the awful road of total war.

KARL E. MUNDT

The speech Douglas MacArthur delivered to the joint meeting of the Houses of Congress upon his return from Korea seems destined to become one of the classics of the English language.

Sitting as I did about twenty feet directly in front of General MacArthur as he stood at the front of the chamber of the House of Representatives I had an opportunity to view at close range the presentation of an oratorical masterpiece which was excelled in its composition only by the skillful prowess with which it was delivered to those who heard it in person and to the many millions who gave it their rapt attention via radio and television. Without any apparent oratorical effort, MacArthur from the very beginning and by the very force of his sincerity and his magnetic personality held the intense attention of the audience he was to go on to inspire and captivate. He was the complete master of the occasion all the way.

What were the superb qualities of the great speaker that MacArthur so vividly exemplified? High on the list of factors contributing to MacArthur's mastery of the situation was the sincerity and the obvious earnestness he radiated. His choice of vivid words, his balanced phraseology, his great reserve power, his facial expressions, and the eye contact he managed to maintain with the audience without doing violence to his manuscript all contributed to the excellence of his delivery and the convincing impact of his message. Even those who were later to disagree with him and to criticize his recommendations were caught in the magnetism of the occasion; there were very few who had temerity enough to offer quick rejoinder to the arguments presented.

My experience as a college speech teacher impelled me to rate Churchill, Roosevelt, and Madame Chiang-Kai-Shek—in that order—as the most impressive speakers I had heard before joint meetings of the Congress in my fourteen years there prior to the MacArthur speech. Without question, and by general agreement of most of us who had heard all four of them in person, Douglas MacArthur stood out spectacularly above them all.

Perhaps it was the near perfect control of his inflections, perhaps his impressive posture and actions, perhaps the emphasis with which he stressed his points without ever appearing to approximate his full powers of expression—whatever it was, no other speaker in our generation has moved strong men of politics to open tears and caused even those who disagreed with his position to praise his oratorical ability with unhesitating superlatives. In brief, the MacArthur address to Congress demonstrated once again the prowess of the spoken word; it gave new proof that men can still be moved and policies determined by those who excel in the arts of speech.

HUBERT H. HUMPHREY

General MacArthur's speech was a masterful presentation by a persuasive man rising at a dramatic occasion to give reason and justification for his life's work and life's reputation. There is no doubt that it affected every member of the Congress who heard him. His manner, poise, language, and the strength of his voice helped create an impression favorable to him and consistent with the myth associated with him and carefully developed over the past few years.

The issues represented by General MacArthur's speech, however, are far more important than the personality questions involved and more significant than the techniques of speech he has so artistically developed. It is to those issues I enter my dissent.

In my judgment, the basic issue involved in the controversy is one of civilian versus military control over our foreign policy. In a democracy, the elected representatives of the people are responsible for determining foreign policy, and this responsibility is not vested in the military leaders. This is one of the essential elements of our historical tradition. It is part of our Constitution. In dismissing General MacArthur, President Truman, as Commander in Chief under our Constitution, had no choice. The General—a brilliant and able military leader—disagreed with our government's foreign policy and with the recommendations of General Marshall and the Joint Chiefs of Staff. No government can exist so divided in policy since no government can be guided by two inconsistent foreign programs. General MacArthur, as an individual, has a perfect right to disagree with our government's foreign policy but he has no right and no prerogative as a military commander to formulate his own policy in opposition to policy established by our government.

I welcomed General MacArthur's arrival in the United States and his address to the Congress. It brought with it a complete re-examination of our foreign policy, particularly as it affected the Far East. There is no doubt in my mind that at the conclusion of the debate, with the fading away of emotions and the supremacy of reason, the American people will come to see that President Truman was correct in removing General MacArthur. It is my hope that, even as they come to disagree with the General's policies and regret his human failings, they will not allow it to interfere with their judgment of him as a great military leader.

ALEXANDER WILEY

The basic standard by which to evaluate a speech is whether or not it actually succeeds in its objective. Does it sell the speaker's ideas, the speaker's personality? Does it win the audience?

Based on that standard, General MacArthur's address to the Congress and to the American people was a masterpiece of effectiveness. It has been stated that at many times during his speech there was hardly a dry eye in the entire audience—so emotional was its impact.

It should be remembered that although the General had the sympathetic admiration of practically all Americans in view of his fifty-two years of honored military service, he faced a seen and unseen audience which was sharply divided (then as now) as to the major policy points he was recommending. Many members of Congress particularly on the Democratic side of the aisle knew that their every favorable manifestation—applause, cheers, etc.,—might be interpreted as an implied slap at their Chief Executive, the head of the Democratic Party. Nevertheless, they gave themselves almost unrestrainedly in rousing general support of the General even though they did not completely reflect Republican enthusiasm for MacArthur's specific suggestions.

Rarely has a divided audience been so attentive to a speech. Judged from every technical standpoint, the General's comments came across with brilliant diction, masterly timing, keen logical sequence, splendid choice of words. Because he was the thorough master of his subject and of the specific phrasing of his speech, he could look up at the television cameras and at the audience in such a way as to maintain perfect rapport.

MacArthur's speech helped, moreover, to disprove many false ideas about him. To those individuals who had swallowed the false line about MacArthur's arrogance, he came to be respected as a man of great humility. To those individuals who were convinced that he was anxious to precipitate a partisan controversy, he emerged as a true statesman who avoided all references to personalities and who gallantly accepted the cruel dismissal action. To other individuals who had assaulted his basic motives, MacArthur's objective approach knocked the ground from under them. Douglas MacArthur in summary, made an historic address which will be reviewed by future generations as one of the great expositions in the history of oratory.

It should be remembered that not just any individual could have made a speech of such stature. It was a great speech, delivered by a great American, at a great time in the history of our country and of the world. Assuming that combination of circumstances, the speech was a masterpiece. Had it been offered by any individual other than MacArthur, and at any other time, under any other circumstances, it would not have "come off." As it is, it has become a classic in American history.

ROBERT J. CORBETT

The address of General of the Army Douglas MacArthur to the Joint Meeting of Congress was one of the outstanding speeches of modern history. This is true, not because of extraordinary eloquence, excellent delivery, masterful phrasing, or thought-compelling philosophy. The speech was great because it met the situation exactly as it was designed to do.

The situation was as tense and drama-packed as any that ever happened. Tens of millions had waited since the hour of his dismissal for this moment. Few had ever seen or listened to this almost mythical person. Here at last he stood in the Halls of Congress after years of absence from the country, and after a long trip, punctuated with tremendous receptions and covered in minutest detail in the press and on the radio. He could fall or triumph. His case could be lost completely. His whole career could end in a sorry flop. Seldom has so much depended on a single speech.

The speech was great because it met that tremendous situation with unbelievable perfection. The speech did what it was supposed to do. It explained the General's point of view clearly and persuasively. It said what was necessary to say and little more. It matched and multiplied the tense emotional feeling that gripped the nation. The speech was the test of the whole man and his whole career. He and it measured up.

I do not believe that MacArthur's speech should be dissected and analyzed. It can't be studied as a thing apart from the whole circumstance with any hope of understanding or appreciation. It was a great speech because it did a great job.

II. Journalist critics

RICHARD H. ROVERE

As a literary critic and political observer, I view the speech solely from the literary and political points of view. I am not qualified to criticize oratory or elocution.

As a piece of composition, the speech seemed to me a good deal but not a great deal better than the general run of public prose in the United States today. MacArthur has eloquence of a kind, but it strikes me as a rather coarse eloquence. He never shades his meanings, never introduces a note of humor, never gives the feeling that he is one man, only one, addressing himself to other men. His language is never flat and bloodless; neither is it flabby and loose-jointed, as so much writing of this sort is. But to me there is rather a fetid air about it. It does not leave me with the impression that a cool and candid mind has been at work on difficult matters of universal concern. Instead, it leaves me with the impression that a closed and in a sense a rather frantic mind has been at work to the end of making an appeal to history—not neglecting to use any of the rule-book hints on how to do it. I think not of history but of second-rate historian as I read the speech.

Form and content are, if not inseparable, very closely related. Politically, MacArthur's speech seemed extremely weak to me. This is not, I think, because I am opposed to his politics; I believe he could have made out a much stronger case for himself. But he never came to grips with the issues. For example, he wanted to have it that he was being persecuted for "entertaining" his particular views. This, of course, is rubbish. He got into trouble not for the political and military views he entertained (no doubt he was right in saying they were entertained by many of his colleagues) but for seeking to usurp the diplomatic function. He never sought to answer the objections to his position that rest on political and economic facts recognized by both sides: that if we followed him, we would be abandoned by several allies; that if Russia invaded Europe, which he has admitted might be an early consequence of his policy, the industrial balance would favor the Communist world; that, like it or not, American power does have its limitations. MacArthur's policy may be sounder than Truman's. But this contention cannot be sustained without facing these stubborn facts about the world today. MacArthur, in his speech, never faced them.

QUINCY HOWE

In a period that produced Winston Churchill and Franklin D. Roosevelt, General MacArthur stands out as perhaps the greatest actor of them all. Churchill and Roosevelt knew how to express many different moods. MacArthur has less versatility, but greater power within his own field. It is perhaps no accident that his first wife chose as her second husband the professional actor, Lionel Atwill, for MacArthur might also have made a great career for himself on the stage. But he had wider interests and abilities and chose soldiering instead. Finally, at the tragic climax of a dramatic career, he found himself called upon to play before both Houses of Congress the part of the old soldier who did his duty as God gave him to see that duty. By a coincidence, rare in the history of drama, the man who acted the part of the old soldier happened himself to be an old soldier whose experiences precisely resembled the experiences of the old soldier whose part he was enacting. The result was a fusion of man and actor, of reality and illusion, unique in the history of politics and drama. The qualities that make a man a great actor require a student of the drama to define. But the student of history with any experience or interest outside his special field can hardly fail to recognize that MacArthur certainly belongs in the company of Edwin Booth and William Jennings Bryan. His position as a statesman seems to this observer measurably lower than that of Harry S. Truman.

WILLIAM T. EVJUE

An injustice is being done to Abraham Lincoln by those who are claiming that General MacArthur's speech to the Congress is "another Gettysburg address." There is a great difference in the two speeches, as there is a great difference in the two men. One was a humble, sincere, and warmly human man of the people. The other is a mighty warrior, a showman conscious of the part he is playing and the destiny which he seeks to fashion for himself. The climax of Lincoln's greatest speech was a deathless expression of the ideal of democracy. The center of Douglas MacArthur's speech was Douglas MacArthur. The climax was a plea for sympathy for an "old soldier" "fading away."

There is a vast difference between the beautiful simplicity of Lincoln's address and the straining for colorful expression found in MacArthur. Some of it is downright hammy and some would not pass muster in a college freshman theme. For example, MacArthur's statement that the last words of the Korean people to him were: "Don't scuttle the Pacific," belongs in the department of statements that were never made. This is corn. In developing his hunch that the Russians would not enter a war on the side of the Chinese, MacArthur said: "Like the cobra, any new enemy will more likely strike whenever it feels that the relativity in military or other potential is in its favor on a worldwide basis." The simile reveals a striving for effect that makes the thought ridiculous. It conjures up the ludicrous picture of a cobra looking over reports from its intelligence service before it strikes to make sure that the "relativity in military or other potential is in its favor on a worldwide basis."

Outstanding in MacArthur's address was the obvious and amazing lack of knowledge of China. The general in the past has been given to speaking of the "Oriental mind"—an expression, incidentally, of which the Orientals deeply disapprove. It is a concept without foundation, just as much as the "Occidental mind," or the "American mind," or the "Wisconsin mind," or the "Madison mind" is baseless in social psychology.

In his speech the general said that the Asian people seek "friendly guidance . . . not imperious direction." But in a letter to the V.F.W. on August 28, 1950, he wrote that it is "in the pattern of the Oriental psychology to respect and follow aggressive, resolute and dynamic leadership." The general said that sixty per cent of the world's resources lie in Asia. Does he include the inaccessible coal and the nonexistent steel? He said that the "war-making tendency [up to 50 years ago] was almost non-existent, as they still followed the tenets of the Confucian ideal of pacifist culture." Any student of Chinese history knows that this "pacifist culture" was chiefly marked by centuries of bloody strife between competing warlords. Actually Confucianism is no more pacifist than Christianity. Would a Chinese speaker be right if he told his people that the Christian nations did not make war because Christ taught the ways of peace?

Students of Chinese history are shocked that the general in his discussion of the unification of China failed to mention the name of Sun Yat-sen. MacArthur gave credit to Chang-Tso-lin, thus choosing a Manchurian warlord in preference to Dr. Sun, who was a great scholar and statesman and whose dream was the establishment of a progressive democracy for his people.

In short, it is inconceivable that his address, with its obvious shortcomings in knowledge of essential historical background, its attention to easy and empty sociological concepts, its emotional preoccupation with vainglory and its regrettable theatrics, could even be compared to any of Lincoln's great masterpieces.

III. Academic critics

W. NORWOOD BRIGANCE

Three times within the past 15 years high army commanders have found themselves in disagreement with their chief executives. The first, Francisco Franco, led the army against the government, overthrew it by civil war, and set up himself as dictator. The second, Erwin Rommel, was handed a pistol by the executive's agent and told to shoot himself, else he with his family would be executed. The third, Douglas MacArthur, returned from the field of action and presented his case to Congress and to the American people without reprisal or threat of reprisal from the Chief Executive. This is the larger setting for MacArthur's speech. It was not merely a momentous speech. It was not merely the first momentous speech to be delivered to a combined television and radio audience in America. It was also a demonstration of public address as a force in a free society.

MacArthur's audience might be classified into four groups. First, was the noncritical mass of people to whom he was an abused war hero. Second, were the Republicans—until now hopelessly divided on foreign policy, with Hoover's American Gibraltar wing at one end and the Dulles' world leadership wing at the other—who suddenly and unexpectedly found an issue and a man behind whom they could unite. Third, were the Democrats, stunned by the public fury over MacArthur's dismissal, definitely on the defensive, yet hoping that MacArthur would discredit himself before Congress and the nation. Finally, were a few thinking critical people who respected MacArthur as a great military leader, but who were half convinced that many years in the Far East had conditioned him to think of issues primarily in terms of Asia only.

Within the first 10 minutes, the Democrats knew that they were in a fight for their survival as a majority party. In a voice that sometimes rasped, seldom rose from a low flat pitch, yet swelled with resonant confidence, he came almost at once to the ultimate issue in the minds of critical listeners. "The issues are global . . . there are those who claim our own strength is inadequate to protect on both fronts, that we cannot divide our effort. I can think of no greater expression of defeatism."

Interrupted by applause some thirty times, he marched with a soldier's precision from point to point . . . the Asiatic background, the Korean invasion, his call for reinforcements and for political decisions, a resulting military campaign that "forbade victory."

The climax of "old soldiers never die" was perhaps overdone for critics who heard the speech by radio. Some sneered at it as "corn." To those who saw it on television, however, it was emotionally effective, if not indeed spine-tingling and "beyond the limits of ordinary present-day oratory."

The President was probably right in his decision to dismiss MacArthur. MacArthur was probably wrong in his claim that his position was supported by the Joint Chiefs of Staff. In the immediate aftermath of the speech neither of these important issues counted for much. By this speech MacArthur had seized the initiative even as he had done by the audacious landing at Inchon.

HERBERT A. WICHELNS

Demosthenes had the problem, too: how much to spell out, how formal and explicit to make his proposals. At times Demosthenes judged it best not to "make a motion," but merely to offer comment and advice at large. MacArthur made a similar choice. In the main he chose not to debate, in the sense of formulating proposals and defending them in full. Instead he indicated the heads for debate, leaving no doubt as to the direction of his policy. Definite proposals were few, and sharply limited to Formosa and Korea. Supporting reasons were very sparingly given, and sometimes confined to bare assertions (as on the extent of China's present military commitment and Russia's probable course). But the call for a harder and more aggressive policy is plain from the beginning ("no greater expression of defeatism").

The chief support for that policy is neither logical argument nor emotional appeal, but the self-portrait of the speaker as conveyed by the speech.

It is an arresting portrait. Certain colors are of course mandatory. The speaker respects Congress and the power of this nation for good in the world. He is free from partisanship or personal rancor. He sympathizes with the South Koreans and with his embattled troops. He prefers victory to appeasement. He seeks only his country's good. He hates war, has long hated it. If these strokes are conventional, they take little time, except for the last, on which the speaker feels he must defend himself.

More subtle characterizing strokes are found in the "brief insight into the surrounding area" which form a good half of the speech. Here the General swiftly surveys the nature of the revolution in Asia, the island-frontier concept and Formosa's place in the island-chain, the imperialistic character of the Chinese communities, the regeneration of Japan under his auspices, the outlook for the Philippines, and the present government of Formosa. All this before reaching Korea. Most of these passages have no argumentative force. But all together they set up for us the image of a leader of global vision, comprehending in his gaze nations, races, and continents. The tone is firmest on Japan ("I know of no nation more serene, orderly and industrious"), least sure on the Philippines, but always positive.

Rarely indeed have the American people heard a speech so strong in the tone of personal authority. "While I was not consulted . . . that decision . . . proved a sound one." "Their last words to me"—it is the Korean people with whom the General has been talking. "My soldiers." The conduct of "your fighting sons" receives a sentence. A paragraph follows on the General's labors and anxieties on their behalf. The pace at which the thought moves, too, is proconsular; this is no fireside chat. Illustration and amplification are sparingly used; the consciously simple vocabulary of the home-grown politician is rejected. The housewife who "understood every word" was mistaken; she missed on *epicenter* and *recrudescence* and some others. But having by the fanfare been jarred into full attention, she understood quite well both the main proposition of the speech—a harder policy—and the main support offered—the picture of a masterful man of unique experience and global outlook, wearing authority as to the manner born.

WILBUR SAMUEL HOWELL

No prominent speech of the post-war era has contained so strong an appeal to emotion as MacArthur's did. Here was the old soldier in the fading twilight of life still seeking at the end of a career of fifty-two years in the Army to serve his country, even though she had deprived him of command, even though he was the reluctant advocate of an expanded war. Here was the veteran warrior recalling his boyish hopes and dreams on the plain at West Point a half-century earlier, and concluding his speech in part from the words of a popular barracks ballad of his youth and in part from the celebrated accents of Lincoln in the peroration of the Second Inaugural Address.

But these dominant and recurrent appeals would have been more persuasive if they had not clashed with that which he more briefly developed when he spoke of America's fighting sons in Korea. "I can report to you without reservation," he said, "that they are splendid in every way." He then mentioned his own anguish and anxiety at the growing bloodshed of the savage conflict in Korea. Such words would have the effect of arousing similar anguish and anxiety in his audience, and these powerful sympathies would cancel out those which he was bent upon creating towards himself as part of his program of advocacy of what might produce still greater bloodshed.

Ethical ambiguities in his speech tend also to weaken the effect he wanted to have. The only one of these that I shall deal with is so plainly at work that one wonders why he or his political advisers did not correct its injurious influence in advance. Those who listened to him on April 19 may have shared in part at least my feeling of elation when he urged America not to pursue "a course blind to reality that the colonial era is now past and the Asian peoples covet the right to shape their own free destiny." Here is an ethical standard to which the wise and just can repair. But hardly had these words reached our ears when he declared that from our island chain between the Aleutians and the Marianas "we can dominate with sea and air power every Asiatic port from Vladivostok to Singapore." We do not have to be Asiatics ourselves to feel at this point that in MacArthur's denunciation of colonialism the voice is Jacob's voice, but in his assertion of our power to threaten Asia the hands are the hands of Esau.

As for logic, MacArthur's speech tends to expand into propositions that are easy to grasp and hard to defend. One of these is that all-out war with Communist China should be risked at once, not avoided as long as we can. MacArthur discounts this risk in eleven words—"China is already engaging with the maximum power it can commit." Does not the General miscalculate his rhetorical strategy when he allots so few troops to such a crucial position? An even more crucial position which his strategy requires him to occupy is that America should deliberately risk war with Soviet Russia at this time. But again he does not man the position in strength. He sees that his four recommendations might cause Russia to intervene on the side of China; and then he deals with that grim eventuality so as to discount its possibility, not to calculate its final result. He merely says, "the Soviet will not necessarily mesh its actions with our moves." Even if this is right so far as it goes, it gives our moves a significance that we as a nation have to estimate in terms more exact than those used by the General. Thus it may happen that, with the applause now over and done with, the General's thesis will seem less and less attractive as time goes on.

HENRY L. EWBANK

It is difficult to imagine a more dramatic speech situation. A great military hero and speaker of unusual power, just relieved from his command for reasons not generally understood, broadcasts over all major networks his criticisms of the Department of State and the President. It couldn't happen in Russia. We are glad it can happen here.

This speech is part of a "great debate" on our foreign policy and who should determine it. In the main, MacArthur stuck to the issues, labelled his opinions as such, avoided *ad hominem* attacks, and presented his case with poise and dignity.

By way of objective analysis I applied Rudolf Flesch's criteria of readability. He has devised two scales: one measuring "ease of reading," the other "human interest." The reading ease score is based on sentence length and the number of syllables per hundred words. Possible scores range from zero (practically unreadable) to 100 (easy for any literate person). MacArthur's average sentence length is 24.5 words. The shortest has six; the longest, eighty. The number of syllables per hundred words ranges from 130 to 190; the average is 161. His score is 46 (difficult) compared with 70 (fairly easy) for the Gettysburg Address. The human interest score is based on the percentages of "personal words" and "personal sentences." Possible scores range from zero (very dull) to 100 (of dramatic interest). MacArthur's score is 20, on the borderline between "mildly interesting" and "interesting." Listeners who rated the speech higher in clarity and interestingness were probably reacting to the speaker's prestige, the content of his speech, and the excellence of his delivery.

The style is uneven. There are direct, skillfully constructed sentences: "It assumes instead the friendly aspect of a peaceful lake"; "We have had our last chance"; "They are blind to history's clear lesson . . ."; "In war there can be no substitute for victory"; "These gallant men will remain often in my thoughts and in my prayers always."

But there are a few words strangers to the average listener, an occasional awkward phrase and some sentences whose precise meaning is not readily apparent: ". . . the whole epicenter of world affairs rotates back toward the area whence it started"; "These political-social conditions . . . form a backdrop to contemporary planning which must be thoughtfully considered if we are to avoid the pitfalls of unrealism"; "China . . . was completely non-homogeneous, being compartmented into groups . . ."; ". . . efforts toward greater homogeneity produced the start of a nationalist urge"; ". . . I formally cautioned as follows"; "The problem . . . involves a spiritual recrudescence. . . ."

One must, it seems, say something about the concluding paragraph. It does not fit our stereotyped picture of Douglas MacArthur, nor has he just faded away. But let him who has not waxed sentimental as he bade his fraternity brothers farewell, or reached the end of his professional career, cast the first stone.

In many ways this was, and is, a great speech. But it will not find an enduring place in our literature as a model of speech composition.

A. CRAIG BAIRD

General Douglas MacArthur will be ranked as one of America's outstanding military orators. Partly because of disciplinary and strategic restraints, few modern soldiers have achieved reputations as outstanding speakers. Exceptions occur when military command and political leadership have merged, or when American public opinion of the present decade has invited nation-wide, untrammeled reports from such five-star heroes as George Marshall, Dwight Eisenhower, and Douglas MacArthur.

General of the Army MacArthur, before the Joint Session of Congress, on April 19, 1951, was deeply eloquent in his Apologia. His defense was in the tradition of Robert Emmet, before the Dublin court that had condemned him.

The general adequately fulfilled the speaking demands of the situation, with its expectancy of powerful eloquence that should exist "in the man, in the subject, and in the occasion." He is an orator by temperament, by habit, and by long exercise. Before Congress he realized Webster's criterion of the orator as one who possesses boldness, manliness, and energy.

The mode of his discourse, in spite of its logical texture, was primarily personal and ethical—a vindication of his intellectual integrity, wisdom, and good will. The historical-philosophical overview, the delineation of the new strategic frontier in the Pacific, the speech structure and movement, the language at times somewhat Churchillian—all these exalted the mature judgment and common sense of the speaker. The general's understanding of the vast Eastern populations, his sympathy for them, his implications of his own destiny strongly enforced his assumptions about his own character.

MacArthur in this dramatic setting was heroic in his bearing, movements, and gestures. His voice was by turns self-confident, convincing, stern, scornful, righteous.

What were his limitations? His sonorous delivery, occasional volatile phrasing, and calculated peroration were defects due to Asian rather than to Attic style. Pericles would presumably have composed and delivered this oration with more artistic subtlety, sense of order, freedom from extravagance, with more intellectual severity and emotional balance.

If MacArthur had not been a soldier for the past fifty-two years, he could have become a statesman of stature. For he has much of the parliamentary grand manner and an eloquence that the age has not outgrown.

When you speak in public, you usually want others to be entertained, to understand, to believe, or to act. To achieve your purpose as fully as possible, you must work for originality—in ideas, their management, their expression, and their presentation. A good original speech is the result of good methods consciously applied, and good methods come from the study of principles, guided application of them, sound criticism of their use, and discriminating observation of how others use them. The moments of actual speaking are few but exacting; the hours of preparation are many and equally exacting.

To be an effective public speaker, you must know how to choose a suitable subject for your speech, determine its overall purpose, and gather materials for it quickly and systematically. You must be able to organize your speech in a clear, coherent pattern; express your ideas in accurate, appropriate, lively language; and deliver your speech in a natural, interesting manner. In this Handbook we will examine some of the basic methods you can use to achieve each of these essential functions.

Choosing a subject

How do you select a subject for a speech? Purposeful observation and thoughtful analysis, combined with a liberal dash of imagination, will help you find suitable subjects and aid you in exploring their possibilities. For example, study the pencil in your hand. It invites you to learn and share new knowledge about graphite, wood, rubber, communication, the art of writing. Even in so simple a subject there will be "news" of interest to most speakers and listeners.

After you unearth a potential subject, you should test it by asking two questions: Does it interest me? Can I make it meaningful to other people? If either answer is negative, you should discard the subject. If your answers are affirmative, test the subject further by examining it in the light of the principles suggested in the Glossary under *Subject* and *Originality*. Always seek your subject early, and seek it carefully and methodically. And do not abandon a promising subject at the first sign of difficulty. Remember that it takes time to command a subject thoroughly and to comprehend all of its facets and trace all of its implications.

Audience analysis and purpose

Next come the twin problems of analyzing the audience and determining the precise nature of the response you want from your listeners. This response becomes the specific purpose of your speech.

Here again, you need to ask the right questions: What do I most want to accomplish in speaking on this subject? What does the audience most need to understand or believe concerning it? The answers to these questions will help point the way toward efficient research, fresh ideas that are significant and useful, and a speech pattern that will be closely adapted to the needs and interests of your listeners.

In determining what you as a speaker most want to accomplish in talking on a given subject, proceed as follows:

1. Decide tentatively which of the *ends of speaking* (see Glossary) is most suitable to your subject, audience, and occasion.

2. Decide whether the audience will be willing and able to respond as you would like. To reach this decision, ask yourself the following questions:

A. What attitudes will my listeners probably have toward me, my subject, and the occasion? (Men in the prime of life seldom relish instruction from youth; minorities are not amused by accounts of their difficulties or peculiarities; wedding parties are not occasions for political advocacy.)

B. Has the audience too little, enough, or too much knowledge to respond as I would like? (Children can be informed about rocks but are little amused by geologists' "inside jokes.") Has the audience the authority or power to act as I wish? (Students can be convinced about foreign policy, but there is little they can do to carry out their convictions.)

C. Will my listeners have a sense of common interest or feel themselves strangers to one another's concerns? (Labor union members might agree unanimously on a proposal affecting their working hours but be widely divided on a political or a religious issue.)

D. Will age, sex, socioeconomic status, or similar factors influence my listeners' readiness to respond to my preferred purpose? (The old are often more cynical than the young; women may be less interested in high finance than men; the poor usually respond to "pocketbook motives" more readily than the well-to-do.)

Above all, remember that as a public speaker you are never entirely the master of your own purpose. Only after studying the probable audience can you decide whether the purpose you prefer is wise and realistic. You may wish to *amuse* by poking fun at modern architecture, but what if your hearers have seen few modern buildings? Or what if some architects will be in the audience? Given these conditions, your "realistic" purpose cannot be to amuse. Some of your listeners know too little about the subject, and others know too much. What can you do? You can modify or adjust your purpose to meet the situation. You might *explain* a layman's reaction to modern architecture. And doubtless you could add some amusing touches that would enliven your expository discourse. In a speech with this modified purpose, there would be "news" for all. A moderate shift of your central idea directs your speech toward the true ground on which you, your subject, and your audience can meet, realistically and to mutual advantage.

Gathering materials

Once you have chosen your subject, analyzed your audience, and located a practical purpose, you must turn researcher. Where are the facts, figures, and arguments you will need to influence your listeners—to win from them the response of understanding, belief, or action which you seek? Sound methods of research will save hours of time and will help uncover the best materials available. There are four great repositories of potentially useful information:

1. The storehouse of your own memory; you must think about your subject and remember what you have already learned about it.

2. The world outside yourself; you must take a look about you.

3. The minds of friends, acquaintances, and available experts; you must talk with them.

4. The vast resources of printed materials; you must read.

Speakers who have the most trouble finding materials for their speeches are usually those who do not explore these repositories systematically. They wish they knew all, but they do not take inventory of the bits of relevant knowledge they already possess. They look without seeing and touch without feeling; they pass by pertinent information insensitively. They talk at random; they do not interview. They read without remembering the purpose of their speeches and the characteristics of their prospective listeners.

What specific method should you use in your search for speech materials? You cannot do better than direct your energies as Emerson urged "The American Scholar" to manage his. Read paragraphs 11 through 17, pages 38-39, of this address. Make "the scholar of the first age" your model in research.

In addition, you will find that you can save much time and confusion by taking careful notes. The extra minutes you spend in recording ideas and their sources, *completely and accurately*, on separate slips of paper or note cards, will be minutes quickly won back when you begin to compose your speech. Here is an example of well-recorded information:

> Persuasion   Common Ground
>
> J. A. Winans, *Speech-Making* (1938), p. 370.
>
> ". . . to persuade a man is largely a matter of *identifying* the opinion or course you wish him to adopt with one or more of his established beliefs or customary courses of conduct." (Italics W's.)

You can take such a note quickly, from a book or during a conversation. If you write your information on a note card, you can file it easily, carry it to the speaker's stand, put it out of the way if unneeded, or save it for later use and refer to it with confidence months or years later. Sheets of miscellaneous and fragmentary notations offer none of these conveniences.

Reading is very important. Since public speeches are often about public affairs, you as a student of public speaking should keep informed about current questions. You will find that reading good sources of information regularly is enjoyable as well as educational. In each geographical region there is a "best" newspaper; it is the paper with the widest and least biased coverage of both world and local news. The one "newspaper of record" in the United States is the New York *Times*, which not only has a comprehensive index but publishes the texts of major, newsworthy documents and speeches. For stimulating and authoritative information also study such magazines as the following: for general information *The*

Atlantic, Harper's Magazine, Yale Review; for conservative opinion on public questions the *U.S. News & World Report* and the *National Review;* for liberal opinion *The Nation, New Republic, The Reporter;* for the viewpoint of business *Business Week* and *Fortune.* Some journals specialize in publishing analyses of public issues: *Vital Speeches of the Day* offers the texts of significant current speeches; the *Congressional Digest* presents analyses of current problems, often in debate form; more authoritative articles on such problems can be found in *The Annals of the American Academy of Political and Social Science* and *Foreign Affairs.*

Planning the speech

If you gather your material carefully, think about it, and apply imagination to it, you will usually be able to produce a clear speech plan that will reflect sound and original views—views you can express in your own best language and can relate to your listeners' lives and experiences. If need be, you will also be able to expand or defend these views, because you will understand how and why you came to hold them. On the other hand, when your knowledge is sketchy, reflection meager, and imagination lacking, your speech plans will probably be cloudy and your ideas shallow. In short, you cannot prepare and organize a speech quickly. Success or failure hangs in the balance as you engage in each of the tasks extending from the first search for raw materials to the final shaping of the finished discourse.

Outlining the body of the speech. These are the basic steps in planning the body of a speech:

1. Give final form to the specific purpose of the speech by stating it in a precise, carefully limited sentence. (See Glossary: *Central Idea, Specific Purpose.*) Sometimes your research will prove that the purpose you selected initially was too inclusive, too narrow, or otherwise unsatisfactory. Not infrequently your opinions will change as your study of the subject continues. You *must,* therefore, re-examine your original intention before turning to the other stages of speech planning.

2. Study the relation of the materials collected to the proposed purpose of the speech in order to determine the leading ideas or main divisions.

    A. As guides to this process read these sections of the Glossary, preferably in the following order: *Analysis, Main Headings, Subheadings, Subordination, Patterns of Organization, Motivated Sequence.*

    B. Discover the arrangement of ideas which best supports or explains the purpose of the speech as finally determined in Step 1. The so-called "standard" patterns of organization are simply the arrangements speakers are most in the habit of using. You must judge by your own intelligence and experience which pattern best serves your needs. How you may arrive at this choice methodically is suggested in the Glossary under *Reflective Thinking.*

3. As a result of Step 2 you should have a rough outline of the body of your speech, one in which the organization of the main headings will probably conform to one of the patterns of organization discussed in the Glossary.

4. With the proposed main headings and, perhaps, some of their subheadings coordinated and subordinated in outline form, fill in any subheadings still needed and insert relevant *supporting material* (see Glossary) from the fund of facts and ideas gathered in research. Ask yourself:

    A. Will the main headings, if the audience believes them all, win assent for the central idea?

    B. What needs to be proved or clarified to win assent for each main heading? The answers will suggest the subheadings and supporting materials that are still needed.

    C. Do unused or previously discarded research materials offer better answers to the questions asked in Step 4B? If so, perhaps a weaker heading or less pertinent piece of supporting material should be discarded and a new one put in its place.

    D. Do the subheadings and supporting materials as now revised prove or clarify the main headings and make them striking enough to command the attention of your audience? Does the speech as a whole strongly support the specific purpose? If not, what additional materials might help? At this point some supplementary facts and figures may have to be gathered or some new and stronger arguments formulated; the first phase of research seldom produces every item actually needed for adequate proof and sufficient motivation.

Checking the main sections. With this done, examine each main section of the speech as finally developed. Test it for:

1. Redundancy. Eliminate excess materials, saving only *enough of the best* to win the specific response proposed. No audience wants to hear in a single sitting all that a competent speaker knows.

2. Lack of variety in supporting material. In some instances examples may be needed to replace statistics, or statistics needed to replace authority. Each main heading should be strongly and variously supported.

3. Motivational and suggestive force. The main headings and their subdivisions must make the hearers *want* to understand, believe, or act. (See Glossary: *Adaptation, Motivation, Emotion, Suggestion, Drive, Attitude, Stereotype, Appeal.)*

It is in making these decisions and choices that superior speakers prove themselves and poor speakers proceed by guess rather than informed judgment. To derive and arrange the materials of a speech requires intelligence, command of method, and sensitivity to the nature of audiences. It is an art that you can learn only through long and dedicated practice.

Introductions and conclusions. As a final step in planning your speech, you must compose an introduction and conclusion, being guided both by the nature of your subject and by the needs of the audience. For the essential requirements of a good *introduction* and *conclusion,* see the Glossary.

Style

When you give a speech extemporaneously, you must develop the wording by experimentation in a series of oral or sub-vocal rehearsals (see the following section, "Extemporaneous delivery"). If you deliver the speech from manuscript, or from memory, you may perfect the stylistic elements as writing and rewriting progress. A fourth and probably ideal procedure is to write the speech in full, from the outline, carefully evaluate and perfect the language used, then destroy the manuscript and rehearse the ideas extemporaneously. With this process you are likely to use the carefully worked out expression of the manuscript naturally in the actual speech without destroying the still greater advantages of flexibility in both style and delivery. For the extemporaneous speaker this process of writing enlarges language resources while repeated rehearsals intensify the sense of plan and direction.

As you write a speech or experiment in rehearsals for extemporaneous speaking, you should work for language that is at once accurate, clear, appropriate, and lively. Your experience with words, your common sense, your good taste, must guide the search. No one can give exact instructions suited to all cases, but you can learn, in advance of making any particular language decision, what kinds of useful language are available and what standards influence the best speakers when they make similar choices. Some of these considerations are discussed in the Glossary under such topics as: *Abstraction, Activity, Clarity, Conciseness, Concreteness, Connotation, Conversational Quality, Emphasis, Figures of Speech, Force, Imagery, Impressiveness, Liveliness, Originality, Style, Suggestion, Variety.*

Good oral style requires plentiful and carefully formulated transitions and internal summaries. It is more difficult to achieve clarity in oral discourse than in written because listeners must grasp the full import of a word or sentence instantaneously. They cannot reflect and re-examine as readers constantly do. You must, then, take special pains to keep the relationships among ideas clear by using frequent transitions and summaries. These tell the listeners where the speaker has been, where he is now, and where he is going. They are not integral parts of the organization of a speech; they are verbal bridges between parts, placed there to aid the listener who otherwise might not be able to make the crossing. Since the transition usually restates part of what the speaker has already said, it functions both as a connective and an internal summary. You should plan such aids to listeners in detail—including them in your outline for the speech and consciously inserting them orally as you rehearse. For examples of such transitional and summary statements, see the Glossary under *Transition.*

Extemporaneous delivery

The extemporaneous speaker is more versatile, more adaptable, and, usually, more convincing than the speaker who has memorized his speech or who reads from manuscript.

Rehearsing the speech. Planning and outlining are the backbone of the extemporaneous method. For good delivery you must have total command of your basic speech plan and must be fortified by a series of thoughtful rehearsals. Thus equipped, you can come to the platform confident of your preparation. Having been through the speech many times and having met its difficulties in different ways each time, you know you have a full, diverse fund of thoughts and a ready supply of words with which to meet any problems that may arise during the presentation. To arrive at this enviable frame of mind, prepare as follows:

1. When the speech plan is complete, read it over several times, from beginning to end, always concentrating on how each idea is related to the idea which precedes it and the one which follows it.

2. Next place the speech plan before you and try to talk through the speech, *aloud if possible.* No matter how much trouble you have at any point, do not pause to correct it but proceed from beginning to end without stopping. To do otherwise will establish a psychological block at the point of difficulty.

3. Having made your way through the speech plan, however haltingly, study it again, working out smoother connections between the ideas and planning clearer, more fitting, more lively ways of expressing each point.

4. Now repeat Step 2 exactly as before, moving from the beginning of the speech to the end without stopping. Then review once more the plan and the manner of handling it, just as you did in Step 3. As you rehearse and adjust the speech, constantly keep in mind the audience you will be addressing and the response you seek.

5. When, after alternating Steps 2 and 3, you feel that the speech plan is firmly fixed in your mind, make a set of brief "speaker's notes," based on the detailed speech outline. These notes should consist of cue words and phrases that will help you recall the order of the main headings and the several subheadings that fall under each. They must be brief enough to be read at a glance. To go with these notes, assemble those quotations, statistics, and other detailed materials which you wish to use in the speech but which it would be difficult or impossible to commit wholly to memory.

6. Finally, rehearse the speech again, this time using only your notes and special reference cards. Make the necessary final adjustments in timing, language, emphasis, and delivery. When you are satisfied with these adjustments, you are ready to face your audience. The leading ideas of the speech and their supporting materials will now be old friends. Moreover, you now know the "marching orders" embodied in the detailed speech plan; you know them so well that as the speech is being delivered to the audience you can make minor changes without destroying its essential character.

Delivering the speech. Before taking the platform, you probably will be nervous. You should be. You will have "butterflies." You should have. Like an athlete, you are keyed to your task—a task important enough to be nervous about. Your salvation, like the athlete's, is that you know what the plays are; most of them are in your well-practiced plan. Your nervous tension is a fact, but no more a fact than your thorough familiarity with the ideas you wish to communicate. And if you have rehearsed the speech as you should have, you already have met and conquered most of the difficulties that can confront you on the platform. This, too, is a fact as significant as your nervousness.

But it is uncomfortable to be nervous while waiting to speak. What can be done to bring a little comfort without destroying the keyed-up feeling so essential to effective extemporaneous speaking? Here are some suggestions:

1. Breathe deeply. More oxygen helps. Also, using the large muscles of the chest and abdomen discharges some of the pent-up energy that contributes to discomfort.

2. Drop the arms; let the hands dangle loosely beside the body; let the head droop too if no one is looking. Concentrating on relaxing takes the mind off the task that is causing nervousness.

3. Remember some of the successes of rehearsals; try to recapture the ideas, feelings, and language of those moments. This encourages you and also provides review.

4. When introduced, walk—don't shamble or rush—to the speaker's stand. Take time—time to recapture one of the several good beginnings made in rehearsal. Keep your mind on the response you wish to win from the audience, and why. *You* are not very important now; your business with the audience is.

5. When you are ready, and not until then, "lean into your audience" and begin working on *them.* A speech is not a "performance"; it is a transaction carried on with other minds. The sooner this business relationship becomes your entire preoccupation, the sooner the tensions of speaking will be channeled out of discomfort-producing paths and into paths that make the body obedient to the mind.

Such is the experience of most effective extemporaneous speakers. Experience does not dull the excitement. Experience does not even make the process of preparation less time consuming. The experienced extemporaneous speaker differs from his less experienced brother chiefly because he knows that careful advance planning can solve most problems. He knows that properly used, his tensions can help, not thwart, him. Convinced of these things, his mind is free to re-create the thoughts of his preparation, and his spirit is free to *mean* them.

Other modes of delivery

Few speakers memorize their speeches today. The hurry of modern living does not allow them time. Happily, nothing of great value is lost in consequence. The only good memorized speeches are those in which every idea is an old and familiar friend. Only when words need not be consciously remembered can ideas be delivered with meaning; so it is not until a speech is completely, flawlessly memorized that one arrives at the equivalent of Step 6 in the extemporaneous speaker's program of rehearsal. From this point on, the speaker with a memorized speech prepares himself and focuses his nervous energies in much the same manner as the extemporaneous speaker. For the extra effort of memorization he earns a more perfect control over style, but he also sacrifices much freedom in adapting ideas and appeals to audience responses.

The speaker who reads from a manuscript may believe that he has chosen the easiest mode of speech preparation and delivery. He hasn't if he means to be effective. He has chosen the quickest path to detailed control over style but the most difficult path to vibrant, communicative delivery. Moreover, if he means to speak with genuine effect, he must struggle with his habits to avoid writing an essay rather than a speech; he must rework his written draft as carefully as the extemporaneous speaker reworks his modes of expression. Unless he is already a well-trained, gifted reader, he must spend much time in rehearsal. President Franklin D. Roosevelt's "War Message" of December 8, 1941, was exceedingly brief (about 45 lines), yet he put it through three written drafts within twenty-four hours, before he was willing to read it to Congress and the nation. Those who propose to speak from manuscript should be guided by the fact that Roosevelt, the finest manuscript speaker in modern American history, normally insisted that each speech be rewritten five to eight times and carefully rehearsed aloud before it was finally delivered.

Effective oral reading is a special art that cannot be examined here, but it is an art that must be mastered if speeches are to be meaningfully delivered from manuscript. That this necessity is seldom met by public figures, painful memories and painful anticipations attest.

Impromptu speaking—that is, speaking without formal preparation—is sometimes necessary. Few, if any, effective speeches have ever been so delivered, however—except on subjects about which the speaker had already thought long and clearly. The test of adequacy in impromptu speaking is simple: Is the speaker so well grounded in the subject and the art of speech composition that not even the unexpected call for a speech upsets his command of substance and method? Impromptu speaking may afford excellent drill in the methods of effective speaking; but except when done by the best informed and ablest speakers, it is usually an imposition upon the listeners.

Physical aspects of delivery

The physical aspects of delivery concern the proper use of voice and body.

The voice. All listeners, but only some speakers, seem to know that the speaker must speak loudly enough to be heard or his breath is wasted. If you have normal vocal equipment, you are capable of speaking so that you can be heard by a hundred listeners in a moderately quiet hall. You can, if you are willing to work at it, establish habits of using the breathing apparatus, the vocal folds, and the resonators efficiently—even pleasingly. This may require drill, but the drills are best conducted as specially prepared exercises, not in the public speaking situation itself.

It is also plain that your pronunciation and articulation of words must be reasonably conventional or understanding will be impaired. Again, if you have unconventional habits or are handicapped by physical or other difficulties so that your speaking manner distracts from the communication of your meaning, you must retrain yourself. This kind of retraining is best undertaken under the supervision of a speech rehabilitation specialist and, except under special circumstances, conducted apart from attempts to learn the art of influencing audiences through public speaking.

The speed or rate at which you speak is a function of the duration of sounds and of the duration of the pauses between those sounds. Up to a point, intelligibility depends more on clear articulation than on the control of rate. Speakers who articulate clearly often can be understood when speaking well over 200 words a minute; some can speak no more than 160 words a minute before listeners begin to complain of their speed. On the other hand, fluent speakers seldom are thought to speak too slowly until they fall well below 100 words a minute. As a public speaker, you must learn by observation, study, and drill what kinds of emphasis and mood can be suggested by changing the duration of words and pauses, thus changing the overall rate of utterance. Here, as everywhere in public speaking, manageable variety is the goal.

Body action. The problem of when and how to use gestures has plagued aspiring speakers for centuries. Charts have been drawn, rules have been proclaimed, taboos have grown up. Elaborate "sciences" or "arts" of gesture have won fanatic followers. But direct, meaningful oral communication has seldom resulted from these efforts. Neither has it come from the opposite extreme—from the purists of the nature-will-take-care-of-you-if-you-only-let-it-alone persuasion. A few propositions about communication through physical movement may, however, be given.

1. People who don't *want* to communicate with others seldom communicate effectively—physically or in any other way. You must have the will to communicate—or a "lively sense of communication," as it has been called—before you can use gestures meaningfully.

2. People strongly bent on communicating with others sometimes use one means in preference to another, and do so effectively. Some speakers prefer to rely much on vocal resources and little on physical movement; some rely on head-and-shoulder emphasis but little on movements of the arms. Always, however, your bodily actions must be motivated by the ideas you seek to communicate. Gestures, bodily movements, muscle tension, and facial expression come from the inside out; they are not superimposed upon the speech by a predetermined formula.

3. Although different styles of physical emphasis and different patterns of gestures may be equally communicative, three qualities are necessary if you expect to reinforce your ideas effectively through bodily action:

A. Your communicative activity must be coordinated. Bodily movements must serve the same meanings as the accompanying verbal language, or they will distract from, rather than add to, what is said.

B. Your bodily activity must be well timed. Our natures seem to dictate that a gesture which is really meant just precedes or exactly coincides with the utterance it reinforces. The wonderfully comic effects of ill-timed movement are sufficient evidence that meaningful gestures have a subtle time relationship to the ideas or feelings that generate them.

C. Your posture and position on the platform must allow expressive movements to develop easily, whenever meaning demands them. This is why you should carry your weight on the balls of the feet, keep your hands free, and stand somewhat away from a lectern.

Self-evaluation. In all aspects of delivery, self-observation and self-criticism are continuously necessary—for the experienced speaker as well as for the inexperienced. Unless you constantly evaluate yourself, you may develop distracting mannerisms in your vocal or bodily behavior. You must learn what your personal resources are, blend them into what is for you the most communicative speaking style, and then guard that style against faulty habits and annoying behaviors. Often this requires self-conscious drill, preferably apart from actual speechmaking. When you are delivering a speech, most of your energies must be concentrated on the meaning of the ideas you are communicating and on the people to whom you are communicating them. Your body will then contribute added meaning insofar as it is trained to serve your mind. Its further retraining may well deserve attention after the speech is over, but you can hardly deliver an effective speech and at the same time pass judgment on the behavior of an arm or leg.

A final word

Studying a textbook, reading a student's handbook, and analyzing the texts of speeches will not, even together, make you an effective public speaker. But these undertakings will furnish you with a body of sound ideas about how men influence others through speech. From such ideas you may learn much that will be of use as you confront audiences in the classroom and in later life. Do not look, however, for sure-fire tricks and devices. There are none. *There is no way to make a good speech without having something to say that is so much worth saying that you want others to know it too.* Given this kind of worthiness in intention, methodical, thoughtful preparation and a well-disciplined body will mediate between your meaning and the listener's experience so that your message is clearly and impressively communicated. The study of speaking and speeches can contribute much to your understanding, method, and principles of discipline; only you can supply the practice that is necessary to turn such knowledge into productive, influential behavior. "The only way that promises success in the long run is to become intelligent about speech-making."[1]

---

1 J. A. Winans, *Speech-Making* (New York, 1938), p. 8.

GLOSSARY OF RHETORICAL TERMS

For the student's convenience, glossary terms are italicized wherever they are referred to in the following discussions.

a

Abstraction Dealing with nonsensory concepts, such as truth, honesty, democracy. See "Remarks on Government Regulation of Broadcasting," p. 120, par. 25; "What Is Truth?" pp. 182-186; "The Challenge of Abundance," pp. 225-226, par. 28 (except the reference to Roosevelt). See also *Concreteness.*

Action Step See *Conclusion, Motivated Sequence.*

Activity Action or movement in communication conveyed through the choice and forms of language as well as through gestures and other physical behavior. Movement or progression can be suggested by the arrangement of ideas and images, as in climactic order; through special arrangements of thought units, as a *periodic sentence;* and through choosing images that suggest things in motion. Listeners pay the most attention to those communications that set pictures moving within their minds. See "The Inner City—Our Shame," p. 247, par. 6, "Like an eddy . . . mainstream of society." See also *Climax, Liveliness.*

Adaptation Generally, the adjustment of all elements of discourse to the capacities and expectations of the listeners. Effective speaking requires that ideas, arrangement, style, and delivery be adapted to the audience, *occasion,* purpose, and speaker—with a view to securing responses favorable to the *end* the speaker has chosen. See an address to jail inmates, "Crime and Criminals," pp. 136-143; address to a potentially hostile audience at a Lincoln Day dinner, "The South Respects the Written Constitution," pp. 143-150; address to an alien audience, "Address to the Russian People," pp. 241-246; see also "The Haven of the Defeated," p. 161, pars. 3, 5, and 8, "Remember, I'm not . . . the same as you and me."

Allegory A somewhat extended communication, usually *narrative,* in which events, characters, or objects have figurative or metaphorical as well as literal meanings. A *parable* is likely to be a metaphorical narrative used as *supporting material,* an allegory is a still more extensive, metaphorical unit that often constitutes the entire *amplification* of a major point. Allegories rarely appear in modern public addresses, though they are sometimes found in sermons and speeches to entertain. John Bunyan's *Pilgrim's Progress* and Jonathan Swift's *A Tale of a Tub* are among the most familiar allegories in literature. See also *Figures of Speech.*

Allusion A brief reference to some fact or event or character to clarify or vivify a thought. "The lesson of Sputnik" alludes concisely to Russian advances in science and to Western concern about them. Here, as with all allusions, the hearer must be able to supply details of the thing alluded to from his own knowledge if he is to understand the reference. See "The Man with the Muck-Rake," p. 103, pars. 2-3, and p. 104, par. 8, "Such laughter . . . to fruition."

Amplification Literally, enlargement or extension. In rhetoric, amplification is usually thought of as the discussion which provides the details, illustrations, and other clarifying material concerning an idea. There is no necessary distinction between that which "proves" a point and that which amplifies it, but the term "amplification" is usually applied to developmental material without regard to its strength as "proof." See "The Inner City—Our Shame," p. 248, pars. 10-14, for an illustration of amplification that "proves" largely by suggestion; "Changing Concepts of Public Service," p. 236, pars. 29-33, for an illustration of a variety of amplifying methods within one segment of a speech; Reuther, "Administered Prices," pp. 201-202, pars. 25-28; p. 206, pars. 109-111; pp. 206-207, pars. 116-133. See also *Allegory, Allusion, Analogy, Anecdote, Concreteness, Definition, Epigram, Evidence, Example, Figures of Speech, Imagery, Parable, Proof, Proverb, Repetition.*

Analogy A moderately extended comparison, either literal or figurative, used either to clarify or to "prove." An extensive figurative analogy is usually called a *parable* or an *allegory.* Analogy connotes a comparison more complex or extensive than a simile or metaphor. See "Crime and Criminals," p. 140, par. 24; "The Case Against Segregated Schools," p. 152, par. 22; "The American Family," p. 155, par. 8; "The Three Parts of Morality," pp. 177-178, pars. 3-4; "The Value of Self-Criticism for Business and Labor," p. 191, par. 78; "The Challenge of Abundance," p. 225, par. 23. See also *Amplification, Figures of Speech.*

Analogy as Argument The use of circumstances existing in one place or sphere of experience as the basis for an inference about the circumstances existing elsewhere. Such argument usually runs: what is true of A must also be true of B since A and B are known to be similar. The validity of such an argument depends (1) on the truth of what we say about A; (2) on the similarity of A and B in all significant respects; (3) on whether the causative forces that work in A are also at work in B. Because of the difficulty of establishing these matters beyond reasonable doubt, argument from analogy is often called the weakest of the forms of argument, yet it is one of the commonest. Many analogies that fail the tests of logical validity contain enough probability to help sustain arguments that are also supported by other methods. See "Remarks on Government Regulation of Broadcasting," p. 118, par. 10; "The South Respects the Written Constitution," p. 147, par. 64; "The Case Against Segregated Schools," p. 151, par. 15; "The Haven of the Defeated," p. 162, pars. 17-19. See also *Argument, Persuasion, Proof.*

Analysis A term used in several senses and contexts. Practically, the term refers to the division of anything into its constituent parts. In rhetoric, analysis is the process by which the discussable aspects of a subject—the *central idea,* the *main headings,* and even the *subheadings*

—are discovered and revealed. Analysis of a subject involves discovering what, of all that it is possible to say about the subject, should be said to a specific audience on a particular occasion. The experience of centuries proves that many subjects can be analyzed by dividing them according to one of several standard patterns. See *Patterns of Organization.*

Anecdote Usually a brief *narrative* supporting or amplifying a thought or *proposition.* Anecdotes used in introducing or concluding a speech or essay should be subordinate to the *central idea* of the discourse. An anecdote may serve either or both of two rhetorical functions: to make the idea more vivid and interesting or to support the idea as a *proof* by providing an illustration. See "Moppet Manipulation," p. 115, par. 9; "The Philosophy of Social Justice Through Social Action," p. 132, pars. 18-20; "The Three Parts of Morality," p. 174, par. 1; "Address to the Russian People," p. 245, par. 64.

Animation In oral or written composition, the quality of *liveliness* or *activity.* Expressive utterance, facial vivacity, and physical movement are the chief elements of animated delivery.

Antithesis A form of expression in which opposing terms or ideas are set against one another. Antithesis is especially valuable in argumentative discourse since it points up the sharp contrast between two viewpoints. In his *Rhetoric* Aristotle makes the point that lively expression in persuasive speech must be especially marked by "antithesis, metaphor, and actuality [the *concreteness*]."

Appeal A term commonly and somewhat loosely used to mean evoking a reasoning or feeling state by means of something said or done. The phrases "emotional appeal" and "logical appeal" are frequently used to describe the process by which a speaker seems to invite a given kind of response from his audience.

By means of ideas, language, and delivery speakers can cause listeners to have mental experiences within themselves; and to these experiences, in turn, the listeners may react—sometimes with much and sometimes with little intellectual calculation. That these reactions are exclusively emotional or rational seems improbable. The same phrase or action may arouse very different experiences in different listeners. There is even evidence to show that trained listeners cannot agree with themselves or with others when they try to identify portions of a communication as "logical" or "emotional."

It is true one can find segments of printed speeches in which the purpose seems to have been to make the listeners feel more than think or vice versa. This tells us the speaker's probable purpose, but not how the listeners reacted—how they translated the "appeal." In general, both speakers and critics must remember that normal respondents react to what they see and hear with mixed, often individualistic, feelings and thoughts; and it is the *effect* to which speaker and critic must pay most attention. To describe a child on an operating table may evoke highly professional calculations in a listening surgeon and deep emotion in the surgeon's wife, though they sit side by side in the same audience. Is the appeal of the description, then, "logical" or "emotional"?

For what would generally be regarded as an emotional type of appeal, see "The South Respects the Written Constitution," p. 150, pars. 100-102. Cf. "The Case Against Segregated Schools," p. 152, par. 20.

In "The Inner City—Our Shame," pp. 248-249, pars. 10-18 appeal for sympathy but also form evidence that action is needed. In "The Moral Bankruptcy of Television," p. 109, pars. 5-7 appeal to a sense of dissatisfaction by offering targets or objects toward which the feeling can be discharged. In "Address to the Russian People," p. 242, pars. 20-21, the appeal is to reason, and also to opinions about what justifies defensive action and to possible feelings of guilt about aggressiveness. In "The City—A Cause for Statesmanship," p. 252, pars. 21-22, the appeal is against an allegedly inconsistent opposition's ethos and, indirectly, to the listeners' belief in their own better logic. See also *Attitude, Emotion, Logic, Persuasion, Proof.*

Appropriateness The quality of being suitable. In rhetoric this term usually refers to *style:* "Effective oral style must be clear, appropriate, and lively." Whatever language is at once suitable to the speaker, his subject matter, the *occasion* on which he speaks, and the particular audience he addresses will be called appropriate. Usually appropriateness, as distinguished from *clarity,* refers to such subjective qualities as propriety, good taste, level of difficulty, etc. See also *Liveliness.*

Argument It is doubtful that any distinction between argument and persuasion is psychologically defensible in rhetoric. Nonetheless, in composing a persuasive communication, one must often concentrate on the discovery and arrangement of *propositions* and the *evidence* for their support. In this phase of creativity the composer is usually said to be developing "arguments." Also, listeners and readers tend to classify as "arguments" those parts of a communication in which extensive reasoning and evidence are introduced. In "Address to the Russian People," p. 243, pars. 27-32, an allegation is refuted chiefly by adducing the evidence of examples; but by repeating "It was rejected by the USSR" at the end of each item of proof, a strong suggestion of blame is injected into the argument. See also *Analogy as Argument, Causal Relationship, Persuasion, Sign, Syllogism.*

Assertion Any statement or declaration for which no support except the authority of the communicator is offered. In rhetoric, unlike scientific discourse, many assertions are entirely acceptable to audiences because experience or common knowledge supplies *proof* to support the assertion. Theodore Roosevelt's "There is nothing more distressing to every good patriot . . . ," p. 104, par. 8, only asserts an alleged fact. In "The Challenge of Abundance," p. 222, par. 8 consists largely of assertions. Note how each listener's political bias will govern the acceptability of these statements. See also *Proposition.*

Attention The act of noticing or becoming aware of something. It is especially important for speakers to remember that (1) a listener's attention must be aroused before ideas can have any influence upon him; (2) human attention is selective, not diffuse—a listener perceives only what seems important or interesting to him at the moment; (3) unless ideas, language, and delivery constantly renew the listener's interest in what is being said, his attention will be lost very quickly. The attention of listeners is even less stable than the attention of readers; therefore, the speaker, even more than the writer, must know and constantly use all the resources of arrangement, style, and delivery to direct his listener's attention to whatever is most important in the speech. See also *Adaptation, Emphasis, Factors of Attention, Interest, Motivation, Persuasion, Variety.*

Attitude A predisposition to respond favorably or unfavorably to a stimulus. Attitudes are learned. Once we have learned them, we are ready to act approvingly or disapprovingly whenever the stimulus that created them recurs. Having formed a distaste for cabbage, we no longer experiment with it; no menu that contains cabbage seems wholly good to us. What is commonly called an *appeal* in speaking is usually an attempt by the speaker to evoke some set of strong attitudes that his listeners share. By this means the speaker hopes to arouse his listeners' feelings, including perhaps a desire to reason. There are several facts about attitudes that are especially important to speakers: (1) each listener possesses attitudes that are inconsistent with one another, but, at any given moment, the attitudes actively influencing a listener will tend to be consistent; (2) people who share similar attitudes tend to congregate together, and often what is called the speech "*occasion*" can be defined best by describing the particular attitudes that made the people gather to hear the speaker; (3) we often have attitudes—even strong ones—that we would rather not put into words, so what people say they favor or disapprove does not always reflect their true attitudes; (4) to create new attitudes or to change old ones is always a slow process, almost never accomplished by a single speech. Note Jonathan Smith's adaptation to both favorable and unfavorable attitudes in "On the Federal Constitution," pp. 270-271, ll. 41-46, "I had been a member. . . . well enough without." See also *Opinion, Persuasion, Suggestion.*

Authority The source from which *opinion* or expert testimony is derived. Although we tend to think of authorities as individual people, agencies such as the Bureau of the Census or the New York *Times* serve as authorities in many speeches. The *credibility* of an authority usually depends on the general *prestige,* the known or demonstrated competence, and the consistency of the source. Thus, whether a speaker introduces direct quotations from his authority or cites the authority indirectly, he ought to state the qualifications of his source unless the authority is already well known to his listeners. The *supporting material* drawn from a well-qualified and eminent authority not only serves as a form of *evidence* but also constitutes a form of *suggestion* because men tend to believe readily and often uncritically those whom they respect. Lincoln paraphrased Jesus when he said, "A house divided against itself cannot stand." The quotation probably had more suggestive than logical force for his listeners; the same opinion is doubly convincing today, for we give it the authority of both Jesus and Lincoln. Who, now, analyzes the evidence behind the quotation? Note the uses of eminent authorities to provide evidence and to lend impressiveness to various topics in "Changing Concepts of Public Service," p. 236, par. 30; p. 237, par. 44; and p. 238, pars. 54-55. See also "The Philosophy of Social Justice Through Social Action," pp. 133-134, pars. 33-45; "The South Respects the Written Constitution," p. 148, pars. 78-80; "The Case Against Segregated Schools," p. 152, pars. 26-28; "Administered Prices," p. 201, pars. 18-21.

b

Body That portion of a speech or essay containing the support or explication of the *central idea* or thesis. A speech or essay will always contain some *proposition,* stated or implied, and a *proof* of the proposition. This proof forms the body of the composition. To the proposition and proof, an *introduction* and a *conclusion* may be appended as the audience requires. "The Challenge of Abundance," pp. 221-226, has no introduction; par. 1 begins the body with proof that there is a problem.

Burden of Proof The responsibility for providing full, affirmative support in argument. In almost all situations those who propose something are expected by their hearers or readers to furnish convincing proofs in favor of their proposal. This is the general burden of proof that goes with initiating ideas, but sometimes there are also special rules or customs that prescribe more exactly where and how the burden of proof shall fall. In United States courts whoever prosecutes is required to prove guilt, while the defendant need only maintain the innocence the law already presumes in his favor. In certain parliamentary situations and in school debate it is the custom to require that those who advocate a change from existing practices shall assume the burden of proving the change better than any alternative. Except where there are special rules of this sort, persuaders must study their audiences to discover just what burdens of proof must be assumed. Since commencement speakers usually praise education—as is almost expected of them—they need not prove to their audience that education is necessary and desirable unless they recommend further education.

c

Causal Relationship The relationship between things or ideas that answers the question "Why?" Persons of Western culture tend to assume that whatever exists must have had a cause and that if any force is exerted some effect must follow. It is therefore necessary in any discourse to be explicit about why alleged effects came into being and what consequences follow from any "cause" that is discussed. The basic conditions to be proved about an alleged causal relationship in *persuasion* are these: (1) that the relationship between the supposed cause and its supposed effect is a steady and invariable one, and (2) that the supposed cause is sufficiently strong to produce the alleged effect. In *exposition* the communicator's chief task is sometimes to show simply and clearly how causes and their effects are interrelated, as when the thrust of a jet engine is to be explained. Even in a *narrative* it is essential to clarify why the events of the narrative flow as they do. Causality, then, is either a relationship that has to be clarified or proved or a relationship that suggests a way of dividing and organizing a discourse. See "The Inner City—Our Shame," p. 248, pars. 10-12, where the speaker amplifies the effects of an alleged cause (overcrowding); "Science and Society," pp. 79-81, pars. 1-12. See also *Patterns of Organization.*

Cause to Effect, Argument from That form of argument in which the communicator first shows that a given force (cause) is at work and then undertakes to prove that some consequence was or will be produced by the cause. See "The Philosophy of Social Justice Through Social Action," pp. 131-132, pars. 12-15; "The Challenge of Abundance," pp. 222-223, par. 9. See also *Causal Relationship, Effect to Cause, Patterns of Organization.*

Central Idea A *proposition* or statement that expresses the essential meaning of an entire communication. To reveal its truth is the function of all *amplification* and *proof* in the discourse. In *persuasion* the central idea is the proposition to be proved; in *exposition* it is the statement to be clarified; in *description* it is a statement characterizing the spatial relations which the discourse will detail. Because of the limitations of auditory *attention,* the central idea of a speech must be especially explicit and frequently deserves repetition. In persuasive discourse, especially when the audience is hesitant or hostile, the central idea may be withheld until the proofs have rendered it acceptable, but it should still dominate the persuader's planning and presentation. Other terms synonymous with central idea are subject sentence, thesis, and theme statement. See Reuther, "Administered Prices," p. 200, par. 3. In "Changing Concepts of Public Service," pp. 233-240, the central idea is stated in different ways in pars. 3, 5, 15, 18, 51, 56. There is no explicit statement of the central idea in "Address to the Russian People," pp. 240-246, a speech to a presumably hesitant or hostile audience.

Character of the Speaker See *Ethos.*

Chronological Pattern See *Patterns of Organization.*

Clarity The quality of being fully understandable. In rhetoric this term is most often used in reference to *style*. Clarity in style is attained through precise and familiar language, conventional usage and word order in grammatical construction, and simplicity and directness in all the functions of composition and presentation. Because of the instability of listeners' *attention* speakers must seek to make all they say so clear that it will be instantaneously intelligible. For an especially luminous style, see "The World of Jazz," pp. 62-72. See also *Appropriateness, Liveliness*.

Classification See *Definition*.

Cliché Any term or phrase that is trite or hackneyed. "Those immutable laws which down the corridors of Time have guided the destiny of man" is pure cliché. *Figures of speech* and *epigrams* are especially likely to become clichés after being so widely used that familiarity destroys the imagery or originality that first made them strikingly communicative. See "Science and Society," p. 83, par. 32, first sentence.

Climax A culmination or high point. In rhetoric the term usually refers to the point in a discourse at which the greatest force or impact is achieved. Although we usually think of a climax as coming late in an experience, there is reason to believe that this is not always desirable in a speech. Experimental studies and speeches themselves show that the point of greatest impact comes sometimes with the first main point of a speech. It is, in any case, impossible to say that the climax of a speech must necessarily appear near the conclusion. In "The Man with the Muck-Rake" the climax of the speech seems to come in pars. 12-13, p. 105; for a climax at the end of the speech, see "The Inner City—Our Shame," pp. 248-249, pars. 16-18. See also *Attention, Interest, Patterns of Organization*.

Coherence Literally, sticking together. In discourse, the quality of relevance—all parts being relevant to the *central idea* and to each other. Note how carefully the sentences and the main divisions are locked together in "Science, Technology, and World Development," pp. 84-89.

Common Ground Any belief or feeling about which speaker and listener have shared *interests* or *attitudes*. Such a belief or feeling is an ideal basis for reasoning or *amplification*: the advocate of better roads should talk more of safety and convenience than of higher taxes. Whenever speakers can show that their knowledge or views are the same as those of the people they address, they may expect arguments and amplifications based on these topics to be favorably received. Note how Eliot in "What Is a Classic?" assumes that his audience is as interested in Virgil as he is. See also his reference to their scholarship, pp. 52-53, pars. 11 and 12. See also "The South Respects the Written Constitution." p. 144, par. 12; "Address to the Russian People," p. 241, pars. 9-10; "The City—A Cause for Statesmanship," p. 254, par. 41, "I know . . . this problem is." See also *Adaptation, Appeal, Attention, Ethos, Identification, Persuasion, Suggestion, Syllogism*.

Concession The voluntary yielding of a disputable point for the sake of gaining a strategical advantage in an argument or in order to win a hearing from listeners who are hostile to the speaker or his proposal. In making concessions, the speaker must take care not to concede any of the major points upon which the case rests nor to concede so many minor points that its strength is impaired. See "The South Respects the Written Constitution," p. 114, pars. 1-7; "The Case Against Segregated Schools," p. 151, par. 16; p. 152, par. 22; "The Challenge of Abundance," p. 224, pars. 16-17. See also *Common Ground, Yes Response*.

Conciseness Compactness of expression. A speech is concise when, because of the precision of the wording, the meaning may be grasped as easily and quickly as possible. The concise speech is not necessarily a brief speech. The speaker wishing to speak briefly cuts down on his ideas and supporting material; the speaker wishing to speak concisely keeps all the ideas and supporting material he thinks necessary for his purpose but communicates them in wording that is as exact and pithy as he can make it. The following sentence fails to be concise because of its many useless words. "In the case of Abraham Lincoln we find that he had a marked tendency to enjoy stories that can best be described as having a humorous character." All it says is that Lincoln enjoyed humorous stories. Words that in one fashion or another mean the opposite of conciseness are wordiness, verbosity, redundancy, and tautology. Note the ultraconciseness in Urey's list of intellectual developments, "Science and Society," pp. 81-82, pars. 16-25. See also "On the Federal Constitution," pp. 266-272.

Conclusion The last of the three major divisions of a speech, and as such to be distinguished from the *introduction* and the *body*. The conclusion usually takes the form of a summary or reiteration of the principal ideas presented in the body, or of an appeal for belief or action based upon those ideas. It should (1) grow out of the body easily and naturally, (2) be relatively brief, (3) touch once again upon the principal interests and concerns of the listeners, and (4) bring the speech to a satisfying termination esthetically as well as logically. For a "summary" type of conclusion, see "Crime and Criminals," pp. 181-182, par. 36. An "appeal" conclusion is exemplified by "The Case Against Segregated Schools," p. 153, par. 31. Cf. "The Haven of the Defeated," p. 163, pars. 26-27.

Concreteness Possessing the power to evoke sense impressions. Considered in absolute terms, concrete expressions evoke sense impressions (sight, hearing, touch, taste, smell) whereas abstract expressions do not. Considered in relative terms, concrete expressions are more specific than abstract terms and hence tend to evoke sense impressions to a higher degree. Notice how this works in the following series in which the words range from the general and abstract to the more specific and concrete: thing—vehicle—automobile—Studebaker—Studebaker hardtop—a white and gold Studebaker hardtop. Abstractions are necessary for ideas and concepts, but concrete words suggest the world of actual experience. Both are necessary in the typical speech. The weakness in many speeches is that the speaker slights the concrete. See "The American Family," p. 155, pars. 4-7; "Address to the Russian People," p. 241 par. 9. Note also the concreteness in Zimmermann's speech, "Mingled Blood," pp. 99-101.

Connotation A complex of associations brought to mind by a word. A connotation is distinct, therefore, from a *denotation*, which is the dictionary definition of a word, stripped of its emotional overtones. The *American College Dictionary* gives the same denotations for "sweat" and "perspire": to excrete watery fluid through the pores. But the connotations of the words are quite different. "Sweat" brings to mind such things as laborers, athletes, horses, and locker rooms. "Perspire," on the other hand, suggests more genteel persons, or at least more genteel activities: a hot night at a dance, a girl with a moist forehead, a man's dress shirt getting wet under the arm.

Connotations can be roughly divided into two classes: group connotations and individual connotations. The first are the connotations common to a large number of people because of shared experience. For example, "Red" suggests danger or communism to many people; "green" suggests "go" or envy; "Cadillac" suggests wealth and refined living. Because of your unique experience, however, "red" may suggest to you alone a red sports car you smashed up the night after buying it. Obviously, speakers cannot capitalize on the individual connotations their listeners have for words, because they do not know what they are. But they can and do capitalize on group connotations. That is, if they want a favorable reaction to a man, they call him a "statesman" instead of a "politician," "firm" instead of "stubborn," "a public servant" instead of "a bureaucrat," "a man who is loyal to his friends" instead of "a tool of the interests that elected him." See "The City—A Cause for Statesmanship," p. 251, par. 7, ". . . the new low-income and minority ghettos"; par. 8, "metropolis"; p. 253, par. 27, "Half a building . . . through it."

Contrast The placing of two opposing ideas side by side in order to make them stand out in vivid opposition. See "The Philosophy of Social Justice Through Social Action," pp. 130-131, pars. 4-8; "Crime and Criminals," pp. 140-141, pars. 27-28; Reuther, "Administered Prices," p. 206, pars. 109-112.

Conversational Quality Having the tone and spirit of an animated conversation as carried on among educated persons. It is generally regarded as being the opposite of an "oratorical" pattern of style or delivery.

Suggesting that a speech should have a conversational quality does not mean that it is to be worded and delivered in exactly the same manner as when one converses. Although good conversation usually has the desirable qualities of directness, spontaneity, and informality, more often than not even the best conversation is marred by slovenly articulation, inadequate projection, imprecise word choice, awkward sentence structure, and the presence of colloquialisms and slang. Conversational quality, as the recommended spirit of good public speaking, does not include these undesirable qualities of conversation but emphasizes its desirable qualities to meet the demands of the more formal public situation.

Many of the elements that make for conversational quality are especially well exemplified in "The World of Jazz," pp. 62-72; "The Philosophy of Social Justice Through Social Action," pp. 129-135; and "Crime and Criminals," pp. 136-143.

Credibility Inherent probability or likelihood. The power of an assertion to win acceptance in its own right and prior to the introduction of any evidence or argument designed to support it.

An assertion may possess credibility because (1) it appears, to the best of the listeners' knowledge, reasonable or true to fact; (2) it is made by a person or a group of persons whose judgment and integrity the listeners respect; (3) the listeners wish to believe it since it attests to their happiness or security, or flatters their ego, or accords with their predispositions and prejudices.

A speaker should carefully gauge the probable degree of credibility an assertion will have for his listeners, and stand ready to introduce proof in support of any statement that does not seem likely to win ready acceptance in and of itself. See also *Probability*.

Cumulation A massing of specific details in an effort to clarify a complex matter, or a heaping up of many independent proofs to accumulate an overwhelming preponderance of evidence in favor of a disputable *proposition*.

Cumulation as a technique for winning assent by "piling on" a preponderance of independent proofs aims at a variety or multiplicity of support, and is to be distinguished from so-called "straight-line" reasoning, in which a speaker advances a single, carefully drawn argument to show that a certain conclusion must inevitably follow from admitted facts. A typical use of cumulation in argument is found in "Address to the Russian People," p. 243, pars. 28-32. See also *Cause to Effect, Deduction, Induction*.

d

Deduction The process of reasoning from two established or admitted propositions to a conclusion. For example, one may deduce that since virtually all humans have some form of spoken language, the people of a little-known Eskimo tribe probably have such a language. If this kind of reasoning is to seem reliable to those who hear it, at least two conditions must be met: (1) the audience must agree that virtually all humans do have some spoken language, and (2) they must accept the tribe in question as one that consists of humans. The full statement of a deduction is called a *syllogism*. Deductions may use premises of various types. In popular speech or writing the materials of deductive reasoning are usually only probably true, and they are generally so familiar to the audience that a part of the syllogistic form may be omitted without causing confusion. The illustration of a deduction given in the second sentence of this definition is of the abbreviated type. See *syllogism* for alternative forms of deduction. See "Remarks on Government Regulation of Broadcasting," p. 119, par. 22; "The South Respects the Written Constitution," pp. 144-145, pars. 12-14; p. 146, pars. 33-34; "Address to the Russian People," p. 244, pars. 49-53. See also *Induction, Logic*.

Definition A clarification of the meaning of an unusual word or phrase, or an explanation of the sense in which a term will be employed. Because communication cannot take place unless language is meaningful, the framing of clear and precise definitions may be an essential part of a speaker's task.

Common methods of definition employed by speakers include:

Definition by classification. Explaining the term to be defined by assigning it to a similar group of items or by dividing it into its natural subgroup. ("Mankind may be defined as consisting of all males and females of the human species.") See "Changing Concepts of Public Service," p. 233, par. 4.

Definition by context. Using the term in such a way that the sentence or passage makes its meaning clear. ("He who is *impetuous* will live to rue his hasty actions.")

Definition by etymology. Explaining the derivation of a term. ("*Propeller* comes from the Latin *pro* meaning 'forward,' and *pellere*, which means 'to drive.' Therefore a *propeller* is something that drives a movable object forward.")

Definition by genus and differentum. Putting the term to be defined into a genus or class and then differentiating it from other things in that class. ("Democracy is that form of government *[genus]* in which sovereignty resides not in a single man or class but in the people as a whole *[differentum]*.")

Definition by negation. Making clear what a term does not mean. ("Socialists, who believe in public ownership of the major means of production, are not to be confused with Communists, who believe in the common ownership of all goods.") See the definition of a "classic" in "What Is a Classic?" pp. 47-48, par. 1, and of "provincial," pp. 55-56, par. 20. See also "The Scarcity of Ideas," p. 228, par. 24.

Definition by synonym. Supplying a word closely related in meaning to the term being defined. ("A campanile, or bell tower.")

Stipulative definition. A definition more or less arbitrarily adopted by a speaker in order to develop a particular line of explanation or argument. ("For purposes of this discussion, let us define 'inflation' as that state of affairs in which too many dollars are chasing too few goods.") See the definition of "maturity" in "What Is a Classic?" pp. 48-49, par. 3; "The American Family," p. 156, par. 19; "The Greatest Invention of Them All," p. 194, par. 6; Reuther, "Administered

Prices," pp. 202-203, pars. 47-52; Curtice, "Administered Prices," p. 209, pars. 26-27; "The Challenge of Abundance," p. 222, par. 7.

Deliberative Speaking Speaking concerned with the formulation of public policy—the selection or rejection of courses of common action to be followed by a community, state, or nation. Characteristically persuasive in nature, oriented toward the future rather than the past, and centering in considerations of cost, feasibility, moral obligation, and the like.

Deliberative speaking is to be distinguished from *forensic speaking,* which deals with the justice or injustice of past actions; from informative speaking, which conveys knowledge or gives instructions; and from *epideictic speaking,* which is essentially "occasional" or ceremonial in nature. "Moppet Manipulation," pp. 113-116, is a deliberative speech which advocates individual and collective action along certain lines; "Remarks on Government Regulation of Broadcasting," pp. 116-121, is deliberative in that it opposes a prospective course of action.

Denotation The dictionary or scientific definition of a word. See *Connotation*.

Description A word picture of a person, scene, event, object, situation, or feeling; a systematic enumeration of the essential qualities of a thing in an effort to make listeners understand how it looks, feels, tastes, smells, or sounds.

In order to convey a picture accurately through language, a speaker must (1) mention crucial rather than trivial details; (2) select words that represent these details precisely, and that can be understood easily by the audience; (3) order the selected details into a systematic pattern (space order, time order, etc.); and (4) observe the traditional requirements of coherence and emphasis. See "Mingled Blood," p. 100, pars. 10-11; "The American Family," p. 155, pars. 4-6; pp. 155-156, par. 10; "The Haven of the Defeated," p. 161, par. 6; pp. 161-162, pars. 9-11. See also *Coherence, Emphasis, Imagery, Narrative*.

Dilemma An argument that poses two equally undesirable alternatives, one of which must, as a practical matter, be selected. ("If you always speak the truth, men will despise you; if you do not, the Gods will despise you.")

The dilemma is frequently used by speakers as a "special method of *refutation*" to show that a policy advocated by an opponent can have only two results, either of which would be undesirable. ("If, as Mr. Jones proposes, we reduce our present air strength, either we shall have to double or triple appropriations for our already expensive rocket development program, or we shall be entirely without means of retaliation in case we are attacked.")

If a dilemma is to have validity as an argument the alternatives to which it points must (1) follow as necessary effects of the policy proposed, (2) be all-inclusive, and (3) be mutually exclusive. Occasionally speakers employ trilemmas. These are like dilemmas in all respects except that they proffer three choices instead of two. See "Remarks on Government Regulation of Broadcasting," pp. 118-119, par. 13; p. 119, par. 15. See also *Causal Relationship*.

Direct Discourse Discourse in which the speech or writing of another person is quoted exactly. It is to be distinguished, therefore, from indirect discourse and paraphrase. Indirect discourse is discourse in which the phrasing of another is imbedded in the speaker's sentence with such adjustments as are necessary to maintain coherence. Paraphrase is a free rendering of the discourse of another.

Direct discourse (in quotation marks). Alexander Pope wrote: "To err is human; to forgive divine." See "Social Morality," p. 179, par. 1.

Indirect discourse. Alexander Pope once wrote that to err is human, to forgive divine. See "Moppet Manipulation," p. 115, par. 9, "Dr. Frances . . . to the store."

Paraphrase. To make mistakes is a consequence of our humanity, but to forgive mistakes is a sign of our divinity. See "The Man with the Muck-Rake," p. 103, par. 2.

Drive Persistent goal-directed behavior, arising from an internal stimulus and terminating when the desired goal is achieved. Often referred to as a "basic wish" or "motive."

Most psychologists classify drives as "primary" or "secondary." Primary drives (hunger, thirst, etc.) arise out of recognized physiological needs; secondary drives (desire for ego satisfaction, security, property, etc.) are socially or environmentally produced. Authors of textbooks in public speaking list "drives" in many different ways, some recognizing only four or five, and others cataloging as many as thirty. Among the drives most commonly named, however, are health and personal well-being, self-advancement, security of property and possessions, sex, and ease and personal enjoyment. These also are probably the drives most frequently invoked in speeches to persuade, stimulate, or actuate.

When a public speaker tries to make use of a drive or motive he says in effect, "Do as I recommend, and you will be secure or rich or happy or healthy or will attain a higher status." For an appeal to "security," see Reuther, "Administered Prices," p. 200, pars. 7-10. See also *Motivation*.

e

Effect to Cause, Argument from That form of argument in which the speaker first points to some result or consequence and then undertakes to show the cause that produced it. See "Crime and Criminals," pp. 138-139, pars. 14-15; "The Case Against Segregated Schools," p. 152, par. 21; "The Haven of the Defeated," p. 162, par. 14; Curtice, "Administered Prices," pp. 210-211, pars. 49-50. See also *Causal Relationship, Cause to Effect, Patterns of Organization*.

Emotion Very loosely, any "feeling." More precisely, an emotion is any response of such strength that it is accompanied by physiological changes such as changes in pulse rate, breathing rate, perspiration, etc. Emotions, understood in this sense, not only change our biological processes (making possible "lie-detecting" instruments), but they also incline us toward more complex behaviors such as sobbing, wringing the hands, running, thinking, speaking. Ideas and even single words can be emotion-producing stimuli; the emotions they produce within us may cause us to seek relief through fearful, angry, affectionate, thoughtful, or other kinds of behavior that relieve the psychological tensions produced by what we hear. When this happens, it is sometimes said that what we heard "appealed" to fear, or to hate, or to love, or to reason. The speaker's business, then, is to try to control the emotional responses of his listeners, for, as Aristotle insisted, an important part of persuasion "is effected through the audience, when they are brought by the speech into a state of emotion; . . . we give very different decisions under the sway of pain or joy, and liking or hatred." See also *Appeal, Attitude, Common Ground, Connotation, Humor, Identification, Motivation, Persuasion, Proof*.

Emphasis Forcefulness; the means by which anything is made to stand out or to seize the *attention*. Modern research suggests that among the most effective ways to achieve emphasis in speaking are: (1) to give an idea the first position in the *body* of the speech; (2) to repeat an idea three or four times, preferably at intervals, during the speech; (3) to call special attention to an idea, as by saying, "This is the point I especially want you to remember"; (4) to give a larger portion of one's time to one idea than to others. Since any change tends to seize the attention, ideas may also be emphasized if they are delivered with gestures, pauses, or other behaviors even slightly out of the ordinary. Any method of emphasis, of course, can become boring or absurd if used too often; hence, there must be *variety* even in methods of emphasis. "Address to the Russian People," p. 243, pars. 29-33, " . . . rejected by the USSR," illustrates emphasis by repetition. In "The Moral Bankruptcy of Television," pp. 109-110, pars. 3-9, the greater time given to the indictment of American tendencies and of TV make the criticism seem more significant than any of the briefly discussed solutions. That the criticism has first position in the address further emphasizes this topic. See Curtice, "Administered Prices," p. 209, par. 20; p. 210, par. 30. See also *Climax, Force, Impressiveness, Patterns of Organization, Repetition, Rhythm, Vividness.*

Ends of Speaking The aims or general purposes for which men speak, called by some writers "the rhetorical purposes." Most writers classify the ends of speaking according to the kinds of audience response a speaker wishes to elicit; thus, one finds the ends of speaking divided in such ways as these: to please, to inform, and to move; to inform, to convince, to persuade, and to entertain; to inform, to stimulate, to actuate, and to entertain; or to report, to inquire, to persuade, and to evoke. Any of these classifications can be useful if it reminds the speaker that he must make some single aim, and only one, dominate each speech.

Epideictic Speaking Literally to show forth; display. The name traditionally given to speaking done on commemorative or patriotic occasions (at dedications and commencement exercises; on Memorial Day, the Fourth of July, etc.), and including speeches of tribute or eulogy. As generally used today, the term "epideictic" also refers to the more specialized "forms" of public address—speeches of presentation, acceptance, welcome, and the like. See also *Deliberative Speaking, Forensic Speaking.*

Epigram A terse witty statement. An epigram can be especially useful in pinning down a point because its ingenuity attracts attention and its brevity makes it easily remembered. The following are two examples from Mark Twain:

"The man who is a pessimist before forty-eight knows too much; if he is an optimist after it, he knows too little."

"Let us so live that when we come to die even the undertaker will be sorry."

See "The Philosophy of Social Justice Through Social Action," p. 133, par. 28, " . . . if they are paternalistic, I am a father." Epigrams in Emerson's "The American Scholar," pp. 36-46, can be numbered by the score.

Ethos The *proof* or persuasiveness that comes from the source of a communication. This influence may spring from the reputation of a speaker or the group he is known to represent; it will always grow or shrivel, depending on his behavior, as he appears before his audience. Aristotle said of these influences, "We might almost affirm that ethos is the most potent of all the means of persuasion." Modern research demonstrates that he was right, at least concerning immediate responses to a communication. Just how "ethical proofs" affect our delayed responses to things said is not yet understood in psychology or rhetoric. The fact of greatest importance to the speaker is that all his behaviors —selection of ideas, their arrangement, their expression in language, and their delivery—inevitably add to or detract from the ethical reinforcement he, himself, gives to his message. In "The Moral Bankruptcy of Television," p. 110, par. 11, "For example . . . Trendex ratings" illustrates a speaker qualifying himself by pointing to his special experience. See also *Attitude, Authority, Credibility, Identification, Motivation, Persuasion, Suggestion.*

Etymology See *Definition.*

Euphemism A mild or prestigious term substituted for one considered unpleasantly direct. We live in a world of euphemisms: "pass away" for "die," "powder room" for "women's toilet," "lower level" for "basement," "mortician" for "undertaker," "plumbing engineer" for "plumber," "recession" for "depression," and so on. Since euphemisms tend to draw a veil over reality, they should be strenuously avoided unless the more direct word is likely to give pain to a listener. See "The Inner City—Our Shame," p. 247, par. 3, "uncles"; "Remarks on Government Regulation of Broadcasting," p. 117, par. 1, "But it . . . the jury's courage" euphemistically refers to recent criticism of broadcasting.

Evidence Those matters of *fact* and *opinion* that underlie and support argument; the data upon which a speaker bases his *proof* of a contention.

As employed in speeches, evidence usually takes one of three forms: *statistics,* quotations from *authorities,* or *examples.* To be of value in proof, evidence must be (1) recent, (2) sufficient in quantity, (3) germane to the point to be established, and (4) derived from a reliable source. Moreover, a speaker has the moral obligation to report fully and fairly the evidence upon which his argument rests. "The City—A Cause for Statesmanship," pp. 252-253, par. 26, "Last week . . . can do this job," illustrates use of statistical evidence within an example that rests on the authority of "a friend." See also *Argument, Supporting Material.*

Example An instance or sample specimen selected from a larger group of items of the same general class. A leaf may be held up as an example of foliage, or the work of a mechanical engineer may be given as an example of what engineers do. Examples of this sort clarify general ideas and are especially useful in *exposition.* Some writers use the term "illustration" for such examples to distinguish them from examples used as *proof.* A single example usually forms a weak proof; audiences are more impressed by several examples than by only one, no matter how representative the single example is shown to be. Only the naïve believe that the first swallow to arrive proves that summer has also come. The rhetorical effectiveness of examples lies primarily in their concreteness. See "Remarks on Government Regulation of Broadcasting," p. 118, par. 10; "Crime and Criminals," pp. 137-138, pars. 5-8; pp. 139-140, pars. 21-24; "The South Respects the Written Constitution," p. 145, pars. 17-22; "The Scarcity of Ideas," p. 227, pars. 15-16.

Exposition The term applied to a class of rhetorical processes and also to the compositions produced by these processes. Exposition processes show the nature or character of something by revealing how its parts are related to each other, how the parts form the whole, how a thing is produced or evolves through a series of interrelated stages, etc. A composition, written or oral, in which the chief object is to inform others by means of these processes is also called an exposition. *Clarity* is the foremost requirement in successful exposition; the special forms of support most commonly used to attain clarity in exposition are comparison, *definition, example, statistics,* and visual aids (such as graphs, charts, pictures, and the like). See "What Is a Classic?" pp. 47-57; Reuther, "Administered Prices," p. 202, pars. 41-45; p. 203, pars. 57-61; p. 204, pars. 70-78; pp. 206-207, pars. 116-133; Curtice, "Administered

Prices," pp. 208-209, pars. 11-15. See also *Amplification, Analogy, Causal Relationship, Central Idea, Patterns of Organization.*

f

Fable A short tale designed to teach a moral. Frequently it uses animals or inanimate objects as characters. Some of the best known are such fables of Aesop as "The Tortoise and the Hare" and "The Fox and the Grapes." Fables are useful in speech to draw attention to moral considerations. Their rather childlike simplicity makes them easy to follow and to remember.

Fact An item of knowledge; something known with reasonable certainty. A fact is capable of objective confirmation and so is to be distinguished from *opinion*. See *Evidence*.

Factors of Attention Special characteristics or qualities of discourse that tend to enhance its interest value and hence to capture the spontaneous attention of listeners. Generally, attention factors include such qualities as *activity*, conflict, novelty, primacy, proximity, and recency. Thus a speaker who gives activity and movement to his ideas, or who brings ideas into conflict, or who deals with novel matters or treats old matters in a new way, or who selects a subject close to the interests of his audience or recent in time, will, as a general rule, hold attention better than one whose ideas are static, or hackneyed, or not immediately related to the concerns of his listeners. See "Address to the Russian People," pp. 243-244, pars. 41-44, in which the speaker uses the listeners' high interest in things American as an attention factor.

Figures of Speech Expressions which make their point not literally and directly but in terms of something else. Consider these two sentences: *She's a very attractive girl* and *She's a doll*. They both mean the same thing, but in the first the words all carry their literal, dictionary meaning. In the second "doll" does not have its literal meaning of a toy puppet but a figurative meaning which colorfully suggests the girl's attractiveness. As this example suggests, figures of speech are useful because they can be vivid and memorable and because they often catch the quality of the object or action much more dramatically and economically than a literal statement can. They have to be used with some caution, however, because (a) if too many of them are used, they call attention to themselves and make a speech seem artificially ornamented, and (b) if they are not reasonably original, they give the speech a dull, hackneyed flavor. (See *Cliché*.) The most common figures of speech are these:

Simile. A stated comparison between things which, except for a particular quality, are essentially dissimilar. Usually a simile is introduced by *like* or *as*. *He kept after me just as if he were a badger. He kept after me like a badger*. See "What Is Truth?" p. 185, par. 22, "Suddenly, true reality . . . finally disappears."

Metaphor. An implied comparison between two essentially dissimilar things. In a metaphor, *like* and *as* are omitted. *The man is a badger if ever I saw one. He badgered me incessantly*. A mixed metaphor is a silly combination of two or more metaphors. *Let's set our helm and stay on this course until we reach the mountain peak of success*. See "What Is Truth?" p. 185, par. 22, "New darknesses . . . by the truth."

Personification. The attribution of human characteristics to animals or inanimate objects. *When a badger is sitting still, thinking about its sins, that's the time to be wary of it*. See "What Is Truth?" p. 185, par. 22, "Or you may be . . . acceptance of yourself"; "The City—A Cause for Statesmanship," p. 254, par. 46, "of everlasting . . . decay," and par. 47, "a Balkanized metropolis." See also *Allegory, Irony, Overstatement, Understatement*.

Force Energy or vigor of expression and, as such, a quality of style, as well as of delivery. In delivery a forceful manner results from appropriate arm and head gestures, alert muscle tension, animated facial expression, a faster than average speaking rate, and a volume adjusted to the meaning and mood of the material being presented. Forcefulness in style depends primarily upon the compelling quality of the speaker's ideas, but it may be enhanced if he employs many concrete words, uses short declarative sentences, casts selected passages into the active voice, omits unnecessary connectives, and uses with restraint and judgment a few epithets, metaphors, hyperboles, and *rhetorical questions*.

Contrary to the opinion sometimes held, force in delivery is not attained simply by shouting, nor does force in style result from exaggeration or bombast or from the uncontrolled use of exclamations and other strong figures. Rather, forcefulness springs from compelling ideas presented in an earnest and animated manner. "The Moral Bankruptcy of Television," p. 110, par. 9, illustrates force springing from the quality of the ideas, marred perhaps by too little restraint in the use of figures of speech and by undue sentence length. Note, on the other hand, in "Address to the Russian People," p. 244, pars. 51-54, how short, balanced statements in series produce forcefulness.

Forensic Speaking A term having two common but different meanings. In the loosest sense, forensic speaking or forensics may mean almost any kind of debate under formal rules. Thus used the term may refer to courtroom speaking, to highly organized parliamentary debate, to school debate, or even to oratory under contest rules.

The older and more exact use of the term refers only to the kind of speaking in which the speaker tries to prove that an accepted rule or code has or has not been broken sometime in the past. Accusing and defending, pleading the justice or injustice of past acts, are the commonest functions of such speaking; courtrooms, hearing rooms, and the like are the places where forensic speaking is most frequently heard. This meaning of the term goes back at least to the time of Aristotle and is the meaning still used in the study of rhetoric. Forensic speaking, in this sense, differs from *deliberative* and *epideictic speaking* in both subject and aim, for the forensic speech treats chiefly past events and "laws" with the object of securing a judgment of "right" or "wrong."

Generalization A statement about a group or class rather than about a particular member of the group or class. ("People seem to care less about the arms race than they used to." "European schools have high academic standards.") See "Science and Society," pp. 79-80, par. 2.

Good Will, Speech of A speech designed to deepen the listeners' appreciation of some profession, organization, or institution, thus unobtrusively securing their support for it. See "The Greatest Invention of Them All," pp. 193-198.

Humor Most broadly conceived, anything that is amusing. Chiefly, humor arises from a sudden perception of the incongruous, provided the perception does not bring a sense of pain. Any joke, therefore, is simply a sudden break in the listener's pattern of expectancy. He expects one thing and gets something quite incongruous to his expectation. Note how this works in an old wheeze used by Freud: Two men met near a European municipal bathing establishment. "Have you taken a bath?" asked one. "Why?" replied the other. "Is one missing?"

The basic uses of humor in speech are these: to entertain, to help explain a point, to affect the listener's thinking or conduct. Inexperienced speakers often find their humor gets no response from the audience. Most frequently the reason is that it has too little bearing on the subject and hence seems forced or that they introduce it too formally. The casual touch is best in handling humor. See "The Philosophy of Social Justice Through Social Action," p. 130, pars. 2-3; "The Value of Self-Criticism for Business and Labor," pp. 189-190, pars. 42-50. See also *Irony, Overstatement, Satire, Understatement*.

i

Identification Literally, the act of showing that one thing is the same as another; hence, in rhetoric the term usually applies to any process by which listeners or readers are brought to see that their interests, goals, or judgments are shared by a speaker or writer. Some writers use the term "identification" as a synonym for *common ground*. Note the repeated identifications of broadcasting and newspaper interests in "Remarks on Government Regulation of Broadcasting," pp. 116-121.

Illustration See *Example*.

Imagery The sensory details of a speech. Imagery includes all specific sensations suggested by a speech, i.e., those of sight, sound, touch, taste, and feeling. These sensations can be suggested either literally or figuratively. Images are useful rhetorically because they inevitably carry emotional overtones and hence help to affect the listener's feelings and attitudes. A speaker arguing for slum clearance, for example, might profitably attempt to evoke in the minds of his audience images of the sights, sounds, and odors characteristic of the local slum. These might well have more rhetorical effect than any amount of well-knit argument. See "Home Decoration," p. 74, par. 10; "The American Family," p. 155, pars. 4-7; "The Haven of the Defeated," p. 161, par. 6, "The Inner City—Our Shame," p. 247, par. 3.

Implication A form of argument (or series of arguments) in which the writer or speaker offers *proofs* without emphasizing the propositions they support. A speaker argues by implication if, without urging that we do the same, he tells us of a community that reduced its juvenile delinquency problem when a group of college students volunteered to assist in its youth centers. Entire speeches and essays are sometimes organized in this way; for example, a speaker wishing to stir enthusiasm for better schools may do so by presenting an *exposition* of conditions in the existing schools. In "Address to the Russian People," p. 245, par. 59 is an indirect or implicative argument about what is the wisest Soviet policy; "The Inner City—Our Shame," pp. 247-250, is also developed chiefly by implication. See also *Amplification, Appeal, Argument, Patterns of Organization, Persuasion, Suggestion*.

Impressiveness That quality of a speech, or of some passage within a speech, which causes it to have a deep and lasting influence upon the listener. Impressiveness does not derive from pompousness or oratorical display, but from significant ideas expressed in a manner appropriate to the topic, the audience, and the occasion. Style or delivery that is exhibitory or highly dramatic may render ideas momentarily striking, but it seldom makes them permanently impressive.

Induction The process of reasoning from specific cases. The reasoning may be from one instance to another, as in *analogy*, or from a number of instances to a general conclusion. The reliability of all such reasoning depends on the representativeness of the cases used and the accuracy of one's information about them. Absolute reliability in inductions is difficult to obtain because completely analagous instances are rare and because generalizations must always be inferred from a selected sample of known instances. The following example illustrates three degrees of reliability in generalizations based on the same data. A study of eight clothing and shoe factories shows all individual workers aged fifty-five to sixty are more productive than the average of the best and fastest group of young workers. From this we may induce that workers aged fifty-five to sixty are more productive than any similar group of young workers in these eight factories. This induction is highly reliable if the facts were correctly gathered. If we reason that in all clothing and shoe factories workers aged fifty-five to sixty are likely to be more productive than young workers, our induction will be fairly reliable if our eight factories are representative of the clothing and shoe production industries. To reason that elderly men make better workers than young men in all factories would be entirely unjustified, for there is no reason to think that our sample is representative of all workers and all factories. In offering inductions as *proofs* speakers must take special pains to satisfy their audiences that (1) the reasoning rests on truly representative cases, (2) the facts about the cases were accurately gathered, and (3) the conclusions offered claim no more than the sample will justify. See "Address to the Russian People," p. 243, pars. 28-33; "The City—A Cause for Statesmanship," p. 252, par. 24. See also *Deduction, Logic*.

Interest The focusing of one's *attention*. Whatever seems even momentarily important or pleasing arouses us—it attracts our attention because it interests us. No feature of speaking is ever without some positive or negative influence upon the listeners' interest in the whole message; hence every speaker should incorporate into his presentation all relevant qualities that arouse and sustain interest. Among the most important of these qualities are those that can be introduced through astute and sensitive composition; a number of such resources are identified above as *factors of attention*. See also *Activity, Common Ground, Imagery, Motivation, Variety*.

Introduction The first of the three major divisions of a speech, the other two being the *body* and the *conclusion*. The purpose of the introduction is to catch the *attention* of the listeners, arouse their interest in the subject under discussion, and prepare them to understand and appreciate the ideas that will be set forth in the body of the address.

An introduction which performs these functions well usually consists of highly concrete material, is striking without being cheap or sensational, and is closely related to the body of the speech in thought and mood. Common methods of developing the introduction include telling a story (serious or humorous), making a startling statement, asking a question or a series of questions, reading a quotation, or making a reference to the subject, audience, place, or occasion. Common faults of introductions are excessive length, abstractness in language or ideas, effusiveness, feigned sincerity, and the absence of an adequate *transition* into the body of the speech. Note how concisely the introduction to "Remarks on Government Regulation of Broadcasting," p. 117, pars. 1-5, makes reference to subject, audience, speaker, and occasion and uses unexpected quotations in startling language. An introduction developed by reference to the speaker's purpose may be found in "The Case Against Segregated Schools," p. 150, par. 1. Questions are used effectively in "The American Family," p. 155, par. 1. "The Value of Self-Criticism for Business and Labor," p. 187, par. 1, begins with a reference to the subject. Place and occasion are mentioned in "The Greatest Invention of Them All," p. 194, par. 1. Another reference to subject occurs in Curtice, "Administered Prices," p. 208, pars. 1-3.

Irony A figure of speech in which for the purpose of derision, however slight, the literal meaning is something other than the intended meaning. Often an ironic statement is the opposite of what is intended. "Let's spend more and more money on athletics so that American education can get better and better." It may, however, simply involve some obvious disparity of *understatement*. Any kind of material can be treated ironically: the light and playful, the deadly serious. The special value of irony is that its indirect approach calls attention to the material and, when ingeniously handled, provides intellectual pleasure at the same time that it persuades rhetorically. Socratic irony is irony in which the speaker pretends to be more naïve or ignorant than he really is. See the comment on coffee cups in "Home Decoration," p. 75, par. 15; "The Scarcity of Ideas," pp. 226-227, par. 9.

l

Liveliness Vivacity or sprightliness of expression; a language pattern marked by animated thought, vivid words, crisp form, and rapid movement. The opposite of a ponderous, unimaginative style.

Liveliness of expression depends ultimately upon a stock of fresh and lively ideas, but it may be enhanced by appropriate stylistic devices, such as metaphor, antithesis, and hyperbole, provided these are used in moderation and always to help communicate ideas rather than to embellish them. See also *Force, Impressiveness, Interest.*

Logic Logic can be practically defined as the science of reasoning reliably. When a connection is alleged to exist between two or more things or events, it becomes important to ask, "How reliable are the thought processes by which this connection was 'discovered'?" This is the basic question that logical rules and procedures explore; for example, one logical procedure for testing whether we may safely reason about A from what we already know about B is to explore the essential likenesses and dissimilarities of A and B. (See *Analogy*.) Some of these methods of testing the ways we think are fairly simple and familiar; others, like those of statistical analysis, are highly complex. Audiences apply at least the simpler logical tests to what they hear, especially in moments of doubt or disagreement with the speaker. With a speaker's help most audiences are also able to follow and to apply moderately complicated logical procedures, a fact of great value to speakers who must offer unfamiliar reasonings in behalf of a cause or who must criticize the logic of an opponent in *refutation*. When a speaker encourages his listeners to use logical procedures in validating conclusions, he is said to be using a "logical appeal."

m

Main Headings Usually, the statements that express the chief divisions of the *body* of the speech or essay. The term derives from the prominence these statements have in an outline, where they are assigned special symbols and indentations. Arrangements of main headings that are especially common are called standard *patterns of organization*. If a speech is organized in topical order, each major statement to be developed constitutes a special "topic" and, hence, is a main heading. If the disease-remedy pattern is used, the statements specifying the need, recommending a solution, and, perhaps, asserting the desirability of a solution will form the main headings. For *clarity* and *coherence* the main headings, taken together, must form a complete and sufficient justification of the *central idea;* the *proofs* and *amplifications* associated with each main heading should justify or clarify the main heading itself. In "Changing Concepts of Public Service," pp. 233-240, main headings are clearly announced in pars. 20, 29, 35, 40, 49.

Motivated Sequence A comprehensive *pattern of organization* based upon "the normal process of human thinking," and for this reason assumed to be particularly effective in motivating listeners to respond to the speaker's purpose.

As developed by its principal exponent, Professor Alan H. Monroe (*Principles and Types of Speech,* 4th ed. [Chicago: Scott, Foresman and Co., 1955]), the motivated sequence provides a basic pattern by which all types of speeches may be organized, "needing only to be modified by omitting or lengthening certain parts according to the particular situation." In speeches to actuate, all five steps of the sequence are present. These bear the functional names of Attention, Need, Satisfaction, Visualization, and Action. The first step catches the "attention" of the listeners; the second points to the existence of a problem or "need"; the third advances a proposal that will "satisfy" this need; the fourth "visualizes" the benefits to be derived from adopting the proposal; and the fifth, drawing upon the groundwork thus laid, makes a direct *appeal* for "action." In speeches to inform, only three steps—Attention, Need, and Satisfaction—are present. The function of the first is again to catch "attention"; the second shows the listeners why they "need" to know the information that is to be presented; and the third "satisfies" this "need" by presenting the information. Speeches to entertain may be either an extended development of the Attention Step or a mock-serious treatment of the speech to inform, convince, or actuate.

Motivation Generally, an inducement or incentive. In rhetoric the terms "motive" and "motivation" usually refer to very broad and overlapping descriptions of the goals for which human beings strive. Thus, it is said that among the strongest and most universal motivations of man are his desires for self-protection, love, admiration, comfort, etc. Such general listings of human motives are always loose and imprecise, but they serve to remind speakers of the predictable tendencies of most listeners. The wise speaker knows his hearers must be motivated by their own desires or *drives;* he should discover what their desires are likely to be, how strong they are, and whether any of them can be gratified by the actions he expects to urge. Franklin Roosevelt, in asking public support for foreign aid, once argued that only a churlish man would refuse the loan of his garden hose when his neighbor's house was on fire; his hint that to refuse the aid would bring ill repute added one more inducement to the case he had already made on England's behalf. A less astute speaker might have rested his case on England's need alone, neglecting to touch the always present desire to be well thought of.

n

Narrative The recounting of a connected succession of events, usually with a description of the persons involved and of the environment in which the events occurred. Occasionally an entire speech—particularly a speech to entertain or inform—may be developed as a narrative. Persuasive speeches often contain one or more narrative passages in which happenings that explain or support the speaker's contentions are related.

Narratives usually possess the attention factors of *activity* and conflict and may also have elements of suspense, *humor*, or surprise. Hence, they are high in interest value and may under appropriate circumstances be used to enliven almost any sort of speech. Listeners, however, are sometimes slow to grasp the point of a narrative or to see how it relates to the ideas and arguments being developed. Whenever a speaker suspects that the significance or relevance of a story may not be evident, he should pause to make these matters entirely clear. See "The South Respects the Written Constitution," pp. 146-147, pars. 49-52; Reuther, "Administered Prices," pp. 204-205, pars. 86-98.

O

Occasion The circumstances in which a speech occurs, including whatever reasons brought the audience together. This term is often used to refer to the entire environment in which a speech is set. Each set of conditions for speaking offers distinctive opportunities and imposes distinctive limitations; each setting affects the expectations and predispositions of the audience and prescribes forms and precedents that speakers may not safely violate. If, for example, the occasion is a legislative debate, the speaker must accomplish his purpose within the rules enforced by the legislative body; on the other hand, legislative speakers may choose their proofs more freely than courtroom pleaders, whose procedures and rules of evidence are more detailed and restrictive. Each ceremonial occasion also prescribes in some degree what may be said and how: the commencement speaker is not free to oppose education or to adopt the tone he might use in addressing a club smoker. Even physical circumstances are influential: the bishop is more impressive and the political fanatic more ridiculous when speaking from beneath an ancient Gothic arch; the highly personal anecdote needs an intimate and conversational setting, while the sonorous phrase sounds best from a somewhat distant platform. All these considerations and more are encompassed in the injunction that every effective speech must be adapted in all its details to its subject matter, audience, and occasion. Contrast the differing requirements of the speaking occasions for "The Place and the Price of Excellence," pp. 26-33; "The Moral Bankruptcy of Television," pp. 108-113; "Crime and Criminals," pp. 136-143; and "Address to the Russian People," pp. 240-246. See also *Adaptation*.

Opinion A judgment grounded in inconclusive evidence and, therefore, dependent, to a greater or lesser extent, upon a subjective evaluation of the meaning and worth of that evidence.

Opinions may be classified as sound or unsound, according to the amount and quality of the evidence on which they are based and the accuracy and objectivity with which that evidence is interpreted. Even the soundest of opinions, however, are disputable in a sense that "facts" are not.

The public speaker who expresses an opinion has the moral obligation of reporting the evidence upon which it rests and of evaluating that evidence as precisely and fairly as possible. For examples of opinions based on the speaker's own experience, see "The City—A Cause for Statesmanship," p. 254, pars. 41-42. For a second sense in which the term "opinion" is commonly used by writers of textbooks on public speaking, see *Attitude*.

Originality Freshness in ideas, interpretations, judgments, or proposals, and in the language in which these are communicated to listeners. The speaker who is original in his thinking does not rehearse facts and conclusions reported by others but, as a result of long study and reflection, advances worth-while creative insights of his own. Original expression conveys ideas in a fresh and sprightly manner and is free of overworked phrases, bromides, and *clichés*. Originality is an important quality in a speech not only because fresh ideas freshly expressed are more likely to prove interesting to listeners, but also because the speaker who thinks creatively makes a greater contribution to the intelligent solution of the problems with which he deals. Theodore Roosevelt's use of the image from *Pilgrim's Progress* met the standards of rhetorical originality and contributed to the lasting influence of the speech "The Man with the Muck-Rake," pp. 102-107.

Overstatement Exaggeration or hyperbole. Overstatement has the same value as caricature: it calls attention to an important aspect of the subject through gross exaggeration. To be successful, overstatement must be gross enough so that it is absurd, and original enough so that it attracts by its ingenuity. Mark Twain described a jack rabbit he shot at in this form: "He dropped his ears, set up his tail, and left for San Francisco at a speed which can only be described as a flash and a vanish! Long after he was out of sight we could hear him whiz." Wilde is probably indulging in overstatement when he says a museum could be filled with the different kinds of water jugs used in hot countries, "Home Decoration," p. 74, par. 10.

Parable A short tale designed to convey a moral truth. Easily the most famous examples are the parables of Jesus, such as that of the prodigal son, the tares and the wheat, or the mustard seed. Although parables oversimplify reality, they are useful in putting across a single, unadorned idea.

Parallel Construction Construction in which ideas of equal worth are given the same syntactical form. That is, two or more ideas are said to be in parallel construction if they appear, for example, as independent clauses, as dependent clauses, as participial phrases, or as words. The connectives most used in parallel construction are *and, but, for, either . . . or,* and *neither . . . nor*. Parallel construction is especially useful in pairing items, in listing a series, or in establishing an *antithesis*. It tends to make prose rhythms more regular than they usually are, and for this reason it is often employed at the end of a speech to provide emotional intensity. For good examples of the extended use of parallel construction, turn to the Lord's Prayer in the King James Version of the Bible or to the Gettysburg Address. See "The Haven of the Defeated," p. 162, par. 14.

Patterns of Organization The structural plan or framework of a speech. In selecting the pattern of organization to be followed in any given speech, the speaker should carefully consider not only the ideas to be communicated but also his purpose (to entertain, inform, persuade, etc.) and the attitude of the audience (friendly, neutral, hostile). Standard patterns, which may be adapted or modified to meet specific speaking situations, include these:

Cause to effect order. Pointing first to a generative or causal force and then to the result it may be expected to produce. ("Wages in the steel industry continue to rise. Therefore, we may expect the price of steel products to increase.")

Chronological order. Describing events in the order in which they occurred, or giving instructions by telling what to do first, what second, etc. ("On the evening of the murder Jones left home at seven o'clock and went to the filling station. From there. . . .")

Deductive order. Urging the acceptance of a controversial claim on the ground that its truth, justice, or practicability follows of necessity from an accepted principle. ("If, as we believe, all Americans are entitled to religious freedom, then members of all religious sects, however unpopular, should be allowed to worship as they please.")

Disease-remedy or problem-solution order. Pointing first to the existence of a problem or evil, and then offering a program to correct it. ("Our city is overrun with slums. We should have an urban renewal program.") The corrective program that is set forth must meet two principal criteria: (1) it must be practicable—that is, capable of being put into effect and of actually eliminating the evil in question; (2) it must be desirable—that is, it must not introduce new and worse evils of its own. The farmer who burns down his barn to rid it of rats adopts a practicable solution but not a desirable one. See "The Haven of the Defeated," pp. 160-164; "On the Federal Constitution," pp. 266-272.

Effect to cause order. Accounting for an existing situation by explaining the cause that produced it. ("Today our military establishment is inadequate and outmoded. Why? Because in recent years we have not made adequate appropriations for defense.")

Elimination order. Sometimes called the "method of residues." Considering all possible interpretations of a subject or all possible solutions to a problem, and then showing that all except one are incorrect, impracticable, or undesirable. ("We could solve the problem of overcrowded schools by increasing the size of classes, running double shifts, making wider use of televised instruction, or by hiring more teachers and constructing more school buildings. Of these possible remedies, however, all except the last would seriously impair the quality of education our children receive.")

Inductive order. Using a number of individual cases or instances as the basis for a generalization concerning additional members of the same class. ("A concentration of funds and research efforts was effective in curbing polio. The same thing happened with tuberculosis, typhoid, and the diseases of infancy. Therefore, in all probability, cancer can be conquered through similar efforts.")

Reflective order. Organizing a speech according to the five steps in "reflective thinking" as outlined by the philosopher John Dewey: (1) recognition of problem; (2) description and delimitation of problem; (3) suggestion of possible solutions; (4) comparative evaluation and testing of solutions; (5) selection of preferred solution. ("1. The sharp drop in farm income poses a problem. 2. This is primarily a problem of overproduction. 3. To solve this problem, we could ship more food abroad, consume more at home, move families off the farm, or continue our policy of price supports. 4. But shipping more food abroad would glut the world market. We cannot consume more at home. Moving families off the farm would seriously disrupt their lives. 5. On the whole, therefore, the best solution is to continue our program of price supports.") See "Science, Technology, and World Development," pp. 84-89.

Space order. Describing how something looks by proceeding systematically from left to right, top to bottom, front to back, etc., mentioning each part or aspect in order. ("At the front of the great hall stands the golden throne. To its left is an impressive Flemish tapestry. Immediately in front of the tapestry is a carved table, and to its right a stool.")

Topical order. Arranging ideas in an order dictated by the subject being discussed. ("Intelligent reading requires understanding the general purpose and structure of a book, as well as mastering the detailed information it presents. Let us consider, first, how to discover a book's purpose and structure; then how to master its details.") See "Changing Concepts of Public Service," pp. 233-240; "Address to the Russian People," pp. 240-246.

Chronological, space, and topical orders lend themselves most naturally to informative speeches; cause to effect, deductive, disease-remedy, effect to cause, elimination, inductive, and reflective orders are best adapted to persuasive speeches. See also *Motivated Sequence.*

Periodic sentence A sentence in which the meaning is not completed until the end. Because they are more formal, periodic sentences are less common to our conversation than loose sentences, which continue after the main clause is completed. But they can be helpful in a speech requiring suspense and great emphasis on the word or words which come last.

Periodic sentence: "Whatever you may say of me or whatever you do to me, I will not retract."

Loose sentence: "I will not retract, no matter what you say about me or what you do to me."

Persuasion In general, any form of discourse that influences others in a predetermined way through some combination of information, reasoning, and *emotion.* To persuade through speech requires that one make his listeners give attention to those ideas, images, words, manners, etc., which will lead them to feel that accepting the recommendations of the speaker will be more satisfying than rejecting them. Some writers on rhetoric and logic seek to distinguish persuasion from *argument* and propaganda, but few are clearly agreed on how these processes differ from one another, if they do. It is generally agreed, however, that discourse ought to be called persuasive if it aims at modifying *attitudes, opinions,* and perhaps conduct. Most authorities also agree that to "be persuaded" of anything, one must have adopted some new way (to him) of responding to a situation or idea. For changes of this kind to occur there must be, somewhere, an incentive or *motivation* strong enough to make the change seem gratifying. These incentives or motivations may be brought to a listener's attention through the reasonings, the *suggestions,* and the *ethos* and *prestige* of the speaker. Thus, whatever meaning is assigned to the term "persuasion," it is clear that when speakers undertake to change any aspect of human behavior, they must find and offer their listeners the kinds of incentives that will make the new behavior seem more satisfying than the old. See also *Appeal, Common Ground, Logic, Proof.*

Precedent A type of *authority* drawn from previous actions or decisions, as of a court of law. See "The South Respects the Written Constitution," p. 145, pars. 22 and 28-29; p. 146, pars. 37-39 and 46. See also *Supporting Material.*

Prestige The power of arousing admiration or esteem that influences acceptance of spoken or written materials. The sources of such prestige include but often go beyond the *ethos* of a speaker. The reputations of those who help a speaker communicate his message and the impressiveness or unimpressiveness of the *occasion* are additional sources of prestige affecting the response to a speaker's message. If, for example, a speaker addresses his audience by radio or television, his prestige may be increased or diminished by the trust people have for these media of communication; also, the prestige of the program on which he appears and the reputation of the broadcasting station or network may add to or detract from his stature. Similarly, speakers gain or lose prestige according to the reputations of those who sponsor their appearances on public platforms. If others are known to have assisted a speaker in preparing his address, their reputations may also affect the esteem in which speaker and speech are held. In the persuasive process called *suggestion,* prestige is the most important single factor determining favorable or unfavorable audience response. The prestige of the presidency gave weight to ideas expressed in "The Man with the Muck-Rake," pp. 102-107; the prestige of religious office reinforced the criticisms in "The Moral Bankruptcy of Television," pp. 108-113; and, probably, the prestige of the Russian broadcasting services affected the credibility of "Address to the Russian People," pp. 240-246, in the eyes of the Russian audience.

Probability A degree of likelihood greater than possibility, but less than certainty; that which is more likely than not to be true, but concerning which we have no absolute assurance.

Since the choices and actions of men cannot be predicted accurately, speakers dealing with problems lying in the realm of human affairs or involving future events cannot be expected to prove their *propositions* conclusively (for example, to show that uniform marriage and divorce laws will *certainly* reduce the divorce rate; or that the introduction of an honor system on a college campus will *certainly* reduce cheating). Even in criminal law, where a man's life may be at stake, only proof "beyond reasonable doubt" is required. A speaker does, however, have the obligation of introducing a preponderance of proof to support any proposition that is not self-evident—the burden of showing that it is more likely than not to be true. His proof should always approach certainty to the fullest extent his subject matter permits. See also *Credibility*.

Proof Broadly, anything about a speech that induces belief or action. This general meaning is common in rhetoric, although in logic and science proof usually refers only to the result of evidence. Aristotle's view that rhetorical proof takes four forms is still widely accepted: there is proof (1) arising from the *logic* of reasoning and *evidence;* (2) arising from the feelings aroused in the audience *(emotion);* (3) arising from the reputation of the speaker and the impressions he creates while speaking *(ethos);* and (4) supplied by the introduction of such aids to argument as documents, witnesses, photographs, and the like. Whether an audience accepts, ignores, or rejects what it is told depends on the weight the hearers give to these classes of proof. While hearing a speech, the listener consciously or unconsciously reacts to the seeming reliability of the logic offered and accordingly tends to accept or reject these reasonings as justifications for belief; he allows the interests, attitudes, and feelings aroused by the speech to tell him whether accepting what he hears will bring him any personal gratification or pain; he judges the speaker to be a reliable or unreliable adviser and accordingly allows his impression of the messenger to color his impression of the message; and he is impressed or unimpressed by whatever documentation the speaker may exhibit and accordingly favors or deprecates the speaker's case. Of course, listeners do not respond as deliberately as this description suggests, but each of the four kinds of reaction to proofs contributes in some measure to the disapproval, indifference, or enthusiasm with which an audience finally responds to a speech. "Remarks on Government Regulation of Broadcasting," pp. 116-121, relies heavily on logic and identification; "The Inner City—Our Shame," pp. 246-250, seeks to arouse the emotion of sympathy as a proof; the speaker's ethos is especially important as proof in "On the Federal Constitution," pp. 266-272.

Proposition A statement, usually in the form of a simple declarative sentence, expressing a point to be discussed. In the design of an *argument* the proposition states what the evidence proves; in the design of an *exposition* the proposition states what the *amplification* clarifies or reveals; in the design of a *description* the proposition characterizes the relationships to be set forth. The *central idea,* each *main heading,* and each *subheading* of persuasive, expository, or descriptive discourse should be capable of expression as propositions, even though they may or may not be uttered in this form when the message is actually delivered or written. The resolutions commonly used in debate are also propositions, despite the parliamentary or judicial form in which they are sometimes phrased; hence, one finds the term "proposition" occasionally used to refer exclusively to the statement of a point for debate. For central idea as proposition see "The Man with the Muck-Rake," p. 103, par. 5; for main heading as proposition see "Address to the Russian People," p. 242, par. 19; for subheading as proposition see "The Challenge of Abundance," pp. 222-223, par. 9. See also *Assertion*.

Proverb A wise saying or useful idea expressed in a brief, ingenious fashion ("A penny saved is a penny earned"). See "Address to the Russian People," p. 242, par. 17.

Rebuttal Literally, a repulsing or driving back. In a speech, the rebuilding of an argument after it has been attacked.

Rebuttal may take the form of (1) a demonstration that the attack leveled against an argument is irrelevant, inadequate, or unfair; (2) the introduction of additional evidence or reasoning to support an argument; or (3) an attack upon an alternative or counterargument advanced by an opponent. See "The Challenge of Abundance," p. 225, par. 23; "The City—A Cause for Statesmanship," pp. 252-253, par. 26. See also *Refutation*.

Reflective Thinking This term refers to the process of inquiry that follows the stages of inductive thought outlined by John Dewey (see *Patterns of Organization, Reflective order.*) Reflective thinking is disciplined, logically ordered thinking about any problem for which a solution is needed. Its opposite is impulsive or emotional decision making. Reflective thinking, thus, is a method of intellectual attack; good speakers use it constantly in research and in planning speeches. A speaker intending to speak on "Crime and Punishment" would (1) need to find out what to say about the subject and what to disregard. If he (2) tried to delimit and describe his problem, he might discover he must know two kinds of things about his subject: (a) the facts about crime and punishment today and (b) what his audience will already know about the subject. His reflection can now move forward another step to (3) review the ways (solutions) by which he can acquire the two kinds of information he needs: reading, interviewing, speculating, visiting penal institutions, making audience surveys, etc. From among these options he may (4) choose what seem to be the most promising courses of action and (5) verify the wisdom of his choices by trying them out. By the same intellectual method speakers explore what *propositions* deserve *proof* and *amplification,* what will be the ideal kind of *evidence,* and many other problems of speech planning and composition. And if it seems best to urge an audience to explore a problem for itself, the reflective order may prove the best available *pattern of organization*.

Refutation An attempt to neutralize or destroy an argument with which one disagrees. To be distinguished from *rebuttal,* which is the process of rebuilding an argument after it has been attacked.

A speaker may refute an argument (1) by showing that the evidence upon which it rests is insufficient, irrelevant, comes from an unreliable or biased source, or has been unfairly reported; (2) by showing that the conclusion drawn from the evidence is unwarranted; (3) by using one or more of the so-called "special methods of refutation"—*dilemma,* elimination, reduction to absurdity, or *turning the tables*.

The destruction of opposing arguments through refutation lends only indirect support to the speaker's own case. In order to establish his own contentions, he must also introduce argumentation to support them. A speaker cannot prove that he is right merely by proving that his opponent is wrong. See "The Moral Bankruptcy of Television," p. 110, par. 11; "The Case Against Segregated Schools," pp. 144-145, pars. 3-29; Curtice, "Administered Prices," pp. 208-210, pars. 4-34; pp. 211-212, pars. 52-72; "The Scarcity of Ideas," p. 226, par. 8.

Repetition The act of saying again. To say anything more than once increases the likelihood that the statement will be perceived and remembered by a listener, but unless repetition is accompanied by *variety*, as in restatement, its power to command *attention* begins to diminish after the third or fourth utterance. "Repetition accompanied by sufficient variety to lend interest but with sufficient uniformity to acquire a constant meaning, produces a genuine cumulative effect" (H. L. Hollingworth, *The Psychology of the Audience* [New York: American Book Company, 1935], p. 144). In this sense repetition becomes a form of *supporting material*, even though it adds no new content or *proof*. Note the number of times identification of broadcasting and newspaper interests is reaffirmed in "Remarks on Government Regulation of Broadcasting," pp. 116-121. For examples of repetition in language for emphasis and clarification, see "The Philosophy of Social Justice Through Social Action," pp. 132-133, par. 25, and p. 134, par. 47; "The Value of Self-Criticism for Business and Labor," p. 188, par. 9, and p. 189, par. 30; Reuther, "Administered Prices," p. 201, par. 26; Curtice, "Administered Prices," pp. 209-210, par. 29.

Reputation The qualities of character and intelligence imputed to any person. See also *Ethos, Prestige*.

Rhetorical Question A question asked for its effect on the audience and not because the speaker wants or needs an answer. It is often used to introduce a speech or a new topic or to emphasize a point. To be effective, a rhetorical question must be asked so that the answer is uncomplicated, obvious, and the same for almost everyone in the audience. "Isn't it clear, therefore, that we should all vote Democratic next Tuesday?" would not be an effective rhetorical question in an audience of Democrats and Republicans, but might be a successful one at a Democratic rally. See "The Moral Bankruptcy of Television," p. 110, par. 11; "The Philosophy of Social Justice Through Social Action," pp. 130-131, pars. 7, 9-10, 13, 15; "The South Respects the Written Constitution," p. 145, pars. 24-26, and p. 146, pars. 32-33. Observe that the questions in "The City—A Cause for Statesmanship," p. 254, par. 38, are not rhetorical questions but express topics for further study.

Rhythm The movement of a speech in terms of sound, accent, tempo, and pauses. All speeches have rhythm, though in some it may be so irregular and jagged as to be hardly worthy of the name; in others it becomes so regular that the speech approaches free verse. Rhythm in speaking is not something to work for directly. An appealing rhythm is one of the happy consequences of correct syntax, variety in sentence structure and beginnings, coherence, and emphasis. It should be added that an appealing rhythm is also one that suits the subject. The rhythm of a call to arms is hardly appropriate for a funeral oration.

Ridicule Discourse designed to make fun of somebody or something. Ridicule ranges broadly from good-humored spoofing to the bitterest kind of jeering. To ridicule, one may, for example, mimic, mock, tease, scoff, deride, taunt, or jeer. Any kind of ridicule in a prepared speech, however, must be used with a deft touch, for applied too heavily it tends to make the speaker rather than the object of his ridicule look silly. See "Home Decoration," p. 74, par. 10; "The Philosophy of Social Justice Through Social Action," p. 133, par. 28.

S

Sarcasm Biting denunciation. Sarcasm may be ironical (that is, it may say one thing while obviously meaning another), or it may be direct. To be effective, sarcasm should be used sparingly. ("What a brilliant diplomat he would make: he thinks the Canary Islands are a bird sanctuary!") See "Crime and Criminals," p. 138, par. 11.

Satire Discourse that, by other than logical means, attempts to influence thought and conduct by exposing human frailties. Based on firm conviction, satire finds its targets in men's pretensions, follies, and vices. Its object is not amusement but indignation and reform. Its chief means are *humor, ridicule, irony, sarcasm,* and invective.

Burlesque is light satire which by distortion makes fun of a class or genre, such as college freshmen, political speeches, or TV westerns. Aiming at men's pretensions rather than their vices, the burlesquer is usually as much interested in providing amusement as he is in affecting thought and conduct.

Parody is light satire on a particular work, such as Poe's "Raven" or Lincoln's "Gettysburg Address." Parody is primarily for amusement and does not necessarily imply any lack of respect for the target of the spoofing.

Travesty is a burlesque in which a lofty subject is treated trivially.

Mock-epic is a burlesque in which a trivial subject is treated in a lofty style.

Sign, Argument from That form of argument in which a speaker claims that some outward mark or symptom is indicative of an inner state or condition. ("X country maintains an army, navy, and air force much larger than it needs for its own defense. This indicates [is a sign] that it has aggressive intentions against its neighbors.")

Signs may be classified as infallible or fallible, depending upon the degree of conclusiveness with which they indicate a state or condition. ("This metal is glowing red; therefore, it is hot." [infallible] "He drives a large car and owns a yacht; therefore, he is wealthy." [fallible]) See also *Cause to Effect*.

Slogan A brief, striking phrase, usually used to epitomize and make memorable the *central idea* of a persuasive speech. ("Millions for defense, but not one cent for tribute." "Fifty-four forty or fight." "We have nothing to fear but fear itself.") For a slogan used to evoke unfavorable attitudes, see "The Moral Bankruptcy of Television," p. 109, par. 6. In "The Philosophy of Social Justice Through Social Action," pp. 129-135, note how the title phrase is repeated at many points throughout the speech.

Specific Purpose The name given by various writers to two somewhat different kinds of purpose statements. As used by some, the term refers to a statement expressing both the *end of speaking* and the *central idea* of a speech. Under this interpretation, "I intend to persuade my audience that the officials of this city do not oppose organized crime with vigor," would be designated a statement of the speaker's specific purpose. Others apply the term to a statement expressing the general response expected from the audience. "I intend to persuade my audience that organized crime still threatens us," would be called a specific purpose statement under the second usage. Those who use the term in this narrower sense assume that the ideas by which the purpose is to be achieved will be epitomized in a second statement designated the subject sentence or central idea. Note that both interpretations presuppose that every speaker must have an exact awareness of his aim and of his major *proposition* if he is to speak with *clarity.* See "Changing Concepts of Public Service," p. 233, par. 3.

Statistics Numbers which express relationships among phenomena or summarize or interpret bodies of data. The forms of statistical information most commonly employed by speakers in explaining or supporting their ideas include means, modes, averages, parts or percentages of a whole, increases, decreases, and concomitant variations. See Reuther, "Administered Prices," p. 203, pars. 62-64.

Stereotype Literally, anything undistinguished by individual marks. A term applied and popularized by Walter Lippmann as a name for the incomplete "systems of thought" and "pictures in our heads" that represent our simplified interpretations of the things about us. We may, for example, simplify a complex system like capitalism into a less complete system which we think of as "competition"; often we also associate visual images with such conceptions—the image of a wealthy tycoon may represent capitalism. These stereotypes, like any other images or systems of thought, evoke favorable or unfavorable *attitudes* and *emotions* whenever they are raised to the level of consciousness. When this happens, we behave as though our stereotypes were true and complete systems or pictures. Speakers can scarcely hope to influence others persuasively unless they deal respectfully with their audiences' stereotypes and attitudes. Neither can be changed swiftly, so the wise persuader associates his cause with his listeners' stereotypes whenever he can and avoids those he would have to contradict were he to deal with them openly. Note the cautious indirection with which Jonathan Smith treats his listeners' stereotypes of lawyers, "moneyed men," and "learned men" in "On the Federal Constitution," pp. 271 and 272. See also *Suggestion.*

Striking Phrase or Statement An expression which because of its unusual stylistic qualities or novel juxtaposition of ideas makes a strong and lasting impression upon a listener. See "The Haven of the Defeated," p. 161, par. 2, "havens of defeat"; "The Value of Self-Criticism for Business and Labor," p. 188, par. 19, "junior-grade South Sea Bubble"; Reuther, "Administered Prices," p. 200, par. 7, "freedom's margin of survival."

Style The distinctive manner of a speech or a speaker. Style is a loosely used word and very hard to define. The expression "a speaker's style" may refer to his appearance, delivery, language, and voice; or it may refer to his language and delivery; or it may simply refer to his language. Whatever its scope, "style" is usually employed to designate the special characteristics of manner, as apart from content, that distinguish one speaker from another. When applied to the use of language, style is employed most specifically to designate the selection and arrangement of words. While there are as many styles as speakers, styles can roughly be divided into two groups: the simple (sometimes called the Attic) style, in which the speaker uses clear, simple words and uncomplicated sentence structure, and (2) the ornate (sometimes called the baroque or Hebraic or Isocratic or Ciceronian, depending on the nature of the ornateness), in which the speaker makes substantial use of *parallel constructions, antitheses,* long and frequent *periodic sentences, figures of speech,* alliteration, and other structural and sound devices. The only thing that can be said arbitrarily about style is that there is no such thing as a good style in any absolute sense. The best style for a speech is the one that permits the speaker to communicate his ideas to a particular audience in the most effective manner possible. For an example of very simple style see "The World of Jazz," pp. 62-72. A more ornate style is illustrated by "What Is Truth?" pp. 182-186. Note the contrasting styles used by the same speaker to express interpretations of facts and aspirations for the future in "The City—A Cause for Statesmanship," p. 254, par. 43 and p. 255, pars. 50-51.

Subheadings The *propositions* that state a point to be proved or clarified in support of a *main heading.* Like a main heading, the subheading gets its name from the position given it in an outline or brief —in this case a subordinate position. The subheadings under a main heading should, together, form a complete and sufficient justification of the main heading. See also *Analysis.*

Subject The topic with which a speech deals; what the speech is about.

In selecting a subject, the speaker should ask: (1) Does it "fit" me as an individual? Is it something I already know a good deal about and concerning which I want to learn more? (2) Does it "fit" the audience? Will they be interested in it and be able to understand it? (3) Does it "fit" the occasion? Can it be dealt with in the time allotted? Is it suitable in tenor and mood?

A common fault is the selection of a subject too broad to be covered in a speech of reasonable length. The best speech subjects usually result when the subject that first occurred to the speaker is carefully narrowed or when a certain segment of it is selected for presentation.

Subordination The process of arranging under each of the *main headings* of a speech those ideas or arguments that explain and support it. Proper subordination requires that subsidiary ideas or *subheadings* be narrower in scope and of less importance than the main heading, and that they directly support the main heading under which they are placed. If subheads vary among themselves in scope or importance, they should be arranged according to the two rules just stated. In "Moppet Manipulation," p. 115, the ideas expressed in par. 9 are plainly subordinated to the one in par. 8. See also "The Haven of the Defeated," p. 162, par. 13.

Suggestion The effect that occurs when a person responds to an idea uncritically or without reflection. The term may also refer to the practice of evoking such responses. Suggestion invites the listener to react automatically rather than to weigh supporting facts and arrive at a reasoned judgment.

Most authorities recognize two basic types of suggestion: direct and indirect. Direct suggestion consists of employing symbols (words, actions, visual effects, etc.) which, because of the previous conditioning of the listeners, tend to arouse predetermined responses the speaker wants. If a speaker repeatedly calls his proposal "patriotic," "economical," or "democratic," his listeners may accept these words at face value and view the proposal favorably; reference to an opposing proposal as "disloyal," "wasteful," or "muddle-headed" may tend to discredit it. Or a speaker may directly suggest that his listeners "Consider the cost in taxes" to change their focus of attention. Indirect suggestion is the process of establishing an idea without open reference to it, by arousing habitual responses to ideas consciously or unconsciously associated with it in listeners' minds. Without directly mentioning taxes, a speaker may call attention to them by saying, "My opponent's plan would increase the costs of government." If the listeners commonly associate governmental costs with taxes, their thoughts will automatically turn to that subject. Similarly, "Moon Glow" might be a good name for a face powder; though it has little meaning, it indirectly suggests beauty and romance. "Scritch," on the other hand, would be a poor choice; indirectly it may arouse the unfavorable responses associated with "scratch" and "itch."

A second important distinction is between positive and negative suggestion. Positive suggestion affirms an idea ("Candidate X is a business expert and is highly respected in Washington"); negative suggestion aims to reject it ("Ignore any rumors you hear that Candidate X bribed Congressmen to secure government contracts. They are malicious and untrue"). The danger in negative suggestion is that it draws attention to the very ideas the speaker hopes to dispel.

Because the speaker who deliberately uses suggestion attempts to short-circuit the reasoning process, the ethics of responsible public address demand that the end he seeks be above reproach and that logical arguments and evidence be combined with suggestion.

See "The Philosophy of Social Justice Through Social Action," p. 134, par. 48. Note the dependence on positive, indirect suggestion in "The City—A Cause for Statesmanship," p. 253, par. 33; see also marginal notes to "On the Federal Constitution," pp. 266-272.

Summary A review or reiteration, generally condensed, of facts and ideas previously presented. In addition to a final summary at the conclusion of his speech, a speaker may employ an "initial summary," in which, as part of his introduction, he announces the points he will cover; and one or more "internal summaries," in which he reviews the ideas and arguments presented up to that point.

In oral discourse the pace is set by the speaker; the listener is given no opportunity to review for himself what has been said earlier. Carefully drawn summaries are, therefore, important aids to comprehension and memory. See "What Is a Classic?" pp. 49-50, par. 5. Internal summaries occur in "Crime and Criminals," p. 138, par. 10; "Changing Concepts of Public Service," p. 238, par. 47; "Address to the Russian People," p. 244, par. 49.

Supporting Material The subject matter or content used to justify or clarify any *proposition* that is a *main heading* or *subheading* in a speech. The kinds of content available to the speaker for this purpose are variously named and classified. In this glossary these materials are identified and explained under the following designations: *analogy, authority, definition, evidence, example, opinion, repetition,* and *statistics*. Visual aids, such as charts, graphs, models, etc., constitute another class of supporting materials; they are introduced during the delivery of a speech but planned as an integral part of the content that supports the leading ideas.

Syllogism A form or scheme in *logic* by which *deductions* may be so expressed as to test their reliability. The syllogistic form tests whether anything must necessarily follow from two premises assumed to be true, and it permits exploration of the necessary relationship between three and only three "terms" or concepts within a single syllogism. Two of several possible variations in syllogistic reasoning are demonstrated by the following syllogisms. All animals have bodies, All men are animals, Therefore all men have bodies (All A have B, All C are A, Therefore, all C have B); Every person here speaks English, Some people here are French citizens, Therefore some French citizens speak English (All A have B, Some A are C, Therefore some C have B). In each case the form used allows us to demonstrate that the conclusion is necessarily true if the premises are true. Syllogisms occur rather infrequently in speaking because the things talked about are often so familiar that uttering the three-stage syllogism would seem pedantic and because the deductions we can make about human affairs are so fraught with uncertainties that their conclusions are at best probable, seldom necessary or certain. For these and other reasons, the deductions that occur in speeches are likely to be expressed so that either a premise or the conclusion is omitted but understood. Such rhetorical syllogisms or enthymemes can usually be reconstructed to fit the standard syllogistic form, but they may still demonstrate no necessary conclusions. The following rhetorical syllogisms can be fitted to the same syllogistic structures as the formal syllogisms illustrated above. "We of the Poets' Guild may share with poets everywhere the assurance that we have experienced insights not known to men in other pursuits"; "We are Americans, so, of course, we understand the history of our land." In each example the first premise is unstated; but even if it were stated and the syllogistic form observed, the conclusion of neither would be necessarily true. One can know only that many poets experience unique insights; it is probable that only some members of the Poets' Guild are true poets. The conclusion is probably true in a limited degree only. In the second case it is probably true that all Americans understand something about their own history, but their understandings are so varied that the conclusion can be highly reliable or highly unreliable, depending on our interpretation of "understand." Still, this argument can be cast into a technically reliable syllogism. As Aristotle first said, we will find in rhetoric a kind of reasoning that is the "counterpart" of the syllogism but seldom a genuine syllogism. This formally incomplete syllogism Aristotle called an enthymeme; others prefer to call it a rhetorical syllogism. See "Address to the Russian People," p. 243, par. 39; "The City—A Cause for Statesmanship," p. 253, par. 34.

Symbol An image or concrete detail that conveys meanings beyond the literal meaning. Thus "night" is used frequently to represent death as well as that period when the sun is down; the cross represents Christianity, the hammer and sickle Communism, green the Irish, and so on. Since these symbols are widely accepted, they are known as conventional symbols. Such symbols are occasionally useful in a speech because they catch attention, make communication easy, are often rich in connotations, and are easily remembered. Sometimes a speaker may use what we might call a private symbol. Such a symbol is one that he invents to help the audience understand and remember his point. Thus a speaker might suggest that an appropriate symbol for his class or club is an armadillo, since the group has such a hard shell that it is impervious to the shafts of truth. (It should be noted that in the broadest sense every word is a symbol; here, however, we are concerned with the symbolism of the images communicated by certain words rather than by words themselves.) Note how Bernstein uses Ivy League clothes, crew cuts, and horn-rimmed glasses as symbols of the well-bred intellectual in "The World of Jazz," p. 71, par. 43.

Topic See *Subject*.

Transition A passage in a speech by means of which two ideas or headings are related, so that the listener can move from one to the other easily and without confusion. A transition may vary in length from a few words to entire paragraphs. Note the transitional elements at the beginnings of each paragraph in "Science, Technology, and World Development," pp. 84-89. See also "The South Respects the Written Constitution," p. 148, par. 69; "The American Family," p. 157, par. 32; "The Greatest Invention of Them All," p. 196, par. 24; "The Haven of the Defeated," p. 161, par. 8. In "The City—A Cause for Statesmanship," pp. 253-254, pars. 36-38 are transitional, connecting one main heading (need for funds) with the next (need for collaborative planning).

Turning the Tables One of the special methods of *refutation*. Accepting an opponent's premise, but drawing the opposite conclusion. ("You say that since our nation needs many highly trained scientists, we should make it possible for more young people to go to college. I admit we need scientists, but I say that is the very reason why we should severely restrict college attendance, accepting only those students showing the most promise.'') See ''The Case Against Segregated Schools,'' p. 152, par. 19; ''The Scarcity of Ideas,'' p. 227, par. 14. See also *Dilemma.*

u

Understatement A statement that makes less of the truth than the facts will allow. Whereas *overstatement* or exaggeration was especially appealing to Americans in the nineteenth century, understatement is preferred now. *Humor,* especially, is more effective today if it is based on understatement. (''A good speaker must have poise, a pleasing voice, and a forceful delivery. It is also helpful if he has an idea or two.'') See ''Remarks on Government Regulation of Broadcasting,'' p. 117, par. 2; ''The Scarcity of Ideas,'' p. 228, par. 24, and p. 229, par. 32.

Unity The cardinal virtue which results from including only those matters in a speech which support its *specific purpose.* Any disregard of the principle of unity—that is, any inclusion of material that does not support the specific purpose—confuses the listener, and thus limits the effectiveness of the speech. ''On the Federal Constitution,'' pp. 266-272, is probably the most tightly unified address in this volume.

v

Variety The cardinal virtue that comes from a vigorous and natural way of speaking. No speaker should work for variety simply for its own sake. The problem is to see that each idea is handled in the most effective way possible. Attention to this principle will automatically result in variety, since ideas normally require different kinds of support, different kinds of sentence structure, different kinds of words, and different kinds of delivery. Monotony not only destroys attention to what is said; it falsifies the material of a speech. While variety as such should not be a direct objective, the worst aspects of monotony can be overcome by conscious effort. Any good speech textbook, or just good common sense, will indicate some of the means by which this can be done.

Vividness The color and brightness a speech acquires as a result of emphasis on such matters as *concreteness* in details and *connotation* in language. See ''The American Family,'' p. 155, pars. 4-6.

y

Yes Response Proceeding through a series of related points and winning agreement upon each in turn to gain the acceptance of some more basic *proposition* which these successive admissions imply. (''Do you want to have the respect of your classmates and instructors? Yes. Do you want to merit the hopes and sacrifices of your parents in sending you to college? Yes. Do you want to get a good job after you have graduated from college? Yes. Then you must study hard day after day.'')

This device is most often employed as the approach step or introduction of a persuasive speech to an apathetic or hostile audience, but it is also useful in other rhetorical situations where persuasion must be effected. See also *Common Ground.*

Note to Instructors: In the table of contents the speeches are classified according to *content.* In the following pages, they are classified according to *purpose* and *occasion.* However, as the editors note, "Any classification of speeches according to purpose or intent is necessarily open to dispute. The precise balance of a speaker's intentions is not always obvious, the terms with which such intentions can be described are numerous, and few speeches exhibit a single, exclusive purpose throughout. Occasions for speechmaking, too, can be variously described. Therefore, the classifications that follow are suggestive only. For other possible systems of classification, see the glossary entries *Ends of speaking,* p. 302, and *Occasion,* p. 306."

Classification of the speeches according to purpose:

1. **Instructive** (speeches designed primarily to inform)

2. **Persuasive** (speeches designed primarily to influence belief or action)

3. **Investigative** (speeches designed primarily to explore a subject)

4. **Evocative and Impressive** (speeches designed primarily to move and to stimulate thought)

Classification of the speeches according to occasion:

3 4 5 6 7 8 9 10 11 12 13 14 15 16 17 18 19 20 21 22 23 24 25 B 70 69 68 67 66 65 64 63